DEPARTMENT OF THE ENVIRONMENT

CW00538837

ENGLISH HOUSE CONDITION SURVEY 1991

ENERGY REPORT

LONDON: THE STATIONERY OFFICE

ISBN 0 11 753201 2

Acknowledgements The analysis of the EHCS energy data and drafting of this Report was the responsibility of the Department of the Environment (Building Stock Research Division) and its executive agency, the Building Research Establishment (Environmental and Health Requirements Division, Scottish Laboratory and Building Energy Efficiency Group). The contribution of other agencies and organisations is acknowledged in two other EHCS reports[1]. For this Report, thanks are due to the electricity companies and British Gas regions for the provision of quarterly consumption data at the addresses in the fuel consumption survey. Thanks are also due to Maggie Davidson (BRE) for the modelling of investment income, to Richard Hartless (BSR) for help with the index and Andy Taylor (DOE, Design Drawing and Print Services) for the camera ready copy.

Authors

Richard Moore	DOE/BSR	(Editor & Ch. 1, 2, 7, 11, 19pt. & 20)
David Smith: Glyn Evans	"	(Ch. 15 & 18: Case studies)
Alan O'Dell: John Mayer	BRE/EHRD	(Ch. 6, 17 & 19: 4, 5 & 7pt.)
Chris Sanders	BRE/SL	(Ch. 10 & 14)
Julie Dunster	BRE/BEEG	(Ch. 4 pt., 9 & 13)

1   *Department of the Environment, English House Condition Survey 1991, HMSO, London, 1993 and 1996 (forthcoming).*

Printed in Great Britain on recycled paper
Designed by DDP Services
B2546 September 1996
95Pubs0364

Contents

Chapter 1

Summary

Introduction

1.1   In England, housing accounts for some 30% of total fuel consumption and a similar proportion of energy-related carbon dioxide emissions. At the same time, cold homes represent the primary health risk associated directly with the condition of the stock. This Report provides the findings of the 1991 English House Condition Survey (EHCS) on the energy efficiency and performance of the housing stock, action by occupants and landlords to improve conditions and the potential for further improvement and energy savings.

1.2   The report refers to data collected in 1991 and 1992. Since then, there has been some improvement in energy efficiency, but the basic nature of the conditions and their patterns of distribution are unlikely to have changed substantially from those described in this Report. Any significant changes will be revealed by the 1996 EHCS Energy Survey, currently underway.

Physical standards

Heating facilities

1.3   The EHCS confirms the increasing monopoly of one particular heating system, over 4 out of 5 dwellings being centrally heated and four fifths of these being gas-fired. Since 1986, with a continued decline in solid fuel and an increase in storage heaters, electricity has overtaken solid fuel as the second most common fuel for space heating. Four fifths of centrally heated dwellings have 'full-house' heating, whereas around half of all other dwellings have fixed heaters in only one or two rooms.

1.4   Owner occupiers generally enjoy higher standards of heating than tenants; only 1 in 10 owner occupied dwellings lack central heating compared to four times this proportion of privately rented properties. The fuel used also varies with tenure, dwelling type and age. While many housing association dwellings have electric heating, over 1 in 5 early post-war semi-detached council houses are still heated by solid fuel, predominantly in open fires. In the private rented sector, 1 in 7 of all converted flats - the most common dwelling type - have no fixed heating.

1.5   Over all tenures, less than 2% of occupied dwellings have no fixed provision. However, some 2% of households who own a central heating system do not use it, most citing the running costs as the reason. Over a third of these use portable heaters instead, adding to those who have no fixed heating.

1.6   There is considerable geographical variation in heating facilities. The proportion of the stock without central heating ranges from less than 1 in 10 in the Northern and Eastern counties to over 1 in 3 in West Yorkshire and, reflecting availability, the use of gas for heating is nearly twice as high in Tyne and Wear as Devon and Cornwall. Suburban areas have the best facilities and urban areas the worst; more than half of private rented dwellings in urban areas are without central heating.

1.7 Like space heating, water heating facilities also vary with tenure and dwelling type. In nearly four-fifths of owner occupied dwellings the main provision for hot water is a gas-fired central heating system; only 14% rely on electric immersion heaters. However, over a quarter of council tenants and a third of those privately renting are provided only with electric, mainly on-peak, immersion heaters.

Thermal insulation

1.8 The thermal insulation of a dwelling depends on its construction as well as any specific insulation measures. Over 60% of all dwellings have cavity walls but 31% have solid masonry walls - mostly 9 inches thick. Around a quarter of cavity walls are insulated, compared with less than a tenth of solid walls. Standards of insulation vary between tenures and regions, reflecting differences in the age and type of stock.

1.9 Nearly 25% of all dwellings have full double glazing and a further 30% have some. The proportion of the owner occupied stock with this measure (70%) is twice that in other tenures. A third of dwellings have draught excluders, these being concentrated in the owner occupied and local authority stocks.

1.10 Nearly 90% of accessible lofts in dwellings are insulated, but an estimated 1.6 million are reported to be without any insulation. Most of these are in the owner occupied stock, although proportionally greatest in the private rented sector. Overall, about three-quarters of dwellings with accessible lofts have insulation meeting the 1976 Building Regulation standard.

1.11 Around 85% of dwellings have hot water cylinders and 92% of these are insulated. The majority have cylinder jackets and a quarter the more efficient foam coated cylinders. In the owner occupied stock under 1 in 15 cylinders remain uninsulated, compared to nearly 1 in 5 of those in the private rented sector.

Energy efficiency

1.12 In the Report, the overall energy efficiency of a dwelling is measured by giving it an 'energy rating' obtained by the Government's Standard Assessment Procedure (SAP). This is an index of the annual cost of heating the dwelling to achieve a standard heating regime and is normally described as running from 1 (highly inefficient) to 100 (highly efficient).

1.13 In England, the average SAP energy rating of the occupied housing stock is 35, the mean varying little between tenures, except in the generally older private rented stock where it is below 22. In total, nearly 3 million dwellings (15%) have SAP ratings under 20, these accounting for over a tenth of owner occupied dwellings, nearly a fifth of those socially rented and well over two fifths of those rented privately.

1.14 The SAP rating is determined by the heat loss from the dwelling and the performance of the heating system. Dwelling age and built form are the predominant factors which determine heat loss; post 1980 flats and mid-terrace houses have, on average, half the rate of loss of pre 1850 detached and semi-detached houses. There is less variation in the performance of heating systems. Here, tenure is the main factor, owner occupiers generally having the best systems and private tenants the worst. In the overall energy rating, dwelling age is the dominant influence, tenure playing an important but secondary role.

1.15 Of the 3 million least efficient dwellings, nearly 90% have high heat losses and a similar proportion inefficient heating systems. Many dwellings have a high 'heating price' because of their reliance on on-peak electric immersion water heaters, although inefficient space heating is the main cause. Over a third have solid fuel or on-peak electric fires and a further 14% rely on portable heating. A minority of the least efficient properties are in poor condition generally; only 1 in 16 are unfit on the present standard.

1.16 There is a regional pattern to energy efficiency, particularly in the council stock where mean SAP ratings range from 24 in Devon and Cornwall to over 43 in Inner London. Generally, in all tenures, the more urban the area the more efficient the dwelling. This is only in part due to differences in the age and type of stock.

Households and standards

1.17 In the owner occupied stock, families and lone parents are generally living in the most efficient housing and lone pensioners in the least, the latter being less well housed than tenants in the social rented sectors. However, all are significantly better off than private tenants, for whom average SAP ratings range from 28 for adult couples to only 11 for over a quarter million lone pensioners.

1.18 For all except those privately renting, the likelihood of occupying relatively energy efficient housing depends more on income than on tenure. Private tenants on the highest income are generally in less efficient accommodation than the poorest households in other sectors. Professional groups have the most efficient housing, having significantly more high rated homes than 'employers and managers' on similar incomes.

1.19 The most vulnerable households appear to be concentrated in the least efficient stock. Around 1 million or 22% of households with heads aged 65 years or more, including a quarter of those aged 75 or older, live in homes with SAP ratings under 20, of which nearly half are rated under 10. Nearly half of these are owner occupiers and a fifth private tenants. Persons with respiratory illnesses and those with mobility problems are also more likely to be found in less energy efficient housing than those without such problems.

1.20 This concentration is due to the association of such groups with the least energy efficient house types, particularly bungalows and older terraced housing, as well as with the least improved dwellings generally. Nearly 90% of all pre 1980 council bungalows (which have an average SAP rating of only 25) are rented by pensioner households. Overall, a half of all council dwellings with SAP ratings under 20 are let to tenants who are pensioners.

Energy consumption

Heating and appliance use

1.21 The extent and duration of heating in the home depends as much on its overall energy efficiency, its type of heating and the controls provided, as on the type of occupants, their lifestyle and general pattern of employment. Thus, for all households not in full-time employment, the proportion who heat their living room intermittently - rather than all-day - increases in dwellings of higher energy efficiency, as the versatility and control of the heating system improves and the rate of heat loss decreases.

1.22   Heating controls are often inadequate or rarely utilised. Amongst households with central heating controls, room thermostats and the override on programmers are most frequently used (both by around 45%) but less than a fifth regularly use the manual valves on their radiators.

1.23   Typically, a third of energy consumption goes on lighting, cooking and other domestic appliances. Some 47% of households use mains gas cookers, 38% electric cookers and 12% dual fuel appliances, predominantly gas hobs and electric ovens. The last are most common amongst affluent, larger households in the owner occupied sector. Around 57% of all households also have a microwave oven.

1.24   Twice as many households have a washing machine (88%) as a tumble drier (44%). Fewer possess a dish washer (17%). Again, more affluent households in the owner occupied sector are most likely to own all three appliances. Families generally are more likely to possess a given appliance than smaller households and the frequency of use also increases with household size.

Fuel consumption

1.25   Virtually all households receive on-peak electricity and most use at least one other fuel, the combinations of fuels and fuel use found in homes being extremely diverse. Over four-fifths of all households use gas, although this is closer to three-fifths for private and housing association tenants, and much lower in older housing. Just over a fifth use off-peak electricity with little variation between tenures and almost as many use solid or other unmetered fuels. There is large variation in the use of gas across the country, ranging from 95% of homes in the West Midlands Metropolitan Area to only 57% of those in Devon and Cornwall.

1.26   Of total domestic energy consumption in England, 68% is made up of gas, 15% on-peak electricity, over 3% off-peak electricity and 14% other fuels. High fuel consumption, with a large proportion being mains gas, is a feature of large, high income families owning older detached or semi-detached houses. Conversely, low consumption is associated with smaller households - especially pensioners - living in rented flats and newer dwellings.

1.27   The least energy efficient homes have the lowest total consumption, but use the highest proportion of on-peak electricity and other fuels. Low rated dwellings are generally smaller and often inadequately heated by their low income occupants. Total consumption rises with increasing SAP ratings, with only a small fall in the highest rated dwellings. It appears that higher standards of heating but low total consumption is found only in these relatively few, modern, most energy efficient dwellings.

1.28   After allowing for differences in external temperatures between 1986 and 1991, total gas consumption is estimated to have increased by 5% and electricity by 1%, possibly reflecting the increased ownership of central heating.

Fuel expenditure

1.29   In 1991/92, average household expenditure on fuel was nearly £660, the mean ranging from under £300 for lone pensioners in housing association dwellings to approaching £1,000 for large families in private housing. However, due to their greater use of electricity and poorer tariff arrangements, tenants generally pay more for their energy (per kWh) than owner occupiers. Per square metre of floor area, mean fuel expenditure is highest for council and private tenants.

1.30   Mean expenditure per square metre decreases only slightly with better energy efficiency. As with fuel consumption, total expenditure increases - due mainly to the larger size of more efficient homes - until the very highest SAP ratings are reached.

1.31   The average proportion of household income spent on fuel is just over 8%, but varies from under 5% for small families in owner occupation to an average of 23% for large families privately renting.

1.32   The adequacy of a household's expenditure on fuel can be assessed against the total costs required in their dwelling to achieve either a standard or a minimum heating regime. The standard regime is that used in the Standard Assessment Procedure (SAP) and assumes full house heating with temperatures of 21°C in the living room and 18°C elsewhere. The minimum regime, designed primarily to safeguard health, assumes only partial heating giving temperatures of 18°C in the living room and 16°C in other heated rooms.

1.33   Due to the poor energy efficiency of their homes and consequent high heating costs, over 1 in 3 households would need to spend at least 10% of their income on fuel to achieve the standard heating regime. The extent of the problem varies widely between households and one in five lone pensioners would require more than 20% of their income to achieve the minimum heating regime. Over 60% of lone pensioners are presently 'under-spending' in relation to this standard.

1.34   Whilst low income and under-occupation are major factors causing lack of affordable warmth, the results confirm the overwhelming importance of energy efficiency in solving the problem. In all tenures, some 9 out of 10 households in homes with SAP ratings of 60 or above are spending sufficient to meet or exceed the minimum heating regime compared with under a fifth of those in homes rated below 10.

Thermal conditions

1.35   The temperatures achieved in a dwelling will depend on the heating regime desired by the occupants in relation to their lifestyle and expectations; the capacity of the heating appliances to maintain the desired regime against the heat losses; and the ability of the household to pay the consequent fuel costs.

Home temperatures

1.36   In early 1992, when the mean external temperature was 11°C, the average spot temperatures recorded by the survey was 19.5°C in the living room and 18.3°C in the hall - a proxy for the mean of all rooms. Home temperatures increase progressively with higher energy efficiency, the average living room and hall temperature being respectively 2°C and 4°C higher in dwellings with SAP ratings of 70 or more than in those rated below 10.

1.37   The average living room and hall temperatures that correspond to households feeling "comfortable" (19.4°C and 18.6°C) are close to average spot temperatures for these rooms. Households with rooms well above 21°C generally regard them as too warm and those with living rooms below

18°C and halls around 16.4°C as too cold, thereby supporting the definition of the standard and minimum regimes.

1.38 On average, pensioner households have homes with a greater temperature difference between the living room and other rooms than other households. Over 1 in 4 heat their living rooms to above 21°C but a greater number have halls under 16°C. Generally, low income households have colder homes than higher income groups.

1.39 Despite the mild winter weather in 1991/92, a large proportion of heated homes were relatively cold. Only 25% of homes fully met the temperatures of the standard regime and only 70% those of the minimum regime. The likelihood of a home failing to achieve these temperatures is governed largely by its energy efficiency, the availability of a comprehensive heating system, the household income and, not least, the external temperature. With the latter below 4°C, the proportion of dwellings failing to achieve the minimum regime increases from under a third in each sector to 50% in the owner occupied stock, 62% in council housing and 95% in the generally inefficient private rented sector.

Damp and mould

1.40 Cold and damp conditions are frequently related, over 20% of private rented dwellings being damp, compared to 5 to 7% of those in other sectors. Damp is associated generally with older dwellings in poor condition, approaching three-quarters of those with rising damp being built before 1919. Penetrating damp affects 30% of the worst condition stock compared to only 1% of the best.

1.41 Condensation and mould is associated as much with social factors as the age and condition of the stock. Over 22% of all households report some condensation or mould growth, but the majority of problems are slight. Both incidence and severity vary significantly between tenures; only 1 in 16 owner occupiers suffer more serious (moderate or severe) outbreaks, compared with nearly 1 in 6 tenants in the social rented sector and well over 1 in 5 of those privately renting. However, with the growth in owner occupation since 1986, over half the dwellings affected are now in this sector.

1.42 Large, low income families in less efficient dwellings are the most likely to suffer problems. Households reporting the most condensation and mould all have dependant children, comprising small families (28%), large families (34%) and lone parents (38%). Despite their low fuel consumption and often cold homes, pensioners are least affected, producing much less water vapour than family households.

1.43 The survey confirms the role of adequate ventilation and heating in controlling condensation and mould growth. Full central heating, of all types, greatly reduces the incidence of problems, while dwellings using individual on-peak electric fires are worst affected.

Satisfaction with heating

1.44 Despite often poor thermal conditions, most households are satisfied with their heating; overall 13% are not, 5% being very dissatisfied. This represents a significant improvement on levels of satisfaction recorded in 1986. As in 1986, dissatisfied households complain most about lack of heat; half of their complaints are about insufficient heat or the limited extent of their heating system. Fewer complain about the cost of heating.

1.45 Contrary to the average efficiency of their homes, pensioners are the most satisfied with their heating and lone parents the least. Those working full time are much more satisfied than those unemployed, many of whom complain about the cost of heating. Low income households with high fuel use account for half of all complaints about the cost of heating. However, as incomes rise, increasing expenditure on fuel is paralleled by increasing satisfaction.

1.46 Owner occupiers are generally more satisfied than tenants, only 1 in 14 having a complaint compared to between 1 in 3 and 1 in 5 of those in the rented sectors. However, the type of heating system has a stronger influence on household satisfaction than either tenure or household characteristics. Less than a tenth of households with central heating are dissatisfied, compared to a third of those without - such dissatisfaction being reflected in the improvements undertaken.

Energy action

Energy related work

1.47 During 1991, the total value of energy related work by householders was some £4.7 billion. This comprised actual expenditure of around £4.0 billion on 'major' and 'minor' works, plus the equivalent labour costs of DIY work. There was a sharp increase in home improvement between 1987 and 1991, the value of work over the full 5 years (£17 billion) being only about 3.6 times that in 1991.

1.48 Amongst owner occupiers, 55% of the total expenditure went on double glazing, only 5% on other insulation measures, and 23% on central heating - 10% going on new installations. In 1991, around 1 in 10 fitted double glazed windows (at an average cost of £1,900) but possibly for reasons other than energy efficiency. Couples and small family owner occupiers, particularly those on higher incomes, tended to do the most work, while pensioner households did the least.

1.49 Between 1987 and 1991, nearly £2 billion was spent by local authorities on energy measures. A third of the capital spend (which averaged around £1,940 per dwelling) went on double glazing and almost half on heating systems. Some 11% of the council stock had new systems installed and a further 6% received improvements to existing ones. Housing associations invested just over £0.2 billion on energy related works and an estimated £0.6 billion to £0.75 billion was spent by private landlords over the same period.

1.50 A few tenants undertook major work. However, the total expenditure by tenants was only £25 per dwelling when averaged over the total rented stock, compared with some £300 for all owner occupiers.

Attitudes to insulation work

1.51 Over three quarters of owner occupiers have improved the insulation of their present home, many installing double glazing and/or other measures in a wide variety of combinations. There is some evidence that owner occupiers install simpler and cheaper measures first (loft and cylinder insulation) and wait longer to install more expensive items, such as double glazing.

1.52   Most owner occupiers whose homes could be improved by the installation of wall insulation or double glazing say they have no intention of installing these in future. They see no need for these measures or can't afford them. Those with the least insulation - lacking even loft and/or cylinder insulation - are most likely to say that they intend to undertake work.

1.53   Under a third of tenants have carried out any work to insulate their home, most of these installing draught excluders alone. They see insulation work as the landlords responsibility, while in the private rented sector, transience (indicated by the frequent reason "moving soon") also limits action.

Improvement potential

1.54   In the Report, improvements in 'energy efficiency' are calculated as the percentage saving in the cost of heating required to achieve the standard heating regime. Unless comparable savings are made in the fuel costs for lighting, cooking and domestic appliances, the saving in the total fuel cost will be significantly less. Energy savings are also not necessarily proportional to the cost savings, as the improvement may involve a change of fuel. Overall, energy savings are likely to be less than cost savings.

1.55   On the above definition, a 30% improvement in 'energy efficiency' over the whole stock could be achieved, for the least cost, by improving all dwellings with a SAP rating below 44 by at least 10 SAP points and also to a minimum rating of 30. The average capital costs of the works required would be around £2,000 per dwelling improved and, for the stock as a whole, some £26 billion. The notional annual saving in fuel expenditure would be around £2.5 billion.

1.56   Almost all of the works required on dwellings with SAP ratings below 20 can be financially justified in that they have a simple 'payback period' of less than ten years. For a capital cost of just over £5 billion, they would permit a notional saving in annual heating expenditure of more than £1.2 billion. However, more extensive programmes are less easy to justify in these terms; of all works on dwellings rated under 50, over half have a 'payback' longer than ten years.

1.57   The above savings and 'paybacks' are based on the assumption that households already heat their homes to the standard regime, but the EHCS shows that, in practice, heating standards in energy inefficient homes are generally far lower. It also shows what is spent by households of similar type and income who are already living in energy efficient properties, and this information can be used to predict actual expenditure savings.

1.58   The prediction suggests that, for the majority of households, expenditure on fuel after improvement will generally be comparable to or even higher than that before. However, while the number of households whose expenditure will rise is greater than the number whose spending will fall, the latter tend to be the higher spenders and savings from this minority should more than offset the increased expenditure of low spenders. However, the aggregate saving is unlikely to exceed 3% over the stock as a whole.

1.59   These predictions are supported by a separate analysis of a sample of dwellings actually improved between 1986 and 1991. These show an average actual increase in fuel consumption after improvement of nearly

20%. In short, improvements in energy efficiency are likely to lead to higher temperatures and levels of comfort rather than a significantly lower fuel expenditure or energy consumption.

1.60 Even relatively modest programmes of energy efficiency, however, would yield important gains in affordable warmth. Capital spending of around £11 billion could halve the number of homes (3 million) where existing fuel spending falls substantially short of that needed for the minimum heating regime. Private tenants and lone pensioners in the worst conditions would secure a proportionally greater improvement in affordable warmth than other groups. However, achieving further improvements would be disproportionately costly.

Overview and conclusions

1.61 There remains considerable scope for improving the energy efficiency of the housing stock. Probably a third or more of heating systems cannot physically meet the standard heating regime, while many older, albeit well heated houses have poor insulation standards. Only 5% of any sector can be said to be energy efficient - having a SAP rating of 60 or over.

1.62 Low energy efficiency combines with low income and, often, under-occupation to deprive many households of affordable warmth, including a majority of lone pensioners and other vulnerable groups. Lack of affordable warmth and low energy efficiency generally, results in poor thermal conditions over much of the stock, insufficient heat rather than the cost of heating being the main source of complaint amongst households.

1.63 In theory, a 30% improvement in 'energy efficiency' could be achieved in a 10 to 15 year period with existing levels of capital spending. In practice, there is a mismatch between the homes in which the majority of works are carried out and those in most need of improvement.

1.64 The opportunities for securing energy savings are nevertheless limited. Improvement often brings new opportunities for whole house heating and lifts the fear of unaffordable fuel bills. Consequently, for many households, fuel spending after improvement tends to be the same as or even higher than that before, and is likely to lead to only a small saving in energy consumption across the stock as a whole. Some savings may be achieved by encouraging economy among households already in efficient housing, but potential savings here are estimated to be less than 5% of total fuel now consumed.

1.65 While improvement of the worst stock would benefit those households most in need, lack of affordable warmth cannot be eradicated by housing improvement alone. As well as very low incomes, this is due to high levels of under-occupation and the fact that over 1 in 5 of all dwellings are not physically capable of being made energy efficient at reasonable cost. It appears that for the medium term the most cost effective strategies would be those that aim to replace the very worst stock, while improving the remaining bulk of older housing to only moderately high standards.

1.66 Over the last two decades, a dramatic growth in central heating has been paralleled by improvements in thermal insulation and the efficiency of appliances to keep average fuel consumption relatively static. In the shorter term, the benefit of improved energy efficiency will continue to lie in preventing the escalation of fuel consumption to fulfil the remaining large potential for higher heating standards. Equally, it should provide affordable warmth, particularly to very many households in the most vulnerable groups concentrated in the least energy efficient housing.

Chapter

Introduction

Background

2.1 In England, housing accounts for some 60% of energy consumption in buildings and 30% of total fuel use and energy-related carbon dioxide (CO_2) emissions. At the same time, cold homes represent the primary health risk in buildings, contributing to a proportion of some 20,000 excess winter deaths each year[1]. This Report describes the housing conditions and patterns of energy use which result in high fuel consumption on the one hand and lack of affordable warmth on the other. It reports the findings of the 1991 English House Condition Survey (EHCS) on the energy efficiency and performance of the housing stock, action by occupants and landlords and the potential for improvement and energy savings.

2.2 The 1991 EHCS is the sixth in the quinquennial series undertaken by the Department, the coverage of energy issues in the EHCS having increased in line with the growing concern for energy conservation and affordable warmth. Since 1976, the survey has included questions on heating, insulation, damp and mould growth. In 1986, these sections were extended and new questions added on fuel consumption, spot temperatures and satisfaction with heating. The 1991 survey covers these issues in further detail and provides new data on energy efficiency ratings, fuel expenditure and household attitudes to energy measures.

2.3 Data generated by the energy questions in the 1991 EHCS have been used to inform Government policies on housing renewal, energy efficiency and CO_2 emissions and to provide guidance to local authorities on strategies for their own stock.[2] The present report provides more detailed statistics and covers all tenures; it is the second in the series, updating the 1986 EHCS Energy Report.[3] The general conduct of the 1991 survey and its findings are described in two other reports[4].

The survey

Table 2.1   Energy related issues covered by the 1991 EHCS

Full physical survey 1991	Household Interview Survey 1992 Full sample	Household Interview Survey 1992 Energy sample	Postal and fuel surveys 1992
· heating facilities	· use of heating	· heating controls	· work/expenditure
· thermal insulation	· thermal insulation	· heating regimes	on measures
· damp and mould	· damp and mould	· air temperatures	· legislation used
· air tightness	· moisture creation	· ventilation/draught	· dwelling or area/
· construction	· appliance use	· fuel consumption	estate action
· form/dimensions	· long-term illness	· fuel expenditure	
· orientation &	· work/expenditure	· attitude to heating	· fuel consumption
shading	on measures	& energy action	· fuel tariffs
sample no. 13,986	*sample no. 9,965*	*sample no. 4,942*	*sample no. 10,750*
			fuel sample 4,179

1   *The total of deaths during December to March which are in excess of the average rate for the year, GJ Raw and RM Hamilton (editors), 'Building regulation and heath', Building Research Establishment Report 289, CRC, London, 1995, p.7.*
2   *Department of the Environment, Energy Efficiency in Council Housing: Strategic Guide, Condition of the Stock, DOE, 1995*
3   *Department of the Environment, English House Condition Survey: 1986 Supplementary (Energy) Report, HMSO, 1991*
4   *Department of the Environment, 1993 and 1996, op.cit.*

The energy questions

2.4   Energy questions in the EHCS were included in a number of linked surveys: a physical survey of dwellings, undertaken in Autumn 1991; a household interview survey including a temperature survey, carried out between February and May 1992; a subsequent postal survey of local authorities and housing associations; and, in summer 1992, a consumption survey involving the electricity companies and British Gas regions. Detailed energy questions, temperatures and permission to obtain fuel data were sought at nearly half of the addresses in the full interview survey, which in turn comprised a sub-sample of addresses in the physical survey. The achieved samples and energy issues covered by each part are listed in Table 2.1.

2.5   In the temperature survey, spot readings were taken outdoors and indoors, generally in the main living rooms and hall/stairs, the latter corresponding closely with the mean temperature of all rooms. Consumption data and tariffs for electricity and gas were obtained from the fuel suppliers and for other fuels from the household. The survey data on heating facilities, insulation and other physical factors were used in the EHCS Energy model - based on the Building Research Establishment's Domestic Energy Model (BREDEM) - to determine energy efficiency ratings on the Standard Assessment Procedure. (Annex C, paras. C.21-28)

Methodological aspects

2.6   The other 1991 EHCS reports contain full copies of the main survey forms, but those pages which include the principal energy questions are also reproduced here, together with the proformae used in the fuel consumption and tariff surveys (Annex B). The methodology and sample structure for the main survey parts are also described in the other reports. The present report describes the conduct of the energy, temperature and fuel consumption surveys, their relationship to the main parts, response rates and grossing for these sub-samples. (Annex C, paras. C.2-20)

2.7   The various samples used in the analysis are grossed to represent the national stock. Depending on the sample sizes, this procedure introduces some uncertainty around the numbers and percentages estimated in this report. An explanation of these confidence limits and other errors associated with the methods of measurement can be found in the other EHCS reports. However, where such errors are particularly relevant to the analysis of the energy data, these are mentioned in the text and discussed specifically. (Annex C)

Table 2.2   EHCS 1991, grossed dwelling and household totals by tenure

thousand dwellings/households

	Owner occupied	Private rented	Local authority	Housing association	Totals
Existing households	12,872	1,700	3,877	662	19,111
Occupied dwellings	12,872	1,626	3,851	591	18,940
New dwellings[1]	122	-	8	15	146
Vacant dwellings	508		113	18	639
Total dwellings	15,128		3,972	624	19,725

1 Not in fieldwork sample

The energy report

Basis of estimates

2.8 All estimates in this report refer to either occupied dwellings or households. Dwelling estimates, relating to physical standards and facilities are based on data generated mainly by the physical or postal surveys. Household numbers relate to the use of facilities by occupants and come from the interview or fuel consumption surveys. Differences between the dwelling and household totals result mainly from houses and flats in multiple-occupation.

2.9 As in the 1986 energy report, the main estimates exclude (a) vacant dwellings, where a full survey - required to determine heating, insulation and energy efficiency - was generally not possible and (b) new dwellings built between the date the sample was drawn and the fieldwork - where no survey was undertaken. The 639 thousand vacant dwellings are likely to include some of the least efficient in the stock, but some 22% were either awaiting demolition, no longer used as dwellings or were long-term vacants. A further 12% were in the process of being modernised. In contrast to vacant dwellings, the 146 thousand new dwellings are probably amongst the most energy efficient in the stock, but due to their relatively small number, their omission has no significant effect on the estimates in the Report. (See Annex C, para. C.17)

Contents of report

2.10 After this general introduction, the report is divided into four main Parts. Part I looks at the energy efficiency of the housing stock and at how households are distributed in this stock. Part II deals with the fuel consumption and fuel expenditure of households. In Part III, the report goes on to examine the resulting thermal conditions, particularly home temperatures, damp and mould growth, and household attitudes to heating. Part IV concludes by looking at work undertaken since 1986 to improve the stock, household attitudes to such measures and the potential for further improvement. The report ends with an overview of the main findings. (Table 2.3)

Table 2.3   Structure of the Energy Report

1 Summary			
2 Introduction			
I Physical Standards	**Energy II Consumption**	**Thermal III Conditions**	**IV Energy Action**
3 Energy rating & case studies	8 Heating regimes & case studies	12 Causal factors & case studies	16 Measuring change & case studies
4 Heating facilities	9 Heating and appliance use	13 Home temperatures	17 Energy measures
5 Thermal insulation	10 Fuel consumption	14 Damp & mould	18 Attitude to measures
6 Energy efficiency	11 Fuel expenditure	15 Satisfaction with heating	19 Improvement potential
7 Households and standards			20 Conclusions

2.11 The way the heating provision and thermal insulation combine to determine the overall energy efficiency of a dwelling and, in turn, interact with the households use of facilities and fuel consumption to produce different thermal conditions, is complex. Such relationships can be more easily understood at the level of the individual dwelling and household than at the level of the total stock. Consequently, following a summary of the principles and measures underlying the analysis in the following chapters, each Part of the report is prefaced by four case studies. Each of these covers all factors, but illustrates particularly the range of conditions covered by the statistical information in that part.

2.12 The central themes in the Report reflect the two main policy concerns in energy efficiency - those of energy consumption on the one hand and affordable warmth on the other. With these concerns in mind, each of the main chapters examines the energy efficiency or thermal performance of the housing stock, firstly in relation to the general characteristics of tenure, dwelling age, type, and condition; and then with reference to household characteristics such as size, household type, income and employment status.

2.13 Where relevant, chapters include a summary of trends since 1986, the 1991 findings being compared with the equivalent estimates from the previous survey. However, as the number of addresses from the 1986 energy sub-sample included in the 1991 sub-sample was only 660 (575 with fuel consumption data), a detailed longitudinal analysis of energy-related factors is not statistically feasible.

2.14 In each main chapter, the text is illustrated with summary tables and figures, while the main tables are presented in Annex A. These tables are prefixed A, followed by the relevant chapter and table number. A comprehensive index to the text, figures and tables in the text and main tables is included at the back of the report. Other annexes at the end of the report reproduce the main energy questions asked in the survey, discuss methodological aspects of the survey and analysis and provide survey definitions.

Trends since 1991

Central heating, insulation and fuel consumption

2.15 Data from the annual GfK Home Audit indicate that improvement in the energy efficiency of the housing stock has continued since the fieldwork for the EHCS energy component was completed in Summer 1992. In this period, the proportion of total households using central heating as their main form of heating has increased by some 1% each year, with a somewhat higher increase in those using gas-fired systems. There has also been a significant increase in the proportion of households with double glazing, but a smaller take up of cavity wall insulation. However, the proportion of the stock with loft insulation and hot water cylinder insulation has remained fairly static since 1991, there being evidence that here saturation has been reached. The total energy demand of the stock has also remained relatively stable in the years following the 1991 Survey.

Table 2.4   Trends in energy efficiency factors since the 1991 EHCS

% of households

Percentage of households	GfK Home Audit & BREHOMES				
	Dec 1991	Dec 1992	Dec 1993	Dec 1994	Dec 1995
using central heating					
all central heating	82	83	84	86	86
gas central heating	63	65	66	69	70
with home insulation					
cavity wall insulation	21	23	22	23	24
some double glazing	51	52	54	59	60
some loft insulation	88	89	90	90	91
insulated HW tanks	95	94	94	95	95
energy use					
fuel consumption (PJ)	1,577	1,542	1,574	1,517	-

2.16 Whilst some of these changes are significant, the Report is concerned not just with the condition of the stock at one point in time, but with the underlying problems and processes at work in domestic energy efficiency. These processes, the basic nature of the problems, their scale of magnitude and patterns of distribution within the housing stock and amongst household groups are unlikely to have changed substantially since 1991/92 from those described in this Report.

The next survey

2.17 Any significant changes since 1991 will be revealed by the 1996 EHCS Energy Survey, currently underway. This covers essentially the same ground as the last survey (see Table 2.1), but includes a larger longitudinal sample to enable a comparison of the energy efficiency and performance of the same dwellings in 1991 and 1996. A follow up survey, based on this longitudinal sample, is also proposed for early 1997. This will collect more detailed information on the temperature regimes achieved and on the distribution of fuel consumption and expenditure between space and water heating, lighting, cooking and other domestic appliances.

Part *I* PHYSICAL STANDARDS

Owner occupied sector

1 1919 - 1944	2 1945 - 1964	3 1965 - 1980	4 1965 - 1980	5 1850 - 1899
Semi-detached	Semi-detached	Detached	Semi-detached	Larger terraced
SAP 32.8	SAP 38.1	SAP 43.4	SAP 41.4	SAP 37.2

6 Post 1980	7 1850 - 1899	8 1965 - 1980	9 1945 - 1964	10 1919 - 1944
Detached	Small terraced	Bungalow	Bungalow	Detached
SAP 52.5	SAP 28.6	SAP 29.6	SAP 30.5	SAP 35.2

Private rented sector

1 1850 - 1899	2 1900 - 1918	3 1850 - 1899	4 1850 - 1899	5 Pre 1850
Converted flat	Converted flat	Small terraced	Larger terraced	Converted flat
SAP 27.4	SAP 26.5	SAP 17.1	SAP 25.7	SAP 34.8

Local authority sector

1 1965 - 1980	2 1945 - 1964	3 1945 - 1964	4 1919 - 1944	5 1919 - 1944
Low-rise flat	Low-rise flat	Semi-detached	Semi-detached	Small terraced
SAP 42.5	SAP 35.2	SAP 27.1	SAP 29.2	SAP 29.6

6 1965 - 1980	7 1945 - 1964	8 1965 - 1980	9 1945 - 1964	10 1945 - 1964
Larger terraced	Small terraced	High-rise flat	Larger terraced	Bungalow
SAP 44.4	SAP 31.1	SAP 49.4	SAP 32.7	SAP 23.7

Housing associations

Average energy efficiency ratings (notes overleaf)

1 1965 - 1980	2 Post 1980	3 1850 - 1899	4 1900 - 1918	5 1965 - 1980
Low-rise flat	Low-rise flat	Converted flat	Converted flat	Larger terraced
SAP 43.0	SAP 47.1	SAP 32.3	SAP 24.4	SAP 44.6

Figure I.1   Average energy efficiency rating for most numerous
              dwelling types in each sector

The frontispiece to Part I shows the average (SAP) energy rating for the
most numerous dwelling types in each tenure; the top ten in the case of the
owner occupied and local authority sectors and the top five in the smaller
private rented and housing association stocks. In total, these types account
for nearly 60% of the national stock. The photographs illustrate typical
examples of each dwelling type, but the particular case shown may not
necessarily have the average SAP rating, all types exhibiting a fairly wide
range of ratings about the mean. These mean SAP ratings may be compared
with the average for the whole stock of 35 and range from nearly 53 for
owner occupied post 1980 detached houses to only 17 for 1850 to 1899
small terraced houses in the private rented sector.

Chapter 3

Energy rating & Case studies

Preamble 3.1 *This first part of the Report profiles the physical standards of energy efficiency in the English housing stock. Chapter 4 describes the facilities available for space and water heating and Chapter 5, the standards of thermal insulation in the stock. Overall standards of energy efficiency are explored in Chapter 6, while the distribution of household types in housing of different efficiencies is discussed in Chapter 7.*

3.2 *Part I starts, however, by outlining the measurement of energy efficiency and showing the relative importance of heating facilities and thermal insulation. A range of relationships between heating facilities, thermal insulation and overall energy efficiency is then illustrated at the level of the individual dwelling in the first set of four case studies.*

Energy rating 3.3 The energy efficiency of an individual dwelling can be described by giving it an 'energy rating'. Generally, an energy rating is a measure of the annual unit cost of heating the dwelling to a standard regime, assuming a certain heating pattern and specific room temperatures. In this report the Government's Standard Assessment Procedure (SAP) is the energy rating used. (See Annex C, paras. C.21-28)

Standard Assessment Procedure

SAP scale 3.4 The SAP rating is on a logarithmic scale, which normally runs from 1 (highly inefficient) to 100 (highly efficient). However, in extreme cases, the formula which defines the rating can result in figures outside this range, and applied to the EHCS sample produces a number of negative ratings. In practice, when issuing SAP ratings such values would be reset to the scale limits. In this Report, however, values produced by the SAP formula that fall outside this range have been retained so as not to distort the profiles of energy efficiency within the housing stock.

Basis of rating 3.5 The SAP rating is designed to reflect the energy efficiency of the dwelling, irrespective of its size, geographical location and characteristics or behaviour of its occupants. The rating therefore measures the cost of heating per unit of floor area. However, because larger dwellings generally have a smaller wall to floor ratio and consequently lower heat losses, they tend to have slightly better SAP ratings than smaller ones built to the same standard. The SAP rating also takes no account of the climatic conditions in which the building is situated. The notional cost of heating on which the rating is based approximates to the actual cost of maintaining the standard heating regime in a building located close to the middle of the country. An identical dwelling in a colder region would have the same SAP rating but, due to higher heat losses resulting from the colder climate, actually require a higher fuel cost to maintain the same heating regime.

3.6 The standardised cost of maintaining a given heating regime in a dwelling, and therefore the SAP rating, depends on two distinct factors:

❑ the rate of heat loss, resulting from the dwelling form, the thermal properties of the building fabric and degree of insulation and level of ventilation; and

❑ the cost of supplying the lost heat, resulting from the efficiency of the heating system, the price of the particular fuel used and any solar gain.

Examples of SAP ratings

Some appreciation of the way the SAP scale relates to standards of heating and insulation as well as the form and size of dwellings, may be gained from Table 3.1.

Table 3.1   Examples of dwellings and their SAP ratings

Semi-detached, 2-storey house, medium sized (90 sq.m), poor insulation (typical interwar standard), with:-	SAP Rating
A) portable heaters, on-peak electric immersion water heater	-19
B) coal fires, on-peak electric immersion water heater	-6
C) gas fires, off-peak electric immersion water heater	30
D) modern gas central heating with hot water system	37

Semi-detached, 2-storey house, medium sized (90 sq.m), modern gas central heating with hot water system, with:-	
E) moderate insulation (to 1976-81 Building Regulations)	57
F) good insulation (to 1990 Building Regulations)	79

Modern gas fires, off-peak electric immersion water heater, moderate insulation (to 1976-81 Building Regulations), in:-	
G) semi-detached bungalow, medium sized	47
H) mid-terrace two storey house, medium sized	58
I) low rise flat, top floor (90 sq.m.) 2 external walls	67
J) low rise flat, mid floor (90 sq.m.) 1 external wall	87

Heat loss & heating price index

3.7 To determine the contribution of the standard of insulation and of the heating system to the overall energy efficiency of a dwelling, the energy model used to estimate SAP ratings has been unpacked to produce separate indices of the 'heat loss' and 'heating price'. The heat loss index represents the total annual heat loss per square metre of floor area, due to ventilation and transmission losses through the building fabric, while the heating price index represents the price of replacing the lost units of energy. In constructing both indices, values for individual dwellings are related to the average value for the stock as a whole, which is given a score of 100. Thus, a value of the heat loss index well above 100 signifies a poorly insulated and 'leaky' dwelling, whilst a high value of the heating price index indicates an inefficient or expensive to run heating system. Figure 3.1 illustrates the relationship between the heat loss and heating price indices for the total stock, the particular examples B, D and F in Table 3.1 being positioned on the plot.

3.8 It is clear that an individual dwelling can have a low SAP rating because it is defective on both of the indices, or because it scores very badly on just one of them. The EHCS shows that dwellings with high SAP ratings gain their advantage mainly because of low heat losses due to their superior insulation, and not because they have particularly efficient heating systems. Dwellings with low SAP ratings tend to have both poor insulation properties and poor heating systems, with the latter generally having the dominant effect. However, in bungalows, the exceptionally high wall/roof to floor ratios generally leads to the heat loss being the predominant factor in a low rating.

Figure 3.1   Relationship between SAP, heat loss and heating price indices

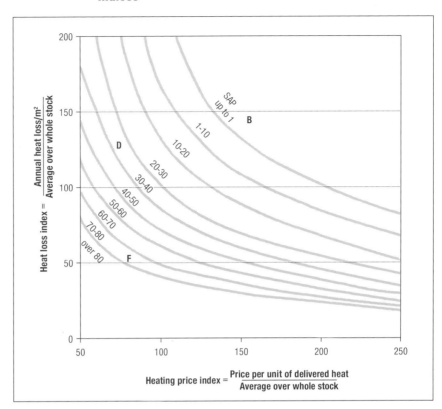

Case studies 3.9 This last point is illustrated in the first of four case studies, which together show a range in heating facilities, thermal insulation, energy efficiency and household composition covered by the statistical material in the following four Chapters. They illustrate how the heating price relates to the heating facilities of a dwelling, the heat loss to the thermal insulation and physical characteristics and how the two factors combine to give a range of SAP ratings. *(Although based on the data recorded in the EHCS, some details not relevant to energy efficiency or fuel consumption have been changed to protect the identity of individual households).*

Case 3.1:
Local authority
1945-1964
Bungalow
(SAP 3)

3.10 This small council bungalow, in a mining town in the East Midlands, demonstrates the particularly poor energy efficiency of a dwelling with high wall and roof to floor area ratios, little insulation and an inefficient central heating system.

3.11 Built as part of a council estate in the early 1960s, the semi-detached bungalow comprises a hall, living/dining room, kitchen, bathroom and a single bedroom. It has a floor area of 36 m². The dwelling is constructed of cavity brick, under a pitched clay-tiled roof. The EHCS surveyor found it to be in generally good condition and satisfactory on all fitness matters.

Physical standards

Heating facilities

3.12 Both space heating and hot water are provided from a back boiler to the open solid fuel fire in the living room, feeding radiators in the hall, bedroom, and kitchen. The fire is the only heating available in the living room, and there is no heating provision in the bathroom. The only controls present are manual valves on the radiators.

Thermal insulation

3.13 The only thermal insulation is 100mm of mineral wool between joists in the loft. The hot water cylinder is unlagged, and although the windows were recently replaced with PVC-U units, they are single-glazed.

Energy efficiency

3.14 The relative inefficiency of the heating system is partially offset by the low cost of solid fuel, resulting in an only slightly higher than average heating price index of 117. However, the form of the bungalow, and the lack of insulation combine to give a much higher than average heat loss index of 172. This very high heat loss together with the higher than average heating price yields a very poor SAP rating - of just **3.** This figure is low both for local authority bungalows of the period and for the type of household. (Tables 3.2 & A3.1)

Household characteristics

3.15 The tenants, an ex-colliery storeman and his wife, have occupied the bungalow since new, and are now pensioners approaching their 70th birthdays. Their annual net income from state and other pensions, of which 16% goes on rent, is slightly above average for pensioner couples in council housing, but falls in the second lowest quintile for household incomes generally.

Energy consumption

3.16 The couple tend to keep the fire lit all day and regulate their heating by turning the radiators on and off. They cook using mains gas. Their total annual fuel consumption is approximately 20,660 kilowatt hours (kWh) and the equivalent fuel cost of £600 is much higher than the average expenditure of pensioner couples in council housing (Tables 3.2 & A3.1). However, as an ex-colliery worker, the tenant receives free smokeless fuel, giving a relatively low actual fuel spending of £420 (6% of net income).

Thermal conditions

3.17 The couple are fairly satisfied with their heating system. On the afternoon of interview, in late March 1992, the house had been heated all-day as usual. The recorded temperatures were 18.5°C in the living room and 18.2°C in the hall, compared to an outside temperature of 8.6°C. This was rated as being "comfortably warm" and the "same as usual".

Energy action

3.18 According to the EHCS postal survey, the house is not subject to or proposed for any kind of action. There is however considerable scope for further energy measures such as hot water cylinder insulation, cavity wall insulation, draught proofing and double glazing. A full package of insulation measures, costing some £3,500, would increase the SAP rating to around 33.

Case 3.2:
Owner occupied
1850-1899
Converted flat
(SAP 27)

3.19 The second case study, an owner occupied flat in a northern London borough, illustrates a better than average heating price more than offset by the high heat loss associated with the poor insulation standards of Victorian housing.

3.20 The ground floor flat, converted from a pre-1900 semi-detached house, is L-shaped and comprises a hall, living room, kitchen/diner, bathroom and one bedroom, giving an overall floor area of 43m². The flat has 9" solid brick walls on three sides, large single-glazed timber windows and suspended floors. The EHCS surveyor found the house to be satisfactory in condition, apart from some minor disrepair.

Physical standards

Heating facilities

Thermal insulation

Energy efficiency

3.21 Heating and hot water are provided from a mains gas central heating system with radiators in all rooms. The system is controlled by a timer and manual valves on the radiators. The only energy measure present in the flat is some draught stripping in the living room. The hot water cylinder is unlagged, the windows single glazed and the solid walls uninsulated. There is also an open chimney in the lounge, adding to the ventilation heat loss.

3.22 The efficiency of central heating and the relatively low cost of gas combine to give a lower than average heating price index of 88. However, the overall heat loss index of 137 is significantly higher than average. The dominance of this high heat loss compared to the reasonably good heating price leaves the dwelling with a lower than average SAP rating of 27. This is relatively low both with respect to converted flats of this period and the type of household. (Tables 3.2 & A3.1)

Household characteristics

3.23 The owner occupiers, a dentist and nurse in their mid-twenties, have only recently moved into the property. Their joint income is high for couples without children in owner occupation, falling well within the highest 20% of all household incomes.

Energy consumption

3.24 The couple generally use morning and evening heating during the week and all day heating at weekends. They cook with electricity. The overall energy consumption of the flat is 26,100 kWh per year, but the annual fuel bill of £650 amounts to under 2% of the total household income.

Thermal conditions

3.25 The interview, in early March 1992, was undertaken during the second heating period of the day. The living room temperature was 20.7°C and that in the hall 18.3°C. The occupants found the conditions to be 'comfortable' but 'warmer than usual'. They were fairly satisfied with their heating system, but regarded the living room as draughty around the windows and floorboards.

Energy action

3.26 The potential for energy action in this dwelling includes lagging the hot water tank, double glazing, further draught proofing measures, dry-lining of the external walls, and better controls on the central heating system. A comprehensive package of measures could double the current SAP rating, for a cost of around £3,500.

Case 3.3:
Owner occupied 1965-1980 Detached house **(SAP 46)**

3.27 This owner occupied house, in the suburbs of an urban area in the Yorkshire and Humberside region, illustrates the relatively low heating price associated with full gas-fired central heating combined with a better than average heat loss.

3.28 The four bedroom detached house, privately built in 1967, has a total floor area of 107 m². It has a concrete tiled pitched roof, cavity walls, with tile cladding to the front elevation and is characterised by large timber framed picture windows, fairly typical of the period.

Physical standards

Heating facilities

Thermal insulation

3.29 The house has a full gas-fired central heating system with radiators in all rooms, controlled by a room thermostat, timer and manual valves. There is also a mains gas fire in the living room and a portable oil-filled radiator in one of the bedrooms. The house has a number of recently installed thermal insulation measures, including cavity wall fill, 100mm of mineral wool in the loft, some PVC-U double glazed replacement windows and secondary glazing to most other windows, draught stripping, and lagging to the hot water tank.

Energy efficiency

3.30 The lower than average heating price index of 89 reflects the relatively efficient and cheap to run heating system. The high level of insulation is offset, in part, by the high window to wall ratio and generally high heat loss of the detached form to give a better than average, but not exceptionally good, heat loss index of 83. These relatively low values of heat loss and heating price combine to give a reasonably good SAP rating of 46. This figure is above average for the type of household, but is fairly typical of owner occupied detached houses of this period. (Tables 3.2 & A3.1)

Household characteristics

3.31 The owner occupiers, a self-employed cabinet maker and his wife in their late fifties, have lived in the house since it was built, although they hope to move within the next five years to a smaller dwelling. The household income is around the national average, but low for non-pensioner couples in owner occupation.

Energy consumption

3.32 The central heating is generally used all day and supplemented occasionally with the gas fire. Cooking is done with mains gas and a microwave oven. The annual energy consumption of the house is 33,450 kWh and the resulting fuel bill of £850, amounts to some 8% of the total household income.

Thermal conditions

3.33 When the householders were interviewed after lunch, in late April 1992, the house had been heated in the early morning and again from 1 o'clock. The temperatures recorded were 20.1°C in the main living room and 18.9°C in the hall, compared to an outside air temperature of 14.3°C. This was considered to be the 'same as usual' and 'comfortable' overall. The central heating was rated as fairly satisfactory.

Energy action

3.34 The central heating system, cavity wall and loft insulation, double glazing and draught stripping were all installed by the owners within the last 5 years, in order to make the house warmer. Other than major alterations to reduce the window ratio, the dwelling offers little scope for further insulation measures. However, the installation of a condensing boiler and temperature zoning controls could increase the SAP rating to over 60.

Case 3.4:
Owner occupied
1965-1980
Low rise flat
(SAP 55)

3.35 The final case study in Part I is an owner occupied purpose built flat in a coastal resort in the South West region. It illustrates the combination of electric heating, and its relatively high heating price, with a better than average heat loss to give a good overall SAP rating.

3.36 The large ground floor corner flat, privately built between 1965 and 1980, is L-shaped in plan and exposed on three sides. It comprises a hall, living room, kitchen, bathroom and two bedrooms, giving a total floor area of 91 m². The external fabric is mainly cavity brickwork and the flat has solid floors, whilst the block has a flat roof with asphalt covering.

Physical standards

Heating facilities

Thermal insulation

3.37 The flat has electric storage heaters in the living room and kitchen, and fixed electric heaters in the living room, bedrooms and bathroom. The storage heaters have overnight charge control and a thermostat. Hot water is provided from an off-peak immersion heater in a jacket insulated tank. Other insulation consists of sealed unit PVC-U double glazed windows, but it is not known whether the walls have cavity fill and assumed not.

Energy efficiency

3.38 The relatively high heating price index of 110 reflects the use of electric heating, although this is mitigated somewhat by using an off-peak tariff. However, the heat loss index of the flat is significantly lower than average, resulting in a good overall SAP rating of 55. This is higher than average for single person households, but not untypical of low-rise purpose built flats of this period. (Tables 3.2 & A3.1)

Household characteristics

3.39 The owner-occupier, who owns a small garage repairs business, has lived in the flat for the past three years. His annual net income is above average for single non-pensioner owner occupiers, falling at the top end of the middle income quintile for all households.

Energy consumption

3.40 The heating tends to be used daily in the living room but not at regular periods, and rarely or never in the bedrooms. Cooking is by electricity, making this an all electric flat. The annual electricity consumption of the flat is 7,537 kWh per year, of which nearly 57% is off-peak. The resulting fuel bill is £417, which amounts to just over 3% of the total household income.

Thermal conditions

3.41 At the time of the interview, in early March 1992, the living room had been heated for about 1 hour. The temperature here was found to be 20.4°C, whilst that of the hall was 20.6°C. These conditions were considered to be 'warmer than usual' and 'comfortably warm'. The owner is very satisfied with his heating arrangements.

Energy action

3.42 There is little scope for further energy action in this dwelling, although conversion to a gas-fired central heating system would reduce the heating price index, thus producing a higher SAP rating. If the cavity walls are not already insulated, then this could be done for around £450, improving the SAP rating to over 70, and paying for itself in 3 years.

Comparison of case studies

3.43 To set these case studies in the context of the national picture described in the following chapters, the energy efficiency and other key characteristics of each case has been compared with the corresponding average figure for the total population and also for the same type of household in the same tenure. The results are given in Table 3.2 and at Annex A in Table A3.1. The mean figures for England are shown in brackets.

Table 3.2   Comparison of case study dwellings with mean for all households of same type, size and tenure

Case study figures/(mean for household type & size in tenure)

	Case 3.1 LA-2 pens	Case 3.2 OO-2p Hhld	Case 3.3 OO-2p Hhld	Case 3.4 OO-1p Hhld	All hholds
Physical standards					
Dwelling size m²	36 (60)	43 (86)	107 (86)	91 (72)	**(83)**
Energy SAP rating	3 (34)	27 (37)	46 (37)	55 (32)	**(35)**
Heating price index	117 (104)	88 (94)	89 (94)	110 (107)	**(100)**
Heat loss index	172 (99)	137 (99)	83 (99)	56 (101)	**(100)**
Energy consumption					
Total consumption MWh	20.7 (15.9)	26.1 (24.8)	33.5 (24.8)	7.54 (18.2)	**(24.0)**
Total expenditure £	600 (488)	649 (661)	850 (661)	417 (517)	**(661)**
Thermal conditions					
Outside temp °C	8.6 (11.3)	- (10.8)	14.3 (10.8)	14.6 (11.1)	**(11.1)**
Living room temp °C	18.5 (19.9)	20.7 (19.5)	20.1 (19.5)	20.4 (18.9)	**(19.5)**
Hall/stairs temp °C	18.2 (18.3)	18.3 (18.4)	18.9 (18.4)	20.6 (17.7)	**(18.3)**
Energy Action					
Target SAP rating	33	53	64	73	-
Improvement cost £	3,430	3,550	2,790	470	-
Simple payback yrs	13	21	14	3	-

Chapter 4

Heating facilities

Preamble

4.1 *This chapter looks at the main type and extent of space heating available in dwellings, the distribution within the stock with particular reference to tenure, dwelling type, location and housing conditions, and the overall adequacy of the facilities. After a summary of trends in space heating since 1986, the chapter concludes with a description of heating controls and provisions for water heating.*

4.2 *Data on types of heating collected both in the Physical Survey and during the Interview Survey have been combined to give a picture of the types of heating comprising the principal heat source. This is generally the primary source in the main living room and, consequently, the availability of electric storage heaters may be underestimated, where these provide a supplementary source.*

Space heating

Type of provision

Mains gas

4.3 Table 4.1 confirms the increasing dominance of central heating and of mains gas as the fuel for both central heating and other fixed heating. Over four out of five dwellings have central heating and four fifths of these systems are gas fired. One specific type of system predominates; a gas-fired dedicated (free-standing or wall hung) boiler heating water to radiators is found in nearly half the housing stock. Individual gas appliances are the main facility in nearly four-fifths of dwellings without central heating. In total, 79% of all dwellings are heated by mains gas.

Table 4.1   Main type of space heating provision, 1986 and 1991

% of dwellings

Type	Fuel	System/appliance	1986	1991
Central Heating	**Mains gas**	· Dedicated boiler & radiators	37.6	48.8
		· Back boiler & radiators	13.6	14.6
		· Ducted air	3.2	3.5
		· Convector heaters	0.3	0.3
	Total mains gas		**54.7**	**67.2**
	Solid fuel	· Dedicated boiler & radiators	1.6	0.7
		· Back boiler & radiators	5.9	3.9
	Total solid fuel		**7.5**	**4.6**
	Electricity	· Off-peak storage heaters	3.3	6.8
		· Other (eg underfloor/ceiling)	2.1	0.9
	Total electricity		**5.4**	**7.7**
	Fuel oil	· All oil systems	**3.6**	**3.3**
	Other systems	· Tanked gas/communal etc[1]	**0.7**	**1.3**
Total central heating			**71.9**	**84.1**
Other Fixed Heating	**Mains gas**	· All gas appliances	**18.6**	**11.6**
	Solid fuel	· Open fires	4.6	1.9
		· Enclosed stove/range	0.7	0.4
	Total solid fuel		**5.3**	**2.3**
	Electricity	· All electric appliances	**3.6**	**0.8**
Total fixed heating			**27.5**	**14.7**
Portable Only		· All portable appliances	**0.6**	**1.2**
Total occupied dwellings (000s)			**17,814**	**18,940**

[1] Some communal systems are included under the fuel type (see para. 4.15)

Other fuel types 4.4 With an increase in off-peak storage heaters since 1986 and a continued decline in solid fuel as the main form of heating, electricity has overtaken solid fuel as the second most common fuel for space heating. However, it accounts for under a tenth of dwellings, 4 out of 5 of these having night storage heaters. Some 7% of all dwellings are heated by solid fuel, of which two thirds are centrally heated mainly from a back boiler to an open fire or stove. Solid fuel remains the second most common fuel for other main heating, 2% of all dwellings having open fires as their principal form of heating. Over 200 thousand or 1.2% of dwellings have no fixed heating.

Extent of heating 4.5 Four out of five dwellings with central heating have 'full house' installations, having radiators, warm air vents or storage heaters etc. in 70% or more of all rooms. A further 15% of systems provide 'half house' central heating, covering between 30 and 70% of rooms. The remaining 5% cover typically only one or two rooms. (Table A4.1)

Central heating 4.6 The extent of central heating varies considerably with the type of system. For gas fired central heating, 9 out of 10 dwellings with dedicated boilers have full house installations and those with back boilers have only slightly less. However, under three-fifths of gas-fired ducted air systems and programmable convectors cover the whole dwelling. For other fuels, some 86% of dwellings with oil-fired central heating have full house heating, compared with about 66% of those with solid fuel fired systems. The extent of heating in electrically centrally heated dwellings is substantially less, with under a third having full central heating.

Other heating 4.7 Where dwellings lack central heating, the extent of fixed heating (of all types) also varies with the main fuel used, but is generally far less extensive than in centrally heated dwellings. Where mains gas or electricity is the principal fuel for heating, just under half of dwellings have fixed appliances in less than 30% of rooms. However, in dwellings relying on solid fuel open fires or stoves, nearly 4 out of 5 have fixed heating in, typically, only one or two rooms.

Figure 4.1   Extent of central heating by heating system

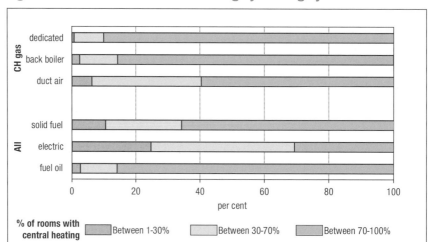

Variation within housing stock 4.8 The type of system and fuel used varies substantially between tenures, reflecting differences in the original provision as well as in the extent of subsequent improvements. Figure 4.2 shows the form and type of heating in the four main tenures. Only some 1 in 10 owner occupied dwellings are still without central heating. Council housing has twice this proportion,

Tenure

whilst the private rented sector has nearly four times as many - 40% of dwellings having no central heating. Moreover, in comparison with only 0.5% of owner occupied dwellings, nearly 2% of council owned properties and over 6% of private rented dwellings have no fixed heating facility whatsoever. (Table A4.2a)

Private sector 4.9 In the private sectors, three-quarters of owner occupied housing has gas-fired central heating, nearly three-fifths of all dwellings having a gas-fired dedicated boiler heating radiators. This sector also has a high incidence of oil-fired central heating, albeit in a little over 5% of the stock. Oil fired systems are as common in the private rented sector, but only just over a third of this stock has gas central heating. Solid fuel is used in nearly a fifth of private rented dwellings, the majority of these lacking central heating. Some 13% of this sector is heated by electricity, mainly with storage heaters, but with over 2% of dwellings relying on individual fixed on-peak appliances - in addition to the 6% reliant on portable heaters alone. (Table A4.2b)

Social rented sector 4.10 Electric central heating is most frequently found in the housing association stock (16%), mainly in the form of electric storage heaters, and this sector also has the highest incidence of 'other' central heating, including communal systems. Council housing makes the most use of gas fired back-boiler and ducted air central heating systems (7%), but also has above average proportions of electric underfloor/ceiling heating (2%) and solid fuel back boiler systems (5%). A further 3% of council dwellings are also heated by open fires and stoves but lack central heating.

Figure 4.2   Type of central and other heating by tenure *(Non-central heating exploded)*

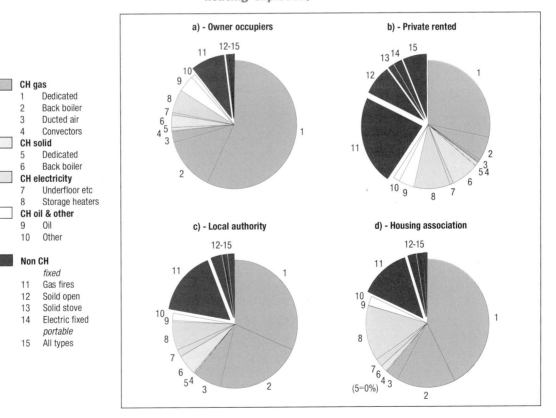

Extent of central heating by sector 4.11 The proportion of private rented and housing association dwellings with central heating having full systems (65%) is slightly less than the local authority stock (71%). Both are considerably less than the owner occupied sector, where 85% of centrally heated properties have full installations. (Table A4.2c)

Figure 4.3   Extent of central heating by tenure

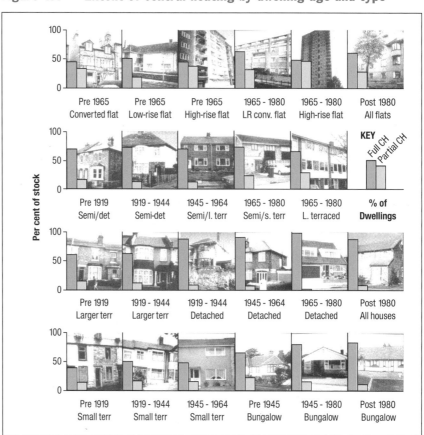

Variation in central heating by dwelling type, age & tenure

4.12   The type of heating is strongly related to the age and, particularly, the type of dwelling. Older and smaller dwellings are less likely to have central heating than larger more modern ones, post 1964 detached houses having the highest proportions. Only around 60% of pre 1965 small terraced houses have central heating compared with around 95% of all post 1964 houses and flats. (Figure 4.4)

Central heating   4.13   The distribution of central heating in different types of dwellings varies with tenure. For owner occupied dwellings it is similar to the total stock, but in the local authority sector, there is a marked difference between pre

Figure 4.4   Extent of central heating by dwelling age and type

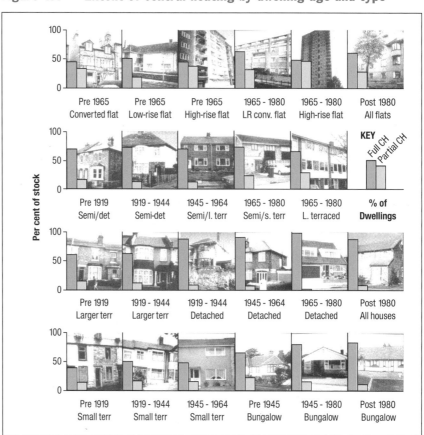

and post 1965 dwellings of all types. Dwelling types built before 1965 tend to have 2 out of 3 dwellings or less with central heating, while generally for those built after this date 9 out of 10 dwellings or more have central heating.

Extent of central heating

4.14 With regard to the extent of central heating, most types of houses have between 75 and 85% of centrally heated dwellings with full central heating. However, centrally heated flats are much less likely to have full systems, most types of flat having between 55 and 65% with full central heating. For the owner occupied stock the distribution is similar to that for the total stock, a greater divergence occurring in the local authority sector.

Variation in type of heating

Communal and electric heating

4.15 The main heating type and fuel also varies widely with dwelling type and age as well as with tenure. The survey estimates that some 550 thousand or nearly 3% of all dwellings have communal or centrally metered heating schemes[1]. Some 55% of these are local authority owned, the remainder being in the housing association and private sector. Nine out of ten are flats, a fifth of all local authority flats having such heating arrangements, compared with a tenth of those in other sectors and well under 1% of houses. As expected, flats also have the highest proportion of electric, mainly night storage, heating systems. Nearly a third of post 1965 flats which are owner occupied and two-fifths of those privately rented have electric central heating. Similarly, in council housing, nearly 30% of pre 1965 high rise flats and 40% of those built between 1965 and 1980 have this type of heating, compared with under 8% of the national stock.

Solid fuel

4.16 Whilst by 1991 the reliance on solid fuel for heating had fallen to less than 7% of all dwellings, it remains common in particular parts of the stock. In the local authority sector, solid fuel - burnt mainly in open fires and stoves - is the main fuel for over 1 in 7 pre 1980 bungalows and over 1 in 5 early post-war semi-detached houses - the third most common type of council dwelling. In the private rented stock, a third of pre 1980 bungalows and nearly half of all pre 1919 detached and semi-detached houses are still heated with solid fuel - most of the latter lacking central heating. (Figure 4.5)

Figure 4.5 **Dwelling types with high proportions of solid fuel heating, electric non-central heating or lacking any fixed heating**

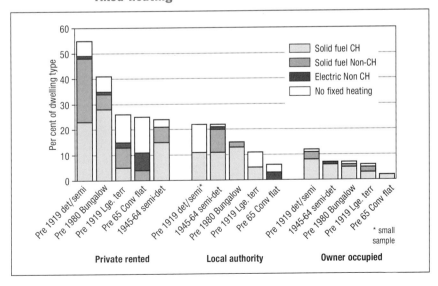

1 *Due to the small sample of addresses actually recorded with communal heating and the large amount of missing data, these particular estimates need to be treated with caution.*

No fixed heating

4.17 Three housing types stand out as having a significant number of dwellings lacking any form of fixed heating. These are pre 1965 converted and purpose built flats and pre 1919 larger terraced houses. In council housing, some 1 in 20 pre 1965 purpose built flats and, in the private rented sector, over 1 in 10 pre 1919 larger terraced houses and 1 in 7 of all pre 1965 converted flats - the most common type in the sector - have, at best, only portable heaters. (Figure 4.5)

Regional variation

Central heating

4.18 The frequency of central heating varies considerably between regions. In the colder Northern and Eastern regions less than 1 in 10 of all dwellings lack central heating, whereas Devon and Cornwall, the West Midlands metropolitan area and Merseyside have more than 1 in 4 dwellings and West Yorkshire over 1 in 3 dwellings without central heating. The regional distribution of types of central heating indicates a greater use of natural gas in the eastern areas of England than in those of the west. The most frequent use of gas systems, in the Tyne and Wear metropolitan area (82%), is approaching twice that of the lowest use - Devon and Cornwall with 44%. (Figure 4.6)

Other main heating

4.19 For dwellings relying on individual appliances for heating, mains gas was the predominant fuel in all regions, apart from the South West where it accounted for less than half of the fuels used. Elsewhere, the distribution in the use of gas tends to follow the distribution of dwellings without central heating, with no discernible regional pattern emerging. While most regions

Figure 4.6   Central heating fuel by administrative and metropolitan area

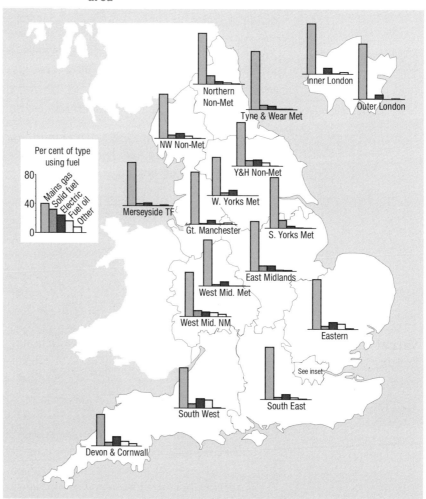

have fewer than 1% of dwellings reliant solely on portable heaters, Outer and Inner London have around 3%, and Devon and Cornwall nearly 5% of dwellings without any fixed heating.

Variation by locality

Central heating

4.20   There is also variation in heating facilities between dwellings in different types of locality. In city centres and other urban areas, just over a fifth of owner occupied, local authority and housing association dwellings are without central heating. For the social rented sectors, the situation is similar in suburban and rural areas, but here well under 1 in 10 owner occupied dwellings lack central heating. More than half of private rented dwellings in urban areas - where the bulk of the stock is located - are without central heating, around a fifth of these lacking any form of fixed heating. (Figure 4.7 & Table A4.3)

Main fuel type

4.21   In rural areas, solid fuel is still the main heating fuel for many dwellings, particularly in the rented sectors. Compared with under 12% of owner occupied properties, over 30% of rural council dwellings have solid fuel as their main heating provision. A third of all private rented dwellings are located in rural areas, and only a fifth of these are heated by mains gas - nearly half are heated by solid fuel, in 9 out of 10 cases burnt in open fires and stoves. (Figure 4.7)

Figure 4.7   Types of central heating *(right of axis)* and non-central heating *(left of axis)* by tenure and dwelling location

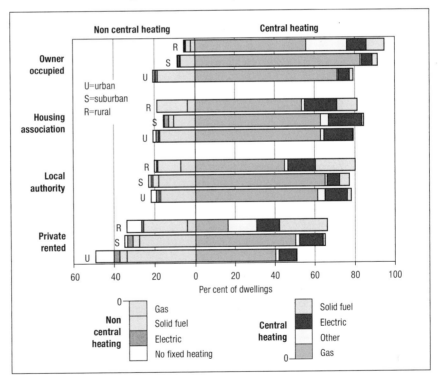

Variation with housing conditions

4.22   There is also a clear relationship between heating provision and the condition of the property in terms of both fitness and repair. Generally, dwellings in poor repair are much less likely to have central heating than those in good repair, and this pattern holds true for most sectors. For example, the proportion of all dwellings with repair costs over £50 per sq m. which have central heating (48%) is around half the proportion (90%) of those with repair costs less than £5 per sq m. In the private rented sector there is greater divergence, nearly 80% of dwellings in good condition having central heating, compared with less than 30% of those in poor repair. (Figure 4.8)

4.23 Over the whole stock, the proportion of fit dwellings with central heating (86%) is also significantly greater than the proportion of unfit dwellings (57%) and an analysis of the best 30% and worst 10% of dwellings, considering both fitness and disrepair, shows a similar result. Over a quarter more dwellings in the best stock have central heating than do the worst stock. The difference is slightly greater in the social rented sectors and considerably greater in the private rented stock, where the incidence of central heating in the best stock (82%) is well over twice that in the worst (37%).

Figure 4.8   Central heating by cost/sq m to make good by tenure

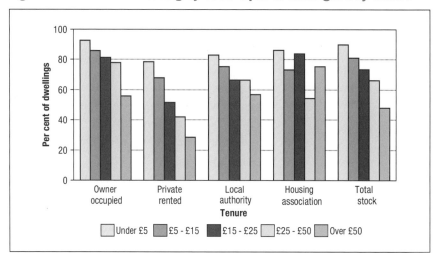

Inadequate provision for heating

4.24 In the following analysis, the few dwellings judged as "unfit" on the grounds of "adequate provision for heating" (about 1%) are combined with those considered "defective" on this requirement but not unfit (under 3%) and together termed 'defective'[2]. There are very few centrally heated dwellings that are defective under this narrow definition (under 1%). However, for dwellings without central heating, some 14% of those with individual gas fires and some 20% of those relying on solid fuel, electric or portable heaters are judged defective. (Figure 4.9)

Figure 4.9   Overall fitness assessment (unfit or defective only) by type of heating by tenure

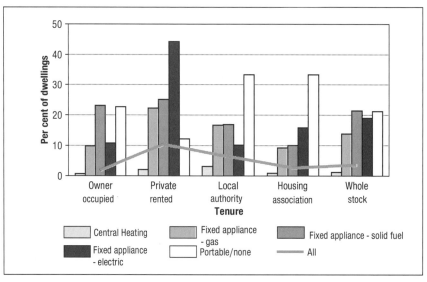

2   *The EHCS surveyors were asked to record the provision for heating in the dwelling as "unfit", "defective", "just acceptable" or "satisfactory". Few provisions were recorded as "unfit"; under the present fitness standard a dedicated electrical socket or gas point may be deemed to satisfy the standard. "Defective" was coded if there were "major problems" which were not sufficient to make the dwelling unfit on this particular matter.*

4.25 Amongst dwellings with central heating, the local authority stock has a higher proportion of dwellings defective on their provision for heating (3%) than any other sector. Around a third of all socially rented dwellings with no fixed heating provision are judged defective, this being higher than the average (21%) for all such dwellings. Overall, the local authority stock has a higher proportion of dwellings defective than the housing association or owner occupied stocks. However, the private rented stock is worse than all other sectors.

Trends in space heating 1986-1991

Central heating

4.26 Changes in the proportion of different heating systems in each tenure occur due to new building, demolition and transfers between sectors as well as the improvement of the remaining housing stocks. Overall, the proportion of dwellings with central heating grew from 72% in 1986 to 84% in 1991. Most of the new installations are gas fired, such facilities having increased disproportionately from 54% to 67%. Although this overall pattern is common, the increase in gas systems has been greatest in council housing.

4.27 The use of electric central heating, mainly storage heaters with their low capital cost, has increased in all sectors - it has more than doubled in the private rented sector and increased by a third in the owner occupied and housing association stocks. Although with no overall change in the proportion of electric central heating, the local authority stock has also experienced a growth in storage heaters, this increase being off-set by a decline in other, less efficient under-floor or ceiling systems. Solid fuel and oil fired central heating also continue to decline, although in the private rented sector solid fuel still accounts for nearly 8% of all central heating. (Figure 4.10)

Other heating

4.28 As central heating has increased, so other heating has declined (from 28% to 15%). This decrease has been greatest in the local authority and housing association stocks, although significant in all sectors. Falls in the reliance on individual solid fuel, open fires and stoves have been particularly marked

Figure 4.10   Trends in heating facilities by tenure, 1986 to 1991

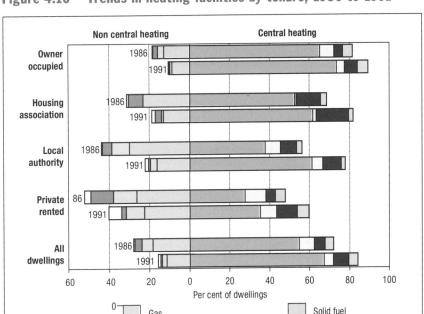

- except in the private rented stock where it still accounts for nearly a tenth of all main heating. (Figure 4.10)

Heating controls

Types of Control

4.29   In the Interview Survey, households were asked about the forms of controls they had over their central and other heating systems. The results have been used to estimate the types of heating controls available in the dwelling stock[3]. Overall, the most common controls recorded were a central time switch/programmer (78%), a manual override on the timer/programmer and manual controls on the radiators or vents (both 69%) and a wall thermostat (59%). (Table A4.4)

Relationship to type of heating

4.30   The possession of different controls varies with the type of central heating. Central time switches/programmers are most commonly found in water-borne systems with gas boilers (92%), propane or butane boilers (97%), oil fired boilers (88%) and gas fired ducted air systems (70%). Wall thermostats are also most frequently found in these systems, although with percentages ranging from 62 to 92% they are not quite as common as programmers. Although far less common than manual controls, thermostatic radiator valves are found in over a third of systems with a solid fuel or oil fired dedicated boiler and in 28% of those with a dedicated gas-fired boiler. (Table A4.5)

Combination of controls

4.31   Some 22% of all dwellings with a central heating system have manual controls on radiators or vents, a wall thermostat, a programmer and a programmer override. Not surprisingly, this combination is most common in water borne systems fired by mains gas, tanked gas or fuel oil. Some 21% of gas ducted air systems have manually controlled vents, a wall thermostat, a programmer and programmer override, although a further 23% have the latter three items without the vent control. Manual controls on radiators is the only control reported by 45% of households in dwellings with a solid fuel back boiler. (Table A4.6)

Level of control

4.32   From the range of heating controls recorded in the Survey, four categories have been defined to describe the level of control householders have over the time of heating, the room temperatures, or both or neither of these. Almost 70% of dwellings have both forms of control on the system, but 12% have neither time nor temperature controls. (Figure 4.11)

4.33   Gas fired systems with dedicated boiler, back boilers or ducted air-systems have a high level of control, 83%, 72% and 73% respectively having both

Figure 4.11   Level of control for central heating systems

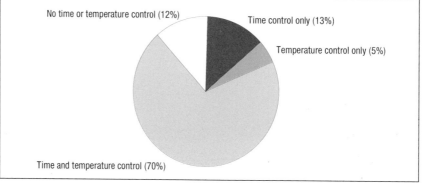

No time or temperature control (12%)

Time control only (13%)

Temperature control only (5%)

Time and temperature control (70%)

3   *As not all households may be familiar with the different types of controls - programmers, thermostats etc - these estimates need to be treated with some caution*

time and temperature controls. Oil fired systems have a similarly high level, with 87% with both forms of control. Less than 4% of any of these systems have neither time nor temperature controls.

4.34   With solid fuel central heating there is a significant difference between dedicated and back-boiler systems. Some 42% of those with dedicated boilers have both time and temperature controls, although just over a quarter have neither. However, only a tenth with back boilers have both forms of control and two-thirds have neither. Nearly a fifth of dwellings with electric underfloor or ceiling heating report both time and temperature controls, but a quarter have neither. Households using storage heaters report even less control, only 1 in 10 reporting both forms and 69% having neither. (Table A4.7)

Water heating

Relationship to space heating

4.35   The final section of this chapter deals with the main provision in the dwelling for heating water. As expected, this depends generally on the type of space heating. Around 9 out of 10 dwellings with a gas, solid fuel, oil and other (including tanked gas) fired central heating system had the facility to use this system to heat water (respectively 96%, 92%, 95% and 85%). Immersion heaters are the main provision in 3 out of 4 dwellings with an electric central heating system.

4.36   Where individual gas fires are the main form of heating, well over two-thirds (69%) have an immersion heater and a further fifth instantaneous heaters as the main provision for water heating. Almost 61% of non-centrally heated dwellings with solid fuel fires and stoves have an electric immersion heater as the main source of hot water, while a further 31% have a solid fuel fired system from a back boiler. The former is the main provision in respectively some 88% and 71% of dwellings heated principally by fixed electric fires or portable heaters. Well under 1% of the stock is without any fixed provision for hot water but this varies with tenure, ranging from 0.2% in the owner occupied to 1.3% in the private rented sector.

Figure 4.12   Type of water heating system by tenure (*on-peak immersion heaters - exploded*)

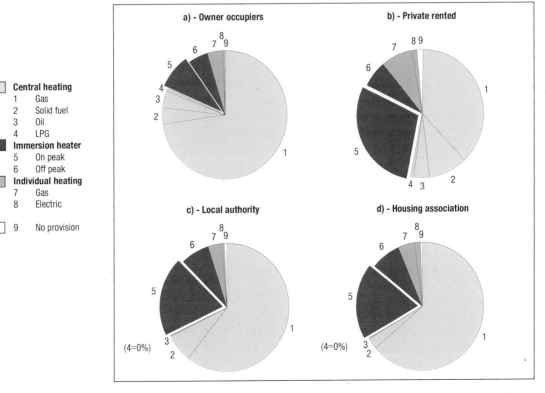

Variation with tenure

Private sector

4.37 In four-fifths of owner occupied dwellings the main provision is the central heating system, and in nearly 9 out of 10 cases this is gas-fired. In contrast, only half of all private rented dwellings are supplied with hot water from a central heating system and, of these, 1 in 3 use fuels other than mains gas. In this sector, the incidence of both immersion and instantaneous water heaters is at least double that in the owner-occupied stock. Some 36% of dwellings rely on electric immersion heaters - over four-fifths using solely on-peak electricity - whilst a further 10% have either gas or electric instantaneous heaters. (Figure 4.12 & Table A4.8)

Social rented sector

4.38 Unlike the two private sectors, the local authority and housing association stocks show similar provisions for hot water. In both sectors. just over two-thirds of dwellings have hot water provided from a central heating system, which is again predominantly gas-fired. The frequency of immersion heaters is also the same, being the primary source of hot water in 27% of dwellings and, in both sectors, just over two-thirds of these use on-peak electricity.

Variation with dwelling type

4.39 Reflecting both tenure and the built form, the main method of water heating varies with both the age and type of dwelling. Central heating, particularly a gas-fired system, is the most common method of water heating in all ages of dwelling. However, the proportion of dwellings with this form of provision increases inversely with dwelling age, from some 71% of pre 1850 dwellings to 92% of those built since 1980. (Table A4.9)

4.40 Some 92% of detached houses of all ages have a central heating system to heat water, compared with only some 61% and 68% of purpose-built and converted flats respectively. A fifth of the latter have electric immersion heaters and almost one third of purpose-built flats have electric immersion heaters as their main provision. As expected, very few flats use solid fuel for water heating, but almost half of all such systems are to be found in semi-detached houses. (Table A4.10)

Geographical variation

Region

4.41 Like facilities for space heating, provision for heating water also shows some variation with region. Dwellings in the Northern region are most likely to have hot water provided by central heating, particularly a gas-fired system (86%, 73% gas) and are least likely to have such facilities in Yorkshire and Humberside (71%, 61% gas) and the South West (72%, 53% gas). With the limited availability of mains gas, dwellings in the South West account for a significant proportion of other fuels used for water heating. Some 15% of dwellings with hot water from a solid fuel central heating system are located in the South West (and 17% in Yorkshire and Humberside); whilst 31% using fuel-oil are located in this region (and 24% in the Eastern region). Electric immersion heaters are also most commonly found in the West Midlands and the South West where they are the main provision in nearly a quarter of the housing stock. (Table A4.11)

Dwelling location

4.42 The proportion of dwellings with a central heating system providing hot water generally increases the more rural the locality. Some 80% of isolated rural dwellings heat their water this way compared to only 62% of those in city centres, Over a fifth of those in city centres use on-peak electric immersion heaters. However, this tendency is reversed if only gas-fired central heating is considered, 23% of isolated rural dwellings having such a hot water system. Some 57% of these rural dwellings heat their water by central heating systems fired by solid fuel, fuel oil or tanked gas - compared with 2% of inner city dwellings. (Table A4.12)

Chapter 5

Thermal insulation

Preamble

5.1 *This third chapter on physical standards analyses the types and extent of thermal insulation, under the headings of wall insulation including forms of construction, double glazing and draught proofing, loft insulation and finally hot water cylinder insulation.*

5.2 *As much thermal insulation is hidden, questions on these elements were asked largely of the occupant. In reporting insulation, many householders, particularly those in modern dwellings, will be specifying insulation included when the building was erected as well as any installed subsequently. However, if installed during construction or by a previous owner, many occupants, particularly tenants, will be unaware of such insulation and this is reflected in the high proportion of 'not knowns' in the insulation data.*

Wall construction and insulation

5.3 The thermal insulation provided by the walls of a dwelling depends on their basic form of construction and any specific insulation installed during construction or subsequently. The information on wall type was collected by the EHCS surveyors in the Physical Survey, while questions on wall insulation - which is generally interstitial - were asked of the householder in a short interview in the Physical Survey and in the subsequent main Interview Survey.

Thermal standards

5.4 In addition, the data from these sources has been combined and used with the age of the property to determine which of the increasingly stringent standards set by the Building Regulations is met by the dwelling. The four standards that have been considered are that below the 1965 Building Regulations, that meeting the 1965-74 standard, the 1975-1981 standard and the requirements of the 1981 amendment to the Building Regulations.

Figure 5.1   **Wall and roof insulation (Building Regulation) standards compared with age of stock**

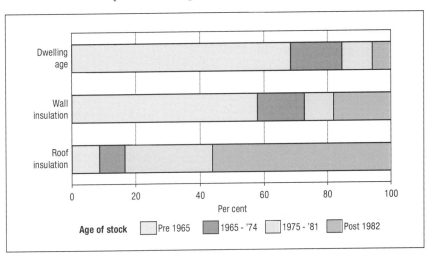

Wall construction   5.5   Most dwellings have cavity walls, this form of construction occurring in over 60% of the stock. Around 31% of dwellings have solid masonry walls (of brick, block or stone), most of these being 9 inches thick. The remaining 6% comprise a wide variety of construction types, such as in-situ and prefabricated concrete and timber frame.

Insulation   5.6   According to householders, around 1 in 5 or some 4 million dwellings have insulated walls. Over 70% of these are reported as having cavity wall insulation and 15% as having either external insulation or internal dry lining, the type of insulation being unspecified in the remaining 15%. Overall, some 3.4 million or over a quarter of all properties with cavity walls have walls that are insulated and similarly around a quarter of non-masonry walls are also insulated. Less than a tenth of dwellings with solid masonry walls have any added insulation.

Overall standard   5.7   Overall some 11 million dwellings or nearly three-fifths of the stock (58%) have walls which are insulated to a standard lower than that required by the 1965 and subsequent Building Regulations. However, since 68% of the stock or nearly 13 million dwellings were built before 1965, this indicates that around two million dwellings of this age have had the insulation of their walls improved. (Figure 5.1)

Figure 5.2   Wall construction and insulation by tenure (insulated exploded)

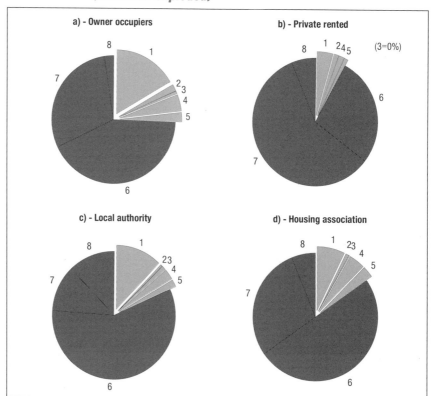

Tenure variation

Wall construction

5.8   Wall construction varies significantly between tenures, reflecting differences in the age and type of stock. More than 70% of local authority dwellings have cavity walls, compared with over 60% of the owner occupied and housing association stock and only a third of private rented dwellings. Conversely, around 60% of the private rented sector and a third of owner occupied and housing association dwellings have solid masonry walls, in comparison with under 13% of the local authority stock. With the greater use of industrialised building in this sector, over 14% of council dwellings have non-masonry solid, mostly insitu and prefabricated concrete walls. Only around 5% of the other sectors have non-traditional forms of construction. (Figure 5.2)

Insulation   5.9   More than a quarter of owner occupiers report the possession of wall insulation. In the rented sectors, 18% of council and 15% of housing association tenants report having such insulation compared to only 8% of those privately renting. In the private rented sector, as many as 83% of dwellings fail the 1965 Building Regulations standard, compared with around 55% of those in other tenures. (Figure 5.2 & Table A5.1)

Dwelling age   5.10   As expected, the proportion of the stock with cavity walls is closely related to the age of the dwelling, increasing progressively from only 13% of dwellings built before 1919 to nearly 90% of the post 1964 stock. Conversely, the frequency of solid masonry walls decreases from 83% of pre 1919 dwellings to less than 5% of those built after the second world war. (Table A5.2)

Wall construction

Insulation   5.11   In line with the increasing number of dwellings with cavity walls, the frequency of wall insulation increases in more recent properties. Only around 9% of pre 1919 dwellings have wall insulation, a half of this being cavity fill. In comparison, wall insulation is found in 36% of the post 1964 stock, two thirds of this being cavity insulation.

Figure 5.3   **Cavity wall and cavity insulation by dwelling age and type**

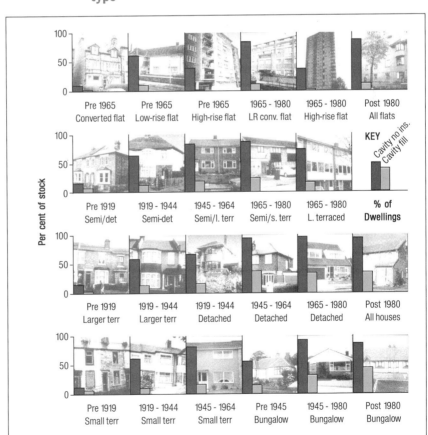

Dwelling type   5.12   Reflecting construction dates, only around a quarter of detached and semi-detached houses have solid masonry walls compared with about half of terraced houses and almost 90% of converted flats. Solid walls are much

Wall construction

less common in purpose built flats; around 75% of low rise have cavity walls and 8% non-masonry walls, whilst as many high rise flats (47%) have non-masonry as cavity brick or block walls, in addition to any structural frame. (Table A5.2)

Insulation

5.13 Detached houses and bungalows have the highest proportion of wall insulation, around 38% being reported as insulated, mainly with cavity fill. Around a fifth of semi-detached houses have insulated walls, again predominantly in cavity walls, whilst only 14% of terraced houses are reported as insulated, a third of these having wall insulation other than cavity fill.

Overall standard

5.14 With its strong association with dwelling age, the type of dwelling is strongly correlated with the standard of insulation. Detached houses and bungalows have very high proportions of dwellings meeting, at least, the 1981 Building Regulations, both having 30% reaching this standard compared with only around 12% for other types. Conversely, only around a third of detached and bungalows fail the 1965 Building Regulation standard compared with more than two thirds of terraced and semi-detached houses and converted flats.

Regional variation

5.15 Cavity wall dwellings are most commonly found in the Northern regions and in the South East, five regions having more than 70% of their stock with cavity walls and three of these having nearly 80% - Tyne and Wear,

Figure 5.4   Wall construction by administrative and metropolitan area

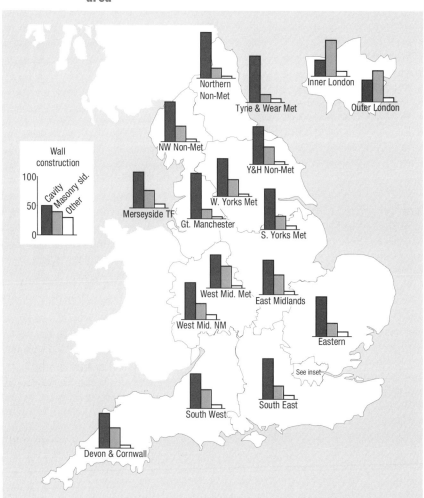

Wall construction	Greater Manchester and the Northern non-metropolitan area. All other regions have more than half the stock with cavity walls, with the exception of Outer London where less than 40% are of this construction and Inner London where only 28% of dwellings have cavity walls. More than a half the dwellings in the London regions have solid walls. (Figure 5.4)
Insulation	5.16 The regions with the highest proportion of wall insulation are generally not those with the most cavity walls. They are the Eastern region, the Midlands and the South West, where more than a quarter of all dwellings were reported to have wall insulation. Outside London, the poorest areas for wall insulation are Merseyside and Tyne and Wear, with only 14% and 16% respectively of dwellings having insulated walls. However, Inner and Outer London have the lowest proportions, only some 8% and 12% of all dwellings having wall insulation of any form.
Double glazing and draught proofing **Extent of provision**	5.17 In the Interview Survey, householders were asked whether any of their windows were double glazed, either with sealed units or with secondary glazing. If they had double glazing, a further question was asked to determine if the whole house was double glazed or, if not, which rooms had double glazing. Other questions were asked to determine whether the dwelling had draught excluders to windows and doors and, if so, the extent of this measure. As dwellings with double glazing are not generally in need of draught excluders, these two measures are discussed together.
Double glazing	5.18 Overall, nearly a quarter of all households say that their dwelling is fully double glazed and a further 30% report some double glazing - under half of the total stock having no double glazing. The extent of double glazing varies with the type fitted. Around 8 million or 40% of dwellings have sealed unit double glazing, roughly equal proportions having full and partial double glazing. Some 2.5 million or 13% have secondary glazing, of which less than 0.5 million have full installations, the majority having this type in only one or two rooms.
Draught excluders	5.19 Over a third of respondents say that they have draught excluders fitted, when questioned on its extent under 6% say that they have full draught exclusion and 30% partial exclusion.
Tenure variation *Double glazing*	5.20 As would be expected, there is a significant difference in the pattern of double glazing between tenures. The local authority, housing association and private rented stocks have similar levels of provision, all three sectors having around a fifth of their stocks with some double glazing. However, in the owner occupied stock, the proportion with some double glazing is well over three times this (73%) and accounts for over 9 million dwellings. (Table A5.3)
	5.21 Over half of owner occupiers have sealed unit double glazing, and of these a half are 'whole house' installations. In the three rented sectors, the local authority and housing association stocks have a higher proportion of dwellings with full sealed units (around 11%) than the private rented sector (7%). However, in the private rented sector, 8% of dwellings have partial secondary glazing - twice that in the social rented sector. (Figure 5.5)

Figure 5.5   Type and extent of double glazing by tenure

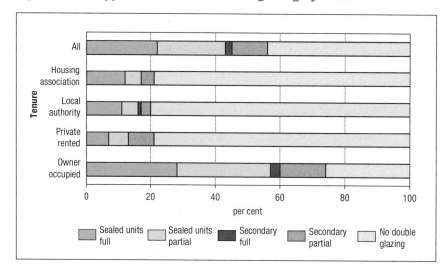

Draught excluders

5.22   There are substantially more dwellings in the two private sectors with fitted draught excluders than in the social rented sectors - around 35% compared with 25%. (Table A5.3)

Dwelling age and type

Double glazing

5.23   Overall, there is some difference in the incidence of double glazing with dwelling age, older properties having about 20% less than modern ones. The variation is greater if the type and extent of double glazing is considered. Only 10% of pre 1919 dwellings have sealed unit double glazing in all main rooms, compared with 20% of those built after 1919 and nearly 30% of the post 1964 stock. However, partial installations of sealed double glazed units can be found in around a fifth of dwellings in any age band.

5.24   Detached houses are most likely to be double glazed, four fifths having some double glazing, compared with 69% of bungalows and nearly 65% of semi-detached houses. Terraced houses and flats have significantly less double glazing, the frequency ranging between 30 and 40%. Full installations of sealed units follow a similar pattern, occurring in around 30% of detached houses and bungalows and over a quarter of semi-detached houses but less than a fifth of terraced houses and flats.

Draught excluders

5.25   Like double glazing, draught excluders are slightly more likely to be found in modern houses than in older ones. Detached houses, bungalows and semi-detached houses again have the highest proportion of installations, all over 35%, whilst terraced dwellings have 30% and flats the lowest proportion - around a quarter of such dwellings having some windows draught proofed.

Regional variation

Double glazing

5.26   There is little pattern in the variation of double glazing between regions. The South East and the Eastern Regions show the highest frequencies, both having over 60% of dwellings with some double glazing. The areas with the least double glazing are Tyne and Wear, where a third of dwellings are reported as having some double glazed windows, and Inner London with less than 30%.

Draught excluders

5.27   The variation between areas in the frequency of draught excluders also shows little pattern; the regions with the highest proportions (all over 40%) including such diverse areas as the Northern and North West non-

Figure 5.6   Double glazing by dwelling age and type

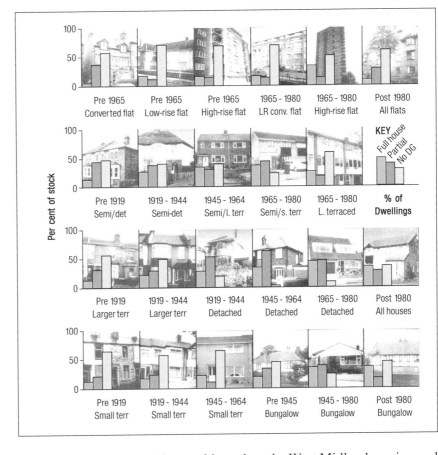

metropolitan areas, the Merseyside region, the West Midlands region and Devon and Cornwall.

Loft insulation

Thermal standards

5.28   In the EHCS Physical Survey, the surveyors were instructed to inspect the loft space of houses wherever access was available and permitted. In these loft inspections, the surveyor recorded whether or not there was insulation and, where present, its type and approximate thickness. In addition, the Interview Survey asked the occupant if their home had any loft or roof insulation. In the following analysis, the reply from the physical survey is taken where possible, but with the response from the interview survey being used wherever data from the physical survey is not available. Lofts in flats were not inspected and, consequently, in the analysis the estimates of the number of accessible lofts, and presence and thickness of insulation, refer to houses only.

5.29   To determine the standard of loft insulation, the surveyor's record of the presence and thickness of loft insulation has been used with the age of the property to determine which of the progressively higher requirements set down by the Building Regulations is achieved by the dwelling. Unless otherwise stated, this separate analysis of Building Regulation standards refers to both houses and flats.

Provision and thickness

5.30   Overall, more than four fifths or some 13.5 million houses have loft insulation. However, nearly 700 thousand or 4% of houses have no accessible loft. As a result, the proportion of houses with accessible lofts that are insulated is greater - around 91%. In addition to the 1.3 million or 9% of houses with no insulation, 35% of those with accessible lofts have insulation less than 100mm, leaving more than half (55%) or 8.2 million dwellings with 100mm or more of insulation. Overall, it is estimated that more than three-quarters of all houses with accessible lofts have insulation meeting, at least, the 1974 amendment to the Building Regulations.[1]

Figure 5.7   Wall and roof insulation (Building Regulation standard) by tenure of dwelling

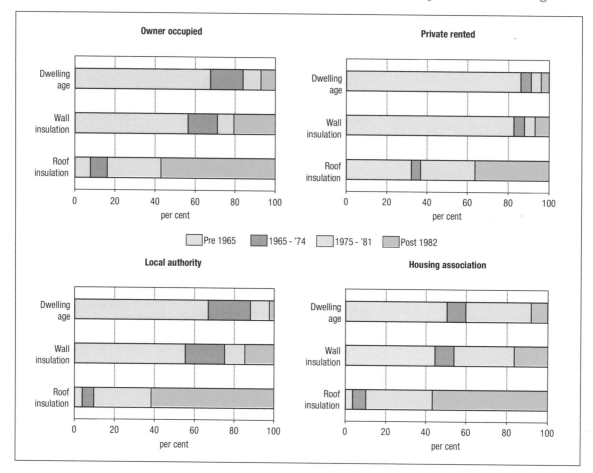

Tenure variation

Provision

5.31   The proportion of houses with accessible lofts and number insulated varies widely between tenures. The local authority and owner occupied sectors have significantly fewer houses with no accessible loft (3 and 4% respectively) than either the housing association sector (9%) or private rented stock (10%). However, in houses with accessible lofts, under 6% of social rented properties and 8% of those owner occupied lack loft insulation, compared with some 30% of privately rented dwellings. Although the owner occupied stock has a small proportion of dwellings lacking insulation, the large size of the sector means that it still accounts for the bulk of all uninsulated dwellings. In all, nearly 900 thousand owner occupied houses with accessible lofts lack insulation, compared with 300 thousand private rented and 150 thousand social rented houses. (see Table A5.4 for all occupied dwelling data)

Thickness

5.32   There are only slight differences between tenures in terms of the thickness of insulation, although the private rented sector stands out in having only 35 % of lofts with insulation of 100 mm or more, compared with 55% of owner occupied and 60% of local authority houses.

1   *Consolidated by the 1976 Building Regulations.*

Figure 5.8   Roof insulation (Building Regulation standard) by dwelling type and age of dwelling

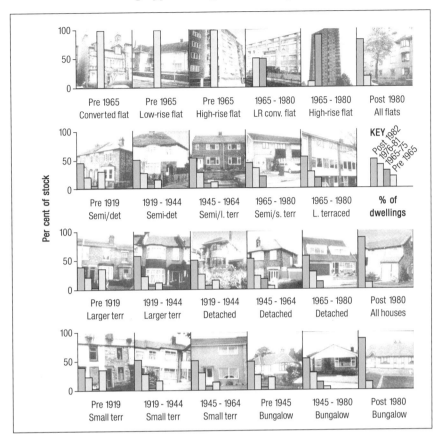

Dwelling age and type

Provision of insulation

5.33   The type of house has little effect on either the presence of a loft or the lack of loft insulation. Nearly two thirds of the 3.4 million flats are not on the top floor, but of the 1.3 million flats that are, 60% were built before 1965 and unless recently upgraded are likely to fall significantly below modern insulation standards. Of the remaining half a million built more recently - many of which will have flat roofs - only 90 thousand built after 1985 are likely to meet the post 1981 Building Regulation standard, having the equivalent of 100mm of roof insulation.

5.34   There is little correlation between the percentage of houses lacking an accessible loft and dwelling age. However, the proportion of accessible lofts lacking insulation increases significantly with the increasing age of the stock, only 2% of those built since 1964 and 9% of those built between the wars having no insulation compared with over 740 thousand or 21% of pre 1919 houses.

Thickness

5.35   Overall, the proportion of houses with 100mm or more of loft insulation is similar for all age bands, suggesting that there has been a considerable amount of topping up of loft insulation. For example, 49% of pre 1919 houses with accessible lofts have 100 mm or more of insulation compared with 55% of interwar houses and those built between 1945 and 1964 and 60% of post 1964 properties.

Regional variation

5.36   Although there is little regional effect on the thickness of insulation, the proportion of houses lacking insulation varies substantially across the country. Inner London, South and West Yorkshire and Devon and Cornwall have the highest proportion of houses with no accessible loft (around 10%).

Inner London also has the highest proportion of lofts lacking insulation - 20% - this being significantly more than in other poor regions such as the North West (14%) and Merseyside (13%). In contrast, some areas such as Tyne and Wear and the Northern non-metropolitan areas, Yorkshire and Humberside, East Midlands and the Eastern region have very high levels of loft insulation with over 93% of accessible lofts being insulated.

Cylinder insulation

5.37   In the Interview Survey, households were asked if their dwelling had an insulated hot water cylinder and if so by what method it was insulated.

Tenure variation

5.38   Some 16 million or around 85% of dwellings have a hot water cylinder and 92% of these (14.7 million) are insulated. Around 10 million (63%) have cylinder jackets, 4.4 million (27%) the more efficient foam coated cylinders and a very small proportion (around 1%) have both. Owner occupied dwellings have the highest proportion of dwellings with cylinders (87%) of which 94% are insulated. By comparison only 71% of private rented properties have hot water cylinders, of which 81% are insulated. (Figure 5.9)

Figure 5.9   Hot water cylinder insulation by tenure

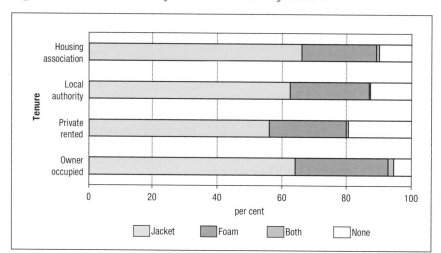

Dwelling age and type

5.39   Dwelling age is the characteristic most closely correlated with cylinder insulation, the proportion of insulated cylinders rising from 83% of pre 1919 dwellings to 92% of those built since 1964. Integral foam insulation is even more closely associated with modern dwellings, the corresponding rise being from 25 to 34%. As with other types of insulation, the properties with the highest proportions of insulated cylinders are detached houses (99%), bungalows (94%) and semi-detached and terraced houses (92%). In comparison, around 87% of purpose built and 63% of converted flats have such insulation.

Regional variation

5.40   There is not much regional variation, but of all regions, Northern region has the lowest proportion of insulated cylinders (82%) and the West Midlands, South West and Eastern regions, the most (93%).

Chapter 6

Energy efficiency

Preamble

6.1   *Chapter 6 looks at the overall energy efficiency of dwellings resulting from the combined effects of the heating systems, forms of construction and thermal insulation, discussed in the previous two chapters. The chapter starts by examining the influence of tenure, building age and built form on the heat loss, heating price and energy (SAP) ratings of the stock and goes on to look at the particular energy characteristics of the least efficient stock. It reports on the variation in energy efficiency between regions and between urban and rural areas and explores the possible reasons behind this variation.*

Tenure, building age and form

6.2   The housing stock in England has an average energy efficiency (SAP) rating of just over 35 and 15% of dwellings with ratings below 20. However, there is significant variation between tenures. The owner occupied sector has the highest average rating (37) and 1 in 10 dwellings of its 12.9 million occupied dwellings rated below 20. The local authority and housing association stocks are not far behind in their mean ratings (34 and 35 respectively) but have a significantly higher proportion of inefficient properties, (with some 18% of 3.9 and 0.6 million respectively below 20). The private rented stock is substantially worse; the average SAP rating is under 22 and over two fifths of its 1.6 million occupied dwellings (43%) fall below a rating of 20. (Table A6.1)

Figure 6.1   Distribution of SAP ratings in four main tenures

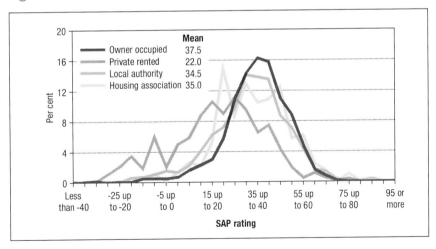

6.3   The physical nature of the sectors are very different - over half of local authority owned properties are flats, compared with under 11% of those owner occupied, and under 4% were built more than 70 years ago, compared with 60% of those privately rented. The extent to which the variation in energy efficiency is merely a product of such differences is explored in Tables 6.1 to 6.3, which show the influence of building age, built form and tenure on the heat loss, heating price and SAP rating (see also Table A6.2). In this analysis, the tenure categories used are owner occupied, private rented and the social rented sector; the relatively few housing association dwellings are grouped with those in local authority ownership.

Heat loss

6.4 For all tenures, the dwelling age and form are the overwhelming factors which determine the heat loss through the building fabric. Many older buildings have been upgraded by the addition of roof and wall insulation, but since 1964, Building Regulations have required progressively higher insulation standards for all new housing. As important as the level of insulation is the proportion of the dwelling envelope exposed to the external weather. In this respect, flats tend to be better than houses, and mid-terrace houses better than semi-detached or detached houses. The importance of both dwelling age and form are clearly shown in Table 6.1. After controlling for these two factors, there is little variation between tenures; although owner occupied dwellings appear to be marginally better than properties in the social rented sectors, which in turn are better than those privately rented.

6.5 Overall, owner occupied flats and mid-terraced houses built since 1980 have, on average, a rate of heat loss which is half that of private rented detached and semi-detached houses built before 1965.

Table 6.1 Relationship between dwelling age, type and tenure and heat loss *(categories listed in order from lowest to highest heat loss)*

Dwelling Age	Dwelling type	Tenure	Mean	Min	Max[1]
Post 1980	mid-terr.	00	66	50	92
Post 1980	all flats	00	67	48	92
Post 1964	all flats	PR	74	46	107
1965-80	mid-terr.	00	79	53	117
1965-80	all flats	00	79	41	138
Post 1980	detached	00	80	54	120
Post 1980	all types	LA/HA	81	34	182
1965-80	all flats	LA/HA	82	33	171
Post 1980	semi-det.	00	82	60	129
1965-80	mid.terr	LA/HA	86	51	155
Pre 1965	pb.flat	LA/HA	91	37	184
Pre 1965	cnv. flat	00	95	43	216
Pre 1965	mid-terr	00	95	51	197
1965-80	semi-det	00	95	57	146
1965-80	detached	00	96	61	152
Pre 1965	pb. flat	00	97	46	217
Below Av. Pre 1965	mid-terr	LA/HA	97	60	191
Above Av. heat loss Pre 1965	pb. flat	PR	100	44	211
Pre 1965	cnv. flat	PR	101	40	208
Pre 1965	cnv. flat	LA/HA	102	33	185
Pre 1965	mid-terr	PR	107	63	210
1850-1964	semi-det	00	108	54	233
Post 1964	all houses	PR	109	72	157
1850-1964	detached	00	109	54	250
Post 1964	semi & det	LA/HA	109	65	170
Pre 1850	detached	00	112	61	195
Pre 1965	semi & det	LA/HA	113	63	236
Pre 1850	semi-det	00	117	57	188
Pre 1965	semi-det	PR	132	68	231
Pre 1965	detached	PR	142	63	235

1 The minimum and maximum values in the EHCS sample represent statistically the range covered, on average, by over 99% of dwellings in the national stock of each type.

Price of heating

6.6 The picture in relation to the price of heating is very different. Tenure appears to be the dominant factor, with a clear separation between dwellings in owner occupation with the best heating systems, those in the social rented sectors with less efficient, more costly heating, and the private rented sector with the worst provision.

6.7 The building age has relatively little influence on the performance of the heating system, since systems are likely to be changed several times during the lifetime of a building. Although built form has no direct impact on the efficiency of the heating, the type of dwelling appears to be significant, particularly among owner occupied properties. Here, it seems that the 'status' of the dwelling type, which is associated with the income of the occupants, influences the heating efficiency, detached houses being superior to semi-detached, which in turn are superior to terraced houses and finally to flats.

6.8 The pattern is not so obvious amongst socially or privately rented properties, although flats generally appear to have high heating prices. However, flats tend to have a lower heat loss and therefore can afford to

Table 6.2   Relationship between dwelling age, type and tenure and heating price *(categories listed in order from lowest to highest heating price)*

Tenure	Dwelling type	Age	Heating Price Index		
			Mean	Min	Max[1]
OO	detached	1965-80	86	69	151
OO	detached	Post 1980	87	75	148
OO	detached	1850-1964	90	69	224
OO	semi-det	1850-1964	93	67	257
OO	semi-det	1965-80	93	70	255
OO	cnv. flat	Pre 1965	93	78	287
LA/HA	mid-terr	1965-80	95	75	170
OO	mid-terr	Post 1980	96	85	179
OO	semi-det	Post 1980	96	82	257
OO	mid-terr	1965-80	96	77	291
LA/HA	semi-det	1965-80	97	73	257
OO	detached	Pre 1850	98	66	257
PR	houses *Av. price*	Post 1964	99	73	144
LA/HA	all types	Post 1980	100	78	193
OO	semi-det	Pre 1850	101	67	228
OO	all flats	1965-80	102	79	195
OO	mid-terr	Pre 1965	103	74	258
LA/HA	semi-det	Pre 1965	104	72	297
LA/HA	all flats	1965-80	107	74	256
LA/HA	mid-terr	Pre 1965	110	74	262
OO	pb. flat	Pre 1965	110	75	295
LA/HA	pb. flat	Pre 1965	114	78	293
LA/HA	cnv. flat	Pre 1965	116	80	287
PR	detached	Pre 1965	118	72	257
PR	mid-terr	Pre 1965	119	76	257
PR	pb. flat	Pre 1965	119	74	256
PR	all flats	Post 1964	119	86	180
OO	all flats	Post 1980	122	89	255
PR	semi-det	Pre 1965	125	77	297
PR	cnv. flat	Pre 1965	130	79	295

1 The minimum and maximum values in the EHCS sample represent statistically the range covered, on average, by over 99% of dwellings in the national stock of each type.

have more expensive heating systems. A clear example of this is seen in post 1980 owner occupied flats, which on average have the second lowest rate of heat loss but stand apart from all other owner occupied types in having the third most expensive to run heating systems. In such flats, electric heating and high insulation are usually designed as an integrated system, and as a result this category of dwelling has the third highest mean SAP rating.

Energy efficiency

6.9   Table 6.3 shows the variation in the overall energy efficiency (SAP ratings) between the different dwelling categories. Overall, the age of the dwelling is the dominant influence, with tenure playing an important but secondary role. The table shows how the dwelling groups fall neatly into three blocks corresponding to the age bands 'post 1980', '1965-1980' and 'pre 1965'. There are only four exceptions to this rule, which can be explained by owner occupied properties rising into a higher SAP block or dwellings from the rented sectors slipping into a lower SAP block. Also within each block there is a fairly clear pattern of owner occupied properties being slightly more efficient than those owned by local authorities or housing associations, with private rented dwellings coming a poor third. (Table A6.3)

Table 6.3   Relationship between dwelling age, type and tenure and energy (SAP) rating *(categories listed in order from highest to lowest mean SAP rating)*

Dwelling Age		Tenure	Type	Energy (SAP) ratings			
				Mean	Min	Max[1]	<10
Post 1980		00		mid-terr	56	21	72	0
Post 1980		00		detached	50	19	71	1
Post 1980		00		all flats	48	21	69	5
Post 1980		LA/HA		all types	47	16	88	0
	1965-80	00		mid-terr	47	-13	70	2
Post 1980		00		semi-det	46	18	63	2
	1965-80	00		all flats	46	15	66	0
	Post 1964		PR	all flats	44	14	66	0
	1965-80	LA/HA		all flats	44	-16	86	2
	1965-80	LA/HA		mid-terr	43	-3	69	1
	Pre 1965	00		cnv. flat	41	-8	77	4
	1965-80	00		detached	41	18	61	0
	1965-80	00		semi-det	39	-20	68	1
	Pre 1965	LA/HA		pb. flat	36	-28	85	8
Above Av	Pre 1965	00		mid-terr	36	-23	71	5
Below Av.	Pre 1965	00		pb.flat	35	-28	75	8
SAP rate	1850-1964	00		detached	34	-24	69	6
	Pre 65	LA/HA		mid-terr	33	-19	65	8
	1850-1964	00		semi-det	33	-27	69	5
1965-80		LA/HA		semi & det.	32	-14	62	7
	Post 1964		PR	all houses	31	3	54	12
	Pre 1965	LA/HA		cnv. flat	30	-27	80	7
	Pre 1965		PR	pb. flat	30	-20	80	17
	Pre 1850	00		detached	30	-23	60	14
	Pre 1965	LA/HA		semi & det	28	-36	60	11
	Pre 1965		PR	conv. flat	27	-41	72	22
	Pre 1850	00		semi-det	27	-15	66	14
	Pre 1965		PR	mid-terr	24	-19	56	18
	Pre 1965		PR	semi-det	13	-38	47	40
	Pre 1965		PR	detached	12	-31	54	38

1 The minimum and maximum values in the EHCS sample represent statistically the range covered, on average, by over 99% of dwellings in the national stock of each type.

6.10 Although using fairly broad housing categories, the table shows average SAP ratings ranging from 56 to only 12. A SAP rating of 56 corresponds to a notional annual heating cost (to achieve a standard heating regime) of around £4.60 per square metre and SAP 12 to a cost of £11.70 per square metre. Therefore, from the best group (owner occupied post 1980 mid-terrace houses) to the worst (private rented pre 1965 detached houses) there is almost a threefold variation in average heating costs. However, the least efficient individual dwellings recorded in the sample (SAP under -30) have typical heating costs of ten times those of the most efficient properties (SAP over 80) - the respective notional costs being around £29.30 and £2.90 per square metre.

Range in efficiency within dwelling types

6.11 As well as showing the mean SAP rating for each dwelling category, Table 6.3 also shows the distribution from the worst to the best in the sample. The final column gives the percentage of dwellings in each group which have SAP ratings less than 10 and thereby fall within the worst 7% of the stock. However, compared to the total stock, many groups are not normally distributed. For example, pre 1965 local authority and housing association converted flats have a mean SAP rating well below the national average but only an average proportion of the worst dwellings.

6.12 The description above shows that there are fairly distinct, if complex, patterns in the energy related characteristics of different sectors of the stock. Some of the main determinants of energy efficiency relate to the basic structure of the dwelling and earlier modifications and are, at least in part, outside the control of the occupants or owners. However, these are the factors which determine what can be done to improve the property and what standard might be reasonably aimed for.

6.13 While the average values of the SAP ratings, heat loss and heating price indices reveal typical differences between dwelling categories, there is nevertheless considerable spread within each category which ensures

Figure 6.2a & b Frequency distribution of SAP ratings by building age and tenure

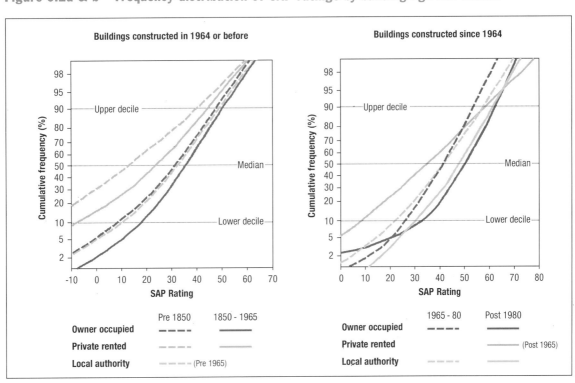

overlap between categories. This can be seen more clearly from the full frequency distributions for different dwelling ages and tenures given in Figures 6.2a & b. For example, Figure 6.2b shows that the lines for local authority dwellings built between 1965 and 1980 and for owner occupied dwellings of the same age have different gradients, indicating differences in the spread of SAP ratings between the two groups. The lines cross at the median level showing that they have the same average SAP rating - of around 42. However, either side of this point the two lines diverge, giving around double the proportion of council dwellings as owner occupied ones with poor SAP ratings (8% and 4% below 20), but also over double those with good ratings (respectively 8% & 3% over 60).

Number of dwellings with low SAP ratings

6.14 In the total stock, there are just over 3.0 million occupied properties with SAP ratings greater than 50 and 5.9 million with ratings below 30, 2.8 million of the latter being rated under 20. As Figure 6.3 shows, the owner occupied stock has the greatest number of inefficient dwellings, but a significantly lower proportion than other sectors. Just over a quarter of owner occupied dwellings have SAP ratings below 30, compared with 35% of local authority or housing association owned properties and 63% of those privately rented. These disparities between sectors increase as the SAP threshold is reduced, a far larger proportion of the private rented stock having SAP values below 10 than the owner occupied sector.

Figure 6.3   Number of dwellings with low SAP ratings

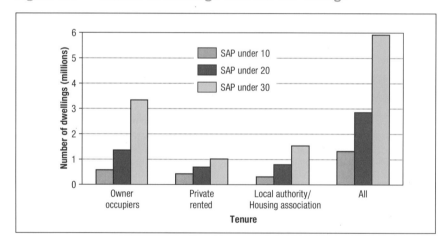

Energy inefficient dwellings

6.15 To provide an insight into the action required on those dwellings most in need of energy efficiency improvements, the characteristic and particular energy related problems of the 15% of stock with SAP ratings below 20 have been analysed in greater detail.

Balance of heat loss and heating problems

6.16 Table 6.4 shows how these come to have low energy ratings. As shown along the top row (with pale shading), 13.4% of these dwellings have no problem with heat loss, having index values less than the average for the total stock, but have a heating price higher than average - in fact at least 30% higher. Conversely, another 10.4% have no problem with the price of heating but higher than average rates of heat loss (first column of pale shading). Some 47% have the two problems in combination, but neither being particularly serious (shown in the table with intermediate shading), while the remaining 30% have both problems with at least one being serious. The worst dwelling encountered in the 1991 survey had a rate of heat loss which was 1.6 times the average and a heating price nearly 3 times the average for the stock.

Table 6.4   Heat loss and price of heating in dwellings with SAP ratings under 20

% of dwellings

Heat loss index		Heating price index					Total
	Average	50-100	100-150	150-200	200-250	250-300	
50-100	*Average*		2.8	4.4	1.7	3.5	13.4
100-150		2.3	46.9	9.2	1.2	4.3	63.9
150-200		7.4	9.1	3.7	0.1	0.9	21.1
200-250		0.7	0.7	0.2	-	-	-
Total		10.4	60.4	17.4	3.0	8.7	100.0

6.17   The balance between heat loss and heating price problems does not vary markedly between tenures. Generally, owner occupied dwellings suffer a little more from problems of heat loss and the social rented sector from inefficient heating; the private rented sector shows more serious problems of both types.

Poor space and water heating

6.18   Figure 6.4 shows the space and water heating systems of those properties with SAP ratings below 20 which also have a high heating price index (over 125). Nearly 14% of these dwellings rely upon portable units for their space heating, and a further 35% on solid fuel fires or fixed electric fires and heaters (not storage). These make up the bulk of the very high costs systems (i.e. all those with a heating price index over 200 and most of those over 150). Gas fires figure significantly among the less costly systems (38%), as do solid fuel and electric central heating (7%), and even gas central heating, including those employing back boilers (7%). (Table A6.4)

Figure 6.4   Space and water heating in dwellings with SAP < 20 and high heating prices

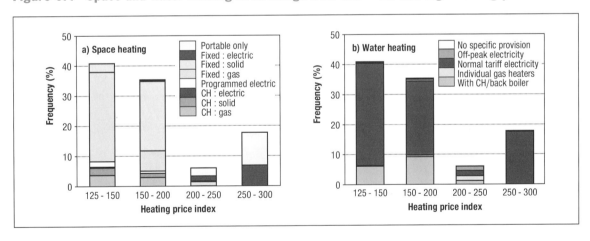

6.19   The explanation for why these last, relatively efficient space heating systems, result in a high heating price lies with the water heating provision. Overwhelmingly, the problem appears to be associated with the use of immersion heaters using on-peak electricity. (Table A6.4)

Poor thermal insulation

6.20   Figure 6.5a describes the insulation characteristics of dwellings with SAP ratings below 20 which have a relatively high heat loss (i.e. index greater than 125). As expected, the problems lie almost exclusively with pre-1965 properties (90% of the affected dwellings) and predominantly with detached, semi-detached and end-terraced houses (81%). Over three-quarters of the dwellings in the group under consideration are of these types and of this age. (Table A6.5)

Figure 6.5   Dwelling type and age and extent of heating among dwellings with SAP < 20 and high heat losses

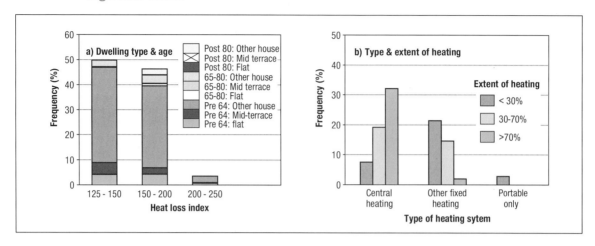

6.21   Since this group of dwellings will lose heat quickly, it is relevant to consider the extent to which there will be parts of the home which cannot be heated to an adequate temperature. Figure 6.5b shows the type and extent of the heating system available in these particular dwellings. Around half have some form of central heating. In approximately a third of the dwellings, virtually the whole of the home can be heated by some form of fixed appliance, but in a further third the heating is limited to under a third of rooms. (Table A6.6)

Relationship with condition of fabric

6.22   The majority of energy inefficient dwellings are otherwise in reasonably good condition. There is nevertheless a strong correlation between poor energy efficiency and housing in poor general condition, both factors being linked to dwelling age. Of the 2.8 million dwellings with SAP ratings below 20, over 700 thousand need repairs costing in excess of £2,500, a tenth of these having repair costs over £10,000. With regard to unfitness, over 300 thousand (23%) of dwellings with ratings below 10, 500 thousand (18%) of those rated under 20 and 760 thousand (13%) of those below 30 are statutorally unfit. A similar pattern is seen with respect to the number of defects contributing to, but not necessarily causing unfitness. That said, most of those with low SAP ratings (622 thousand of the 1.3 million with ratings below 10 and 1.5 million of the 2.8 million rated under 20) are not defective on any of the current fitness requirements. (Tables 6.5 & A6.7 to A6.9)

Table 6.5   Dwellings defective on fitness requirements by energy (SAP) rating

Number of fitness defects	SAP < 10		SAP < 20		SAP < 30	
	% with SAP<10	Number (thousand)	% with SAP<20	Number (thousand)	% with SAP<30	Number (thousand)
Nil	4.5	622	10.6	1,470	25.2	3,503
1	7.2	198	18.8	469	40.4	1,012
2	15.2	187	31.0	379	50.8	622
3	18.0	95	30.1	160	47.6	253
4	27.0	206	45.2	345	62.1	473
Total dwellings	6.9	1,308	14.9	2,824	31.1	5,863

6.23   This relationship between energy efficiency and poor general condition holds through all tenures as may be seen from Figure 6.6.

Figure 6.6   Dwellings with low SAP ratings defective on fitness requirements by tenure

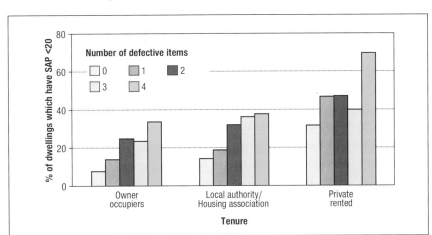

Geographical variation

Regional patterns

Social rented sector

6.24   There is considerable variation in the range of domestic energy efficiency across the country, but there is no clear overall pattern. Any patterns which do exist vary from tenure to tenure. The sample sizes for the private rented sector do not allow detailed analysis by region, but reliable estimates are available for the other sectors. (Table A6.10)

6.25   The strongest regional pattern occurs within the social rented sector. This is shown in Table 6.6 and Figure 6.7 which give the proportion of dwellings of high and/or low energy efficiency in the Government's administrative regions broken down by their metropolitan and non-metropolitan areas. The areas are ordered according to their average SAP rating, from the highest average of 41.9 in Inner London to the lowest of 24.4 in Devon and Cornwall. Above average areas are those of Greater London and the Eastern regions and the North and North West. The poorer regions are

Table 6.6   Incidence of lowest and highest rated dwellings in largest sectors by administrative region and metropolitan area *(mean SAP order)*

Social rented	Mean SAP	% of dwellings			Owner occupied	Mean SAP	% of dwellings		
		<10	<20	50+			<10	<20	50+
Inner London	41.9	4	9	33	South West (rest)	39.6	5	8	21
Gt. Manchester	39.6	2	6	20	South East	39.5	3	8	23
Tyne & Wear	37.7	1	8	13	Inner London	39.2	6	12	24
Outer London	36.9	8	16	21	Eastern	39.0	4	10	22
Eastern	35.4	6	14	15	Northern Non-met	37.7	3	10	16
N.W. Non-met	35.1	5	15	17	Tyne and Wear	37.2	3	7	11
Northern Non-met	34.9	5	12	13	W. Mids. Non-met	36.9	4	11	17
Merseyside TF	34.4	8	16	15	S. Yorkshire Met	36.8	1	7	16
Y & H Non-met	34.3	6	20	17	Outer London	36.8	3	7	14
East Midlands	33.5	7	17	14	N.W. Non-met	36.5	9	15	15
S. Yorkshire Met	32.9	11	22	14	East Midlands	36.5	4	8	15
South East	31.7	8	25	10	Y & H Non-met	36.2	8	14	19
W. Mids. Non-met	30.3	12	24	11	Gt. Manchester	35.5	7	12	18
South West (rest)	30.3	13	26	14	W. Midlands Met	34.8	5	13	12
W. Midlands Met	30.1	10	28	12	W. Yorkshire Met	34.1	5	15	8
W. Yorkshire Met	30.1	8	30	12	Devon & Cornwall	33.1	6	22	18
Devon & Cornwall	24.4	21	36	5	Merseyside TF	32.8	5	16	4

— — — National average for sector

Figure 6.7a   Incidence of lowest rated dwellings by administrative
region and metropolitan area - Social rented stock

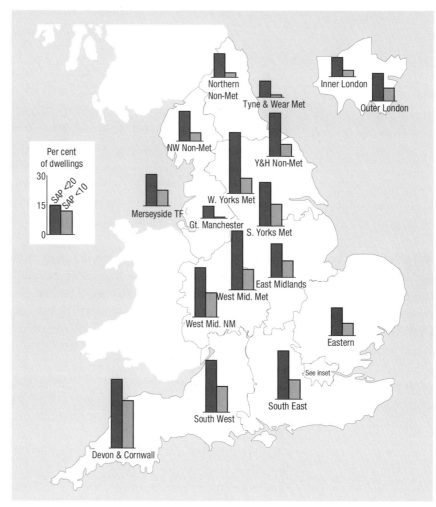

the South West, the West Midlands and the West Yorkshire metropolitan areas. Generally, the metropolitan counties within a region come out worse than the non-metropolitan areas.

6.26   In the social rented sector, there is a reasonably strong correlation between the average value of SAP rating and the proportion of dwellings with ratings below 20, and a slightly weaker correlation with the proportion rated below 10 or 50 or more. Thus, if the areas were ranked on the proportion of energy efficient or inefficient dwellings rather than on the average SAP, their order would not change substantially.

Owner occupied sector   6.27   The owner occupied sector shows a slightly less diverse range of average SAP values, from 39.6 in the South West region to 32.8 in Merseyside. There are some similarities to the rank ordering of the social-rented sector, in that Inner London and the Eastern Region are again above average amongst the most efficient areas and Devon and Cornwall and the West Midlands and West Yorkshire metropolitan areas are amongst the least energy efficient. However, there are also clear differences; the rest of the South East and, particularly, the rest of the South West make a much better showing within the owner occupied sector. Conversely, Greater Manchester moves from second best to fifth worst, whilst Merseyside falls from an average to the worst position.

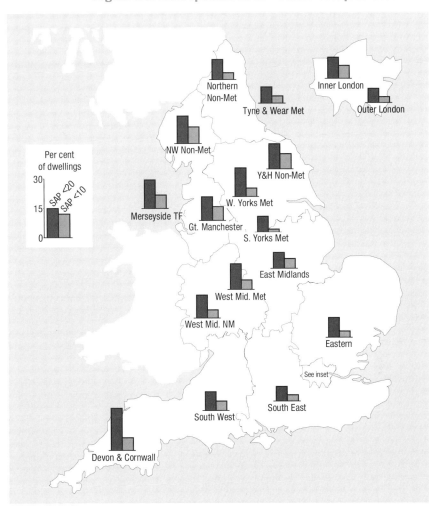

Figure 6.7b Incidence of lowest rated dwellings by administrative region and metropolitan area - Owner occupied stock

6.28 Again there is a correlation between the average SAP values and the proportion of good or poor energy efficient dwellings, but it is much weaker than within the social rented sector. If ranked on the proportion of inefficient dwellings, South Yorkshire, Outer London and the East Midlands would make a far better showing, whilst if ranked on the proportion with SAP ratings above 50, both Greater Manchester and Devon and Cornwall would be more average.

Impact on regional variation of stock composition

6.29 It was shown earlier that energy efficiency is strongly associated with building age and type and consequently the possibility that geographical variations are explained largely by differences in the composition of the

Table 6.7 Effects of building age and type on regional variation in SAP ratings

		Regional mean SAP ratings		
		Lowest	Highest	Mean
SAP ratings	Owner occupied	32.8	39.6	37.3
	Social rented	24.4	41.9	34.5
	Private rented	-	-	21.7
Modified SAP rating	Owner occupied	32.7	39.0	36.9
to remove effect of building	Social rented	23.0	38.0	32.6
age and type variation	Private rented	-	-	22.4

stock has been examined. This has been done by recalculating the average SAP values on the assumption that in each region the building age and type profiles are identical to those in the stock as a whole. A summary of the results of this calculation is shown in Table 6.7.

6.30 The relative positions in the rank ordering of the different regions are not greatly affected. In both the owner occupied and social rented sectors, the overall range of mean SAP ratings between regions falls, but by less than 15%, indicating that a real 'geographical' difference exists over and above any stock differences.

6.31 There is also a small but noticeable shift in the relationship between tenures after the influence of building age and type is controlled for. The mean SAP rating within the social rented sector worsens slightly in comparison with the owner occupied sector, whilst that in the private rented sector marginally improves.

Impact of 'rurality' on SAP ratings

6.32 Irrespective of its geographical situation, the type of locality in which the dwelling is situated (i.e. the nature of the immediate environment as judged by the Surveyor) provides a significant pointer to its energy efficiency. Table 6.8 shows, for each of the main tenures, the mean values of SAP for dwellings in different types of locality, together with the proportions of the stock which fall below 10 and below 20.

Table 6.8   Variation in SAP rating by type of locality and tenure

		City centre	Urban	Sub-urban	Village centre	Rural residential	Rural isolated
Local authority							
% of dwells	SAP<10	4.0	5.4	6.9	8.9	15.4	12.6
with:-	SAP<20	12.9	13.6	17.1	21.9	33.1	41.5
Mean SAP		40.4	37.5	34.1	28.9	26.6	22.8
indexed to	Actual	1.18	1.10	1.00	0.85	0.78	0.67
suburban	Modified	1.06	1.06	1.00	0.84	0.79	0.69
Owner occupied							
% of dwells	SAP<10	4.4	4.9	3.2	8.3	6.1	8.9
with:-	SAP<20	9.6	12.1	7.9	20.5	12.3	20.1
Mean SAP		37.4	36.2	38.1	32.7	37.6	35.5
indexed to	Actual	0.98	0.95	1.00	0.86	0.99	0.93
suburban	Modified	1.01	0.98	1.00	0.88	0.95	0.96
Private rented							
% of dwells	SAP<10	13.3	19.5	14.6	56.1	39.5	46.5
with:-	SAP<20	24.4	34.6	33.4	66.2	54.1	65.5
Mean SAP		29.5	27.1	26.3	(3.3)	15.1	10.5
indexed to	Actual	1.12	1.03	1.00	(0.12)	0.57	0.40
suburban	Modified	1.04	0.99	1.00	(0.29)	0.47	0.53

Locational variation within tenures

6.33 It is apparent that whatever the measure of efficiency used, there is a clear distinction between 'rural' and 'urban' properties in all tenures. Particularly in local authority and private rented sectors, the more urban or densely developed the area the more efficient the dwelling. For both tenures in the private sector, dwellings in a village centre perform the least well. Private rented dwellings in rural areas generally, many of which are 'tied-cottages', have very poor energy efficiency, with typically 2 in 3 dwellings with SAP ratings below 20 and an average rating of 15 or less.

6.34 This variation with the type of environment owes something to differences in the composition of the stock in the different areas, particularly between city centres, urban and suburban environments. For all tenures, the removal of the effects of building age and type systematically reduces the variation. However, as shown by the last row for each tenure in Table 6.8 (where SAP ratings are 'modified' to remove these effects), this is by no means the full explanation.

Locational variation by region for council stock

6.35 That the effect is general and not generated by the particular circumstances in a few dominant regions is seen from Table 6.9. This Table - for the local authority sector, where the variation is most pronounced - shows the mean values of SAP modified to remove the variation in dwelling age and type. It shows for each main region the energy efficiency of dwellings in different types of location in relation to those in suburban residential areas within each region. Some of the figures (those in brackets) are based on small samples and therefore unreliable, but for the table as a whole the evidence for the poor performance of rural council housing relative to its urban counterparts is overwhelming. Only the South East Region runs counter to the trend; in this region the 'rural' areas follow the normal pattern, but council housing in 'urban' locations, particularly in city/town centres, also performs less well in comparison with that in suburban areas.

Table 6.9   Variation in energy efficiency of LA stock by type of locality by tenure *(after controlling for stock differences)*

Region	Modified SAP indexed to suburban locality					
	City centre	Urban	Suburban	Village centre	Rural residential	Rural
Inner London	1.15	1.20	1.00	-	-	-
Northern	(1.16)	1.01	1.00	(0.74)	0.72	-
Outer London	(1.09)	1.01	1.00	-	-	-
North West	1.00	0.92	1.00	-	(0.69)	-
South East	0.72	0.97	1.00	(1.13)	0.84	(0.86)
East Midlands	(0.99)	1.00	1.00	(0.63)	0.78	-
West Midlands	(1.32)	1.02	1.00	-	0.86	(0.85)
East Anglia	-	(1.09)	1.00	-	0.73	-
Yorks/Humber	1.07	1.14	1.00	(0.60)	0.85	-
South West	-	1.04	1.00	-	0.62	(0.54)
All regions	1.06	1.06	1.00	0.84	0.79	0.69

6.36 The poor showing of rural areas can be explained, at least in part, by the more limited availability of mains gas and the consequent use of more expensive fuels and, as seen in Chapter 3, the West Country generally suffers most in this respect. However, while there is some correlation between high heating prices and the lack of mains gas, the relatively good showing of rural owner-occupied housing suggests that this is not the full explanation. In fact, it appears that a lack of central heating is more significant than the availability of gas, albeit that these are often associated.

Regional variation relative to locational differences

6.37 Table 6.10 shows for both the local authority and owner occupied stock how much of the variation between regions can be explained by differences in the types of locality which make up the region. The first column for each tenure shows the overall variation between regions, after controlling for differences in dwelling age and type, while the second column shows the variation for suburban areas only. With reference to the previous table, a significant difference between the two figures in any region will generally indicate the extent to which that region is dominated by urban housing of relatively high energy efficiency or conversely inefficient rural properties.

Table 6.10 **Variation in energy efficiency between regions and between suburban and total stocks in each region (after controlling for stock differences)**

Modified SAP mean indexed to whole country	Local authority sector		Owner occupied sector	
	All localities	Suburban only	All localities	Suburban
Inner London	1.17	0.99	1.06	1.02
Northern	1.08	1.09	1.00	1.03
Outer London	1.08	1.06	1.02	0.99
North West	1.07	1.11	0.97	0.95
South East	1.02	1.06	1.04	1.05
East Midlands	1.00	1.06	0.96	0.98
West Midlands	0.91	0.90	0.98	1.00
East Anglia	0.91	0.96	0.96	1.01
Yorkshire/ Humberside	0.90	0.89	0.97	0.98
South West	0.79	0.86	0.99	0.96
All regions	1.00	1.00	1.00	1.00

6.38   For the local authority stock, the two distributions are similar, the only significant difference occurring for Inner London, due to the predominance of 'urban' and 'city centre' housing which tends to be associated with high energy efficiency. The conclusion to be drawn is that broad geographical variations in SAP within the local authority sector owe little to differences in levels of 'rurality' (or to building type and age, since the table has been constructed to remove the effect of these factors). The same conclusion can be drawn for the owner occupied sector, although for this tenure the variation between regions is appreciably less.

6.39   The fact that geographical variation cannot be fully explained by differences in the composition of the stock, by the levels of 'rurality' or by the availability of gas, suggests that in the local authority sector it arises to a large degree from differences in the historical policies and actions of individual councils. This is partly confirmed by the 1991 Census findings[1] on the substantial variation in the availability of central heating between different local authority districts - ranging from over 99% to only 33% of the local council stock.

Impact of climate on SAP ratings

6.40   The geographical variation may, to some extent, be related to the demands of the local climate, council housing in the Northern region, for example, having a generally higher standard of energy efficiency than the warmer South West.

6.41   The extent to which the geographical variation matches the climatic differences and consequent differential heat losses is illustrated in Figure 6.8. This plots the notional annual costs of heating against SAP ratings for properties located in the extreme South West, in central England and in the extreme North East. For example, it shows that while a dwelling in

1   *See DOE, Energy Efficiency in Council Housing, Condition of the Stock, 1995, op.cit,. page 12*

the South West with a rating of 30 can be heated to a standard regime for a cost of some £750, a dwelling in the North East would need a SAP of nearly 40 to achieve the same heating regime for the same cost.

Figure 6.8   Relationship between notional annual heating costs and SAP ratings for the South West, central England and the North East

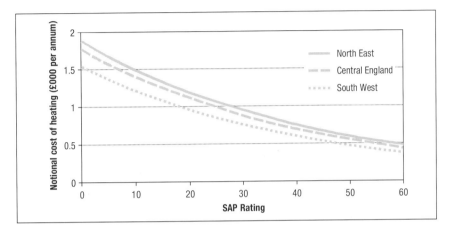

6.42   The information in these plots has been used to estimate the 'equivalent central England SAP rating' for the council stocks of Devon and Cornwall and the Northern metropolitan and non-metropolitan areas, to indicate how these stocks would perform were they to be transplanted to the middle of the country. The results are shown in Table 6.11. The stock from the Northern areas would still cost less to heat than that from Devon and Cornwall, but the difference is far less than suggested by the actual SAP ratings. There is also a corresponding reduction in the variation in the proportion of dwellings with low SAP ratings.

Table 6.11   Comparison between South West and Northern areas, for actual and equivalent central England SAP ratings

Region	Mean SAP rating		% of dwellings with SAP<10		% of dwellings with SAP<20	
	Actual	Equiv. CE	Actual	Equiv. CE	Actual	Equiv. CE
Devon and Cornwall	24	30	20	12	36	25
Northern non-met.	35	32	5	8	15	20
Tyne and Wear	37	34	1	3	8	11

Chapter 7

Households and standards

Preamble

7.1 *This concluding chapter in Part I describes how households are distributed in housing of different physical standards. With particular reference to tenure, it looks first at the variation in the energy efficiency and heating of homes occupied by households of different composition and different socio-economic status. It then goes on to analyse the housing standards of the most vulnerable groups and concludes by looking specifically at those in the most and least efficient parts of the housing stock.*

7.2 *For sake of brevity, in this Chapter dwellings with SAP ratings less than 20 are termed 'inefficient', while those rated under 10 are coined 'very inefficient'. In a number of the tenure comparisons and accompanying figures and tables, all tenants in the social rented sectors are taken together, the relatively small sample of housing association tenants showing broadly similar SAP rated homes to those of council tenants.*

Household composition

Household size

7.3 Domestic energy efficiency is strongly related to the composition of the household. This is apparent when considering the size of the household and age of the head as well as the type of household. However, the pattern varies with tenure. In all sectors, domestic energy efficiency tends to increase with household size, with single person households occupying the least efficient properties. In the social rented sector, the general increase with household size is less pronounced. Here, large households of 6 or more persons are the best housed, whilst in the private rented stock such households, albeit relatively few, appear amongst the worse off in terms of energy efficiency. (Figure 7.1 & Table A7.1)

Figure 7.1 Mean SAP ratings and % of homes rated below 20 by size of household and tenure

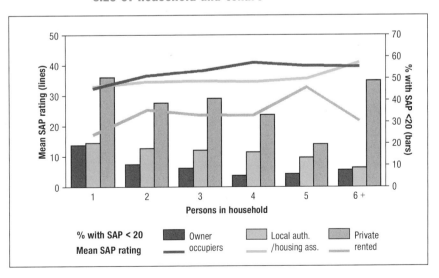

Age of head of household

7.4 The efficiency of homes generally decreases with the age of the head of household, although there is some variation with tenure. The youngest owner occupiers have slightly more inefficient homes than those in middle age and the oldest private tenants marginally less than those with heads aged between 60 and 75. However, overall, the correlation between low efficiency and age of the head of household is stronger in the private than in the socially rented sectors. (Figure 7.2)

Figure 7.2   Mean SAP ratings and % of homes rated below 20 by age of head of household and tenure

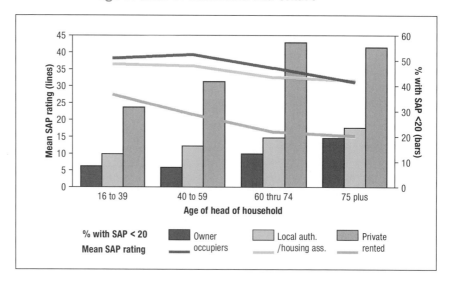

Household types

7.5   The patterns for size of household and age of head are reflected in the pattern for the energy efficiency of homes of different types of household, as shown for the whole stock and within each housing sector in Figure 7.3 and Table 7.1 respectively. (see also Table A7.2)

Energy efficiency of different groups

7.6   Families with children generally live in more energy efficient homes than do all-adult households. Over the whole stock, small and large families are generally the best housed with less than 1 in 10 living in inefficient homes. However, this proportion ranges widely with tenure - from around 6% in the owner occupied stock to 33% in the private rented sector. Lone parents come third in the total population. They generally have the highest average SAP ratings in each individual tenure, but compared to other families are more likely to live in the poorer private rented sector. Although mainly on lower incomes, this group tends to occupy smaller flats or are recent movers, both attributes which predisposes them to have more efficient homes than others in the same sector.

Figure 7.3   Energy efficiency (SAP) ratings by household type *(in mean SAP order)*

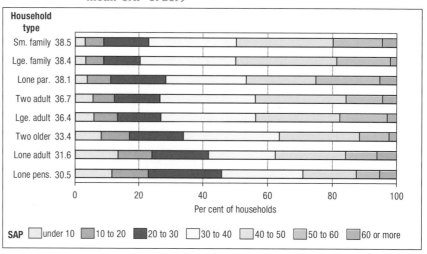

7.7 Lone pensioners and lone adults generally occupy the least efficient dwellings, with nearly a quarter living in energy inefficient properties. In the owner occupied and local authority stocks, around a fifth of both groups live in such dwellings. In the private rented sector nearly 38% of lone adults, 48% of pensioner couples and no fewer than 63% of lone pensioners live in homes with SAP ratings below 20 - two thirds of the latter being very inefficient dwellings. (Table A7.2)

Rank ordering of types by tenure

7.8 Table 7.1 lists the types of household in each tenure in order of the average energy efficiency of their accommodation. The range of average SAP ratings varies in the owner occupied stock - from 42 for lone parents to 32 for lone pensioners - the latter being generally less well housed than public sector tenants. Both tenure groups are well above those of private tenants where average SAP ratings range from 28 for two adults to only 11 for over quarter of a million lone pensioners.

Table 7.1 Mean SAP ratings, heat loss and heating price index, % of homes rated <20 and >50 by household type and tenure *(in mean SAP order)*

Owner occupiers	LA/HA tenants	Private tenants	Mean SAP	Mean HLI	Mean HPI	% with SAP <20	% with SAP >50	Total thous.
lone parent			42.1	92	91	6	37	272
small family			40.4	95	91	6	22	2,498
large family			39.5	95	92	7	20	1,505
large adult			38.2	97	93	9	19	1,698
two adults			37.9	99	94	9	16	2,505
	lone parent		37.8	94	102	11	21	365
	large family		37.4	96	99	13	17	370
	two adults		36.2	95	106	16	18	312
	one adult	(stock mean)	35.5	94	117	20	24	333
two older			34.9	102	96	13	11	2,132
	small family		34.3	100	102	16	15	481
	large adult		34.2	95	108	21	16	365
one adult			32.8	101	108	21	16	827
	two older		32.4	101	107	21	12	698
	lone pensioner		32.4	102	109	20	14	953
lone pensioner			32.2	106	102	19	14	1,439
		two adult	27.9	107	117	36	7	371
		lone parent	26.1	107	114	32	4	71
		small family	26.0	116	105	33	8	224
		large adult	23.4	112	113	40	5	168
		one adult	23.2	108	129	38	7	328
		large family	22.3	112	121	31	0	101
		two older	20.7	117	120	48	9	181
		one pensioner	11.1	129	137	63	1	255
All OO types			37.2	99	95	11	18	12,872
	All LA/HA		34.4	98	107	18	16	4,539
		All PR types	22.4	114	121	42	8	1,700
All tenures			**35.3**	**100**	**100**	**15**	**16**	**19,111**

7.9 As indicated by the mean values for the heat loss (HLI) and heating price (HPI) indexes, the group of owner occupiers in the most efficient housing gain their advantage by generally having homes which have both heat losses and, particularly, heating systems which are better than average. Most tenants socially renting have higher than average heating prices, but in homes of above average SAP ratings this is offset by the lower heat losses associated with flats or newer dwellings. Private tenants suffer from both high heat losses and particularly inefficient heating systems.

Heating provision

7.10   Considering the heating provision specifically, small families and lone parents are generally the best provided, over 85% of these having central heating. Single adult households, including lone pensioners, have the worst provisions, a fifth to a quarter being without central heating. The household types with the highest and lowest proportion of central heating in each tenure are shown in Figure 7.4. In the two private sectors, these correspond to the best and poorest mean heating price index, but for lone pensioners socially renting a high proportion of electric systems results in them having the second poorest index in the sector.

Figure 7.4   **Household types with greatest and least central heating provision in each tenure** *(non central heating shown to left of axis)*

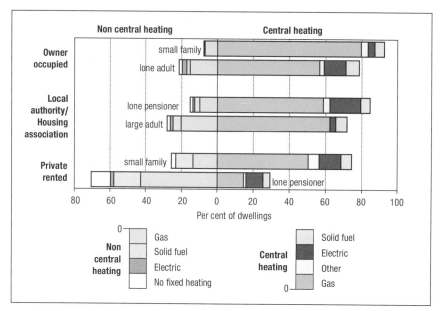

7.11   Overall, the availability of central heating ranges from small family owner occupiers, under 8% of whom are without such heating, to lone pensioners privately renting; 71% of the latter lack central heating, 17% have only on-peak electric or open solid fuel fires and a further 11% lack any form of fixed heating. (Table A7.3)

Thermal insulation

7.12   Lone pensioners and single adults also tend to occupy homes with the lowest levels of all types of thermal insulation. Lone parents also have generally low standards of home insulation compared to other family households. (Table A7.4) However, because of the high proportion of such households living in flats with their low external wall areas (40% of all single adults compared to 7% of other families), these differences are less clearly reflected in the variation in overall heat losses.

Length of residence

7.13   A similar pattern is apparent in the relationship between energy efficiency and length of residence of the household. In the total stock, households in the least efficient housing tend to be those who have lived in the accommodation a long time or a very short time. Over two-fifths of those living in very inefficient homes have had the same address for over 20 years, compared with well under a tenth of those in dwellings with a SAP rating of 60 or more. The propensity for short term residents to be in inefficient housing is only significant in the private rented sector. However, the proportion of long term residents (20 years or more) in inefficient homes is roughly double that of those of 2 to 4 years standing in every sector, ranging from 18% in owner occupied to 66% in private rented dwellings. (Figure 7.5 & Table A7.5)

Figure 7.5   Mean SAP ratings and % of homes rated below 20 by length of residence and tenure

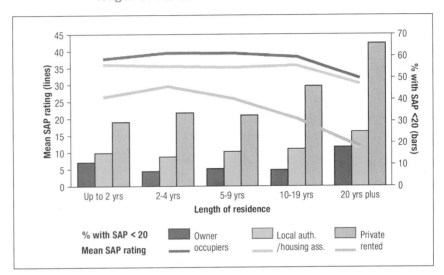

Multiple occupation

7.14   Households in dwellings in multiple occupation - nearly half of whom are lone adults and a quarter lone pensioners - are particularly poorly housed in terms of energy efficiency. Such accommodation, virtually all of which is rented, has an average SAP rating of only 15, two thirds is rated under 20 and a quarter has no fixed heating.

Socio-economic factors

Household income

Energy efficiency

7.15   In contrast, households with high annual incomes, those with persons in full time employment and those with 'white collar' jobs tend to be advantaged in the energy efficiency of their homes. Generally, there is a progressive increase in the efficiency of the home with rising household income - from a mean SAP of 32 for those with the lowest 20% of incomes (lowest quintile) to nearly 42 for those in the highest quintile. There is a corresponding drop in the proportion of inefficient properties from some 22% down to 4%. Although with few tenants in the highest income group, the same is generally true of the social rented sector and particularly so in the private rented sector, where the mean SAP rating nearly doubles from 18 to 33. (Table A7.6)

7.16   Table 7.2 shows that for all except private tenants, the likelihood of households living in relatively energy efficient housing is related far more closely to their income than their tenure. That said, for households on average or above average income, owner occupiers are consistently, if only slightly, better off than tenants in the same income band, whilst for those on below average income the reverse is true. For private tenants, the tenure is the dominant factor, even those on the highest income generally having less efficient homes than households on the lowest income living in the owner occupied and public sectors. Apart from private tenants, those on the lowest incomes are marginally better housed than those in the same tenure on more average incomes.

Table 7.2   Mean SAP ratings and % of homes rated <20 and >50 by net household income and tenure (*in mean SAP order*)

	Net household income (quintiles)					Energy efficiency			Total
	£19,500 plus	£13,500 - 19,500	£8,500 - 13,500	£4,500 - 8,500	under £4,500	Mean SAP	% with SAP<20	% with SAP>50	hholds thous.
	OO					42.0	4	24	3,431
	LA/HA					41.1	8	27	63
		OO				38.7	7	18	3,268
		LA/HA				37.1	11	19	308
	mean		OO			35.3	14	14	2,560
					LA/HA	34.2	18	17	1,918
			LA/HA			34.1	19	16	691
				LA/HA		33.9	19	15	1,558
					OO	33.2	19	18	1,582
				OO		33.1	16	10	2,032
	PR					32.8	21	10	152
		PR				26.6	30	11	226
			PR			23.6	46	13	347
				PR		20.6	44	6	462
					PR	18.5	48	3	511

Heating provision

7.17 Figure 7.6 compares the types of heating of households in the highest and lowest income groups. Compared with less than 4% of households in the highest group, 26% of those on the lowest incomes are without central heating, over 1 in 3 of the latter relying on solid fuel fires, on-peak electric or portable heaters.

Figure 7.6   Type of heating of households with highest and lowest 20% of incomes (*non-central heating exploded*)

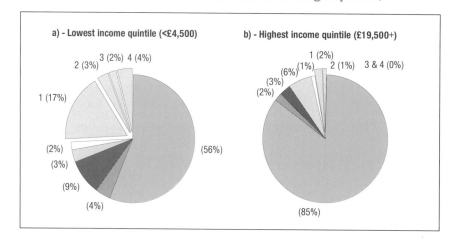

Thermal insulation

7.18 There is also a strong correlation between income and the standard of all forms of thermal insulation. Households on the highest 20% of incomes have twice as many homes with wall insulation, double glazing or full draught proofing and less than half the proportion of houses with uninsulated lofts as those in the lowest income quintile. (Table A7.7)

Employment status

7.19 Overall, there is a marked difference between the energy efficiency standards of those in employment and those who are unemployed or retired. However, the tendency for single person households to be relatively poorly housed holds true regardless of working status. On average, single persons in full-time employment occupy similarly efficient properties to unemployed

Figure 7.7   Energy efficiency (SAP) ratings by working status of household *(in mean SAP order)*

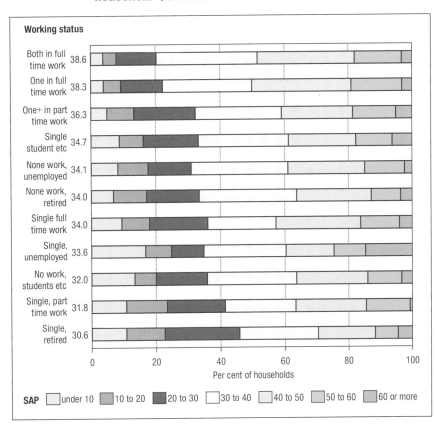

and retired households of two or more, whilst those in part time employment or retired are the worst housed, nearly 1 in 4 living in inefficient homes. However, the single unemployed have the highest proportion of both inefficient and reasonably efficient properties, a half of this group being split between dwellings with SAP ratings under 20 and over 50. (Figure 7.7)

Variation with tenure   7.20   The pattern varies with tenure. The proportion of inefficient properties ranges from only 6% for two owner occupiers in full time employment to over 60% for the single retired in the private rented sector. In the social rented sectors, those in full time employment are the best housed and those retired the worst - regardless of the number of adults. In the private rented sector, the divergence with household size is also less pronounced than in the owner occupied stock. Here, larger unemployed households share with the single unemployed the second least efficient stock (mean SAP rating of 15), above the single retired with their average SAP rating of 12. (Table A7.8)

Socio-economic groups   7.21   As with income, there is an equally strong correlation between domestic energy efficiency and the socio-economic group of the head of household. Interestingly, professionals head the field with 27% of homes with SAP ratings of 50 or over. This is significantly more than the figure for the similarly high earning employers and managers (under 19%) and over twice that for both skilled and semi-skilled manual workers (around 12%). The pattern is reversed for less efficient dwellings and holds true for all tenures. Under 6% of professionals own inefficient homes compared with over 60% of semi-skilled manual workers who rent privately. (Figure 7.8 & Table A7.9)

Figure 7.8   Energy efficiency (SAP) ratings by socio-economic group (*in mean SAP order*)

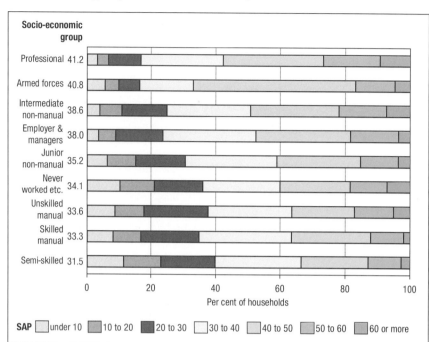

Vulnerable households

7.22   Households living in homes with poor heating and low energy efficiency are most likely to lack affordable warmth and suffer cold conditions. The next section of this chapter examines the extent to which the most vulnerable households - those with young children, elderly, sick or less mobile members - are found in such accommodation.

Young children

7.23   Households with children under the age of 11 are relatively well housed. Less than 1 in 10 live in dwellings with SAP ratings less than 20 compared with 17% of the remainder of the population. However, the proportion varies with tenure, over 14% of council tenants with very young children and 26% of those in private rented accommodation living in such homes. In total, over 400 thousand households with children under 11 years have energy inefficient homes, nearly two-fifth of these being in the social rented sectors and a further fifth privately rented. Well over half the total include children under 4 years old. (Table A7.10)

Figure 7.9   Mean and distribution of SAP ratings by age of children

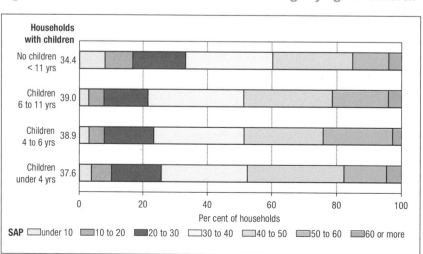

Elderly persons

7.24 In contrast to households with young children, those with elderly persons tend to be housed in less energy efficient accommodation than the rest of the population. Moreover, the older the head of household the more likely they are to live in inefficient dwellings. This pattern applies generally to all tenures, with typically 1 in 4 persons of over 85 years living in dwellings with SAP ratings less than 20. However, in comparison to the owner occupied stock, the correlation is less strong in the social rented sectors where there are more younger households in poor housing, while in the private rented sector all elderly age groups have more than 1 in 2 households in inefficient dwellings. (Figure 7.10 & Table A7.11)

Figure 7.10   Mean and distribution of SAP ratings by age of head of household

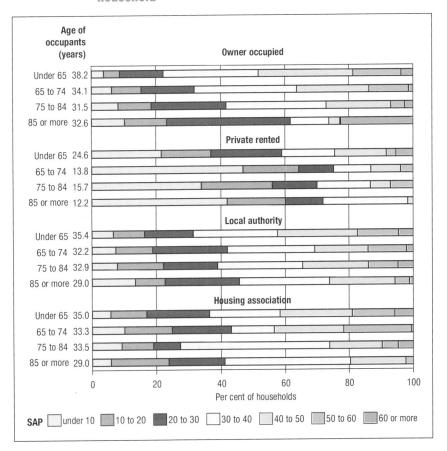

7.25 Overall, around one million or 22% of households with heads of household of 65 years or more - including some 600 thousand (24%) aged 75 or older - live in homes with SAP ratings under 20, of which nearly a half are rated under 10. Nearly a half of these are owner occupiers and a further fifth private tenants.

Respiratory and mobility problems

7.26 Generally, households which include persons with mobility problems and particularly those with respiratory illnesses are in less energy efficient housing than those without such problems. In total some 413 thousand or 16% of households including persons with mobility problems and 462 thousand (18%) with respiratory ailments live in dwellings with SAP ratings under 20, compared with around 14% of all other households. However, certain groups such as households with more than one person with a respiratory ailment are better housed than the rest of the population.

7.27 The situation also varies with tenure. In the social rented sector, tenants aged 75 or more with mobility problems are generally in better housing than other such elderly tenants, particularly those with respiratory problems. In the owner occupied stock, nearly 1 in 4 elderly households suffering from respiratory problems also live in energy inefficient dwellings, compared with under half this proportion of those with mobility problems. However, in the private rented sector, persons with mobility problems are the worst housed; 4 out of 5 homes housing elderly persons with such problems have SAP ratings below 20. (Figure 7.11 & Table A7.12)

Figure 7.11   Percentage of vulnerable groups living in energy inefficient dwellings *(SAP<20)* by tenure

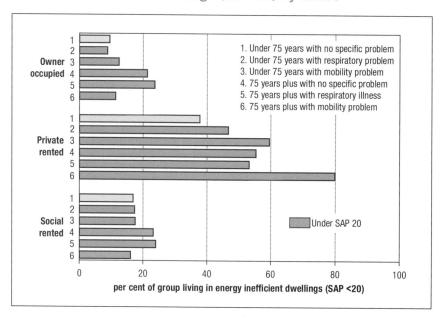

1. Under 75 years with no specific problem
2. Under 75 years with respiratory problem
3. Under 75 years with mobility problem
4. 75 years plus with no specific problem
5. 75 years plus with respiratory illness
6. 75 years plus with mobility problem

Under SAP 20

per cent of group living in energy inefficient dwellings (SAP <20)

Households in best and worst stock

7.28   The remaining part of the Chapter looks at the particular profile of the households in the most and least energy efficient housing. It looks first at household distribution in the 16% of the stock with SAP ratings of 50 or above and the similar proportion rated below 20, then with reference to the most and least efficient dwelling types and finally at variation within the most common types.

High and low energy rated homes

Household composition

7.29   The 4% of homes with SAP ratings of 60 or more have an above average proportion of small households, reflecting the relatively high energy efficiency of flats. The larger stock of properties with SAP ratings between 50 and 60 has a smaller proportion of single persons, being lived in mainly by families and large adult households. In this respect, it is more akin to the bulk of housing with more average energy ratings.

7.30   Although of greater number, dwellings of low energy efficiency are similar to the best stock in having a particularly high proportion of small households. Nearly 37% of those with a SAP rating below 20 and 41% below 10 accommodate only one person. The majority of these are elderly persons, around 1 in 4 of all energy inefficient homes housing lone pensioners and a further 1 in 5 pensioner couples. A half of the heads of household are aged 60 years or more, a fifth being 75 years old or older. (see Figure 7.12 - width of stock indicates size of stock)

Household composition by tenure

7.31   There are very few efficient homes in the private rented sector and over 72% of properties rated over 50 are owner occupied. Half of the latter are owned by families and large adult households and only a quarter by

Figure 7.12   Household types in most and least energy efficient dwellings by SAP rating

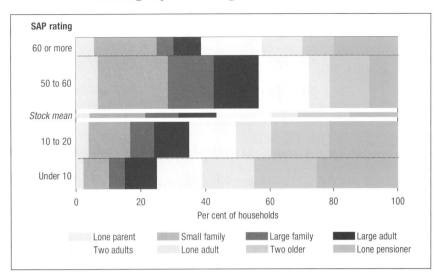

pensioner households and lone adults. Pensioner households are twice as likely to be found in reasonably efficient housing in the social rented sectors. All sectors have a high proportion of elderly households in the worst stock, but the concentration is greatest in the social rented sectors. Here 20% of such homes accommodate pensioner couples and a further 27% lone pensioners. (Figure 7.13 & Table A7.13) In such housing, around 3 in 5 heads of household are 60 years or more and 1 in 4 at least 75 years old.

Figure 7.13   Household types in most and least efficient dwellings by tenure

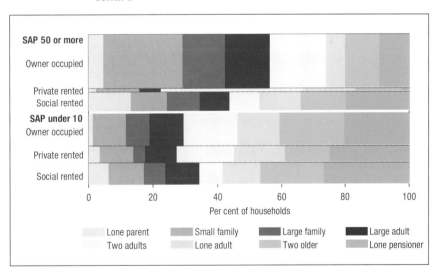

Socio-economic factors

7.32   Three fifths of all households living in least efficient homes are in the lowest two income quintiles, with two fifths gaining more than three-quarters of their income from state benefits. Approaching 2 in 3 heads of household are or had been manual workers, compared with around a half of the total population.

Households in most and least efficient dwelling types

7.33   The housing standards of different groups is a product largely of the tenure, type and age of dwellings that they occupy. Figures 7.14 and 7.15 show the distribution of households in the most and least efficient dwelling types. For the purpose of the analysis, these are defined as those types in each tenure that have a mean SAP rating of over 42 or 29 or below, both of these accounting separately for some 3.8 million homes or 20% of the

Figure 7.14 Household types in the most and least efficient dwelling types in the owner occupied sector

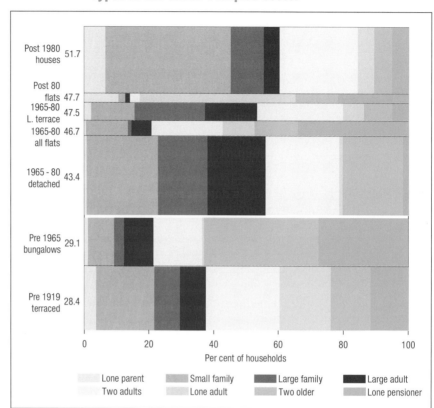

total stock[1]. The owner occupied sector has the largest stock of efficient dwelling types. Conversely, the rented sectors have the most inefficient types, with nearly 1.5 million such homes in the social rented sectors,

Figure 7.15 Household types in the most and least efficient dwelling types in the private rented sector

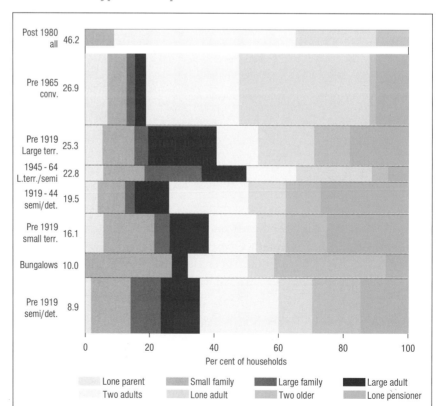

1 *For sake of clarity some dwelling types with very similar mean SAP ratings are grouped together*

over 1.3 million in the private rented stock and just over 1 million owner occupied. (Table A7.14)

Owner occupied sector

7.34   In the owner occupied stock, the occupation of the most efficient houses - large terraced properties built since 1965 and all post 1980 types - is dominated by small families and younger couples. Lone adults and older couples (40% in the total population) own less than a fifth of this stock. The latter groups are much more frequently found in flats built since 1965, albeit these are relatively few. Older couples are better represented in the large stock of detached houses built between 1965 and 1980, but inevitably these contain very few single households. Household distribution is very different in the most inefficient dwelling types, with an above average proportion of lone adults owning pre 1919 small terraced properties and over 60% of pre 1965 bungalows owned by pensioner households.

Private rented sector

7.35   The few efficient, modern properties in the private rented sector are rented mainly by adult couples. There is a more diverse range of inefficient dwelling types and spread of households than in other tenures. However, the proportion of lone adults in pre 1964 converted flats is five times the national average and, typically, between a third and two fifths of the least efficient types - pre 1919 and inter-war houses and bungalows - are privately rented by pensioner households.

Social rented sectors

7.36   Lone pensioners, lone adults and to a lesser extent older couples are much more likely to be accommodated in the most efficient parts of the housing stock in the social rented than in the private sector. (Figure 7.16) For example, some 64% of tenants in the large stock of low-rise flats built between 1965 and 1980 are single persons, over 45% being lone pensioners. However, the same household groups are also frequently over-represented

Figure 7.16   Household types in the most and least efficient dwelling types in the social rented sector

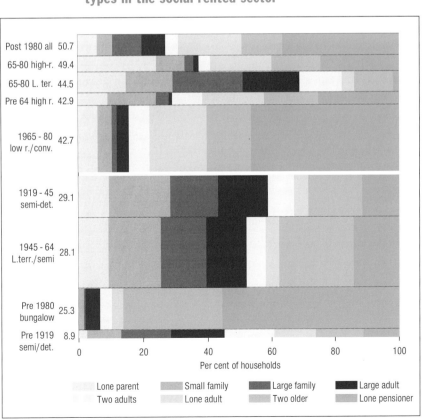

in the least efficient social housing. Nearly 1 in 4 tenants in inter-war semi-detached and large terraced houses built in the early post-war years are pensioner couples. Over 86% of those in the even poorer stock of pre 1980 bungalows are pensioner households, 56% being lone pensioners.

Households in best and worst homes of a specific type

7.37 While the dwelling types analysed above are generally the most and least energy efficient in the stock, they each account for only around half of all dwellings with SAP ratings of 50 or above and under 20. As shown in the previous chapter, most dwelling types have a wide range of efficiencies, and the question remains as to the extent to which, within any specific type, households also differ with varying standards. To answer this question the most common dwelling types in the owner occupied and social rented sectors are considered - namely the 1.4 million inter-war semi-detached houses and 0.65 million low rise flats built between 1965 and 1980. The household distributions in the most and least efficient dwellings of these two types are shown in Figure 7.17. (see also Table A7.15)

Figure 7.17 Household types in the most and least efficient homes from the most common owner occupied and social rented dwelling types

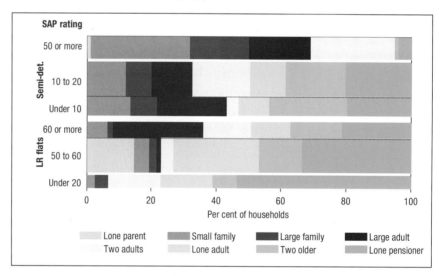

Owner occupied 1919-1945 semi-detached houses

7.38 For owner-occupied semi-detached houses built between the wars, the mean SAP rating of 33 is just under that for the stock as a whole. However, this type has nearly three times as many inefficient dwellings (13%) as efficient ones. Over 96% of the latter have gas central heating, while a quarter of the least efficient have solid fuel central heating and a further two-thirds lack any central system. Over two thirds of the most efficient homes are owned by families and large adult households and only 5% by pensioner households and lone adults. In contrast, these households own 50% of all inter-war semis with ratings under 20.

Social rented 1965-1980 purpose built low-rise flats

7.39 Socially rented low rise flats built between 1965 and 1980 have a mean SAP rating of 43 and over four times as many efficient dwellings (32%) as inefficient ones. Some 85% of the former have gas central heating, while nearly a third of the inefficient flats have on-peak electric underfloor or ceiling heating with a further quarter relying on individual electric fires or portable heaters. The efficient stock is rented predominantly by lone parents, lone adults and pensioner households. However, the last group are even more likely to be found in the least efficient flats of this type; well over half are rented by lone pensioners.

Part II ENERGY CONSUMPTION

Owner occupied sector

1 1919 - 1944
Semi-detached
£728

2 1945 - 1964
Semi-detached
£650

3 1965 - 1980
Detached
£837

4 1965 - 1980
Semi-detached
£633

5 1850 - 1899
Larger terraced
£682

6 Post 1980
Detached
£740

7 1850 - 1899
Small terraced
£585

8 1965 - 1980
Bungalow
£613

9 1945 - 1964
Bungalow
£657

10 1919 - 1944
Detached
£1000

Private rented sector

1 1850 - 1899
Converted flat
£560

2 1900 - 1918
Converted flat
£644

3 1850 - 1899
Small terraced
£511

4 1850 - 1899
Larger terraced
£585

5 Pre 1850
Converted flat
£760

Local authority sector

1 1965 - 1980
Low-rise flat
£396

2 1945 - 1964
Low-rise flat
£474

3 1945 - 1964
Semi-detached
£581

4 1919 - 1944
Semi-detached
£607

5 1919 - 1944
Small terraced
£557

6 1965 - 1980
Larger terraced
£625

7 1945 - 1964
Small terraced
£571

8 1965 - 1980
High-rise flat
£442

9 1945 - 1964
Larger terraced
£607

10 1945 - 1964
Bungalow
£455

Housing associations

Average total fuel expenditure (notes overleaf)

1 1965 - 1980
Low-rise flat
£339

2 Post 1980
Low-rise flat
£275

3 1850 - 1899
Converted flat
£448

4 1900 - 1918
Converted flat
£553

5 1965 - 1980
Larger terraced
£645

Figure II.1   **Average total fuel expenditure for the most numerous dwelling types in each sector**

The frontispiece to Part II shows the average total fuel expenditure for each of the most numerous dwelling types in the four sectors of the housing stock. Each figure represents the sum of the annual household fuel bills for electricity, mains gas and any non-metered fuels used, such as coal, oil or paraffin gas. For each dwelling type, total fuel expenditure will vary with the efficiency of the dwelling and particular household, but the mean expenditure also shows considerable divergence. Compared with an average for all households of around £660 per annum, this ranges from £1,000 for owner occupiers living in detached houses built between the wars to only £275 for housing association tenants living in post 1980 purpose built, low rise flats.

Chapter

Heating regimes & Case studies

Preamble

8.1   *This second part of the Report deals with energy consumption. It examines, in Chapter 9, how the heating facilities and other appliances, described in Part I, are used by households. Chapter 10 goes on to analyse how much fuel is consumed as a result and, finally, Chapter 11 analyses the consequent fuel expenditure of households. This Part starts, however, with a description of how levels of energy consumption can be assessed relative to the physical standards of the dwelling. This is followed by the second set of case studies.*

Heating regimes

Factors determining consumption

8.2   Patterns of energy consumption vary considerably within the housing stock, but typically two thirds of total consumption is used for space and water heating, and the remaining third for lighting, cooking and other domestic appliances. The main determinants of energy consumption in a dwelling, therefore, are the physical and social factors which affect heating, being primarily the:

❑   Heating regime -   the duration and time of the heating, the extent of the heating in the dwelling and temperatures achieved.

❑   Energy efficiency -   the efficiency of the heating system in providing heat for a set amount of fuel and the capacity of the building fabric to retain that heat.

❑   Dwelling size -   the total floor area affecting the heating requirement.

8.3   Other energy consumption is determined by the use and efficiency of the lighting, cooking and other appliances in the home but, being largely dependent on the size and type of household, this is also generally reflected in dwelling size.

8.4   While dwelling size and energy efficiency are set by the existing physical characteristics of the dwelling, the heating regime is more changeable, being determined by the household's lifestyle and behavioural attitudes and resulting use of their heating facilities and controls. As such, regimes differ widely with different household types and resources. Some households clearly waste energy, whilst others starve themselves of heat to maintain affordable fuel bills.

Thermal comfort and health risks

8.5   For the purposes of assessing levels of energy consumption in the stock, therefore, it is useful to determine what might be reasonably considered as fully satisfactory and minimum heating regimes. Research has shown[1] that most people begin to feel cold at temperatures below 18°C, but that there are no serious health risks until 16°C or below. There is then serious discomfort and an increased risk of respiratory illness. Below 12°C there is a more severe problem of increased cardiovascular disease and a risk of hypothermia below 9°C (Figure 8.1).

1   *GJ Raw and RM Hamilton, 1985, op.cit.*

Standard and minimum regimes

8.6 These temperatures suggest that a household's actual energy consumption may be measured against that required to achieve one of two heating regimes - the standard SAP regime providing thermal comfort and used when designing energy efficiency improvements - and a lower minimum standard safeguarding health, more appropriate for targeting action for improvement. (Table 8.1)

Figure 8.1   Room temperatures and possible health risks

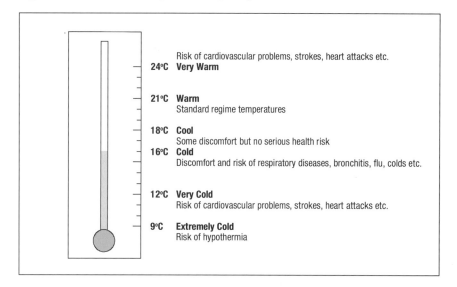

8.7 The standard heating regime used in calculating SAP ratings assumes temperatures for thermal comfort of 21 degrees Centigrade in the living room and 18°C in other rooms. The minimum regime provides for 18°C in the main living room and 16°C in other heated rooms when the outside temperature is -1°C (the design temperature of heating systems) and aims to maintain the 16°C and 12°C health thresholds during particularly cold weather. Because of the vulnerability of infants and elderly households, it provides for all-day heating. However, unlike the standard regime, only partial heating is allowed for - typically to the ground floor alone recognising that such homes are often under-occupied and that it is a 'minimum' regime.

Table 8.1   Specification of Minimum and Standard heating regimes

Heating regimes	Minimum	Standard
Room temperatures		
Living room	18°C	21°C
Other heated rooms	16°C	18°C
Duration of heating	All-day	Morning & evening
Extent of heating	Half-house	Full-house
References	*DOE Circular 6/90*	*Standard for SAP*

Examples of fuel expenditure

8.8 How the energy consumption and expenditure relates to different heating regimes, standards of energy efficiency and sizes of dwelling may be seen in Table 8.2. This assumes normal levels of occupancy for the size of the dwelling, and average use of lighting, cooking and other appliances, and that the location is in the centre of the country giving an average exposure and climate.

Table 8.2   Examples of homes and their fuel expenditure

Medium sized dwelling (70 sq.m.), with average SAP rating of 35 and heated to the:-		Annual fuel cost (£)
A) Minimum heating regime	(18°C & 16°C, half-house, 16 hours)	610
B) Standard heating regime	(21°C & 18°C, full-house, 9 hours)	700
Medium sized dwelling (70 sq.m.), heated to the standard regime, with:-		
C) very low energy efficiency	(SAP rating of -6)	1,415
D) low energy efficiency	(SAP rating of 17)	930
E) average energy efficiency	(SAP rating of 37)	680
F) good energy efficiency	(SAP rating of 57)	515
G) very good energy efficiency	(SAP rating of 79)	410
Standard heating regime in dwelling with average SAP rating of 35 and a:-		
H) small floor area of 40 sq. m.		445
I) average floor area of 80 sq. m.		780
J) large floor area 120 sq. m.		1,120
K) very large floor area of 160 sq. m.		1,455

Case studies

8.9   In practice, dwellings are often under-occupied, households make different use of appliances and heating regimes and local climates vary. How such factors affect energy consumption is explored in more detail in the second set of case studies. These illustrate the range in the use of heating and appliances, fuel consumption and fuel expenditure covered by the statistical material in the following three Chapters. (*Although based on data recorded in the EHCS, some details have been changed to protect the identity of individual households.*)

Case 8.1:
Owner occupied
1965-1980
Larger-terraced
(Fuel bill £767)

8.10   This former council house is located on a suburban, local authority built estate in a market town in the South East region. It illustrates the typical use of a full central heating system in a largish house of relatively high energy efficiency, but the maintenance of high room temperatures and heavy use of on-peak appliances, resulting in a slightly higher than average total fuel consumption and expenditure.

8.11   The modern 3 bedroom mid-terraced house was built in the 1970s, but has been subject to considerable improvement in recent years. This has included the erection of a single storey room extension, giving the dwelling a total floor area of 85 m². The main structure is of cavity brick under a pitched concrete tiled roof. The EHCS surveyor judged the house to be fully satisfactory, except for some condensation and mould growth.

Physical standards

8.12 Water and space heating is provided by a gas-fired boiler, feeding radiators in every room. The system is controlled by a timer, a room thermostat and thermostatic radiator valves. The cavity walls are insulated, as is the loft, the latter with 150mm of mineral wool. Overall, a half of the windows are double-glazed, and the hot water cylinder is insulated with a jacket. There are no extract fans in the dwelling. The SAP rating is 65.

8.13 The house has been occupied for the past two decades by the same family. Originally council tenants, the family became the owners in the eighties under the Right to Buy scheme. Both parents are working, the husband as a shop manager and wife as a receptionist, and the two teenage children are still at school. The annual household income is slightly below average for small families in owner occupation, but falls into the second highest quintile of household incomes generally.

Energy consumption

Heating and appliance use

8.14 The family use the central heating daily for two periods, from 7.30 to 8.30 in the morning and 5.00 to 9.30 in the evening, and rarely or never alter any of the controls. Cooking facilities comprise an electric oven and hob and a microwave, and the family also has a dishwasher which is used 4 times a week and a washing machine used daily, with the clothes being dried inside on a clothes horse or on radiators. All appliances are run using on-peak electricity.

Fuel consumption

8.15 The annual energy consumption is some 27,500 kWh, of which 83% is gas and 17% standard tariff electricity. After controlling for an above average floor area, this gives a unit fuel consumption of 324 kWh/m^2, which is fairly average for four person families in the owner occupied sector.

Fuel expenditure

8.16 While the family's overall fuel cost is average (2.80 p/kWh), the relatively large dwelling size results in an above average total fuel bill. This amounts to nearly £770, split equally between gas and electricity, although representing under 5% of the household's income. However, because of the relatively high SAP rating, this is 22% more than required to maintain the standard heating regime of full-house heating with temperatures of 21°C in the living room and 18°C elsewhere.

Thermal conditions

8.17 The family are very satisfied with their central heating system. On the afternoon of the interview, in mid April 1992, the occupants had been in the house for 1 to 2 hours, but the heating had remained off since 8.30 that morning. Despite this and an outside temperature of only some 11°C, the recorded home temperatures were 22.2°C in the living room and 21.4°C in the hall, these being rated by the household as "comfortable" but "colder than usual".

Energy action

8.18 Since 1986, the family have improved the energy efficiency of the dwelling, installing a new gas-fired water borne central heating system, a new damp-proof course, some replacement PVC-U double glazed windows and a new cylinder jacket. The dwelling offers little scope for further energy measures, except possibly for a 'white meter' to run appliances off-peak.

However, reducing temperatures in the living rooms to 21°C and elsewhere to 18°C would reduce the existing fuel consumption and total fuel bill by around 15%.

Case 8.2:
Owner occupied
Pre 1850
Detached house
(Fuel bill £1,127)

8.19 This owner occupied detached house, near a small village in the Devon and Cornwall sub-region, illustrates average energy efficiency but a higher than average total fuel consumption typical of large detached, older rural properties with oil-fired heating.

8.20 The large, 4 bedroom house dates from before 1850, but has a small pre-war single storey kitchen extension, giving a total floor area of 120 m². The fabric is of 9" solid brick, with a pitched, clay tiled roof and a mixture of wooden and metal framed single glazed windows. The EHCS surveyor found the property to be unfit due to extensive internal and external disrepair, structural problems and penetrating damp.

Physical standards

8.21 Space heating and hot water is provided by an oil-fired boiler feeding radiators in all rooms, the system being controlled by a timer, a room thermostat and thermostatic radiator valves. The loft is insulated and the hot water cylinder also has an insulation jacket. Draught excluders are fitted in the hall. The SAP rating is calculated to be 34.

8.22 The house has been occupied for the past 25 years by the same family, which now comprises a middle aged couple and their teenage daughter. Both parents are employed in the farming industry but the household income is low for owner occupiers with small families, although still falling within the second highest income quintile.

Energy consumption

Heating and appliance use

8.23 During the week the family use the central heating for two periods, from 6.30 to 8.30 in the morning and then again from 12.30 to 10.30 pm. At the weekend they heat the house all day between 8.00 am and 10.30 pm. They rarely or never alter any of the controls. Cooking facilities include an electric hob and oven and a microwave. The family also has a washing machine which is used 5 times per week, the clothes generally being dried on a line in the kitchen. All appliances are run using on-peak electricity.

Fuel consumption

8.24 The annual energy consumption is some 59,200 kWh, of which 84% is oil and 16% standard rate electricity. After controlling for an above average floor area, this gives a unit fuel consumption of some 498 kWh/m², which is high for 3 person families in the owner occupied sector, but not untypical of large detached, rural properties with oil-fired central heating.

Fuel expenditure

8.25 The total fuel bill of £1,130, of which 68% is electricity, is also relatively high, although the combination of a large floor area and low unit fuel cost (1.90 p/kWh) results in a fairly average unit expenditure of 9.47 £/m². The family are spending nearly 7% of their total income on fuel, which represents 94% of the amount required to maintain the full standard heating regime, but more than required for the minimum regime.

Thermal conditions

8.26 The family are very satisfied with their central heating system, but are distressed by the severe condensation and mould growth in the dining room, kitchen and bathroom, and find the house to be draughty. On the afternoon of the interview the occupants had been at home for 2 to 4 hours and the house heated as usual for a weekday. The recorded temperatures were 18.9°C in the living room and 19.7°C in the hall, with an outside temperature of 11.3°C. These were rated by the household as "comfortably warm" and "the same as usual".

Energy action

8.27 The dwelling offers some scope for further energy measures, particularly as substantial repair of the building fabric is needed. A package of measures including further draught stripping, secondary double glazing, roof insulation topped up to 150mm and upgraded heating controls would increase the SAP rating of the house to over 50.

Case 8.3:
Local authority
1919-1944
Semi-detached
(Fuel bill £675)

8.28 This council house is located on a suburban council estate in an industrial town in the West Yorkshire metropolitan area. It illustrates the morning and evening use of a partial central heating system and inefficient water heating in a dwelling of low energy efficiency. This results in a fairly average fuel consumption and expenditure, which nevertheless falls short of that required to achieve even the minimum heating regime.

8.29 The inter-war semi-detached house, modernised between 1965 and 1980, has a total floor area of 75 m². The accommodation comprises a hall, living room and kitchen on the ground floor and 3 bedrooms and bathroom on the first. The walls are of cavity brickwork to the ground floor and rendered precast concrete panels above, with wooden single-glazed casement windows. The roof cover is natural slate. The surveyor considered the dwelling to be in need of external repair and recorded condensation and mould in the bedrooms and bathroom.

Physical standards

8.30   Heating provision consists of a mains gas fire, with back boiler, in the living room serving radiators in the hall, kitchen and bathroom. The bedrooms have no heating provision at all. The gas fire and central heating have controls although the type is not recorded. Hot water is supplied by an on-peak electric immersion heater to a jacket insulated cylinder. The only other insulation present is 50mm of mineral wool between joists in the loft, and there are no extract fans in the dwelling. The SAP rating is calculated to be 19.

8.31   The tenant of the property for the past eight years has been a jobbing gardener, who is currently unemployed. The family of four are receiving state benefits, having an annual income below average for small families in council housing and in the second lowest income quintile for all households.

Energy consumption

Heating and appliance use

8.32   The family use the partial central heating system daily, heating the house from 7.00 to 8.15 in the morning and from 6.20 to 11.00 in the evening during the week and from 9.00 to 11.30 am and 5.30 to 11.00 pm at weekends. The controls provided are rarely or never changed, and they use no heating at all in the bedrooms. The family cook with a mains gas hob and oven, and have a washing machine which is used once per week, with the clothes being dried on a line in the kitchen.

Fuel consumption

Fuel expenditure

8.33   Both the annual fuel consumption at 25,630 kWh (86.3% gas, 13.7% electricity) and the total fuel bill at £675 (55% gas, 45% electricity) are fairly average for the stock nationally. However, this resulted from a high fuel use (346 kWh/m^2) combined with an average floor area and below average fuel cost (2.63 p/kWh). The household, who are receiving state benefits due to the permanent ill-health of the head, are spending just under a tenth of their income on fuel. This amounts to under 80% of that required to maintain a minimum heating regime giving temperatures of 18°C in the living room and 16°C in other downstairs rooms.

Thermal conditions

8.34   On the afternoon of the interview, in early April 1991, neither the living room nor hall temperature (13.2°C and 13.8°C respectively) were much above the outside temperature of 12.9°C, the heating having been off since 8.15 that morning and the family having been in for less than half an hour. However, this was judged to be the 'same as usual', and 'comfortably cool' overall. The family are fairly satisfied with the heating, although the condensation and mould growth is causing some inconvenience and the house is considered to be draughty.

Energy action

8.35   According to the EHCS postal survey, the house is not subject to or proposed for any kind of action. There is however considerable scope for further energy measures such as extra loft insulation, cavity wall insulation, double glazing and draught stripping. There is also scope to extend the central heating system to the upstairs rooms, although this would probably necessitate the replacement of the boiler as well. A comprehensive package of heating and insulation measures could raise the SAP rating to over 70, at a cost of about £7,400 and with a payback period of 13 years.

Case 8.4:
Housing
association
1919-1944
Semi-detached
(Fuel bill £468)

8.36 This council built house, located in a coastal area in the North Eastern region, is in housing association ownership. It is a more extreme example of lack of affordable warmth, illustrating the under-occupation of a house of very poor energy efficiency. Here, irregular heating results in a relatively low fuel expenditure, which is nevertheless very high in relation to income.

8.37 The inter-war semi-detached house, of 94 m², comprises a hall, 2 receptions and a kitchen on the ground floor, and 3 bedrooms and a bathroom on the first. Built of cavity brick, the property has a pitched roof, refurbished with clay tiles in the 1960s, and replacement single glazed wooden casement windows, installed in the 1980s. The surveyor found the house, although not unfit, to be defective in its provision of amenities, in disrepair and with some evidence of penetrating damp.

Physical standards

8.38 Heating is provided by an open solid fuel fire in the main living room and 4 portable electric heaters elsewhere. Hot water is supplied by a back boiler to an uninsulated tank, and backed up by an on-peak electric immersion heater. The only insulation measure is 100mm of mineral wool insulation to the loft. The SAP rating is calculated to be 5.

8.39 The tenant, a female office cleaner approaching retirement age, has lived in the house for 30 years, and is currently unemployed and receiving state benefits. Her income is below average for single adults renting from a housing association, falling well within the lowest 20% of household incomes.

Energy consumption

Heating and appliance use

Fuel consumption

Fuel expenditure

8.40 The heating is used on a daily basis but not at regular periods, and water is heated when needed, using the back boiler in winter and the immersion heater in summer. Cooking is done using an electric hob and oven, and the tenant also has a washing machine which is used once a week, with the clothes generally being dried outside.

8.41 The low annual energy consumption of 17,630 kWh (21% on-peak electricity, 79% solid fuel) and relatively low fuel bill of £470 (71% electricity, 29% solid fuel) resulted from a low unit fuel use (188 kWh/m²) and an average overall fuel cost (2.65 p/kWh.). However, due to her particularly low income, the occupant was still spending well over a fifth (22%) of her income on fuel, although this represented under 40% of the amount required to maintain the minimum heating regime.

Thermal conditions

8.42 The occupant considered the heating to be very satisfactory. When interviewed in late February, however, she had not used the heating that day despite having been in the house for more than 7 hours. As a consequence, the temperatures of the living room and hall were not much more than 1°C higher than that outside, both being around 13°C. The occupier found this to be 'comfortably cool' and similar to the usual temperature.

Energy Action

8.43 According to the EHCS postal survey, the house is not subject to or proposed for any kind of action. There is however considerable scope for further energy measures. A comprehensive package of heating and insulation work could raise the SAP rating to over 80, at a cost of about £10,500, giving a payback period of 10 years.

Comparison of case studies

8.44 Table 8.3 compares the energy consumption and other key characteristics of each of the second four case studies with the average figures (in brackets) for the same type of household in the same sector, as well as for all households. Further comparative statistics are given in Table A8.1.

Table 8.3   Comparison of case study dwellings with mean for all households of same tenure, type and size

Case study figures/(mean for household type & size in tenure)

	Case 1 00 - 4p family	Case 2 00 - 3p family	Case 3[2] LA - 4p family	Case 4 HA - 1p adult	All house-holds
Physical standards					
Dwelling size sq.m.	85 (95)	119 (82)	74 (66)	94 (65)	**(83)**
Energy SAP rating	65 (43)	34 (37)	19 (33)	5 (18)	**(35)**
Energy consumption					
Total consumption MWh	27.5 (29.2)	59.2 (26.0)	25.6 (22.6)	17.6 (16.5)	**(24.0)**
Unit consumption kWh/m²	324 (324)	498 (329)	346 (353)	188 (304)	**(303)**
Unit fuel cost p/kWh	2.78 (2.90)	1.90 (2.97)	2.63 (3.15)	2.66 (3.14)	**(3.23)**
Total expenditure £	767 (787)	1,127 (731)	675 (677)	468 (480)	**(661)**
Unit expenditure £/sq.m.	9.02 (8.95)	9.47 (9.29)	9.12(10.41)	4.98 (9.35)	**(8.68)**
Adequacy of spend[1]	122 (94.5)	94.2 (97.4)	67.8 (94.6)	32.3 (91.3)	**(87.7)**
Thermal conditions					
Outside temp °C	11.4 (10.9)	11.3 (11.5)	12.9 (10.6)	11.9 (12.3)	**(11.1)**
Living room temp °C	22.2 (19.4)	18.9 (19.8)	13.22 (19.7)	13.0 (18.2)	**(19.5)**
Hall/stairs temp °C	21.4 (18.5)	19.7 (18.8)	13.82 (18.0)	13.0 (17.0)	**(18.3)**
Energy action					
Target SAP rating	65	51	81	86	-
Improvement cost £	0	3,930	7,410	10,480	-
Simple payback yrs	-	14	13	10	-

1 Adequacy to achieve standard heating regime
2 Household in home less than 1 hour

Chapter 9

Heating and appliance use

Preamble

9.1 *Domestic energy consumption depends on both the physical characteristics of a dwelling and the life-styles of the occupants. In this Chapter, we examine how households use their space and water heating facilities, including the controls available on their heating. The Chapter concludes by looking at other major sources of energy consumption, namely the use of cooking and washing appliances in the housing stock - these also being a cause of condensation.*

Use of heating

9.2 In the Interview Survey, households were asked if they own a central heating system and whether they use it, and if not the reasons why. Table 9.1 compares the main type of space heating available in the home with the heating used by households during the winter.

Table 9.1   Comparison between heating used and main type of space heating available

thousand households/%

	Main type available[1]		Type used		Difference of use	
	No. of hh	% of hh	No. of hh	% of hh	No. of hh	% change
Central Heating						
Mains gas	12,709	66.5	12,546	65.6	- 163	- 1.3
Solid fuel	900	4.7	868	4.5	- 32	-3.6
Electric	1,492	7.8	1,453	7.6	- 39	- 2.6
Fuel oil	594	3.1	585	3.1	- 9	- 1.5
Communal etc	309	1.6	272	1.4	- 37	-12.0
All CH systems	16,004	83.7	15,724	82.2	- 280	- 1.7
Non-CH						
Mains gas	2,297	12.0	2418	12.7	+ 121	+ 5.3
Solid fuel	453	2.4	467	2.4	+ 14	+ 3.1
Electric	133	0.7	176	0.9	+ 43	+ 32.3
Portable/none	225	1.2	326	1.7	+ 101	+ 44.9
All non-CH	3,107	16.3	3387	17.7	+ 280	+ 9.0
All households	19,111	100.0	19,111	100.0		

1 Where homes have both central heating and individual appliances, the former is taken as the main type available

Non-use of central heating

9.3 Some 280 thousand or just under 2% of all households owning a central heating system do not use it. However, this proportion is nearer 3 and 4% for those with electric and solid fuel systems and 12% for 'other' central heating, including communal systems. Instead of their central heating, over 43% of these households use a gas fire in their living room and almost as many (over 36%) a portable heater or no heating source. As a result, over 100 thousand more households are relying on portable heaters or use no heating than the 225 thousand who lack fixed heating. (Table 9.1)

Characteristics of non-users

9.4 Households who possess but do not use their central heating comprise a greater proportion of tenants than would be expected from the distribution of central heating by tenure. Some 30% are local authority tenants, although the council stock accounts for less than a fifth of all centrally heated homes. Over a third are lone parents and two-thirds are amongst those with the lowest 40% of incomes, the corresponding figures for the total centrally heated stock being only 7% and 25% respectively.

Reasons for
non-use

9.5 Almost 55% of households who do not use their central heating, cite the running costs - "expensive/can't afford to run" - as a reason for not using it, and in over 38% of all cases this is the only reason given. Other reasons coded are that the central heating needs repair or is too old (9%), is too hot or too cold (6%) or has other problems. (Table A9.1)

9.6 All lone parents who own a central heating system but do not use it give the running costs as the reason, as do over three-quarters of large adult households and two-thirds of small families. However, lone pensioners and older couples are more likely to give other than financial reasons for not using their central heating. However, no-one picked "controls too difficult/complicated" as a reason.

Figure 9.1 **Percentage of households owning but not using central heating by tenure**

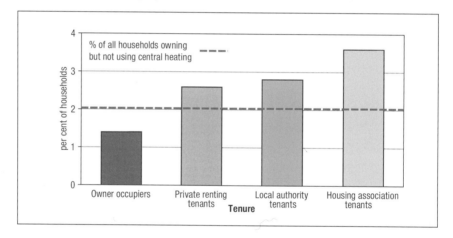

Use of heating
controls

Central
heating

9.7 All households with central heating were asked what type of controls they have on their system, whether this enabled them to switch off their heating completely and how often they change these. Over 2% of households said that they cannot switch off their heating completely. Almost two-thirds of these have solid fuel central heating, mainly with a back-boiler to an open fire, although the remaining 73% of households with such systems do not record this complaint.

9.8 Table A9.2 shows the percentage of households that possess each type of control and the percentage that change these "at least once a week" or "rarely or never". In most cases, the control is "rarely or never" changed during the winter; for example, less than 1 in 5 households regularly use the manual valve on their radiators. However, both wall thermostats and the manual override on a programmer are used at least once a week by over 44% of the households that have them.

Other heating
systems

9.9 All households that did not have central heating or that did not use it, were similarly asked to identify the controls they had on their main heating appliance and the frequency with which they changed these during the winter. Table A9.3 summarises the number of households with each control and the percentage who alter their control settings during the winter "at least once a week" or "rarely or never". Heat output and other controls were adjusted regularly, some 80% of households that had either of these controls adjusted them at least once a week. The remainder of the controls were more likely to be "rarely or never" changed than be changed "at least once a week".

Heating patterns

Classification of

9.10 The EHCS Interview Survey included questions on the times and duration when heating is used in the living rooms and in bedrooms. A distinction is made between weekdays, Saturdays and Sundays, recognising that during the week many homes are unheated whilst their occupants are at work and that occupancy patterns may also differ between Saturday and Sunday. If the living room or main bedroom is heated regularly, the times at which the heating is switched on and off during the day was recorded to determine the heating pattern. Previous studies[1] have identified typical heating patterns used by British householders as:-

- ❑ All day/night · · · · typically 16 hours
- ❑ Morning and Evening · · · · typically 2 hours in the morning and 6 hours in the evening
- ❑ Evening only · · · · typically 6 hours in the evening

9.11 According to when the heating was switched on and off, the EHCS data has been allocated to one of these categories, where possible. In practice, the average number of hours homes are heated 'all-day' and in the 'morning-and-evening' are found to be somewhat higher than the typical duration quoted above, whilst in the case of 'evening-only' heating they are slightly lower. For households who do not heat their home regularly, the pattern was coded as "daily but not regularly", "less than daily, but occasionally" or "rarely or never". To accommodate these other cases, two further main categories - "no regular heating pattern" and "no heating in the named room" - have been added to the 3 listed above.

Weekly variation

9.12 Only a minority of households change their heating pattern during the week. Approaching two thirds (63%) have the same pattern in their living room on all 7 days. Around 14% have the same pattern on Saturdays and Sundays but a different one on weekdays, while a further 9% change the pattern only on Sunday. Finally, some 13% have different patterns on Saturday, Sunday and weekdays. Even less variation was recorded for the main bedroom, over three quarters (78%) maintaining the same heating pattern throughout the entire week. (Table A9.4)

9.13 Clearly, any change in the duration of heating reflects the households' change in occupancy. Where the heating pattern in the living room remains the same during the whole week, all-day heating is the most frequent pattern used. However, where a different pattern is used over the weekend or on Sunday, morning-and-evening heating is the most common during the week with the living room being heated all-day on Saturday and/or Sunday.

Stock characteristics

Tenure

9.14 Heating patterns vary substantially between tenures, reflecting not only differences in the age and employment status of those housed but between the types of heating and levels of control available. Heating the living room in the morning-and-evening is the most frequent pattern used by owner occupiers,

1   *BREDEM - BRE Domestic Energy Model: Background philosophy and description. B. R. Anderson et al. BRE Report, Garston, 1985.*

albeit with a noticeable increase in all-day heating at the weekend. In contrast, heating all day during the week is the most common pattern in all the rented sectors. For local authority and private tenants, morning-and-evening heating is slightly more common than evening only heating, although the reverse is the case for tenants renting from a housing association. In all tenanted sectors, the proportion of households heating all-day increases at the weekends, especially on Sundays. (Figure 9.2 & Table A9.5)

Figure 9.2   Heating pattern *(in living room on weekdays)* by tenure

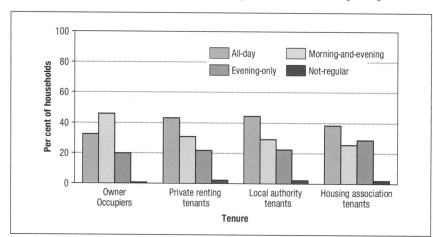

9.15   Over three times as many council and private tenants (19%) and over twice as many housing association tenants (15%) have unheated bedrooms as do owner occupiers (6%). In all tenures, households who heat their living room morning-and-evenings or evening only, tend to have the same heating pattern for their main bedroom. However, only half the owners and a third of the tenants who heat their living room all day heat their bedroom for as long. In contrast to the living room, a significant proportion of households in all tenures heat their bedroom irregularly.

Dwelling type etc   9.16   Reflecting differences in tenure, standards and heating facilities and in the social composition of households, there are also significant differences in the distribution of heating patterns found in different dwelling types and ages, in different regions and dwelling locations and amongst dwellings of different general condition. (see Tables A9.6, A9.7 & A9.9)

Energy characteristics

Central heating   9.17   In centrally heated dwellings, the most common heating pattern adopted in the living room varies with the fuel used and probably reflects the ease with which the systems can be controlled to provide intermittent heating. For gas and oil fired systems, morning-and-evening heating is the most frequently used, with respectively 50% and 54% of households adopting this pattern during the week. However, with both these fuels, there is a noticeable increase in all-day heating at the weekend, particularly on Sundays, when less than a third maintain a morning-and-evening regime. For electric and solid fuel central heating the situation is very different. During the week, all day heating is the most frequent in each case (59% and 71% respectively), and there is less divergence between weekday and Sunday patterns. (Figure 9.3)

9.18   Only 4% of main bedrooms in all centrally heated dwellings are not heated. However, some 12% of households with electric central heating and 7% with communal and other systems do not heat their bedroom, compared with under 3% of those using gas or oil-fired central heating. (Table A9.8)

Figure 9.3   Heating patterns *(in living room on weekdays)* by central heating fuel

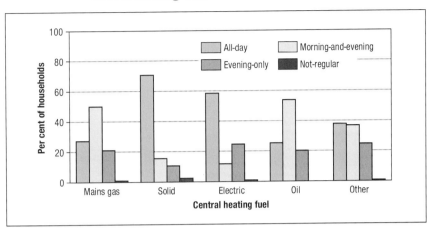

Central heating controls

9.19   Heating patterns are closely related to the level of heating control. Table A9.10 shows the patterns used in the living room during the week in centrally heated dwellings by the level of time and temperature control available. The influence of time controls is clearly evident. Only 16% of households who had neither time nor temperature control and some 21% of those with only temperature control had morning and evening heating. In contrast, almost a half of those who had time control only and over a half with both forms of control had this pattern.

9.20   Although heating the living room all day increases at the weekend irrespective of the level of control, the percentage still heating the living room in the morning and evening is significantly lower for those with no time control. The percentage changing their heating pattern at the weekend is also significantly higher for those with only a time control (30%) and both time and temperature control (27%) than for households with only temperature control (18%) or neither form of control (17%).

Other heating systems

9.21   For dwellings without central heating, all-day heating is the most frequent pattern employed in the living room during the week, with 44% of households using electricity, 53% using mains gas and 64% with solid fuel heating using this regime. However, the main difference in non-centrally heated homes is that nearly 40% of main bedrooms go unheated - compared to only 4% of those in centrally heated dwellings. (Figure 9.4 & Table A9.8)

Figure 9.4   Heating patterns *(in living room on weekdays)* by non-central heating fuel

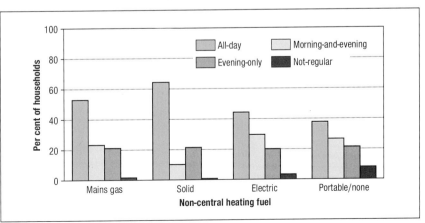

SAP energy ratings

9.22 Figure 9.5 shows the relationship between the living room heating pattern used during the week and the dwellings SAP energy rating. As the SAP rating rises, the proportion of households heating their home all-day decreases, whilst those using a morning-and-evening heating pattern increase. In part, this result may be explained by the fact that those in work who only require morning-and-evening heating tend to occupy better housing than the retired and unemployed who are at home all-day. However, a repeat of the analysis excluding those households in full-time work, shows a similar picture. By retaining heat longer and having heating systems and controls which readily permit intermittent heating, more efficient dwellings allow the more frequent use of more flexible and shorter heating regimes. (Table A9.11)

Figure 9.5   The influence of SAP ratings on heating patterns *(in living room on weekdays)*

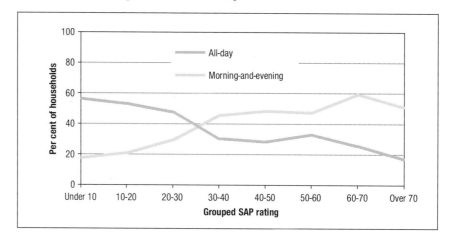

Household characteristics

Household type

9.23 Heating patterns vary with the type of household reflecting general differences in their working status as well as their heating facilities. Heating the living room all-day during the week was more common (53%) for lone pensioners than any other type of household. However, some 47% of older couples and 43% of lone parents also had this pattern. Lone parents and lone adults were most likely to leave the main bedroom unheated, some 21% and 16% respectively not heating this room. As the size of household increases, the frequency of all-day heating in the living room tends to decrease while that of morning-and-evening heating increases - only 29% of large families using the former pattern and 52% the latter. (Table A9.12)

Employment status

9.24 As expected, heating patterns follow closely the employment status of the household. Thus, heating the living room in the morning and evening during the week was more frequent (58%) in households where 2 people were in full-time employment than in any other category. Conversely, heating the living room all day was particularly common, both during the week and on Sundays, for two person and single households not in work. However, 16% of the latter did not heat their bedroom, compared to under 5% of households with 2 persons in full-time work. (Table A9.13)

9.25 Where 2 members are in full-time work, the percentage of households using a morning and evening heating pattern in the living room during the week varies significantly with the level of control. Where households have no time or temperature controls or only a temperature control, 30% and 27% respectively employ this pattern. In contrast, where there was time control or both time and temperature control, 56% and 66% respectively employed a morning-and-evening pattern. If the example of two members of the household not working is considered a similar result emerges; a significantly smaller percentage of households lacking any time control employ a morning and evening heating pattern than those with time control.

Household
income

9.26 There is also a strong relationship between heating patterns and household income. As incomes rise, the number of households heating their living room morning-and-evening increases progressively, whilst the number with all-day heating decreases. Similarly, the number using a morning-and-evening pattern in the bedroom also rises and the percentage of bedrooms left unheated falls - from 18% to under 2% for those on the lowest and highest 20% of incomes. (Figure 9.6 & Table A9.14)

Figure 9.6 **Heating pattern** *(in living room on weekdays)* **by household income**

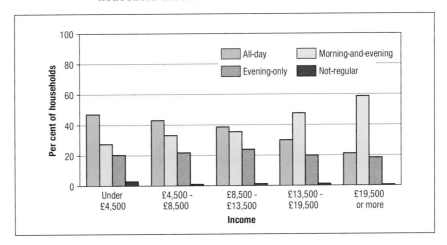

Income support

9.27 Not surprisingly, households with an income at or below income support level have similar heating patterns to those in the lowest 20% of incomes. Most heat their living rooms all day during the week, 47% adopting this pattern compared to 31% heating morning-and-evening and 19% in the evening only. This is in contrast to all other households where the most common heating pattern is morning-and-evening heating. In comparison with 9% of all households, 17% do not heat their main bedroom. (Table A9.15)

Trends, 1986
to 1991

9.28 The EHCS findings indicate that there have been some changes in the heating patterns used by households between 1986 and 1991. The most significant change is the reduction in the number of main bedrooms that remain unheated. In 1986 some 22% of main bedrooms were not heated, but by 1991 this figure had dropped to just under 10%. This characteristic is evident across all tenures with less than one fifth of local authority homes having no heat in the main bedroom in 1991 compared with over a third in 1986. There has also been a significant increase in the number of households heating their main bedroom in the morning and evening. In 1986 some 13% of households with central heating did not heat their bedroom compared with only 4% in 1991. For those households without central heating, in 1986 some 45% did not heat their main bedroom whereas in 1991 this percentage had dropped to 38%.

9.29 If the weekday heating pattern in the living room is considered, it is also clear that the percentage of households having irregular heating patterns has also decreased. This characteristic is common to all tenures but is particularly striking in the local authority and private rented stock. In 1986 some 11% of council tenants did not heat their living rooms regularly whereas by 1991 this percentage had dropped to just over 2%.

Use of water heating

9.30 Around 2.2 million or 12% of all households use a different method of heating their water in summer from that used in winter, and in the vast majority of cases the change is from a central heating system to an electric immersion heater. In winter just over 73% of households use their central heating system to heat their water, but in summer this drops to just under 61%. Conversely, use of electric immersion heaters increases from just over 18% during the winter to some 28% in summer. (Table A9.16)

9.31 In over 9 out of 10 cases, the switch is to an on-peak immersion heater, in summer over three-quarters of such heaters being run on the standard tariff compared with two thirds of those used during the winter. By comparison, the use of gas and electric instantaneous water heaters remains fairly constant. The proportion of households switching to a different system in summer, depends largely on the type of fuel used in winter. Only some 8% of households with gas central heating change to an immersion heater in summer, compared with 29% of those using tanked gas, 30% with oil and 62% with solid fuel central heating.

Cooking facilities

9.32 Cooking is estimated to account for typically nearly 5% of domestic energy consumption[2]. In the Interview Survey, households were asked whether they had exclusive or shared use of a "proper" cooker (3 or more rings and an oven), a small cooker (at least 2 rings and a grill) or a microwave oven. For those having a cooker, the type of fuel used for the hob and for the oven was recorded.

9.33 Almost 98% of all households had use of a proper cooker, nearly 3% a small cooker and 57% a microwave. In a small number of cases, under half a percent of households, a microwave was the only cooking appliance recorded. However, just under 1% of households, mainly in the private rented sector, shared cooking facilities with others.

Cooking fuels

9.34 Some 16 different combinations of fuels used for the hob and main oven were identified in the EHCS sample. However only half of these each accounted for more than 0.1% of all cases and these are listed, with the remaining combinations banded into two small groups, in Table 9.2. Some

Table 9.2 Fuels used for cooker hob and oven

Cooking fuel for hob and oven	% of households	% of hh also with microwave
Mains gas hob and oven	46.7	51.6
Electric hob and oven	38.4	56.4
Bottled gas hob and oven	1.5	58.2
Solid fuel hob and oven	0.4	45.7
Oil fired hob and oven	0.3	53.9
Mains gas hob and electric oven	11.5	81.6
Bottled gas hob and electric oven	0.5	85.9
Electric hob and any other oven	0.3	57.1
Other combinations	0.1	85.9
No cooker	0.5	68.7

2   *L D Shorrock and J H F Bown, Domestic Energy Fact File 1993 update, HMSO, 1993*

47% of all households use mains gas cookers and 38% use electric cookers. Of the remainder, bottled gas was used by almost 2% and solid fuel, oil and other fuel by just under 1%. Some 12% of households had dual fuel cooking facilities and in over 90% of these mains gas was used to fuel the hob and electricity the oven. Over four fifths of these households also owned a microwave, compared to just over half of those using cookers fuelled only by mains gas.

Stock characteristics

Tenure

9.35 Gas cookers were more common in owner occupied (44%) and local authority properties (59%) whilst electric cookers were more frequently found in housing association (53%) and private rented homes. Dual fuel cookers were characteristic of owner occupied homes, almost 94% being found in this sector and over 17% of owner occupiers having such facilities. In contrast, under 2% of housing association tenants had a dual fuel cooker. Microwaves were also more common amongst owner occupiers, 65% of households possessing one compared with only 39% of housing association tenants. (Figure 9.7 & Table A9.17)

Figure 9.7 Cooking fuels by tenure *(types accounting for less than 1% not labelled)*

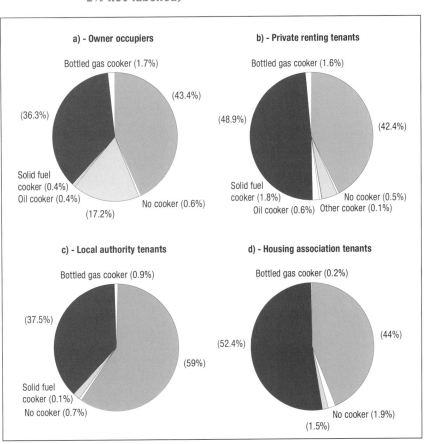

Dwelling type and age

9.36 Electric cookers were more common in flats, both converted (53%) and purpose built (46%), than in any other dwelling type. Mains gas cookers were most frequently found in mid-terraced houses (60%) whilst some 63% of households living in temporary dwellings used a bottle gas cooker. Almost 41% of dual fuel cookers were found in detached houses and some 30% in semi-detached ones, these being more likely to be modern than older dwellings. Conversely, the less common cooking fuels, solid, fuel oil and other, were more frequently found in older properties. Microwaves were less commonly available in converted (27%) and purpose built flats than in other house types, and although not generally correlated with dwelling age were most frequently found in the post 1980 stock. (Table A9.17)

Dwelling location

9.37 As expected, as the location of the dwelling changes from city centre to rural isolated sites, there is a decrease in the incidence of gas cookers and increase in the use of electricity and bottled gas. There is a similar increase in the frequency of solid fuel, oil and other fuels for cooking, for which there are no recorded cases in city centres. Dwelling location has less influence on the ownership of microwave ovens, although these are somewhat less common in city centres and urban locations. In all areas other than Greater London, a household is more likely to have a microwave than not. (Table A9.17)

Region

9.38 These locational differences are reflected generally in the regional picture. The South West region where the supply of natural gas is most limited, has the lowest proportion of gas cookers (35%) and highest proportion of electric ones (51%). Almost 30% of all solid fuel cookers, 41% of oil fired cookers and 50% using 'other' fuels are also to be found in this one region.

Household characteristics

Household type

9.39 Lone pensioners are more likely to have an electric cooker (47%) than any other type of household. However, lone parents were least likely to cook by electricity (31%), having the greatest incidence of 'all gas' cookers (53%). Dual fuel cookers were most common in larger households, while over half of those that lacked a cooker were single person households and a further quarter 2 person households. The proportion of households owning a microwave increases with household size, from some 32% for single person households to 72% for households of 5 or more. However, only some 1 in 4 lone pensioners have microwaves compared with about 3 in 4 large families. Lone pensioners, lone adults and older couples are more likely to lack a microwave than own one, whereas the reverse is true for all other households.

Employment status

9.40 The type of cooker that a household has reflects their employment status. Households where the main members are not in work are more likely to cook by gas than other households. Such households are least likely to have dual fuel cookers (5%), these being most common where a minimum of one member is in full-time work (20%). These latter households are also the most likely to use solid fuel, oil or other fuelled cookers. The highest incidence of microwaves is recorded where two people are in full-time employment (79%), whilst the lowest incidence is for a single person not working (31%). (Table A9.18)

Household income

9.41 The proportion of households cooking by gas tends to decrease as incomes rise, just over a third of those in the highest 20% of incomes using gas compared with a half of those in the lowest quintile. (Figure 9.8) Some 56% of households that own an oil-fired cooker and 44% of those with dual fuel cookers are in the highest quintile, only 10% of the latter falling in the lowest income group. The ownership of microwaves similarly increases with income, over three-quarters of those in the highest income group having them compared with a third of those in the lowest group. (Figure 9.9 & Table A9.18)

Figure 9.8   Type of cooker by household income

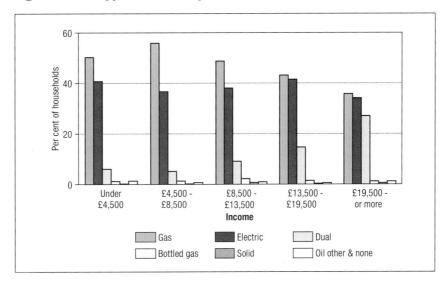

Figure 9.9   Use of microwave oven by household income

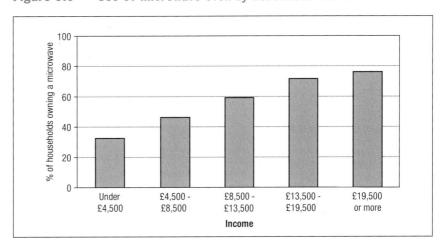

Washing appliances

9.42   In a typical home, the use of washing appliances can account for up to 14% of domestic electricity consumption attributable to lights and appliances.[3] The EHCS asked households if they had exclusive or shared use of a washing machine (including washer-dryers), a tumble drier or a dishwasher. Those owning appliances were further questioned about how often they use them in winter, whether they have 'economy 7' and if they run their appliances in the off-peak period.

Use of appliances

9.43   Washing machines are the most commonly owned 'washing' appliance, with 88% of household having one; half this number (44%) have a tumble drier while only 17% possess a dishwasher. Some 12% have all three, 31% a washing machine and tumble drier and 40% a washing machine alone. Less than 1% of households share a washing machine or tumble drier and no one was recorded as sharing a dishwasher. (Table A9.19)

Loads per week   9.44   On average, washing machines and dishwashers are used around 5 times a week and tumble driers some 3 times a week. Not surprisingly, the larger the household the more often each appliance is likely to be used - families of 5 or more washing an average of over 10 loads of clothes each week. (Figure 9.10) However, whilst there is a similar correlation with the type

3   *L D Shorrock and G Henderson, Energy use in buildings and carbon dioxide emissions, BRE, Garston, BR.170.*

Figure 9.10   Washing appliances, loads in last week by household size

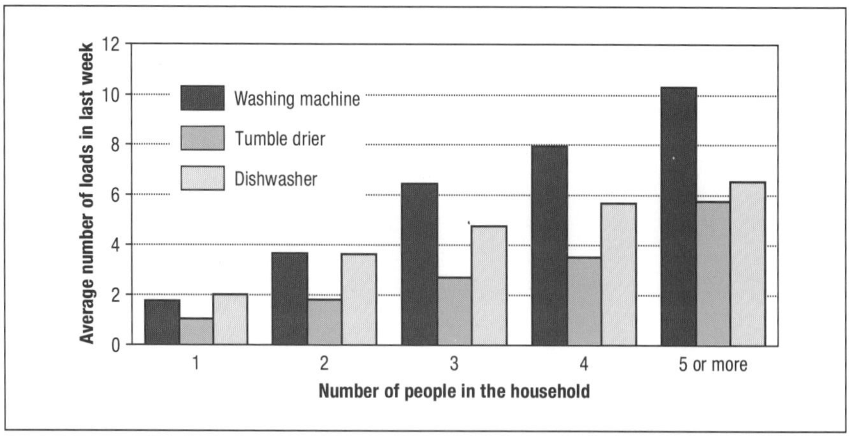

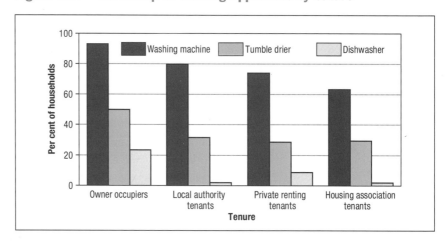

of household, older couples and lone pensioners tend to use their washing machines and tumble driers less often than other households of the same size. (Table A9.20)

Use of
economy 7

9.45   Nearly three-quarters of households with a dishwasher and around 1 in 5 of households with a tumble drier or washing machine have economy 7. Of the latter, 27% always use their washing machine in the off-peak period, 30% occasionally and 37% never. Tumble driers are used less often with economy 7, but 57% of households always run their dishwasher at the lower tariff. (Table A9.21)

Stock
characteristics

Tenure

9.46   Washing machines, tumble driers and dishwashers are found most frequently in the owner occupied sector and least frequently in housing association dwellings. For example, nearly a quarter of owner occupiers have dishwashers compared with only 2% of housing association tenants. Furthermore, some 17% of owner occupiers have all three appliances, these accounting for 94% of all such cases; under 0.5% are accounted for by housing association tenants. (Figure 9.11 & Table A9.22)

Figure 9.11   Ownership of washing appliances by tenure

Dwelling type
and age

9.47   All three appliances are most commonly found in detached houses and are least available in flats. Whilst washing machines are found in equal numbers in all ages of dwellings, dishwashers are most frequently present in the very oldest (pre 1850) and most recent (post 1980) properties. (Table A9.22)

Location and region

9.48 The more rural the location the more likely households are to own a washing appliance, 87% of households in isolated rural housing having a washing machine, 53% a tumble drier and 30% a dishwasher. By comparison, in city centres where households tend to be smaller and launderettes more common, 76% have a washing machine, 29% a tumble drier and 12% a dishwasher. (Figure 9.12) Reflecting this, households living in Greater London are least likely to have a washing machine or tumble drier. However, dishwashers are least common in the Northern Region. (Table A9.22)

Figure 9.12   Ownership of washing appliances by dwelling location

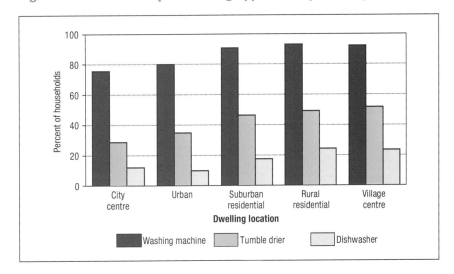

Household characteristics

Household type and employment status

9.49 As with frequency of use, the ownership of each of the three appliances is related closely to the size of the household. Single person households have the lowest proportion, 64% having washing machines, 19% tumble driers and 3% dishwashers. These contrast with figures of 96%, 61% and 32% respectively for households of 5 or more. Similarly, family households are most likely to own these appliances and lone pensioners least likely. Generally, washing appliances are least frequently owned by single person households not in work. Conversely, households with one or more persons in full-time employment are most likely to have a washing machine and tumble drier and those with 2 members in work to have a dishwasher. (Table A9.23)

Figure 9.13   Ownership of washing appliances by household income

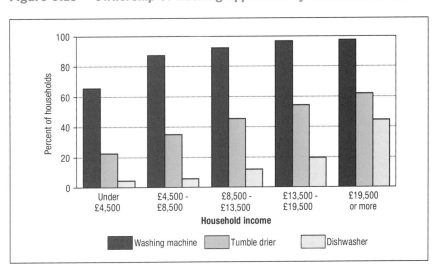

Household income

9.50 As expected, the ownership of each of the appliances also increases with household income. For the 1 in 5 households on the highest incomes, 98% own a washing machine, 63% a tumble drier and 45% a dishwasher, whilst for the fifth on the lowest incomes the respective percentages are 66%, 23% and 5%. Over half the households who own all three appliances are in the fifth of households on the highest incomes, whilst over half lacking all three are in the fifth on the lowest incomes. (Figure 9.13 & Table A9.23)

Chapter 10 Fuel consumption

Preamble

10.1 *After outlining the EHCS fuel consumption survey, this Chapter looks first at the use of mains gas, electricity and other non-metered fuels and how these are combined for use in heating, cooking, lighting and running domestic appliances. It illustrates the consumption profiles of these fuels and how their use in the four main tenures contributes to domestic fuel consumption nationally. It analyses the average consumption of households in housing with different stock, energy and household characteristics and finally, determines the distribution of the lowest and highest fuel users in terms of both total consumption and consumption relative to dwelling size. It ends with a comparison of findings from the 1986 and 1991 fuel surveys.*

10.2 *During the Interview Survey, householders were asked permission for the Department to approach the local fuel companies to obtain their electricity and, where relevant, gas consumption. To gain information about other, non-metered fuels used, occupants were asked to estimate the amounts they spent on various solid fuels, fuel oil, bottled gas or paraffin. (Details of the 1991 EHCS fuel consumption survey are given in Annex C, paras. C.7-14)*

Use of fuels

Mains gas

Variation within stock

10.3 Nationally, over four fifths (82%) of households use mains gas. Owner occupiers and council tenants are close to this average, but fewer than two-thirds of private and housing association tenants use gas. (Figure 10.1 & Table A10.1) There are wide variations in usage between dwellings of different age and type, with nearly 96% of post 1980 houses using gas, compared with only 44% of older homes built before 1850. Generally, fewer flats than houses use gas, only 50 to 60% of those higher than 5 storeys using this fuel. (Figure 10.2) Reflecting this difference, smaller households are less likely to use gas than larger ones, under three-quarters of one person households using this fuel compared to over 92% of those with 6 persons or more.

Figure 10.1 Use of individual fuels by tenure

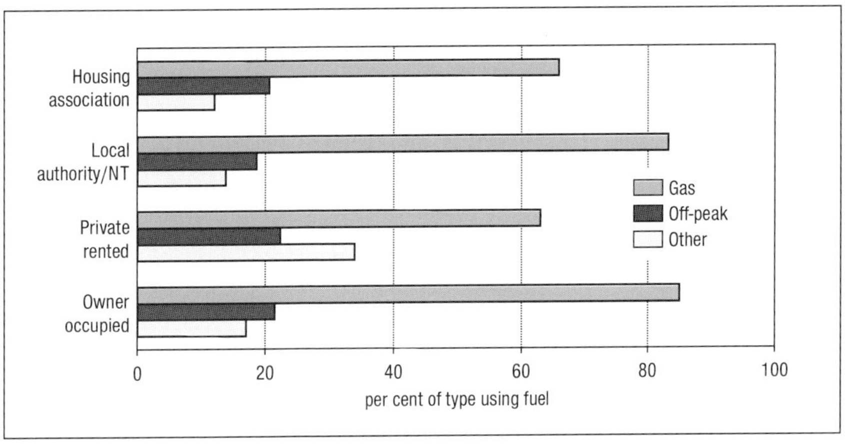

Region and location

10.4 As already suggested by the distribution of heating and cooking fuels, there are very marked variations in the use of mains gas between regions and between urban and rural localities. For example, gas is used by 95% of households living in the West Midlands Metropolitan Area, compared to only 57% of those in Devon and Cornwall. About 90% of households use gas in urban or suburban areas compared to under 50% in villages and only 12% in isolated rural locations, clearly reflecting the difficulties of supply in more remote areas. (Table A10.1)

Figure 10.2   Use of individual fuels by dwelling type and age

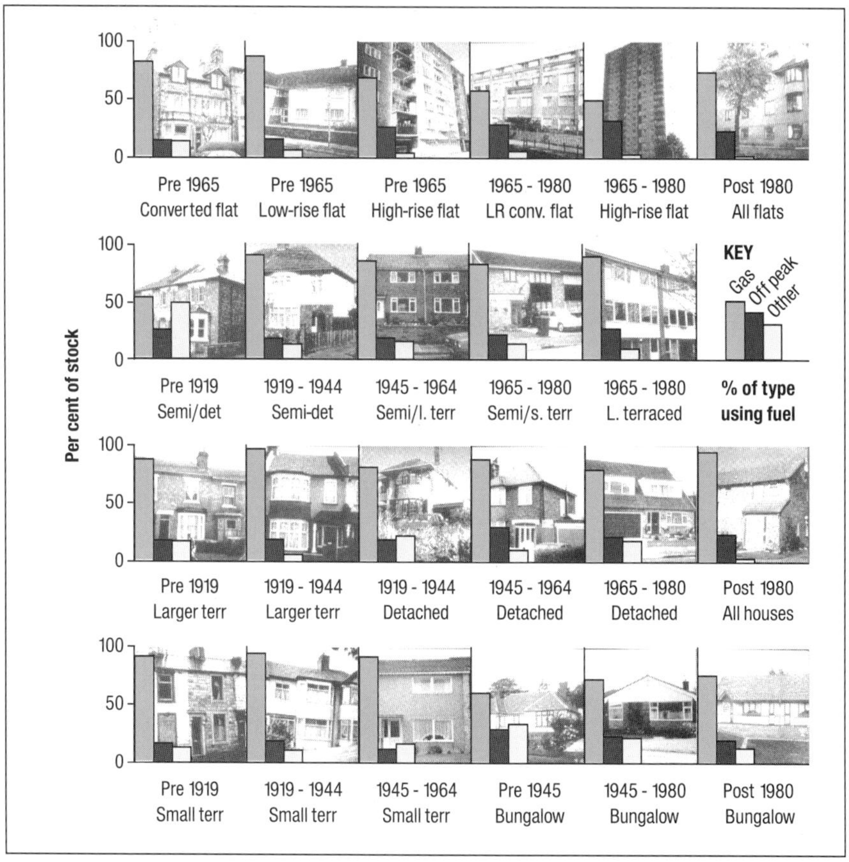

Electricity

On-peak

10.5 Virtually all households use on-peak mains electricity[1] but only just over 3% use on-peak electricity alone. However, this proportion is much higher in the rented sectors, rising to nearly 16% in housing association property. Half of the households using solely on-peak electricity lie in the lowest quarter of household incomes, with well over a third (37%) being lone pensioners.

Off-peak

10.6 Just over a fifth (21%) of households also use off-peak electricity, with little variation between tenures or with family size and income. Generally, this tariff is used more in flats built since 1965 and in houses built after 1980 than in earlier dwellings. However, it is most likely to be found in the oldest dwellings built before 1850 (37%), and those in rural areas. There are considerable differences between the usage in different regions, ranging from under 2% in the West Yorkshire Metropolitan Area to nearly 47% in the East Midlands; this probably reflecting the historic policies of the local electricity companies. (Figure 10.3)

---

1   *The 3 sample dwellings recorded with no mains electricity are all from the West Midlands suggesting possible data errors in these particular cases.*

Other unmetered fuels

All other fuels

10.7 Some other non-metered fuel is used by nearly 18% of all households, with almost twice as many private tenants (34%) and somewhat fewer council tenants (14%) and housing association tenants (12%) using another fuel. Perhaps surprisingly, there is little variation in usage between different household types and income. However, as expected, households living in older houses are much more likely to use these fuels than those in flats and newer dwellings. Again there are major differences in usage over the country and between urban and rural areas, reflecting not only the limited availability of mains gas but the availability of fuels such as wood and coal. (Figure 10.4)

Figure 10.3   Use of individual fuels by region

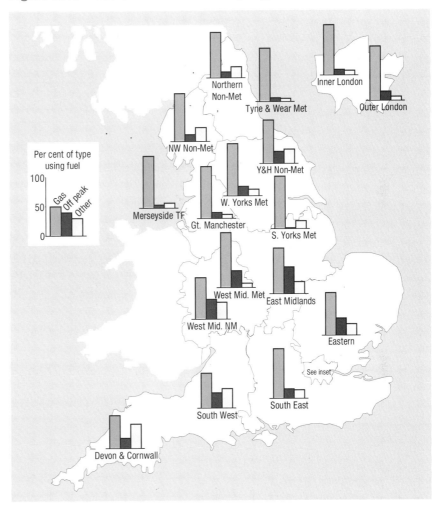

Individual types

10.8 Of the various unmetered fuels, coal is used by 7% of all households, smokeless fuels by 4%, wood by nearly 3% and bottled gas is used by nearly 6% of all households. However, the proportion of private tenants using these fuels is well over double these figures in all cases. Paraffin is used by under 1% and fuel oil by 3% of all households, almost all from the two private sectors.

Combined uses of fuels

Most common combinations

10.9 Despite the dominant use of mains gas for heating, the combinations of fuels and fuel use found in homes is extremely diverse. Table 10.1 shows the fifteen combinations of fuels used by households for space and water heating, cooking, lighting and appliances which account individually for more than 1% of the stock. Electricity is divided into on-peak supplies alone and those also with off-peak tariffs and unmetered fuels includes all solid fuels and all tanked/bottled fuels. Whether the fuel is (a) the main

Figure 10.4 Use of individual fuels by dwelling location

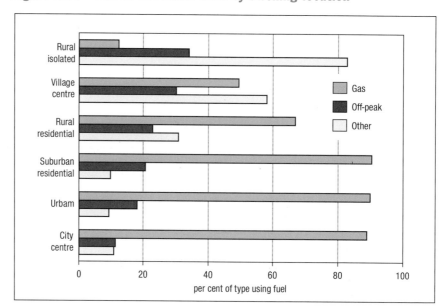

fuel used for each purpose, or (b) is a supplementary fuel (that used only in summer in the case of water heating) or (c) is used equally with other fuels (e.g. the two fuels used in dual fuel cookers) is indicated by the notation A, B and C respectively.

Table 10.1   Fifteen most common combined uses of fuels

Fuel and uses in home	Most common combinations of fuels and uses														
	1	2	3	4	5	6	7	8	9	10	11	12	13	14	15
Mains gas															
Space heating	A	A	A	A	A	A	A			A	A	A	A		
Water heating	A	A	A	A	A					A	A	A	A		
Cooking	A		C	A		A	A			A	A	C	A		
Mains electricity															
Space heating on peak				B	B	B						B		B	B
heating off-peak															A
Water heating on peak						A	A	B			B			B	
heating +off peak															A
Cooking*		A	C		A			A	A	A		C		A	A
Lighting	A	A	A	A	A	A	A	A	A	A	A	A	A	A	A
Appliances on peak +off-peak	A	A	A	A	A	A	A	A	A		A	A		A	A
ances +off-peak													A		
Unmetered fuels															
Space heating								A	A	B				A	
Water heating								A	A					A	
Cooking															
% of households using combination	23.2	12.8	7.2	6.5	4.1	2.4	2.2	2.2	2.0	1.7	1.6	1.5	1.2	1.1	1.1

Notes: A = main fuel used; B = secondary or summer fuel use; C = equal/dual use with other fuel
* excludes microwave ovens which are treated as appliances

10.10 Only two combinations account individually for more than a tenth of the stock. These are the use of mains gas for space, water heating and cooking and on-peak electricity for lighting and appliances, with no supplementary fuel use (23%) and the same combination except for the use of electricity for cooking (13%). Of the 15 most common combinations, the majority use just gas and electricity. Only one uses more than two fuels and one is all electric.

All combinations

10.11 In total, these 15 combinations account for some 71% of all homes, while the remaining 29% of homes have more than 300 combinations of main and secondary fuel uses. Nearly two thirds of these combinations include unmetered fuels, the greatest diversity of uses occurring where all three fuel types are used. A summary of the fuels used for all the combinations found in the stock is given in Table 10.2.

Table 10.2   Combination of fuel types

% of all households

Fuel used for space, water heating or cooking	Off-peak electricity all uses	On-peak electricity only for heating or cooking	On-peak electricity only appliances & lighting only	Total with combination
Electricity only	4.4	3.1	-	7.5
Mains gas	11.7	40.0	23.2	74.9
Other fuels	3.6	6.3	0.7	10.6
Gas and other fuels	1.2	4.1	1.7	7.0
All fuels	20.9	53.3	25.8	100.0

Mean fuel consumption

Distribution profiles

10.12 Figures 10.5 and 10.6 provide the consumption profiles for mains gas, on-peak and off-peak electricity and other fuels for those households that use each type, together with the distribution profile for total fuel consumption over the whole stock. All the distributions are skewed towards low consumption - that for the consumption of other fuels being markedly so.

Figure 10.5   Distribution of on-peak and off-peak electricity consumption

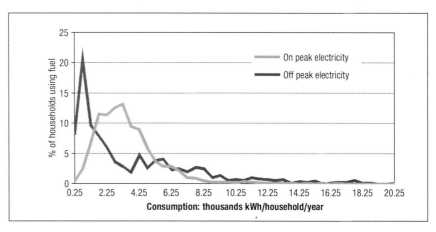

Figure 10.6   Distribution of gas, other fuels and total consumption

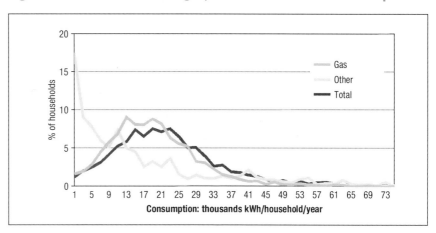

10.13 Five percent of owner-occupiers are using nearly 57,000 kWh/year, whereas in contrast, ten percent of housing association tenants are using less than 1,500 kWh/year. Table A10.2 gives the mean consumption in kilowatt hours per year for households with the lowest and highest fuel consumption, broken down by tenure and for each type of fuel. There is wide variation in the lowest and highest total fuel consumption both within and between tenures.

National consumption

10.14 The best estimate from the 1991 EHCS of the total annual domestic energy consumption for England is some 1,650 Peta-Joules[2]. Of this total over two-thirds is made up of gas, 15% on-peak electricity, 3.5% off-peak electricity and 14% other un-metered fuels. Figure 10.7 shows that by far the largest consumption, by fuel and tenure group, is the use of gas by owner-occupiers. This accounts for over half of the national consumption of all fuels. In total, owner occupiers - who comprise two-thirds of all households - account for over three-quarters of all fuel consumption. (Table A10.3)

Figure 10.7   National consumption (PJ) of different fuels by tenure

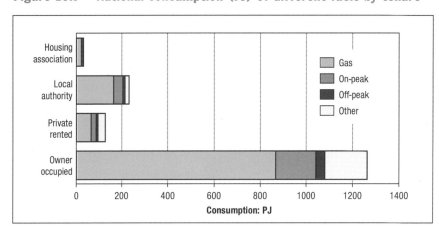

Stock characteristics

Tenure

10.15 If the annual consumption per household is considered, owner occupiers use on average more fuel (27,200 kWh per household) than any other tenure group and twice that used by housing association tenants (13,600 kWh). Gas accounts for 65 to 70% of the mean consumption in all tenures except in the private rented sector where it represents only half. Here, the difference is made up largely from other unmetered fuels, which account for almost a quarter of the mean compared to only 14% in the owner occupied stock and 5 to 7% in the other rented sectors. (Figure 10.8 & Table A10.4)

Figure 10.8   Mean annual consumption of fuels by tenure

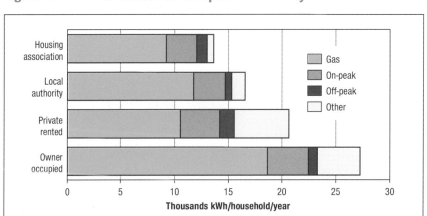

2   *The EHCS figure agrees closely (within 5%) with estimates made from other sources such as the Family Expenditure Survey and the Building Research Establishment energy stock model BREHOMES. (The PJ is a common unit of national consumption and equals 278 million kWh.)*

Dwelling type   10.16 With their small floor and external wall areas, flats use less fuel than other dwelling types and, with fewer open chimneys and fuels, also less other fuels (under 2% of their total consumption). Conversely, they use more on-peak electricity (21%) than other types. At the other extreme, detached houses use most fuel and, after the small group of temporary dwellings, use most other fuel (26% of their total). (Figure 10.9)

Figure 10.9   Mean annual consumption of fuels by type of dwelling

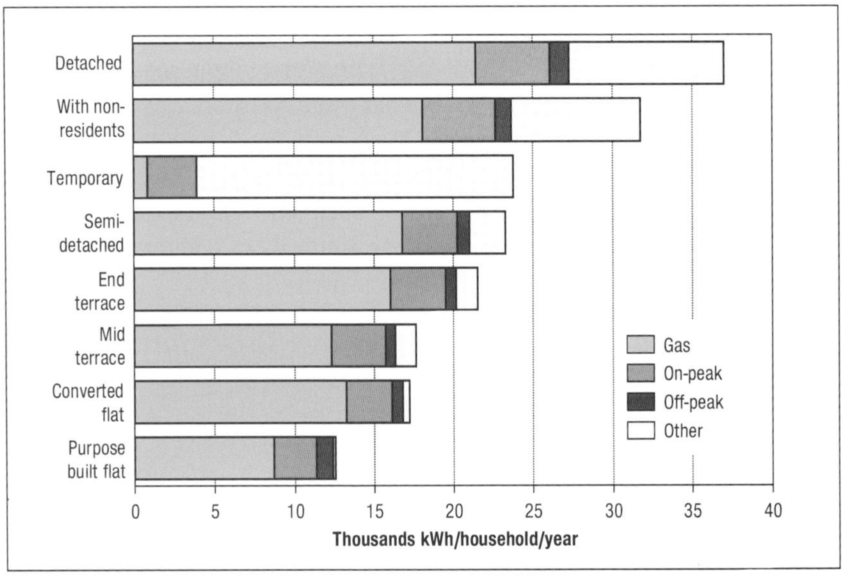

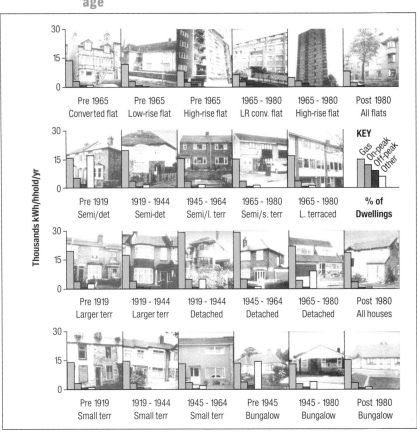

Dwelling type and age   10.17 The mean consumption of different dwelling types (by age and built form) is shown in Figure 10.10. The types with the highest totals, which also use the highest proportion of other fuels, are all the older houses. All flats, especially those more recently built, have the lowest consumption and use virtually no other fuels.

Figure 10.10 Mean annual consumption of fuels by dwelling types and age

Region &
metropolitan
area

10.18 The consumption of each fuel in each of the metropolitan and non-metropolitan areas of England is shown in Figure 10.11. The total annual fuel consumption varies from under 19 thousand kWh per household in the Merseyside Task Force area to over 27 thousand kWh per household in the neighbouring North West Non-Metropolitan Area. There is little or no evidence of general increases in consumption with a colder climate, as Outer London, Devon and Cornwall and the South East are all towards the high consumption end of the scale, and Merseyside and Tyne and Wear towards the lower end. The relative contributions of the different fuels to the total vary from area to area - gas varying from 83% of the total in the Tyne and Wear metropolitan area down to only 38% in Devon and Cornwall. Other unmetered fuels vary inversely from 41% in the latter area to only 1% in Inner London. On-peak electricity is more or less constant falling between 14 and 17% in all areas, but off-peak varies from nearly 8% in the South West to under 1% in South Yorkshire. (Table A10.6)

Figure 10.11 Mean annual consumption of fuels by metropolitan and non-metropolitan areas within each region

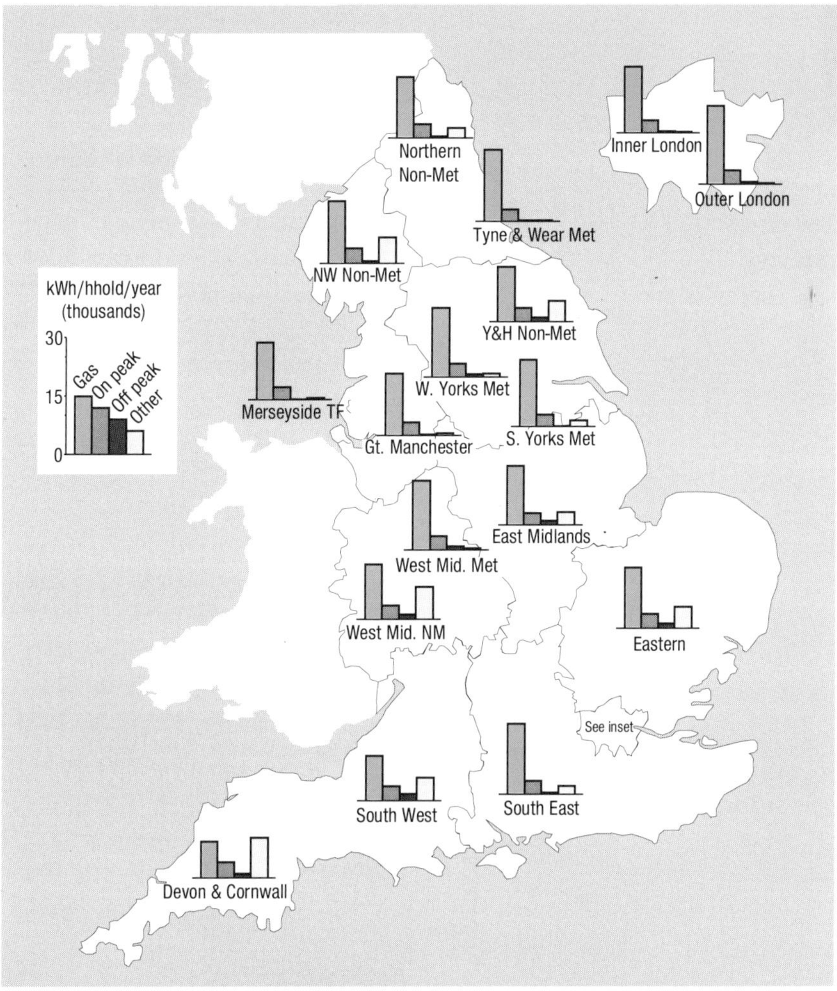

Dwelling
location

10.19 In terms of the type of locality, there is a systematic increase in total consumption away from inner cities towards rural areas. Out to the suburbs this is made up of increasing gas consumption, but in increasingly rural areas the contribution of gas falls again, while that of electricity and, particularly, other non-metered fuels rise.

Dwelling
condition

10.20 The overall condition of the dwelling makes little difference to the total consumption. However, the relative contributions of the various fuels is significantly different, with gas making up only 56% in unfit homes and 68% in fit ones and conversely, non-metered fuel contributing 23% and 13% respectively. The contribution of different fuels also varies significantly with respect to the adequacy of the provision for heating to satisfy the fitness standard. Gas accounts for nearly 70% of total consumption in homes judged by the EHCS surveyors to have satisfactory provision compared to 55% in those failing this particular fitness requirement. In the former case, on-peak electricity accounts for 14% of total consumption compared to 22% in those judged unfit. (Figure 10.12 & Table A10.5)

Figure 10.12 Mean annual consumption of fuels by provision for heating

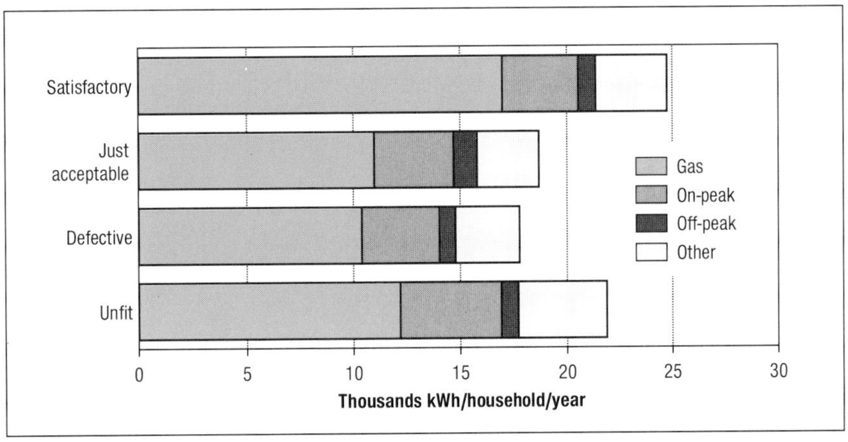

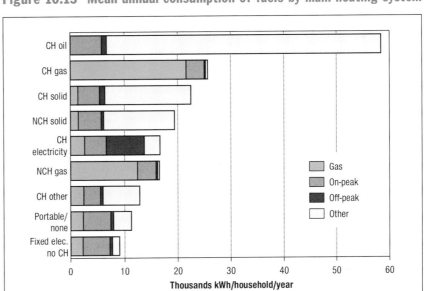

Energy characteristics

Type of heating

10.21 Figure 10.13 shows the consumption of fuels broken down by the main heating system used by the household. Gas accounts for 84% of the fuel used in homes with gas central heating, while other fuels make up 72% of the consumption in those with solid fuel systems. The particularly high consumption of fuel oil in homes with oil-fired central heating needs to be treated with caution as it is based on the occupants estimates of expenditure. However, the same is true of the other non-metered fuels which appear to give a more reasonable consumption. Dwellings with oil-fired central heating may genuinely have a very high fuel consumption, for the EHCS shows them typically to be very large, old detached houses owned by large families on high income.

Figure 10.13 Mean annual consumption of fuels by main heating system

Energy efficiency

10.22 As described in Chapter 3 of the report, the energy rating has two main components, a 'heating price index' increasing with the inefficiency of the heating system and price of fuel used, and a 'heat loss index' dependent on the insulation values and external surface area of the dwelling. Figures 10.14 and 10.15 show the mean consumption of each fuel for homes with heating price and heat loss indices ranging (in five equal bands or quintiles) from the lowest to highest.

Heating price

10.23 There is a marked fall in total annual fuel consumption with the increasing price of heating, homes with the lowest values using twice the fuel (30,000 kWh) than those with the highest (15,000 kWh). Inevitably, the proportion of total consumption derived from mains gas falls from 76% in homes with the lowest heating price to 43% in those with the highest. Conversely, the proportion derived from expensive on-peak electricity and unmetered fuels associated with inefficient heating systems each rise from around 11% to 25% or more. (Figure 10.14)

Figure 10.14 Mean annual consumption of fuels by 'heating price' index

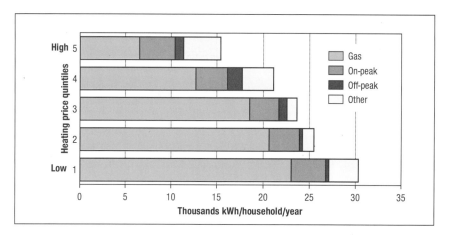

Heat losses

10.24 In contrast to the heating price, there is relatively little variation in fuel consumption with different indices of heat loss - both the lowest and highest bands having annual consumption of between 21 and 22 thousand kWh. However, there is a significant difference in the proportion of different fuels used - gas accounting for three-quarters of the total in homes with the lowest heat loss compared to only 56% in those with the highest. (Figure 10.15)

Figure 10.15 Mean annual consumption of fuels by 'heat loss' index

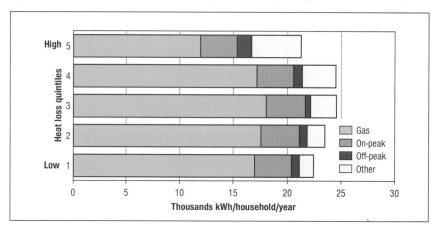

SAP energy rating

10.25 Figure 10.16 shows the fuel consumption and the relative contribution of different fuels in relation to the overall energy efficiency (SAP) rating of the dwelling, derived from the heating price and heat loss indices. Households living in dwellings with the lowest SAP ratings use on average under 17,000 kWh of fuel per year, of which only 23% is gas and 45% is other non-metered fuels. By comparison, those with the highest SAP rating use nearly 22,000 kWh per year of which 83% is gas and under 1% 'other' fuels. (Figure 10.16 & Table A10.5)

Figure 10.16 Mean annual consumption of fuels by SAP rating

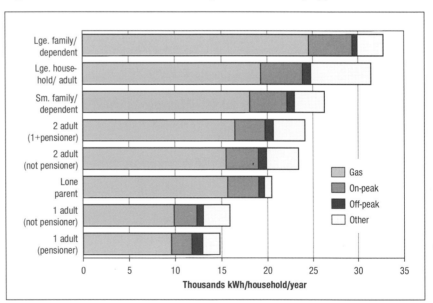

Household characteristics

Household type

10.26 Not surprisingly there is a steady increase in energy use with household size and this is reflected in the consumption by different types of household. Lone parents use significantly less fuel than other households with children and gas, the cheapest main fuel, contributes to over three-quarters of their total consumption - the highest proportion of any household type. As expected, lone adults and lone pensioners use the least fuel. (Figure 10.17 & Table A10.7)

Figure 10.17 Mean annual consumption of fuels by type of household

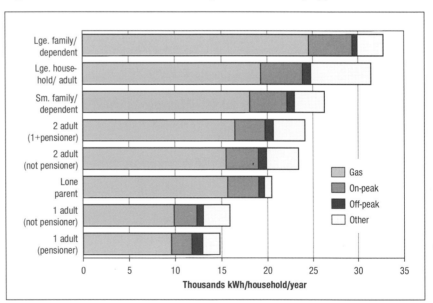

Household income

10.27 As expected also, there is a systematic increase in total consumption with increasing household income. However, the contribution of each fuel remains more or less constant over all the income quintiles. (Figure 10.18 & Table A10.7) Other measures of low income give similar results - households with three-quarters or more of their income deriving from state benefits use 18,000 kWh (67% of which comes from gas) compared to the 25,000 kWh (68% from gas) used by other households.

Figure 10.18 Mean annual consumption of fuels by household income

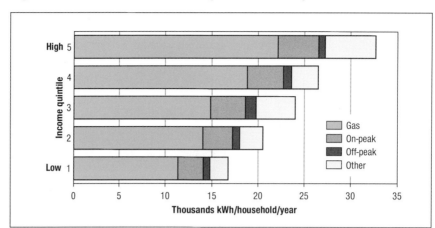

**Low and high
fuel
consumers**

**Fuel
consumption**

10.28 The remainder of this Chapter considers those households at both ends of
the spectrum of fuel consumption. It looks first at the 20% of all households
with the lowest total fuel consumption and 20% with the highest total.
Households consuming unusually small amounts of fuel may be living in
very small or very energy efficient dwellings, but alternately may not be
able to afford more fuel and so lack affordable warmth. At the other end
of the scale, those with the highest total consumption may be large families
in very large houses, but may also be living in poorly insulated houses
with inefficient heating systems.

10.29 Compared with more average consumers, there is a marked variation in
the use of different fuels by the lowest and highest consumers. For the
former, gas accounts for only 44% of the energy used, compared to 76%
for average and 61% for the highest fuel consumers. For those with the
lowest consumption, the most important fuel is electricity accounting for
48%, with on-peak electricity contributing 34% of the total. Clearly as
well as using the least fuel, low fuel users are also paying the most for
what they use. For the highest consumers, other fuels such as oil and coal
are used most after gas, these accounting for a quarter of the total. (Figure
10.19 & Table A10.8)

Figure 10.19 Percentage contribution of different fuels by total consumption

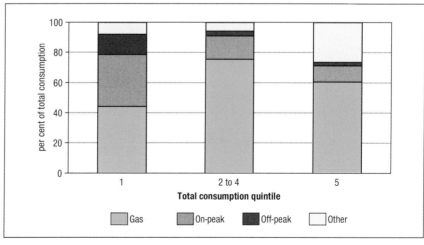

Dwelling size 10.30 One of the major determinants of total consumption is the size of the
dwelling, reflected in its floor area. The mean total floor area rises from
68 sq.m. for homes with the lowest energy use to 132 sq.m. for those with

the highest fuel consumption. Some 70% of households living in homes with the 10% largest floor areas are in the highest consumption quintile. Conversely, 61% of homes with the smallest floor areas are in the lowest quintile. (Figure 10.20)

Figure 10.20 Distribution of fuel consumption by floor area

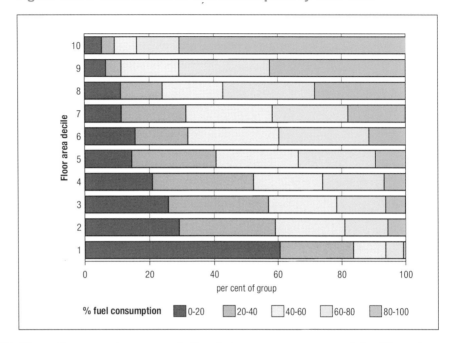

Low consumers

10.31 Given the very strong correlation between energy use and dwelling size, fuel consumption per square meter gives a better indication of those households whose consumption of fuel is intrinsically high or low. In the remaining analysis, the 20% and 10% of all households with the lowest unit consumption are termed 'low' and 'very low' consumers respectively, while the 20% and 10% with the highest figures (kWh/sq.m) are referred to as having a 'high' and 'very high' fuel consumption.

Tenure variation

10.32 All rented sectors accommodate higher proportions of low fuel consumers than the owner-occupied stock. Compared with 7% of owner occupiers, 14% of local authority tenants, 17% of private tenants and as many as 24% of housing association tenants are very low fuel consumers. (Figure 10.21 & Table A10.9)

Figure 10.21 Distribution of highest and lowest fuel consumption per unit floor area by tenure

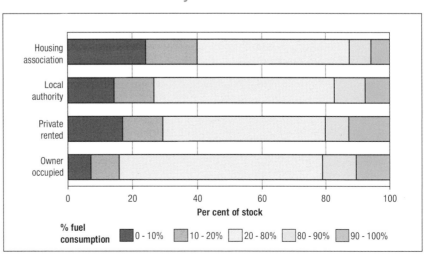

Dwelling age and type

10.33 Reflecting both dwelling and household size, flats are most likely to have a very low fuel consumption - over a third of pre 1965 and as many as 47% of post 1965 high rise flats falling in this category. By comparison, under 3% of post 1980 built houses have a very low consumption. (Table A10.9)

Dwelling location

10.34 Households living in city centres and rural locations are both more likely to be low consumers than those in suburban areas. Low energy consumption in the city centre, where 21% of households are very low consumers, results from a combination of small households on low income and a high proportion of flats. A low fuel consumption in rural areas, where 19% are very low consumers, is associated with low income alone as houses in rural areas are generally older, detached properties with low overall energy efficiency. (Figure 10.25 & Table A10.9)

Type of heating

10.35 There is a very marked difference between the proportion of low consumers in homes with gas central heating (4%) and those with other forms of heating. Households with central heating other than gas are more likely to be very low consumers - 17% with oil, 21% with electricity and 27% with solid fuel, whilst households without central heating are much more likely - 27% with solid fuel, 50% with portable heaters and 56% with fixed electric fires. (Figure 10.22 & Table A10.10)

Figure 10.22 Distribution of highest and lowest fuel consumption per unit of floor area by main heating system

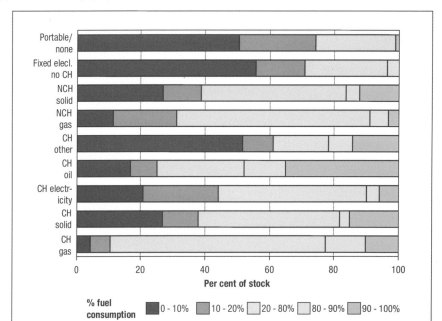

Price of heating and heat losses

10.36 Over 1 in 5 households with the most inefficient heating systems (in the top 20% on the 'heating price index'- see para. 3.7) are very low fuel consumers, compared to only 3% of those with the lowest fuel prices and most efficient heating systems. The other component of SAP, shows the opposite trend, with a fall in the number of low consumers as the heat loss increases.

SAP ratings

10.37 The association between energy efficiency (SAP) ratings and low fuel consumption is not as straightforward as might be expected. Nearly a quarter of homes with the lowest SAP ratings (below 10) have a very low fuel consumption, compared to between 5 and 6% of homes with SAP ratings ranging from 30 to 60. However, more households (11%) in homes with ratings above 60 are very low consumers, suggesting that only in the highest rated homes is improved energy efficiency affecting fuel consumption. (Figure 10.23 & Table A10.10)

Figure 10.23 Distribution of highest and lowest fuel consumption per unit of floor area by SAP rating

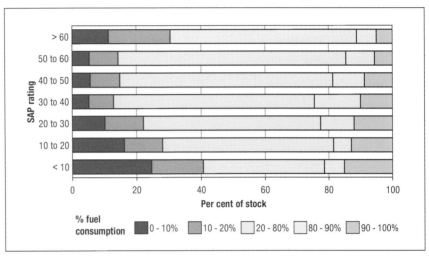

Household size and income

10.38 Single person households are very much more likely to be low consumers, 1 in 5 being very low consumers, than larger families - less than 1 in 20 families of 4 or more having a very low fuel consumption. (Figure 10.24) There is also a progressive fall in the likelihood of families being low consumers with increasing household income. Only 7% of families in the highest income group (top quintile) are very low fuel consumers compared to 18% of those on the lowest incomes. (Table A10.11)

Figure 10.24 Distribution of highest and lowest fuel consumption per unit of floor area by household size

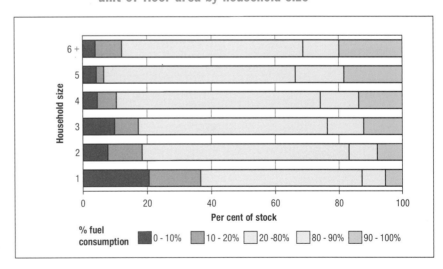

Significance of factors

10.39 The various factors discussed above all interact in complex ways. To take account of all these interactions, a multiple regression model has been constructed to relate the chance of a household being a low fuel consumer to all the relevant factors. The parameters that emerge as significant are summarised in decreasing order of importance in Table 10.3. The three most important factors are the lack of gas-fired central heating, a small household size and low energy efficiency.

Table 10.3   Factors affecting low fuel consumption

Variable	Beta	T
No gas central heating	0.362	44.20
Small household size	0.122	15.92
Low SAP rating	0.100	11.77
Flat	0.070	9.09
In Devon & Cornwall	0.061	8.86
City centre	0.050	7.22
Low household income	0.059	7.08
Not detached house	0.023	3.26
Rented	0.019	2.39

High consumers

Tenure

10.40 In comparison with low consumers, there is relatively little variation between tenures in the proportion of households who are high consumers, once differences in dwelling size are taken into account. The private sector has the highest number of very high consumers (13%) and the housing association stock the lowest (6%).

Dwelling age and type

10.41 Older homes are most likely to have a high fuel consumption - 22% of those built before 1850 having a very high consumption compared to under 3% of those built after 1980. Far fewer flats have a high consumption than houses. The variation is even greater when both the age and type of dwelling is considered. Only 1 in 100 households living in houses built after 1980 are very high consumers compared to 1 in 4 of those living in bungalows built before 1965. (Table A10.9)

Dwelling location

10.42 There is a general increase in the incidence of high consumption from urban to rural areas. Only just over 8% of suburban households are high consumers compared to nearly 24% of those in isolated rural houses. The lack of availability of mains gas and the likelihood of the dwelling being an older, rambling detached property combine to increase fuel consumption in rural areas. (Figure 10.25 & Table A10.9)

Figure 10.25 Distribution of highest and lowest fuel consumption per unit of floor area by dwelling location

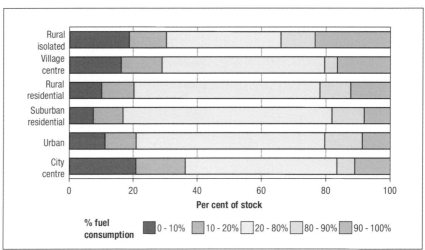

Type of heating

10.43 In terms of high consumption, the outstanding heating system is oil fired central heating - over a third of households with this system being very high fuel consumers compared to only 10% of those with gas central heating, 6% with electric central heating and even less for those lacking central heating. (Table A10.10)

SAP ratings   10.44 As with low consumers, there is a progressive decrease in the proportion of high consumers with increasing SAP ratings. Over 15% of homes with a SAP rating of below 10 have a very high consumption compared to only 5% of those rated 60 or more. Heat loss appears to be the most important component of energy efficiency with regard to high fuel consumption; the proportion of homes with a very high consumption rises steadily from under 4% for those with the lowest heat losses to nearly 19% of those with the highest. The price of heating seems to be less important - the proportion of high consumers only falling from 11 to 7% across the range of heating prices.

Household type   10.45 There is a consistent increase in the proportion of very high fuel consumers
and income   with increasing household size. Only 1 in 20 of single person households are in the highest consumption group compared with 1 in 5 households of six or more people. The correlation with income is lower; under 12% of households in the highest income quintile are high consumers compared to nearly 7% of those in the lowest. (Figure 10.26 & Table A10.11)

Figure 10.26   Distribution of highest and lowest fuel consumption per unit of floor area by household income

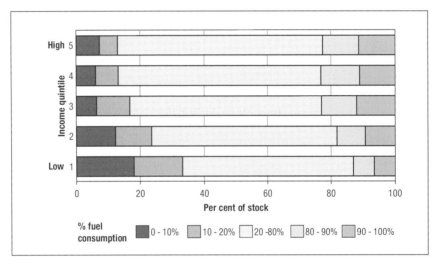

Significance of   10.46 As for low consumers, the various factors interact in complex ways. A multiple
factors   regression analysis has again been undertaken to relate the chance of a household being a high fuel consumer to the relevant factors. The parameters that emerge as significant are somewhat different from those for low consumers and are listed in descending order of importance in Table 10.4 below.

Table 10.4   Factors affecting high fuel consumption

Variable	Beta	T
Large household size	0.153	19.00
Bungalow built before 1965	0.130	17.27
Oil central heating	0.103	13.68
Low SAP rating	0.080	10.39
High household income	0.070	7.80
Not detached house	0.028	3.56
Built before 1850	0.019	2.61

10.47 Household size, which was second in the factors for low consumption, is the most important for high fuel consumption, living in an older bungalow and having oil fired central heating being the second and third most significant factors.

Trends in fuel consumption 1986 - 1991

10.48 Although varying with tenure, the total domestic consumption of gas and electricity in 1991/92 was lower than that recorded in 1986/87. However, annual fuel consumption fluctuates with weather conditions and 1991/92 was significantly milder than 1986/87, which included a particularly cold winter. During the 12 months over which the fuel data were collected for the 1986 survey, the outdoor temperature was 0.6°C lower than the long term average for the years 1975 to 1995, while during the first quarter of 1987 it was nearly 2°C lower than the average first quarter figure. In comparison, the temperature was 0.5°C above average, for the fuel data collected for the 1991 survey.

Tenure variation

10.49 Using a methodology developed by the Building Research Establishment the mean annual gas and electricity consumptions for the two years have been corrected to the long term mean external temperature (see Annex C, paras C.36-39). The results are shown for each tenure in Table 10.5 and Figure 10.27. (Due to the small 1986 fuel sample for housing associations, the two social rented sectors have been combined).

Table 10.5   Average consumption of gas and electricity in 1986 and 1991 by tenure *(corrected to long-term mean temperature)*

	Uncorrected mean kWh		Temperature corrected mean kWh		%
	1986	**1991**	**1986**	**1991**	**change**
Gas consumption					
Owner occupied	22,393	21,987	21,515	22,644	+5.2
Private rented	15,593	16,730	14,981	17,230	+15.0
Social rented	13,501	14,096	13,292	14,532	+11.9
Total stock	**20,162**	**19,789**	**19,371**	**20,380**	**+5.2**
Electricity consumption					
Owner occupied	4,690	4,640	4,613	4,675	+1.3
Private rented	4,441	5,000	4,368	5,037	+15.3
Social rented	3,895	3,369	3,823	3,394	-11.2
Total stock	**4,466**	**4,420**	**4,393**	**4,453**	**+1.4**

Figure 10.27   Consumption of gas and electricity in 1986 and 1991 by tenure *(corrected to long term mean temperature)*

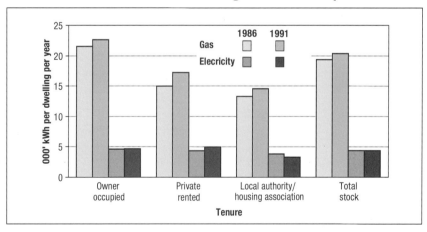

10.50 After allowing for the differences in external temperatures, there has been a rise of over 5% in gas and 1% in electricity consumption, suggesting that the more widespread use of central heating, particularly gas-fired systems, is reflected in increased consumption, despite energy efficiency measures having some effect. The greatest increase has occured in the rented sectors, particularly in the least thermally efficient private rented stock.

Chapter 11

Fuel expenditure

Preamble

11.1 *This Chapter deals with household expenditure on fuel for domestic heating, cooking, lighting and appliances. It looks first at the pattern of actual fuel expenditure, the total amounts spent and the distribution of fuel spending with respect to dwelling size, fuel costs, energy efficiency and household income. It then goes on to examine the important issue of 'affordable warmth', defining the term and assessing the extent of the problem in relation to the compounding factors of low income, poor energy efficiency and under-occupation.*

Existing spending

Total expenditure

Tenure variation

11.2 In 1991/92, average household expenditure on all fuels for domestic use was nearly £660 - amounting to a national annual domestic fuel bill of some £12.6 billion. Total fuel expenditure varies with tenure. All tenures have a similar pattern of expenditure but the profiles are displaced, giving progressively higher means for council tenants, private tenants and owner occupiers than those renting from a housing association. All profiles show a long tail of households spending over £1,000 per year on fuel - the 13% of owner occupiers so spending accounting for nearly a quarter of the total expenditure in this sector. (Figure 11.1)

Figure 11.1 Total fuel expenditure - mean and distribution by tenure

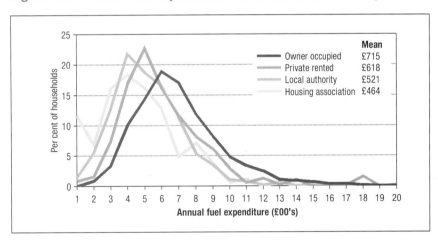

Household type

11.3 As expected, total fuel expenditure is closely related to the type of household. Lone pensioners and other lone adult households have the lowest expenditure, less than a fifth spending more than £600 per annum on fuel. Although the third lowest, lone parents are spending significantly more, their average expenditure being over £600. With averages of £810 and £874 respectively, the highest spenders are large adult households and large dependent families - a quarter of the latter spending more than £1,000 a year on fuel. (Figure 11.2)

11.4 A breakdown of household type by tenure shows a greater divergence, average total expenditure ranging from under £300 for lone pensioners in housing association accommodation to over £980 for large families privately renting. However, there is a wide range of spending amongst all types of household, to the extent that in every tenure there are some lone pensioners with total fuel costs of over twice those of some large families. (Table A11.1)

Figure 11.2   Total fuel expenditure by household type

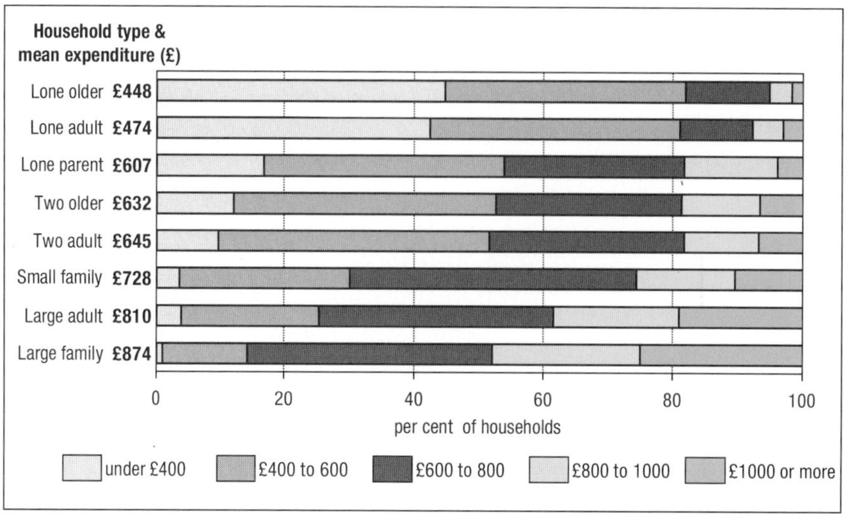

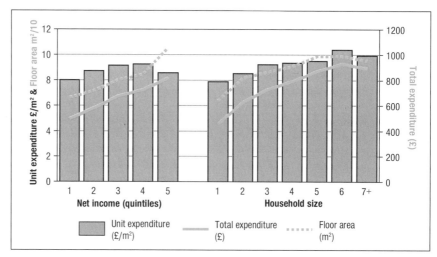

Household income and size

11.5   Mean total fuel expenditure rises progressively with income in line with the increasing size of household accommodation. The increase in the expenditure per unit of floor area is less pronounced and drops for the highest income group, where dwellings are on average substantially larger. The pattern for fuel expenditure by household size is similar with a progressive rise in total expenditure and, to a lesser extent, expenditure per square metre. However, with the very largest households, both unit and total expenditure also decline with a drop in dwelling size. (Figure 11.3)

Figure 11.3   Mean fuel expenditure by household size and income

Expenditure relative to dwelling size

11.6   Although related to household size, total fuel expenditure is more closely correlated with the size of the dwelling (the respective correlation coefficients being 0.41 and 0.58). On average, fuel spending increases from only some £350 in dwellings of less than 30 sq.m. and rises to some £1,500 in the very largest properties. Nevertheless, in the latter, expenditure per square metre is a third of that of the smallest dwellings - unit expenditure generally falling with increasing dwelling size. (Figure 11.4)

Figure 11.4 Mean fuel expenditure by dwelling size

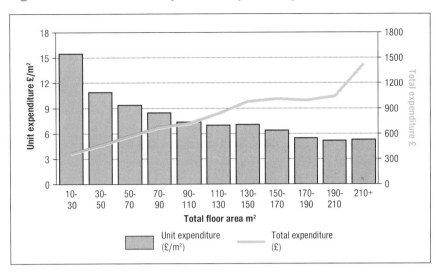

11.7 The lower expenditure of tenants is due mainly to their smaller accommodation - for example, council dwellings are on average a third smaller than owner occupied properties - and to a lesser extent their smaller energy use per se - typically only some 10% less per square metre than that of owner occupiers. After controlling for dwelling size, mean fuel expenditure is very similar across all tenures, but marginally highest for those renting from a council or private landlord. (Figure 11.5)

Figure 11.5 Mean fuel expenditure and consumption by tenure

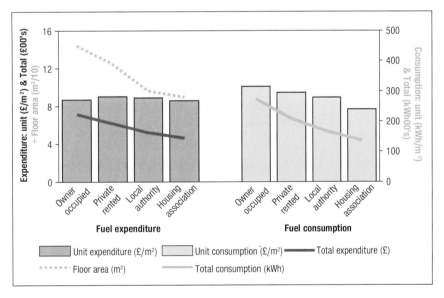

11.8 In the total population, large family households have the highest unit expenditure overall whilst, amongst low income groups, lone adults are generally spending the most in relation to floor area and lone pensioners the least. In relation to tenure, such expenditure ranges from an average of £10.50/sq.m. or more for large families in the social rented sector to £7.20/sq.m. for lone pensioners owning their homes. (Figure 11.6 & Table A11.2)

Unit fuel costs

Tenure variation

11.9 The overall unit fuel cost, measured in pence per kilowatt-hour (p/kWh), depends mainly on the extent to which householders use cheaper fuels, mains gas and solid fuel, rather than more expensive ones such as on-peak electricity. However, for each fuel, high consumers also generally have lower unit costs due to the lower proportion taken by standing charges

Figure 11.6   Mean unit fuel expenditure *(£/sq m)* by household type

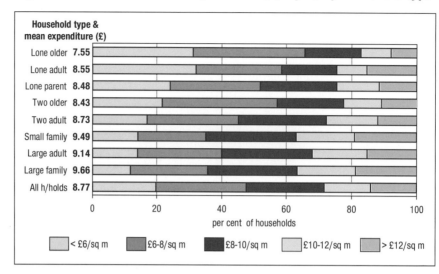

Legend: < £6/sq m | £6-8/sq m | £8-10/sq m | £10-12/sq m | > £12/sq m

and, increasingly, their better tariff arrangements. With their smaller fuel consumption, tenants generally need to spend more than owner occupiers for each unit (kWh) consumed. With their large proportionate use of electricity, housing association tenants are paying particularly highly for their energy - on average nearly 60% more per kWh than owner occupiers. (Table 11.1)

Table 11.1   Mean fuel costs* and fuel use by tenure

p/kWh/(% of total consumption)

Tenure	Mains gas		Electricity			Other fuels		All fuels used	
	cost p/kWh	use %	cost p/kWh	on-peak %	off-peak %	cost p/kWh	use %	cost p/kWh	use %
Owner occupied	1.82	(70)	8.55	(18)	(4)	1.42	(8)	3.02	(100)
Private rented	1.91	(51)	8.68	(24)	(7)	1.58	(18)	3.57	(100)
Local Authority	2.15	(64)	9.24	(24)	(6)	1.87	(6)	3.77	(100)
Housing association	1.92	(53)	9.21	(34)	(9)	2.43	(4)	4.75	(100)
All households	1.90	(66)	8.73	(20)	(5)	1.54	(9)	3.28	(100)

* inclusive of standing charges

Household type   11.10 Of all household types, large families enjoy the lowest unit fuel costs, due to the high consumption of gas in their homes and their generally favourable tariff arrangements. Lone pensioners, who are generally much more dependent on electricity and have lower total fuel consumption, are paying the most for their fuel. On average, their fuel costs an extra 1p per kWh or 36% more than that of large family households. Amongst all household types and tenures, average unit fuel costs range from under 3p/kWh for all family households in owner-occupation to well over twice this cost (7p/kWh) for lone pensioners renting from a housing association. (Tables 11.2 & A11.3)

Relationship between factors   11.11 Whilst in each tenure and household group, total expenditure varies with a wide range of circumstances, the most characteristic relationships between unit fuel costs (p/kWh), fuel use (kWh/sq.m.), dwelling sizes and total spending are shown for each group in Table A11.4. For families in owner occupation, low fuel costs are generally more than overtaken by the demands of high fuel use and large dwellings to give high total expenditures. In contrast, for single person households in the social rented

Table 11.2   Mean fuel costs* and fuel use by household type

p/kWh/(% of total consumption)

Tenure	Mains gas		Electricity			Other fuels		All fuels used	
	cost p/kWh	use %	cost p/kWh	on-peak %	off-peak %	cost p/kWh	use %	cost p/kWh	use %
large family	1.78	(74)	8.46	(18)	(2)	1.57	(6)	2.93	(100)
large adult	1.78	(66)	8.39	(19)	(4)	1.38	(11)	3.06	(100)
small family	1.82	(70)	8.42	(18)	(4)	1.44	(8)	3.05	(100)
two adults	1.82	(67)	8.60	(20)	(4)	1.56	(9)	3.21	(100)
two older	1.87	(66)	8.72	(18)	(5)	1.51	(11)	3.12	(100)
lone parent	1.95	(71)	8.90	(22)	(4)	2.13	(3)	3.46	(100)
lone adult	2.14	(60)	9.42	(22)	(7)	1.66	(11)	3.71	(100)
lone older	2.22	(58)	9.33	(24)	(10)	1.66	(8)	3.98	(100)
All households	1.90	(66)	8.73	(20)	(5)	1.54	(9)	3.28	(100)

* inclusive of standing charges

sector, high fuel costs are combined typically with low fuel use and small dwellings to produce low overall fuel spending. This is particularly so in housing association dwellings, where the lowest fuel expenditures stem from very low fuel use and very small dwellings countering the highest fuel costs resulting from the predominant use of electric heating.

Energy characteristics

Heating

11.12 With space and water heating accounting typically for nearly two-thirds of total fuel costs, the type of heating system is a major factor in determining the fuel expenditure in all housing sectors. Households reliant on electric heating or portable heaters - predominantly electric fires - are generally spending the most per unit of floor area. Those heating with solid or other non-metered fuels have, on average, the lowest total unit expenditure. However, most of their fuel expenditure still goes on electricity - as is the case for all households without gas central heating. (Figure 11.7)

Figure 11.7   Mean fuel expenditure (£/sq m) by type of heating

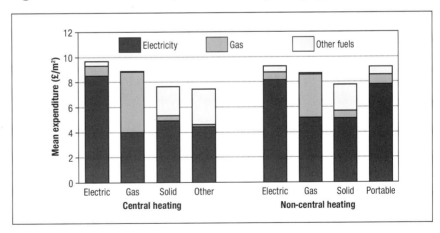

Energy efficiency

11.13 As a result of their poor heating systems, the fuel costs in the least efficient homes are typically twice those in properties having average to high energy ratings. After an initial rise, this is reflected in a general decline in fuel expenditure per sq. metre as energy efficiency improves. However, this is more than offset by the progressively larger floor size of higher rated homes, total fuel expenditure increasing with better energy efficiency; no overall saving occurs until the average floor area ceases its rise and the highest SAP ratings are reached. (Figure 11.8)

Figure 11.8 Mean fuel expenditure, fuel costs and floor area by SAP rating

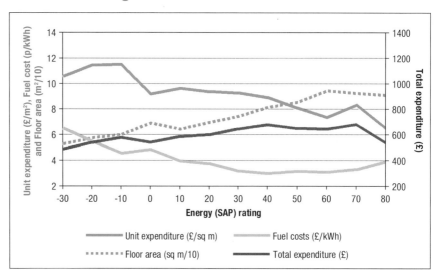

Fuel expenditure relative to income

11.14 In the total population, the average proportion of net household income spent on all fuels is 8.3%. However, this proportion varies considerably, the differences in fuel expenditure being generally far smaller than differences in income. For example, whilst the richest 10% of households have an average net-income of 15 times that of the poorest 10%, their total fuel expenditure is under twice that of this lowest income group. Generally, there is a progressive fall in the proportion of income spent on fuel as net incomes rise - from nearly 23% to under 3%. (Figure 11.9)

Figure 11.9 Fuel expenditure by net household income

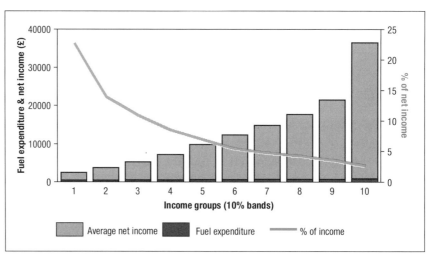

Tenure profiles 11.15 With the concentration of low income groups in the tenanted sectors, this pattern is reflected in the tenure profiles of fuel expenditure when expressed as a percentage of income. The profiles of tenants - particularly those in the social rented sectors - are far flatter than that of owner occupiers, their total fuel expenditures all averaging a tenth or more of net income. (Figure 11.10)

Household type 11.16 The pattern is similarly reflected in the proportion of net income spent on fuel by different types of household. Generally, households comprising two adults or with small families spent the smallest proportion - on average under 6% - two thirds spending under 5% of their income on fuel. Single pensioners and lone parents spend the most, less than a sixth of such

Figure 11.10 Fuel expenditure as % of household income by tenure

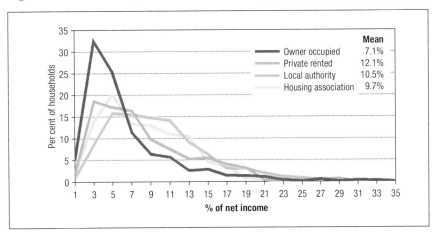

households devoting less than 5% and lone parents averaging as much as 16% of their net income. The variation is even greater when tenure is also considered, the proportion of income spent on fuel ranging from under 5% for small families in owner occupation to an average of 23% for large families renting from a private landlord. (Figure 11.11 & Table A11.5)

Figure 11.11 Fuel expenditure (% of income) by household type

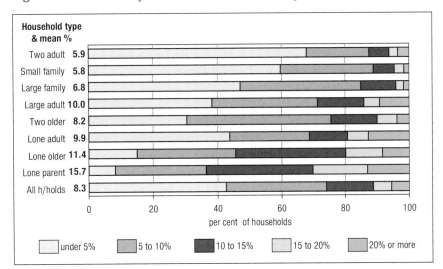

Affordable warmth

11.17 Many households are spending a high proportion of their income on domestic fuel without achieving satisfactory thermal conditions - in short, they lack 'affordable warmth'. Because the energy efficiency (SAP) rating is an indicator of the cost of heating a dwelling to a set standard, it can be used with fuel expenditure to assess levels of affordable warmth. The actual fuel expenditure of the household can be compared with that required to achieve heating regimes that provide full thermal comfort or, at the very least, safeguard health. For the purposes of the following analysis, these are taken as the standard and minimum heating regimes specified in Chapter 8. Non-heating costs for lighting, cooking and domestic appliances are assumed to be average for the dwelling size, number of occupants and overall level of fuel consumption. (see Annex C, paras. C.29-32)

Expenditure targets relative to income

11.18 What level of fuel expenditure is affordable for any heating regime will depend largely on a household's income after tax. A widely accepted target for affordable warmth is that a household's total fuel costs should not exceed 10% of disposable income[1]. In 1991, over 1 in 4 of all households

1   *BRECSU 'Energy efficient refurbishment of existing housing', Energy Efficiency Office Good Practice Guide 155, BRE, January 1995, p.7.*

were spending more than this, but even amongst tenants where the average expenditure was over 10%, relatively few were spending much more than 15%. Consequently, 10% and 15% may be considered as target and maximum fuel expenditures for the purposes of assessing affordable warmth.

Tenure
variation

11.19 For the total population, the average fuel expenditures required to achieve the minimum and standard heating regimes are close to the 10% target, accounting for 9.4% and 10.8% of income respectively. However, the requirements vary with tenure, both averages being under 10% of income for owner occupiers and both over the target cost for tenants, particularly those in the private rented sector. (Table 11.3)

Table 11.3   Mean fuel expenditure *(% of income)* **and that needed for minimum and standard heating regimes by tenure**

| Household type | Actual mean in 1991/92 | Mean to achieve regime:- | |
		Minimum	Standard
Owner occupiers	7.1	7.7	8.9
Private tenants	12.1	16.5	19.6
Council tenants	10.5	11.5	13.3
HA tenants	9.7	11.6	13.4
All households	8.3	9.4	10.8

Household type

11.20 Generally, younger couples and families can achieve both regimes with spending significantly below 10%. In 1991, their average expenditure was the same as that for the minimum regime and nearly 90% of that required for standard heating. For the latter, all other groups would generally need to spend more than 10% of income and in the case of lone parents and pensioners, an average of around 18% is called for. Controlling for tenure increases the divergence between household types. The spending of small families in owner occupation, at under 5% of income, is above the average required for the minimum regime, whilst the 11% spent in private rented accommodation by lone pensioners is little more than half the average expenditure they need. (Tables 11.4 & A11.6)

Table 11.4   Mean fuel expenditure *(% of income)* **and that needed for minimum and standard heating regimes by household type**

| Household type | Actual mean in 1991/92 | Mean to achieve regime:- | |
		Minimum	Standard
two adults	5.9	6.0	6.9
small family	5.8	5.8	6.6
large family	6.8	6.9	7.8
large adult	10.0	11.3	13.0
one adult	9.9	12.1	14.2
two older	8.2	9.0	10.5
one older	11.4	14.9	17.6
lone parent	15.7	16.6	18.9
All households	8.3	9.4	10.8

11.21 Nearly 70% of all households can achieve the minimum heating regime with a fuel expenditure of under a tenth of their net income, but this proportion also varies widely with household type. It is nearly 90% of households in the case of younger couples and small families, but under 30% for lone parents and pensioners. Nearly two-fifths of the latter two groups would need to spend over 15% - one in five lone pensioners requiring more than 20% of their income to achieve the minimum regime.

11.22 Under two thirds of all households are able to achieve the standard heating regime for less than 10% of their net income. Moreover, a half of all lone pensioners would require to spend more than 15% and nearly a third over 20% of their income to achieve this standard. The situation again varies between tenures, a much higher proportion of lone pensioners requiring such high levels of spending in the private sector, particularly the private rented sector (57%), than in the social rented sector (around 17%). (Figure 11.12 & Table A11.7)

Figure 11.12 Fuel expenditure required to achieve standard heating regime by household type

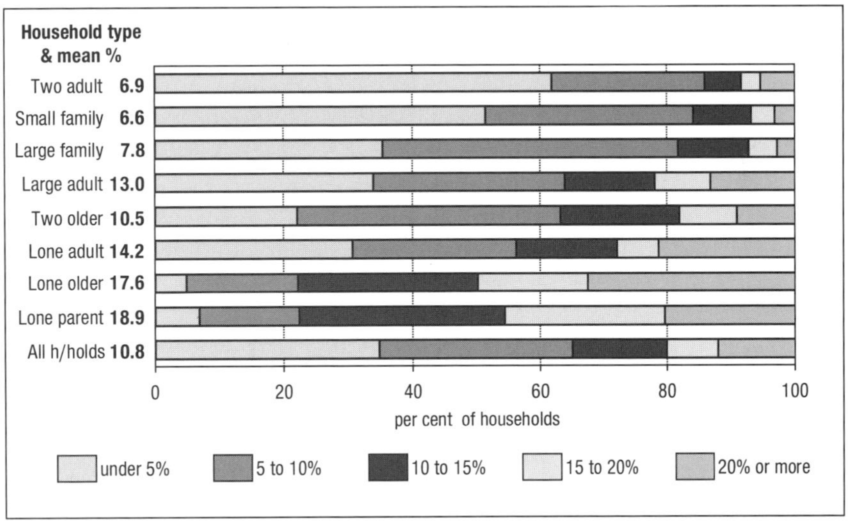

Household type & mean %

Household type	mean %
Two adult	6.9
Small family	6.6
Large family	7.8
Large adult	13.0
Two older	10.5
Lone adult	14.2
Lone older	17.6
Lone parent	18.9
All h/holds	10.8

per cent of households

under 5% | 5 to 10% | 10 to 15% | 15 to 20% | 20% or more

Adequacy of existing spending

11.23 In practice, what level of fuel expenditure is affordable will depend not only on a household's net income but their many other commitments. For some low income households even 10% of income may not be affordable, whilst for higher income groups in large inefficient homes such a level of spending may also represent unacceptably large costs. Consequently, an alternative way of assessing 'affordable warmth' is to determine the extent to which actual fuel expenditure exceeds or falls below that required to achieve the minimum and standard heating regimes, irrespective of the proportion of income this represents.

11.24 Over 55% of all households are spending less than that required to achieve the full standard regime, but under 40% are under-spending relative to the minimum regime[2]. However, the former is a design standard and, in practice, many households may choose a somewhat lower, albeit still healthy heating regime. Consequently, whilst it is appropriate to assess whether homes can achieve the standard regime with target spending of, say, less than 10% of income, it is more meaningful to gauge the adequacy of actual expenditure against the minimum heating regime.

---

2 *Actual fuel spending within 10% of the theoretical costs required are assumed to be 'about adequate' and, in practice, to give broadly comparable heating regimes.*

Household type   11.25 The adequacy of fuel expenditure varies with the type of household. Over 70% of younger couples and young families have adequate fuel spending for the minimum regime. With their relatively high fuel expenditure, some 60% of lone parents are also meeting or exceeding the costs required - more than any other low income group. The 2.7 million lone pensioners are least likely to have adequate expenditures. Over 60% are clearly 'under-spending' relative to the minimum regime, 1 in 3 lone pensioners spending less than 70% of the costs required. (Figure 11.13)

Figure 11.13   Adequacy of expenditure to achieve minimum regime by household type

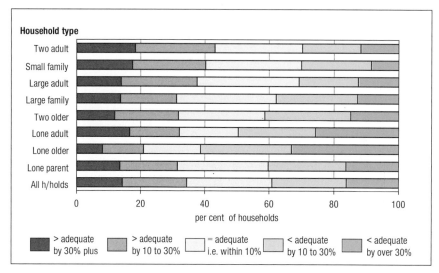

Tenure variation   11.26 In relation to tenure, nearly two-thirds of all owner occupiers are spending enough to meet the costs of the minimum regime, compared to under two-fifths of private tenants. Within tenures, the likelihood of various household groups meeting these costs ranges from nearly 3 out of 4 for small families in owner occupation to only 1 in 6 lone pensioners in private rented accommodation. (Table A11.8)

11.27 The proportion of households significantly 'under-spending' varies little with the percentage of income devoted to fuel, the proportion exceeding 30% even amongst those households spending over a fifth of their net income on fuel. (Figure 11.14)

Figure 11.14   Actual expenditure by extent of 'over/under-spending' to achieve minimum heating regime

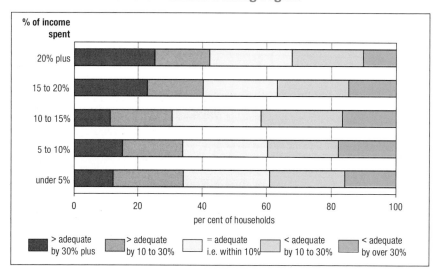

Adequacy of spending relative to % of income spent

11.28 This suggests the further classification of household fuel expenditure by combining the proportion of income spent with the extent of 'over or under-spending'. Some 62% of younger couples and small family households are meeting the minimum regime costs with fuel expenditures of under 10% of income. Some 43% of all lone parents are achieving such heating costs only by committing more than a tenth of their income to fuel. Nearly 30% of lone pensioners are spending more than a tenth of their income on fuel and are still falling significantly short of the costs of the minimum heating regime. (Figure 11.15)

Figure 11.15   Fuel expenditure and its adequacy to achieve minimum regime by household type

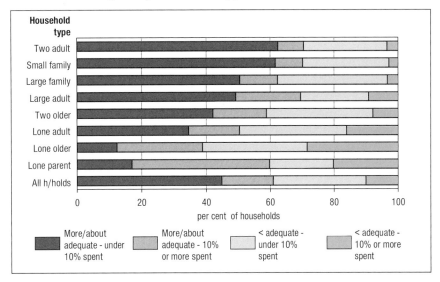

Heating characteristics

Heating patterns

11.29 Pensioner households are the largest group lacking affordable warmth despite their frequent use of all-day heating. The correlation between actual heating patterns and the adequacy of fuel expenditure is far less than simple logic would suggest. In fact, householders who heat their home all-day are, with those who have no regular heating pattern, the most likely to be significantly under-spending on fuel - over 40% spending less than three-quarters of the fuel costs required for the standard heating regime. Those who heat morning and evenings only are the least vulnerable, only some 20% under-spending to the same extent.

Figure 11.16   Adequacy of expenditure to achieve minimum regime by type of heating

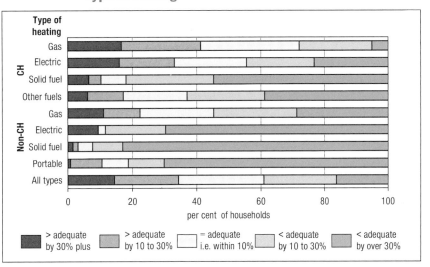

Heating provision

11.30 There is, however, a strong correlation between the main type of heating used and the adequacy of household fuel expenditure to achieve the minimum and standard regimes. Nearly three-quarters of all households with gas central heating are meeting or exceeding the costs of the former, compared with 1 in 10 or less of those who rely on individual electric or solid fuel fires. Over 80% of the latter, and 70% of households reliant on fixed electric or portable heaters are under-spending by over 30% relative to the costs required for the minimum heating regime. (Figure 11.16)

Energy efficiency and affordable warmth

11.31 A strong relationship between the energy efficiency of a dwelling and the ability of the household to achieve affordable warmth might be expected. In practice, however, the relationship is complicated by the tendency of more efficient dwellings in the stock to be larger properties with higher total consumption.

Expenditure relative to heating costs

11.32 For the above reason, expenditure per unit of floor area gives a better picture than total fuel expenditure of the overall relationship between energy efficiency and adequacy of actual fuel spending. Whilst average spending per square metre falls only slightly with increasing energy efficiency, there is a much sharper drop in the unit costs of achieving either the minimum or standard heating regimes. However, average fuel expenditure only becomes sufficient to achieve the minimum heating regime in homes with SAP ratings above 30, and only meets the costs required for the full standard regime in homes rated 50 or more. (Figure 11.17)

Figure 11.17   Mean fuel expenditure and that required for minimum and standard heating regimes by SAP rating

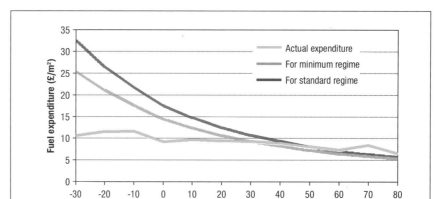

Household income

11.33 In part, this result is due to the general occupancy of more efficient dwellings by higher income households with larger fuel consumption per square metre. However, in homes of low energy efficiency, even households in the highest 20% of incomes are substantially 'underspending' on fuel in relation to the costs of both the minimum and standard heating regimes - despite having a particularly high total expenditure - on average, some £803 per year. Compared with the general population, these high income 'under-spenders' are much more likely to be owner occupiers or private tenants under-occupying large, old detached houses with poorer heating systems. Over 70% of their homes have floor areas of over 100 sq.m., compared with 20% of all homes and only 14% of those on equally high incomes who are meeting the costs of the standard regime.

11.34 Overall, the highest income group still requires a SAP rating of 40 or more for their average expenditure to meet the full cost of the standard regime. For those in the lowest 20% of incomes, with their lower fuel expenditure, a mean energy rating as high as 60 is needed. (Figure 11.18)

Figure 11.18 Actual fuel expenditure and that required for standard regime by SAP rating for highest and lowest income groups

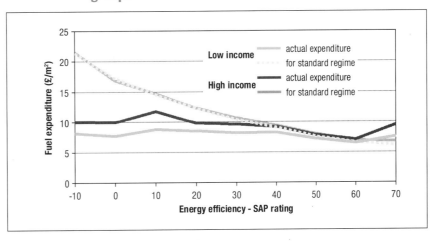

Proportion of income spent and needed

11.35 Whilst the pattern of unit expenditure relative to the energy efficiency rating is similar for both high and low income households, the proportion of income spent remains very different. In the highest income households, those in the least efficient homes are, despite their high expenditure, generally devoting only a marginally larger proportion of their income to fuel than those in better housing - still well under 4%. In contrast, in the lowest income group, those in the least efficient housing are spending, on average, nearly 17% of their incomes on fuel - although still under half that required for the standard heating regime. Low income households in more efficient housing - who tend to have even lower incomes but larger homes than the group generally - are devoting even more, on average nearly 23%, yet uniquely amongst those in better housing, are still falling short of the costs of the standard regime. (Figure 11.19)

Figure 11.19 Mean fuel expenditure *(actual and required)* by income and SAP ratings

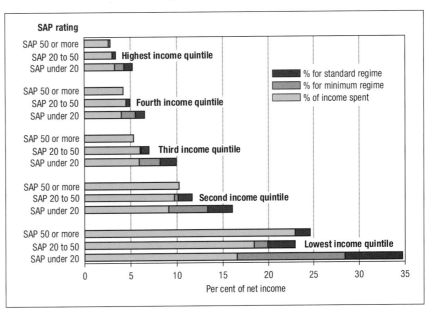

Adequacy of
fuel
expenditure

11.36 Leaving aside the proportion of income spent, there is a more straightforward relationship between energy efficiency and the adequacy of actual fuel expenditures to achieve the minimum or standard heating regimes. For example, the number of households with fuel spending sufficient to achieve the minimum heating regime decreases progressively with falling energy efficiency - from some 9 out of 10 households living in homes with SAP ratings of 60 or above to less than 1 in 5 of those with ratings under 10. Nearly two-thirds of the latter are spending under 70% of that required for the minimum regime. (Figure 11.20)

Figure 11.20 Adequacy of expenditure to achieve minimum regime by SAP rating

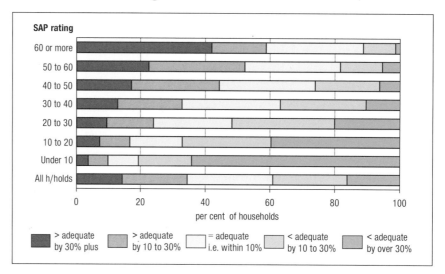

Local authority
stock

11.37 The relationship is also more straightforward in the local authority stock where households with different incomes, albeit all relatively low, are more evenly distributed across housing of variable efficiency. Here, over two-thirds of tenants renting homes with SAP ratings of 60 or above are able to fully achieve the standard heating regime with a fuel expenditure of less than a tenth of their income. The figure is under 13% for those in dwellings rated below 10, over 50% of these tenants needing to spend over a fifth of their income to achieve such heating. (Figure 11.21)

Figure 11.21 Fuel expenditure required in LA stock for standard heating regime by SAP rating

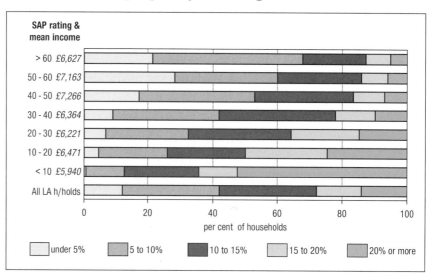

Under-occupation and affordable warmth

11.38 In addition to low income and poor energy efficiency, the under-occupation of dwellings is another major factor affecting the lack of affordable warmth. In the total stock, some 83% of households who are living at or below the 1968 'Parker Morris' space standards are approaching or exceeding the fuel costs of the standard heating regime. By comparison, of all households whose space standards are more than double this, under half (45%) have an equally adequate level of fuel spending.

Local authority stock

11.39 The problem of under-occupation can be seen most clearly - as well as most appropriately - in the local authority stock where there are less divergent dwelling sizes and household incomes. Some 54% of council tenants occupying dwellings at or below the 'Parker Morris' standard are able to achieve the full standard regime with a fuel expenditure of less than a tenth of their income, compared with only 17% of those with space standards of over twice this. Over 46% of the latter would need to spend over a fifth of their net income to achieve this standard. (Figure 11.22)

Figure 11.22 Fuel expenditure *(% of income)* required for standard heating regime by extent of under-occupation - LA tenants

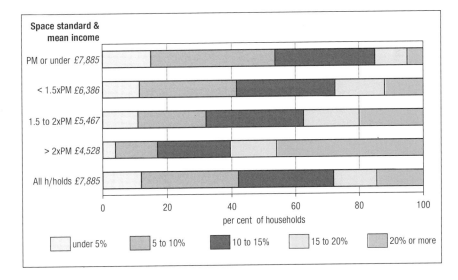

Household types

11.40 The problem is exacerbated, however, by most cases of under-occupation in council housing, and to a lesser extent in the private sector, occurring amongst lower income groups. Over 70% of the 300 thousand council tenants living at over twice the 'Parker Morris' space standard are dependent on state benefits - compared with nearer 60% in the council stock as a whole - well over half (55%) being lone pensioners. In the owner occupied stock, some 3 million households are living at equally high space standards and of these just under half (47%) are pensioner households, 23% being lone pensioners.

Part III THERMAL CONDITIONS

Owner occupied sector

| 1 1919 - 1944 Semi-detached **18.2°C** | 2 1945 - 1964 Semi-detached **18.3°C** | 3 1965 - 1980 Detached **19.0°C** | 4 1965 - 1980 Semi-detached **18.5°C** | 5 1850 - 1899 Larger terraced **17.7°C** |

| 6 Post 1980 Detached **19.1°C** | 7 1850 - 1899 Small terraced **17.9°C** | 8 1965 - 1980 Bungalow **18.5°C** | 9 1945 - 1964 Bungalow **18.7°C** | 10 1919 - 1944 Detached **18.4°C** |

Private rented sector

| 1 1850 - 1899 Converted flat **18.6°C** | 2 1900 - 1918 Converted flat **20.0°C** | 3 1850 - 1899 Small terraced **17.5°C** | 4 1850 - 1899 Larger terraced **16.3°C** | 5 Pre 1850 Converted flat **18.3°C** |

Local authority sector

| 1 1965 - 1980 Low-rise flat **19.9°C** | 2 1945 - 1964 Low-rise flat **18.4°C** | 3 1945 - 1964 Semi-detached **17.2°C** | 4 1919 - 1944 Semi-detached **17.1°C** | 5 1919 - 1944 Small terraced **17.3°C** |

| 6 1965 - 1980 Larger terraced **19.2°C** | 7 1945 - 1964 Small terraced **16.9°C** | 8 1965 - 1980 High-rise flat **20.3°C** | 9 1945 - 1964 Larger terraced **17.7°C** | 10 1945 - 1964 Bungalow **18.5°C** |

Housing associations

Average home temperatures *(notes overleaf)*

| 1 1965 - 1980 Low-rise flat **20.1°C** | 2 Post 1980 Low-rise flat **22.3°C** | 3 1850 - 1899 Converted flat **21.5°C** | 4 1900 - 1918 Converted flat **17.7°C** | 5 1965 - 1980 Larger terraced **18.3°C** |

Figure III.1   Average home temperature for the most numerous dwelling types in each sector

The frontispiece to Part III shows the average home temperature for each of the most numerous dwelling types in each sector. The temperature given is that of the hall, this having been found to be a good proxy for the mean of all rooms. For the total stock, the average living room temperature is a little over 1°C higher than the hall temperature of 18°C, but the difference between rooms tends to be less than this in dwellings with high energy ratings and greater in those with low ratings. On average, the warmest dwellings - post 1980 low-rise flats in the housing association sector, with a hall temperature of over 22°C - are those with the lowest fuel expenditure and third highest energy rating (mean SAP 47.1). The coldest homes - larger terraced houses in the private rented sector with a mean temperature of just above 16°C - are generally amongst the least energy efficient (mean SAP 25.7).

Chapter

Causal factors and Case studies

Preamble

12.1 *This third part of the Report deals with the thermal conditions resulting from the interaction of the physical standards described in Part I of the Report with the use of heating and appliances and energy consumption of households described in Part II. Chapter 13 describes the distribution of home temperatures achieved in the housing stock, whilst Chapter 14 goes on to look at the incidence of damp and mould growth. Finally, Chapter 15 considers the satisfaction of households with their heating. The part begins, however, by examining some of the causal factors in thermal conditions and with the third set of case studies.*

Causal factors

12.2 The thermal conditions, particularly the home temperatures actually achieved in a dwelling, will depend largely on:

Main determinants

❑ Heating regime - (desired) — the heating regime desired by the occupants in relation to their lifestyle and customs.

❑ Energy efficiency - the capacity of the heating appliances to maintain the desired regime against the heat losses of the building fabric.

❑ Fuel expenditure - the ability of the household to pay the consequent fuel costs.

Heating regimes

12.3 With respect to heating regimes, we saw in Part II that the extent, time and duration of heating varies widely with household type, employment status and income. As also mentioned, most people begin to feel cold - particularly if sedentary - when home temperatures drop below 18°C, but between 18°C and 22°C preferences differ. Elderly people, however, are physiologically less sensitive to temperatures and are more likely to live with cold (under 16°C) or excessively warm rooms (over 24°C) - both of which present health risks.

12.4 Regardless of the desired heating regime, actual temperatures around the home can be determined by the type, extent and capacity of the heating system, with - as will be shown in Chapter 15 - lack of heat being a more common complaint than the cost of heating. However, fuel expenditure is a constraint for many low income households, frequently resulting in a less than satisfactory, often irregular heating regime.

Effect on home temperatures

12.5 How these factors affect actual home temperatures can best be seen in the individual case studies. Table 12.1 shows the living room and hall temperatures against the SAP energy rating, heating regime and fuel expenditure for each of the case studies, in Parts I, II and III of the report, where the household had been at home for 1 hour or more when the outside temperature was less than 16°C. Ordered by the adequacy of the households' annual fuel expenditure to achieve the standard heating regime, this shows how this 'under-spending/over-spending' is generally reflected even in the random spot temperatures taken on the day of interview.

Table 12.1   Comparison between heating systems, regimes, fuel expenditure and achieved temperatures in case studies

Case No.	SAP rating	Heating system	Heating on day of interview	Annual fuel spend	% cost of standard regime	Living room °C	Hall temp. °C	Outside temp. °C
8.4	4	Coal NCH	Not heated	468	32	13.0	13.0	11.9
12.3	24	Gas NCH	3hrs earlier	632	81	13.8	13.6	8.5
12.2	21	Gas CH	Not heated	1,110	91	16.3	13.9	14.5
3.1	2	Coal CH	All-day	600	93	18.5	12.2	8.6
8.2	34	Oil CH	2 periods	1,127	94	18.9	19.7	11.3
3.3	45	Gas CH	2 periods	850	102	20.1	18.9	14.3
3.2	25	Gas CH	2 periods	650	114	20.7	18.3	n.k.
8.1	65	Gas CH	2 periods	767	122	22.2	21.4	11.4
12.1	46	Communal	24 hours	665	224	25.6	23.4	13.3

Case studies

12.6   The last of the examples listed is the first of the four case studies in this part. These illustrate the range in the home temperatures, damp conditions and satisfaction with heating covered by the statistical material in the following three Chapters. They show the various ways thermal conditions can relate to the physical standards and energy consumption, described in Parts I and II of the Report. (*Although based on data collected in the EHCS, some details have been changed to protect the identity of individual households*).

Case 12.1:
Local authority
1965-1980
High rise flat
(Hall 23.4°C)

12.7   This council flat, on a town centre estate in the North West, illustrates the maintenance of excessively high temperatures by a lone pensioner in a communally heated dwelling of better than average energy efficiency.

12.8   The 30 m² flat is on the third floor of a high-rise block, built in the early 70s to provide accommodation for elderly tenants. Its construction is of cavity masonry on a concrete frame, under a flat roof. The windows are single glazed with metal frames. The flat surveyed comprises a hall, a living room with balcony, one bedroom, a kitchen and a bathroom. The surveyor found the flat to be in good condition, and satisfactory on all fitness matters.

Physical standards

12.9   Heating and hot water are provided communally via a district heating scheme. Radiators are provided in all rooms except the hall, and the system controlled by a room thermostat, central programmer and individual manual controls on the radiators. The only insulation measures present are draught excluders to the windows, and there are extract fans in the kitchen and bathroom. The SAP rating is calculated to be 46.

12.10 The sole tenant, an 80 year old ex-docker, has lived in the flat for five years. His income, mainly from state benefits, is somewhat below average for lone pensioners in council housing, falling well within the lowest 20% of all household incomes.

Energy consumption

12.11 The tenant uses the communal system to provide 24 hour heating in the living room, but rarely or never heats the bedroom. The timer and wall thermostat are regularly adjusted in winter, but the manual radiator controls are rarely or never changed. He has an electric cooker and uses the extract fan in the kitchen regularly, but not the one in the bathroom.

12.12 Having communal heating, the dwelling's gas consumption is not known, but the annual electricity consumption is some 1040 kWh, the cost of which represents 23% of the total fuel bill. The rent for the property includes a sum of over £10 per week for heating and hot water, which, together with an annual electricity bill of £125, results in an annual fuel spend of £665. This is equivalent to a fifth of the pensioner's income, but amounts to more than twice the amount required to maintain a standard heating regime in the flat.

Thermal conditions

Home temperatures

12.13 On the morning of the interview, in early May 1992 when the weather was relatively mild (14.3°C outside), the heating had been on continuously in the living room for more than seven hours, and the temperature recorded was 25.6°C, whilst that of the unheated hall was 23.4°C. This was rated by the occupant to be 'comfortably warm' and was judged to be the 'same as usual'. These temperatures are much higher than average, and suggest a lack of advice and control.

Damp and mould

Satisfaction with heating

12.14 The occupier is very satisfied with his heating system. However, he is not entirely happy with the running costs of the flat, and this is perhaps a reflection of the high proportion of his income going on fuel. Otherwise, he is generally satisfied with the flat and its surroundings and reports no particular problems with its condition. He does not suffer any problems with draughts, damp, condensation or mould growth.

Energy action

12.15 According to the EHCS postal survey, the flat was not subject to or proposed for any kind of action. There is obviously scope for reducing energy consumption through a reduction in the room temperatures to more normal levels, although in this case expenditure on fuel would not decrease unless the saving was passed on to the tenant with a reduction in the rent. The provision of secondary double glazing and further draught stripping could increase the SAP rating to over 60, and potentially reduce the fuel bill by a quarter.

Case 12.2:
Owner occupied
1900-1918
Larger terraced
(Hall 13.9°C)

12.16 This owner occupied house is located in the West Midlands metropolitan area, in an urban centre of mixed residential and commercial buildings. It shows a large adult household who are dissatisfied because they can not afford to use the central heating provision. Instead they use individual gas fires and an on-peak electric immersion heater, although the resulting fuel expenditure is still high, particularly in relation to the household's income.

12.17 The three bedroom end terrace house was built around the turn of the century. The house is basically rectangular in shape with a recently refurbished extension at the rear, giving a total floor area of 90 m². The walls are constructed of solid 9" brick, with a mixture of wooden sash and casement single-glazed windows. The pitched roof has natural slate tiles. The EHCS surveyor found the house satisfactory on all of the fitness matters and requiring only minor repairs.

Physical standards

12.18 Heating provision consists of a gas-fired central heating system with radiators in all rooms served from a back boiler in the lounge. Controls include a room thermostat, timer and manual controls on the radiators. Fixed gas fires are also available in the two downstairs living rooms, along with a portable electric heater in the kitchen. Hot water is provided from the boiler via a jacket insulated cylinder, with an on-peak electric immersion heater as backup. The only other form of insulation is 100mm of mineral wool between joists in the roof space. The SAP rating of the dwelling is calculated to be 21.

12.19 The owner-occupiers, a couple, their pensioner mother and a teenage son, have only recently moved into the house. The head of the household is a hospital porter, his partner works part-time as a cleaner and their mother receives a state pension. The household income is low for such owner occupiers, falling in the second lowest income quintile.

Energy consumption

12.20 They use the central heating only if the weather gets really cold, and then only for a few hours at a time. The gas fire in the living room is the only heating used regularly, from 4.00 to 8.30 pm on weekdays and between 2.00 and 8.30 pm at the weekend, with a portable electric heater also used in the kitchen. The on-peak immersion heater is used to heat the water both during the winter and in summer. Cooking facilities include an electric hob and oven and a microwave, and the occupants also have a washing machine used daily and a tumble drier, used 5 times per week.

12.21 The annual energy consumption was 35,900 kWh, of which 77% was gas and 20% on-peak electricity. The annual fuel bills come to over £1,100 (41% gas, 59% electricity), representing 18% of the main household income, but only roughly the amount required to provide the house with a minimum heating regime.

Thermal conditions

Home temperatures

12.22 On the day of the interview, in early March 1992, the occupants had been at home for more than 7 hours, although no heating at all had been used that day. The house temperatures recorded were 16.9°C in the lounge and 13.9°C in the hall, compared with an outside temperature of 14.5°C. This was felt to be the 'same as usual' but rated as 'much too cool' by the interviewee.

Damp and mould growth

12.23 The occupants found the house to be draughty throughout, with the doors and windows perceived to be the main culprits. They were also being caused some discomfort by serious condensation, damp and mould growth, and reported a number of problems ranging from steamed up windows in most rooms, to mould growth on the walls and furnishings in three rooms, the dining room being the worst affected. The problems persist all year, and they tend to deal with the mould growth by cleaning it off as it appears.

Satisfaction with heating

12.24 The occupiers expressed themselves to be unhappy with the heating system and running costs of the house. Although having access to full central heating, the occupiers could not afford to use it very often, leaving them very dissatisfied. As well as running costs, reasons for their dissatisfaction were that the house was difficult to heat due to a lack of insulation ("the heat just goes out of our windows") and that the output from the system was poor.

Energy action

12.25 According to the EHCS postal survey, the house was not subject to or proposed for any kind of action. The occupants did not intend to install any further energy measures as they wished to move soon because they could not afford to live there. There is however scope to improve the energy efficiency of the dwelling, by for example dry-lining external walls and installing double glazing and draught excluders. A full package of insulation measures and upgraded heating controls would provide the occupants with affordable warmth, but the total cost of over £10,000 would not be recovered from lower fuel bills for 17 years.

Case 12.3:
Local authority
1919-1944
Small terraced
(Hall 13.6°C)

12.26 This council house is located on a suburban council estate in the Greater Manchester metropolitan area. It illustrates a dwelling of generally low energy efficiency, which is cold, draughty and condensation ridden, due to the poor heating provision and high levels of moisture generation by the young tenant family.

12.27 The inter-war mid-terraced house, refurbished in the late 1960s or 70s, is rectangular in shape, and has a total floor area of 65 m². The accommodation comprises a hall, lounge and kitchen/diner on the ground floor and three bedrooms and a bathroom on the first. The external walls are of 9" solid brick, mostly rendered, with single-glazed, wooden-framed casement windows. The pitched roof is tiled with natural slate. The EHCS surveyor found the house to be in good condition generally, the only problem being some external disrepair.

Physical standards

12.28 The surveyor considered the dwelling to be defective in terms of its provision for heating, with only one fixed mains gas heater in the living room, and a further fixed electric heater in one of the bedrooms. One portable electric heater is also available for use. Hot water is provided by an on-peak electric immersion heater with an uninsulated tank. The only form of insulation present is 100mm of mineral wool between joists in the loft. The SAP rating is calculated to be 26.

12.29 The tenants, a couple in their thirties with two children of primary school age have been living in the house for two years. The father is a bricklayer and his spouse is currently unemployed. The household income, although near the top of the second lowest income quintile, is below average for small families in council housing.

Energy consumption

12.30 During the week, the living room is generally heated in the morning and evening, and all-day at weekends. The bedrooms are rarely heated at all and the immersion heater is generally left on all the time to provide hot water. Cooking facilities comprise a mains gas cooker and a microwave. The family also have a washing machine which is used 12 times per week, and an unvented tumble drier. All appliances are run on on-peak electricity.

12.31 With the head of household working, the family are spending nearly 8% of their income on fuel bills, which is 95% of that required to maintain a minimum heating regime in the house, and 81% of that required to maintain a standard regime. Annual energy consumption is 14,830 kWh (64% gas, 36% electricity) and the fuel bill £630 (29% gas, 71% electricity).

Thermal conditions

Home temperatures

12.32 The household was interviewed in late March 1992, on an afternoon when the outside temperature was between 8°C and 9°C. Although the occupants had been at home for more than 7 hours, the heating had been off since 10.00 am that day. The temperature of the living room was only 13.8°C and that of the hall 13.6°C. The living room temperature was considered to be 'colder than usual', whilst that of the hall 'warmer than usual', but both perceived to be 'much too cool'.

Damp and mould growth

12.33 The occupants found the house to be draughty throughout, citing the doors and windows to be causing the main problems. They were also distressed by condensation on the walls and windows in most rooms, although there was no mould growth reported.

Satisfaction with heating

12.34 The family are very dissatisfied with the house in general, and with the heating system in particular. The house is perceived to be difficult to heat and the heating system inadequate and too expensive to run. They particularly mentioned the lack of central heating to be a problem.

Energy action

12.35 The EHCS postal survey revealed that although the area was currently included in an Estate Action Scheme, there were no works planned for this particular dwelling. No expenditure on energy measures was envisaged by the tenants, as this was not felt to be their responsibility. The potential for energy action in this house is large, and could include the provision of central heating, lagging of the hot water tank, dry-lining, double glazing and draught proofing. A central heating system with condensing boiler and temperature zoning controls would cost about £2,200 and could increase the SAP rating to the high 60s.

Case 12.4:
Owner occupied
1965-1980
Low rise flat
(Hall 19.2°C)

12.36 This owner occupied flat, located in a southern Inner London borough is situated on a predominantly low-rise council built estate. It illustrates problems of severe condensation and mould growth, probably due to 'cold bridging', in a dwelling of average energy efficiency and despite an average expenditure on fuel by the young family household.

12.37 The 1965-80 purpose-built maisonette is rectangular in shape and exposed on all sides. The dwelling has a total floor area of 62 m^2, and comprises a hall, living room and kitchen/diner on the first floor and two bedrooms and a bathroom on the second floor. The walls are cavity brick on an in-situ concrete frame, and the dwelling has a flat roof and metal framed single glazed windows. Although judging the dwelling to be fit, the EHCS surveyor found it defective due to serious condensation/mould growth in all rooms. There was also some evidence of differential movement leading to cracking at the external corners.

Physical standards

12.38 Heating is provided by a gas central heating system to radiators in all rooms apart from the hall and kitchen, and is controlled by a roomstat, timer and manual valves on the radiators. Hot water is provided from the boiler to a jacket insulated tank, with an electric immersion heater for back-up. No other insulation measures were recorded, although the status of the roof and the walls were unknown. There are no extract fans in the flat. The SAP rating of the dwelling is calculated to be 41.

12.39 The flat has been occupied for the past four years by a couple in their early thirties and their two pre-school children. Originally council tenants, the family became the owners in the early 1990s under the Right-to-Buy scheme. The husband is a civil servant, and the family income is around the national average, although low for a small family in owner occupation.

Energy consumption

12.40 The family use the central heating regularly in the morning and evening during the week, and all-day at weekends. The only control normally used is the manual override on the timer. The boiler is used to provide hot water in the winter, whilst the on-peak immersion heater is used in summer. Cooking facilities consist of a mains gas cooker and microwave, and the washing machine is used 3 times per week, with the clothes being dried inside on the radiators or a clothes horse.

12.41 The annual energy consumption for the flat is 28,770 kWh, of which 89% is gas and 11% on-peak electricity, resulting in a fuel bill of £732 (62% gas, 38% electricity). With the head of household working, the family are spending 7% of their income on fuel, which amounts to 18% more than should be required to maintain a standard heating regime in the dwelling.

**Thermal
conditions**

*Home
temperatures*

12.42 The household was interviewed in mid May 1992, on a warm evening when the outside temperature was just above 16°C. Although the family had been at home for more than 7 hours, no heating had been used on the day. The temperatures recorded were 19.4°C in the living room and 19.2°C in the hall, the conditions being judged by the interviewee as being the 'same as usual' and 'comfortable'.

*Damp and
mould growth*

12.43 Condensation, damp and mould growth are causing the family some distress, with all rooms except the bathroom being affected. The problems include steamed up windows, wet walls, damage to paint on windows, and mould growth on the walls and floors. The problems persist throughout the year and is worst in the main living room. The mould is dealt with by cleaning as it appears and occasional redecoration. Although there are no extract fans in the flat, the hall, kitchen and living room are identified as being draughty, particularly around doors and windows.

*Satisfaction
with heating*

12.44 The family are fairly satisfied with their heating system, although at the start of the interview they identified heating as something they were unhappy with.

Energy action

12.45 According to the EHCS postal survey, the property was not subject to or proposed for any kind of action. The owners also had no plans to install any further energy efficiency measures. However, there is some potential for action. A complete package of insulation measures would cost about £3,300 and could improve the SAP rating to over 70, saving £200 a year on fuel and paying for itself in 16 years.

**Comparison of
case studies**

12.46 Along with other key characteristics of the case studies, Table 12.2 compares their home temperatures and a severity index for any mould growth (see Annex C, paras. C.44-49) with the corresponding averages (in brackets) for the same type of household in the same tenure. (See also Table A12.1)

**Table 12.2   Comparison of case study dwellings with mean for all
households of same type, size and tenure**

Case study figures/(mean for household type & size in tenure)

	Case 12.1 LA -1 pension	Case 12.2 OO -4p Hhold	Case 12.3 LA -4p family	Case 12.4 OO -4p family	All hholds
Physical standards					
Dwelling size m²	30 (50)	90 (109)	65 (66)	62 (95)	**83**
Energy SAP rating	46 (31)	21 (37)	26 (33)	41 (43)	**35**
Energy consumption					
Total consumption MWh	- (11.6)	35.9 (41.9)	14.8 (22.6)	28.7 (29.2)	**24.0**
Total expenditure £	665 (380)	1,110 (941)	632 (677)	732 (787)	**661**
Thermal conditions					
Outside temp °C	14.3 (10.9)	14.5 (10.9)	8.5 (10.6)	16.3 (10.9)	**11.1**
Living room temp °C	25.6 (20.0)	16.3 (19.7)	13.8 (19.7)	19.4 (19.4)	**19.5**
Hall/stairs temp °C	23.4 (18.5)	13.9 (18.8)	13.6 (18.0)	19.2 (18.5)	**18.3**
Mould growth index[1]	0.0 (0.16)	2.5 (0.19)	1.0 (0.96)	3.5 (0.26)	**0.34**
Energy action					
Target SAP rating	64	72	67	72	
Improvement cost £	275	10,690	2,210	3,274	
Simple payback yrs	5	17	6	16	

1 slight mould (0.5 to 1.0), moderate (1.5 to 2.5) and severe (3 and over)

Chapter

Home temperatures

Preamble

13.1 *In Chapter 11 we looked at those households whose annual fuel expenditure was insufficient for them to maintain the minimum and standard heating regimes. This Chapter profiles those homes which were failing or achieving the minimum and standard regime temperatures at the time of the survey and examines how their numbers are affected by colder weather. However, the Chapter starts with an examination of the average home temperatures achieved in the housing stock, followed by a description of household attitudes to their room temperatures. The Chapter ends with a comparison of the temperatures recorded in 1991 with those of the 1986 survey.*

13.2 *In the EHCS Temperature Survey, interviewers were instructed to take two internal and one external spot temperature outside the building. The first reading was generally taken in the living room used by the occupant and the second in the hall, the latter being a good proxy for the mean of all rooms. (see Annex C, paras. C.5-6)*

Average temperatures

13.3 Temperatures were measured during a relatively mild period of four months from February to May 1992, the average external temperature of 11°C comparing with an average of 6.3°C in the 1986 survey. (Table A13.1 gives the mean external, living room and hall temperature for each month). For the total period, the average temperature achieved in the living room was 19.5°C and for the hall 18.3°C. (See Table A13.2 for averages in individual rooms) The distribution of the living room, hall and external temperatures are all fairly normal as shown in Figure 13.1.

Figure 13.1   Distribution of living room, hall and external spot temperatures

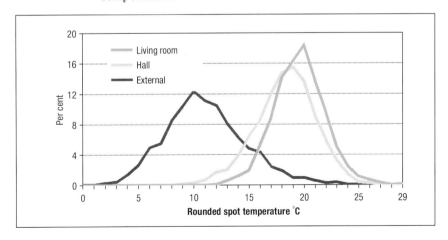

Stock characteristics

Tenure

13.4 On average, living room temperatures in homes rented from housing associations (20.5°C) and local authorities are warmer than those in owner occupied homes (19.4°C), although halls in the latter are generally warmer than those in local authority tenancies. Private tenants have the coolest average living room and hall temperatures. (Figure 13.2 & Table A13.3)

Figure 13.2   Mean living room and hall spot temperatures by tenure

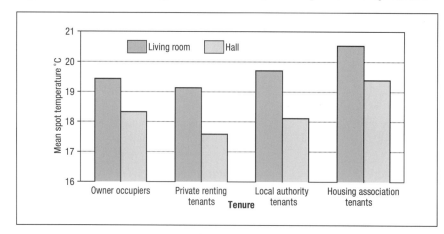

Dwelling age and type

13.5   Not surprisingly, older dwellings are found to be colder. Living rooms in pre 1850 dwellings are about 1°C cooler on average than post 1980 dwellings. The average temperature difference between the living room and hall also increases with age. In terms of dwelling type, purpose built flats have the warmest average living room and hall temperatures (20.2°C and 19.4°C respectively), while temporary dwellings are found to be the coldest, with average living room and hall temperatures of only 18.4°C and 14.5°C. (Table A13.3)

Region and locality

13.6   There appears to be no significant differences in room temperatures between regions. The warmest average living room temperature is 20.0°C recorded in the East Midlands and the coolest 19.1°C recorded in the West Midlands. The average temperature difference between the living room and hall was also greatest in the West Midlands and smallest in Greater London. Despite the general uniformity of room temperatures across the regions, the average living room and hall temperature tends to decrease as the dwelling location becomes more rural, while conversely the average difference between the living room and hall temperatures tends to increase. Both of these trends reflect, amongst other things, the lower frequency of gas central heating in homes in more rural locations. (Table A13.3)

Housing condition

13.7   Home temperatures were related to dwelling condition, particularly to the fitness of a dwelling. The average living room and hall temperatures recorded in fit dwellings were significantly warmer than in those judged unfit by the EHCS surveyors. (Table A13.3) A correlation was also found between home temperatures and the surveyors assessment of the adequacy of the provision for heating. Both the average living room and hall temperature increases as the fitness category of the heating system moves from "unfit" to "satisfactory", while the difference between the two temperatures decreases. (Figure 13.3 & Table A13.5)

Energy characteristics

Central heating

13.8   Dwellings with a central heating system are generally significantly warmer than those without central heating. On average, the living room in a centrally heated home is just under 1°C warmer than in one not centrally heated, while halls are on average over 2°C warmer. Reflecting this, the average temperature difference between the living room and hall is just over 1°C in centrally heated homes, but as high as 2.2°C in those with no central heating. (Table A13.4)

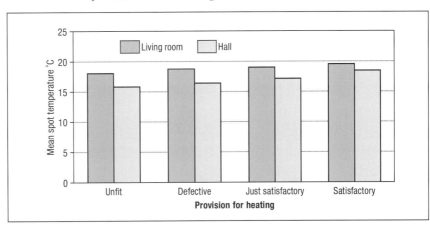

Figure 13.3 **Mean living room and hall spot temperatures by provision for heating**

Type of heating 13.9 Differences are also found between the living room temperatures in dwellings with different forms of heating and fuel use. Living rooms with 'other' central heating, including communal systems, and with electric central heating, are generally warmer than those with gas fired central heating, the first type achieving a mean of 20.5°C and the latter 19.7°C. Homes with a solid fuel central heating system were recorded as having colder living rooms than any other centrally heated homes, their mean temperature being 19.1°C. However, the coldest living rooms were those heated by solid fuel fires and stoves where there was no central heating system. Here the mean was only just over 18°C. (Table A13.5)

Heating patterns 13.10 As one would expect, there is a relationship between the temperature in the living room and the heating pattern employed in that room. Those households that have a regular heating pattern and heat their living room all day had the highest average living room temperature (19.7°C), followed by those who regularly heat the room in the morning and evening (19.5°C) and in the evening only (19.2°C). Those without a regular heating pattern recorded the lowest average spot temperature in the living room (18.5°C). (Table A13.5)

Time of day 13.11 The time of day when a spot temperature is recorded is important as it reflects both the duration and period of heating. In the following analysis only those households where the heating has been on in the living room for an hour or more have been included. Figure 13.4 plots the average indoor temperature readings against the time of the interview for households using central heating and those using other forms of heatings and shows the influence of the type of heating used.

13.12 There were few evening readings particularly in non-centrally heated homes. In centrally heated homes the increase in room temperatures during the day is clearly evident. In these dwellings, temperatures tend to peak at 1200 hours, 1500 hours and 1800 hours, suggesting that dependent on their lifestyles certain groups of the population switch their heating on at these times. In dwellings without central heating, there is an unexpected decrease in average temperature in the latter part of the day. It is possible that the data are less reliable for this time due to the relatively few evening readings obtained for this part of the sample. However, it may reflect a genuine fall in room temperatures with falling external temperatures in dwellings which, as well as lacking central heating, are often less well insulated.

Figure 13.4   Average living room and hall temperatures for centrally and non-centrally heated dwellings by time of day

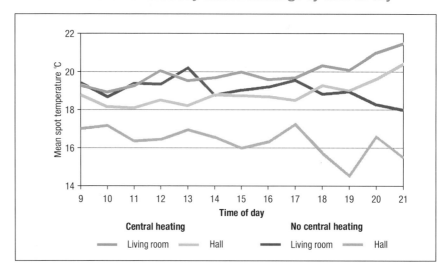

SAP ratings

13.13 The greater the overall energy efficiency, the generally warmer the dwelling; the average living room and hall temperatures increasing progressively with higher SAP ratings. Hall temperatures show the steepest gradient, the temperature difference between the living room and hall decreasing significantly with increasing efficiency. (Figure 13.5 & Table A13.5)

Figure 13.5   Mean living room and hall spot temperatures by SAP ratings

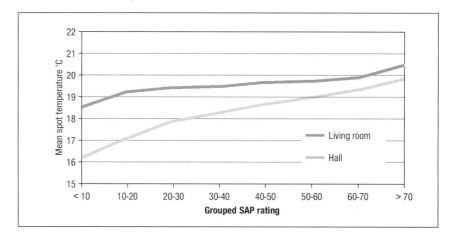

Household characteristics

Household type

13.14 Lone adult non-pensioners are found to have the coldest average living room and hall temperatures. On average, lone pensioners and older couples have the warmest living rooms, but also the largest average temperature difference between their living room and hall - indicating that one room is often heated to a significantly higher standard than the rest of the house. In contrast, large family households have the smallest temperature difference between their living room and hall. (Table A13.6)

Employment status

13.15 Of households where the employment status is known, those with two people in full-time employment generally have the warmest living room temperatures (19.6°C). The average temperature difference between the living room and hall is smallest for single people in full-time work and greatest in households where two people are not working. (Table A13.6)

Household income

13.16 The average hall temperature increases progressively with increasing income, while the average temperature difference between living room and hall decreases. The 20% of households with the lowest incomes have a mean hall temperature of under 18°C compared to nearly 19°C for the 20% with the highest. (Table A13.6)

Comfort rating 13.17 In order to gain an assessment of household attitudes to room temperatures, the occupant was asked to describe the current temperature in the living room and hall in terms of a 7 point 'comfort' scale ranging from "much too cool" to "much too warm". As shown in Figure 13.6, the distribution of responses was skewed towards the warmer end of the scale in the case of living rooms, with 30% of households rating their room as "comfortably warm". With halls, the reverse was the case with significantly more households considering their halls "too cool" than "too warm". (Table A13.7)

Figure 13.6   Comfort rating for living room and hall with mean temperatures

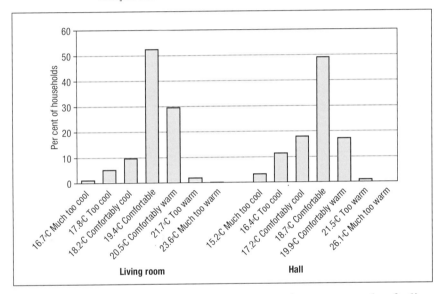

Living room and hall 13.18 The average living room and hall temperatures that correspond to feeling "comfortable" (19.4°C and 18.6°C respectively) are close to the average temperatures for all living rooms and halls (19.5°C and 18.3°C), although there is significant deviation around the means. While most households consider their homes comfortable, households with rooms well above 21°C generally regard them as too warm and those with living rooms around 17.8°C and halls around 16.4°C as too cold.

Overall 13.19 Households were also asked to assess the overall temperature of their home on the same comfort scale, while for comparison the interviewer recorded his or her overall assessment. Although slightly less skewed, the distribution of household responses tends to be closer to the living room profile than that of the hall, but the reverse is true of the interviewers assessments. In just over 56% of cases the householder's and interviewer's assessment is the same. (Table A13.8)

Usual temperature 13.20 To indicate whether the spot temperatures were representative of the thermal conditions normally achieved in the home, householders were asked if the living room and hall was "colder, warmer or about the same as it usually is". Some 70% of households said the temperature in the living room was the same as usual, while 18% said it was colder and some 12% warmer than usual. In the case of the hall, 77% of households said the temperature was the same, 12% judging it to be colder and 10% warmer than usual. (Table A13.9)

13.21 Compared to those identified as the same as usual, the average living room and hall temperatures were significantly lower in those rooms said to be colder than usual. Conversely, temperatures in rooms judged warmer than usual were appreciably higher. Similarly, rooms judged colder or warmer than usual had respectively a lower and higher comfort rating (on the 7 point scale) than those considered the same as usual.

Minimum & standard temperatures

13.22 The average temperatures achieved in those living rooms and halls (the proxy for all rooms) identified by households as too cold or too warm largely supports the use of the 18°C and 16°C minimum thresholds and 21°C and 18°C standard design temperatures used in the analysis of affordable warmth in Chapter 11. This current Chapter continues with an estimate of the proportion of households actually achieving the temperatures required for the minimum and standard heating regimes at the time of the interview. This analysis is limited to those households whose heating has been on for an hour or more in, at least, the living room where the spot temperature was taken, thereby eliminating any homes which may be cold merely because the household has only recently returned home.

Households achieving temperatures

13.23 For the analysis, three exclusive categories have been defined, as follows, according to whether both the living room and hall temperatures meet those of the standard or minimum regimes:

1) Both meet Standard   Living room at 21°C or above <u>and</u> hall at 18°C or above.

2) Both meet Minimum   Living room at 18°C or above <u>and</u> hall at 16°C or above, but one or both below the standard regime temperatures.

3) Below Minimum   Living room below 18°C <u>or</u> hall below 16°C.

Figure 13.7   **Percentage of households achieving minimum and standard regime temperatures** *(after heating living room and/or hall for 1 hour or more)*

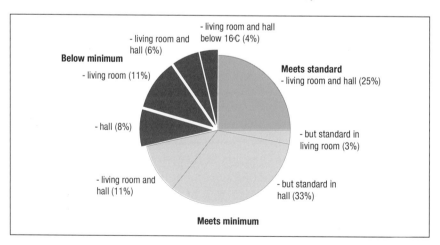

13.24 Despite the relatively mild weather, a large proportion of homes were found to fail these temperatures. Overall, nearly 1 in 4 households have home temperatures which meet or surpass those of the standard regime, 47% meet those of the minimum regime, 19% fail to meet one and 10% fail both of the minimum regime temperatures. Of all those failing, 28% fail only on the hall, 37% fail on the living room alone and 34% fail on both temperatures. Nearly half of the latter (16%) have both living room and hall below 16°C. (Figure 13.7)

Tenure

13.25 The private rented sector had the greatest proportion of homes failing to meet the minimum temperatures and the housing association sector the smallest. Only 22% of housing association properties failed the minimum standard, compared to 28% of those owner occupied, with respectively just under and just over 9% of each sector failing on both temperatures. Some 31% of local authority homes and 33% of those privately rented failed, with over 1 in 10 and nearly 1 in 6 of the total stocks failing both temperatures. Conversely, the private tenants have the lowest proportion of homes that reach the standard regime temperatures - only some 22% compared to 26% of council tenants and 40% of housing association tenants.

Heating facilities

13.26 Dwellings with central heating were almost twice as likely to reach the standard temperatures as those without central heating. Well over a half (53%) of the latter did not achieve both minimum temperatures, nearly 1 in 4 homes failing on both. This compares with under a quarter (24%) of centrally heated homes of which only 8% failed both temperatures. Households using portable heaters are most likely to fail the minimum regime temperatures, some 73% failing at least one temperature and 24% both, these figures being three times those for homes with gas-fired central heating. The full standard regime temperatures were met by 41% of those with communal or 'other' central heating, 31% with oil fired systems, 26% with gas central heating and 23% with either electric or solid fuel central heating.

SAP rating

13.27 Some 48% of dwellings with a SAP rating below 20 failed to meet the minimum standard and just under a half of these fail on both temperatures. In contrast, only 27% of dwellings with a rating greater than 20 fail, a third of these failing on both temperatures. The proportion of households failing to reach the minimum temperatures decreases as household income increases, while conversely the proportion reaching those of the standard regime increases.

Figure 13.8   Influence of external temperatures on achieving minimum and standard regime temperatures

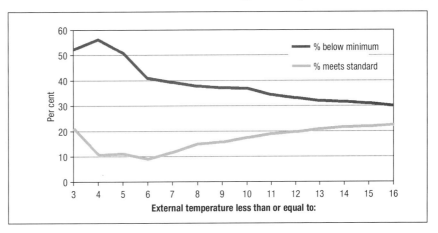

Effect of cold weather

13.28 Figure 13.8 illustrates the influence of external temperatures on the internal temperature readings. Clearly, as the external temperature drops the proportion of households failing to achieve the minimum temperatures increases and the proportion failing to achieve the minimum temperature in both living room and hall increases. Thus, where the external temperature is some 16°C or below, some 30% of households failed to achieve the minimum regime temperatures, a third of these failing in both the living room and hall. This proportion increases to some 53% of households when the external temperature was 3°C or below. The proportion of households meeting the standard temperatures also decreases with falling external temperature but increases again with external temperatures of 3°C and below. This increase in home temperatures during colder weather is thought to result from many households over-compensating with their heating controls. The large proportion of households reported in Chapter 9 as changing their thermostat at least once a week supports this conclusion. (see also Table A13.10)

Tenure variation

13.29 The effect of external temperature on the ability to achieve the standard and minimum temperatures is evident in all tenures, but is greater in the private rented and local authority sectors than in the owner occupied stock. The colder the weather the greater is the divergence between the proportion of owner occupiers and proportion of tenants achieving these temperatures. When the external temperature was 16°C or below (mean about 10°C), 30% of owner occupiers failed to achieve the minimum temperatures but this proportion increased to 50% when the external temperature dropped to 4°C or below. However, for local authority tenants the corresponding increases were from 32% to 62% and for private tenants from 32% to 95% of households below the minimum regime.

13.30 When the external temperature reaches 3°C or below, the percentage of owner occupiers achieving the high temperatures of the standard regime almost doubles - from 12% when the external temperature was 4°C or below to 22% in even colder weather. This suggests that in many owner occupied homes, room temperatures generally fall as the weather gets colder but that in particularly cold spells, owners respond by over-compensating with their heating controls. A similar response is shown by local authority tenants, the percentage achieving the standard regime temperatures increasing from 11% when external temperatures were at 4°C or below to 18% in even colder weather. (The sample of homes in the private rented and housing association sectors with particularly cold external temperatures are not sufficient for a comparable analysis). (Table A13.11)

Type of heating

13.31 Figure 13.9 shows the influence of outside temperatures on those indoors in homes possessing and lacking central heating. The proportion of households using central heating but failing to achieve the minimum temperatures tends to increase as the external temperature falls, and the same is true for those lacking central heating. However, the proportion failing the minimum standard at any given external temperature is over half that in homes with central heating than in those without.

13.32 Where the outside temperature is 3°C or below, for example, some 48% of centrally heated homes fail the lower standard compared to all other recorded homes. The proportion of households achieving the standard regime temperatures also decreases with colder weather, whether or not central heating is used. However, centrally heated homes are again over twice as good as others on this measure. Where the external reading is 3°C or below, 23% of houses with central heating meet this standard compared with none of those without. (Table A13.12)

Figure 13.9   Influence of external temperature on achieving temperature standards by central heating

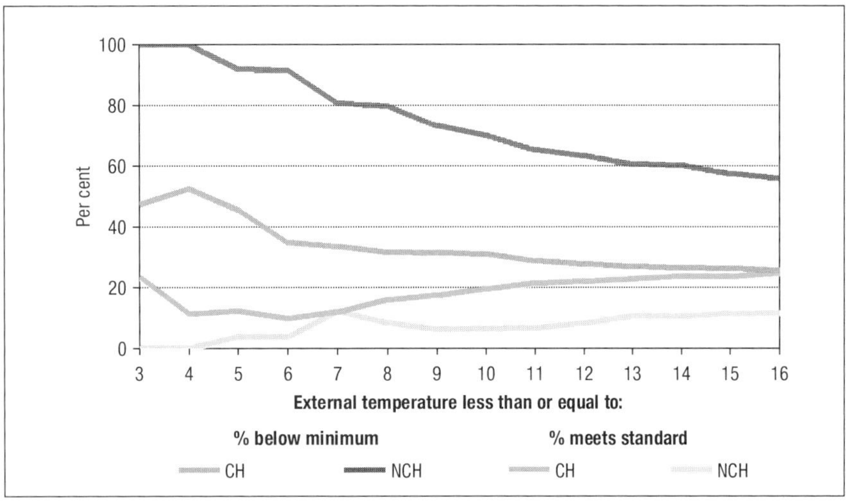

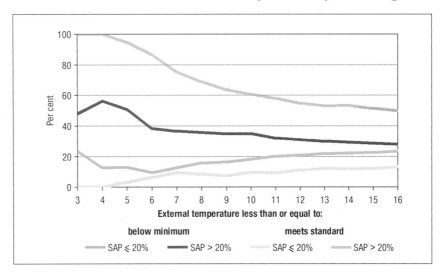

Energy (SAP) rating

13.33 Reflecting their poor heating and insulation, the percentage of households failing to meet the minimum temperatures at different external readings, is significantly larger for dwellings with low SAP energy ratings than for those with higher values. For example, where the external temperature was 3°C or below, all recorded homes with a SAP rating below 20 failed the minimum temperatures compared with under half of those with a rating of 20 or more. The proportion of households achieving the standard regime temperatures also generally decreases with falling outside temperatures for both dwellings above and below a rating of 20, but in the more efficient dwellings this trend is reversed when the outside temperature reaches 3°C or below. Again this can be attributed to households over-compensating with temperature controls, which the households with the lower SAP ratings will often lack. (Figure 13.10 & Table A13.13)

Figure 13.10   Influence of external temperature on achieving the minimum and standard temperatures by SAP rating

Household income

13.34 The influence of external temperature on achieving adequate temperatures is also evident across all income groups, although significantly more important for those on the lowest incomes. With a fall in the mean outside temperature from 16°C to 3°C or less the number of high income households (i.e. highest 20%) failing the minimum temperatures increases by under a third to 35%, while the number on below average income (lowest 40%)

more than doubles to affect nearly 4 out of 5 such households. With such outside temperatures, there are no recorded cases of those on the lowest incomes (i.e. lowest 20%) reaching the standard temperatures, but the proportion of those on high income meeting this standard stays the same (26%). (Table A13.14)

State benefits   13.35 As pensioner households and lone parents account for well over a third of all households where three-quarters or more of the income derives from state benefit, this group has also been considered. The proportion of households reliant on benefits who are failing to achieve the minimum temperatures increases by an even greater amount (from 33% to 86%) over the same range of external temperatures. Conversely, the number of recorded cases meeting the standard regime temperatures falls from 23% to zero. By comparison, the proportion of households not reliant on benefits who are failing the minimum standard increases by a half (from 30 to 45%) while the number achieving standard temperatures increases slightly (to 24%). (Table A13.15)

Figure 13.11   Influence of external temperature on achieving minimum and standard temperatures by households on state benefit

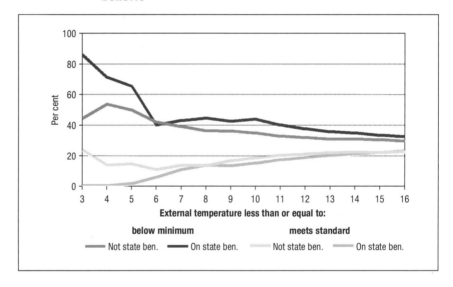

Trends, 1986 to 1991   13.36 The 1986 Survey was undertaken between December 1986 and March 1987 and included a particularly cold January when outside temperatures were below freezing in most places at all times. Where the outside temperature was below 5°C, the survey revealed a large number of particularly cold homes, those with the warmest room (usually the living room) below 16°C and the coldest room (generally the hall) below 12°C being classed as "cold" and those with both rooms below 12°C being termed "very cold". Despite generally being heated for one hour or more, some 2.3 million homes or 13% of the stock were found to be "cold homes", of which 400 thousand, or over 2%, were "very cold".

13.37 The 1991 Temperature Survey, which was undertaken between February and May 1991 in a period of fairly mild weather, found only 3% of the stock to be "cold" on the 1986 definition. However, the 1991 Survey has again demonstrated the strong influence of outside temperatures on home temperatures, particularly in certain sections of the stock. In 1991/92, the average external temperature recorded by EHCS interviewers was about

11°C, whereas in the 1986/87 fieldwork period it was only some 6°C and averaged zero during the particularly cold snap.

13.38 A comparison of indoor spot temperatures shows that home temperatures were significantly warmer in the 1991 survey than in 1986, the average living room temperature being 1°C warmer and that in the hall approaching 2°C warmer. Despite the clear effect of cold weather on home temperature shown in both surveys, the differences in room temperatures are weakly correlated with the difference in outside temperatures. However, whereas in 1986 persistent cold weather affected the heat loss throughout the day, in 1991 cold external temperatures tend to be limited to early morning or evening readings taken after homes had already benefited from lower heat losses during the day.

13.39 To overcome such factors and directly compare the temperatures recorded during the 1986 and 1991 surveys, an analysis has been carried out using simple linear regression of a common sample of addresses that were included in both interview surveys and which had valid living room and hall temperatures for both years. (see Annex C, paras C.40-43) This analysis shows that, despite some individual improvements, there is no evidence to suggest that the internal home temperatures measured in 1991 would have been significantly different from the lower standards recorded in 1986 had the same weather prevailed.

Chapter 14

Damp and mould growth

Preamble

14.1 *This third chapter on thermal conditions is concerned with damp and mould growth. It first examines rising and penetrating damp as assessed by the surveyors, these primarily physical matters being included here because of their close association with mould. The bulk of the chapter concerns condensation and mould growth as reported by respondents in the Interview Survey. It maps the distribution of mould growth and concludes by using regression analysis to explore the causal factors in its incidence.*

Rising and penetrating damp

14.2 As part of the Physical Survey, the surveyor assessed whether any of seven rooms, including the kitchen, bathroom and circulation area had defects caused by rising or penetrating damp. In the analysis that follows the percentages of the stock with rising damp refer to only those dwellings with a ground floor or basement (16.9 million), while those for penetrating damp refer to all occupied dwellings (18.9 million).

Overall incidence

14.3 Overall, nearly 1.1 million dwellings (7% of the relevant stock) are affected by rising damp in one or more rooms. Most of these have the problem in only one room (4% of the stock) with smaller numbers (under 2%) affected in two rooms and a little over 1% in three or more rooms. Penetrating damp occurs in 1.6 million properties (8% of the stock); 5% being affected in only one room, 2% in two rooms and over 1% in three or more rooms. There is no significant difference in the incidence of either problem between various types of room.

Stock characteristics

Tenure

14.4 Figures 14.1 and 14.2 show the incidence of rising and penetrating damp respectively, broken down by tenure and age of construction. The overall incidence of both problems is much higher in the private rented stock (21% with rising damp and the same percentage with penetrating damp) than in the other three tenures (about 5% with rising damp and 7% with penetrating damp). The age of the private rented sector - 64% were built before 1918 - has combined with poor maintenance to exacerbate problems in this sector. (Table A14.1)

Figure 14.1   Rising damp to ground floor by dwelling age and tenure

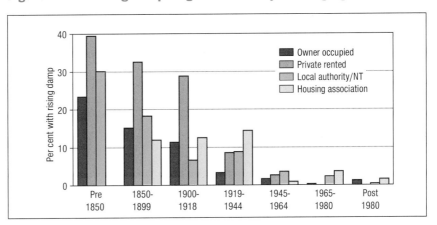

Dwelling age

14.5 Both damp problems are concentrated in the older stock, over 71% of rising damp problems occur in dwellings built before 1919 with a further 16% in those built between the wars; the corresponding figures for penetrating dampness are some 61% and 17% respectively. The older stock, especially those built before 1919, will be more likely to have solid walls with no damp proof courses and will also be in a poorer state of repair.[1]

Figure 14.2   Penetrating damp by dwelling age and tenure

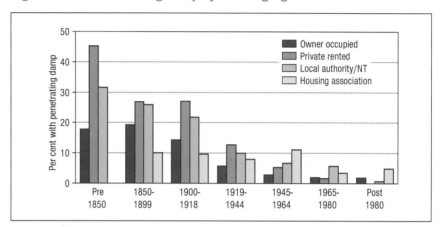

Dwelling location and region

14.6 Figure 14.3 shows the incidence of rising and penetrating damp by the different type of localities. Table A14.2 shows the same data together with the percentage of the stock in each group that were built before 1919. As with other factors, there is a strong association with age of construction. The high level of penetrating damp in urban and city centre housing (over 13% and 12% respectively) - the group most likely to be sheltered from driving rain - is associated with the fact that over 45% were built before 1919. This compares to the much more exposed rural and suburban residential housing with only 5 and 6% respectively with problems and 16% and 11% of dwellings built before 1919.

Figure 14.3   Rising and penetrating damp by type of locality

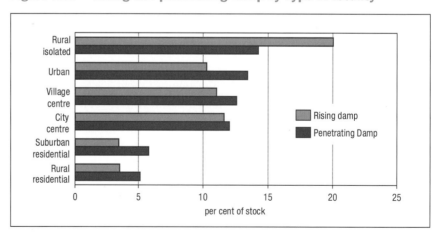

14.7 This situation is reflected on the regional scale, Inner London, probably the area least exposed to driving rain but with 50% of its stock built before 1919 has rain penetration in nearly 14% of its stock, compared to Devon and Cornwall, the most exposed area, with 30% of older dwellings and only 9% of the stock affected.

Dwelling condition

14.8 As part of the Physical Survey the surveyors assessed whether the damp proof course (DPC) was faulty or incomplete - 58% of dwellings with a

1 *The number of local authority dwellings built before 1919 is very small.*

faulty DPC have rising damp, compared to 3% with an apparently satisfactory DPC. Also, as shown in Figure 14.4, dwellings in poor condition overall are much more likely to have both forms of damp. Rising damp affects over 24% of the worst ten percent of the stock and only 1% of the best thirty percent. The difference for penetrating damp is even more marked, with nearly 30% of the worst stock affected compared to only 1% of the best.

Figure 14.4   Stock affected by rising and penetrating damp by overall condition

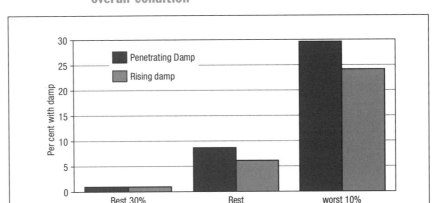

Household characteristics

Income

14.9 There is a marked relationship between low household income and damp - nearly 13% of dwellings occupied by households in the lowest income quintile have penetrating damp, compared to only some 5% in the highest quintile. The corresponding figures for rising damp are 10% and 4% respectively. However, those in the bottom quintile live in poorer quality dwellings irrespective of dwelling age - over 15% are in the worst 10% of the stock, compared to only 5% in the highest income quintile.

Household type

14.10 There is relatively little difference in the incidence of damp in dwellings with different household types except for those occupied by lone parents (11% with rising damp and the same number with penetrating damp) and especially single adults (over 15% and 8% respectively). The dwellings occupied by single adults combine both the features that tend toward problems - 40% were built before 1918 and nearly 18% are in the worst 10% of the stock. Households with vulnerable persons - pensioners or young children - are no more likely than average to live in a damp dwelling. (Table A14.3)

Condensation and mould growth

14.11 Condensation and mould growth are caused by an interaction between the structure of the dwelling - likely relevant factors being poor insulation, local thermal bridges and inadequate provision for heating and ventilation - and the way that it is used by the occupants. Problems are generally more common in homes in which the occupants have difficulty in affording heating; that is, in rented housing in general and in the local authority stock in particular.

Survey questions

14.12 During the Interview Survey the occupants were asked a number of questions concerning the incidence of condensation and mould growth in their home, how much it concerns them and which rooms are affected. To provide an objective comparison, they were also asked which of three photographs of mould most resembled the problem in their home. (See below)

Photograph 14.1 Photographs of mould used in Interview Survey

Incidence and rooms affected

14.13 Over 22% of householders report some sort of problem with condensation and mould, but the incidence varies significantly between tenures, with only 17% of owner occupier homes affected, compared to over 28% of housing association, 33% of local authority and 37% of those in private rented housing. (Table A14.5)

14.14 The rooms most severely affected are, with little variation between tenures, those likely to have high moisture productions or low heat inputs, i.e. the bathroom (the worst affected in a quarter of dwellings with a problem), the main bedroom (20%) and the kitchen (17%). Living rooms, which are generally relatively well heated, are the worst affected room in under a tenth of the affected stock.

Distress of households

14.15 Figure 14.5 shows that, while over 21% of owner occupiers with problems of condensation and mould find it 'discomforting' or 'distressing', the corresponding figures for tenants are over 40% in private rented, nearly 50% in local authority and 53% in housing association homes. However, it should be recognised that the fact that tenants have an identifiable landlord means that they may be more likely to complain about problems such as mould growth than owner occupiers who may feel that they are personally responsible for any such problems in their home. (Table A14.4)

Figure 14.5 Household distress caused by mould by tenure

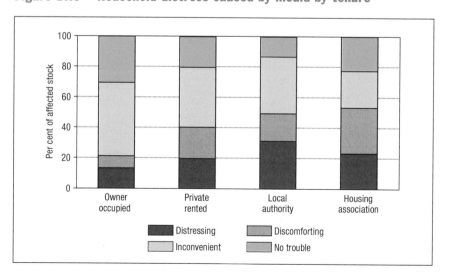

14.16 That said, both the occupants perception of the problem and the mould photograph identified, suggest that besides being more widespread, the problems in rented housing are genuinely more severe than those in the owner occupied stock. The most severe mould photograph was identified in only just over 1% of owner occupied homes, compared to over 3% of housing association, 5% of local authority and nearly 9% of private rented dwellings. (Table A14.5)

Severity index

14.17 To further the discussion of the nature and distribution of problems amongst the various sectors of the housing stock, the responses to the various EHCS questions concerning condensation and mould have been combined to classify the severity of problems into 'slight', 'moderate' and 'severe'. The general circumstances represented by these three categories are specified in Table 14.1. (The full calculation of the index is described in Annex C, paras. C.44-49)

Table 14.1   Severity of condensation and mould growth

Slight	Condensation on windows and/or limited mould in bathrooms and kitchens
Moderate	Larger areas of mould especially in bedrooms and/or widespread condensation
Severe	Widespread mould, especially in living rooms

Stock characteristics

Tenure

14.18 Using this classification, Figure 14.6 shows the distribution of condensation and mould growth between the tenures. Overall, tenants are affected more severely than owner occupiers. Their lower incomes and often poorer housing means that their rooms are less well heated, although as mentioned earlier, there may also be perceptual differences between tenants and owners. In the rented sectors, the local authority stock lies between private rented housing, which partly because of its age is generally in much poorer condition, and the housing association stock, which comprises a mixture of older, renovated buildings and new build. (Table A14.5)

14.19 Because of the size of the sector, however, over half of all homes with mould growth are owner occupied (52%), compared to the 30% accounted for by the local authority stock. Condensation and mould growth is no longer overwhelmingly a problem of rented housing as it was perceived to be in the 70s and early 80s; but most of the severe problems (67%) are still in the rented sectors. (Table A14.6)

Figure 14.6   Severity of mould growth by tenure

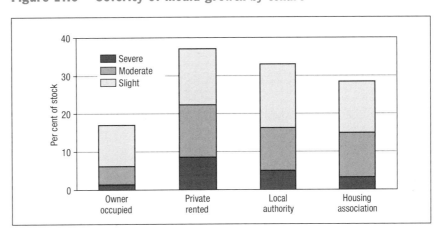

Dwelling age

14.20 As with the other forms of damp discussed earlier, condensation and mould growth problems are more common in older properties. Only 15% of dwellings built since 1980 have any problems and well under 1% have severe problems. The incidence of any type of problem rises to 24 -27% in dwellings built between 1850 and 1964, with 3 - 5% suffering from severe problems; there is a sharp rise to 32% with problems in the oldest group. The effect of the increases in the insulation standards brought about in successive revisions to the Building Regulations since 1975 and the almost universal installation of central heating in new dwellings, have combined to improve thermal and comfort standards within the home. The oldest dwellings generally have solid, poorly insulated walls and are less likely to have central heating. (Table A14.7)

Dwelling type

14.21 In principle, detached dwellings should be most vulnerable to condensation and damp problems as they have a maximum number of exposed surfaces from which they can lose heat. However, because they are relatively uncommon in the rented sectors and tend to be occupied by more affluent families, they show fewer problems (17% with any problem, 2% with severe problems) than end terraced (28% and 4%) and converted flats (28% and 6%) which are much more common in the rented, especially the private rented sectors.

14.22 Figure 14.7 shows these factors combined in the distribution of the severity of problems in different ages and types of property. The groups with fewest problems tend to be modern dwellings and flats - only 9% of detached dwellings built between 1965 and 1980 and 12% of flats built after 1980 have any problems, with very small proportions with severe problems. Post war bungalows, many of whom are occupied by pensioners, are also

Figure 14.7   Severity of mould growth by dwelling age, size and type

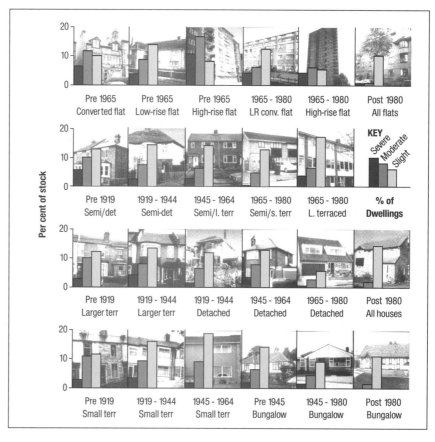

close behind with problems in only 12 - 15% of the stock. At the other end of the scale, older terraced dwellings and converted properties are much more widely affected - more than 28% have problems of some sort. (Table A14.7)

14.23 The most interesting contrast is between the worst group, pre 1965 high rise flats (36% with any problem, 11% with severe problems) and post 1965 high rise flats which are near the top (16% and 4%). The high rise flats from the late sixties often have good insulation standards and small external wall areas from which to lose heat, many blocks having been improved with external cladding. (Table A14.7)

Regional variation

14.24 The variation in the incidence of condensation and mould problems between the different metropolitan and non metropolitan regions (shown in Figure 14.8) is not very marked, ranging from 19% with some form of problem in Outer London to 29% in the West Midlands Metropolitan Area. Although the four least affected regions are all in the south east of England, with a relatively mild climate and little exposure to driving rain, this geographical and climatic pattern is not reflected in the other regions. Northerly regions such as the South Yorkshire Metropolitan Area and Northern Non-Metropolitan Area are toward the bottom of the range while Devon & Cornwall, with the mildest climate, and the West Midlands Metropolitan Area, also a sheltered area, are at the top. Factors such as the age of the

Figure 14.8   Severity of mould growth by region and administrative area

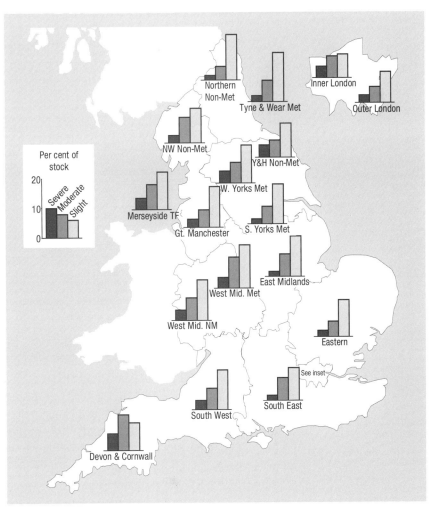

stock, the provision of efficient central heating (as shown in Chapter 4, Devon & Cornwall has the lowest ownership of gas central heating of any area) and the overall affluence of areas such as the South East, are more important. (Table A14.7)

Locality

14.25 The incidence in different types of locality varies from 30% with any problems in isolated rural areas and 26% in urban areas to 19% in residential rural areas and 21% in suburban areas, again reflecting differences in availability of heating fuels and family income.

Energy characteristics

Type of heating

14.26 The main heating system in the home has a very strong effect on the incidence of condensation and mould growth. Under 15% of dwellings with oil central heating (as noted in Chapter 10 these tend to be large expensive homes occupied by families with a high income) have any problems - 3% having severe problems. Homes with gas central heating - by far the largest group - have severe problems in only 2% of cases and any problems in 20%. At the other end of the scale, 43% of homes with direct on-peak electric heating have some degree of problem. As noted previously these tend to be occupied by families on low incomes - many in the private rented sector. Homes with solid fuel central heating and those relying solely on portable heaters stand out as having a particularly high incidence of severe problems - 9% and 7% respectively. (Table A14.8)

14.27 Overall, 21% of dwellings with any form of central heating have some form of condensation or mould growth problem - over 2% having a severe problem. This compares to over a third of dwellings with no central heating with problems, 5% being severe. (Figure 14.9 & Table A14.8)

Figure 14.9   Severity of mould growth by main heating

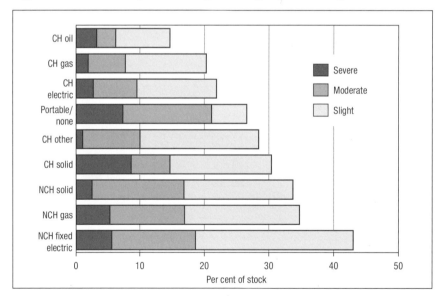

SAP energy ratings

14.28 Turning to the overall energy efficiency of the home, Figure 14.10 shows the distribution of mould growth by different SAP ratings. There is a steady reduction in the incidence and severity of mould growth as homes become more energy efficient - 36% of dwellings in the lowest group having some form of problem, compared to only 17% in the most efficient group. The two components of SAP - the heat loss index of the dwelling and the heating price of the heating system both increase with increasing mould growth - the former is 8% higher in dwellings with severe mould growth compared to those with no problem and the latter 13% higher.

Figure 14.10 Severity of mould growth by energy (SAP) rating

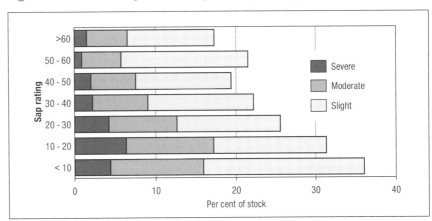

14.29 There is little variation in fuel consumption with increasing mould growth. Homes with no mould growth are using, on average, almost 274 kWh per square metre compared to the 295 kWh per square metre used by those with a severe problem. One significant difference occurs in the proportions of the different fuels used to make up the total. Homes with no mould growth are taking 69% of their energy consumption from gas, mainly for gas central heating, compared to only 55% in those with severe mould growth. The proportion of consumption supplied by electricity remains fairly constant but the proportion made up from other, unmetered fuels rises from 13% with no mould growth to 27% in dwellings with a severe problem. (Figure 14.11 and Table A14.9)

Fuel consumption

Figure 14.11 Severity of mould growth by consumption of different fuels

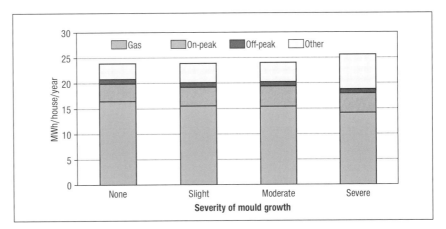

Household characteristics

Household type

14.30 Household type and size is an important determinant of condensation problems, as shown in Figure 14.12, in which the different household types have been ordered by the incidence of any problem. The three households with most problems: small families (28% with problems), large families (34%) and lone parent families (38%, 7% with severe problems), all have dependent children. This will lead to increased moisture load on the home due to washing clothes, bathing etc. Households with pensioners are least likely to suffer from any problems - they will tend to be continuously heated and have relatively low levels of moisture production. (Table A14.10)

Household income

14.31 Taken overall, total household income has relatively little effect on the incidence of condensation and mould growth - 21% of households in the lowest income quintile have some degree of mould growth (over 3% with

Figure 14.12   Severity of mould growth by household type

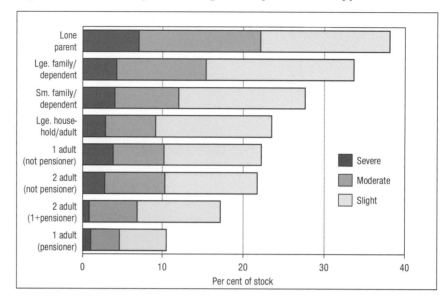

a severe problem) compared to under 18% in the highest quintile (2% with a severe problem). However, this picture is distorted by the general position of pensioners on low income - as discussed above.

Household type by income

14.32 Figure 14.13 shows the severity of mould growth by total household income for three different family types - lone adults (non pensioners), families with children, and pensioners. 'Adult' households show a consistent reduction in income with increasing mould growth - the average income of those with severe mould is only 80% of those with no mould at all. This is even more marked in the case of families with children - those with severe mould have only 60% of the income of those with none. In contrast, there is no variation of pensioners' income with increasing mould severity.

Figure 14.13   Severity of mould growth by household type by income

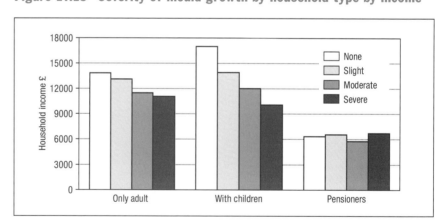

Significant variables

14.33 As many of the factors discussed above interact in complex ways, multiple regression analysis was carried out on a series of variables. The results of this analysis, in the form of a list of the most significant coefficients, are given in Table 14.2 opposite.

Trends in condensation and mould, 1986 - 1991

14.34 The 1986 EHCS contained information on the proportion of the stock with condensation, generally steamed up windows with no mould growth, and mould growth on walls and/or on furniture in one or more rooms. The comparable figures calculated from the 1991 survey are shown broken

Table 14.2   Ten significant variables in mould growth *(in order of importance)*

Order	Coefficient	Significant variable
1.	0.166	Rented dwelling
2.	0.109	dwelling not occupied by pensioners
3.	0.099	household not satisfied with heating
4.	0.097	family with children
5.	0.060	low SAP rating
6.	0.032	dwelling built before 1965
7.	0.024	no central heating
8.	0.023	dwelling condition in the worst 10%
9.	0.031	dwelling condition not in the best 30%
10.	0.024	built before 1918

down into three tenure groups in Table 14.3 and Figure 14.14, housing associations being grouped with private rented as in the previous survey.

Table 14.3   Incidence of condensation and mould growth by tenure as reported in 1986 and 1991

(% of households)

Tenure	Condensation		Mould Growth	
	1986	1991	1986	1991
Owner Occupied	23.1	31.6	14.8	12.8
Local Authority	23.8	46.3	28.2	24.5
Private rented/HA	12.5	41.1	35.6	29.1
All tenures	22.2	35.7	20.5	17.1

14.35 Between the two surveys, there has been a marked rise in the incidence of the reporting of condensation on windows. This may be caused by a rise in internal vapour pressure due to a reduction in infiltration caused by energy conservation measures, including draught stripping, as well as greater moisture generation through the more frequent ownership and use of washing appliances, showers etc. It is also possible that occupants may report condensation on new double glazing that previously they would have taken for granted on single glazed windows.

Figure 14.14   Incidence of condensation and mould growth by tenure as reported in 1986 and 1991

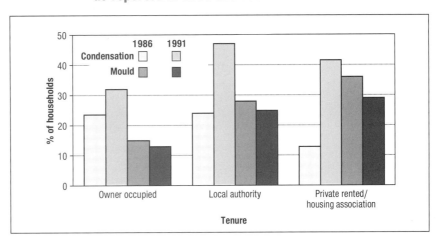

Tenure

14.36 The incidence of mould growth has fallen significantly in all tenures, particularly the private rented stock, between the two surveys. The increasing use of central heating and improved insulation standards in more recent housing, will work to raise temperatures, opposing the possible trend towards higher vapour pressures suggested above.

14.37 Table 14.4 shows the distribution of problems between tenures in the 1986 and 1991 surveys. Due to the rise in owner occupation, more than half of the mould growth reported is now in this sector, with just under 30% in the local authority stock and just over 20% in other rented housing.

Table 14.4   Distribution of homes with condensation and mould growth between tenures in 1986 and 1991

(Column %)

Tenure	Condensation		Mould Growth	
	1986	1991	1986	1991
Owner Occupied	65.4	60.0	45.6	50.6
Local Authority	29.1	26.3	37.5	29.1
Private rented/HA	5.5	13.7	17.0	20.2
All with problem	100	100	100	100

Chapter 15

Satisfaction with heating

Preamble

15.1 *This chapter examines household satisfaction with heating and reasons for complaint. After describing the total extent of satisfaction and complaints, the chapter looks first at its variation in different parts of the housing stock and related to different standards of energy efficiency and then with respect to different household characteristics. It concludes with an analysis of changing levels of satisfaction since the previous survey.*

15.2 *During the Interview Survey, households were asked: "In general, how satisfactory is your heating?". Those who said it was "fairly unsatisfactory" or "very unsatisfactory" were asked "How is it unsatisfactory" and to specify their particular complaints. If they listed more than one, they were further asked: "What is most unsatisfactory about it?"*

Extent and nature of dissatisfaction

15.3 The survey findings show a high level of satisfaction with heating facilities. Half of all households are "very satisfied" with their heating and a further 37% are "fairly satisfied". However, the remaining 13% or 2.4 million households are not satisfied and these include nearly 0.9 million households (5%) who are very dissatisfied. Compared to the 1986 survey, 7% more households are fairly satisfied with their heating and 3% less are very dissatisfied. (Table 15.1)

Table 15.1   Satisfaction with heating 1986 to 1991

(k households/col %)

Satisfaction with heating	1991		1986	
	Hholds	%	Hholds	%
Very satisfied	9,556	(50.0)	9,110	(50.4)
Fairly satisfied	7,161	(37.4)	5,508	(30.5)
Fairly unsatisfied	1,521	(8.0)	1,953	(10.8)
Very unsatisfied	873	(4.6)	1,360	(7.5)

Reasons for complaint

15.4 Amongst households dissatisfied with their heating, there are generally more complaints about lack of heating than about the cost of heating. However, many have more than one complaint. One third find their homes "difficult to heat" and almost as many complain that there is "not enough heat" or that their home has "insufficient radiators/only partial heating". Just under a third complain that their heating system is "expensive to run", but 14% of all those dissatisfied say that they "can't afford to use heating". (Table 15.2)

Main complaint

15.5 The main complaint of nearly a fifth of all those dissatisfied is that they have insufficient radiators or only partial heating. For some 14% the main problem is that there is "not enough heat" and similarly for 11% that their home is "difficult to heat". The expense of running the heating is the main complaint for a further 14%, and 6% cite primarily that they "can't afford to use" their heating.

Grouped complaints

15.6 The various responses suggest four main types of complaint as reasons for households being dissatisfied with their heating. Households are complaining essentially about: (1) the lack of warmth or 'insufficient heat' produced by their heating; (2) the limited extent of their heating or 'partial heating'; (3) problems with their system (such as it being dirty, dusty or difficult to control) and; (4) about its running costs and expense.

15.7 Most complaints - almost half of all main complaints - concern the need for more heat; either the home is difficult to heat or the heating system is not extensive enough (partial heating). Problems with the heating system account for just over one quarter (27%) of main complaints. Another fifth of main complaints concern cost and affordability of heating, either "expensive to run" or "can't afford to use". (Table 15.2)

Table 15.2   Reasons for complaint *(all complaints, main complaints and grouped complaints)*

(Col %/k households)

Complaint and grouped complaints	All Complaints*		Main Complaint			
	% all hholds	% all dissatisfied	% all hholds	% all dissatisfied	% dissatisfied Very	% dissatisfied Fairly
House difficult to heat	4.2	33.6	1.4	11.2	37.8	62.2
Not enough heat	3.9	31.2	1.7	13.7	39.5	60.5
Other-drafts/insulation	0.3	2.5	0.1	0.7	33.6	66.4
All insufficient heat	*7.1*	*57.1*	*3.2*	*25.6*	*38.6*	*61.4*
Partial heating only	3.6	28.9	2.3	18.4	41.3	58.7
Want central heating	0.5	3.8	0.4	3.0	51.1	48.9
All partial heating	*3.9*	*31.7*	*2.6*	*21.3*	*42.7*	*57.3*
H'ting not working properly	2.5	19.9	1.4	10.9	38.1	61.9
Heating side effects	0.8	6.4	0.5	4.0	23.5	76.5
Wrong fuel/system	1.9	15.1	0.9	7.0	28.1	71.9
Can't control heat	1.3	10.8	0.5	3.7	11.9	88.1
Problems with controls	0.6	4.5	0.2	1.8	0.0	100.0
All problems with system	*5.5*	*44.4*	*3.4*	*27.3*	*27.4*	*72.6*
Expensive to run	4.0	32.4	1.7	14.0	32.8	67.2
Can't afford to use	1.7	13.7	0.8	6.2	40.4	59.6
All cost of heating	*4.7*	*37.6*	*2.5*	*20.2*	*35.1*	*64.9*
Reason not stated	0.4	3.2	0.7	5.6	48.1	51.9
Total dissatisfied %	**12.6**	**100.0**	**12.6**	**100.0**	**36.2**	**63.8**
Households		(2,375)		(2,375)		

(* Some households cited more than one complaint)

Extent of satisfaction and heating complaints

15.8 Households who complain of insufficient heat - partial heating or not enough heat - are more dissatisfied (43% and 39% respectively being very dissatisfied) than those complaining about cost of heating or problems with their heating systems (35% and 27% being very dissatisfied). (Table 15.2) This is also true of individual main complaints. For example, over half of those who "want central heating" are very dissatisfied, compared to only 24% of those who complain of heating side effects, or 12% of those who "can't control" their heating.

Number of complaints

15.9 Of households with complaints, nearly two fifths have only one, a third two and just under one fifth have three complaints; only 4% have five or more. However, as the number of complaints increase, so does dissatisfaction with heating. (Figure 15.1 and Table A15.1) The greater the number of complaints, the more likely is the household to identify cost of heating as the main complaint - 36% of those with four complaints compared to only 17% of those with one complaint. Almost half of those with 5 or more complaints lack central heating.

Figure 15.1   Dissatisfaction with heating and number of complaints

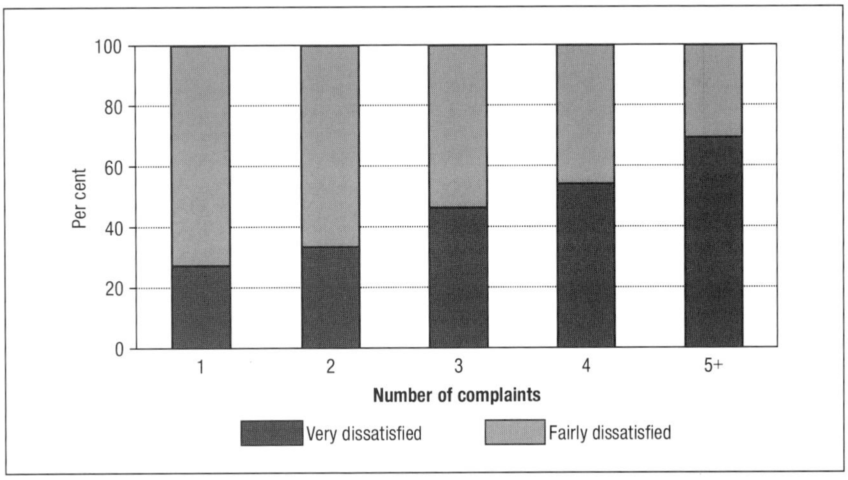

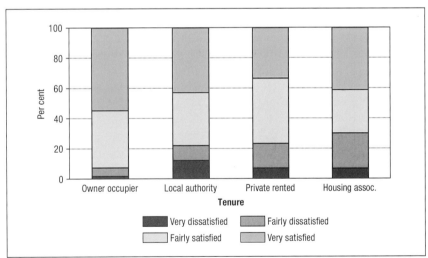

Satisfaction within stock & population

Tenure and dwelling characteristics

15.10 Satisfaction with heating varies with tenure. Owner occupiers are more likely to be satisfied than households in other sectors; only 1 in 14 are dissatisfied compared to some 1 in 5 council tenants, 1 in 4 private tenants and nearly 1 in 3 of those renting from a housing association. (Figure 15.2 and Table A15.2) Complaints also vary, one main set of complaints predominating in each tenure. For housing association tenants the main complaint is partial heating, a third citing this problem. (Table A15.3)

Figure 15.2   Satisfaction and tenure

Dwelling age and type

15.11 Reflecting differences in heating systems and insulation as well as tenure, satisfaction also varies with the age and type of dwelling. Not surprisingly, households living in the most recent stock are the most satisfied with their heating, only 3 and 5% respectively of those in houses and flats built since 1980 being dissatisfied. (Table A15.2) Households living in bungalows are also very satisfied (only 5% dissatisfied), but this reflects their frequent occupancy by pensioner households rather than the quality of heating. The least satisfied households live in high-rise flats, nearly 30% of those residing in blocks built before 1980 expressing dissatisfaction. Nearly a quarter of the 1.8 million households in the 'worst' 10% of the stock in terms of condition are also dissatisfied with their heating.

15.12 In most dwelling types, owner occupiers are more satisfied with their heating than other households. In the private rented sector, more than half of households living in dwellings built before the war are dissatisfied. The local authority sector has the most households who are very dissatisfied with their heating, dissatisfaction being greatest in flats. In houses, the most dissatisfied live not in the oldest stock but in small terraces and semi-detached houses built between 1965 and 1980. Tenants in bungalows are the least dissatisfied, being mainly elderly households. The most dissatisfied households of all, almost two thirds of them, are housing association tenants living in converted flats.

Region and locality

15.13 Household satisfaction with heating varies region by region. The least satisfied households are found in Greater London (where 16% are dissatisfied) and the most satisfied in the rest of the South East (where only 10% are dissatisfied). Households in city centre and urban locations are generally more dissatisfied (17 or 16%) than those in suburban or rural areas (11 and 12% dissatisfied). (Table A15.2)

15.14 Cost of heating is complained about most often in Northern, North West and South East regions (27%, 24% and 24% respectively), while households in Yorkshire and Humberside complain most about lack of heat or partial heating (60% of their complaints). In general, lack of heat is the most frequent complaint for households in city centre and rural locations, accounting for about half of all complaints. Households in urban and rural areas have the most complaints about cost of heating (about one quarter of their complaints). (Table A15.3)

Heating facilities

15.15 As expected, there is a clear relationship between satisfaction with heating and the type of heating. Only 7% of the 16 million households with central heating express any dissatisfaction with their heating, while around one third of the 3 million households without central heating are dissatisfied (Figure 15.3). Less than 7% of households with full central heating are dissatisfied, compared with 16% of households with partial central heating.

Figure 15.3   Satisfaction and main heating

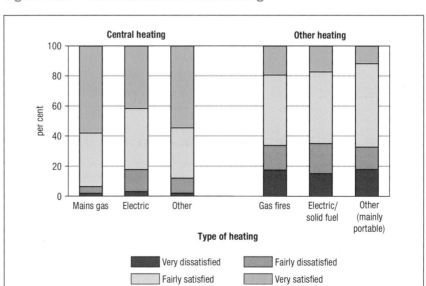

(Table A15.4) Overall, households without any central heating account for the largest share (43%) of all complaints. (Table A15.5)

Central
heating

15.16 Satisfaction is greatest for the small minority with oil fired central heating, only 2% being dissatisfied. Only some 7% of the majority of households with mains gas central heating are dissatisfied and 5% of those with water borne systems using a single purpose boiler. Gas ducted air and programmable convectors are much less popular (27% and 22% being dissatisfied respectively). For electric and solid fuel central heating, 18% are dissatisfied in each case. As with gas systems, households are most satisfied with the most common electric system, off-peak storage heaters (17% dissatisfied), 23% being dissatisfied with electric under-floor/ceiling heating. However, for solid fuel systems, households prefer single purpose boilers to the more common back boiler systems. (Table A15.4)

Other heating

15.17 Around one third (32 to 37%) of those with gas fires - the most common form of other heating - fixed electric fires and those reliant solely on portable heating are dissatisfied. The least popular form of heating is solid fuel open fires, where 40% of households are dissatisfied. (Table A15.4)

15.18 Different heating systems give rise to different sets of complaints. Central heating produces complaints about the system: "lack of control", "wrong fuel or system", "heating side effects" (Figure 15.4a and Table A15.5

Figure 15.4a Heating systems and main complaints

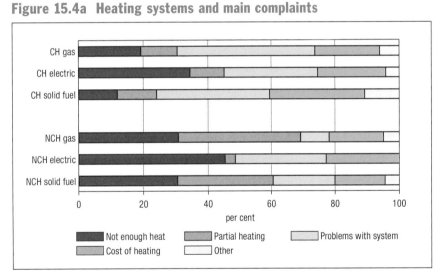

Figure 15.4b Extent of central heating and main complaints

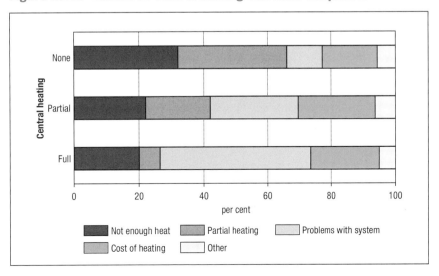

show grouped complaints). The main single complaint is that the "system doesn't work properly" (18%, compared to 2% of those without central heating). Only a small proportion (6%) find their homes difficult to heat. Compared to those with full central heating, households with partial installations are less concerned with problems with the system and understandably complain more about having insufficient heat and partial heating. (Figure 15.4b and Table A15.5)

15.19 Households without central heating also complain mainly about insufficient heat. Their main single complaints are: problems of "partial heating" (mentioned by 21%), or that the home is "difficult to heat" (by 18%, three times higher than for homes with central heating). Some 6% complain they "can't afford to use" their heating - similar to those with central heating.

Tenure, heating systems and main complaints

15.20 There is a distinction between dissatisfied owner occupiers and tenants in terms of availability of central heating. Of owner occupiers who complain, nearly three-quarters have central heating. They complain most about problems generated by these systems (two fifths of their complaints). In the rented sector, complaints arise predominantly from poor (non-central heating) facilities giving insufficient heat or only partial heating. In the private rented sector, only just over a quarter of those dissatisfied have central heating. Of such tenants complaining of insufficient heat (38%) and partial heating (22%), some 62% and 93% respectively lack such provision. Similarly, the main complaints of council tenants are partial heating (29%), insufficient heat (25%) and cost of heating (21%). Of the first two groups, 60% are without central heating. (Table A15.3)

15.21 Complaints also differ with the type of fuel. Households with electric heating - both central heating and fixed appliances - complain more about insufficient heat than complainants with other heating systems. Those with gas central heating from a back boiler and with mains gas or solid fuel fires complain more about partial heating. Gas ducted air central heating systems have the strongest association with complaints about the system, particularly with "heating side effects" (45%). With their high incidence amongst low income groups, solid fuel central heating, particularly of the back-boiler type, and portable heaters, are most closely associated with complaints about the cost of heating. (Table A15.5)

Figure 15.5   Satisfaction by age of heating system

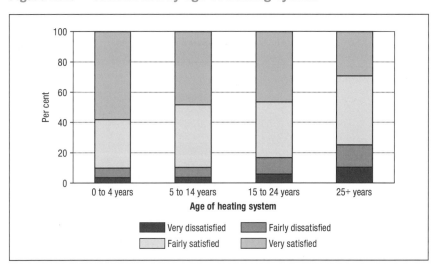

Age of heating system

15.22 Households with older heating systems (more than 25 years old) are least satisfied with their heating, over 1 in 4 being dissatisfied compared with less than 1 in 10 of those with systems under 5 years old. (Figure 15.5 and Table A15.4) Those with central heating this old have two, very specific complaints: either their heating is not working properly (41%) or there is not enough heat (39%). Non-central heating arrangements this old produce a wider variety of complaints, although over two-fifths also complain of not enough heat.

Provision for heating

15.23 In assessing housing fitness, the EHCS surveyors recorded the adequacy of the provision for heating on a four point scale: "satisfactory", "just acceptable", "defective" and "unfit". Only 10% of households with "satisfactory" provision for heating are dissatisfied with their heating, increasing progressively to 44% of those in homes with an "unfit" provision. (Table A15.4) There is also a tenure relationship here in that only 3% of all dissatisfied owner occupiers have defective or unfit provision for heating, compared to 6% of housing association households, 14% in the local authority and 18% in the private rented sectors.

Energy efficiency

15.24 Satisfaction with heating is also closely related to the overall energy efficiency of the home. Only 7% of households in relatively energy efficient homes (SAP of 50 or more) are dissatisfied, compared with 11% of those in homes of average efficiency (SAP 20 up to 50) and more than 25% of those living in the lowest rated homes (SAP less than 20). (Figure 15.6 and Table A15.6) The last group complain most about a lack of heat (home difficult to heat, not enough heat, partial heating etc.), over half voicing these complaints. (Table A15.5) Of the few in high SAP rated homes who are dissatisfied, most (46%) have problems with their heating system. Complaints about the cost of heating remain around one fifth of the total in each SAP category.

Figure 15.6   Satisfaction and SAP ratings

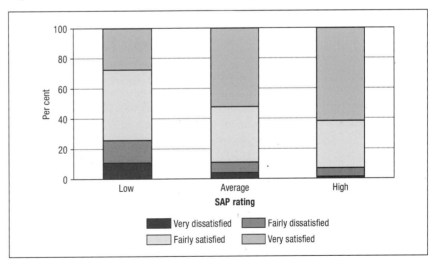

Relative to heating

15.25 Low SAP rated homes without central heating complain most that their homes are difficult to heat (20%), of partial heating (16%) and that their heating is expensive to run (16%). Inefficient homes with central heating complain of insufficient heat (28%) and of heating that is expensive to run (20%), reflecting the difficulties of heating a low energy efficient home even with central heating.

*Tenure, SAP
and
satisfaction*

15.26 In homes with low SAP ratings, only 16% of owner occupiers are dissatisfied with their heating, compared with 35% of private rented, 34% of local authority and 28% of housing association tenants. Again, owner occupiers complain most of problems with their systems (36%). Private rented and housing association complaints focus on lack of heat (37% and 42% respectively). Local authority tenants complain about partial heating (35%).

*Heat loss and
heating price*

15.27 The two main components of energy efficiency, heat loss and heating price both have an effect on satisfaction with heating. (Figure 15.7 and Table A15.6) In homes where the heat loss is above average, households are more dissatisfied but have no predominant type of complaint. Where the price of delivered heat is 10% or more above average there is a more marked increase in dissatisfaction. Half of these households have individual gas fires and one fifth solid fuel or electric central heating. Four main complaints account for two thirds of all their complaints: partial heating (24%), home difficult to heat and heating expensive to run (both 16%) and not enough heat (12%).

**Figure 15.7   Satisfaction and heat loss, heating price indices
(quintiles)**

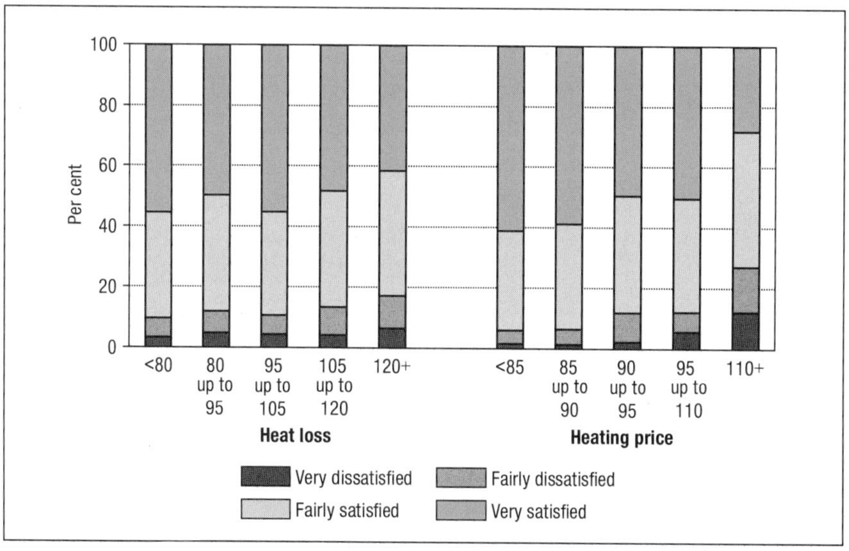

**Household
characteristics**

*Age and length
of residence*

15.28 As well as reflecting different physical conditions, satisfaction with heating also varies with different household characteristics. Dissatisfaction declines with age of the head of household. Younger heads (aged 16 to 39) are two to three times more dissatisfied (21%) than older groups. (Table A15.7) Dissatisfaction similarly decreases with length of residence. Nearly a fifth of those resident for less than two years are dissatisfied, while of those resident for 10 years or more only a tenth are dissatisfied. The longer the residence, the more likely heating problems will have been tackled or the household will have adjusted to them.

Income

15.29 Around a fifth of households receiving benefits or at or below the income support level, are dissatisfied with their heating. This is broadly similar to the 17% dissatisfied who have net household incomes of less than £4,500 per annum.

*Household
types*

15.30 Reflecting tenure and their generally high fuel expenditure relative to income, lone parent households are more dissatisfied (30%) with their heating than other groups (almost three quarters of dissatisfied lone parents are local authority or housing association tenants). Their main heating complaint is partial heating, mentioned by over a third, and cost of heating, mentioned by a quarter. Of those concerned with cost, two thirds say that their heating is expensive to run, whilst the remaining third cannot afford to use their heating. (Table A15.7 & A15.8)

15.31 Of younger adult households and households with dependent children, 14% are dissatisfied in each case. Families with children most often mention lack of heat (28%) and problems with their heating systems (32%). Pensioner households are the least dissatisfied (8%) and have no one single, predominant complaint. Insufficient heat, partial heating, and cost of heating each account for some 22% of their complaints. Problems with the heating system account for slightly more (28%), pensioner households being more concerned with heating side effects (11%) than any other household type.

Employment status

15.32 Households where the household head or partner is unemployed are much less satisfied with their heating (about one third dissatisfied) than households where both work full-time (11% dissatisfied). Not surprisingly, households where two partners work full-time complain less about heating costs than other household types, 8% compared with 43% of single households in part-time employment and 32% where at least one partner is unemployed. Some 12% of the latter say that they "can't afford to use" their heating. This is above the level for pensioners (8%) and compares with less than 1% where two partners work full-time.

Fuel consumption and income

Mains fuels

15.33 Satisfaction relative to fuel consumption varies with the type of fuel. The most satisfied gas users are those with the highest fuel consumption and expenditure. Only 8% of the largest consumers (highest quintile) are dissatisfied with their heating, but this rises to 25% for those households in the lowest quintile. (Table A15.9) Similarly, for the 15.3 million households whose main heating system is gas-fired, only 6% of high consumers are dissatisfied compared to 22% of the lowest fuel consumers (Figure 15.8). Gas users with low consumption complain mainly about partial heating (a third of complaints), whilst those with the highest gas bills complain mostly (about half) of problems with the heating system.

Figure 15.8   Satisfaction and consumption of fuel for heating

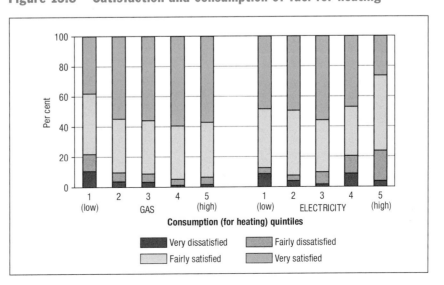

Complaints about the cost of heating are fairly constant across all consumption quintiles (a fifth to a quarter of complaints).

15.34 For electricity users, dissatisfaction with heating is highest in the top quintiles (where 17% are dissatisfied), but otherwise is not related to the size of consumption or fuel bills. This reflects the diverse (non-heating) uses to which electricity is put in the home, with only the highest consumers generally including those with electric heating systems. For the 1.8 million households who use electricity for their main heating, dissatisfaction tends to increase as electricity bills rise, from 13% dissatisfied in the lowest quintile to 24% in the highest consumption quintile. However, there is no clear pattern in the nature of complaints, although insufficient heat accounts for around a third of complaints in most quintiles.

15.35 As incomes rise, total expenditure on fuel, and satisfaction with heating, both increase, 17% being dissatisfied in the lowest income quintile compared with only 6% in the top quintile. Some 28% of households on the lowest incomes identified cost of heating as their main complaint, compared to only 12% of the highest income group. (Figure 15.9 and Table A15.7)

Proportion of income spent

15.36 The proportion of income spent on fuel is particularly relevant here. Households in the bottom two income quintiles who spent 10% or more of their income on fuel (about one quarter of all households) account for almost half of all complaints about the cost of heating. By comparison, households with the same income but who spent less than 10% on fuel (16% of all households) account for only just over a fifth of these complaints. Households in the top two income quintiles (40% of all households), almost all of whom spent less than 10% on fuel, generate only 14% of complaints about heating costs.

Figure 15.9   Income and heating complaints

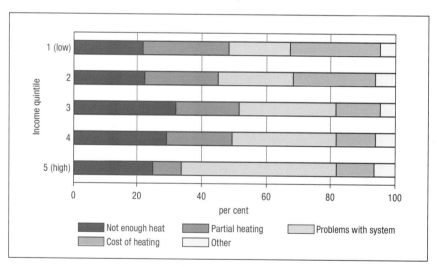

What determines satisfaction with heating?

15.37 Satisfaction with heating is clearly related both to the quality of the heating system and the characteristics of the household, including the type of tenure. To assess whether heating or household characteristics exert the strongest influence on satisfaction, one common house type (with average SAP ratings, to limit diversity) was analysed in more detail. The results suggest that the heating system has a more marked effect on satisfaction than other characteristics.

Heating

15.38 Of households living in average SAP rated semi-detached houses built before 1965, overall 11% are dissatisfied with their heating. Only 7% in homes with gas central heating are dissatisfied, compared to 15% of those with electric central heating and 29% of those with gas fires as their main heating source.

Household

15.39 Controlling further, for only households with gas central heating in these homes, allows assessment of the effects of household factors. Tenure has some effect - only 5% of owner occupiers are dissatisfied with their heating, compared to 9% of tenants renting privately and 18% of local authority tenants. Income appears to have little effect - 6% of those in the lowest income quintile are dissatisfied, compared to 7% in the highest quintile, though there is some variability in between. Length of residence also has a limited effect - 4 or 7% are dissatisfied for four of the residence categories (although the figure is 16% for residents of 2 to 4 years). Age of household head has some effect - younger households (10% of those aged 16 to 39) are more dissatisfied than older households (5 to 7% dissatisfied). Pensioners are the least dissatisfied household type (5%), families with children and lone parents the most dissatisfied (9% and 14% respectively). However, none of this variability is as great as for the type of heating.

Home temperatures

Meeting standard and minimum regimes

15.40 As would be expected, satisfaction with heating generally reflects the thermal conditions achieved in the home. As described in Chapter 13, households can be categorised as meeting one of three temperature regimes - they meet those of the standard regime, of the minimum regime, or fall below the minimum. The last category can be further divided into those below minimum temperatures in the living room or in the hall, and those below in both rooms. Only 8% of 'standard regime' households are dissatisfied with their heating and 10% of 'minimum regime' households. However, 18% of those below minimum in one room and 22% of those below in both are dissatisfied. For this last group this also indicates that four fifths are satisfied with their heating; about two fifths are very satisfied. (Figure 15.10 and Table A15.10) There is some association with type of heating. Of all households not achieving the minimum regime, the largest single group (38%) have individual gas fires - under half have central heating.

Figure 15.10 Satisfaction and home temperatures

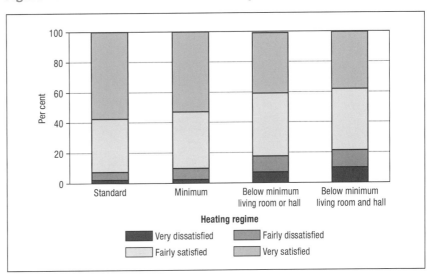

15.41 Households failing to meet the minimum regime in both rooms have the most complaints about cost of heating (30% of their complaints compared to 10% for standard regime households). They also have twice the level of complaints about insufficient heat (29% compared to 13%) but only half the level of complaints about partial heating. (Table A15.11)

Households in cold homes

15.42 Of households not achieving the minimum regime temperatures in the living room or hall, over two thirds assess their homes as "comfortable" or "comfortably warm". Most of these, about 85%, are satisfied with their heating, as are 83% of those who felt their home was "comfortably cool". Only 16% of this group define their homes as "too cool" or "much too cool". However, less than half of these are satisfied with their heating.

15.43 Pensioner households in cold homes are the least dissatisfied; only 12% are not satisfied with their heating. Adult households under pensionable age are around average for the level of satisfaction with cold homes (22% are dissatisfied). Households with children living in cold homes are much more likely to be dissatisfied with their heating, 28% of two parent families and 50% of lone parents being dissatisfied.

Condensation and mould growth

15.44 As the number of rooms affected by condensation or mould increases, dissatisfaction with heating also increases. (Figure 15.11 and Table A15.12) In households unaffected by condensation, 8% are dissatisfied with their heating. This increases to 17% dissatisfied in homes where 1 to 3 rooms are affected and to 26% where 4 or more rooms are affected by condensation. For mould growth, only 9% of households are dissatisfied in homes where there is no mould growth, increasing to 27% where 1 to 4 rooms are affected and to 52% where 5 or more rooms are affected - most of the latter being very dissatisfied. Considering the overall severity of the problem, some 22% of households with 'slight' problems are dissatisfied, increasing to 32% of households with 'moderate' problems and to 34% if 'severe' problems, many of the latter cases being caused by factors other than poor heating.

Figure 15.11 Satisfaction and condensation/mould growth

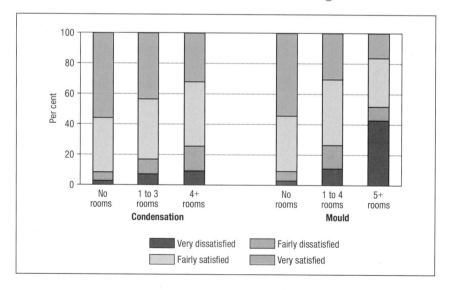

15.45 Where condensation is widespread, however, there is some association with heating system and type of complaint. Homes where 4 or more rooms are affected by condensation have a variety of heating systems but the largest single group (38%) have individual gas fires. The main complaint is cost of heating (31% of those dissatisfied, of whom 1 in 3 say that they "can't afford" heating).

Trends 1986 to 1991

15.46 As mentioned at the beginning of the Chapter (Table 15.1), satisfaction with heating increased between the 1986 and 1991 surveys. This is linked to the 12% increase in households with central heating over the same period, households without central heating being markedly more dissatisfied - two fifths being dissatisfied in 1986 and one third in 1991 - compared to less than 10% of those with central heating who were dissatisfied in either survey.

15.47 There were also some differences between the two surveys in the reasons for dissatisfaction[1]. There was little change in the proportions of households claiming their heating was "expensive to run" between 1986 and 1991 but there was a rise in those who said they "can't afford to use" their heating, from 10% to 14%. Complaints of "partial heating/not enough radiators" also increased from 10% to 29% but there was a big drop in complaints of "not enough heat" from 54% of all complaints in 1986 to 31% in 1991. However, as well as real improvements in heating and insulation, this may equally reflect the much milder prevailing weather in the winter of 1991/92.

15.48 The improvement in satisfaction has not occurred uniformly across all tenures. Owner occupiers are the most satisfied in both surveys (11% dissatisfied in 1986, 7% in 1991). Tenants are much more dissatisfied but have also made progress since 1986. One third of local authority tenants were dissatisfied in 1986, falling to one fifth in 1991. Similarly, 28% of tenants in the private rented sector were dissatisfied in 1986, compared to 23% in 1991. Overall, housing association tenants had made least progress, being similar to local authority tenants in 1986, but still with over 30% dissatisfied with their heating in 1991.

15.49 In 1991, the more complaints a household had about their heating, the more dissatisfied they were. This was true also in 1986, although the data are not directly comparable - Figure 15.12. In 1986, the more dissatisfied

Figure 15.12   **Per cent dissatisfied with heating by number of complaints and tenure**

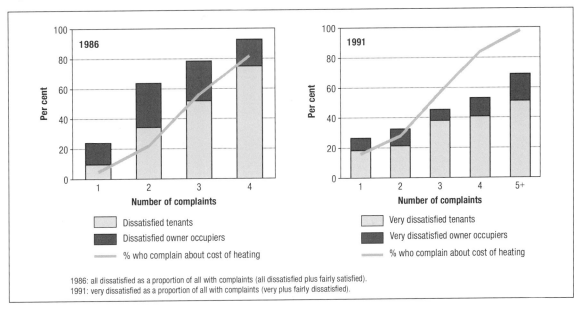

1986: all dissatisfied as a proportion of all with complaints (all dissatisfied plus fairly satisfied).
1991: very dissatisfied as a proportion of all with complaints (very plus fairly dissatisfied).

1   *Changes in the questions on satisfaction between the surveys, including some changes in the complaint categories, means that caution is required when looking at the type of complaint.*

the household the more likely they were to complain about the cost of heating - 5% of those with one complaint, 82% of those with four complaints. This was also true in 1991. In both surveys, tenants were more likely than owner occupiers to be the complainants.

Part *IV* ENERGY ACTION

Owner occupied sector

1 1919 - 1944	**2** 1945 - 1964	**3** 1965 - 1980	**4** 1965 - 1980	**5** 1850 - 1899
Semi-detached	Semi-detached	Detached	Semi-detached	Larger terraced
£238	**£258**	**£245**	**£259**	**£176**

6 Post 1980	**7** 1850 - 1899	**8** 1965 - 1980	**9** 1945 - 1964	**10** 1919 - 1944
Detached	Small terraced	Bungalow	Bungalow	Detached
£106	**£121**	**£194**	**£277**	**£268**

Private rented sector

1 1850 - 1899	**2** 1900 - 1918	**3** 1850 - 1899	**4** 1850 - 1899	**5** Pre 1850
Converted flat	Converted flat	Small terraced	Larger terraced	Converted flat

Local authority sector

1 1965 - 1980	**2** 1945 - 1964	**3** 1945 - 1964	**4** 1919 - 1944	**5** 1919 - 1944
Low-rise flat	Low-rise flat	Semi-detached	Semi-detached	Small terraced
£134	**£249**	**£187**	**£222**	**£201**

6 1965 - 1980	**7** 1945 - 1964	**8** 1965 - 1980	**9** 1945 - 1964	**10** 1945 - 1964
Larger terraced	Small terraced	High-rise flat	Larger terraced	Bungalow
£153	**£173**	**£307**	**£125**	**£206**

Housing associations

Average spending on energy measures *(notes overleaf)*

1 1965 - 1980	**2** Post 1980	**3** 1850 - 1899	**4** 1900 - 1918	**5** 1965 - 1980
Low-rise flat	Low-rise flat	Converted flat	Converted flat	Larger terraced

Figure IV.1   Average spending on energy measures for the most
numerous dwelling types in each sector

The frontispiece to Part IV shows the value of annual spending between 1987 and 1991 on all major energy measures, including double glazing, for each of the most numerous dwelling types in the owner occupied and local authority sectors (the sample of work done in the private rented and housing association stock is too small for comparable estimates). This is calculated as the mean expenditure over every dwelling in that particular part of the stock, and not just those receiving improvement, and therefore provides a comparable measure of the total investment in each type. Excluding modern properties, this investment ranges in the owner occupied stock from £121 per year for small terraced houses built between 1850 and 1899 to £277 for early post-war bungalows. The average for this sector was £207 per annum. Spending on the local authority stock shows an even greater divergence between types. Comparison of these figures with those shown in the frontispieces to Parts I, II and III suggests that investment is often poorly distributed in relation to the needs of the stock.

Chapter 16 Measuring change and Case studies

Preamble

16.1 *This final part of the Report concerns action to make the housing stock more energy efficient. Chapter 17 reports on the detailed energy measures undertaken by owner occupiers and landlords in 1991 and more generally for the five year period between 1987 and 1991, while Chapter 18 reports on the attitudes of households who have and have not installed insulation measures. Chapter 19 examines the potential for further improvements in energy efficiency and energy savings in the housing stock and, finally, Chapter 20 provides an overview and draws some conclusions. This part commences, however, with a discussion of the options for measuring actual and potential changes in energy efficiency and with the final series of case studies now focusing on energy action.*

Measuring change

Alternative measures

16.2 The improvement in the 'energy efficiency' of housing resulting from the provision of more efficient heating systems or the installation of thermal insulation can be described in a number of ways. The simplest is just to record the improvements undertaken or the financial investment made, and this approach is followed in Chapters 17 and 18. However, this gives little quantitative information on the benefits obtained - which is needed if different improvement options are to be compared.

16.3 The increase in SAP ratings following improvement gives a measure of the increase in energy efficiency, but generally the logarithmic scale which is the basis for the rating makes interpretation difficult. If the main interest is in environmental matters, then the change in energy consumption or the reduction in CO_2 and other emissions are likely to be the preferred measures. For many purposes, the change in fuel costs resulting from improved heating or insulation offers distinct advantages as the primary measure: first, it allows alternative improvement schemes to be appraised in a financial cost-benefit analysis; secondly, it allows household resources to be taken into account within the concept of 'affordable warmth'; and thirdly, it offers a reasonable proxy for the change in energy usage following improvement. This is the approach taken in the first part of Chapter 19.

Reduction in heating costs

16.4 The main measure used here to show the impact of improvement is *the percentage reduction in the cost of achieving the standard heating regime in a dwelling*, as given by:

$$\left[\frac{\text{Cost of space and water heating before upgrading - cost after upgrading}}{\text{Cost before upgrading}} \right] \times 100$$

It is important to note that this is a theoretical measure; it is based on the premise that the standard heating regime prevails both before and after improvement, and takes no account of the likely household behaviour in adjusting home temperatures according to cost. In this sense it is a measure of the improvement in the 'energy efficiency' of a dwelling, rather than a realistic measure of the expenditure saving on heating.

16.5 Two further points need to be made about this measure. First, it relates only to space and water heating, and not to lighting and other domestic appliances. Heating generally accounts for around two thirds of total fuel costs, so a saving of 30% in heating costs will typically imply a saving of around 20% in total fuel costs. Significant savings in fuel use for lighting, cooking and other appliances are possible as the use of low energy lighting and efficient appliances becomes more widespread, but these are not evaluated in this Report. Secondly, it should be borne in mind that energy savings are not necessarily proportional to cost savings, since improvement may involve a switch to a cheaper (or more expensive) fuel or a change in standing charges. Calculations show that schemes which emphasise improved insulation tend to give a better energy than cost saving, while work aimed mainly at improving the heating system has the reverse effect. Overall, it appears that cost savings are likely to be a few percent greater than energy savings.

30% saving in energy consumption

16.6 Because energy savings are generally less than cost savings and heating costs only around two thirds of total energy costs, a saving in total energy consumption of 30% would require a reduction in heating costs of some 50% without improvements in the energy efficiency of lighting, cooking or other domestic appliances.

Examples of improvements

16.7 Table 16.1 compares the change in the theoretical heating and total fuel costs for two dwellings (both with a floor area of 60 m^2 and two occupants) with a low and average existing SAP rating and for different standards of improvement.

Table 16.1 **Examples of improvements in energy efficiency and notional savings in fuel costs**

| | SAP rating | | Fuel cost of standard regime | | | | | |
| | | | Heating cost only (£) | | | Total fuel cost (£)* | | |
	Before	After	Before	After	% fall	Before	After	% fall
LA/HA Flat	17	30	640	485	24%	820	665	19%
(60 m²;2 adults)		50		320	50%		505	39%
		70		220	66%		400	51%
LA/HA Flat	35	50	435	320	26%	620	505	19%
(60 m²;2 adults)		70		220	50%		400	35%

* assuming no change in standardised non-heating fuel costs

Actual fuel savings

16.8 As shown in previous chapters, in practice relatively few unimproved dwellings are heated to the standard regime, either with respect to the extent of their heating or their room temperatures. After improvement, households are more likely to approach the standard heating regime, having taken some or all of their fuel cost savings in achieving more comfortable thermal conditions. Consequently, an alternative and in some respects more relevant way of measuring the effect of energy measures is to estimate the actual saving in fuel consumption or expenditure after improvement. This is the approach used in the final parts of Chapter 19.

Case studies

16.9 The final set of case studies looks at individual improvements in the energy efficiency of the housing stock and some of the common barriers to action. The first two cases look at the benefits of installing central heating and insulation, whilst the final two illustrate reasons why some owner occupiers and tenants do not carry out work to improve the energy efficiency of their homes. *(Although based on data collected in the EHCS, some details have been changed to protect the identity of individual households).*

Case 16.1:
Local authority
1945-1965
Low rise flat
(Improved)

16.10 This council flat is located in a commuter suburb in the Eastern region, in a residential area of mixed tenure and dwelling type. It shows the eradication of mould growth and improvements in home temperatures and satisfaction derived from the installation of central heating, and the resulting increase in fuel consumption. However, this is offset by a change in the fuel split in favour of gas over electricity, resulting in a broadly similar fuel expenditure.

16.11 The two bedroom, first floor flat with a 53 m² floor area, was originally built around 1950, but has undergone considerable modernisation in more recent years. The wall construction is steel-framed with cavity brick infill, with PVC-U framed double glazed windows, and the roof is pitched with concrete tiles. The EHCS surveyor found the property to be in generally good condition, but with minor disrepair and some penetrating damp.

Physical standards

16.12 Heating and hot water are provided by a dedicated gas fired central heating boiler feeding radiators in all rooms, and an additional gas fired heater in the living room. The system is controlled by a room thermostat, timer and manual valves on the radiators, and the hot water cylinder is foam insulated. The flat has 100mm mineral wool insulation in the loft, and cavity fill, as well as the double glazing, resulting in a SAP rating of 49.

16.13 The tenant, who has lived in the flat since it was built, is a 70 year old widow. A school cook before retirement, her annual income, mostly from pensions, is above average for lone pensioners in council housing, falling within the second lowest income quintile for all households.

Energy consumption

16.14 The occupier uses the central heating daily from 7.00 to 10.30 in the mornings and again from 5.00 to 10.30 in the evenings. She also uses the gas fire in the living room as a boost, and rarely or never alters any of the system controls. She has a mains gas cooker, but no other recorded appliances. The current fuel bill for the flat is some £500 per year (64% gas and 36% electricity), and although this amounts to about 10% of the pensioner's income, it is also nearly 20% more than required to maintain a standard heating regime. The annual energy consumption is 20,068 kWh, of which 90% is gas.

Thermal conditions

16.15 The tenant is very satisfied with her heating system, and reports no problems at all with draughts or condensation and damp. On the afternoon of the interview in late April 1992, she had been in all day and the flat was heated as normal. The temperatures recorded were 24.3°C in the living room and 22.1°C in the kitchen. These were rated to be 'comfortably warm' and the 'same as usual'.

Energy action

Energy measures

16.16 The flat has benefited from a wide range of energy measures in recent years. However, it is the installation of central heating, since the last survey in 1986, that has made the greatest difference to the living conditions of the tenant. In 1986 the flat only had a gas fire in the lounge, electric heaters in the kitchen and bathroom, and an on-peak electric immersion heater for hot water. The flat was cold (12.2°C in the lounge and 10.7°C in the kitchen), despite the tenant having been in all day with the heating on, and suffered from condensation and mould growth. The annual energy consumption then was 11,760 kWh, of which 32% was electricity. Since the central heating was installed the overall consumption has risen by 70%. However, the use of electricity has almost halved giving the benefit of a lower heating price index. At 1991 prices, the current and previous fuel bills are about the same.

Attitudes to measures

16.17 The installation of central heating has changed the tenant's perception of her heating from 'fairly unsatisfactory', due to not having enough heat, to 'very satisfactory'. She now appears to have a much more comfortable and healthy home.

Potential action

16.18 The dwelling now offers little scope for further energy measures. However, a better use of controls, reducing temperatures in the living room to 21°C and elsewhere to 18°C could reduce the existing fuel consumption by about a quarter. Alternatively, the provision of temperature zoning controls, costing about £150, could pay back the capital outlay in two years and increase the SAP rating to the high 60s.

Case 16.2:
Owner occupied
1965-1980
Larger terraced
(Improved)

16.19 This former council house is located on a suburban estate in the South Yorkshire metropolitan area. It shows the energy savings and other benefits achievable from improved insulation in an all-electric home with a relatively inefficient heating system.

16.20 The four bedroom end terrace house was built by the local authority in the late sixties. Rectangular in shape and with a total floor area of 97 m², the

house is built of cavity brick under a pitched concrete tiled roof. The EHCS surveyor found the house to be in good condition, apart from some minor internal disrepair and differential movement.

Physical standards

16.21 Heating to the downstairs rooms is provided by an off-peak electric underfloor heating system. This is controlled by means of a timer, wall thermostat and manual controls on the outlets. There is a further fixed electric heater in the living room, but no heating at all upstairs. An off-peak electric immersion heater provides hot water to a jacket insulated tank. The walls and roof are also insulated and the windows are double glazed PVC-U sealed units. The SAP rating of the dwelling is calculated to be 41.

16.22 The occupiers, a middle aged car salesroom manager and his wife, have lived in the house since it was built. Originally council tenants they have recently purchased the house under the Right-to-Buy scheme. They are both working and have an annual household income which is above average for two adult households in owner occupation and just within the highest 20% of all household incomes.

Energy consumption

16.23 During the week, the off-peak heating is charged between 7.30 pm and 8.00 am the following morning, and again between 1.30 and 4.00 in the afternoon. At weekends the heating is left on all day. The fixed electric heater in the lounge is used as a boost, and the only controls regularly used are the wall thermostat for the central heating and the output control on the fixed heater. The couple have an electric cooker and microwave oven, and use their washing machine 6 times per week, occasionally taking advantage of the off-peak tariff. The hot water is heated exclusively off-peak.

16.24 The annual consumption of this all-electric house is 11,150 kWh, of which nearly three quarters is off-peak. The annual bill comes to £290, only 1.5% of the family income, but is less than half the amount estimated to be required to provide the house with a standard heating regime.

Thermal conditions

16.25 When interviewed in the early afternoon in late April 1992 the occupants had been in for almost 2 hours and the house heated as usual for a weekday. The temperature of the lounge was 20.0°C and the hall 18.5°C, when the outside temperature was 15°C. These were felt to be the 'same as usual' and 'comfortably warm'. However, the couple are very dissatisfied with their heating, saying that it wasn't the type of system they wanted, that it was expensive to run and only provided partial heating.

Energy action

Energy measures

Attitudes to measures

16.26 Since assuming ownership of the house in the mid 1980s, the occupiers have insulated the loft and cavity walls, so as to 'reduce fuel bills' and installed double glazing to 'keep the house warmer'. They had previously insulated the hot water tank to 'keep the water hot'. As a result of these energy measures the 1991 consumption was some 35% lower than that recorded in the 1986 EHCS (17,268 kWh), although three grown-up children have also left the household since then, which may account for some of the difference. The house also appears to be more comfortable. The temperatures in the two surveys are not strictly comparable, but in 1986 the dining room was at 16.2°C and the kitchen at 13.7°C, at an outside temperature of 4.1°C.

Potential action

16.27 There seems to be little further scope for insulation measures in this house. The most obvious outstanding improvement would be the installation of a full central heating system. Such an installation, with a condensing boiler and temperature zoning controls, would cost about £2,700 and raise the dwelling's SAP rating to 75. The 'pay-back' period would be 8 years.

Case 16.3:
Owner occupied
1850 -1899
Larger terraced
(Unimproved)

16.28 This owner occupied house is located in a southern Outer London borough in a mixed residential and commercial area. It illustrates a dwelling of low energy efficiency where the household lacks the resources to install energy measures.

General characteristics

16.29 The three bedroom mid-terraced house was built in the late 19th century. It is L-shaped, having a two-storey rear extension, and has a total floor area of 142 m². The dwelling has solid 9" brick walls and wooden single-glazed sash windows. The roof of the main part of the house is pitched with a natural slate roof, whilst the extension has a flat roof. The EHCS surveyor found rising and penetrating damp and some external and internal disrepair, but did not find the dwelling unfit.

Physical standards

16.30 Heating provision consists of a fixed gas fire in the main living room, electric storage heaters, with charge control, in the hall and second living room, a fixed electric heater in the bathroom, and portable paraffin and electric heaters in the main bedroom. Hot water is provided by an instantaneous gas heater. No insulation measures were present in the house, leaving it with a SAP rating of around 37.

16.31 The owner is a 71 year old former self-employed watch repairer, who has lived in the house for 30 years. In the past he has sublet part of the house, but is now the sole occupier. His annual income from state pensions is well below average for lone pensioner owner occupiers, falling well within the lowest 20% of household incomes generally.

Energy consumption

16.32 The two electric storage heaters are generally charged for 8 hours overnight, and the rest of the heating, including the paraffin heater, is used daily, but not at regular times. The occupant rarely or never alters any of the controls. He cooks using mains gas, but has no other recorded appliances.

16.33 The annual fuel bill of £290 (33% gas, 55% electricity and 12% paraffin) amounts to almost 10% of the householder's income, but only a third of the amount estimated to be required to maintain a minimum heating regime in the house. This is probably due to the fact that the occupier uses only a small portion of this large house. The annual energy consumption is 7,450 kWh, of which 48% is gas, 4% peak rate electricity, 30% off-peak electricity and 18% paraffin.

Thermal conditions

16.34 The house had not been heated at all on the day of the interview, despite the occupier having been in all day, and the temperatures recorded were 16.6°C in the living room and 15.5°C in the hall, when the outside temperature was nearly 11°C. This was rated to be the 'same as usual' and 'comfortable', and the owner was fairly satisfied with the heating. He found the house to be draughty in parts, particularly around the windows of the living room, but reported no problems with damp, other than "steamed up" windows in the kitchen.

Energy action

Energy measures

16.35 The house has not been subject to any energy action. The EHCS Postal Survey shows that the owner had applied for a Home Improvement Grant to cover fabric repairs, but that this did not cover any energy measures.

Attitudes to measures

16.36 The owner did not intend to install any insulation measures in his house as he couldn't afford to do so.

Potential action

16.37 There is considerable scope for energy action in this dwelling, the most obvious being loft insulation and draught proofing, both of which would currently attract a HEES grant. The cost of this work would be around £800, and in raising the SAP rating to nearly 60 could pay for itself in under 2 years. The installation of a central heating system and double glazing would also improve the energy efficiency of the house, although the owner's lack of resources would be a problem.

Case 16.4:
Private rented
1900-1919
Small terraced
(Unimproved)

16.38 This privately rented house is located in the West Midlands non-metropolitan area in an urban centre of mixed residential and light industrial use. It illustrates a house of low energy efficiency that would clearly benefit from improvement, but also shows the limitations on economic improvement dictated by the inherent form and structure of the dwelling.

16.39 The main part of this three bedroom end-terrace dwelling was built between 1900 and 1918, with a rear extension being added later, giving a total floor area of 63 m². The walls are of 9" solid brick, the windows single glazed and the roof pitched with asbestos cement tiles. Whilst judging the house to be fit, the EHCS surveyor found the house to be defective in terms of internal and external fabric disrepair, structural stability, and rising and penetrating damp.

Physical standards

16.40 Heating provision consists of fixed mains gas fires to the living rooms and bedrooms and a fixed electric heater in the bathroom, all with heat output control. Hot water is provided by an instantaneous gas heater. There are no insulation measures provided in the dwelling, resulting in a SAP rating of just 9.

16.41 The tenants, who have been renting the property from a private landlord for two years, are a couple in their mid-twenties and their two pre-school children. The husband is a part-time clerk and the household income from this and state benefits is only half the average for small families privately renting. Overall, it falls within the second lowest income quintile.

Energy consumption

16.42 The family use the heating daily, from 7.00 am to 10.00 pm in the main living room and from 10.00 to 11.00 pm in the bedrooms, but rarely or never change any of the control settings. They cook using mains gas and use a washing machine about 5 times per week. Analysis of the fuel bills shows that the annual energy consumption is 34,217 kWh, of which 93.5% is gas and the rest standard tariff electricity. The annual fuel bill is £740 (72.1% gas, 27.9% electricity), which amounts to 12% of the household income, but is only 81% of that needed to maintain a minimum heating regime in the house.

Thermal conditions

16.43 When interviewed, just after lunch in early March 1992, the respondent had been in for less than half an hour, although the heating had been on in the living room since 7.00 am. The recorded temperatures were 18.9°C in the lounge and 14.1°C in the unheated hall, at an outside temperature of around 10°C. This was considered to be the 'same as usual' and 'comfortably cool', and the family are fairly satisfied with the heating. The house is draughty throughout, particularly around doors and windows, and severe damp and mould growth in the kitchen and bathroom are causing some inconvenience in winter.

Energy action
Energy measures

16.44 The house has not been subject to any kind of energy action, either by the landlord or the tenants.

Attitudes to measures

16.45 The current tenants did not intend to install any energy measures as they did not feel it was their responsibility, an attitude common in the private rented sector.

Potential action

16.46 There is considerable scope for energy action in this dwelling, the most obvious being loft insulation and draught proofing, which may attract a HEES grant. The installation of a central heating system and double glazing would also improve the energy efficiency of the house. However, insulating the extensive external walls is likely to be uneconomical, effectively limiting the extent to which the dwelling can be improved. A complete package of heating and insulation measures, excluding the solid walls, could increase the SAP rating to 45 at a cost of over £5,000. The improvements could save the occupants over £450 a year in fuel bills.

Comparison of case studies

16.47 Table 16.2 compares aspects of energy action and other key characteristics of each of the final four case studies with the average figures (in brackets) for the same type of household in the same sector and for all households. Further comparative statistics are provided in Table A16.1.

Table 16.2 Comparison of case study dwellings with mean for all households of same type, size and tenure

Case study figures/(mean for household type & size in tenure)

	Case 16.1 LA - 1 pension		Case 16.2 OO - 2p Hhold		Case 16.3 OO - 1 pension		Case 16.4 PR - 4p family		All hholds
Physical standards									
Dwelling size m²	53	(50)	97	(86)	203	(78)	63	(88)	**83**
Energy SAP rating	49	(31)	41	(37)	37	(29)	9	(23)	**35**
Energy consumption									
Total consumption MWh	20.1	(11.6)	11.2	(24.8)	7.5	(18.5)	34.2	(32.2	**24.0**
Total expenditure £	501	(380)	287	(661)	292	(523)	742	(858)	**661**
Thermal conditions									
Outside temp °C	16.7	(10.9)	15.0	(10.8)	10.8	(11.0)	9.8	(11.0)	**11.1**
Living room temp °C	24.3	(20.0)	20.0	(19.5)	16.6	(19.4)	18.9	(19.5)	**19.5**
Hall/stairs temp °C	22.1	(18.5)	18.5	(18.4)	15.5	(18.1)	14.1	(18.6)	**18.3**
Energy action									
Target SAP rating	66		75		59		45		-
Improvement cost £	150		2,660		810		5,160		-
Energy saving[1] kWh	375		12,765		13,060		21,595		-
Cost saving[1] £	95		330		530		468		-
Simple payback yrs	2		8		2		11		-

1 assuming standard heating regime and normal energy use for dwelling and household size

Chapter 17

Energy related work

Preamble

17.1 *This Chapter concerns the extent and nature of energy related improvement work undertaken in the housing stock. It reports first on the estimated value of work undertaken in 1991 by occupants, both owner occupiers and tenants, and then on the detailed nature of these works. After looking at the factors influencing work by occupants, the Chapter goes on to report on the energy work undertaken by occupants between 1987 and 1991. It concludes by describing the value and nature of work by landlords, in the local authority, housing association and private rented sectors, over the same five year period.*

17.2 *There is some difficulty in specifying precisely what works are 'energy measures' since some jobs, such as the installation of double glazed replacement windows, have implications for the thermal insulation of a dwelling but are often carried out primarily for other reasons. For the purposes of this Report, all works which might have a bearing on energy efficiency are considered[1]. In the EHCS, apart from being classified by the type of job undertaken, work is also categorised into 'major' and 'minor' according to its value: a job which would cost more than £500 if done by a contractor would be regarded as 'major'.*

Work by occupants during 1991

Value of work

17.3 During 1991, the total expenditure by individual households on 'major' energy related repairs and improvements was £3.8 billion; representing 23% of all major works. However, the real <u>value</u> of the work was higher since some jobs were undertaken by the occupants themselves, and DIY carries no explicit labour costs. If calculations are made as though the work had been contracted out, the estimated value of major work approaches £4.4 billion. The estimated value of all minor works was around £0.3 billion, bringing the total for energy related repair and improvement during the 12 month period to £4.7 billion. (Table 17.1)

Table 17.1 Energy related *(major + minor)* works by occupants during 1991 by tenure

Tenure	Total value of energy related work (£ billion)				Mean expenditure by household (£)	
	Major works	Minor works	All works	As % of all work	Over all hholds-	Of all with e.r. works
Owner occupied	4.2	0.3	4.5	19.4	298	1,091
Private rented	0.1	-	0.1	19.5	39	592
Local authority	0.1	-	0.1	12.5	18	375
Housing association	-	-	-	-	26	762
All tenures	4.4	0.3	4.7	19.1	209	1,040

1 *For this reason, the EHCS estimates for 'energy related' works are substantially higher than those given by the Housing Investment Programme returns for energy efficiency measures, where much of the work on heating systems etc. is excluded.*

17.4   Not surprisingly, the vast bulk of the work commissioned by individual households occurs in the owner occupied sector. In 1991, the average expenditure on energy related work over all households in this sector was £298, compared with £25 for all tenants. However, the proportion of total spending which went on energy related work was approximately the same for owner occupiers and private tenants, but slightly lower in the social rented sectors where there is much more energy related work by landlords. (Table 17.1)

Types of work   17.5   Table 17.2 shows the relative importance of the different types of work undertaken, distinguishing between owner occupiers on the one hand and tenants in all rented sectors on the other.

17.6   The two most frequent jobs might not be motivated by a desire to reduce fuel bills or to improve thermal comfort. The installation of replacement double glazed windows is usually driven by the need to deal with existing defective timber windows or to reduce future maintenance, although it does have some effect on energy efficiency. The removal and possible replacement of old fireplaces is often undertaken for decorative purposes, and the opening up of open fires and chimneys may actually reduce energy efficiency.

Table 17.2   Type of work *(major and minor)* done by occupants during 1991

Type of work	% of households doing job of total population[1]		% of households doing job of all with energy work		Mean value of job over all doing energy work	
	Owner occupier	Tenants	Owner occupier	Tenants	Owner occupier	Tenants
Insulation						
Double glazing	10.1	0.3	37	6	710	89
Loft insulation	3.3	0.3	12	6	26	14
Wall insulation	0.9	0	3	0	16	2
Draughtproofing	1.1	0.5	4	9	2	5
Secondary DG	0.6	0.1	2	2	4	2
Other heating						
Work on open/electric fires	6.1	2.3	23	44	87	147
Install solid fuel stove	0.5	0	2	1	8	3
Install gas fire/convector	3.8	1.2	14	23	40	61
Insert chimney lining	0.9	0	3	1	17	1
Central heating						
Install (non-electric) CH	2.6	0.5	10	10	132	195
Extend (non-electric) CH	1.6	0	6	1	29	1
Replace CH boiler	3.4	0.1	12	3	94	20
Replace CH distribution	3.0	0.1	11	3	21	5
Install electric CH	0.3	0	1	0	10	5
Replace/install CH controls	1.8	0.1	7	1	14	1
Water heating						
Install/replace immersion/ instantaneous heater	1.1	0.4	4	7	3	6
Install/replace HW cylinder	1.3	0.2	5	3	11	8
Other items						
Service heaters/boilers	4.1	0.2	15	5	24	5
Fit extractor fans	1.8	0.3	7	7	8	7
Install/extend gas supply	2.7	0.5	10	10	23	23
All jobs	27.1	5.3	100	100	1,279	605

1 Some households undertake more than one job

Tenure differences

17.7 Owner occupiers are about five times more likely to carry out work than tenants, but the pattern of jobs is fairly similar. Where there are differences they arise from the propensity of tenants to undertake relatively simple tasks which increase thermal comfort, such as draughtproofing, and their lesser involvement in the servicing of appliances (normally the province of the landlord) and in large structural projects such as the replacement of windows. However, a few tenants do report large jobs initiated and paid for by themselves.

Insulation

17.8 Amongst owner occupiers, approximately 55% of the value of energy-related work during 1991 involved the installation of double glazing with only 5% going on other insulation measures. Amongst tenants, some 15% of the value of work related to double glazing and 4% to other insulation. Around 1 in 10 owner occupiers fitted double glazed windows at an average cost of £1,900 per dwelling but, perhaps surprisingly, some tenants also undertook this measure at an average cost of £1,500.

Heating

17.9 Tenants were also involved in the installation of heating systems: 0.5% put in central heating at an average cost of £1,950, 1.2% fitted gas fires or convectors at an average of £260; and 2.3% did work on fireplaces. Overall, amongst tenants, 38% of the value of work was attributable to heating. Within the owner occupied sector, some 23% of the value of work related to central heating, 10% to new installations and 13% to the upgrading or repair of existing systems. Around 2.6% of all owner occupiers installed central heating during 1991 and 3.8% put in gas fires and convectors.

Factors influencing work

Dwelling type and age

17.10 How energy-related work by owner occupiers depends on the characteristics of the dwelling is shown in Figures 17.1 to 17.3. The first of these plots the average value of all energy-related work (calculated over all relevant parts of the stock whether or not the occupants undertook work) for different types of dwelling and dates of construction. It shows a clear distinction between houses and flats, with spending on flats being about half that on houses, and some variation between the various house types and with dwelling age. (Table A17.1, also A17.3 for work by tenants)

Figure 17.1   Mean value of energy related work *(over whole stock)* by owner occupiers in 1991 by dwelling type and age

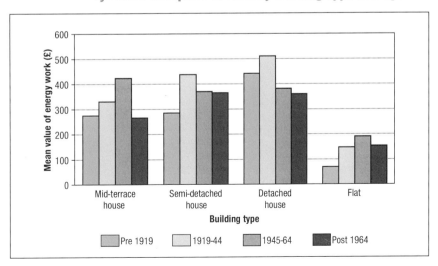

17.11 More variation with the date of construction appears when a distinction is drawn between work on insulation measures and work on installing or

Figure 17.2   Mean value of insulation work *(including double glazing)* in owner occupied stock in 1991 by dwelling type and age

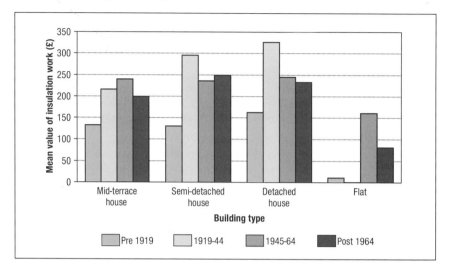

Figure 17.3   Mean value of work on central heating systems in owner occupied stock in 1991 by dwelling type and age

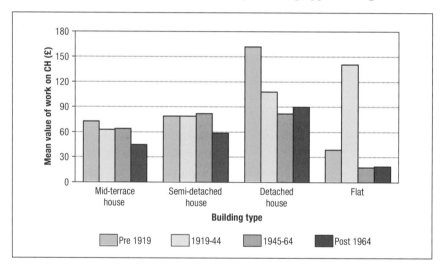

Figure 17.4   Energy inefficient dwellings in owner occupied stock by dwelling type and age

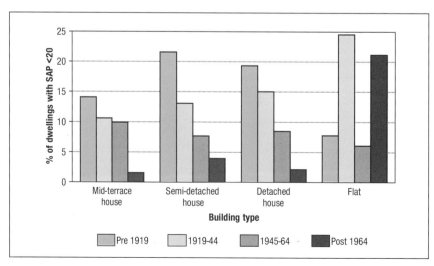

upgrading a central heating system. (Figures 17.2 and 17.3) Insulation work occurs predominantly amongst modern and inter-war properties, particularly detached and semi-detached houses. However, as shown in Figure 17.4, these are dwelling types which already tend to be reasonably energy efficient. Work on central heating systems tends to be more frequent in pre 1919 and interwar properties, and hence is more in line with what is required to improve the least energy efficient stock, although the degree of concentration on older properties is still much less than is needed.

Household type and income

17.12 Not surprisingly, there is a tendency for more work, or work of greater value, to be done by those owner occupiers with higher incomes, although there is considerable variation about this trend (Figures 17.5 and 17.6). Couples and small families tend to do the most work, whilst lone pensioners do the least. (Table A17.2, also A17.4 for work by tenants)

Figure 17.5   Mean value of insulation work *(including double glazing)* in owner occupied stock in 1991 by household type and income

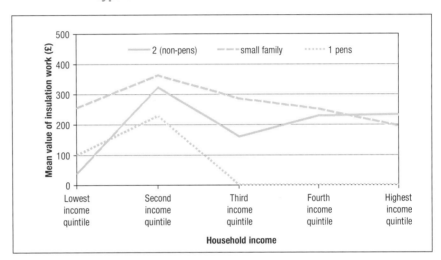

Figure 17.6   Mean value of work on central heating in owner occupied stock in 1991 by household type and income

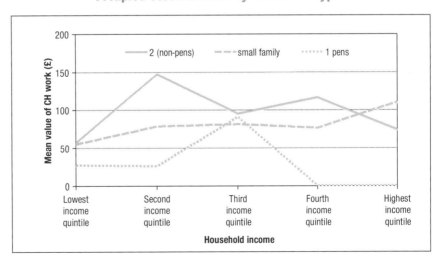

17.13 As seen from Figure 17.7 this pattern is in clear opposition to what is needed to have a significant impact on the energy efficiency of the stock; there is a clear correlation between low energy efficiency and low income and, amongst owner occupiers, pensioners live in by far the least efficient accommodation.

Figure 17.7   Energy inefficient dwellings in owner occupied stock by household type and income

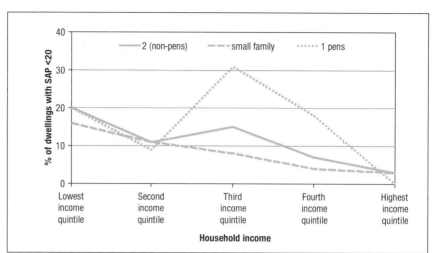

17.14 A similar pattern is just discernible in work undertaken by tenants, but the small sample sizes and the variation within the data, particularly between the private and public sectors, makes it impossible to draw reliable conclusions here.

Works by occupants 1987 to 1991

17.15 To allow comparison with the work undertaken by landlords, it has been necessary to analyse the information which is available from the EHCS on work done by occupants over the five year period 1987 to 1991. This information is limited to 'major works' (i.e. jobs costing more than £500 if done by a contractor) making any comparison with the above data for the single year 1991 not wholly straightforward.

Trend during period

Value of work

17.16 All the evidence from the Survey (and from the Family Expenditure Survey) suggests that there was a fairly steep increase in home improvements and repair between 1987 and 1991. The total value of major energy related works by owner occupiers over this period was £14.8 billion (at 1991 prices) compared with £4.2 billion invested in 1991 - giving a ratio of 3.6 rather than the 5.0 which would have been expected if the work rate had remained constant over these years.

Table 17.3   Energy related 'major' works by occupants during 1987 to 1991 by tenure

	Total value of energy related major works		Mean expenditure by household (£)	
	Value (£ billion)	As % of all work	Over all households	Of those with e.r. works
Owner occupied	14.82	20.2	1,037	2,164
Private rented	0.17	16.2	85	1,457
Local authority	0.20	12.5	41	765
Housing association	0.03	14.8	45	1,134
All tenures	15.22	20.0	716	2,104

Tenure variation

17.17 This growth in the annual volume of work is reflected in Tables 17.3 and 17.4, which show for the five year period 1987 to 1991 the same breakdowns included in Tables 17.1 and 17.2 for the single year 1991. The 1987 to 1991 figures reflect the fewer households involved per year and the higher average costs per job resulting from the exclusion of the cheaper minor works, as well as the possibility that individual households may undertake work in several different years within the five year period. Bearing in mind these differences, Tables 17.4 and 17.2 show, for example, that the proportion of owner occupiers undertaking energy related work during the five year period was some 48%, compared with 27% who undertook work in 1991. For tenants, however, the comparable figures are both around 5%, the additional households covered by the longer time period being balanced by those lost by the exclusion of minor works - a higher proportion of jobs by tenants being minor works.

Table 17.4   Major work by occupants during 1987 to 1991

	% of households doing job of total population[1]		% of households doing job of all with energy work		Mean value of job over all doing energy work	
	Owner occupier	Tenants	Owner occupier	Tenants	Owner occupier	Tenants
Insulation						
Double glazing	28.2	0.6	59	10	1,469	181
Loft insulation	5.1	0.4	11	7	30	31
Wall insulation	2.3	0.1	5	1	32	6
Draughtproofing	1.2	0.1	2	1	8	1
Secondary DG	1.0	0.1	2	1	11	9
Other heating						
Work on open/electric fires	11.4	2.6	24	48	124	264
Install solid fuel stove	0.9	0.3	2	6	12	33
Install gas fire/convector	7.4	1.3	15	25	49	80
Insert chimney lining	1.7	0.1	3	1	20	6
Central heating						
Install (non-electric) CH	7.3	1.2	15	23	288	444
Extend (non-electric) CH	3.1	0.1	6	2	65	13
Replace CH boiler	8.0	0.2	17	4	141	33
Replace CH distribution	2.9	0.1	6	2	23	5
Install electric CH	0.8	0.1	2	1	16	18
Replace/install CH controls	2.6	0	5	2	18	0
Water heating						
Install/replace immersion/ instantaneous heater	1.4	0.3	3	6	5	16
Install/replace HW cylinder	1.7	0.2	4	3	10	7
Other items						
Service heaters/boilers	2.4	0.1	5	1	22	6
Fit extractor fans	3.2	0.2	7	4	10	6
Install/extend gas supply	4.5	0.8	9	15	32	43
All jobs	47.9	5.4	100	100	2,402	1,193

1 Some households undertake more than one job

Work by landlords 1987 to 1991

17.18 The remainder of this chapter looks at the work undertaken by landlords, both public and private, over the same five year period 1987 to 1991. However, care needs to be taken when using the 'value of work' to compare the volumes of activity in the public and private sectors, as this value is dependent on the relevant market prices for work and these may vary significantly between sectors.

Local authority sector

17.19 Over the five year period from 1987 to 1991, approximately £5.1 billion was spent by local authorities on all major capital works to their own

Capital expenditure

stock. Of this sum, around 38% went on energy related improvements, including heating systems. This proportion compares with 29% spent on work to the external fabric, 15% on work to the interior (including the fabric, amenities and services, but excluding heating), 7% on works to the curtilage, 6% on structural modifications and adaptations and 5% on common areas in flat blocks. Overall, just over a quarter of the local authority stock was included in that part of the capital programme which involved energy related work.

Type of work

17.20 The breakdown of capital expenditure on energy related improvements is given in Table 17.5. A third of the total went on the provision of double glazed windows. While double glazing has an impact on energy efficiency, this tends to be small unless the dwelling is already very efficient, and in most instances the main purpose of such new windows is to replace rotten or otherwise obsolete ones and to reduce maintenance costs. Consequently, the true proportion of all spending which should be attributed to energy related measures is less than 38%; a figure of around 30% perhaps being more appropriate. (also Table A17.5)

17.21 By far the largest proportion of energy related spending went on heating systems (almost half of the 38% and a greater proportion of 30%). The installation of new central heating systems takes almost three quarters of this. In all, some 11% of the stock had new systems installed and a further 6% received improvements to existing systems in this period.

17.22 Less than a quarter of what was spent on heating systems was invested in improved insulation levels. Around 4 to 5% of the total expenditure was used for overcladding.

Table 17.5   Energy related work in capital programmes undertaken by local authorities during 1987-91

Type of work	Value of work			Dwellings affected	
	Value (£m)	% of all capital spend	% of all energy spend	Number (000s)	As % of stock
Overcladding	70	1.5	3.6	38	1
Double glazing, secondary glazing	650	12.8	33.2	309	8
Roof, cavity and wall insulation	60	1.3	3.1	424	11
Insulation to water tanks & pipework	20	0.4	1.0	232	6
Other and non-specified insulation	120	2.3	6.1	77	2
Improvements to heating systems	270	5.2	13.8	232	6
New heating systems	650	12.7	33.2	424	11
Other & non-specified measures	120	2.2	6.1	77	2
All energy measures	1,950	38.4	100.0	1,003	26

Revenue expenditure

17.23 In addition to those undertaken under capital programmes, some energy related works on the local authority stock are carried out under cyclical maintenance programmes or as responsive repairs. The EHCS suggests that over the five year period, 1987 to 1991, around £0.4 billion was spent under the headings listed in Table 17.5, but does not provide reliable information on its breakdown. However, it is estimated that approximately £23 million was spent over the period on servicing heating appliances and systems as part of the regular programme of cyclical maintenance, around a fifth of the local authority stock being included.

Inpact on stock

17.24 From a comparison of the results from the 1986 and 1991 EHCS, it would appear that the availability of central heating in council housing grew dramatically over this period, from about 56% to 78% of homes. At first sight this growth rate is higher than implied by the numbers in Table 17.5, but the figures are confounded by the substantial movement of properties between tenures in recent years and by the possibility that some tenants (rather than landlords) organised the work. Nevertheless, there is no doubt that the changes have been substantial and that overall the gap between the owner occupied and local authority sectors in the provision of central heating is narrowing.[2]

Housing association sector

Programme expenditure

17.25 During 1987 to 1991, around 12% of the housing association stock received work which contributed to the improvement of energy efficiency. Double glazing, roof and wall insulation and upgrading of heating systems were undertaken in roughly equal proportions, with many dwellings receiving several of these measures. The lower level of activity may reflect the relatively recent construction or comprehensive refurbishment of the majority of properties in this sector.

Revenue expenditure

17.26 Some additional work will have been undertaken as responsive repairs and minor works but, as with the local authority stock, no breakdown is available. However, around £3.3 million was spent on servicing heating facilities as part of the cyclical maintenance programme, affecting 18% of the housing association stock.

Table 17.6   Energy related work in programmes undertaken by housing associations during 1987-91

	Value of work			Dwellings affected	
	Value (£m)	% of all rehab. spend	% of all energy spend	Number (000s)	As % of stock
Overcladding	0	0	0	0	0
Double glazing, secondary glazing	81.4	9.3	37.9	39	6.3
Roof, cavity and wall insulation	15.2	1.7	7.1	34	5.4
Insulation to water tanks & pipework	3.5	0.4	1.6	29	4.6
Other and non-specified insulation	9.4	1.1	4.4	5	0.8
Improvements to heating systems	42.9	5.0	20.0	23	3.7
New heating systems	35.4	4.0	16.5	25	4.0
Other & non-specified measures	26.7	3.0	12.4	12	2.0
All energy measures	214.5	25.0	100.0	74	11.8

Private rented sector

Value of work and data sources

17.27 As the 1991 EHCS did not collect data directly from private landlords, it is necessary to use the information supplied by tenants on the work they believe their landlords have carried out. It is known from the EHCS Postal Surveys of local authorities and housing associations that this procedure results in a gross under-estimation of the true value of work done (by a factor of 6 for local authority work and 8 for housing association schemes undertaken between 1987 and 1991). However, assuming that private tenants have similarly under-estimated the work by private landlords, the total value of all work in the private rented sector over the period 1987 to 1991 can be estimated at between £3.7 billion and £5.0 billion.

2 *The 1991 Census, however, suggests that the extent of this gap varies substantially between authorities, the ownership of central heating in the council stock being half that of owner occupied housing in some districts.*

17.28 An independent EHCS 'follow-up' survey gives an estimate for the value of all work in this sector during 1991 of £1.4 billion. If this figure is multiplied by 3.6 (the factor relating work by occupants during 1987 to 1991 to work in 1991), a five year estimate of some £5.0 billion is again arrived at. This appears, therefore, to be a reasonably reliable, if somewhat crudely determined, estimate of the value of all work in the private rented sector.

Proportion of total expenditure

17.29 The proportion of this total expenditure committed by private landlords to energy-related work is estimated to be around 15%, compared with proportions in the social rented sectors of more than one third. The approximate breakdown between different types of work is given in Table 17.7.

Table 17.7   **Energy related work undertaken by private landlords during 1987-91**

	Type of work		Value of work
	Value (£ billion)	% of all rehab. spending	% of all energy spending
Overcladding	0	0	0
Double glazing, secondary glazing	0.36	7.2	48
Roof, cavity and wall insulation	0.02	0.3	2
Insulation to water tanks & pipework	0	0	0
Improvements to heating systems	0.10	2.1	14
New heating systems	0.18	3.6	24
Other & non-specified energy measures	0.09	1.8	12
All energy measures	0.75	15.0	100

Chapter 18

Attitudes to insulation work

Preamble

18.1 *This chapter examines the reasons given by households for installing thermal insulation - wall, loft/roof and hot water cylinder insulation, double glazing and draught excluders - and reasons for non-installation. Owner occupiers are considered independently of tenants, not least because the issue of owner/landlord responsibility is a major influence on household attitudes in these different sectors.*

18.2 *For the purpose of the analysis, households were divided into three main groups. 'Improvers' (11.2 million households) are households who have added to, replaced or installed any of five types of thermal insulation. The 'already efficient' (1.4 million households) are those who already have SAP ratings of 50 or more and have made no improvements. The third group 'non-improvers' (6.5 million households) have also not improved home insulation but their SAP ratings (below 50) suggest they might benefit from further measures.*

Insulation and tenure

18.3 Over three quarters of owner occupiers are improvers. In all other tenures, more than two thirds of households are non-improvers. (Figure 18.1 and Table A18.1a) Owner occupiers also install the most insulation, many improving several features (Figure 18.2) and in a large variety of combinations.

Figure 18.1   Improvers and non-improvers by tenure

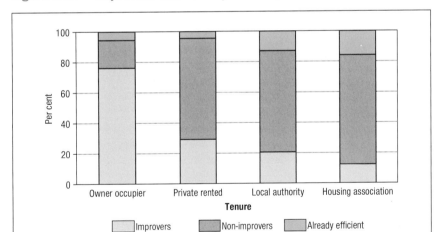

18.4 Landlords have also improved insulation. Tenants are the main beneficiaries; only 2% of owner occupiers (leaseholders etc.) report improvements carried out by others on their behalf, compared to one fifth of tenants renting privately, almost a third of housing association and half of local authority tenants. (Table A18.2) Landlord improvements are considered in more detail in the section which looks at tenants.

Figure 18.2   Improvers: number of insulation features improved

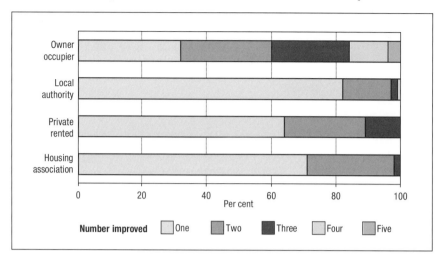

Insulation and location

18.5   Improvers are more likely to live in rural areas than in city centre or urban locations. (Figure 18.3 and Table A18.1b) However, this is not simply a function of dwelling location. Average incomes are higher in these rural areas, and, except in isolated rural areas, there are proportionately more owner occupiers. Conversely, there are more already efficient homes in urban areas. In most regions around two thirds of households are improvers, slightly less (half of all households) in Northern and London regions. (Table A18.1c)

Figure 18.3   Insulation and location

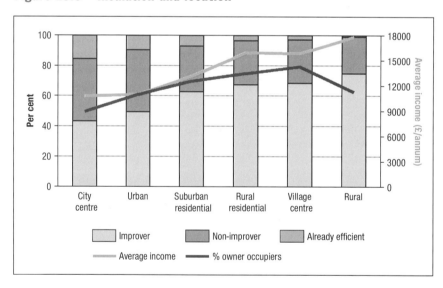

18.6   Households with least insulation appear most likely to carry out future improvements. Overall, 1.8 million households (10%) intend to install insulation in the future. However, 12 to 14% of those with two or less insulation features intend to do so, compared to only 4% of those already with four of the five insulation measures.

18.7   Not all insulation has been installed recently, and the accuracy of the respondents recall is likely to decrease with time. The analysis that follows includes some detail of all insulation installed, but like the previous Chapter focuses on that installed in the five years before the survey.

Owner occupiers

18.8   Overall, 9.8 million owner occupiers report that they have improved the insulation of their present home. In many cases owners have installed more than one measure, but ten combinations account for almost three quarters

Improvers

of their improvements. None of these combinations include wall insulation, but six include double glazing. (Figure18.4) The main reason for improving insulation tends to be to make the home warmer rather than to reduce the cost of heating.

Figure 18.4   Improvements by owner occupiers, most common combinations

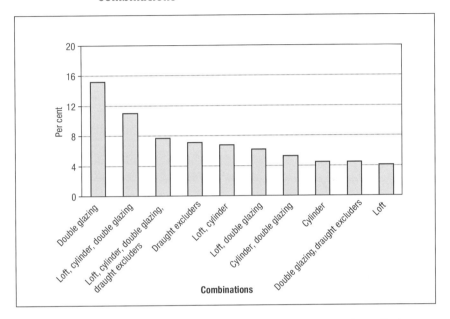

Single improvement, since 1986

18.9   Since 1986, 6.4 million owner occupier improvers have installed some insulation. A third of these have installed double glazing alone. Over half (57%) do so to make their homes warmer, other reasons, such as ease of maintenance, being less common. Just over 11% installed draught excluders only and 6% loft insulation only, again to make the home warmer (91% and 78% respectively). Of those insulating their hot water tank/cylinder only, two thirds do so "to keep water hot" and less than one fifth to reduce fuel bills. (Table A18.4)

Multiple improvements, since 1986

18.10   Many improved more than one feature between 1986 and 1991, most commonly double glazing plus one other type, for example with draught excluders (9%), with cylinder insulation (6%) and with loft insulation (5%). (Table A18.3)

All improvements, when installed

18.11   For all owner occupier improvers, Figure 18.5 shows when the ten main insulation combinations were installed. Most loft and cylinder insulation was installed more than five years before the survey, while double glazing, and also draught excluders, show more recent installation, much having been installed since 1986. Some progression is also evident, in that households which have installed most insulation have been resident at the same address longest. One explanation is that households install simpler and cheaper insulation first (loft and cylinder insulation) and wait longer to install more expensive items, such as double glazing.

Reasons for not insulating

18.12   Not all improvers have all five forms of insulation and the extent to which these owner occupiers say they intend to undertake further work varies with the particular measures lacking. (Figure 18.6) Almost 4 million improvers with cavity walls have no wall insulation, but only 3% firmly intend to install it in future. However, up to 15% intend to install double glazing and for those lacking loft insulation, almost a quarter (23%) say that they plan to install it. (Table A18.5a)

Figure 18.5   Owner occupier combinations: when installed

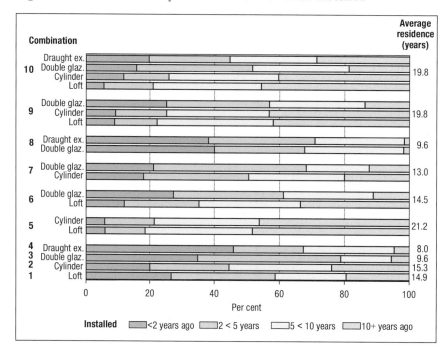

18.13 For each type of insulation there is a group who see no need for it. In the case of draught excluders, 79% of owner occupiers see no need or have never considered them, often preferring double glazing. Similarly, 71% have no interest in wall insulation. Another group say that they can't afford further insulation - almost half of those without double glazing and one third of those with no loft insulation. Of those lacking cylinder insulation, most (58%) see no need for it. (Table A18.5a)

Figure 18.6   Owner occupier improvers: households without insulation

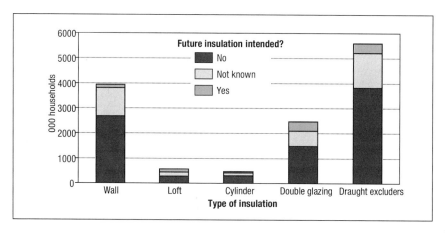

Non-improvers

18.14 Two groups of owner occupiers have not improved home insulation: 0.7 million in 'already efficient' homes and 2.4 million households who could derive benefits from further insulation.

Reasons for not insulating

18.15 Of the 'already efficient', few intend future insulation, and only double glazing (by 6%) and draught excluders (by 6%) is likely to be installed[1]. (Figure 18.7 and Table A18.5b) Of those who do not intend to install, almost two thirds (64%) 'can't afford' double glazing and one third can't afford wall insulation. Another 43% also see no need for double glazing.

1   *Loft and cylinder insulation has been excluded in this analysis as so few of these households lack it.*

More than three quarters see no need for or have never considered draught excluders. For wall insulation, 38% thought it was not their responsibility, many being flat dwellers or leaseholders. (Table A18.5b)

18.16 Compared to the 'already efficient', more of the 'non-improvers' intend to install insulation in future (for example, almost one third of those without loft insulation, 16% of those without double glazing, but only 3% of those without wall insulation). (Figure 18.7) However, depending on the type of insulation, half to two thirds or more say that they do not intend to insulate. Almost two thirds of those without wall insulation or draught excluders see no need, have never considered, or simply do not want these types of insulation. Some 43% say that they "can't afford" double glazing. (Table A18.5c)

Figure 18.7   Owner occupier non improvers without insulation

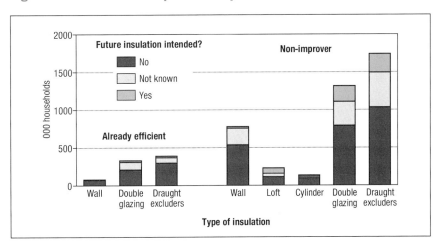

Dwelling and household characteristics

Improvers

18.17 Some significant differences are found between the dwelling and household characteristics of 'improvers', those in 'already efficient' homes and 'non improvers'. Over two fifths of improvers live in detached or semi-detached houses built before 1980 and one fifth live in bungalows. Most (56%) are in full-time employment, being generally in non-manual occupations and having above average incomes - over half earning within the top two income quintiles. There does seem to be a life cycle component to insulation, in that owner occupiers who have insulated since 1986 tend to be younger (29% of household heads under 40) and to be family households (37%). Many have recently moved, 28% within the five years prior to the survey. (Figure 18.8) However, there are also many older, more established households who continue to install insulation. (Tables A18.7 & A18.8)

Figure 18.8   Owner occupiers: length of residence

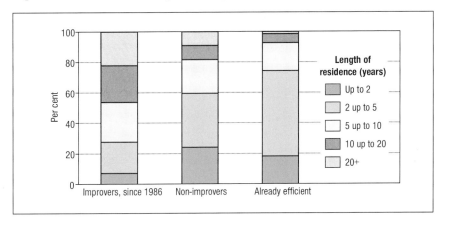

*Already
efficient*

18.18 The 'already efficient' are an even more affluent group who have moved home since 1986, almost three quarters being resident less than five years. Not surprisingly, over half live in the most efficient dwelling types, houses or flats built since 1980. Their household heads are younger, two fifths being under 40 and many (48%) are small or large families - younger, child-rearing households. They have the highest average annual income of any group, almost three quarters earning within the top two income quintiles. They are most likely (79%) to be in full-time employment, mostly in non-manual occupations.

Non improvers

18.19 'Non-improvers' most commonly live in terraced housing, over two fifths being in such properties. They have the lowest average incomes amongst owner occupiers, although still above the national average. Over two-thirds are in full-time employment and most (55%) have non-manual occupations. Again, they are recently established households, younger than the improvers, 45% of household heads being under 40 and three fifths being resident less than five years. Two fifths are single or two adult households (without children).

Tenants

18.20 As expected, tenants put in less insulation than owner occupiers. (Figure 18.9) Draught excluders are the predominant installation in each sector. These provide a cheap alternative to double glazing and are also least likely to be seen as a landlord responsibility. Since 1986, almost half a million local authority tenants and quarter of a million tenants renting privately have installed some insulation, again draught excluders being the predominant measure. (Table A18.3) Tenants also insulate mainly to make their homes warmer. (Table A18.4)

Improvers

Figure 18.9   Improvements by tenants, most common combinations

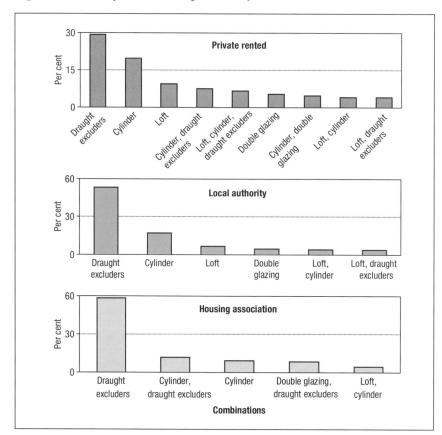

Single improvement, since 1986

18.21 The main tenant improvements to insulation since 1986 have been to single features. The vast majority, who install draught excluders alone, do so to keep their homes warmer - as do the much smaller numbers who put in loft insulation only. Cylinders are insulated to keep water hot (60-70%) and to reduce fuel bills (20-30%). (Table A18.4)

Landlord improvements

18.22 For about a half of local authority improvers and a quarter of improvers renting privately, the landlord also made improvements. Most commonly, these were to loft or cylinder insulation. For local authority tenants, almost a quarter have improvements done which include wall insulation. (Table A18.10)

Reasons for not insulating

18.23 As with owner occupiers, many tenant improvers still lack one or more forms of insulation. (Figure 18.10) For example, almost four fifths of local authority improvers have no double glazing. Few intend themselves to install features they lack; the most likely installations are cylinder insulation in the local authority sector (but only by 8%), double glazing in the housing association sector (by 10%) and in the private rented sector (loft insulation by 18%). The main reason for not insulating is that, as tenants, they see this as a landlord responsibility. This is given as a reason by over 70% for many features in the local authority and housing association sectors, but less in the private rented sector. (Table A18.6a) Other reasons were cost, mentioned by over 30% of council tenants for double glazing, and "moving soon", mentioned by a tenth or more for most features in the private rented sector. "No need", which was often mentioned as a reason for not insulating by owner occupiers, was cited much less often by tenants, and by council tenants in particular.

Figure 18.10 Tenant improvers without insulation: future insulation intentions

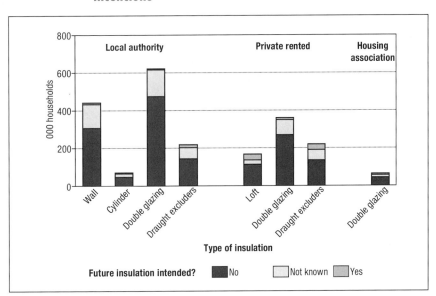

Non-improvers

18.24 The largest groups of tenants are non-improvers (2.6 million local authority households, 1.1 million tenants renting privately, and almost 0.5 million housing association households). Households in 'already efficient' homes are much fewer in number: only 490 thousand in the local authority, 74 thousand in the private rented and 104 thousand in the housing association sectors.

Reasons for not insulating

18.25 Few tenants in 'already efficient' homes intend to insulate in future and, in many cases, their homes may not need further insulation. However, most local authority households in this group lack double glazing and draught excluders, and the most likely further insulation is the latter (mentioned by 4% of housing association and 6% of local authority tenants). (Figure 18.11 and Table A18.6b) Many private tenants have never considered or see no need for insulation.

Figure 18.11 "Already efficient" tenant households: future insulation intentions

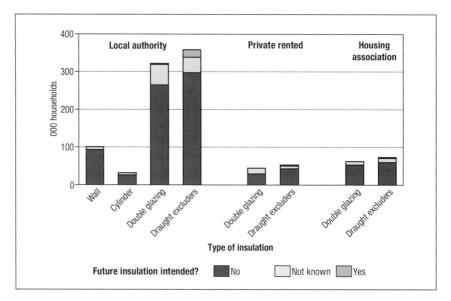

18.26 More 'non-improvers' intend to insulate in future, but again the numbers are small; depending on the sector 7 to 9% propose to put in draught excluders. (Figure 18.12 and Table A18.6c) However, the vast majority have no intention of insulating their home. For example of the 1.1 million (60%) non-improvers in local authority dwellings with cavity walls who lack cavity wall insulation, only 1% intend to insulate.

Figure 18.12 Non-improver tenant households: future insulation intentions

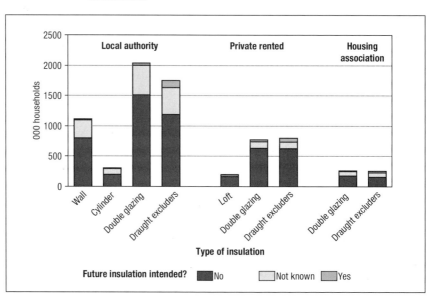

18.27 For most types of insulation, the main reason for non-installation is again that insulation is seen as a landlord responsibility. (Table A18.6c) Cost was more important than for the 'already efficient' group, being mentioned by 25% of the local authority and 26% of the housing association groups as a reason for not installing double glazing. In the private rented sector, "moving soon" features as a reason, reflecting the more transient population in this sector.

Landlord improvements

18.28 Many 'non-improvers' have had insulation installed by their landlords (over half of the local authority tenants, one third of housing association tenants, and almost one fifth of the private rented sector tenants). For local authority tenants, loft or cylinder insulation, singly or in combination, are the most common improvements (42%), though there are a large variety of combinations. With more modern properties, less (41%) of the 'already efficient' have received landlord improvements, and their most common improvements are to single features: double glazing (16%), cylinder insulation (13%) and draught excluders (12%). (Table A18.10) For the housing association, and particularly the private rented stock, landlord improvements also comprise mainly loft and cylinder insulation.

Dwelling and household characteristics

18.29 As with owner occupiers, there is significant variation in the dwelling and household characteristics of improvers, the 'already efficient' and 'non-improvers' in the different rented sectors. About four fifths of local authority improvers live in houses, the largest group in medium/large terraces and semi-detached houses built in the early post-war years, while in the housing association sector more live in houses built between 1965 and 1980. Private rented improvers live in older homes, three quarters in those built before 1945. (Table A18.7)

Improvers

18.30 Improvers have the highest average incomes of all tenants. Even so, three quarters of the local authority group have incomes in the bottom two quintiles nationally. They are most likely to be in manual socio-economic groups, these accounting for three quarters of the local authority group and two thirds of those privately renting. Also in these two sectors, households who have insulated since 1986 are younger (35% of local authority household heads being aged under 40 compared with 45% of those in the private rented sector). They are also family households, 42% having dependent children in both sectors. Many (38% of local authority and 45% of private tenants) had moved within the five years before the survey. Housing association improvers differ slightly. Fewer heads of household are aged under 40 (19%), they are much more likely to consist of large families with dependent children (21%) and half have been resident at the same address for 10 years or more. In all tenures there is a large sub-group of longer-term residents who are improvers. (Figure 18.13 and Table A18.9)

Already efficient

18.31 Tenant households in 'already efficient' homes have some things in common. They mostly live in flats (74% of the housing association group, 69% of the local authority and three fifths of the private rented groups). Around two fifths of household heads are under 40 (three fifths in the private rented sector). They are the most recent movers, around half those in the social rented sector had moved home in the five years prior to the survey and three fifths of those in the private rented sector had been resident less than two years. However, there are also differences. 70% of the local

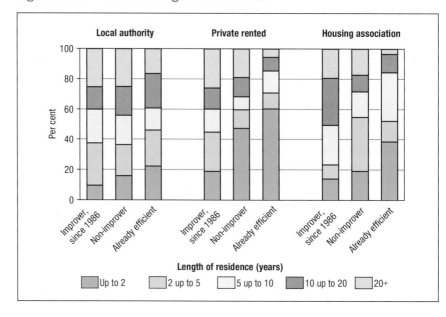

Figure 18.13 Tenants: length of residence

authority tenants are not working, only slightly fewer in the housing association sector and most are defined as in manual socio-economic groups. By contrast, the private rented group are mostly (57%) in full-time employment. This group may consist of people renting prior to buying a first home and may be fairly transient. In the private rented sector, one third of households comprise small families, while nearly a quarter of the housing association households in 'already efficient' homes are lone parents. (Tables A18.7 and A18.9)

Non improvers 18.32 Tenant 'non-improvers' have the lowest incomes in their respective tenures - for example, 77% of the local authority group have incomes in the bottom two quintiles. In the private rented sector, most of these households live in older houses, built pre-war. Most in the local authority sector are also in houses, although one third live in flats. Of the housing association group most live in flats, the largest group in conversions.

18.33 There are two distinct groups of 'non-improvers'. One group are younger households and recent movers. In each rented sector, a large group have been resident less than five years, and half of the private rented group have been resident less than two years. Many of these could become improvers in time, although there may be constraints - many in the housing association sector are lone parent families (20%). The second group is an older, retired group - half the local authority group and almost as many in the housing association sector have household heads aged 60 or more. Many of these have been resident ten years or more and are unlikely to become improvers. (Tables A18.7 and A18.9)

Chapter 19 Improvement potential

Preamble

19.1 *This penultimate chapter of the Report examines the potential for improvements in energy efficiency. After describing a range of works directed at upgrading the stock, the chapter analyses the options for achieving a significant improvement in energy efficiency in each tenure and across the stock as a whole. It goes on to examine the costs and benefits of selected options, particularly in relation to household resources and notional 'pay-back' periods. The chapter concludes by analysing the actual savings in fuel expenditure likely to be achieved by households after improvement works and the scope for reducing 'wastage' of energy irrespective of any upgrading. It ends by examining the gains in affordable warmth which are achievable through improvements in the energy efficiency of the stock.*

Improvement options

Criteria used

19.2 As described in the earlier section on 'measuring change' (Chapter 16, paras. 16.3-16.6), the main measure used in this chapter to show the impact of improvement is the percentage saving in the cost of space and water heating required to achieve the standard heating regime in a dwelling. Across the stock as a whole, savings will depend on the number of dwellings improved, the energy efficiency now and new energy efficiency after improvement. To explore the savings achieved by different improvement options, calculations have been made to show the effect of:-

- ❏ action on increasing proportions of the stock, aimed at improving all dwellings with an existing SAP rating:- (1) below 10; (2) below 20; (3) below 30; (4) below 40; or (5) below 50;

- ❏ a range of increasingly higher targets, aimed at giving each dwelling after improvement a minimum SAP rating of:- (a) 30; (b) 40; (c) 50; (d) 60; or (e) 70; and

- ❏ a general criterion that the energy rating of each dwelling included for improvement shall be raised by at least 10 SAP points.

19.3 In those cases where the particular characteristics of the dwelling do not allow the target standard to be readily achieved, the maximum which can be obtained is accepted provided this represents an increase in the SAP rating of at least 10 points.

Improvement packages

19.4 The energy measures selected for any particular dwelling are those which can achieve or get closest to the required target standard for the minimum cost. The implementation costs used for this purpose are, necessarily, broad averages. Precise costs will depend on a number of factors which cannot be treated here: the method of implementation, market conditions and so on. In the analysis, eight standard target packages are used, each comprising a combination of up to thirteen different individual energy measures. The particular measures included in each target package are shown in Table 19.1.

Table 19.1   Specification of eight target improvement packages

Individual energy measures	Target packages							
	1	2	3	4	5	6	7	8
Upgrade heating controls (TRVs, programmer, thermostat)	*	*			*		*	
Install high grade heating as appropriate	*	*	*		*		*	
Install basic grade heating as appropriate				*				*
Fit cylinder thermostat; insulate primary water heating pipework	*	*				*		
Provide cylinder with 100mm jacket	*	*	*	*		*	*	*
Make up roof insulation to 150mm (target U-value 0.25)	*	*	*	*		*	*	*
Insulate ground floors (target U-value 0.7)	*	*				*		*
Fill all cavity walls (target U-value 0.55)	*	*				*		*
Dry line all solid walls (target U-value 0.8)	*					*		
100% double glazing (low emissivity; target U-value 2.3)	*					*		
100% double glazing (sealed units; target U-value 2.8)		*						*
100% double glazing (secondary; target U-value 3.0)			*					
Reduce air change rate (100% draughtproofing; trickle vents only)	*	*	*	*		*	*	*

Summary of target packages
1 Heating and insulation to highest standard
2 Heating and insulation to high intermediate standard
3 Heating and insulation to low intermediate standard
4 Heating and insulation to minimum standard
5 Heating only to highest standard
6 Insulation only to highest standard
7 Heating to high intermediate and insulation to minimum standard
8 Heating to minimum and insulation to high intermediate standard

19.5   Where a particular measure already exists in the dwelling, the package is implemented without that facility with a consequent reduction in installation cost. In this way, the combination of additional measures is tailored to each individual dwelling, so that the number of actual packages is far more than the eight.

Potential savings in heating costs

19.6   The following paragraphs present results from the study of this range of improvement options. Figures 19.1 and 19.2 (a) to (c) plot, for the total

Figure 19.1   Reduction in heating costs for a range of renewal options - owner occupied sector

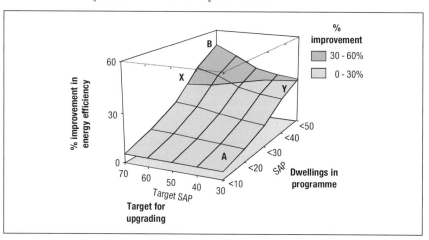

Savings by tenure

stock within each tenure, the percentage reduction in standard heating costs - on the vertical axis - for different sets of dwellings improved and different improvement targets - on the horizontal axes. (see also Table A19.1)

Figure 19.2   Reductions in heating costs for a range of renewal options - rented sectors

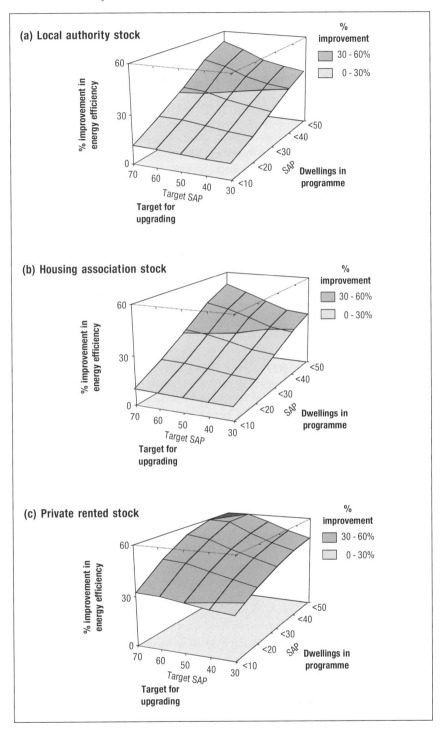

19.7   The resulting surface for the owner occupied stock (Figure 19.1), for example, shows the overall reduction in heating costs ranging from less than 5% to 50%, corresponding to renewal options ranging from (A) improving to a SAP rating of 30 all those dwellings with a rating below 10, to (B) improving to over 70, where possible, all those with a current rating below 50. The contour line (XY) connects all options giving a saving of 30% in the heating cost of the sector as a whole. These options range from (X) improving all dwellings with a SAP of less than 35 to a target of 70, to (Y) improving all those rated under 50 by at least 10 SAP points to a minimum of 30.

19.8   In Figures 19.1 and 19.2 the area above the 30% contour line (in the darker shading) represents all options giving a reduction in heating costs greater than 30%. By comparing the size of this area between tenures, it can be seen that the options for a saving of 30% are more limited in the owner occupied sector than they are in either of the two socially rented sectors. However, because of its existing particularly poor energy efficiency, the task is much easier in the private rented sector - here almost any of the options would achieve over a 30% improvement. (Figure 19.2c)

Savings over whole stock

19.9   Figure 19.3 shows the surface representing the percentage reduction in heating costs achievable in the stock as a whole. It gives contour lines for savings of 10%, 20%, 30%, 40% and 50%. In principle it would just be possible to achieve a theoretical saving in heating costs of 50% within the range of options - by upgrading all dwellings rated below 50 to a target value of 70. (Table A19.1)

Figure 19.3   Reductions in heating costs for a range of renewal options - total stock

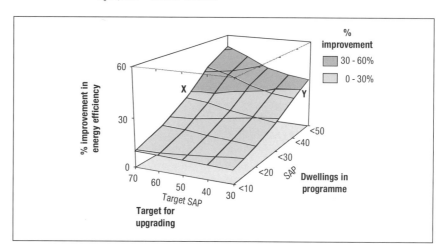

Capital costs

All options

19.10 The various improvements giving the same level of heating cost savings (for example, as represented by the 30% contour line) do not necessarily bear the same capital costs. Figure 19.4 plots, on the vertical scale, the improvement cost per dwelling (averaged over the whole stock, not just those dwellings improved) for the complete range of improvement options - on the horizontal scales. (For the costs for each tenure, see Table A19.2)

19.11 Superimposed on this surface are dotted lines connecting all those improvements which would achieve heating cost reductions of 10%, 20%, 30% and 40%. All these lines run down the slope of the implementation cost surface as the proportion of dwellings included in the programme increases and the target SAP rating decreases. It appears, therefore, that the least expensive way of securing a given reduction in heating costs is to choose the option which improves more dwellings to a relatively modest standard rather than one which improves fewer dwellings to a high standard.

Figure 19.4   Average implementation cost per dwelling in the stock
for the range of renewal options - total stock

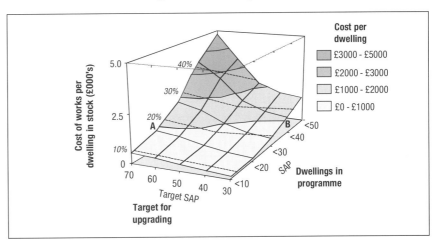

*Least expensive
options*

19.12 Using the least expensive option in each case, Table 19.2 shows the cost of achieving a 30% reduction in heating costs in each of the main tenures, as well as savings of 10%, 20%, 30% and 40% over the total stock. In 'cost-benefit' terms, the greatest potential gains can be made amongst privately rented dwellings since these tend to be the least energy efficient; improvement is most costly in the owner occupied sector where the options are more limited.

Table 19.2   Estimated cost of least expensive options to secure
selected levels of savings in heating costs

Improvement in heating cost (%)	Sector	Size of occupied stock (000s)	Estimated cost of option	
			Per dwelling in stock (£)	Whole stock (£b)
30	Owner occupied	12,872	1,600	20.6
	Private rented	1,626	650	1.1
	Local authority	3,851	1,000	3.9
	Housing association	591	900	0.5
10	All tenures	18,940	190	3.6
20			650	12.3
30			1,370	26.0
40			>2,000	>40

19.13 To secure a 30% reduction in heating costs over the whole stock would require an estimated capital expenditure of over £26 billion, of which some £20.6 billion would be required for the owner occupied stock and £3.9 billion for council housing. To put these sums into perspective, the annual energy-related expenditure (including that on double-glazed windows) by owner occupiers in the single year 1991 was £4.6 billion, whilst the equivalent expenditure on the local authority stock was £0.4 billion. To draw another comparison, the annual domestic fuel bill for the total stock is around £12.6 billion.

**A detailed look
at some limited
options**
*Upgrading
methods*

19.14 The following paragraphs look in a little more detail at the improvements tested and their impact on the stock. Discussion is restricted to those options aiming for a minimum SAP rating of 30. Table 19.3 shows, for different sets of dwellings improved, the packages giving this target SAP rating at least cost. Package 5, which involves only the installation of the most efficient heating appropriate to the dwelling (normally a gas fired condensing boiler, where gas is available) is the most economic option for the majority of dwellings in all tenures. Though relatively expensive, this offers considerable savings in fuel expenditure and is particularly appropriate in older, solid walled dwellings where the opportunities for low cost insulation measures are limited.

19.15 The effectiveness of this package is particularly apparent where the programme includes only those dwellings with SAP ratings below 10. Here a large improvement is generally needed to achieve the target rating, and this is not always available from other measures. Among dwellings with higher current SAP ratings, which often already have a reasonable heating system, improved insulation has a bigger part to play, as do the packages involving smaller, cheaper measures which can just lift these higher ratings by the required 10 SAP points. (Table 19.3) Nevertheless, even in those options involving all dwellings with SAP ratings up to 50, the installation of a more efficient heating system is still the dominant package, although slightly less so in the social rented sector than in the owner occupied stock. (Table A19.3)

Table 19.3   Percentage of dwellings requiring particular improvement packages for different options with target of 30 - owner occupied stock

Dwellings in programme	SAP <10	SAP <20	SAP <30	SAP <50
1) Heating and insulation to highest standard	0.0	0.0	0.0	0.1
2) Heating and insulation to high intermediate standard	2.4	1.0	0.5	0.7
3) Heating and insulation to low intermediate standard	1.2	0.9	1.5	1.6
4) Heating and insulation to minimum standard	4.3	13.6	16.6	14.2
5) Heating only to highest standard	80.8	70.7	60.1	56.7
6) Insulation only to highest standard	2.0	2.2	5.7	3.2
7) Heating to high intermediate/insulation to minimum	6.6	4.4	2.1	1.6
8) Heating to minimum/insulation to high intermediate	2.8	7.2	13.6	22.9

Upgrading costs

19.16 Because the preferred upgrading package is most frequently the installation of a highly efficient heating system, the estimated cost of works per dwelling improved is generally in the region of £1,800 to £2,000. The full distribution of costs for different improvement options in the owner occupied sector is shown in Figure 19.5. The distributions for other sectors are very similar. (see Table A19.4)

Figure 19.5   Distribution of costs of improving owner occupied dwellings for different options

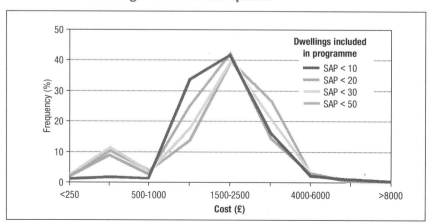

Benefits to energy efficiency

19.17 Figure 19.6 shows the 'benefits' of the improvements on the energy efficiency of the stock. The first gives the distribution of SAP rating after improvement for just those dwellings improved. The second gives the same distribution, but for all dwellings in the stock whether included for improvement or not. Figure 19.6 shows that, following upgrading, the majority of dwellings in the smaller programmes record a relatively modest increase in SAP rating to around 30 to 40. However, there are some where the minimum package of works required to achieve the target of 30 actually raises the dwelling to a SAP rating of 60 or over. (Tables A19.5 & A19.7 for each tenure)

Figure 19.6   Distribution of SAP ratings after upgrading to target of 30

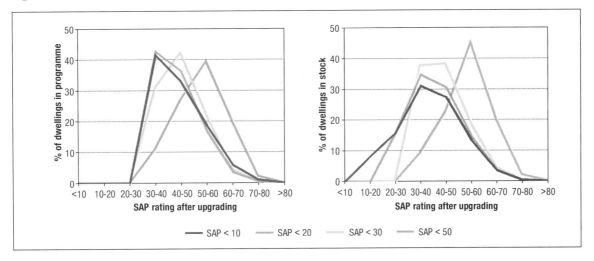

Summary of costs and benefits

19.18 The impact of these improvements is summarised in Table 19.4. The smallest option lifts the mean SAP rating for the stock from 35.4 to 38.4 and leaves just under a quarter of dwellings below the target rating of 30, at a total cost of £2.4 billion. The largest option considered raises the mean SAP rating to 53.2, leaves no dwellings with a rating below 30 and costs £31.1 billion.

Table 19.4   Summary of costs and impact of improvements to achieve a target SAP rating of 30

Rating of dwellings in programme		SAP <10	SAP <20	SAP <30	SAP <50
Number of dwellings improved (000s)		1,241	2,844	5,840	16,089
% of stock included		6.5	14.9	30.6	84.3
Mean cost per dwelling improved (£)		1,964	1,804	1,857	1,933
Total capital cost (£b)		2.4	5.1	10.8	31.1
Mean SAP rating	} dwellings improved	-2.8	7.5	17.0	31.4
before improvement	} over whole stock	35.4	35.4	35.4	35.4
Mean SAP rating	} dwellings improved	43.7	42.9	44.9	52.5
after improvement	} over whole stock	38.4	40.6	43.9	53.2
% of dwellings not	} dwellings improved	0	0	0	0
reaching target	} over whole stock	24	16	0	0
% notional stock saving in heating costs[1]		8	13	19	33

1 On the assumption that the standard heating regime is used both before and after improvement

Funding the improvement

Income constraints

19.19 As was seen in Chapter 7, a large proportion of the households living in dwellings in need of improvement are on low incomes. Figure 19.7 shows the range of improvement costs per dwelling as a proportion of the net income of owner occupiers for the different improvement options summarised in Table 19.4. It indicates that the greater the number of more efficient dwellings included for improvement, the greater the percentage of households who may be able to fund the improvement works from their income, either directly or by securing a loan.

19.20 As would be expected, households in the least efficient dwellings are likely to experience the most difficulty in funding improvements. Of all owner occupiers in dwellings with SAP ratings below 50, around 18% rely on state benefit for more than three quarters of their income and some 6% are at the level of income support. However, for those in dwellings rated below 10, over 1 in 3 are reliant on benefit, and nearly 1 in 10 on income support. For most households dependent on benefit, and others where the cost of the works is high in relation to annual income, renovation grants or loans secured on the equity of the property may be required to achieve significant improvements. (Table A19.6)

Figure 19.7   Improvement costs in relation to household resources of owner occupiers for different improvement options

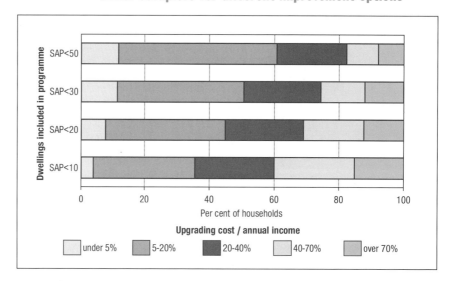

Pay-back period

19.21 For those owner occupiers able to fund improvements, the motivation to improve their homes is likely to come mainly from the desire for increased comfort, since many complain of lack of heat. However, some might be looking primarily for savings in fuel costs. A measure of the latter can be obtained by dividing the cost of the works by the potential annual saving in fuel expenditure (assuming a standard heating regime both before and after improvement) to give the simple payback period for each dwelling. Figure 19.8a shows, for the owner occupied stock, the distribution of these payback periods corresponding to the range of options to achieve a target rating of 30.

19.22 What might be considered a reasonable 'payback period' is probably related to the life of the improvement and to length of residence of the household. The life of an average heating system is usually taken as between 15 and 20 years, with insulation lasting much longer. However, households move relatively frequently, with a typical period at one address being between 5 and 15 years - less than the lifetime of the heating system. So in investment

Figure 19.8   Payback periods for different improvement options with target SAP rating of 30

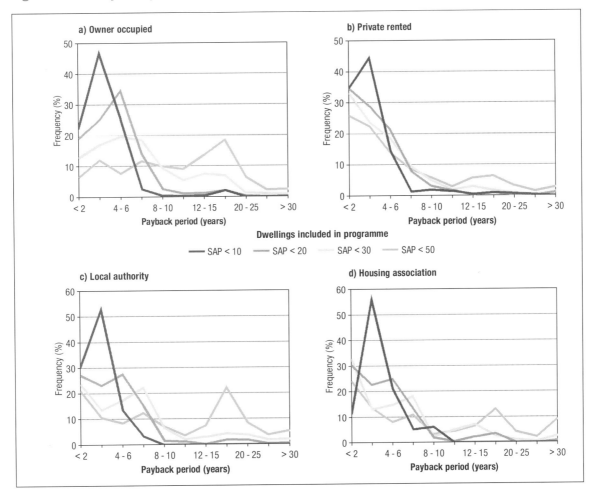

terms, a household would generally wish to recover its outlay in, say, less than 15 years. This time equates to a simple 'pay-back' period of around 10 years, as the latter is not 'discounted' and does not allow for the opportunity costs of spending in advance to make future savings. In short, although many are attracted to double glazed windows despite their long payback period, in financial terms, improvements with a 'pay-back' period of more than 10 years are likely to be unattractive to many households.

19.23 With this criterion, Figure 19.8a shows that almost all of the works required on dwellings with SAP ratings below 20 can be justified financially. However, for all dwellings with ratings under 30 around 22% have a 'pay-back' period longer than 10 years, while for dwellings rated up to 50 the equivalent proportion is over 50%. So if the motivation were largely financial, a significant proportion of owner occupiers might be unwilling to subscribe to an upgrading programme. (For payback periods for other tenures, see Figures 19.8b to c and Table A19.8)

Impact on energy consumption

19.24 The foregoing analyses, including the examination of 'pay-back' periods, are based on the assumption that households would achieve the standard heating regime both before and after improvement. However, as the chapters on fuel expenditure and home temperatures, as well as many of the case studies clearly demonstrate, the heating achieved by many households falls well below this standard.

19.25 For these dwellings, the actual fuel saving after improvement is likely to be significantly lower than that assumed for the purposes of calculating

Household behaviour following improvements

notional savings in heating costs and the notional 'pay-back' period. In some cases, improvements are likely to be associated with an increase in energy consumption, as householders - no longer fearful of high fuel bills - find themselves for the first time within striking distance of achieving whole house heating.

Predicting real fuel savings

19.26 We know, from the EHCS Fuel Consumption Survey, what is spent by households who have the same social characteristics and income as those in energy inefficient homes, but who already live in more efficient dwellings. We can make use of this information to estimate the change in fuel consumption and expenditure which is likely to accompany the improvement of the dwelling.

19.27 A multivariate statistical procedure (multiple linear regression) was used to model the relationship between the characteristics of households and their dwellings, the energy efficiencies of the dwellings and expenditure on fuel. Separate models were constructed to establish the relationship between the annual expenditure on fuel by owner occupiers and tenants in dwellings with different SAP ratings. A number of dwelling and household characteristics were examined; those found to have the greatest influence on fuel expenditure in each housing and tenure group are listed in Table 19.5.

19.28 The two dominant influences on fuel expenditure are the size of the dwelling and number of persons in the household. This holds true for both sectors and for all moderate and higher levels of SAP ratings considered, with floor area being more important in owner occupied properties and household size in rented dwellings. Amongst owner occupied dwellings with moderate SAP ratings, building characteristics which affect heat loss, such as the dwelling type and age, are important, as is income which may limit what can be spent on heating. As the energy efficiency increases and the heating costs become less important in the total fuel bill, building factors and income lose their importance. Amongst rented dwellings, income does not appear explicitly as an important factor, although the working status of the household (number of earners and whether in full or part-time work) appears to play a similar role.

Table 19.5   Household and dwelling characteristics which influence expenditure on fuel, listed in order of significance

| | Energy efficiency of housing | | | |
	SAP 30 to 40	SAP 40 to 50	SAP 50 to 60	SAP 60 to 80
Owner occupied	floor area household size household income dwelling type dwelling age	floor area household size household income dwelling type	floor area household size SEG working status	household size floor area
Rented	household size floor area working status	household size floor area working status	household size floor area age of HoH	household size building age

Projected savings in fuel expenditure

19.29 The models were used to predict the likely fuel expenditure of households after the improvement of their dwellings, and the results of the analysis are shown in Table 19.6. They suggest that with improvement to a target

SAP rating of 30, as many households (owner occupiers and tenants) will experience an increase in their expenditure on fuel as will experience a fall. For owner occupiers, expenditure is predicted to rise on average by 2% and by up to 10% for those in the least efficient dwellings. A similar pattern of change is predicted for tenants, except that they are likely to see an even greater rise, by perhaps 9% on average and up to 20% in the least efficient properties. (Table 19.6)

Table 19.6   Ratio of actual expenditure on fuel before improvement and estimated expenditure after improvement

	ratio of:-	estimated household expenditure after improvement actual household expenditure before improvement			
		Mean of ratios	lowest decile	Median	highest decile
Owner occupiers	SAP <10	1.10	0.73	1.03	1.80
	SAP <20	1.07	0.68	1.00	1.73
	SAP <30	1.08	0.72	1.03	1.49
	SAP <50	1.02	0.71	0.97	1.39
	All Owners	1.02	0.71	1.00	1.36
All tenants	SAP <10	1.20	0.61	0.87	2.59
	SAP <20	1.19	0.67	1.06	1.80
	SAP <30	1.13	0.67	0.98	1.65
	SAP <50	1.09	0.69	1.00	1.45
	All tenants	1.09			

19.30 Paradoxically however, although households will on average experience an increase in expenditure following improvement, there is likely to be a reduction in the aggregate expenditure in absolute terms. While the number of households whose expenditure will rise is greater than the number whose expenditure will fall, the latter tend to be the higher spenders and savings from this minority more than offsets the total increase in expenditure from the majority of lower fuel spenders. As is shown in Table 19.7, the best estimate of this aggregate saving in fuel expenditure varies with the energy efficiency of the existing dwellings, but the savings are unlikely to exceed 3% over the stock as a whole.

Table 19.7   Predicted total savings on heating and total fuel costs of improvements to achieve a target SAP rating of 30

Rating of dwellings in programme		SAP <10	SAP <20	SAP <30	SAP <50
% notional stock savings in heating costs		8	13	19	33
Predicted actual % savings on heating[1]	} dwellings in programme	11	5	5	5
	} over whole stock	0	0	1	3
Predicted total % savings in fuel costs[2]	} dwellings in programme	9	4	3	4
	} over whole stock	0	0	1	3

1 Estimated from the regression based relationships
2 Assuming the non-heating components of fuel remain unchanged

19.31 These limited savings are a consequence of the low levels of expenditure before improvement, which on average (and indeed for the vast majority of the dwellings) is appreciably less than is required to achieve the standard heating regime. That these households suffer a standard of heating which is below that aspired to as the norm is confirmed by an examination of the temperatures in their homes (see Chapter 13). However, the analysis suggests that there would be a substantial improvement in heating after improvement, with the standard regime being achieved in the majority of homes.

Examples of recent actual improvements

The sample

19.32 These results derive from a theoretical approach; however, the predictions are not contradicted by the actual behaviour of a group of households followed up since the previous EHCS in 1986. The sample of 172 homes comprises those which were improved (to a range of standards) between 1986 and 1991, and for which comparable data on both home temperatures and fuel consumption are available for the two survey years. As the consumption of unmetered fuels such as coal was not calculated in the earlier survey, the cases are limited to those using only gas and electric heating in 1986. The upgrading, however, is not restricted to improved insulation: some dwellings have seen individual gas or electric fires replaced by gas central heating. To ensure that meaningful conclusions can be drawn about temperatures, the sample is further confined to households who had been at home for more than one hour prior to each interview.

Changes 1986 to 1991

19.33 The sample includes a higher than average proportion of dwellings from the rented sectors, nearly 42% compared with under 32% for the stock as a whole. As energy ratings were not calculated in the 1986 EHCS, the original energy efficiency of the sample is unknown. However, the fact that 31% lacked central heating in 1986, and four fifths are pre 1964 dwellings with three-quarters of these built before the war, suggests generally low pre-improvement ratings. By 1991, only 15% remained without central heating. Their mean SAP rating of 37 was now above average, particularly for their age and tenure, although somewhat below that achievable with the improvement options described above.

19.34 Table 19.8 shows that in nearly two thirds of cases, the post-improvement spot temperatures of 1991 were higher than those recorded in 1986. A similar proportion had higher fuel consumption and fuel expenditure in 1991, around 70% of these also having higher temperatures. Overall, the mean living room and hall temperatures were some 1°C and 1.5°C higher respectively. Despite warmer weather in 1991 than 1986, the average annual fuel consumption was around 24,000 kWh or nearly 20% higher after improvement, the main increase being in the use of gas. (Figure 19.9)

Table 19.8 **Comparison of actual energy consumption and temperature changes**

sample number/(% of total sample)

	Main living room temperature		Hall/ stairs temperature		Total sample
	1991<86	1991>86	1991<86	1991>86	
Fuel consumption					
1991>86	31 (18)	78 (45)	33 (19)	76 (44)	109 (63)
1991<86	32 (19)	31 (18)	32 (19)	31 (18)	63 (37)
Fuel expenditure					
1991>86	31 (18)	74 (43)	37 (22)	68 (39)	105 (61)
1991<86	32 (19)	35 (20)	28 (16)	39 (23)	67 (39)
Total sample	63 (37)	109 (63)	65 (38)	107 (62)	172 (100)

Figure 19.9   Comparison of average temperatures and energy consumption in 1986 and 1991

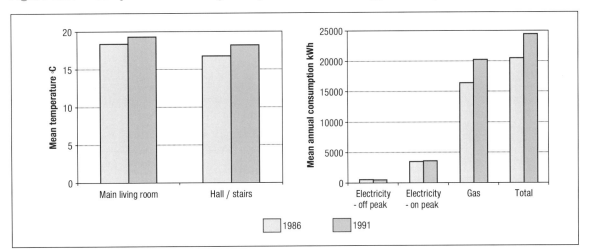

Household changes

19.35 Just over a quarter of households were new residents on generally above average income. These dwellings show the greatest increase in fuel consumption, expenditure and overall home temperatures, the previous generally low income occupants having had low room temperatures and a particularly low mean fuel consumption in 1986. On average, existing households were using 14% more fuel in 1991 than in 1986, but because many had switched to cheaper fuels, their increase in fuel expenditure was less. (Table 19.9)

Table 19.9   Mean fuel consumption, expenditure and temperatures before improvement (in 1986) and after (in 1991) by length of residence in 1991

Fuel use and temperatures in 1986 & 1991		Length of residence in 1991		Total house- holds
		New households Up to 4 years	Existing households 5 years or more	
Mean fuel	1986	16,996	21,777	20,536
consumption	1991	23,399	24,852	24,472
(kWh)	*% increase*	*37.6*	*14.1*	*19.2*
Mean fuel	1986[1]	452	585	550
expenditure	1991	589	627	617
(£)	*% increase*	*30.3*	*10.7*	*12.2*
1991 mean income (£)		17,068	12,307	13,552
Mean hall	1986	16.1	17.1	16.8
temp. (°C)	1991	18.3	18.2	18.3

1 at 1991 prices

A look at more comprehensive improvements

19.36 Whilst targeting dwellings of below average SAP ratings and bringing them up to a moderate standard would clearly achieve a significant improvement in energy efficiency and thermal comfort, the analysis above suggests that it is unlikely in the short term to contribute significantly to any campaign to reduce domestic energy consumption. The question remains, however, whether improving the stock to a much higher standard than was achieved in this EHCS sample, or would be achievable with the limited options dealt with earlier, could yield significant real energy savings.

Summary of costs and benefits

19.37 Table 19.10 summarises the likely impacts and costs of more comprehensive upgrading, aiming for target SAP ratings of 70 or 100.

Several different options are considered for the first of these, taking in dwellings with initial ratings below 10, below 20, below 30 and below 50: for the second it is assumed all dwellings in the stock would be included.

19.38 A target rating of 70 gives in the best case a theoretical saving in heating costs of 52%: this compares with 33%, which is the best that can be achieved with a target rating of 30. (see Table 19.4) This saving derives from the dramatic improvement in mean SAP rating for the stock as a whole from 35.4 to 69.3 which leaves not much more than a third of the stock below the target rating of 70. However, the total capital cost of improvement goes up dramatically - from around £31 billion to £92 billion.

Table 19.10   Summary of costs and impact of improvement programmes to achieve target SAP ratings of 70 and 100

Target SAP rating		70			100
SAP rating of dwellings in programme	<10	<20	<30	<50	<100
Number of dwellings in programme (000s)	1,241	2,844	5,840	16,089	19,086
% of stock in programme	6.5	14.9	30.6	84.3	100.0
Mean cost per dwelling in programme (£)	5,864	5,880	5,948	5,700	7,075
Total cost of programme (£b)	7.3	16.7	34.7	91.7	135.0
Mean SAP rating before improvement } dwellings in programme	-2.8	7.5	17.0	31.4	35.4
} over whole stock	35.4	35.4	35.4	35.4	35.4
Mean SAP rating after improvement } dwellings in programme	68.9	69.8	69.6	71.6	75.9
} over whole stock	40.1	44.6	51.5	69.3	75.9
% of dwellings not reaching target } dwellings in programme	43	37	37	26	99
} over whole stock	96	90	81	37	99
% notional stock savings in heating costs	10	17	27	52	59
Predicted actual % savings on heating[1] } dwellings in programme	13	3	4	5	4
} over whole stock	0	0	1	4	4
Predicted total % savings in fuel costs[2] } dwellings in programme	17	4	5	7	4
} over whole stock	0	0	1	6	6

1 Estimated from the regression based relationships
2 Assuming the non-heating components of fuel remain unchanged

19.39 Analysis taking into account occupants behaviour, however, suggests that these theoretical savings are unlikely to be realised in practice. A target of 70 gives a real saving in energy among those dwellings improved, which is slightly greater than that predicted for a target of 30 (Table 19.7). However the benefit for the stock as a whole is not significantly greater.

Comprehensive improvement of whole stock

19.40 The most comprehensive of all improvements examined, which aims for a target rating of 100, could achieve a theoretical saving in heating costs of almost 60% (Table 19.10). The regression approach to the prediction of changes in expenditure following upgrading becomes dubious in this instance since there are so few dwellings with very high SAP ratings in the current stock on which to base predictions. However, the evidence that expenditure on fuel does not vary much with rating in this region (see Figure 19.10) suggests that there will not be dramatic savings to be made. Following the use of even the most comprehensive packages, many dwellings would remain well below the target of 100, the final rating for the whole stock of 76 being not that much greater than the 69 achieved with a SAP target of 70. Yet the total capital cost would be around £135 billion.

19.41 The conclusion has to be drawn that massive upgrading programmes relying upon the sort of energy saving measures which are currently in use will improve the energy efficiency of the stock dramatically. But they are unlikely to bring about a corresponding reduction in energy usage, and would be very costly.

Reducing energy 'wastage'

19.42 A potentially more cost effective approach to achieving energy conservation and reducing CO_2 emissions might be to target 'over-consumption' - that is the wastage of energy by careless usage, the adoption of excessively high room temperatures and use of inefficient appliances.

Actual expenditure compared to heating and other costs

19.43 The expenditure on fuel required for space and water heating can be calculated from the SAP rating and floor area and represents the sum needed to maintain the standard heating regime, given the dwelling's current heating system and thermal characteristics. The expenditure required for lighting, cooking and other appliances can be estimated from the floor area and/or number of persons in the household using the relevant equations in the Building Research Establishment Domestic Energy Model (BREDEM-12). (see Annex C, paras C.29-32)

Absolute costs

19.44 These two theoretical annual expenditures, one for heating and one for appliances, are shown in Figure 19.10, together with the actual total fuel expenditure of households, against the SAP rating of the dwelling. The mean theoretical heating cost per household falls sharply as the energy rating increases (as by definition it must), while the mean expenditure on appliances rises gradually. The mean actual expenditure of households is fairly constant over the range of SAP ratings, and is in fact slightly lower at the lowest values. Far from 'wasting energy', the average household spends appreciably less on fuel than is required to meet the standard heating regime and make reasonable use of appliances. Households living in the least efficient part of the stock do not spend enough to support the heating regime alone. (Table A19.9)

Figure 19.10   Mean actual fuel expenditure compared with appliance and heating costs for standard regime

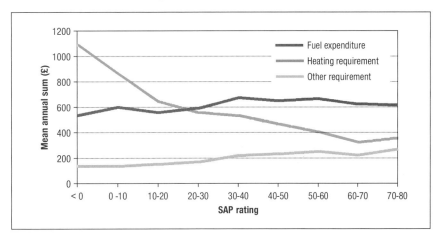

Average 'under-spending' on fuel

19.45 The average level of 'under-spending' by households is shown in Figure 19.11. Only households in dwellings with SAP ratings above 50 tend to spend more than might be expected, and even then the mean difference is slight. Households whose homes are rated below 10 spend on average at least £400 less than required to meet the standard regime. (Table A19.9)

Figure 19.11 Surplus of fuel expenditure over requirement (mean values over all households)

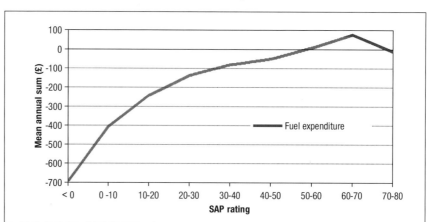

19.46 Figure 19.12 shows the proportion of households in each energy rating band who spend more than the expected sum. Only around 5% of those households in the least efficient housing meet the expectation, but at SAP ratings above 50 the proportion rises to above 50% and peaks at around 70% for households in dwellings rated between 60 and 70. (Table A19.9)

Figure 19.12 Proportion of households spending more on fuel than notional requirement by SAP rating

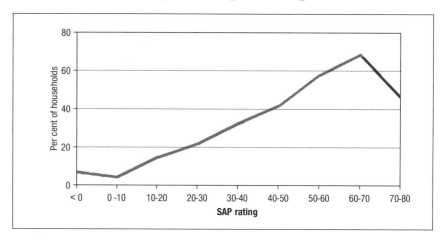

19.47 Figure 19.13 shows for low, intermediate and high SAP ratings the range of 'surplus' expenditure on fuel - that is the actual expenditure less the expenditure required to maintain the standard regime. As energy efficiency improves, the variation in fuel expenditure narrows markedly; with an increasing proportion of households spending close to the required amount. Less than 5% of households in dwellings rated above 60 spend more than £400 a year above that required for the standard heating regime. (Table A19.10)

Total fuel spending relative to costs

19.48 An indication of the possible impact of 'energy wastage' on the stock as a whole may be obtained from Figure 19.14. This shows the total sums of money spent relative to the required costs over the whole stock, rather than the household averages. It therefore sets those relatively few dwellings with very high and very low SAP ratings in the correct perspective, and shows that the overall picture of expenditure is dominated by homes in the SAP range between 30 and 50. Separate plots are shown for those households spending more than the expected sum, and those spending less. The intermediate plot which represents the net spending, shows that the 'under-spend' outweighs any 'over-spend'. The total net 'under-spend'

Figure 19.13 Surplus of actual fuel expenditure over required expenditure

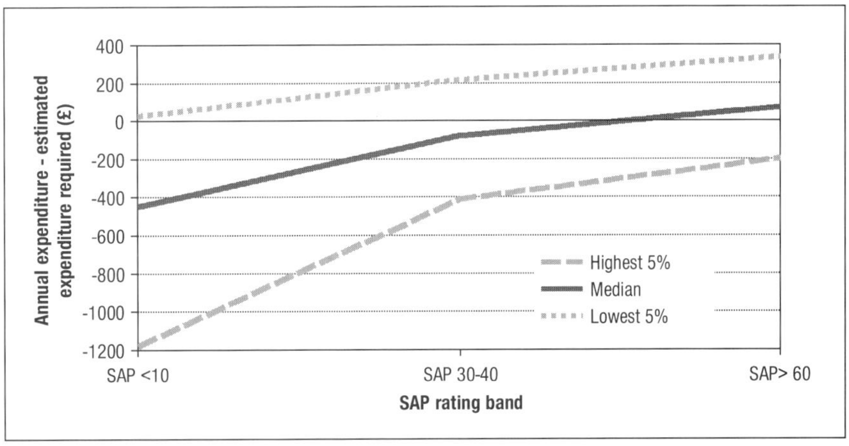

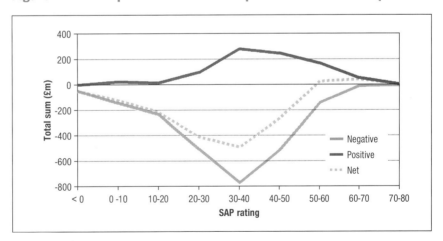

against the cost of the standard regime, for the stock as a whole, amounts to £1,515 million per year and is equivalent to almost 11% of the notional expenditure required.

Scope for energy savings

19.49 If it were possible to achieve energy savings by reducing all high expenditures to just the costs required for the standard heating regime and standard appliance use (that is bringing the uppermost plot in Figure 19.14 to lie along the zero cost line), the annual savings would be around £885 million, equivalent to only a little over 6% of the total expenditure on the stock. Moreover, in practice, a proportion of this 'excess' expenditure has to be regarded as normal variation in the particular requirements of households, which is off-set by some of the 'under-expenditure'. Consequently, any achievable savings would be expected to be considerably less. (Table A19.11)

Figure 19.14 Surplus of annual fuel expenditure over that required

19.50 The fact that there is considerable net 'under-spending' even amongst households whose homes are reasonably efficient (with SAP ratings of 40 or more), suggests that many occupants are already economising by accepting lower standards of heating than might be regarded as reasonable, or by making less use of standard household appliances.

Gains in affordable warmth

19.51 Whilst the opportunities for energy conservation appear limited and greatest in homes of already above average SAP ratings, in the least efficient housing even moderate improvements in energy efficiency would provide affordable warmth to many of the most vulnerable households.

Benefits relative to household income

19.52 Table 19.11 shows the gains in affordable warmth provided by the four improvement options (in Table 19.4), aimed at raising the SAP rating of all dwellings to a minimum of 30. It shows the effect of improving all dwellings with existing SAP ratings below 10, 20, 30 and 50 respectively. Lack of affordable warmth is measured in terms of the % of households who would need to spend more than 10 or 15% of their income to meet the total fuel costs associated with the standard heating regime. The mean % of income needed is also given (in brackets), as is the average SAP rating of the total stock before and after improvement, and the total capital cost of the works in each case.

Table 19.11   Potential impact on the % of income needed for the standard regime of a range of improvement options

(mean %) column % of households		Before improv- ement	After improving all dwellings with existing SAP ratings:-			
			< 10	< 20	< 30	< 50
% of income for standard regime *(Mean % income needed)*		*(10.8)*	*(9.5)*	*(9.1)*	*(8.6)*	*(7.6)*
% of hholds needing:-	10 to 15% of income	15.0	14.7	14.9	15.1	13.1
	15% plus of income	20.1	16.4	14.6	12.1	9.5
Average SAP for all stock		35.4	38.4	40.6	43.9	53.2
Capital costs (£b)			**2.4**	**5.1**	**10.8**	**31.1**

Overall gains

19.53 The greater the number of dwellings included for improvement, the larger the number of households provided with affordable warmth, although there are diminishing returns. For example, improving all dwellings with ratings below 20 reduces the number of households needing to spend 15% or more of their income on fuel by over a quarter (from 20 to under 15%). However, to halve this number (to under 10%) requires the improvement of all dwellings rated below 50.

Gains by tenure

19.54 For any particular option, the reduction in heating costs and consequent gains in affordable warmth varies with tenure. (Table A19.12) Figure 19.15 shows the proportion of households in each tenure who would need to spend 15% or more of their income, and how this declines as the SAP

Figure 19.15   Percentage of households in each tenure needing over 15% of income to achieve standard heating regime for each programme

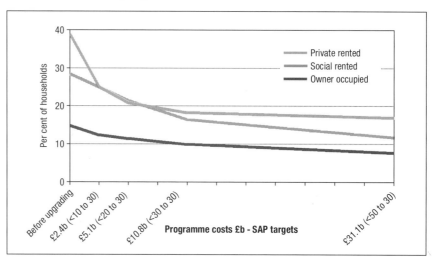

rating is raised. In all tenures, achieving a progressive reduction becomes increasingly more costly. For example, whilst dealing with all dwellings with ratings below 20 almost halves the number of private tenants who would need to spend more than 15% of their income, the more extensive programmes achieve increasingly disappointing gains in affordable warmth.

Benefits relative to fuel expenditure

Overall gains

19.55 As discussed in Chapter 11, affordable warmth may also be measured in terms of the adequacy of present actual fuel expenditure relative to the expenditure required to achieve the minimum heating regime. Because of its lower heating standard and the large number of households already spending over 10% or 15% of their income on fuel, this is generally a less stringent test than that concerned with the proportion of income required to achieve the standard regime. On this criterion, even the smallest programmes show significant benefits in affordable warmth.

19.56 Table 19.12 shows the benefits of the improvements set out in Table 19.11 in terms of the proportion of households 'over-spending' or 'under-spending' relative to the fuel costs of the minimum heating regime.[1] Improving only those dwellings with ratings below 10 reduces by nearly 30% the total number of homes (over 3 million) where existing fuel spending falls severely (over 30%) below the required costs. As the number lacking affordable warmth declines, so the percentage of households spending significantly (over 10%) more than required for the minimum regime increases, enabling these households to achieve higher, more comfortable home temperatures for the same fuel expenditure.

Table 19.12 Potential impact on the adequacy of existing fuel expenditure of a range of improvement programmes

column % of households		Before improv-ement	After improving all dwellings with existing SAP ratings:-			
			< 10	< 20	< 30	< 50
Adequacy of spend for min. regime						
% of Hholds spending	Over 10% more	34.3	40.9	43.4	48.8	64.9
	Within 10%	26.5	26.1	26.4	26.0	21.1
	10 to 30% less	22.9	21.4	20.7	17.9	9.5
	Over 30% less	16.3	11.6	9.5	7.3	4.5
Average SAP for all stock		35.4	38.4	40.6	43.9	53.2
Capital costs (£b)			**2.4**	**5.1**	**10.8**	**31.1**

Gains by type of household

19.57 The extent of potential gains also varies with the type of household, the greatest benefit from any particular improvement programme being generally amongst those originally in the worst conditions. Figure 19.16 shows for the groups least and most lacking affordable warmth (small families and lone pensioners respectively), the potential reductions in the number of households whose fuel expenditure is more than 30% below the total costs required for the minimum heating regime. Improving only dwellings rated below 10 reduces the number of small families so 'under-spending' by a fifth, but reduces the much larger problem experienced by lone pensioners by a third (from 33 to 22%). However, to reduce the extent of 'under-spending' by such pensioners by a further third (from 22 to

1 *For the purposes of this analysis, it is assumed that the actual fuel expenditure of households, including the non-heating costs, remain unchanged after improvement - there is some evidence that this happens in practice.*

15%) would require the improvement of all dwellings below 30 and by yet a further third (from 15 to 10%) improvement of all those below 50.

Figure 19.16 Percentage of lone pensioners and small families under-spending by over 30% re. the minimum heating regime for each programme

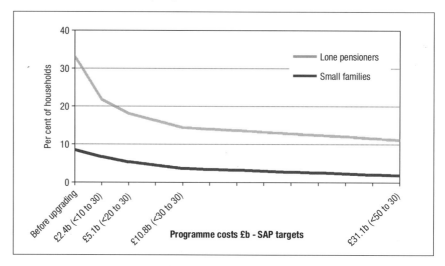

19.58 For each set of dwellings improved, raising the target SAP rating, for example from 30 to 70, increases the number of households provided with affordable warmth, but by no means in proportion with the much higher capital costs involved. (Table A19.13)

Conclusion

19.59 The conclusion to be drawn is that, in the shorter term, the main benefit from improving the energy efficiency of the housing stock will probably lie in providing affordable warmth, particularly to those households currently in the least efficient housing. The benefits of improvements in energy efficiency generally are likely to be taken in higher home temperatures and increased comfort with, at best, small savings in energy consumption. Some further savings in consumption may be achieved by reducing waste among those households, mainly in already reasonably efficient dwellings, who are the highest consumers.

Overview and conclusions

Preamble

20.1 *This final chapter provides an overview of the survey findings, bringing together the main issues examined independently in the previous parts and chapters of the Report, and draws some conclusions. It starts by summarising the scope for improving the energy efficiency and thermal performance of the housing stock. The chapter goes on to compare the potential improvement costs with existing levels of spending. It concludes by examining the potential for energy savings and gains in affordable warmth and ends with a brief, longer-term view.*

Scope for improvement

20.2 It is clear from the findings of the 1991 EHCS that there remains, in all tenures, considerable scope for improvement in the energy efficiency and thermal performance of the housing stock. This is demonstrated throughout the Report in a number of separate analyses: of heating facilities and thermal insulation; energy efficiency; household standards, fuel expenditure and affordable warmth; home temperatures; damp and mould and satisfaction with heating.

Physical standards

Heating facilities and insulation

20.3 Whilst over 4 out of 5 dwellings now have central heating systems, around a quarter of these are older, ducted air, under-floor or solid fuel systems, lacking controls and/or are only partial, usually 'half-house' installations. Nearly 0.3 million systems (under 2%) are not actually used. When these are added to dwellings without central heating, the majority of which have either inefficient or only partial heating, it is probable that a third or more of the total stock has heating facilities which, in practice, cannot physically meet the demands of the standard, full-house, heating regime. Even where the heating system is efficient, heat losses are often high, most of the stock falling well below modern insulation standards; some 30%, including many large dwellings owned by higher income households, have uninsulated solid masonry walls.

Energy efficiency

20.4 With an average SAP rating of only 35, the vast majority of the existing housing stock falls well below modern Building Regulation standards of energy efficiency which typically give SAP ratings of 70 or above. Apart from the private rented stock, around 1 in 6 dwellings in each sector have relatively high SAP ratings of 50 or above. However, less than 6% of any sector could be said to be energy efficient, having ratings over 60. (Figure 20.1)

20.5 Much of the stock is particularly inefficient. Although the owner occupied sector fares well in relative terms, it nevertheless has the highest number of properties with SAP ratings below 20 of any tenure - over 1.3 million. Together, however, the three rented sectors have a higher number of such dwellings. The local authority and housing association sectors account respectively for some 0.7 and 0.1 million of the least efficient dwellings, whilst the private rented sector includes a further 0.7 million dwellings with SAP ratings below 20.

Figure 20.1   Relative size of stocks with different SAP ratings by tenure

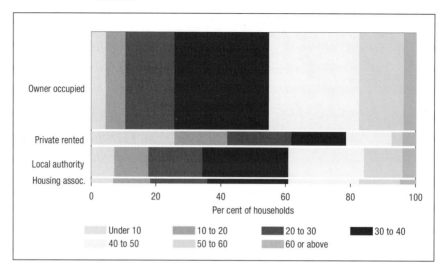

Households and standards

20.6 With a mean SAP rating of under 22, the private rented sector stands out as being exceptionally inefficient, more than half of the total urban stock being without central heating and around a fifth of these lacking any form of fixed heating. This sector houses a significant number of vulnerable households; for example, over a quarter million homes (15%) are privately rented by lone pensioners. These have an average SAP rating of only 11; 70% lack central heating and 10% are without any fixed heating.

20.7 In all sectors, pensioner households and lone adults tend to live in less energy efficient homes than family households and younger couples. This is due to their concentration in the least energy efficient house types, such as bungalows and older terraced houses, as well as their over-representation in the least improved dwellings of any particular type. However, such households stand a better chance of being housed in more energy efficient housing, particularly in newer houses and flats, in the social rented than in the private sector.

Thermal performance

Fuel expenditure and affordable warmth

20.8 Many households in all sectors lack affordable warmth and, in large part, this is attributable to the poor energy efficiency of the stock. The majority of households (over 55%) are spending less than is required to achieve the full standard regime, and nearly 2 out of 5 are 'under-spending' relative to the low standard of the minimum regime. The proportion of households under-spending is directly related to the energy efficiency of their homes; only 10% of those in dwellings with SAP ratings of 60 or above are significantly under-spending relative to the minimum regime, compared to over half of those in homes rated between 20 and 30 and over 80% in homes rated under 10. There is some evidence that even high earners are 'under-spending' if they live in inefficient housing. The same pattern holds true in the social rented sectors where there is generally less divergence in income between those in high and low energy efficient dwellings.

20.9 Many of those in inefficient homes avoid using much fuel, often adopting irregular heating regimes, either due to force of habit or more consciously for fear of incurring very high fuel bills. These include many pensioners, who are most at risk not only because of their increased frailty but also because their age makes them physiologically less sensitive to cold. In total, over 60% of such households are clearly 'under-spending' relative to the minimum heating regime, 1 in 3 lone pensioners spending less than 70% of the costs required to achieve the standard. Other low income households, particularly lone parents, appear more willing to commit a substantial proportion of their income to fuel (16% on average) although even then not always achieving adequate heating regimes.

Home
temperatures

20.10 The lack of adequate spending relative to the two notional heating regimes is directly reflected in the spot temperatures recorded during the survey. Even after being heated for over 1 hour, under 1 in 4 homes fully met the temperatures of the standard regime. Nearly 30% of all homes, where the heating had been on for an hour or more, 'failed' the temperatures of the minimum regime. Again the likelihood of the household meeting these temperatures very much depends on the energy efficiency of their home, nearly half of those with SAP ratings under 20 failing the home temperatures specified by the minimum regime, compared with under a tenth of those rated 50 or over.

20.11 Generally, thermal conditions have improved as a result of energy measures carried out since 1986. However, it is clear that, despite the relatively mild weather during the 1991 survey, there remains a very strong correlation between internal and external temperatures. For example, with a fall in the external temperature from under 10°C to under 4°C, the proportion of dwellings failing the minimum regime increases from under a third in each sector to 50% in the owner occupied stock, 62% in council housing and 95% in the, generally inefficient, private rented sector.

Damp and
mould

20.12 Much of the stock still suffers from damp and mould growth. Rising and penetrating damp occurs predominantly in the older, poorer stock; affecting 20% of private rented dwellings compared to only between 5 to 7% of the other sectors. Condensation and mould is associated as much with social factors. Large, low income families in less efficient dwellings are the most likely to report the problem. Over half the dwellings affected are now owner occupied, although the incidence of mould growth remains highest in the rented sectors.

Satisfaction
with heating

20.13 Although there is a correlation between cold homes and dissatisfaction with heating, the overall level of satisfaction is high given the generally poor thermal conditions in the stock. It is clear that owner occupiers are often not inclined to complain and, in all tenures, this is particularly true of pensioner households who generally spend very little on fuel and have some of the coldest homes. Where households are dissatisfied, their overwhelming complaint is about the lack of heat, nearly a half complaining about insufficient heat or only partial heating and a further quarter about problems with the system, most of which could affect its output. By comparison only 20% of those dissatisfied are primarily concerned with the cost of heating.

Improvement
costs and
current
spending

20.14 Despite the considerable investment in energy related work over the last twenty years, it is clear that there remains a great deal left to be done. The Survey findings suggest that a 30% reduction in standardised heating costs - but not in actual energy consumption - could be achieved, at least in the rented sectors, in 10 to 15 years with existing levels of expenditure - provided this was appropriately targeted.

Table 20.1   Capital expenditure required for 30% improvement in notional heating costs (*minimum cost options*)

	Local authority	Housing association	Owner occupied	Private rented
Major spending 1987-91				
Av. dwellings affected per year (000s)	200.6	14.8	1,233.1	-
Total energy related work (£b)	1.95	0.21	14.8	0.75
Relevant annual spend (£b)	**0.3**	**0.03**	**1.6**	**0.1**
Minimum cost option				
Dwellings improved (000s)	2,300	340	10,000	500
Costs per dwelling in stock (£)	1,000	900	1,600	650
Total improvement costs (£b)	**3.9**	**0.5**	**20.8**	**1.1**
Duration at present levels of spending (yrs)	13	16	13	11

Social rented sector

20.15 In the five years 1986 to 1991, local authorities spent £1.95 billion or some 38% of the total capital expenditure on their own stock on energy-related works. However, some £0.65 billion of this went on double glazing and was probably aimed primarily at replacing rotten or other obsolete window frames. Assuming only a third of this item was truly energy related, the average annual expenditure is reduced to some £0.3 billion. At such a level of spending, a 30% improvement in energy efficiency - costing £3.9 billion - would take around 13 years to achieve. With the same assumptions, a similar 30% improvement in the housing association stock could be achieved with 1986 to 1991 levels of spending in just over 16 years. These crude calculations, however, assume that all local authorities and housing associations adopt the same minimum cost strategy - tackling the majority of their dwellings (with SAP ratings below 40) and improving them up to only a moderate rating (generally between 30 and 50) at an average cost of around £900 to £1,000 per dwelling in the sector. (Table 20.1)

Owner occupied sector

20.16 Between 1986 and 1991, owner occupiers spent around £14.8 billion on energy related 'major' works, but nearly two thirds of this went on double glazing and fireplaces. Again assuming only a third of this item was truly energy-related, reduces the average annual spend to some £1.6 billion, although there is evidence that spending increased over this period. The ratio of this spend to the potential programme costs of £20.8 billion is 1/13 - similar to that for the local authority stock. However, in the owner occupied sector there is not only a greater mismatch between the distribution of spending and the needs of the stock, but also little or no opportunity for a direct redistribution of such expenditure.

Private rented sector

20.17 Spending by private landlords on all energy related works between 1986 and 1991 is estimated at £0.75 billion, of which £0.36 billion was for double glazing. Again reducing the latter as for the other tenures, gives a relevant average spending of some £0.1 billion per annum, compared to the potential programme costs for the sector of £1.1 billion. Due to the generally low efficiency of the stock, the mismatch between spending and needs is likely to be less here, and the significantly lower overall improvement costs (£650 per dwelling in the stock compared with £1,600 per owner occupier) may also improve the possibilities for appropriate action.

Household motivation and finances

Other work

20.18 Generally, it will be most cost effective to carry out energy efficiency measures as part of other work, the latter sometimes presenting the real motivation for improvement. Thus, in the owner occupied sector, works such as extensions and loft conversions as well as the replacement of old window frames with double glazed units are likely to contribute to improved energy efficiency, albeit undertaken primarily for other reasons. In the social rented sectors over two thirds of energy conservation expenditure currently takes place within wider schemes of general modernisation and repair. That said, in much of the stock, the major problem is poor energy efficiency alone. Although unfitness and substantial disrepair correlate with poor efficiency, only one in six of all dwellings with SAP ratings below 20 are unfit, and half have no defects at all relevant to unfitness or serious disrepair.

Payback periods

20.19 Except for those households in the least energy efficient dwellings there is likely to be little financial motivation to undertake energy improvements per se. Energy measures on dwellings with SAP ratings greater than 20 generally have 'simple payback periods' (for the recovery of implementation costs by savings in fuel expenditure) of 10 years or more. Such periods are unlikely to be judged as offering a realistic return on investment.

Thermal comfort

20.20 The motivation for improvement, therefore, has to come from the desire for increased comfort. The nature of energy related work in recent years, particularly the growth of central heating, as well as the attitudes of householders, does suggest that for many the main motivation is increased warmth rather than any savings in fuel bills. This may suggest changes to the way energy measures are promoted, with a greater emphasis being placed on the benefits in comfort and convenience rather than on savings in fuel consumption and expenditure.

Energy conservation

Impact of improvements

20.21 Theoretical calculations have suggested that there are considerable savings in energy consumption and CO_2 emissions to be had from improvements in energy efficiency. However, these largely assume that the same standard heating regimes are employed both before and after improvement. The findings from the 1991 EHCS show that, in practice, the opportunities for energy conservation in the domestic sector are very limited.

Fuel expenditure

20.22 Figure 20.2 shows, for different levels of energy efficiency, the spread in total fuel spending either side of the mean (lowest and highest quintile ranges), and compares this with the equivalent costs of achieving a heating standard within plus or minus 10% of the standard regime. Although there is somewhat less spread in the better stock, the level of spending per square metre remains remarkably constant throughout, the majority of households spending between some £6 and £12/sq. m., regardless of the efficiency of their home.

Expenditure after improvement

20.23 The vast majority of households living in homes of below average efficiency are spending substantially less than that required to achieve the standard heating regime, many having sub-standard home temperatures. Evidence suggests that when these homes are improved to average or moderately high SAP ratings, overall spending tends to fall by only a very small margin. On improvement, households with previously below average expenditure tend to increase their spending with new opportunities for whole house

Figure 20.2   Actual fuel expenditure and expenditure needed to achieve the standard heating regime and run standard appliances, by energy efficiency

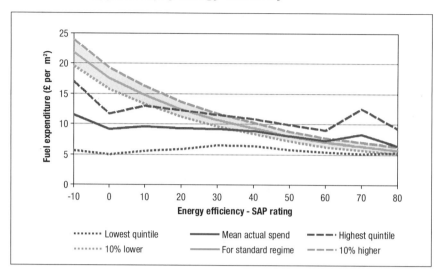

heating and the fear of excessively high fuel bills removed. Such households, including many who have traditionally been content to live with inefficient heating facilities and low thermal standards, appear more than willing to maintain, or even raise their level of spending to achieve the comfortable conditions now within their grasp. However, such increases are offset by savings amongst those currently allocating very high proportions of their income to fuel (generally those above the £12 horizontal in Figure 20.2).

Cost of higher standards

Costs per dwelling

20.24 Only if dwellings are improved to well above average efficiency might it be possible to achieve the standard regime with reduced levels of fuel spending, and so allow a saving in energy consumption. However, higher improvement standards would have major cost implications. Figure 20.3 shows that the average improvement cost per dwelling generally trebles from under £2,000 for a target rating of 30 to around £6,000 for a rating of 70.

Figure 20.3   Average improvement cost per dwelling for increasing improvement standards

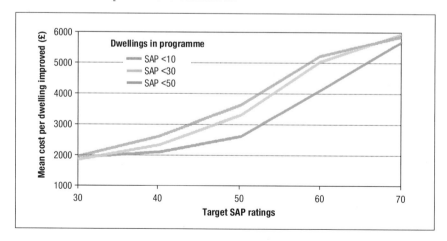

Costs over whole stock

20.25 The cost of attempting to achieve a high level of energy efficiency within the stock as a whole is shown in Figure 20.4. This plots the total improvement costs against the percentage reduction in notional heating costs over the whole stock for five sets of improvement programmes, involving all dwellings with SAP ratings (1) under 10 to (5) under 50, and for target improvement levels ranging from SAP 30 at the bottom of each curve to SAP 70 at the top. As shown on the figure, a theoretical reduction in fuel costs for heating of 30% could be obtained (by improving all dwellings with a SAP rating below 40 to a target rating of around 45) for a cost of under £27 billion. A reduction of 50%, giving a notional 30% saving in total energy consumption, would cost over £80 billion. The greater the total reduction sought, the greater the 'unit cost', the above two options corresponding to around £0.8 billion and £1.5 billion respectively for every percentage reduction in the notional heating cost. (Table A20.1)

Figure 20.4   Total programme costs by notional savings in heating costs

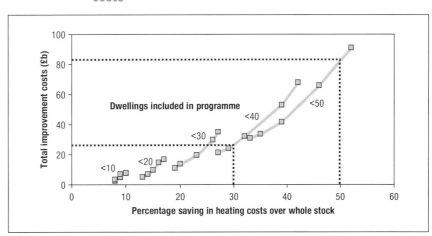

Energy savings

20.26 How the dramatic improvements in energy efficiency which could be obtained from a massive investment in the stock would, in practice, translate into real savings in energy consumption is difficult to assess - there is so little information on the behaviour of occupants of very efficient dwellings. However, what evidence there is (see Figure 20.2) suggests that fuel expenditure holds up even in dwellings with SAP ratings of 70 or over, which would indicate that energy savings are likely to be disproportionately poor.

Reducing 'wastage'

Motivation for savings

20.27 Some fuel savings might be possible by reducing energy 'wastage'. However, only in dwellings of already above average efficiency are a substantial proportion of households currently spending more than required for the standard heating regime. Whilst a saving in energy consumption might be possible here, there is likely to be little motivation for either behavioural changes or further improvements - lack of heat rather than the cost of heating being the main concern of all but the lowest income households. Households in this portion of the stock are, with the exception of those in the best social rented housing, generally those on high incomes, who despite their very warm homes, heavy use of appliances and large fuel bills, are usually spending a relatively small amount of their income on fuel - on average between only 5 and 8%.

20.28 The lack of motivation of this group is confirmed by the recorded attitudes of householders. Well over 90% of those in dwellings with SAP ratings over 50 and two thirds of all others say they have no intention of undertaking future action. Whilst tenants do not regard it as their responsibility, most owner occupiers have already improved their insulation in some way and see no need for further action or cannot afford more expensive measures.

Higher heating standards

20.29 Satisfaction with heating is generally very high and the implication is that the majority of households in the most efficient housing, who can easily achieve warm homes at relatively low cost, have expectations of home temperatures higher than those of even the standard regime. This conclusion is supported by the distribution of living room and hall spot temperatures in homes of different energy efficiency. (Figure 20.5). Whilst even in the most efficient housing the average living room falls below 21°C, the hall - and by implication the far larger heating zone comprising the rest of the dwelling[1] - is generally being heated to a higher temperature than a standard 18°C. In part, this may reflect the increasing tendency in many higher income households, for each individual member, particularly younger members, to effectively use their bedrooms as 'living rooms', with their own television, computer and other appliances.

Figure 20.5   Mean living room and hall spot temperatures by SAP ratings

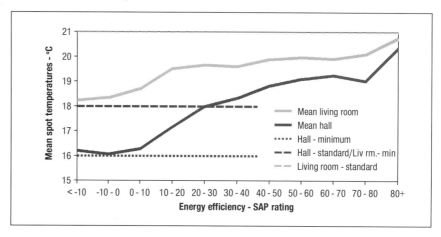

Savings from heating

20.30 That said, the survey also shows a relatively poor provision of heating controls, their inefficient use by owners and tenants as well as the occasional incidence of excessively high home temperatures. With a view to further energy savings, this clearly suggests the need for better controls, combined with increased advice and awareness amongst households in all sectors of the stock. However, potential savings are small, due to the relatively few households who are in such warm properties and/or who are spending substantially more than required for the standard heating regime. In total, around a third of the total population are spending more, but most only marginally so, and if all reduced their heating requirements to that of the standard regime, the overall saving in fuel expenditure would be no greater than 6% - well under 5% probably being a more realistic saving.

Other possible savings

20.31 In order to maximise energy saving, it will be necessary to also reduce the non-heating component of fuel usage. While the power taken by lighting and domestic appliances makes a relatively small contribution to overall fuel usage among the least efficient dwellings (less than 20% for those with SAP ratings below 20), it can account for more than a half in very efficient dwellings.

---

1   *The hall is the normal location of any room thermostat and has been shown to provide a proxy for the mean of all rooms (see Annex C, para. C.5)*

Affordable warmth

20.32 The two central aims of energy efficiency policies - of achieving energy conservation on the one hand and affordable warmth on the other - tend to affect very different sectors of the housing stock. Even moderate improvements in energy efficiency would yield very important benefits in terms of providing affordable warmth to the poorest homes.

Overall gains

20.33 Figure 20.6 shows the gains in affordable warmth across all households provided by four potential improvements aimed at giving the improved dwellings a minimum SAP rating of 30. In this graph, affordable warmth is measured in terms of the number of households whose existing fuel expenditure falls significantly (over 10%) short of that required to achieve the minimum heating regime. On this criterion, even the most modest improvements show very large benefits in affordable warmth. For example, improving only those dwellings with ratings below 10 to a target rating of 30 reduces the total number of households whose existing fuel expenditure is inadequate by nearly 1.2 million.

Figure 20.6   Potential impact on affordable warmth of a range of improvements to achieve a target SAP rating of 30

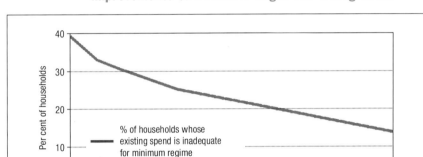

20.34 Generally, the more extensive the improvement the larger the number of households provided with affordable warmth. However, as Figure 20.6 demonstrates, there are diminishing returns as more dwellings with higher SAP ratings are included. While improving all homes rated below 10 reduces by over 16% the proportion of households whose fuel expenditure is inadequate, improving all those rated below 30 (well over four times as many) little more than doubles this figure.

Gains by tenure and type of household

20.35 The extent of potential gains also vary with tenure and the type of household, the greatest benefit from any particular improvement being generally amongst the lowest income households in the least efficient stock. Proportionally, the smallest gains occur in the owner occupied sector and the largest in the private rented stock. In respect of the type of household, the least benefits are to small families and the greatest to lone pensioners. Improving only dwellings rated below 10 would reduce by a third - from 33 to 22% - the large number of lone pensioners severely underspending on fuel (by over 30%) in relation to the total costs of the minimum heating regime.

Implications for housing strategies

20.36 Lack of affordable warmth, however, is by no means eradicated even with the most extensive improvements. As well as very low incomes, this is due to the high levels of under-occupation in much of the stock and the fact that many existing dwellings are not physically capable of being made energy efficient.

Housing management

20.37 As shown in Chapter 11, under-occupation is a major factor contributing to the large number of households lacking affordable warmth. This problem appears particularly acute in council housing, where most cases occur in lower income groups, particularly amongst lone pensioners. This and the fact that many vulnerable tenants are also concentrated in the least energy efficient house types, suggests that allocation policies and housing management may also have a significant role to play in achieving affordable warmth, in addition to any physical improvement of the stock.

Renewal strategies

20.38 The findings show that much of the existing stock is not physically capable of being brought up to a high SAP rating with the heating and insulation measures readily available. For example, whilst even the least efficient dwellings can be improved to a minimum target SAP of 30, over 1 in 5 of all dwellings are not capable of improvement to a SAP rating of 70. Taking all dwellings, only 1% could achieve a full target SAP of 100.

20.39 This problem and the fact that, overall, even the most extensive improvement programmes are unlikely to achieve a substantial reduction in energy consumption, would appear to add weight to the arguments, at least in energy terms, for redevelopment rather than renovation of the worst housing. For the remaining bulk of older housing, all the evidence points to the most cost effective strategies generally being those that aim to improve more dwellings to a moderate standard of energy efficiency, rather than fewer dwellings to a very high standard.

Longer term trends

The last 20 years

20.40 The findings of the 1991 EHCS on the limited opportunities for energy savings are largely supported by longer term trends in energy use, which show a steady increase in fuel consumption over the last 20 years of more than 20%. However, this reflects an increase in the number of households. Energy consumption per household has remained relatively level, albeit fluctuating widely with weather conditions, due to the poor insulation standards. (Figure 20.7) These trends have accompanied a dramatic increase in central heating ownership from only some 35% in 1971 to well over 80%, as well as a substantial growth in the use of domestic appliances.

20.41 Without parallel improvements in insulation standards and in the efficiency of heating and other appliances, it is estimated that fuel consumption could have risen by a further 50%[2]. However, in practice, the extent to which households would be prepared to increase their heating standards, without improvements in energy efficiency to contain their fuel expenditure, is debatable. The EHCS findings suggest that higher heating standards are more the consequence of, rather than the trigger for, improved energy efficiency.

Energy measures

20.42 In the future, the first time installation of full central heating in the existing stock is likely to slow down as ownership reaches saturation, thereby reducing any consequent increase in fuel consumption. However, by the

2   *J. E. Dunster et al, Energy use in the housing stock; Building Research Establishment, Information Paper IP20/94, BRE, 1994*

Figure 20.7   Mean fuel consumption compared to increases in central heating and insulation 1971-1994

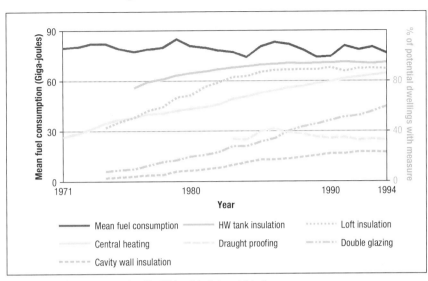

Source: BRE Domestic energy fact file, 1996 update (to be published)

same token, it may also be difficult to sustain the dramatic improvement in insulation standards achieved over the last two decades. In 1976 barely half of all accessible lofts were insulated but within ten years this had risen to 87%. Since 1986 saturation has been reached and the proportion has remained relatively static. The same is true of hot water cylinder insulation. The take-up of cavity wall insulation has been much slower, while the ownership of draught excluders has declined in recent years with the installation of double glazing and other new windows. (Figure 20.7)

20.43 Apart from double glazing, which if often acquired for reasons other than energy efficiency, many owners express reluctance to install further more expensive measures, having already improved their loft and cylinder insulation. Future reductions in fuel costs resulting from a more competitive fuel supply market, while possibly assisting affordable warmth, may further decrease the financial incentive of owners to invest in greater energy efficiency.

CO$_2$ emissions

20.44 While mean energy consumption has remained virtually constant, CO_2 emissions attributable to the domestic sector have steadily declined over the last 20 years, mainly as a result of a switch in fuels for heating away from solid fuels to natural gas. However, whereas in 1971, 1 in 4 homes still had solid fuel as their main form of heating, by 1991 this had dropped to only 1 in 15 - again leaving more limited opportunities for future improvement by this means.

Overall conclusions

20.45 The overall conclusion for energy conservation is that, in the shorter term at least, the main benefit of improved energy efficiency will continue to lie in preventing an escalation in fuel consumption as the result of greater appliance use and the demand - and remaining large potential - for higher heating standards. However, improvements in energy efficiency clearly also have an important role to play in continuing to secure more healthy and comfortable thermal conditions for the very large number of households - many pensioner households and other vulnerable groups in every sector of the housing stock - who continue to lack affordable warmth.

A n n e x

Main tables

Sample sizes

A.1 In the tables, the accuracy of the estimates depends largely on the sample sizes used in the analysis. The code at the foot of each table indicates the total sample size to which the particular estimates refer (See Table AA.1 overleaf). However, because of stratified sampling, this sample number is not necessarily distributed within each table in proportion to the grossed figures.

A.2 In a number of tables, individual cells contain small numbers. Although reliable conclusions cannot be drawn from very small cell sizes, these have been included for completeness. Appendix C of the first EHCS Report[1] provides an indication of the confidence limits associated with different estimates derived from the physical and full interview surveys. A description of the survey samples, grossing procedure and treatment of estimates used specifically in the analysis of the energy data is given in Annex C (paras C.2-20) of this report.

Conventions used

A.3 All dwelling and household numbers have been rounded to the nearest thousand and, consequently, there may be small differences in some tables between the sum of the constituent numbers and the grand totals shown. Because of rounding, row or column percentages may also not add up to 100% precisely.

A.4 In the tables, the following symbols are used

-   Category not applicable

*   Sample is too small for estimate to be produced

0   No cases found in the survey, stock estimates less than 0.05%

---

1 *Department of the Environment, 1993, op.cit.*

AA.1 Description and size of samples used in analyses for main tables

Code	EHCS survey part	Sample description	Sample number[1]
For dwelling estimates			
P1	Physical sample	all occupied dwellings (dwelling totals only)[2]	20,292
P2		occupied dwellings with full survey	13,986
P3		occupied houses with full survey	10,749
Hp1	Interview sample[3]	all occupied dwellings	9,910
Ep1	Energy sub-sample[3]	all occupied dwellings	4,933
Ep2		occupied dwellings with central heating	3,975
Sp1	SAP model sample[3]	all occupied dwellings	9,199
Sp2		occupied dwellings with SAP rating <10	730
Sp3		occupied dwellings with SAP rating <20	1,619
Sp4		occupied dwellings with SAP rating <30	3,197
Sp5		occupied dwellings with SAP rating <50	7,991
Q1	LA postal sample	LA dwellings with work done	3,112
Q2	HA postal sample	HA dwellings with work done	513
For household estimates			
H1	Interview sample	all households[2]	9,965
H2		households in most and least efficient dwellings	3,765
H3		households in most common dwelling types	1,098
H4		households with washing appliances	8,643
H5		households with Economy 7	1,501
H6		households in homes with mould growth	2,525
H7		all owner occupiers	5,535
H8		all tenant households	4,430
E1	Energy sub-sample	all households	4,942
E2		households with central heating	3,981
E3		households without central heating	981
E4		households not using central heating	70
E5		households with heating complaint	741
E6		households, all 'improvers'	2,563
E7		households, 'improvers' since 1986	1,626
E8		all owner occupiers	2,763
E9		all tenant households	2,180
E10		landlord 'improvers' (for tenants)	912
F1	Fuel survey sample[4]	all households	4,938
F2		households using off-peak electricity	997
F3		households using mains gas	4,029
F4		households using other fuels	789
T1	Temperature sample	all households	4,788
T2		households with living room and hall readings	4,297
T3		as T2 and with attitude ratings	4,253
T4		as T2 and with external readings	4,206
T5		as T2, heated homes with low external readings	3,044
T6		as T5 and with heating complaint	543
S1	SAP model sample	all households	9,210
S2		households in energy sub-sample	4,595
S3		households in temperature sample T2	3,994
S4		households with heating complaint	706
S5		all owner occupiers	5,176

[1] The total sample may include a small % of missing data for some variables

[2] In most tables, total numbers are generated by the full physical or interview surveys (see Annex C, paras. C.15-16)

[3] Some estimates from the Interview Survey have been converted to dwelling estimates (see Annex C para C.18)

[4] Includes imputed fuel consumption data (See Annex C, paras. C.11-12)

A3.1   Comparison of case study dwellings with mean for all households of same type, size and tenure

Case study figures/(mean for household type & size in tenure)

	Case 3.1 LA - 2 pens	Case 3.2 OO - 2p Hhld	Case 3.3 OO - 2p Hhld	Case 3.4 OO - 1p Hhld	All hholds
Physical standards					
Dwelling size m^2	36 (60)	43 (86)	107 (86)	91 (72)	**83**
Space heating	Coal CH	Gas CH	Gas CH	Elec. CH+NCH	
Water heating	Coal CH	Gas CH	Gas CH	Electric NCH	
Insulation^3	L	De	W,L,C,Dg,De	C,Dg	
Energy SAP rating	3 (34)	27 (37)	46 (37)	55 (32)	**35**
Heating price index	117 (104)	88 (94)	89 (94)	110 (107)	**100**
Heat loss index	172 (99)	137 (99)	83 (99)	56 (101)	**100**
Energy consumption					
Cooking fuel	Mains gas	Electricity	Mains gas	Electricity	
Total consumption KWh (000s)	20.7 (15.9)	26.1 (24.8)	33.5 (24.8)	7.54 (18.2)	**24.0**
Unit consumption kWh/m^2	574 (271)	608 (308)	313 (308)	83 (281)	**303**
% gas	10 (63)	90 (69)	88 (69)	0 (61)	**66**
% electricity	20 (29)	10 (23)	12 (23)	100 (30)	**26**
% other fuel	70 (8)	0 (8)	0 (8)	0 (9)	**8**
Unit fuel cost p/kWh	2.90 (3.68)	2.48 (3.02)	2.54 (3.02)	5.53 (3.26)	**3.23**
Total expenditure £	600 (488)	649 (661)	850 (661)	417 (517)	**661**
Unit expenditure £/m^2	16.67 (8.44)	15.09 (8.64)	7.94 (8.64)	4.58 (7.94)	**8.68**
% gas	12 (40)	60 (45)	59 (45)	0 (41)	**43**
% electricity	58 (56)	40 (51)	41 (51)	100 (54)	**53**
% other fuel	30 (4)	0 (4)	0 (4)	0 (5)	**4**
Thermal conditions					
Outside temp °C	8.6 (11.3)	- (10.8)	14.3 (10.8)	14.6 (11.1)	**11.1**
Living room temp °C	18.5 (19.9)	20.7 (19.5)	20.1 (19.5)	20.4 (18.9)	**19.5**
Hall/stairs temp °C	18.2 (18.3)	18.3 (18.4)	18.9 (18.4)	20.6 (17.7)	**18.3**
Mould growth index	0.0 (0.30)	0.0 (0.22)	0.0 (0.22)	0.0 (0.22)	**0.34**
Energy Action					
Adequacy of spend^1	64.8 (84.2)	114.3 (93.9)	101.8 (93.9)	76.0 (83.6)	**87.7**
Target SAP rating	33	53	64	73	-
Improvement cost £	3,430	3,550	2,790	470	-
Energy saving^2 kWh	4,050	6,755	7,655	2,475	-
Cost saving^2 £	271	170	195	135	-
Simple payback yrs	13	21	14	3	-

^{1} Adequacy to achieve standard heating regime

^{2} Assuming standard heating regime and normal energy use for dwelling and household size

^{3} Insulation: W=cavity wall fill, L=loft insulation, C=cylinder insulation, Dg=Double glazing, De=draught stripping.

A4.1 **Main type of heating by extent of heating**

(Row %/k dwellings)

	Percentage of rooms with heating:			Occupied Dwellings
	1 up to 30%	30 up to 70%	70 to 100%	
Central heating				
Mains gas dedicated boiler	0.7	9.3	90.0	9,252
Mains gas back-boiler	2.4	12.0	85.6	2,772
Mains gas ducted-air/conv.	6.3	34.0	59.7	710
All solid fuel	10.6	23.6	65.9	868
All electric	24.8	44.5	30.7	1,443
All other CH	2.6	11.6	85.8	880
Total	**4.8**	**14.7**	**80.5**	**15,925**
Other fixed heating				
Mains gas	47.0	45.2	7.8	2,204
Solid fuel	77.6	20.6	1.8	435
Electric	45.7	42.8	11.5	143
Portable	80.3	14.3	5.4	233
Total				**3,015**

Sample: P2

A4.2 **Main type of heating and extent of heating by tenure**

(Column %/k dwellings)

	Owner occupied	Private rented	Local authority	Housing association	All tenures
a) Heating					
Central heating	89.1	59.7	77.9	81.9	84.1
Fixed appliances	10.4	34.0	20.5	17.2	14.7
Portable or none	0.5	6.4	1.7	1.0	1.2
b) Type of heating					
Central heating					
Mains gas dedicated boiler	56.9	28.3	31.7	42.6	48.8
Mains gas back-boiler	13.5	6.1	22.0	15.4	14.6
Mains gas ducted-air/conv.	3.0	0.8	7.4	3.6	3.7
All solid fuel	4.0	8.2	5.5	1.7	4.6
All electric	6.4	10.4	9.1	16.0	7.6
All fuel oil	5.4	5.8	2.0	2.4	4.6
Non central heating					
Mains gas	8.8	22.6	16.4	13.2	11.6
Solid fuel	1.1	9.3	3.2	3.1	2.3
Electric	0.5	2.2	0.9	0.9	0.8
Portable	0.5	6.4	1.7	1.0	1.2
c) Extent of heating (% of rooms)					
Central heating					
1 up to 30%	4.0	10.7	5.8	6.4	4.8
30 up to 70%	11.0	23.9	23.6	29.3	14.7
70 up to 100%	85.0	65.4	70.7	64.3	80.5
Fixed appliances					
Between 1 & 30%	42.3	54.7	66.3	45.7	51.7
Between 30 & 70%	47.5	41.2	29.4	50.3	41.2
Between 70 & 100%	10.2	4.0	4.3	4.0	7.1
Portable or none					
Between 1 & 30%	79.6	79.8	82.4	74.2	80.3
Between 30 & 70%	20.4	9.8	14.7	25.8	14.3
Between 70 & 100%	0.0	10.4	2.9	0.0	5.4
Occupied dwellings	**12,872**	**1,626**	**3,851**	**591**	**18,940**

Sample: P2

A4.3 Heating type and extent of central heating by location by tenure

(Column %/k dwellings)

	Urban	Suburban	Rural	All locations
Owner Occupier				
a) Heating type				
Central heating	79.3	92.6	91.1	89.1
Fixed appliances	19.9	7.1	8.2	10.4
Portable or none	0.8	0.3	0.8	0.5
b) Extent of central heating				
In 1 to 30% or rooms	4.4	3.6	6.1	4.0
In 30 to 70% of rooms	16.9	9.2	10.3	11.0
In 70 to 100% of rooms	78.7	87.2	83.6	85.0
Private Rented				
a) Heating type				
Central heating	50.7	65.7	65.5	59.7
Fixed appliances	40.2	31.1	27.7	34.0
Portable or none	9.1	3.2	6.8	6.4
b) Extent of central heating				
In 1 to 30% or rooms	2.9	9.3	24.4	10.7
In 30 to 70% of rooms	31.3	18.7	22.6	23.9
In 70 to 100% of rooms	65.8	72.0	53.1	65.4
Local Authority				
a) Heating type				
Central heating	78.3	77.5	82.5	77.9
Fixed appliances	19.1	21.3	16.4	20.5
Portable or none	2.6	1.2	1.1	1.7
b) Extent of central heating				
In 1 to 30% or rooms	5.2	5.7	17.8	5.8
In 30 to 70% of rooms	26.7	22.3	11.3	23.6
In 70 to 100% of rooms	68.1	72.1	70.9	70.7
Housing Association				
a) Heating type				
Central heating	79.5	85.5	81.2	81.9
Fixed appliances	18.9	14.2	18.8	17.2
Portable or none	1.6	0.3	0.0	1.0
b) Extent of central heating				
In 1 to 30% or rooms	8.8	4.1	6.4	6.4
In 30 to 70% of rooms	24.6	33.4	57.1	29.3
In 70 to 100% of rooms	66.6	62.5	36.5	64.3
Occupied dwellings	**5,791**	**9,211**	**3,938**	**18,940**

Sample: P2

A4.4   **Central heating controls**

(Column %/k dwellings)

Central heating control	% of dwellings with central heating with named control
Manual valves on radiators/vents	68.6
TRV's	22.2
Appliance thermostat	15.6
Appliance heat output	7.6
Appliance time switch	9.8
Wall thermostat	59.2
Programmer	78.2
Programmer override	69.3
Over night charge control	2.6
Occupied dwellings with CH	**15,925**

Sample: Ep2

A4.5   Central heating controls by heating system

(Column %/k dwellings)

Heating system/ controls	Gas				Solid		Electric		Oil	Com-	L.P.G.
	dedi-cated boiler with rads	back boiler with rads	duct. air	conv-ectors	dedi-cated boiler with rads	back boiler with rads	other eg under floor/ ceiling	storage		munal and other	
Manual valves on radiators/vents	74.5	77.6	39.2	14.3	63.0	84.2	13.0	18.1	77.4	57.1	88.0
TRV's	28.3	15.3	4.4	3.3	36.0	8.8	5.1	5.9	33.6	21.3	28.8
Appliance thermostat	17.3	14.9	7.2	3.3	26.8	7.5	17.2	10.4	22.3	10.0	22.5
Appliance heat output	6.8	5.6	6.2	0	15.4	7.4	14.8	17.1	10.0	1.5	4.7
Appliance time switch	11.4	8.6	5.5	3.3	9.8	3.1	14.8	6.1	13.1	0	19.8
Wall thermostat	67.9	62.0	7.5	23.6	22.2	15.5	53.5	5.7	72.5	44.2	91.5
Programmer	91.3	91.8	69.5	20.3	50.4	11.6	5.7	17.1	87.5	34.2	97.2
Programmer override	83.1	80.3	59.3	20.3	43.9	10.6	1.9	7.1	75.2	8.1	81.8
Over night charge control	0.4	0.5	2.3	0	2.6	0.4	12.4	23.1	1.6	1.7	0
Occupied dwellings with CH	**9,252**	**2,772**	**659**	**51**	**134**	**734**	**162**	**1,281**	**631**	**136**	**113**

Sample: Ep2

A4.6   **Most common combination of heating controls by central heating system**

Central heating system	Most common combination of heating controls	% having the most common combination
Gas - dedicated boiler with radiators	Manual valve, wall stat, programmer and programmer override	31.5
Gas - back boiler with radiators	Manual valve, wall stat, programmer and programmer override	30.0
Gas - ducted air	Wall stat, programmer and programmer override (manual valve, room stat, programmer and programmer override)	23.4 (21.1)
Gas - convectors	Nothing	68.3
Solid fuel - dedicated boiler with radiators	Manual valves (TRV's, programmer and programmer override)	10.7 (10.3)
Solid fuel - back boiler with radiators	Manual valves	44.9
Electricity - other eg underfloor/ceiling	Wall stat	30.7
Electricity - storage heaters	Nothing	45.7
Oil	Manual valve, wall stat, programmer and programmer override	25.9
Communal and other	Manual valves	29.1
LPG	Manual valve, wall stat, programmer and programmer override	51.6

Sample: Ep2

A4.7   **Level of heating control by central heating system**

(Row %)

Heating system	Neither time nor temperature control	Time control only	Temperature control only	Time and temperature control
Gas - dedicated boiler with rads.	2.1	12.2	2.3	83.4
Gas - back boiler with radiators	1.7	24.0	2.1	72.2
Gas - ducted air	2.8	4.2	20.5	72.5
Gas - convectors	76.4	0	0	23.6
Solid fuel - dedicated boiler with radiators	25.4	12.8	19.8	42.0
Solid fuel - back boiler with radiators	67.3	6.5	16.5	9.7
Electricity - other eg underfloor /ceiling	23.8	1.9	55.7	18.6
Electricity - storage heaters	68.9	11.2	9.5	10.4
Oil	3.8	7.6	1.8	86.8
Communal and other	33.2	1.2	31.2	34.4
L.P.G.	0	2.4	0	97.6

Sample: Ep2

A4.8   **Main provison for water heating by tenure**

(Column %/k dwellings)

Main provision for water heating	Owner occupied	Private rented	Local authority	Housing association	All tenures
Gas central heating	72.5	37.8	60.7	63.8	66.9
Solid central heating	4.2	10.0	7.0	2.8	5.2
Oil central heating	4.2	4.2	0.2	0.1	3.2
LPG central heating	0.7	0.8	0	0	0.6
On peak immersion	8.6	29.2	19.9	19.0	13.0
Off peak immersion	5.1	6.7	7.5	7.8	5.8
Individual gas heater	4.0	8.3	3.5	4.5	4.2
Individual electric heater	0.5	1.4	0.6	1.5	0.6
No provision	0.2	1.3	0.6	0.6	0.4
No information	0	0.3	0.1	0	0.1
Occupied dwellings	**12,872**	**1,626**	**3,851**	**591**	**18,940**

Sample: Ep1

A4.9   **Main provison for water heating by dwelling age**

(Column %/k dwellings)

Main provision for water heating	Pre-1850	1850-1899	1900-1918	1919-1944	1945-1964	1965-1980	Post-1980
Gas central heating	36.4	55.2	58.4	70.3	65.6	74.3	81.6
Solid central heating	14.7	4.0	5.8	5.4	7.1	3.6	2.3
Oil central heating	17.5	5.4	3.7	1.0	1.3	4.2	1.1
LPG central heating	2.7	0.4	0.1	0.4	0.9	1.5	6.8
On peak immersion	13.9	19.8	19.5	12.8	17.0	14.9	5.0
Off peak immersion	8.7	4.1	4.0	4.3	6.8	8.6	1.6
Individual gas heater	5.9	8.6	7.4	4.8	3.6	3.2	0.4
Individual electric heater	0.3	1.3	0.6	0.6	0.3	0.9	0
No provision	0	1.0	0.5	0.2	0.4	0.3	0
No information	0	0.2	0	0.1	0	0.4	0
Occupied dwellings	**569**	**2,727**	**1,591**	**3,797**	**4,135**	**4,577**	**1,543**

Sample: Ep1

A4.10   **Main provision for water heating by dwelling type**

(Column %/k dwellings)

Main provision for water heating	End terr.	Mid terr.	Semi-det.	Det-ached	Temp-orary	Conv-erted flat	PB flat	Dwelling with non resident
Gas central heating	64.2	60.5	70.8	75.2	13.2	61.5	59.4	52.5
Solid central heating	6.0	4.2	8.1	4.5	32.5	0.2	1.0	16.7
Oil central heating	0.8	0.2	1.1	11.0	0	6.7	0.8	1.8
LPG central heating	0.1	0.3	0.4	1.1	35.8	0	0	2.0
On peak immersion	16.3	20.6	10.7	3.5	18.5	18.3	17.8	15.3
Off peak immersion	5.2	5.8	5.0	2.9	0	3.9	14.6	6.8
Individual gas heater	6.7	6.7	3.2	1.5	0	7.2	4.6	4.8
Individual electric heater	0.6	0.9	0.4	0.1	0	1.5	1.1	0
No provision	0	0.8	0.3	0.2	0	0.3	0.7	0
No information	0	0.1	0	0	0	0.4	0.1	0
Occupied dwellings	**1,841**	**3,716**	**5,705**	**3,599**	**55**	**1,207**	**2,751**	**65**

Sample: Ep1

A4.11 **Main provision for water heating by Government region**

(Column %/k dwellings)

Main provision for water heating	North	Yorks/ Humb	North West	East Mids.	West Mids.	South West	East- ern	Greater London	South East
Gas central heating	73.0	60.6	65.3	68.3	61.8	52.6	71.7	73.7	72.4
Solid central heating	10.6	8.7	3.4	8.7	6.1	7.8	4.0	0.4	4.2
Oil central heating	1.8	1.8	1.9	2.0	3.1	10.0	6.8	0.3	2.4
LPG central heating	0.5	0.1	0.8	0.4	0.9	1.5	0.6	0	0.6
On peak immersion	6.3	16.2	18.5	9.8	17.0	14.9	8.1	12.1	10.1
Off peak immersion	3.5	5.6	4.9	7.5	6.8	8.6	6.3	5.3	4.3
Individual gas heater	3.5	5.1	4.4	1.9	3.6	3.2	2.0	7.2	5.0
Individual electric heater	0.4	1.3	0.3	0.8	0.3	0.9	0.3	0.7	0.6
No provision	0.4	0.4	0.6	0.5	0.4	0.3	0.2	0.4	0.3
No information	0.1	0	0.1	0	0	0.1	0	0	0.2
Occupied dwellings	**1,042**	**1,926**	**2,706**	**1,535**	**2,032**	**1,906**	**2,193**	**2,825**	**2,775**

Sample: Ep1

A4.12 **Main provision for water heating by location**

(Column %/k dwellings)

Main provision for water heating	City centre	Urban	Suburban residential	Rural residential	Village centre	Rural isolated
Gas central heating	60.0	64.5	75.4	63.7	44.5	22.5
Solid central heating	1.8	1.8	3.5	10.0	18.1	21.0
Oil central heating	0.3	0.4	0.4	6.9	13.9	31.1
LPG central heating	0	0	0.1	1.6	1.9	4.9
On peak immersion	22.9	18.3	10.9	8.8	11.1	11.8
Off peak immersion	5.0	5.1	5.7	7.0	7.5	6.9
Individual gas heater	8.0	8.3	3.3	1.2	1.4	0.4
Individual electric heater	1.1	0.9	0.5	0.4	0.6	0.9
No provision	0.9	0.6	0.2	0.4	1.0	0.5
No information	0	0.1	0	0	0	0
Occupied dwellings	**773**	**5,018**	**9,211**	**2,437**	**646**	**855**

Sample: Ep1

A5.1 **Building Regulation insulation standards by tenure**

(Column %/k dwellings)

	Owner Occupied	Private Rented	Local Authority	Housing Association	All tenures
a) Dwelling Age					
Pre-1965	67.5	86.0	66.9	50.3	68.4
1965-75	16.4	5.0	21.3	9.4	16.2
1976-81	9.0	4.9	9.4	32.1	9.5
Post-1982	7.1	4.0	2.4	8.1	5.9
b) Wall Insulation					
Pre-1965 Standard	56.3	82.7	55.2	44.4	57.9
1965-74 Standard	14.7	5.2	19.9	9.5	14.8
1975-81 Standard	8.4	5.2	10.3	29.6	9.2
Post-1982 Standard	20.6	6.9	14.6	16.5	18.1
c) Roof Insulation					
Pre-1965 Standard	7.7	32.2	3.8	3.6	8.6
1965-74 Standard	8.5	4.6	5.8	6.7	7.9
1975-81 Standard	26.7	26.9	28.7	32.9	27.2
Post-1982 Standard	57.1	36.3	61.7	56.8	56.3
Occupied dwellings	**12,872**	**1,626**	**3,851**	**591**	**18,940**

Sample: P2 & Hp1

A5.2 **Wall construction and insulation by stock characteristics**

(Row %/k dwellings)

	Wall construction			Additional insulation			Occupied Dwellings
	Cavity	Masonry Solid	Other	Cavity Fill	Non-cavity	None	
a) Tenure							
Owner occupied	63.0	33.1	3.9	18.9	6.6	74.5	12,872
Private rented	33.0	60.6	6.4	5.1	2.6	92.3	1,626
Local authority	72.4	12.9	14.7	13.9	4.2	81.8	3,851
Housing assoc.	61.2	31.9	6.9	10.1	5.2	84.7	591
b) Dwelling Age							
Pre 1919	13.5	83.0	3.5	4.6	4.2	91.2	4,887
1919 - 1944	61.6	36.1	2.3	11.7	3.1	85.2	3,797
1945 - 1964	84.6	5.9	9.5	21.3	3.1	75.6	4,135
Post 1964	87.4	3.2	9.4	25.8	10.6	63.6	6,120
c) Dwelling Types							
Small Terrace	47.8	46.2	6.0	10.6	4.9	84.5	2,550
Med/large Terr	44.0	49.6	6.4	9.6	4.0	86.4	2,758
Semi-detached	70.5	24.3	5.2	17.0	4.1	78.9	5,165
Detached	73.2	23.3	3.5	27.8	10.1	62.1	2,738
Bungalow	84.1	6.5	9.4	30.2	7.5	62.3	1,705
Converted flat	10.5	86.8	2.7	1.9	4.9	93.2	1,272
PB flat-low rise	75.2	16.5	8.3	10.7	5.4	83.9	2,390
PB flat-high rise	39.9	13.5	46.6	1.7	6.4	91.9	361
All dwellings	**62.3**	**31.3**	**6.4**	**16.4**	**5.8**	**77.8**	**18,940**

Sample: P2 & Hp1

A5.3   Double glazing and draught proofing by stock characteristics

(Row %/k dwellings)

	Double Glazing			Draught Proofing			Occupied dwellings
	Full	Partial	None	Full	Partial	None	
a) Tenure							
Owner occupied	30.6	42.5	26.9	6.0	31.8	62.2	12,872
Private rented	6.8	14.1	79.1	5.5	29.4	65.0	1,626
Local authority	12.8	8.3	78.9	2.8	20.5	76.6	3,851
Housing assoc.	12.7	9.3	78.0	3.6	24.1	72.3	591
b) Dwelling Age							
Pre 1919	10.8	32.7	56.5	2.3	28.2	69.5	4,887
1919 - 1944	23.3	34.2	42.5	4.9	31.8	63.4	3,797
1945 - 1964	30.2	29.8	40.0	5.6	32.1	62.3	4,135
Post 1964	32.3	31.6	36.1	8.9	29.2	62.0	6,120
c) Dwelling Types							
Small Terrace	17.3	23.4	59.3	6.6	28.2	65.2	2,550
Med/large Terr	19.1	25.0	55.9	3.1	27.5	69.5	2,758
Semi-detached	28.3	36.5	35.2	4.3	33.0	62.7	5,165
Detached	34.6	47.3	18.1	7.1	39.3	53.6	2,738
Bungalow	33.6	35.6	30.8	9.4	28.6	62.0	1,705
Converted flat	5.0	35.4	59.6	0.6	24.0	75.3	1,272
PB flat-low rise	16.1	15.2	68.7	5.7	22.1	72.2	2,390
PB flat-high rise	25.3	13.7	61.0	2.3	20.3	77.4	361
Occupied dwellings	**24.4**	**32.0**	**43.6**	**5.6**	**30.1**	**64.3**	**18,940**

Sample: Hp1

A5.4   Loft insulation by stock characteristics

(Row %/k dwellings)

	No Insulation	Loft insulation	No loft	Flat on top floor	Flat not on top floor	Occupied dwellings
a) Tenure						
Owner occupied	6.8	80.6	3.8	3.6	5.2	12,872
Private rented	18.8	43.0	6.7	14.6	17.0	1,626
Local authority	3.6	58.9	1.7	12.4	23.4	3,851
Housing assoc.	2.1	37.6	3.8	24.7	31.7	591
b) Dwelling Age						
Pre 1919	15.0	56.2	6.9	9.2	12.7	4,887
1919 - 1944	8.0	83.7	1.4	3.0	4.0	3,797
1945 - 1964	4.5	76.8	2.1	5.7	10.8	4,135
Post 1964	1.6	72.8	3.4	8.6	13.6	6,120
c) Dwelling Types						
Small Terrace	11.8	83.8	4.4	-	-	2,550
Med/large Terr	11.1	80.3	8.6	-	-	2,758
Semi-detached	8.2	89.4	2.4	-	-	5,165
Detached	7.1	89.4	3.6	-	-	2,738
Bungalow	3.8	90.3	5.9	-	-	1,705
Converted flat	-	-	-	41.7	58.3	1,272
PB flat-low rise	-	-	-	41.6	58.4	2,390
PB flat-high rise	-	-	-	14.3	85.7	361
Occupied dwellings	**7.0**	**71.5**	**3.6**	**7.0**	**10.8**	**18,940**

Sample: P2

A5.5   **Thickness by type of loft insulation** *(houses only)*

(Column %/k dwellings)

Depth of loft insulation	Per cent	Type of insulation:			
		Mineral wool	Granules	Other	Not specified
No loft	4.4	-	-	-	-
No insulation	8.6	-	-	-	-
Insulation: 1-45 mm	7.3	8.5	19.6	12.5	2.5
46-90 mm	24.2	28.0	46.2	33.4	18.2
91-140 mm	41.4	52.2	26.4	38.2	11.1
141-500 mm	7.3	9.1	2.1	11.6	3.0
Unknown thickness	6.8	2.2	5.7	4.3	65.2
Occupied dwellings **(houses only)**	**14,916**	**11,255**	**405**	**193**	**1,127**

All occupied flats (4024 dwellings) are excluded.
Sample: P3

A6.1   **Distribution of SAP ratings by tenure**

(Column %/k dwellings)

SAP	Owner occupier	Private rented	Local authority	Housing association	Occupied dwellings
<1	2.0	17.0	4.6	2.4	3.8
1-10	2.4	9.3	2.7	3.7	3.1
10-20	6.1	16.3	10.5	12.0	8.0
20-30	15.2	20.5	16.6	18.4	16.0
30-35	14.2	9.0	12.4	14.4	13.4
35-40	15.2	8.3	14.1	9.6	14.2
40-45	16.4	7.4	13.0	12.3	14.8
45-50	11.1	5.5	10.2	9.6	10.4
50-60	13.5	2.9	12.3	12.5	12.2
60-70	3.7	3.2	3.6	3.4	3.5
70+	0.2	0.5	0.9	1.8	0.4
Occupied dwellings	**12,872**	**1,626**	**3,851**	**591**	**18,940**

Sample: Sp1

A6.2 Mean and distribution of SAP ratings by dwelling type by tenure

(SAP rating/row %/k dwellings)

Dwelling type	Mean SAP	% of dwellings with SAP ratings of:							Occupied dwellings
		<10	10-20	20-30	30-40	40-50	50-60	60+	
Owner occupier	**37.3**	**4.5**	**6.1**	**15.2**	**29.4**	**27.5**	**13.5**	**3.9**	**12,872**
Small terrace	37.3	7.3	11.3	18.5	24.4	23.4	11.1	4.0	1,639
Med/lge terrace	33.8	3.0	4.6	12.3	27.4	31.8	17.5	3.4	1,973
Semi-detached	39.6	3.1	5.8	14.5	36.7	27.6	11.1	1.2	4,000
Detached	41.2	2.7	3.2	10.0	27.0	31.0	22.4	3.6	2,589
Bungalow	30.2	10.1	8.3	24.4	31.2	22.6	3.0	0.4	1,272
Converted flat	41.1	5.4	3.1	23.3	13.1	24.1	6.7	24.3	636
All PB flats	41.9	3.5	5.6	12.3	21.4	25.0	18.8	13.4	763
Private rented	**21.7**	**26.3**	**16.3**	**20.5**	**17.3**	**13.0**	**2.9**	**3.8**	**1626**
Small terrace	19.0	27.9	22.8	21.8	14.8	9.1	3.6	0	230
Med/lge terrace	26.4	17.1	7.5	27.2	27.8	17.2	3.2	0	219
Semi-detached	16.3	32.2	22.3	15.9	19.9	9.8	0	0	259
Detached	22.9	38.5	14.9	21.8	16.4	7.4	1.0	0	123
Bungalow	10.6	47.0	16.5	18.4	8.9	9.2	0	0	86
Converted flat	30.1	19.1	12.1	15.1	16.3	17.4	7.7	12.3	464
All PB flats	31.3	11.6	13.3	29.8	11.0	19.5	2.3	12.4	245
Local authority	**34.4**	**7.3**	**10.5**	**16.6**	**26.5**	**23.2**	**11.7**	**4.1**	**3851**
Small terrace	31.9	7.9	12.5	17.5	29.5	23.3	9.0	0.3	598
Med/lge terrace	39.0	4.7	7.0	15.0	15.0	33.8	21.2	3.4	507
Semi & detached	28.6	10.2	15.2	18.4	34.5	17.2	4.6	0	880
Bungalow	26.4	9.3	16.6	33.5	26.8	12.0	1.8	0	321
Converted flat	35.4	5.2	11.5	14.9	28.7	22.2	12.6	4.9	82
PB low rise flat	39.3	6.4	6.2	11.5	23.5	26.7	17.4	8.2	1184
PB high rise flat	47.1	0.9	1.9	7.3	21.2	27.5	19.0	22.1	279
Housing association	**34.8**	**6.0**	**12.0**	**18.4**	**24.0**	**21.9**	**12.5**	**5.2**	**591**
Small terrace	34.0	8.7	9.6	18.6	17.7	30.6	10.6	4.2	83
Med/lge terrace	38.0	8.9	10.5	4.6	20.6	34.0	14.7	6.6	59
Semi & detached	25.9	11.5	12.9	38.0	28.8	4.5	4.3	0	52
Bungalow	25.4	7.0	18.0	23.2	51.8	0	0	0	26
Converted flat	28.8	7.4	24.7	17.9	24.6	15.5	6.1	4.0	90
PB low rise flat	41.4	1.3	7.3	14.7	22.5	23.7	22.5	8.0	263
PB high rise flat	44.4	0	0	6.6	21.6	56.6	0	15.2	18

Sample: Sp1

A6.3 Mean and distribution of SAP ratings by age of dwelling by tenure

(SAP rating/row %/k dwellings)

Dwelling age	Mean SAP	% of dwellings with SAP ratings of:							Occupied dwellings
		<10	10-20	20-30	30-40	40-50	50-60	60+	
Owner occupier	**37.3**	**4.5**	**6.1**	**15.2**	**29.4**	**27.5**	**13.5**	**3.9**	**12,872**
Pre 1850	29.4	12.6	12.3	19.7	29.3	18.9	6.1	1.2	402
1850-99	35.0	7.3	8.8	16.5	28.5	23.3	8.5	7.2	2,008
1900-18	33.9	5.1	9.0	24.6	27.5	23.4	8.0	2.3	1,151
1919-45	33.0	5.4	8.4	19.6	38.3	22.0	5.7	0.5	2,706
1945-64	36.7	3.3	5.0	16.1	33.7	29.8	10.4	1.7	2,413
1965-80	40.9	1.9	2.4	10.0	29.4	33.4	19.9	3.0	2,998
1980+	48.5	0	1.1	3.2	5.2	36.4	39.7	14.4	1,194
Private rented	**21.7**	**26.3**	**16.3**	**20.5**	**17.3**	**13.0**	**2.9**	**3.8**	**1,626**
Pre 1850	13.6	46.1	10.0	23.2	8.0	7.8	3.9	1.0	154
1850-99	21.0	28.2	16.5	20.7	16.9	12.9	3.1	1.8	518
1900-18	16.5	34.4	17.7	18.2	15.0	8.7	5.1	1.0	315
1919-45	20.1	23.2	21.6	22.0	22.7	8.9	1.6	0	218
1945-64	28.0	12.3	19.5	16.6	24.0	20.7	0.9	5.8	156
1965-80	32.7	10.1	6.9	19.2	27.0	32.1	2.2	2.6	187
1980+	38.5	0	9.0	27.7	9.3	11.4	30.0	12.7	77
Local authority	**34.4**	**7.3**	**10.5**	**16.6**	**26.5**	**23.2**	**11.7**	**4.1**	**3,851**
Pre 1919	34.0	7.8	14.2	22.7	20.6	18.4	9.9	6.4	160
1919-45	30.2	7.7	15.3	18.8	35.0	16.8	6.1	0.3	812
1945-64	31.2	10.4	11.5	20.4	25.3	21.5	8.7	2.2	1,514
1965-80	41.0	3.5	5.1	9.8	24.7	30.7	17.5	8.7	1,161
1980+	46.5	0	1.5	7.5	9.8	32.2	36.4	12.7	204
Housing association	**34.8**	**6.0**	**12.0**	**18.4**	**24.0**	**21.9**	**12.5**	**5.2**	**591**
Pre 1919	32.3	6.1	17.1	18.2	24.9	20.4	8.3	5.0	179
1919-45	29.0	8.4	14.7	31.8	25.7	8.9	9.1	1.5	60
1945-64	22.6	22.4	19.2	22.7	28.1	6.4	1.2	0	53
1965-80	41.1	0	5.3	15.8	25.2	28.2	18.4	7.0	231
1980+	47.1	0	1.3	3.9	13.3	43.8	25.8	11.8	68

For local authority and housing association dwellings, the first three age categories are combined as pre-1919 dwellings.
Sample: Sp1

A6.4   Dwellings with SAP <20 and above average heating prices: % of these dwellings with given space and water heating

(% of total group)

	Heating price				
	1.25-1.5	1.5-2.0	2.0-2.5	2.5-3.0	All ≥ 1.25
Space heating					
CH : gas	4	3	0	0	7
CH : solid	3	1	0	0	4
CH : electric	0	0	0	0	0
Programmed electric	2	1	0	0	3
Fixed : gas	30	7	1	0	38
Fixed : solid	3	23	0	0	26
Fixed : electric	0	0	2	7	9
Portable only	0	0	3	11	14
Totals	**42**	**35**	**6**	**18**	**100**
Water heating					
With CH/back boiler	6	9	1	0	17
Individual gas heaters	0	1	2	0	2
Normal tariff electricity	34	25	2	18	78
Off-peak electricity	0	1	2	0	2
No specific provision	0	0	0	0	1
Totals	**40**	**36**	**7**	**18**	**100**

Sample: Sp3

A6.5   Dwellings with SAP <20 and high heat losses: % of these dwellings falling into different age and type categories

(% of total group)

Dwelling type	Heat loss			
	1.25 - 1.5	1.5 - 2.0	2.0 - 2.5	All ≥ 1.25
Pre 1964 : Flat	4	4	1	9
Pre 1964 : Mid-terrace	5	3	0	8
Pre 1964 : Other house	38	33	3	74
1965-80 : Flat	0	1	0	1
1965-80 : Mid-terrace	0	0	0	0
1965-80 : Other house	3	3	0	6
Post 1980 : Flat	0	0	0	0
Post 1980 : Mid-terrace	0	0	0	0
Post 1980 : Other house	0	2	0	2
Totals	**50**	**46**	**4**	**100**

Sample: Sp3

A6.6   Dwellings with SAP <20 and high heat losses: % of these dwellings with given heating type

(% of total group)

Type of heating	Extent of heating			
	< 30% of rooms	30-70% of rooms	>70% of rooms	All
Central heating	7.6	19.2	32.2	59.0
Other fixed heating	21.5	14.6	2.0	38.1
Portables only	2.9	0	0	2.9
All	**32.0**	**33.8**	**34.2**	**100.0**

Sample: Sp3

A6.7 **Dwellings within given SAP rating bands which are defective on a number of items contributing towards unfitness, or are unfit**

(Column %/k dwellings)

	SAP<10		SAP<20		SAP<30	
	%	No (000)	%	No(000)	%	No (000)
Defective items						
0	47.6	622	52.1	1,470	59.7	3,503
1	15.1	198	16.6	469	17.3	1,012
2	14.3	187	13.4	379	10.6	622
3	7.3	95	5.7	160	4.3	253
4	15.7	206	12.2	345	8.1	473
Fitness						
Fit	76.7	1,004	82.5	2,330	87.1	5,107
Unfit	23.2	303	17.5	494	12.9	756
Totals	**100.0**	**1,308**	**100.0**	**2,824**	**100.0**	**5,863**

Sample: Sp4

A6.8 **Dwellings with SAP <20 with given repair costs (all tenures)**

(Column %/k dwellings)

Repair cost (£)	%	No (000)
<500	31.5	901
500-2500	43.8	1,251
2500-5000	15.4	439
5000-10000	6.9	197
>10000	2.4	70
All	**100.0**	**2,858**

Sample: Sp3

A6.9 **Dwellings with SAP <20 by tenure, which are defective on a given number of fitness items**

(Column %/k dwellings)

No. of defective	Owner Occupier		LA/HA		Private rented	
	%	No (000)	%	No (000)	%	No (000)
0	58.1	795	55.8	445	35.1	243
1	15.4	211	17.8	142	17.9	124
2	12.0	164	13.6	108	16.0	111
3	5.0	68	5.6	45	7.1	49
4	9.5	130	7.2	57	24.0	166
Totals	**100.0**	**1,368**	**100.0**	**797**	**100.0**	**693**

Sample: Sp3

A6.10 Mean and distribution of SAP ratings by region by tenure

(Row %/k dwellings)

Region (met & non met)	Mean SAP	<10	10-20	20-30	30-40	40-50	50-60	60+	Occupied Dwellings
Owner occupier	**37.3**	**4.5**	**6.1**	**15.2**	**29.4**	**27.5**	**13.5**	**3.9**	**12,872**
Tyne & Wear met	37.2	3.1	4.3	11.4	39.8	30.2	10.1	1.1	231
Northern non met	37.7	3.2	6.4	12.7	31.5	30.0	13.5	2.7	378
S Yorks met	36.8	1.4	7.4	16.2	36.5	22.6	13.4	2.5	327
W Yorks met	34.1	5.1	9.7	18.9	28.6	29.3	6.7	1.7	490
Y & H non met	36.2	8.4	5.6	13.9	22.7	30.8	17.2	1.3	445
Gt Manchester	35.5	6.9	4.9	16.3	30.0	24.0	17.1	0.9	662
NW non met	36.5	8.5	6.1	14.5	25.4	30.6	9.2	5.5	838
Merseyside TF	32.8	5.0	11.3	22.1	28.2	29.5	3.6	0.5	333
East Midlands	36.5	3.9	4.3	18.8	33.1	25.4	11.3	3.3	1,083
W Mids met	34.8	5.0	8.3	18.1	32.2	24.2	11.8	0.3	624
W Mids non met	36.9	3.7	7.1	17.1	29.1	25.8	16.7	0.5	723
South West	39.6	4.5	3.8	14.9	21.3	35.1	11.2	9.3	938
Devon & Cornwall	33.1	5.9	15.8	18.1	29.7	13.0	12.0	5.6	412
Eastern	39.0	3.6	6.4	12.8	26.7	28.8	16.8	5.0	1,591
Inner London	39.2	6.2	5.6	12.1	23.8	28.7	15.0	8.6	431
Outer London	36.8	3.0	4.0	18.7	34.6	25.7	10.2	3.8	1,260
South East	39.5	3.2	4.6	10.5	30.8	27.8	18.3	4.7	2,106
Private rented	**21.7**	**26.3**	**16.3**	**20.5**	**17.3**	**13.0**	**2.9**	**3.8**	**1,626**
Tyne & Wear met	31.8	5.2	21.1	3.0	39.7	24.7	6.2	0	31
Northern non met	20.2	14.7	37.7	21.5	7.3	15.9	2.9	0	39
S Yorks met	23.4	18.5	25.6	17.7	19.3	15.9	3.1	0	38
W Yorks met	22.4	14.4	40.6	10.6	14.1	20.3	0	0	49
Y & H non met	26.7	20.3	10.4	26.9	11.2	29.5	1.6	0	57
Gt Manchester	28.3	2.8	30.3	21.4	36.0	9.5	0	0	74
NW non met	18.2	27.1	21.1	27.6	20.2	2.0	0	2.0	93
Merseyside TF	22.3	32.3	16.2	33.2	0	0	0	18.2	35
East Midlands	28.4	27.5	4.5	27.3	6.2	8.8	0.7	25.0	113
W Mids met	19.9	21.3	22.1	22.1	27.1	1.8	5.6	0	78
W Mids non met	11.7	45.6	13.7	16.8	12.2	9.5	2.3	0	89
South West	18.6	36.6	11.2	14.0	11.0	19.7	7.0	0.4	179
Devon & Cornwall	2.7	68.9	10.7	1.8	15.2	0	3.3	0	61
Eastern	15.7	32.3	20.2	27.2	7.5	11.7	1.1	0	146
Inner London	32.9	18.5	6.4	14.7	15.0	27.0	8.3	10.0	157
Outer London	23.7	17.7	15.0	33.4	20.5	7.4	3.3	2.7	156
South East	24.7	19.6	15.0	17.8	29.6	14.5	0.9	2.6	231
Social rented (LA & HA)	**34.5**	**7.2**	**10.7**	**16.8**	**26.2**	**23.0**	**11.8**	**4.3**	**4,442**
Tyne & Wear met	37.7	1.1	6.4	13.5	39.6	26.5	10.5	2.3	174
Northern non met	34.9	4.7	7.6	21.5	25.8	27.6	12.2	0.7	188
S Yorks met	32.9	11.4	10.4	15.2	29.3	19.4	10.4	3.8	186
W Yorks met	30.1	8.3	21.8	20.0	19.5	18.9	8.6	2.9	204
Y&H non met	34.3	5.6	14.1	21.3	24.2	18.3	9.0	7.6	130
Gt Manchester	39.6	1.5	4.5	10.9	34.8	28.0	16.6	3.8	299
NW non met	35.1	4.7	10.3	18.7	25.5	24.3	15.8	0.8	206
Merseyside TF	34.4	7.7	8.5	18.1	27.3	23.8	10.6	4.0	165
East Midlands	33.5	6.6	10.0	20.3	30.0	19.5	11.3	2.2	339
W Mids met	30.1	9.6	18.0	19.7	23.2	17.3	9.5	2.7	311
W Mids non met	30.3	11.5	12.2	18.0	31.4	16.2	10.0	0.7	208
South West	30.3	13.4	12.6	16.0	25.6	18.8	9.0	4.7	225
Devon & Cornwall	24.4	20.8	15.2	24.1	27.5	7.8	4.1	0.3	93
Eastern	35.4	5.8	8.1	17.9	23.9	29.3	12.0	3.0	454
Inner London	41.9	3.7	5.2	12.9	21.1	24.3	21.2	11.5	462
Outer London	36.9	8.1	7.8	12.6	26.5	24.1	12.1	8.8	359
South East	31.7	8.4	16.3	16.8	21.8	27.2	6.1	3.4	439

Sample: Sp1

A7.1 Mean and distribution of SAP ratings by size of household by tenure

(SAP rating/row %/k households)

| Tenure and household type | Mean SAP | % of households with SAP ratings of:- | | | | | | | All h/holds |
		< 10	10-20	20-30	30-40	40-50	50-60	60 +	
Owner Occupier	**37.2**	**4.5**	**6.0**	**15.2**	**29.2**	**27.7**	**13.6**	**3.9**	**12,872**
1 person	32.4	10.5	8.9	22.8	24.1	18.8	7.0	7.8	2,266
2 persons	36.6	4.1	6.4	15.3	31.9	28.2	11.1	3.0	4,750
3 persons	38.2	2.5	6.2	14.6	30.3	27.7	16.8	1.9	2,280
4 persons	40.9	2.4	2.9	10.1	27.0	34.0	18.9	4.7	2,475
5 persons	39.9	2.4	3.7	9.7	33.3	28.1	20.3	2.4	825
6 or more	39.7	1.7	6.1	12.1	24.9	35.8	18.8	0.6	277
Private tenants	**22.4**	**25.7**	**16.2**	**20.0**	**16.8**	**13.9**	**3.3**	**4.2**	**1,700**
1 person	17.3	31.9	18.6	18.9	13.9	12.5	3.6	0.5	583
2 persons	25.4	27.1	11.6	19.3	12.7	17.1	3.9	8.3	589
3 persons	23.7	21.8	19.0	20.5	21.9	9.3	1.6	5.8	220
4 persons	23.6	16.2	17.1	23.9	28.0	10.8	2.3	1.7	226
5 persons	32.8	3.4	16.3	19.1	26.8	29.8	4.5	0	48
6 or more	21.8	7.8	41.1	20.8	19.8	10.5	0	0	34
Council tenants	**34.4**	**7.2**	**10.5**	**16.7**	**26.4**	**23.1**	**11.8**	**4.2**	**3,877**
1 person	33.3	8.6	11.5	19.1	25.2	19.3	11.9	4.5	1,286
2 persons	34.5	7.5	10.4	14.7	28.1	23.6	11.7	4.0	1,171
3 persons	34.6	6.0	10.9	18.5	24.6	24.4	10.7	4.9	614
4 persons	34.6	6.2	10.2	15.3	28.6	25.3	12	2.4	450
5 persons	35.4	7.0	7.3	14.1	24.7	32.6	12.6	1.8	239
6 or more	41.0	1.9	7.3	13.9	26.8	23.9	16.9	9.3	11
HA tenants	**34.4**	**6.8**	**11.5**	**17.6**	**25.1**	**21.6**	**12.6**	**4.9**	**662**
1 person	32.2	7.4	14.4	16.1	27.0	22.5	10.4	2.1	320
2 persons	35.4	6.8	10.8	24.9	19.7	14.4	15.0	8.3	175
3 persons	36.8	6.3	11.3	11.2	27.1	16.7	17.5	9.8	74
4 persons	34.9	5.9	7.4	11.1	40.2	24.6	10,8	0	54
5 persons	38.0	6.1	1.3	20.0	1.3	61.8	2.8	6.7	27
6 or more	40.6	0	4.6	8.6	33.6	29.2	24.1	0	11
All households	**35.3**	**6.9**	**8.0**	**16.1**	**27.5**	**25.2**	**12.3**	**4.0**	**19,111**

Sample: S1

A7.2   Mean and distribution of SAP ratings by household type by tenure

(SAP rating/row %/k households)

Tenure and household type	Mean SAP	% of households with SAP ratings of:-							All h/holds
		< 10	10-20	20-30	30-40	40-50	50-60	60 +	
Owner Occupier	**37.2**	**4.5**	**6.0**	**15.2**	**29.2**	**27.7**	**13.6**	**3.9**	**12,872**
lone parents	42.1	1.2	5.1	15.3	23.2	18.8	32.0	4.5	272
two adults	37.9	2.9	5.9	13.6	32.9	29.3	12.4	3.1	2502
small family	40.4	1.6	3.9	12.1	27.5	32.8	17.1	4.9	2498
large family	39.5	2.5	4.3	10.2	30.3	32.4	18.9	1.4	1505
large adult	38.2	3.8	5.0	13.2	31.2	27.4	17.3	2.1	1698
lone adult	32.8	12.6	8.4	17.2	22.8	22.9	8.0	8.0	827
two older	34.9	5.6	7.4	17.0	30.9	27.7	9.0	2.4	2132
lone older	32.2	9.3	9.2	26.0	24.9	16.5	6.4	7.7	1439
Private tenants	**22.4**	**25.7**	**16.2**	**20.0**	**16.8**	**13.9**	**3.3**	**4.2**	**1,700**
lone parents	26.1	17.3	14.3	20.9	36.7	7.0	3.7	0	71
two adults	27.9	25.0	10.5	18.0	12.2	18.6	3.4	12.2	371
small family	26.0	14.7	18.5	27.0	20.1	12.3	2.0	5.5	224
large family	22.3	14.1	17.3	20.6	32.2	15.8	0	0	101
large adult	23.4	19.1	21.0	20.1	25.1	9.8	2.0	2.8	168
lone adult	23.2	22.4	16.0	24.9	9.1	20.5	6.0	1.1	328
two older	20.7	35.1	12.9	17.8	8.6	16.8	5.5	3.3	181
lone older	11.1	42.0	21.4	12.6	19.0	4.1	1.0	0	255
Council tenants	**34.4**	**7.2**	**10.5**	**16.7**	**26.4**	**23.1**	**11.8**	**4.2**	**3,877**
lone parents	37.8	3.7	6.9	16.4	25.0	26.9	13.9	7.2	365
two adults	36.2	7.2	8.6	14.6	21.6	30.2	12.7	5.2	312
small family	34.3	5.5	10.3	19.0	26.4	24.0	12.4	2.5	481
large family	37.4	4.2	8.6	13.5	28.0	28.5	13.0	4.4	370
large adult	34.2	9.0	11.8	13.6	23.7	26.3	10.2	5.5	365
lone adult	35.5	10.6	8.9	12.7	23.3	20.8	16.6	7.0	333
two older	32.4	8.7	12.0	15.5	32.1	19.6	10.2	1.9	698
lone older	32.4	7.8	12.4	21.4	25.9	18.7	10.1	3.6	953
HA tenants	**34.4**	**6.8**	**11.5**	**17.6**	**25.1**	**21.6**	**12.6**	**4.9**	**662**
lone parents	35.8	1.4	12.9	25.2	19.0	17.5	20.3	3.7	71
two adults	36.7	12.8	7.4	23.8	19.5	8.2	7.0	21.2	39
small family	34.5	5.6	9.6	12.8	39.1	20.2	12.7	0	68
large family	37.0	4.2	4.0	20.3	14.3	41.7	11.0	4.6	41
large adult	38.2	8.5	9.8	3.3	20.6	32.5	8.8	16.4	38
lone adult	30.0	6.9	21.9	18.4	21.3	17.8	11.7	2.0	125
two older	35.3	8.0	9.5	22.6	22.6	14.2	17.8	14.5	85
lone older	33.7	7.8	9.6	14.6	30.7	25.5	9.6	2.2	195
All households	**35.3**	**6.9**	**8.0**	**16.1**	**27.5**	**25.2**	**12.3**	**4.0**	**19,111**

Sample: S1

A7.3 Main type of heating by household type by tenure

(k households/col % by tenure)

Type of heating and tenure		lone parent	two adults	small family	large family	large adult	lone adult	two older	lone older	All hhold types
					Col % of household type in each tenure with heating type					
Owner Occupiers		**272**	**2,502**	**2,498**	**1,505**	**1,698**	**827**	**2,132**	**1,439**	**12,872**
Mains gas	dedicated boiler	65.6	58.2	62.1	64.4	57.3	49.1	56.1	40.9	56.9
CH	back boiler	14.0	14.9	13.8	14.9	15.7	6.3	11.4	13.1	13.5
	ducted air etc	0.9	3.5	3.7	2.4	2.3	1.1	4.0	2.8	3.0
Soild fuel	all CH types	3.8	3.4	5.4	2.4	4.5	7.5	3.3	3.3	4.1
Electric	underfloor etc	0.4	0.7	0	0.7	0	2.0	0.3	0.9	0.5
	night storage	4.3	4.8	3.5	2.2	2.9	10.1	8.0	12.6	5.8
Oil/LPG	all CH types	0.9	5.4	3.7	4.3	6.5	1.6	5.3	8.4	5.1
Communal & other		0.8	0.2	0.3	0.2	0.1	0.7	0.2	0.8	0.3
Total central heating		90.9	91.2	92.6	91.5	89.4	78.4	88.7	82.7	89.1
Mains gas	fires etc	8.6	7.5	6.8	6.9	8.3	15.4	9.0	12.6	8.7
Solid fuel	fires/stoves	0	0.5	0.5	0.8	1.9	1.9	1.5	1.8	1.1
Electric	fires etc	0.2	0.1	0.1	0.4	0.2	2.5	0.8	1.2	0.5
Total fixed other heating		8.8	8.1	7.3	8.1	10.4	19.8	11.3	15.6	10.4
No fixed heating		0.3	0.7	0.1	0.4	0.2	1.8	0.1	1.6	0.5
Private tenants		**71**	**371**	**224**	**101**	**168**	**328**	**181**	**255**	**1,700**
Mains gas	dedicated boiler	34.0	35.1	45.8	38.6	32.7	22.3	14.1	8.7	27.8
CH	back boiler	6.1	4.2	3.9	5.3	5.4	11.6	5.7	1.8	5.7
	ducted air etc	0	0.4	0.6	0	0	0.5	0	4.2	0.9
Soild fuel	all CH types	1.6	10.5	5.9	4.3	7.6	4.0	16.4	3.8	7.2
Electric	underfloor etc	1.8	0.3	0	4.0	0	0.2	5.2	0.2	1.0
	night storage	9.5	7.7	12.1	4.5	9.5	12.2	11.0	9.4	9.8
Oil/LPG	all CH types	0	5.0	1.3	9.1	5.5	4.2	10.8	1.3	4.5
Communal & other		0	0.5	4.6	0	0	0	0	0	0.7
Total central heating		53.1	63.7	74.2	65.7	60.7	55.1	63.2	29.3	57.6
Mains gas	fires etc	31.4	15.4	13.7	21.4	25.2	15.3	22.7	42.8	22.0
Solid fuel	fires/stoves	11.8	11.7	9.6	4.1	9.2	1.1	9.2	15.0	8.9
Electric	fires etc	1.8	4.2	0	0	0.8	12.5	2.4	1.9	4.0
Total fixed other heating		44.9	31.3	23.3	25.5	35.1	28.9	34.3	59.7	35.0
No fixed heating		2.0	5.0	2.4	8.8	4.1	16.1	2.5	11.0	7.5
LA tenants		**365**	**312**	**481**	**370**	**365**	**333**	**698**	**953**	**3,877**
Mains gas	dedicated boiler	33.4	33.5	30.2	31.8	34.5	33.7	27.7	32.4	31.7
CH	back boiler	19.3	23.8	24.0	30.0	20.7	19.2	23.4	18.8	22.0
	ducted air	9.8	6.4	4.8	9.3	5.8	6.1	8.1	7.6	7.3
Soild fuel	all CH types	2.2	4.8	6.5	4.7	6.9	2.1	8.1	5.9	5.6
Electric	underfloor etc	0.9	1.2	1.1	0.4	0	4.3	1.6	3.2	1.8
	night storage	5.1	7.2	5.9	1.2	2.8	6.6	7.1	13.5	7.3
Oil/LPG	all CH types	0	0.6	0	0.5	0.3	0.5	0.2	0.5	0.3
Communal & other		3.8	0.7	0.5	0.4	0	3.1	2.2	2.1	1.7
Total central heating		74.7	78.3	72.9	78.3	71.0	75.7	78.3	83.9	77.8
Mains gas	fires etc	14.8	16.4	20.0	22.7	16.7	20.9	15.7	10.8	16.3
Solid fuel	fires/stoves	3.1	2.2	1.6	3.3	3.0	4.3	4.1	3.0	3.2
Electric	fires etc	1.5	0.9	0.2	0.4	1.3	1.8	0.8	0.6	0.9
Total fixed other heating		21.8	19.5	26.3	21.0	27.1	19.4	20.6	14.4	20.3
No fixed heating		4.9	2.3	3.6	0.8	0.7	1.9	1.1	1.7	1.9
HA tenants		**71**	**39**	**68**	**41**	**38**	**125**	**85**	**195**	**662**
Mains gas	dedicated boiler	39.5	39.5	38.6	60.0	21.3	49.4	43.0	43.0	43.0
CH	back boiler	17.5	15.7	21.9	13.2	35.6	6.0	18.8	11.7	14.9
	ducted air	1.3	0	7.0	2.6	16.6	0.8	4.4	3.1	3.6
Soild fuel	all CH types	0	2.7	3.8	3.0	0.8	0.5	0.5	1.0	1.3
Electric	underfloor etc	5.4	0	0.4	0	0	1.4	2.1	2.1	1.8
	night storage	2.1	5.7	5.6	3.2	4.7	29.9	9.6	19.1	14.1
Oil/LPG	all CH types	0	0	0	0	0	0	0.7	0.7	0.3
Communal & other		0.8	2.5	0	0	0	0.3	0	8.5	2.8
Total central heating		66.7	66.1	77.3	81.9	79.0	88.3	79.0	89.2	81.7
Mains gas	fires etc	29.2	30.2	18.7	13.2	14.3	9.4	13.4	5.8	13.7
Solid fuel	fires/stoves	4.1	2.5	3.3	0	6.7	0	7.5	2.1	2.9
Electric	fires etc	0	0	0	4.9	0	0.8	0	1.3	0.8
Total fixed other heating		33.3	32.7	21.9	18.1	21.0	10.2	21.0	9.2	17.4
No fixed heating		0	1.2	0.7	0	0	1.5	0	1.6	0.9

Sample: H1

A7.4 Wall construction and all types of insulation by household type

(Column %/k households)

Construction & additional insulation		lone parent	small family	large family	large adult	two adults	lone adult	two older	lone older	All hholds
Wall construction										
	Cavity	52.7	66.5	61.2	62.9	60.2	47.6	67.2	63.1	61.9
	Masonry solid	34.3	28.5	32.9	30.5	33.9	37.9	26.5	30.9	31.2
	Other	13.0	4.9	5.9	6.6	5.9	14.5	6.4	6.1	6.9
Wall insulation										
	Cavity fill	9.8	19.0	19.4	18.2	17.3	10.1	18.5	11.4	16.3
	Non-cavity ins	5.0	8.3	6.3	4.4	5.4	7.8	4.6	4.0	5.7
	None	85.2	72.7	74.3	77.4	77.3	82.1	76.9	84.5	77.9
Double glazing										
	Full	19.7	29.9	28.8	26.8	28.5	14.2	24.4	14.4	24.2
	Partial	21.5	33.7	33.7	34.0	34.5	16.9	36.6	29.6	31.8
	None	58.8	36.4	37.5	39.2	37.0	68.9	39.0	56.0	44.0
Draught proofing										
	Full	7.3	4.8	4.9	4.2	5.8	2.6	6.6	2.7	4.8
	Partial	24.1	24.8	24.1	28.1	28.8	22.0	28.9	23.2	26.0
	None	68.6	70.4	71.0	67.8	65.4	75.4	64.5	74.1	69.2
Loft insulation										
House with	loft insulation	62.7	83.0	82.1	82.1	75.1	39.7	75.8	51.8	71.2
	no insulation	5.8	5.7	8.5	8.0	6.8	7.4	6.7	8.0	7.1
	no loft	2.3	2.7	5.2	4.6	2.4	7.0	3.5	3.2	3.7
Flat	on top floor	9.3	4.6	1.8	2.7	7.2	22.5	5.3	10.5	7.2
	not top floor	19.9	4.1	2.5	2.5	8.5	23.4	8.7	26.5	10.8
All households		779	3,270	2,017	2,270	3,223	1,613	3,096	2,842	19,111

Sample: H1

A7.5 Mean and distribution of SAP ratings by length of residence by tenure

(SAP rating/row %/k households)

Tenure and household type	Mean SAP	< 10	10-20	20-30	30-40	40-50	50-60	60 +	All h/holds
Owner Occupier	**37.2**	**4.5**	**6.0**	**15.2**	**29.2**	**27.7**	**13.6**	**3.9**	**12,872**
Up to 2 years	37.8	4.2	6.9	13.9	27.7	28.8	13.1	5.4	1.191
2-4 years	39.5	3.4	3.6	12.7	29.0	28.3	17.7	5.3	2,488
5-9 years	39.4	3.7	4.4	11.6	27.6	31.2	17.1	4.4	2,992
10-19 years	38.4	2.6	5.0	16.9	28.1	30.1	12.5	4.8	3,082
20 or more	32.0	8.0	10.0	19.3	32.6	21.2	8.1	0.8	3,119
Private tenants	**22.4**	**25.7**	**16.2**	**20.0**	**16.8**	**13.9**	**3.3**	**4.2**	**1,700**
Up to 2 years	26.4	20.4	9.2	22.4	20.9	17.7	5.4	4.0	651
2-4 years	29.6	15.5	18.4	17.6	19.1	12.7	1.8	14.9	256
5-9 years	26.1	16.9	15.8	27.3	13.0	15.4	6.7	4.8	170
10-19 years	20.1	24.7	21.5	21.3	10.5	20.8	1.1	0	214
20 or more	11.8	43.8	22.1	14.1	14.4	4.7	0.9	0	409
Council tenants	**34.4**	**7.2**	**10.5**	**16.7**	**26.4**	**23.1**	**11.8**	**4.2**	**3,877**
Up to 2 years	36.1	6.6	9.4	17.5	22.0	24.1	13.0	7.5	617
2-4 years	35.6	6.5	7.4	16.9	24.9	28.3	12.3	3.6	769
5-9 years	35.3	4.8	11.3	15.1	29.6	23.8	11.9	3.5	704
10-19 years	35.9	5.8	10.1	15.5	27.1	21.8	14.7	5.1	808
20 or more	30.5	11.1	13.4	18.3	27.7	18.9	8.4	2.2	979
HA tenants	**34.4**	**6.8**	**11.5**	**17.6**	**25.1**	**21.6**	**12.6**	**4.9**	**662**
Up to 2 years	35.3	4.3	7.5	17.8	36.7	19.7	10.7	3.3	141
2-4 years	36.8	5.4	6.7	19.6	23.2	25.7	13.5	5.8	178
5-9 years	38.6	5.9	8.6	8.4	26.5	23.9	19.2	7.5	154
10-19 years	32.6	4.2	22.6	20.1	12.2	24.5	11.6	4.9	116
20 or more	24.0	17.9	16.0	26.2	26.2	8.9	3.8	1.0	73
All households	**35.3**	**6.9**	**8.0**	**16.1**	**27.5**	**25.2**	**12.3**	**4.0**	**19,111**

Sample: S1

A7.6 Mean and distribution of SAP ratings by net household income by tenure

(SAP rating/row %/k households)

Tenure and household type	Mean SAP	< 10	10-20	20-30	30-40	40-50	50-60	60 +	All h/holds
Owner Occupier	**37.2**	**4.5**	**6.0**	**15.2**	**29.2**	**27.7**	**13.6**	**3.9**	**12,872**
Under £4,500	33.2	10.2	9.0	21.0	26.0	15.5	8.9	9.4	1,582
£4,500-£8,500	33.1	7.6	8.6	18.7	31.1	23.6	8.7	1.7	2,032
£8,500-£13,500	35.3	5.2	8.6	18.7	27.0	26.5	11.5	2.5	2,560
£13,500-£19,500	38.7	2.0	4.7	13.2	31.4	30.4	16.3	2.1	3,268
£19,500 or more	42.0	1.6	1.9	9.0	29.1	34.9	17.9	5.6	3,431
Private tenants	**22.4**	**25.7**	**16.2**	**20.0**	**16.8**	**13.9**	**3.3**	**4.2**	**1,700**
Under £4,500	18.5	31.6	16.2	17.1	20.7	11.1	2.9	0.4	511
£4,500-£8,500	23.6	27.4	18.6	15.7	11.5	14.1	1.6	10.9	347
£8,500-£13,500	20.6	25.7	18.2	21.0	13.5	15.9	3.6	2.1	462
£13,500-£19,500	26.6	17.6	12.7	34.3	16.0	8.5	4.6	6.4	226
£19,500 or more	32.8	12.7	7.9	16.0	29.0	24.5	5.6	4.3	152
Council tenants	**34.4**	**7.2**	**10.5**	**16.7**	**26.4**	**23.1**	**11.8**	**4.2**	**3,877**
Under £4,500	34.3	7.6	9.8	18.7	25.4	21.7	11.5	5.4	1,605
£4,500-£8,500	33.6	7.1	12.3	16.3	29.4	21.1	10.7	3.2	1,354
£8,500-£13,500	34.4	7.8	11.2	13.9	22.8	28.0	12.6	3.7	610
£13,500-£19,500	37.4	5.5	5.3	16.3	24.9	28.1	16.8	3.0	258
£19,500 or more	40.4	2.8	4.3	3.9	33.1	33.3	18.9	3.6	50
HA tenants	**34.4**	**6.8**	**11.5**	**17.6**	**25.1**	**21.6**	**12.6**	**4.9**	**662**
Under £4,500	33.1	8.0	13.0	14.8	27.1	21.2	12.9	3.1	313
£4,500-£8,500	36.4	5.9	11.2	21.5	19.0	22.2	12.3	8.0	204
£8,500-£13,500	31.4	6.9	12.3	22.0	32.4	15.9	10.5	0	80
£13,500-£19,500	35.4	4.2	5.6	15.1	24.8	33.1	14.6	2.5	51
£19,500 or more	43.7	4.9	7.0	5.2	33.4	4.4	12.1	32.9	13
All households	**35.3**	**6.9**	**8.0**	**16.1**	**27.5**	**25.2**	**12.3**	**4.0**	**19,111**

Sample: S1

A7.7 Wall construction and all types of insulation by net household income

(Column %/k households)

Construction & additional insulation		Under £4,500	£4,500 to £8,500	£8,500 to £13,500	£13,500 to £19,500	£19,500 or more	All hholds
Wall construction							
	Cavity	56.9	61.3	60.2	65.4	66.2	61.9
	Masonry solid	32.8	31.1	32.7	28.9	30.2	31.2
	Other	10.4	7.6	7.2	5.7	3.5	6.9
Wall insulation							
	Cavity fill	9.8	13.8	15.2	20.8	22.8	16.3
	Non-cavity	4.9	4.6	5.9	6.3	7.1	5.7
	None	85.3	81.7	79.0	72.9	70.0	77.9
Double glazing							
	Full	14.8	17.6	23.4	33.2	33.3	24.2
	Partial	21.1	27.4	33.0	35.4	43.4	31.8
	None	64.1	55.0	43.6	31.4	23.3	44.0
Draught proofing							
	Full	3.2	4.0	5.0	5.7	6.4	4.8
	Partial	22.1	27.5	25.2	26.1	29.3	26.0
	None	74.7	68.5	69.8	68.2	64.1	69.2
Loft insulation							
House	loft insulation	51.5	67.0	72.8	83.6	82.7	71.2
with	no insulation	8.1	7.7	9.4	5.1	5.1	7.1
	no loft	4.1	4.1	4.0	2.5	3.8	3.7
Flat	on top floor	12.6	8.6	6.3	4.1	3.9	7.2
	not top floor	23.7	12.7	7.4	4.7	4.5	10.8
All households		**4,011**	**3,938**	**3,713**	**3,803**	**3,646**	**19,111**

Sample: H1

A7.8   **Mean and % of low and high SAP ratings by employment status by tenure**

(SAP rating/row %/k households)

Employment status by tenure	Mean SAP	% of homes < 20	% of homes 50 +	Total thous	Mean SAP	% of homes < 20	% of homes 50 +	Total thous
Private sector	Owner occupiers			(nk 30)	Private tenants			(nk 6)
Two+ 2+ full time	39.4	5.9	18.5	2,308	25.1	35.0	7.8	219
adults only 1 full time	39.9	6.4	20.4	4,158	24.4	34.2	8.0	315
part time only	36.8	10.2	17.9	671	34.9	33.7	3.4	94
2 unemployed	36.9	10.2	16.7	415	15.8	53.9	1.5	102
2 retired	35.3	12.9	12.7	1,959	24.6	45.9	10.7	127
2 students etc	28.9	23.7	11.7	108	23.3	38.5	0	20
Lone full time work	35.6	14.3	17.0	1,013	23.6	36.4	6.1	245
adult part time	33.0	21.7	18.5	275	19.4	47.2	2.5	65
unemployed	38.8	17.0	35.1	131	14.8	57.2	0	77
retired	32.1	18.1	12.1	1,418	12.1	62.5	1.3	233
student etc	35.6	14.6	19.0	385	25.9	32.2	7.6	198
Social sector	Council tenants			(nk 11)	HA tenants			(nk 1)
Two+ 2 full time work	38.5	11.2	18.3	124	42.3	6.8	38.8	29
adults only 1 full time	35.2	15.4	16.5	504	32.4	17.8	9.7	63
part time only	34.4	14.5	12.3	177	42.8	10.2	33.3	24
2 unemployed	35.4	17.0	16.5	289	38.1	12.5	15.7	20
2 retired	31.6	23.7	12.5	620	35.9	17.1	22.3	81
2 students etc	34.9	14.7	16.7	130	41.3	14.5	28.0	19
Lone full time work	39.1	13.9	27.3	157	31.7	21.2	7.7	34
adult part time	34.8	17.8	12.0	141	30.7	20.4	13.0	24
unemployed	34.2	22.6	22.3	160	35.0	22.8	28.7	33
retired	32.7	19.5	13.7	945	31.3	26.1	10.6	194
student etc	36.5	13.1	19.5	620	35.0	11.5	18.5	139

Sample: S1

A7.9   **Mean and % of low and high SAP ratings by socio-economic group by tenure**

(SAP rating/row %/k households)

Economic status by tenure	Mean SAP	% of homes < 20	% of homes 50 +	Total thous	Mean SAP	% of homes < 20	% of homes 50 +	Total thous
Private sector	Owner occupiers				Private tenants			
Professional	41.9	5.7	28.1	1,191	31.4	18.9	4.9	71
Employer or manager	38.8	7.0	19.2	3,381	27.1	36.3	5.2	223
Intermed. non-manual	39.3	8.9	21.7	1,719	33.9	27.4	29.5	171
Junior non-manual	36.7	10.7	14.6	1,141	20.6	42.4	4.4	166
Skilled manual	34.9	12.8	12.3	3,681	18.8	47.0	1.8	457
Semi-skilled	33.2	17.0	13.1	1,112	13.3	60.1	2.4	305
Unskilled manual	35.7	13.9	21.0	355	22.1	41.0	11.3	122
Armed forced	42.4	9.4	19.4	114	35.8	7.0	9.0	57
Never worked etc	37.1	17.9	27.1	180	28.0	29.4	11.2	129
Social sector	Council tenants				HA tenants			
Professional	39.0	18.8	28.1	28	37.3	10.9	30.9	8
Employer or manager	36.1	14.3	18.8	235	32.3	15.3	17.9	44
Intermed. non-manual	37.4	12.5	18.3	166	35.9	11.2	14.9	35
Junior non-manual	36.9	15.0	20.8	370	31.6	30.6	20.2	85
Skilled manual	33.4	18.2	15.3	1,369	33.4	19.0	12.4	198
Semi-skilled	33.8	20.4	15.0	1,056	36.0	15.6	18.3	182
Unskilled manual	34.1	15.5	14.0	508	40.3	10.7	35.6	55
Armed forced	28.5	46.8	0	3	0	0	0	1
Never worked etc	35.9	19.1	16.2	143	29.0	19.0	3.4	54

Sample: S1

A7.10   Mean and distribution of SAP ratings by age of children in household by tenure

(SAP rating/row %/k households)

Tenure and childrens age	Mean SAP	< 10	10-20	20-30	30-40	40-50	50-60	60 +	All h/holds
Owner Occupier	**37.2**	**4.5**	**6.0**	**15.2**	**29.2**	**27.7**	**13.6**	**3.9**	**12,872**
None under 11 yrs	36.3	5.3	6.8	15.9	29.2	26.9	12.1	3.8	9,776
Some 6 to 10 yrs	40.1	1.9	3.3	12.3	31.2	28.9	18.5	3.9	1,193
Some 4 to 5 yrs	41.1	1.9	2.9	13.3	28.9	24.1	26.0	2.8	488
Some under 4 yrs	39.7	2.1	3.9	13.3	27.4	33.6	15.1	4.6	1,416
Private tenants	**22.4**	**25.7**	**16.2**	**20.0**	**16.8**	**13.9**	**3.3**	**4.2**	**1,700**
None under 11 yrs	21.1	28.8	16.6	18.5	14.6	13.9	3.5	4.2	1,371
Some 6 to 10 yrs	25.6	15.3	18.1	39.3	11.1	13.3	0	2.9	46
Some 4 to 5 yrs	25.1	10.8	14.7	39.3	22.9	7.2	4.9	0	44
Some under 4 yrs	28.8	12.4	13.6	20.6	30.5	15.6	2.3	5.0	239
Council tenants	**34.4**	**7.2**	**10.5**	**16.7**	**26.4**	**23.1**	**11.8**	**4.2**	**3,877**
None under 11 yrs	33.7	8.2	11.3	16.7	26.8	21.8	11.3	4.0	2,835
Some 6 to 10 yrs	36.9	5.1	8.3	15.4	27.5	23.7	14.7	5.3	283
Some 4 to 5 yrs	37.2	3.6	6.1	16.2	30.1	25.9	15.3	2.8	164
Some under 4 yrs	35.9	5.0	9.2	17.9	23.2	27.9	11.9	5.0	595
HA tenants	**34.4**	**6.8**	**11.5**	**17.6**	**25.1**	**21.6**	**12.6**	**4.9**	**662**
None under 11 yrs	33.8	8.1	12.8	16.8	23.9	21.3	11.2	5.9	504
Some 6 to 10 yrs	39.5	0	7.3	18.0	26.9	24.9	20.9	2.0	39
Some 4 to 5 yrs	34.4	5.8	13.3	13.8	11.4	43.3	6.7	5.7	34
Some under 4 yrs	34.8	3.7	6.5	22.9	35.7	12.5	18.2	0.6	86
All households	**35.3**	**6.9**	**8.0**	**16.1**	**27.5**	**25.2**	**12.3**	**4.0**	**19,111**

Sample: S1

A7.11   Mean and distribution of SAP ratings by age of elderly occupants by tenure

(SAP rating/row %/k households)

Tenure and household type	Mean SAP	< 10	10-20	20-30	30-40	40-50	50-60	60 +	All h/holds
Owner Occupier	**37.2**	**4.5**	**6.0**	**15.2**	**29.2**	**27.7**	**13.6**	**3.9**	**12,872**
All under 65	38.2	3.8	5.0	13.5	29.3	29.7	15.0	3.7	10,445
65-74 years	34.1	6.3	9.2	16.4	31.7	22.7	12.3	1.4	1,165
75-84 years	31.5	8.3	10.2	23.1	31.3	20.2	4.3	2.6	924
85 or more	32.6	10.3	13.0	38.4	12.2	3.4	0.3	22.5	338
Private tenants	**22.4**	**25.7**	**16.2**	**20.0**	**16.8**	**13.9**	**3.3**	**4.2**	**1,700**
All under 65	24.6	21.6	15.3	22.1	16.7	16.1	3.0	5.3	1,364
65-74 years	13.8	46.8	17.4	11.0	11.7	9.2	3.9	0	118
75-84 years	15.7	33.9	22.0	14.0	16.8	6.2	7.1	0	141
85 or more	12.2	41.9	18.2	11.7	26.5	1.7	0	0	76
Council tenants	**34.4**	**7.2**	**10.5**	**16.7**	**26.4**	**23.1**	**11.8**	**4.2**	**3,877**
All under 65	35.4	6.7	9.6	15.1	26.1	25.1	12.7	4.6	2,625
65-74 years	32.2	7.4	11.4	23.1	27.3	16.7	12.0	2.1	575
75-84 years	32.9	7.9	14.3	16.7	26.3	20.7	9.2	4.8	525
85 or more	29.0	13.5	9.2	22.9	28.4	20.4	4.5	1.2	152
HA tenants	**34.4**	**6.8**	**11.5**	**17.6**	**25.1**	**21.6**	**12.6**	**4.9**	**662**
All under 65	35.0	5.8	11.1	19.4	21.9	22.8	13.2	5.8	447
65-74 years	33.3	10.1	14.8	18.2	13.3	21.8	21.2	0.5	90
75-84 years	33.5	9.2	9.8	8.4	46.5	16.4	4.9	4.8	101
85 or more	29.0	5.9	17.9	17.3	39.3	17.2	2.4	0	23
All households	**35.3**	**6.9**	**8.0**	**16.1**	**27.5**	**25.2**	**12.3**	**4.0**	**19,111**

Sample: S1

A7.12 Mean and % of low and high SAP ratings by vulnerable occupants by tenure

(SAP rating/row %/k households)

Vulnerable group by tenure		Mean SAP	% of homes < 20	50 +	Total thous	Mean SAP	% of homes < 20	50 +	Total thous
Private sector		**Owner occupiers**			**12,872**	**Private tenants**			**1,700**
Under 75 yrs with:-	no special problem	37.9	9.5	19.0	9,939	24.4	37.7	8.5	1,259
	respiratory illness	37.5	8.8	13.9	1,391	19.9	46.6	5.1	200
	mobility problem	35.5	12.4	7.7	280	20.0	59.5	0	23
75 yrs or older with:	no special problem	32.3	21.3	14.0	937	15.8	55.3	5.6	176
	respiratory illness	31.3	23.6	6.9	109	8.3	53.2	0	22
	mobility problem	29.5	11.3	0.3	216	9.5	79.8	0	20
Social sector		**Council tenants**			**3,877**	**HA tenants**			**662**
Under 75 yrs with:-	no special problem	35.0	16.7	17.5	2,237	35.7	17.1	21.8	390
	respiratory illness	34.7	16.8	16.4	765	31.6	21.1	14.2	125
	mobility problem	34.1	17.9	10.5	198	36.6	13.5	6.5	23
75 yrs or older with:	no special problem	32.3	24.2	14.5	418	33.8	16.2	12.5	74
	respiratory illness	31.1	22.8	7.0	126	31.9	31.0	0	26
	mobility problem	32.5	15.8	10.7	134	30.0	18.1	5.8	24

Sample: S1

A7.13 Distribution of household types in homes of particular SAP ratings by tenure

(Row %/k households)

Tenure and SAP rating	lone parent	two adult	small family	large family	large adult	lone adult	two older	lone older	All h/holds
Owner Occupier									**12,872**
under SAP 10	18.3	12.7	0.6	7.0	6.3	10.6	20.7	23.9	577
10 to 20	9.1	19.6	1.9	12.8	8.1	10.6	20.3	17.7	766
20 to 30	7.4	17.8	2.2	15.6	7.5	11.0	18.6	19.8	1,948
30 to 40	5.1	22.3	1.7	18.4	11.7	13.5	17.5	9.8	3,765
40 to 50	5.4	20.9	1.5	23.1	13.2	12.5	·16.5	6.9	3,573
50 to 60	3.8	18.1	5.2	24.7	15.7	16.1	11.0	5.5	1,749
60 or over	13.4	15.7	2.6	24.6	4.1	6.6	10.3	22.7	494
Private tenants									**1,700**
under SAP 10	15.1	20.3	3.0	7.6	2.7	7.6	16.9	26.8	444
10 to 20	17.2	13.5	4.0	15.2	5.2	13.2	9.9	21.8	273
20 to 30	21.8	18.8	4.7	18.0	5.0	10.3	11.1	10.4	338
30 to 40	9.5	15.2	9.9	15.9	9.4	15.2	6.3	18.6	284
40 to 50	25.7	27.8	2.3	11.7	5.5	7.1	15.0	4.8	240
50 to 60	32.3	22.1	5.2	8.1	0	6.4	20.9	5.1	56
60 or over	4.4	61.2	0	17.7	0	6.9	9.7	0	65
Council tenants									**3,877**
under SAP 10	12.9	8.0	4.9	9.5	5.7	11.7	21.7	25.7	280
10 to 20	7.5	6.6	6.2	12.4	8.0	10.7	20.6	28.1	404
20 to 30	6.7	7.0	9.3	14.3	7.9	7.7	16.7	30.4	643
30 to 40	7.8	6.6	9.0	12.6	10.4	8.5	21.9	23.3	1,023
40 to 50	7.9	10.5	11.1	13.1	12.1	10.8	15.3	19.3	900
50 to 60	12.3	8.7	11.1	13.2	10.7	8.1	15.6	20.2	462
60 or over	14.8	10.0	16.3	7.4	10.3	12.4	8.1	20.7	165
HA tenants									**662**
under SAP 10	17.0	12.3	2.6	9.8	4.2	8.6	15.8	29.7	37
10 to 20	31.8	4.2	13.7	9.8	2.3	5.8	10.9	21.4	67
20 to 30	17.5	8.8	17.5	8.5	7.8	1.3	17.1	21.4	110
30 to 40	14.3	5.1	9.2	18.3	3.9	5.6	12.0	21.6	166
40 to 50	13.8	2.5	9.9	11.0	13.1	10.3	8.8	30.6	155
50 to 60	15.6	3.6	19.7	11.9	5.9	4.8	18.8	19.7	91
60 or over	7.0	28.2	9.4	0	6.3	23.0	14.5	11.6	36
All households	**35.3**	**6.9**	**8.0**	**16.1**	**27.5**	**25.2**	**12.3**	**4.0**	**19,111**

Sample: S1

A7.14 Distribution of household types in the most and least efficient dwelling types in each tenure

(SAP rating/row %/k households)

Best and worst dwelling types in each tenure	Mean SAP	Row % of household type in dwelling type								Total h/holds
		lone parent	small family	large family	large adult	two adults	lone adult	two older	lone older	
Owner Occupied	High									
Post 1980 all houses	51.7	6.6	38.7	10.3	4.9	23.9	5.0	5.6	5.1	858
Post 1980 all flats	47.7	10.6	2.1	0	1.5	3.0	48.0	13.0	21.7	136
1965-80 large terrace	47.5	2.2	13.4	21.7	16.2	26.3	6.4	8.8	5.0	230
1965-80 all flats	46.3	0.5	13.0	1.2	6.2	21.8	9.9	13.4	34.0	207
1965-80 detached	43.4	0.7	22.1	15.3	18.0	22.5	1.1	18.5	1.8	1,020
	Low									
Pre 1965 bungalows	29.3	1.1	8.2	3.1	9.1	14.9	0.6	35.3	27.6	638
Pre 1919 small terr.	28.4	3.7	18.1	7.8	8.0	22.7	15.6	12.3	11.7	846
Private rented	High									
Post 1980 all types	46.2	0	9.1	0	0	56.1	24.7	10.1	0	82
	Low									
Pre 1965 conv	26.2	7.0	5.9	2.6	3.5	28.6	40.4	1.9	10.1	344
Pre 1919 large terrace	24.5	5.4	9.9	4.4	21.1	12.8	17.4	10.9	18.1	192
1945-64 large ter/semi	22.8	5.6	12.9	17.7	13.8	15.4	23.2	5.1	6.3	81
1919-44 semi & det.	19.1	1.4	3.8	2.6	13.3	23.5	14.1	12.7	28.7	117
Pre 1919 small terrace	16.1	5.7	15.8	4.7	12.1	14.6	9.1	12.8	25.0	202
All bungalows	10.0	0	27.0	0	4.9	18.4	8.3	34.4	7.0	103
Pre 1919 semi & det.	8.9	1.8	12.4	9.4	12.0	24.4	10.5	14.8	14.8	265
Social rented	High									
Post 1980 all types	50.7	5.9	4.8	9.1	7.4	3.8	19.7	12.8	36.5	194
1965-80 high rise flats	49.4	24.3	8.7	2.7	1.6	3.6	19.2	15.5	24.4	148
1965-80 large terrace	44.5	14.9	14.5	21.6	17.8	13.4	3.9	12.0	1.9	203
Pre 1965 high rise	42.9	9.2	15.0	3.9	1.1	9.2	19.3	17.2	25.0	102
1965-80 low rise/conv.	42.7	6.0	4.4	1.6	3.7	6.4	17.6	13.9	46.4	638
	Low									
1919-45 semi	29.1	9.5	19.1	14.8	15.6	8.1	4.5	17.0	11.5	418
1945-64 large ter./semi	28.1	9.3	16.2	14.0	12.5	6.1	4.2	23.4	14.2	681
Pre 1980 bungalows	25.3	0	1.6	0.5	4.5	3.6	3.6	30.4	55.6	368
Pre 1919 semi & det.	20.0	2.7	11.3	9.7	17.6	16.8	13.8	16.1	12.0	22

Sample: S2

A7.15 Distribution of household types by SAP rating in most common dwelling type in owner occupied and social rented sector

(SAP rating/row %/k households)

Most common type and SAP bands	Row % of household types in homes of set SAP rating								Total hholds
	lone parent	small family	large family	large adult	two adults	lone adult	two older	lone older	
Owner occupied									
1919-1945 semi-D									1,369
50 or more	1.3	31.7	19.0	19.5	1.3	25.4	1.3	1.8	65
40 to 50	1.6	26.5	20.7	17.1	16.1	1.1	12.2	4.7	282
30 to 40	2.2	20.7	12.7	16.7	20.2	3.9	15.0	8.7	596
20 to 30	2.4	21.0	8.8	14.5	19.1	7.0	14.6	12.5	251
10 to 20	0	12.7	7.5	13.1	20.2	11.6	13.5	21.4	110
Under 10	0	13.7	10.0	21.8	3.6	9.7	24.4	16.8	65
Social Rented									
1965-80 low rise flats									638
60 or more	0	6.3	1.6	27.3	14.4	11.8	17.8	20.8	60
50 to 60	14.3	4.5	2.2	1.3	4.5	26.0	12.9	34.4	147
40 to 50	10.1	3.9	0	1.1	11.7	13.5	9.0	50.7	171
30 to 40	4.9	5.7	3.3	2.8	3.4	19.3	21.7	38.9	158
20 to 30	0	1.6	3.0	0	0	40.5	9.4	46.5	56
Under 20	0	2.9	2.9	0	14.3	14.3	5.7	60.0	46

Sample: S3

A8.1 Comparison of case study dwelling sizes and energy efficiencies with mean for all households of same tenure, type and size

Case study figures/(mean for household type & size in tenure)

	Case 1 OO - 4p family	Case 2 OO - 3p family	Case 3 LA - 4p family	Case 4 HA - 1p adult	All h/holds
Physical standards					
Dwelling size m²	85 (95)	119 (82)	74 (66)	94 (49)	**83**
Space heating	Gas CH	Oil CH	Gas CH+NCH	Coal+elec. NCH	
Water heating	Gas CH	Oil CH	Electric NCH	Coal NCH	
Insulation³	W,L,C,Dg	L C De	L C	L	
Energy SAP rating	65 (43)	34 (37)	19 (33)	5 (32)	**35**
Heating price index	82 (90)	73 (95)	120 (105)	162 (124)	**100**
Heat loss index	60 (91)	128 (99)	113 (99)	114 (93)	**100**
Energy consumption					
Cooking fuel	Electricity	Electricity	Mains gas	Electricity	
Total consumption					
KWh (000s)	27.5 (29.2)	59.2 (26.0)	25.6 (22.6)	17.6 (11)	**24.0**
Unit consumption					
kWh/m²	324 (324)	498 (329)	346 (353)	188 (238)	**303**
% gas	83 (74)	0 (68)	86 (67)	0 (36)	**66**
% electricity	17 (21)	16 (24)	14 (24)	21 (57)	**26**
% other fuels	0 (5)	84 (8)	0 (9)	79 (7)	**8**
Unit fuel cost					
p/kWh	2.78 (2.90)	1.90 (2.97)	2.63 (3.15)	2.66 (4.70)	**3.23**
Total expenditure £	767 (787)	1127 (731)	675 (677)	468 (404)	**661**
Unit expenditure					
£/m²	9.02 (8.95)	9.47 (9.29)	9.12 (10.41)	4.98 (9.35)	**8.68**
% gas	50 (47)	0 (44)	55 (41)	0 (22)	**43**
% electricity	50 (51)	68 (52)	45 (55)	71 (75)	**53**
% other fuels	0 (2)	32 (4)	0 (4)	29 (3)	**4**
Thermal conditions					
Outside temp °C	11.4 (10.9)	11.3 (11.5)	12.9 (10.6)	11.9 (11.1)	**11.1**
Living room temp °C	22.2 (19.4)	18.9 (19.8)	13.2 (19.7)	13.0 (18.8)	**19.5**
Hall/stairs temp °C	21.4 (18.5)	19.7 (18.8)	13.8 (18.0)	13.0 (18.1)	**18.3**
Mould growth index	1.0 (0.26)	3.5 (0.33)	2.0 (0.96)	0.0 (0.70)	**0.34**
Energy Action					
Adequacy of spend¹	122 (94.5)	94.2 (97.4)	67.8 (94.6)	32.3 (91.3)	**87.7**
Target SAP rating	65	51	81	86	
Improvement cost £	0	3,930	7,410	10,480	-
Energy saving² kWh	4,000	14,440	22,130	41,760	-
Cost saving² £	120	275	585	1,110	-
Simple payback yrs	-	14	13	10	-

¹ adequacy to achieve standard heating regime

² assuming standard heating regime and normal energy use for dwelling and household size

³ Insulation: W=cavity wall fill, L=loft insulation, C=cylinder insulation, Dg=Double glazing, De=draught stripping.

A9.1 Reasons for not using the central heating system

(Column %/k households)

Reason for not using central heating	%	H/holds
Expensive/can't afford to run	38.4	107
Needs repair/system too old	3.5	10
Expensive/can't afford to run and needs repair/system too old	5.3	15
Too hot	1.8	5
Too hot and expensive/can't afford to run	3.4	9
Too cold	0.7	2
Other	38.2	106
Other and expensive/can't afford to run	7.6	21
No reason given	1.1	3
Total	**100.0**	**279**

Sample: E4

A9.2 Central heating controls and their usage

(Row %/k households)

Central heating control	% changing named control at least once a week	% rarely or never changing control in winter	% of households with central heating and the named control	H/holds with central heating and the named control
On radiators or vents: manual control	12.5	81.3	68.7	10,799
On radiators or vents: thermostatic valves	24.0	71.2	22.6	3,549
On other appliances: thermostats	16.0	76.6	15.7	2,466
On other appliances: heat output control	28.1	65.3	7.6	1,201
On other appliances: time switches	14.6	76.6	9.8	1,542
Wall thermostat	46.1	49.1	58.8	9,254
Central time switch/ programmer	18.0	76.2	78.6	12,352
Manual override on timer/ programmer	44.4	49.1	69.9	10,985
Overnight charge control on central unit	6.4	85.3	2.5	387
Other	32.7	58.8	2.4	380

Sample: E2

A9.3 Non-central heating controls and their usage

(Row %/k households)

Named control	% of h/holds changing control at least once a week	% of h/holds rarely or never changing control during winter	H/holds
Over night control	39.3	49.7	42
Heat output	79.5	19.0	2,253
Time switch	24.0	76.0	114
Thermostat	34.2	60.7	397
Other	81.4	10.5	17

Sample: E3

A9.4   Saturday heating patterns

(Column %/k households)

Saturday heating pattern same as:	Living room		Bedroom	
	%	Numbers	%	Numbers
Weekday and Sunday pattern	63.2	12,095	78.5	14,712
Sunday pattern only	14.3	2,736	11.3	2,119
Weekday pattern only	9.2	1,750	4.0	7,48
Neither weekday or Sunday	13.2	2,530	6.2	1,165
Households	**100.0**	**19,111**	**100.0**	**19,111**

Sample: E1

A9.5   Heating patterns by tenure

(Row %/k households)

Pattern	All day	Morning and evening	Evening only	Not regular	Don't know	No heat	Room does not exist	H/holds
Owner occupiers								
Living room weekdays	32.6	46.0	20.0	0.9	0.4	0	0	12,872
Living room Sundays	53.8	28.9	15.7	1.2	0.4	0	0	
Bedroom weekdays	16.4	43.8	19.3	13.5	1.2	5.7	0	
Bedroom Sundays	25.7	37.1	17.3	13.8	0.3	5.7	0	
Private renting tenants								
Living room weekdays	43.2	31.0	21.8	2.4	1.5	0	0	1,700
Living room Sundays	58.9	21.9	13.5	3.0	2.8	0	0	
Bedroom weekdays	12.2	27.6	17.3	20.1	3.2	18.5	1.1	
Bedroom Sundays	19.7	25.4	12.6	21.7	1.7	18.0	0.9	
Local authority tenants								
Living room weekdays	44.5	29.2	22.5	2.4	1.2	0.3	0	3,877
Living room Sundays	57.7	17.8	19.7	3.3	1.3	0.3	0	
Bedroom weekdays	14.2	23.0	21.0	20.2	2.3	19.2	0.1	
Bedroom Sundays	17.8	22.0	19.4	20.5	0.9	19.3	0.1	
Housing association tenants								
Living room weekdays	38.5	25.6	28.8	2.2	4.8	0.1	0	662
Living room Sundays	48.7	15.3	27.8	3.3	4.8	0.1	0	
Bedroom weekdays	15.9	23.1	21.9	19.7	0.6	14.4	4.4	
Bedroom Sundays	19.4	18.5	23.6	19.9	0.3	13.8	4.4	

Sample: E1

A9.6   Living room weekday heating pattern by dwelling age and type

(Row %/k households)

Dwelling age and type	All day	Morning and evening	Evening only	Not regular	Don't know	No heat	H/holds
Pre-1965 converted flat	37.5	36.1	21.4	1.7	3.3	0	1,037
Pre-1965 PB low-rise flat	39.2	31.6	24.8	3.9	0.2	0.3	943
Pre-1965 PB high-rise flat	56.3	21.8	21.8	0	0	0	129
1965-80 PB low-rise/conv. flat	40.5	31.4	19.0	3.6	4.5	1.0	886
1965-80 PB high-rise flat	48.1	22.3	20.9	3.1	5.6	0	158
Post-1980 all flats	57.2	26.3	14.6	0	1.8	0	291
Pre-1945 bungalow	52.6	36.5	10.9	0	0	0	280
1945-80 bungalow	47.1	36.1	16.4	0.1	0.3	0	1,335
Post-1980 bungalow	49.9	29.7	20.4	0	0	0	256
Pre-1919 small terrace	37.4	34.0	26.1	1.6	0.8	0	1,140
Pre-1919 medium/large terrace	30.7	36.9	27.2	4.7	0.5	0	1,286
Pre-1919 semi/detached house	38.1	42.1	18.0	1.3	0.5	0	1,420
1919-44 small terrace	42.6	33.9	23.2	0	0.3	0	623
1919-44 medium/large terrace	30.1	37.8	31.5	0.1	0.6	0	351
1919-44 semi-detached house	36.3	42.1	19.5	1.1	0.8	0.2	1,871
1919-44 detached house	27.7	55.3	15.1	1.5	0.4	0	500
1945-64 small terrace	36.4	36.1	26.4	1.1	0	0	401
1945-64 med/large terr./semi	33.3	38.5	27.0	0.8	0.4	0	2,095
1945-64 detached	20.6	68.1	9.7	1.6	0	0	394
1965-80 small terrace and semi	34.4	41.4	22.4	1.3	0.5	0	1,233
1965-80 medium/large terrace	34.4	48.3	16.0	0.2	1.2	0	456
1965-80 detached	23.5	56.9	19.2	0	0.4	0	1,046
Post-1980 all houses	31.3	56.1	12.4	0.3	0	0	980
Households	**36.2**	**40.5**	**21.0**	**1.4**	**0.8**	**0**	**19,111**

Sample: E1

A9.7   Living room weekday heating pattern by region (met and non met)

(Row %/k households)

Region (met and non met)	All day	Morning and evening	Evening only	Not regular	Don't know	No heat	H/holds
Tyne & Wear met	35.9	36.0	25.2	1.9	1.0	0	397
Northern non met	37.7	37.2	24.4	0.2	0.5	0	649
South Yorks met	37.1	34.3	26.2	2.0	0.5	0	583
West Yorks met	39.1	42.4	16.6	1.1	0.9	0	752
Yorks. & Humb. non met	35.3	37.5	26.0	1.2	0	0	603
Greater Manchester	30.1	42.1	26.1	1.4	0.3	0	1,019
North West non met	35.2	38.6	24.6	1.1	0.5	0	1172
Merseyside TF	36.6	40.9	21.0	1.0	0	0.6	526
East Midlands	45.4	35.3	16.4	1.8	0.9	0.1	1,548
West Midlands met	43.1	30.5	25.0	0.5	1.0	0	963
West Midlands non met	43.8	35.1	18.5	1.4	1.2	0	1,096
South West	38.1	38.9	21.6	1.0	0.4	0	1,310
Devon & Cornwall	34.2	33.7	29.9	1.8	0.3	0.1	602
Eastern	31.8	47.0	20.7	0.4	0	0	2,211
Inner London	38.1	37.1	20.4	2.8	1.3	0.2	1,059
Outer London	31.4	42.6	21.4	2.9	1.3	0.3	1,804
South East	32.4	49.6	15.2	1.3	1.6	0	2,819
Households	**36.2**	**40.5**	**21.0**	**1.4**	**0.8**	**0**	**19,111**

Sample: E1

A9.8   Heating patterns by main type of heating used

(Row %/k households)

Pattern	All day	Morning and evening	Evening only	Not regular	Don't know	No heat	Room does not exist	H/holds
CENTRAL HEATING								
Gas central heating								
Living room weekdays	27.2	50.1	21.1	1.1	0.4	0	0	12,546
Living room Sundays	48.7	32.1	16.9	1.6	0.6	0	0	
Bedroom weekdays	14.6	47.3	22.0	11.6	1.7	2.7	0	
Bedroom Sundays	24.1	40.7	20.0	11.9	0.6	2.6	0	
Solid fuel central heating								
Living room weekdays	70.7	15.7	10.8	2.5	0.3	0	0	868
Living room Sundays	77.2	10.2	9.4	1.0	2.2	0	0	
Bedroom weekdays	39.5	24.6	11.6	18.1	1.2	5.0	0	
Bedroom Sundays	47.7	23.6	7.7	16.1	0	4.9	0	
Electric central heating								
Living room weekdays	58.5	11.9	24.8	1.1	3.8	0	0	1,453
Living room Sundays	65.4	8.3	22.3	1.1	2.9	0	0	
Bedroom weekdays	24.7	20.8	15.4	23.6	1.7	12.0	0	
Bedroom Sundays	26.1	18.5	15.0	26.1	0.5	11.9	1.8	
Oil central heating								
Living room weekdays	25.3	53.9	20.2	0	0.6	0	0	585
Living room Sundays	47.0	32.7	18.9	0	1.4	0	0	
Bedroom weekdays	18.4	55.3	9.5	10.7	4.3	1.8	0	
Bedroom Sundays	30.4	47.4	8.3	11.1	0.8	1.9	0	
Other central heating								
Living room weekdays	37.9	36.7	24.6	0.8	0.1	0	0	272
Living room Sundays	63.0	28.1	8.8	0	0.1	0	0	
Bedroom weekdays	28.3	34.7	14.3	0.1	8.1	0	0	
Bedroom Sundays	30.6	35.1	11.7	15.2	0.1	7.3	0	
All central heating								
Living room weekdays	32.6	44.5	20.9	1.1	0.7	0	0	15,724
Living room Sundays	52.0	28.7	16.9	1.4	0.9	0	0	
Bedroom weekdays	17.3	43.7	20.2	13.1	1.7	3.8	0.2	
Bedroom Sundays	26.0	37.9	18.3	13.5	0.5	3.7	0.2	
NON-CENTRAL HEATING								
Gas non-central heating								
Living room weekdays	52.9	23.3	21.3	1.8	0.8	0	0	2,418
Living room Sundays	67.7	11.2	16.8	3.6	0.7	0	0	
Bedroom weekdays	7.4	7.4	16.7	27.9	0.7	39.2	0.7	
Bedroom Sundays	11.6	5.6	14.4	28.4	0.3	39.1	0.6	
Solid fuel non-central heating								
Living room weekdays	64.6	10.4	21.4	2.8	0.8	0	0	467
Living room Sundays	76.5	3.1	16.0	3.6	0.8	0	0	
Bedroom weekdays	2.3	10.2	12.6	36.6	3.2	35.1	0	
Bedroom Sundays	2.6	8.1	12.6	40.3	0.6	35.8	0	
Fixed electric non-central heating								
Living room weekdays	44.3	29.6	20.1	3.5	2.5	0	0	176
Living room Sundays	63.6	15.6	8.6	9.7	2.5	0	0	
Bedroom weekdays	12.8	15.1	21.4	29.5	1.0	18.8	1.5	
Bedroom Sundays	19.0	10.7	19.6	29.5	1.0	18.8	1.5	
Portable heating								
Living room weekdays	37.8	26.7	21.4	8.3	3.1	2.7	0	326
Living room Sundays	59.8	20.3	10.3	3.8	2.1	2.7	0	
Bedroom weekdays	13	9.0	16.1	11.9	1.5	46.9	1.6	
Bedroom Sundays	13.4	11.2	10.7	11.9	1.5	49.7	1.6	
All non central heating								
Living room weekdays	52.6	22.1	21.3	2.6	1.1	0.3	0	3,387
Living room Sundays	67.9	11.2	15.6	3.9	1.1	0.3	0	
Bedroom weekdays	7.5	8.3	16.3	27.6	1.1	38.3	0.7	
Bedroom Sundays	11.0	6.7	14.1	28.4	0.5	38.6	0.6	

Sample: E1

A9.9 Living room weekday heating pattern by dwelling fitness and provision for heating

(Row %/k households)

Fitness assessment	All day	Morning and evening	Evening only	Not regular	Don't know	No heat	Room does not exist	H/holds
Dwelling fitness								
Fit	35.3	41.3	21.2	1.4	0.8	0.1	0	17,698
Unfit	48.1	31.3	17.7	1.9	0.9	0.2	0	1,414
Provision for heating								
Unfit	61.4	12.9	15.1	6.4	2.1	2.2	0	191
Defective	59.4	23.7	14.0	1.8	1.1	0	0	540
Just acceptable	46.9	25.3	24.8	1.5	1.5	0.1	0	1,733
Satisfactory	34.2	42.9	20.8	1.3	0.7	0.1	0	16,647

Sample: E1

A9.10 Heating pattern in centrally heated dwellings by level of control

(Row %/k households)

Pattern	All day	Morning and evening	Evening only	Not regular	Don't know	No heat	Room does not exist	H/holds
living room weekday heating pattern								
No time or temperature	60.2	15.5	17.5	2.6	4.1	0.1	0	1,886
Time only	26.7	48.8	23.1	1.0	0.4	0	0	2,075
Temperature only	58.6	21.1	17.7	1.1	1.0	0.4	0	776
Time and temperature	27.2	50.4	21.3	0.9	0.2	0	0	10,986
living room weekend heating pattern								
No time or temperature	67.2	10.0	16.7	1.6	4.4	0.1	0	1,886
Time only	46.3	32.8	18.6	1.4	1.0	0	0	2,075
Temperature only	70.9	14.7	11.1	1.3	1.5	0.4	0	776
Time and temperature	49.2	32.1	17.1	1.4	0.3	0	0	10,986

Sample: E2

A9.11 Living room weekday heating pattern by SAP rating

(Row %/k households)

SAP rating	All day	Morning and evening	Evening only	Not regular	Don't know	No heat	Room does not exist	H/holds
< 10	56.4	17.7	20.8	3.9	0.9	0.2	0	1,318
10-20	53.2	20.8	23.3	1.4	1.1	0.2	0	1,527
20-30	47.8	29.4	20.8	1.2	0.8	0	0	3,071
30-40	30.4	45.6	22.0	0.9	1.0	0.1	0	5,275
40-50	28.4	48.4	21.8	1.1	0.4	0	0	4,822
50-60	33.1	47.4	17.3	2.0	0	0.2	0	2,342
60-70	25.8	59.4	11.0	3.1	0.7	0	0	677
70 +	17.1	51.0	29.3	0	2.6	0	0	79

Sample: S2

A9.12 Heating patterns by household type

(Row %/k households)

Pattern	All day	Morning and evening	Evening only	Not regular	Don't know	No heat	Room does not exist	H/holds
Single (non pensioner)								
Living room weekdays	34.8	30.4	28.3	4.5	1.5	0.4	0	1,613
Living room Sundays	50.5	18.8	20.5	6.6	3.3	0.4	0	
Bedroom weekdays	15.1	26.5	22.3	17.5	2.1	16.3	0.3	
Bedroom Sundays	20.8	24.0	18.7	17.8	1.6	16.8	0.2	
Couple (non pensioner)								
Living room weekdays	24.6	49.0	23.9	1.9	0.4	0.1	0	3,223
Living room Sundays	55.9	26.4	14.7	2.3	0.6	0.1	0	
Bedroom weekdays	10.7	45.2	22.6	13.3	1.1	7.0	0	
Bedroom Sundays	24.5	37.9	17.0	13.3	0.6	6.7	0	
Lone parent								
Living room weekdays	42.9	31.1	24.2	0.8	0.9	0	0	779
Living room Sundays	54.5	20.9	19.2	4.6	0.9	0	0	
Bedroom weekdays	21.5	24.3	24.7	8.1	0	21.4	0	
Bedroom Sundays	23.8	25.1	18.7	10.7	0	21.7	0	
Small family								
Living room weekdays	30.5	50.7	17.2	0.8	0.8	0	0	3,270
Living room Sundays	53.1	28.4	16.4	1.2	0.9	0	0	
Bedroom weekdays	13.1	45.2	20.0	11.5	1.1	9.1	0	
Bedroom Sundays	21.6	37.1	20.4	11.6	0.5	8.7	0	
Large family								
Living room weekdays	28.6	52.0	18.0	1.1	0.2	0	0	2,017
Living room Sundays	54.5	29.5	15.2	0.6	0.2	0	0	
Bedroom weekdays	12.8	46.4	16.2	14.3	2.0	8.2	0	
Bedroom Sundays	26.6	34.6	15.9	14.6	0	8.3	0	
Large adult								
Living room weekdays	33.0	43.5	22.5	0.4	0.7	0	0	2,270
Living room Sundays	56.3	25.9	16.7	0.4	0.8	0	0	
Bedroom weekdays	15.8	40.8	19.3	11.9	2.2	10.0	0	
Bedroom Sundays	23.8	37.2	16.1	12.1	0.7	10.0	0	
Couple (1 + pensioner)								
Living room weekdays	46.9	31.7	20.0	0.8	0.5	0	0	3,096
Living room Sundays	54.1	27.6	17.5	0.7	0.2	0	0	
Bedroom weekdays	18.1	30.7	19.0	22.5	1.9	7.5	0.3	
Bedroom Sundays	20.9	29.8	18.5	22.9	0.1	7.5	0.2	
Single pensioner								
Living room weekdays	52.5	25.1	19.0	1.6	1.7	0.1	0	2,842
Living room Sundays	58.1	20.8	17.0	2.3	1.7	0.1	0	
Bedroom weekdays	22.0	26.4	15.5	21.3	1.9	11.4	1.5	
Bedroom Sundays	25.3	23.9	15.1	22.4	0.7	11.1	1.6	

Sample: E1

A9.13 Heating patterns by employment status of household

(Row %/k households)

Pattern	All day	Morning and evening	Evening only	Not regular	Don't know	No heat	Room does not exist	H/holds
2 full time								
Living room weekdays	18.1	58.0	22.3	1.1	0.5	0.1	0	2,680
Living room Sundays	56.5	26.7	15.5	0.6	0.1	0	0	
Bedroom weekdays	9.2	51.5	22.9	9.4	2.0	5.0	0	
Bedroom Sundays	26.2	39.8	18.8	9.8	0.6	4.8	0	
Minimum 1 full time								
Living room weekdays	31.4	48.4	19.3	0.8	0.2	0	0	5,039
Living room Sundays	54.5	29.5	15.1	0.7	0.2	0	0	
Bedroom weekdays	13.6	45.8	18.7	13.7	1.2	6.9	0	
Bedroom Sundays	23.5	38.2	17.7	13.6	0.2	6.7	0	
Single full time								
Living room weekdays	27.8	41.0	26.9	3.1	0.7	0.4	0	1,450
Living room Sundays	53.7	23.4	13.8	5.9	2.7	0.4	0	
Bedroom weekday	14.9	25.3	21.5	16.0	1.1	11.0	0	
Bedroom Sundays	23.0	33.3	15.1	16.9	0.9	10.8	0	
Minimum 1 part time								
Living room weekdays	31.2	44.7	21.4	2.2	0.5	0	0	1,471
Living room Sundays	53.5	23.4	17.8	3.1	0.5	0	0	
Bedroom weekdays	16.0	37.1	16.2	15.0	1.4	14.0	0.3	
Bedroom Sundays	22.9	33.1	15.5	14.1	0.5	13.8	0	
2 not working								
Living room weekdays	45.3	32.9	20.0	0.7	1.0	0	0	3,883
Living room Sundays	53.9	25.8	18.3	1.2	0.8	0	0	
Bedroom weekdays	18.1	30.6	20.1	19.6	2.2	9.1	0.2	
Bedroom Sundays	21.6	29.7	18.5	20.4	0.4	9.2	0.2	
Single not working								
Living room weekdays	49.0	26.6	20.8	2.1	1.4	0.1	0	4,539
Living room Sundays	56.2	21.1	18.3	2.9	1.4	0.1	0	
Bedroom weekdays	19.5	26.2	18.0	18.5	1.3	15.5	1.0	
Bedroom Sundays	23.2	23.3	16.8	19.5	0.5	15.5	1.0	
Don't know								
Living room weekdays	43.6	4.4	28.5	0	23.6	0	0	48
Living room Sundays	31.6	4.4	40.5	0	23.6	0	0	
Bedroom weekdays	5.6	4.4	51.2	9.3	23.6	6.0	0	
Bedroom Sundays	22.3	4.4	40.5	9.3	23.6	0	0	

Sample: E1

A9.14　Heating patterns by household income

(Row %/k households)

Pattern	All day	Morning and evening	Evening only	Not regular	Don't know	No heat	Room does not exist	H/holds
Under £4,500								
Living room weekdays	47.1	27.4	20.6	2.9	1.8	0.1	0	4,011
Living room Sundays	56.0	20.2	18.5	3.2	2.0	0.1	0	
Bedroom weekdays	19.2	24.5	18.8	17.1	1.6	17.7	1.0	
Bedroom Sundays	21.9	21.9	18.5	17.9	1.0	17.7	1.0	
£4,500 - £8,500								
Living room weekdays	43.0	33.3	21.8	0.9	1.1	0	0	3,938
Living room Sundays	54.5	23.3	18.7	2.4	1.1	0	0	
Bedroom weekdays	13.2	29.4	19.4	21.2	2.2	14.3	0	
Bedroom Sundays	18.0	28.0	17.0	21.7	0.6	14.3	0.3	
£8,500 - £13,500								
Living room weekdays	39.0	35.7	23.7	1.1	0.3	0.1	0	3,713
Living room Sundays	53.9	25.5	17.6	2.1	0.9	0.1	0	
Bedroom weekdays	15.9	31.5	23.7	18.1	1.5	9.1	0.1	
Bedroom Sundays	21.5	29.9	20.4	18.6	0.3	9.3	0	
£13,500 - £19,500								
Living room weekdays	29.7	47.5	21.0	1.3	0.4	0.1	0	3,803
Living room Sundays	53.4	30.0	15.3	1.1	0.2	0.1	0	
Bedroom weekdays	14.6	46.6	19.3	12.1	1.1	6.3	0	
Bedroom Sundays	25.6	39.3	17.0	12.1	0.2	5.7	0	
£19,500 or more								
Living room weekdays	21.8	59.3	17.8	0.7	0.3	0.1	0	3,646
Living room Sundays	56.6	28.8	13.5	0.5	0.6	0.1	0	
Bedroom weekdays	14.8	55.2	16.6	9.9	1.7	1.8	0	
Bedroom Sundays	29.2	42.1	14.6	10.1	0.5	1.8	0	

Sample: E1

A9.15　Heating patterns by households at or below level of income support

(Row %/k households)

Pattern	All day	Morning and evening	Evening only	Not regular	Don't know	No heat	Room does not exist	H/holds
Living at or below level								
Living room weekdays	46.6	31.2	19.3	1.5	1.3	0.1	0	1,979
Living room Sundays	57.0	22.0	17.4	2.1	1.4	0.1	0	
Bedroom weekdays	19.7	27.1	18.6	15.4	1.9	17.2	0	
Bedroom Sundays	22.9	24.0	18.8	15.7	0.8	17.8	0	
Living above level								
Living room weekdays	35.0	41.6	21.2	1.4	0.7	0.1	0	17,132
Living room Sundays	54.6	26.0	16.6	1.8	0.9	0.1	0	
Bedroom weekdays	15.1	38.6	19.6	15.7	1.6	9.1	0.3	
Bedroom Sundays	23.4	33.4	17.4	16.1	0.5	8.9	0.3	

Sample: E1

A9.16 Main method of water heating during the winter and summer

(Column %/k households)

Method of heating water	Winter	Summer
CH - gas	63.1	57.0
CH - LPG	0.6	0.4
CH - solid	6.0	2.0
CH - oil	2.9	2.0
Immersion on peak	11.5	20.3
Immersion off peak	6.9	7.8
Individual gas	7.5	7.5
Individual electric on peak	0.8	1.0
Individual electric off peak	0.1	0.1
No provision	0.6	0.7
No information	0.0	1.0
Households	**19,111**	**19,111**

Sample: E1

A9.17 Type of cooker by stock characteristics

(Row %/k households)

	Gas cooker	Bottled gas cooker	Electric cooker	Solid fuel cooker	Oil cooker	Dual fuel cooker	None	H/hlds	Micro-wave
a) Tenure									
Owner occupiers	43.4	1.7	36.3	0.4	0.4	17.2	0.6	12,872	65.0
Private rented	42.4	1.6	48.9	1.8	0.6	4.1	0.5	1,700	40.5
Local authority	58.9	0.9	37.5	0.1	0	1.8	0.7	3,877	41.9
Housing association	44.0	0.2	52.5	0	0	1.5	1.9	662	38.5
b) Dwelling type									
End terrace	53.1	0.9	35.0	0.4	0.4	9.4	0.8	1,853	60.2
Mid terrace	60.4	1.3	29.6	0.1	0.1	7.9	0.6	3,760	55.8
Semi detached	48.7	1.1	37.1	0.7	0.1	11.8	0.6	5,948	62.7
Detached	29.6	1.9	41.8	1.0	1.0	24.1	0.4	4,020	68.7
Temporary	7.8	63.2	10.5	0	0	18.5	0	86	71.6
Converted flat	35.7	0.9	53.4	0	0	9.6	0.5	1,034	27.1
Purpose built flat	47.8	0.5	45.8	0	0	4.7	1.1	2,353	36.0
Dwelling with non- resident	64.4	2.0	28.1	0	0	3.4	2.2	58	81.1
c) Dwelling age									
Pre 1850	23.2	4.3	52.9	5.3	4.1	10.1	0	604	54.6
1850-1899	51.2	1.7	32.6	1.0	0.4	12.4	0.7	2,701	50.7
1900-1918	46.5	1.1	41.2	0.2	0.7	9.2	1.1	1,759	51.3
1919-1944	56.7	0.8	29.9	0.3	0.1	11.7	0.5	3,821	58.4
1945-1964	52.0	1.0	37.0	0.2	0.2	8.8	0.7	4,206	57.7
1965-1980	39.0	1.7	46.5	0	0	12.3	0.5	4,491	60.3
Post 1980	28.6	3.0	38.8	0	0	28.7	0.9	1,527	63.7
d) Dwelling location									
City centre	59.9	0.8	31.1	0	0	7.4	0.9	706	44.2
Urban	55.6	0.9	33.0	0	0	9.8	0.6	4,931	49.1
Suburban residential	50.2	1.1	34.2	0	0	13.6	0.8	9,298	60.9
Rural residential	31.1	2.9	48.4	0.7	0.6	16.2	0.2	2,657	63.0
Village centre	19.5	2.2	64.4	1.8	1.9	9.7	0.4	575	67.3
Rural isolated	11.4	4.4	66.3	5.4	3.1	9.0	0.4	944	51.6
e) Region									
Northern	45.4	1.0	43.2	0.2	0.2	9.6	0.4	1,046	60.7
Yorks/Hum	48.5	1.0	36.3	0.5	0.3	12.8	0.6	1,937	63.9
North West	47.1	2.1	36.3	0.1	0.3	13.0	1.2	2,718	58.2
East Midlands	49.1	1.1	38.4	0.2	0	10.7	0.5	1,548	59.8
West Midlands	50.3	1.6	34.5	0.7	0.2	12.6	0.4	2,059	60.5
South West	35.2	2.5	51.0	1.3	1.2	8.3	0.4	1,912	50.4
Eastern	39.6	1.1	46.9	0.5	0.3	11.3	0.3	2,211	61.5
Greater London	56.6	0.2	30.5	0	0	12.0	0.6	2,863	46.1
South East	43.5	2.6	34.7	0.6	0.2	17.5	1.0	2,819	59.5

Sample: H1

A9.18 Type of cooker by household characteristics

(Row %/k households)

	Gas cooker	Bottled gas cooker	Electric cooker	Solid fuel cooker	Oil cooker	Dual fuel cooker	None	H/hlds	Micro-wave
a) Household type									
1 adult (not pens)	42.5	3.7	43.5	0.3	0.2	8.0	1.8	1,613	44.8
2 adults (not pens)	41.7	1.5	39.9	0.5	0.1	15.9	0.4	3,223	68.9
Lone parent	52.7	1.5	30.9	0.5	0	14.0	0.4	779	52.4
Small family/dep	44.2	1.5	33.3	0.6	0.3	19.7	0.4	3,270	73.2
Large family/dep	48.3	0.8	33.1	0.3	0.2	17.1	0.3	2,017	74.5
Large adult	49.8	1.4	32.2	0.8	0.9	14.9	0.2	2,270	71.5
2 adult (1+ pens)	50.7	1.3	40.5	0.4	0.1	6.5	0.4	3,096	44.9
1 pensioner	46.8	1.1	47.1	0.2	0.3	3.2	1.4	2,842	24.1
b) Household size									
1 person	45.2	2.0	45.8	0.2	0.3	4.9	1.5	4,455	31.6
2 people	46.4	1.4	40.0	0.4	0.1	11.2	0.5	6,685	57.0
3 people	49.0	1.5	32.7	0.6	0.3	15.7	0.1	3,189	69.0
4 people	42.0	1.2	34.7	0.6	0.6	20.4	0.4	3,205	74.6
5 people or more	54.3	0.7	27.8	0.4	0.6	15.8	0.4	1,578	72.2
c) Employment status									
2 full time	39.9	1.0	38.0	0.6	0.5	19.8	0.2	2,680	79.1
Minimum 1 full time	42.0	1.6	35.3	0.7	0.4	19.7	0.3	5,039	75.9
Single full time	42.7	3.2	38.7	0.2	0.3	13.0	1.9	1,450	53.2
Minimum 1 part time	47.4	2.4	35.5	0.7	0.1	13.5	0.4	1,471	64.6
2 not working	52.8	1.5	38.7	0.4	0.2	6.0	0.4	3,883	48.0
Single not working	50.7	0.9	41.9	0.1	0.2	4.9	1.2	4,359	30.8
Unknown	56.0	0	33.4	0	0	7.2	3.3	48	32.4
d) Net household income									
Under £4,500	50.9	1.2	40.2	0.2	0.2	6.0	1.2	4,011	33.2
£4,500 - £8,500	55.2	1.5	37.2	0.2	0.1	5.1	0.6	3,938	46.3
£8,500 - £13,500	48.2	2.1	38.8	0.7	0.2	9.3	0.6	3,713	60.4
£13,500 - £19,500	41.8	1.5	40.9	0.4	0.2	14.9	0.3	3,803	72.0
£19,500 or more	35.3	1.2	33.8	0.9	0.8	27.8	0.4	3,646	77.0

Sample: H1

A9.19 Combination of washing appliances

(Column %/k households)

Appliance combination	Per cent	Households
None	11.4	2,180
Dish washer	0.1	19
Tumble drier	0.7	138
Dish washer and tumble drier	0.1	10
Washing machine	39.9	7,620
Washing machine and dish washer	4.9	945
Washing machine and tumble drier	30.9	5,904
Washing machine, tumble drier and dish washer	12.0	2,294

Sample: H1

A9.20 Number of loads in last week by appliance by household characteristics

(Loads/week)

	Washing machine load/week	Tumble drier load/week	Dish washer load/week
a) Number in h/hold			
1 person	1.77	1.05	2.03
2 persons	3.68	1.82	3.64
3 persons	6.46	2.70	4.78
4 persons	7.95	3.53	5.68
5 or more persons	10.31	5.77	6.54
All	**5.27**	**2.82**	**4.88**
b) Household type			
Single person (non-pensioner)	1.24	2.12	1.75
2 adults (non-pensioners)	2.02	4.22	4.00
Lone parent	2.92	6.75	4.93
Small family	3.49	7.72	5.35
Large family	4.87	9.58	6.18
Large adult h/hold	2.78	6.37	5.21
2 adults (1+ pensioners)	1.54	2.91	3.20
Single pensioner	0.88	1.54	2.34
All	**5.27**	**2.82**	**4.88**
c) Net income			
Under £4,500	3.33	1.78	4.22
£4,500 - £8,500	4.43	2.58	3.49
£8,500 - £13,500	5.56	2.74	4.21
£13,500 - £19,500	6.23	2.81	4.88
£19,500 or more	6.25	3.44	5.33
All	**5.27**	**2.82**	**4.88**

Sample: H4

A9.21 Use of Economy 7

(Column %/k households)

Use of Economy 7	Washing machine %	Tumble drier %	Dish washer %
Always	27.2	21.3	57.4
Occasionally	30.2	23.2	18.8
Never	37.4	49.7	19.4
Other	4.2	3.1	2.4
No answer	0.9	2.5	0.7
Households with Economy 7	**3037**	**1646**	**731**

Sample: H5

A9.22 Ownership of washing appliances by stock characteristics

(Row %/k households)

	Washing machine	Tumble drier	Dish washer	Households
a) Tenure				
Owner occupied	93.1	50.0	23.5	12,872
Private rented	74.2	28.7	8.8	1,700
Local authority	79.9	31.6	2.0	3,877
Housing association	63.5	29.6	2.0	662
b) Dwelling type				
End terrace	89.8	41.0	11.1	1,853
Mid terrace	88.5	38.4	9.2	3,760
Semi detached	93.6	47.9	13.8	5,948
Detached	97.0	58.2	44.0	4,020
Temporary	82.5	35.8	18.5	86
Converted flat	58.2	27.7	4.3	1,034
Purpose built flat	67.2	25.2	2.2	2,353
Dwelling with non-resident	86.4	73.4	30.3	58
c) Dwelling age				
Pre 1850	90.3	47.1	31.4	604
1850-1899	81.0	39.4	12.4	2,701
1900-1918	78.5	37.8	17.3	1,759
1919-1944	91.7	43.7	16.6	3,821
1945-1964	90.4	44.0	13.8	4,206
1965-1980	88.6	46.3	18.5	4,491
Post 1980	89.3	47.7	26.0	1,527
d) Dwelling location				
City centre	75.7	28.8	12.1	706
Urban	80.1	34.9	9.9	4,931
Suburban residential	90.9	46.4	17.5	9,298
Rural residential	93.2	49.3	24.3	2,657
Village centre	92.4	51.7	23.6	575
Rural isolated	87.4	52.9	30.0	944
e) Government region				
Northern	92.0	39.2	10.5	1,046
Yorks/Humb	92.9	44.1	15.2	1,937
North West	88.3	41.8	12.1	2,718
East Midlands	91.7	50.1	14.2	1,548
West Midlands	90.1	44.7	13.7	2,059
South West	85.8	46.2	15.6	1,912
Eastern	92.4	49.3	24.3	2,211
Greater London	78.5	33.4	16.8	2,863
South East	85.2	46.8	25.3	2,819

Sample: H1

A9.23 **Ownership of washing appliances by household characteristics**

(Row %/k households)

	Washing machine	Tumble drier	Dish washer	Households
a) Household size				
1 person	63.6	19.0	3.3	4,455
2 persons	92.8	41.0	15.2	6,685
3 persons	96.3	52.9	19.3	3,189
4 persons	98.4	65.4	30.9	3,205
5 or more persons	95.5	61.4	31.8	1,578
b) Household type				
Single (non-pensioner)	70.7	24.7	4.5	1,613
Couple (non-pensioners)	94.1	44.9	18.7	3,223
Lone parent	91.1	48.0	15.2	779
Small family	98.2	63.0	27.7	3,270
Large family	96.8	65.0	33.3	2,017
Large adult household	96.1	51.6	20.1	2,270
Couple (1+ pensioners)	91.8	36.6	11.8	3,096
Lone pensioner	59.5	15.8	2.7	2,842
c) Employment status				
2 full-time	96.5	58.3	31.8	2,680
Minimum 1 full-time	98.4	61.8	27.1	5,039
Single full-time	82.8	33.6	11.3	1,450
Minimum 1 part-time	93.5	45.6	14.6	1,471
2 not working	93.2	38.6	12.1	3,883
Single not working	65.7	21.9	4.3	4,539
Unknown	83.9	35.2	19.4	48
d) Net income				
Under £4,500	66.3	22.8	4.5	4,011
£4,500 - £8,500	87.3	35.3	5.9	3,938
£8,500 - £13,500	92.4	45.3	12.3	3,713
£13,500 - £19,500	96.7	54.5	19.7	3,803
£19,500 or more	97.6	62.7	45.3	3,646
e) At or below income support				
At or below level	72.4	30.4	7.6	1,979
Above level	89.5	45.2	18.2	17,132

Sample: H1

A10.1 Percent of households using individual fuels by tenure and region

(Row %/k households)

	Gas	On peak	Off peak	Other	Households
a) Tenure					
Owner occupied	84.9	99.9	21.4	16.9	12,872
Private rented	62.9	99.9	22.3	33.8	1,700
Local authority/nt	83.2	100.0	18.5	13.7	3,877
Housing association	65.8	100.0	20.6	12.0	662
All tenures	**81.9**	**99.9**	**20.9**	**17.6**	**19,111**
b) Met/non-Met. regions					
W Mids Met	95.3	99.8	29.2	7.6	963
Outer London	94.1	100.0	16.0	7.2	1,804
Tyne & Wear Met	92.1	100.0	6.5	5.7	397
W Yorks Met	90.5	100.0	16.6	11.8	752
Gt Manchester	90.4	100.0	10.5	7.4	1,019
S Yorks Met	90.3	100.0	1.8	13.5	583
Merseyside TF	89.8	100.0	5.7	8.9	526
Inner London	87.6	100.0	10.4	8.7	1,059
South East	85.7	100.0	16.5	14.6	2,819
NW Non-Met	83.0	100.0	11.7	23.9	1,172
East Midlands	79.0	100.0	46.5	21.2	1,548
Northern Non-Met	78.6	100.0	10.1	19.2	649
Y&H Non-Met	75.2	100.0	20.9	24.8	603
Eastern	74.0	100.0	30.0	19.9	2,211
W Mids Non-Met	72.0	99.2	34.7	29.5	1,096
South West	60.5	100.0	26.7	33.8	1,310
Devon & Cornwall	57.2	100.0	18.1	42.2	602

Sample: F1

A10.2 **Distribution of consumption (lowest, median and highest percentiles) by fuel type by tenure**

(Thousand kWh/hhold/yr)

Percentiles	Owner occupied	Private rented	Local authority	Housing association	All stock
Gas					
5	6.7	4.3	2.2	5.4	5.1
10	9.4	6.4	4.9	7.0	4.7
20	12.9	9.0	8.0	7.7	11.0
50	20.2	14.5	13.4	13.0	18.2
80	28.9	23.2	19.9	19.8	26.6
90	34.8	29.2	23.3	22.6	32.3
95	42.5	32.8	26.9	27.3	38.9
On peak electricity					
5	1.4	1.2	0.9	1.0	1.2
10	1.7	1.5	1.1	1.1	1.5
20	2.2	1.9	1.5	1.4	1.9
50	3.4	3.2	2.6	2.4	3.2
80	4.9	4.8	4.0	4.0	4.8
90	6.2	6.2	5.1	5.4	6.0
95	7.3	7.6	6.7	6.5	7.2
Off peak electricity					
5	0.4	0.6	0.4	0.7	0.4
10	0.5	0.8	0.6	1.1	0.5
20	0.7	1.4	0.8	1.8	0.8
50	2.1	5.3	2.0	3.6	2.2
80	6.9	10.1	6.1	6.4	6.7
90	9.2	16.7	7.3	9.4	9.2
95	12.5	17.9	8.7	11.5	12.6
Other fuels					
5	0.7	1.4	0.6	0.5	0.7
10	1.3	1.7	0.9	1.0	1.4
20	3.5	3.6	1.7	1.4	2.8
50	12.9	11.6	6.9	2.0	11.2
80	41.3	22.2	16.0	10.2	33.5
90	59.0	37.7	22.8	14.0	50.8
95	85.8	47.5	29.3	21.3	69.8
Total consumption					
5	8.1	4.8	3.0	1.4	5.5
10	11.3	6.7	5.3	1.4	8.6
20	15.3	9.6	9.4	4.4	12.6
50	23.7	17.7	15.6	12.1	21.3
80	34.9	28.0	23.3	22.1	31.6
90	44.0	36.3	27.4	25.4	40.1
95	56.8	44.7	31.3	29.6	50.7

Sample: F1-4

A10.3 National consumption of each fuel by tenure

(PJ/k hholds)

Tenure	Gas	On peak	Off peak	Other	Total	House-holds
Owner occupied	865.5	176.3	39.0	181.4	1262.1	12,872
Private rented	65.0	22.5	8.3	31.6	127.5	1,700
Local authority	163.8	41.3	8.5	17.2	230.8	3,877
Housing assoc.	21.1	6.5	2.2	1.4	31.2	662
All stock	**1115.4**	**246.6**	**58.0**	**231.6**	**1651.5**	**19,111**

Sample: F1

A10.4 Mean consumption of all fuels by stock characteristics *(in order of total consumption)*

(thousands kWh/hhold/yr)

	Gas	On peak	Off peak	Other	Total (% of owned)	House-holds
a) Tenure						
Owner occupied	18.66	3.80	0.84	3.91	27.21 (100%)	12,872
Private rented	10.53	3.65	1.35	5.12	20.65 (76%)	1,700
Local authority	11.74	2.96	0.61	1.23	16.54 (61%)	3,877
Housing assoc.	9.21	2.82	0.95	0.62	13.60 (50%)	662
b) Dwelling type						
Detached	21.42	4.64	1.18	9.73	36.97	4,020
With non res.	18.06	4.61	1.00	8.08	31.75	58
Temporary	0.83	3.08	0.00	19.87	23.78	86
Semi detached	16.75	3.46	0.77	2.30	23.28	5,948
End terrace	15.98	3.52	0.66	1.33	21.49	1,853
Mid terrace	12.30	3.37	0.62	1.30	17.59	3,760
Converted flat	13.22	2.83	0.70	0.43	17.18	1,034
PB flat	8.67	2.67	1.02	0.16	12.52	2,353
c) Dwelling type and age						
Pre 1919 semi/det	15.8	5.1	1.8	17.0	39.7	1,420
1919-44 det	29.0	4.9	0.8	5.0	39.7	500
1945-64 det	29.1	5.0	0.8	1.3	36.2	394
1965-80 det	21.9	4.3	0.8	9.1	36.0	1,046
Pre 1945 bung	13.8	3.8	2.2	14.7	34.5	280
Pre 1919 m/l-ter	19.4	3.7	0.6	2.6	26.4	1,286
1919-44 semi	19.8	3.5	0.6	1.6	25.4	1,871
Post 1980 all houses	18.5	3.5	0.5	0.7	23.1	980
1919-44 m/l-ter	17.4	4.0	0.9	0.4	22.7	351
1965-80 m/l-ter	16.9	3.5	0.6	1.1	22.1	456
1945-64 m/l-ter/semi	15.5	3.5	0.6	1.8	21.5	2,095
1945-1980 bung	13.2	3.0	1.1	4.0	21.3	1,335
1965-80 s-ter/semi	15.2	3.5	0.8	1.4	20.9	1,233
Post 1980 bung	15.6	3.4	0.7	1.1	20.7	256
1919-44 s-ter	14.9	3.3	0.9	0.7	19.8	623
1945-64 s-ter	13.4	3.6	0.2	1.9	19.1	401
Pre 1919 s-ter	14.3	3.2	0.5	1.0	18.9	1,140
Pre 1965 conv	13.6	2.9	0.7	1.0	18.3	1,037
Pre 1965 pb-low	11.7	2.8	0.8	0.2	15.5	943
Pre 1965 pb-high	8.3	2.5	1.2	0.1	12.1	129
Post 1980 all flats	8.1	2.3	0.6	0.0	11.1	291
1965-80 pb-low/conv	6.3	2.6	1.2	0.2	10.3	886
1965-80 pb-high	4.9	3.1	1.8	0.2	10.0	158
All households	**16.21**	**3.58**	**0.84**	**3.37**	**24.00**	**19,111**

Sample: F1

A10.5 Mean consumption of different fuels by energy characteristics

(thousands kWh/household/year)

	Gas	On peak	Off peak	Other	Total	House-holds
a) Heating system						
CH gas	21.56	3.38	0.23	0.39	25.56	12,709
CH solid	1.41	3.98	0.96	16.09	22.44	900
CH electricity	2.60	4.00	7.07	2.93	16.60	1,492
CH oil	0.01	5.77	0.91	51.69	58.39	594
CH other	2.43	3.06	0.46	6.83	12.77	309
NCH gas	12.37	3.47	0.33	0.32	16.49	2,297
NCH solid	1.45	4.25	0.42	13.27	19.38	453
Fixed elect no ch	2.27	4.96	0.49	1.31	9.03	133
Portable/none	2.33	5.06	0.54	3.31	11.24	225
b) SAP rating						
< 10	3.82	4.08	1.29	7.66	16.85	1,318
10 - 20	8.24	3.67	1.46	5.03	18.40	1,527
20 - 30	13.52	3.45	1.38	2.70	21.05	3,071
30 - 40	19.06	3.45	0.55	2.20	25.26	5,275
40 - 50	19.28	3.40	0.53	1.42	24.63	4,822
50 - 60	19.57	3.40	0.58	1.91	25.46	2,342
> 60	18.55	3.30	0.39	0.02	22.26	756
c) Provision for heating						
Unfit	12.12	4.79	0.82	4.12	21.85	191
Defective	10.36	3.65	0.77	3.01	17.79	540
Just Acceptable	10.96	3.73	1.10	2.90	18.69	1,733
Satisfactory	16.96	3.56	0.82	3.42	24.76	16,647

Sample: F1 & S1

A10.6 Mean consumption of different fuels by region and dwelling location

(thousands kWh/household/year)

	Gas	On peak	Off peak	Other	Total	House-holds
a) Met/non-Met region						
Merseyside TF	14.77	3.33	0.14	0.57	18.80	526
Gt Manchester	15.82	3.38	0.32	0.65	20.16	1,019
Inner London	16.95	3.28	0.46	0.26	20.95	1,059
Tyne & Wear Met	18.38	3.06	0.23	0.35	22.02	397
S Yorks Met	17.35	3.14	0.12	1.60	22.21	583
Northern Non-Met	15.80	3.62	0.40	2.60	22.42	649
W Mids Met	17.89	3.53	1.00	0.39	22.82	963
East Midlands	15.23	3.18	1.07	3.39	22.87	1,548
W Yorks Met	17.87	3.60	0.74	0.94	23.15	752
South West	11.66	3.77	1.79	6.18	23.40	1,310
Y&H Non-Met	14.05	3.60	1.09	5.35	24.09	603
South East	18.18	3.64	0.54	2.32	24.69	2,819
Devon & Cornwall	9.36	4.01	1.16	10.29	24.83	602
Outer London	20.22	3.63	0.63	0.38	24.88	1,804
Eastern	15.58	3.89	1.40	5.55	26.42	2,211
W Mids Non-Met	14.13	3.50	1.27	8.32	27.22	1,096
NW Non-Met	16.09	3.92	0.68	6.68	27.38	1,172
b) Location						
City centre	14.78	3.15	0.49	0.36	18.78	706
Urban	16.49	3.31	0.58	0.71	21.09	4,931
Suburban residential	17.94	3.44	0.68	0.82	22.87	9,298
Rural residential	15.22	3.88	1.09	6.36	26.55	2,657
Village centre	10.79	4.07	1.54	11.07	27.48	573
Rural isolated	4.00	5.75	3.07	32.34	45.16	944

Sample: F1

A10.7 Mean consumption of different fuels by household type and income

(thousands kWh/household/year)

	Gas	On peak	Off peak	Other	Total	House-holds
a) Household type						
1 adult (pens)	9.54	2.27	1.13	1.80	14.73	2,842
1 adult (not pens)	9.85	2.48	0.69	2.86	15.89	1,613
Lone parent	15.64	3.37	0.62	0.79	20.42	779
2 adult (not pens)	15.45	3.55	0.86	3.52	23.38	3,223
2 adult (1+ pens)	16.45	3.28	0.89	3.48	24.11	3,096
Small fam/dep	18.05	4.09	0.80	3.33	26.27	3,270
Large hhold/adult	19.25	4.59	0.92	6.60	31.36	2,270
Large fam/dep	24.54	4.81	0.55	2.83	32.73	2,017
b) Net income						
Under £4,500	11.37	2.71	0.71	1.98	16.77	4,011
£4,500 - £8,500	14.04	3.18	0.79	2.47	20.48	3,938
£8,500 - £13,500	14.83	3.78	1.15	4.23	23.99	3,713
£13,500 - £19,500	18.81	3.90	0.88	2.88	26.47	3,803
£19,500 or more	22.11	4.40	0.70	5.45	32.65	3,646

Sample: F1

A10.8 Mean consumption of individual fuels by total consumption quintiles

(thousands kWh/household/year)

Consumption quintile group	Gas	On peak	Off peak	Other	Total	House-holds
1 Lowest 20%	3.56	2.75	1.08	0.63	8.02	3,832
2	11.10	2.95	0.74	0.86	15.65	3,812
3	15.83	3.43	0.76	1.21	21.23	3,825
4	21.63	3.66	0.52	1.55	27.36	3,821
5 Highest 20%	28.96	5.14	1.13	12.58	47.81	3,821

Sample: F1

A10.9   Distribution of deciles of total consumption per unit floor area by stock characteristics

(Row %/k households)

	0 to 10%	10 to 20%	20 to 80%	80 to 90%	90 to 100%	House-holds
a) Tenure						
Owner occupied	7.1	8.7	63.1	10.6	10.5	12,872
Private rented	16.9	12.4	50.5	7.4	12.8	1,700
Local authority/NT	14.3	12.3	56.0	9.7	7.7	3,877
Housing association	24.1	15.8	47.6	6.7	5.9	662
b) Dwellling type and age						
1965-80 Detached	2.4	5.4	75.2	6.7	10.3	1,046
Post 1980 Bungalow	2.6	9.1	62.5	18.2	7.6	256
Post 1980 All houses	2.6	14.0	80.3	2.0	1.1	980
1945-64 Small terrace	3.9	12.0	61.5	11.1	11.5	401
1919-44 Med/lge terrace	4.6	11.7	79.0	2.5	2.3	351
1945-80 Bungalow	5.6	9.2	53.8	14.6	16.9	1,335
1919-44 Semi-detached	5.7	5.7	61.6	14.3	12.7	1,871
Pre 1945 Bungalow	5.8	7.5	36.5	9.2	41.0	280
1919-44 Small terrace	6.3	7.4	53.7	17.3	15.3	623
1965-80 Small terr/semi	7.6	8.0	70.7	8.9	4.8	1,233
1945-64 Detached	7.7	9.2	64.0	6.8	12.3	394
Pre 1919 Small terrace	7.9	11.0	55.0	11.8	14.3	1,140
1919-44 Detached	9.3	2.0	62.8	14.4	11.4	500
1945-64 Med/lge terr/semi	10.7	8.8	65.3	9.7	5.5	2,095
1965-80 Med/lge terrace	10.9	9.7	73.0	5.2	1.1	456
Pre 1919 Med/lge terrace	12.5	14.6	59.2	7.1	6.6	1,286
Pre 1965 PB low rise flat	12.7	12.3	53.4	11.8	9.9	943
Pre 1965 Converted flat	13.2	12.0	51.5	8.6	14.8	1,037
Pre 1919 Semi detached	14.2	11.8	48.2	10.4	15.4	1,420
Post 1980 All flats	19.2	9.1	46.3	22.8	2.5	291
Pre 1965 PB high rise flat	26.1	25.7	28.8	8.5	11.0	129
1965-80 PB l. r. flat/conv.	33.9	14.0	44.6	4.6	3.0	886
1965-80 PB high rise flat	47.0	16.8	24.9	10.0	1.3	158
c) Location						
City centre	20.8	15.5	47.1	5.5	11.1	706
Urban	11.1	9.8	58.6	11.6	8.8	4,931
Suburban residential	7.5	9.3	65.0	10.0	8.2	9,298
Rural residential	10.1	10.1	57.9	9.5	12.4	2,657
Village centre	16.3	12.6	50.6	4.0	16.5	575
Rural isolated	18.8	11.5	35.7	10.5	23.5	944

Sample: F1

A10.10 Distribution of deciles of total consumption per unit floor area by energy characteristics

(Row %/k households)

	0 to 10%	10 to 20%	20 to 80%	80 to 90%	90 to 100%	House-holds
a) Heating system						
CH gas	4.2	6.3	66.9	12.4	10.2	12,709
CH solid	26.8	11.1	43.9	3.1	15.1	900
CH electricity	20.8	23.2	46.1	3.9	6.0	1,492
CH oil	16.9	8.2	26.9	12.8	35.2	594
CH other	51.5	9.5	17.2	7.5	14.3	309
NCH gas	11.4	19.7	59.8	5.7	3.3	2,297
NCH solid	27.0	11.7	44.9	4.3	12.1	453
Fixed elect no ch	55.6	15.1	25.6	3.7	0.0	133
Portable/none	50.4	23.7	24.6	0.0	1.2	225
b) SAP rating						
< 10	24.6	16.0	37.9	6.2	15.2	1,318
10 to 20	16.1	11.9	53.5	5.6	12.9	1,527
20 to 30	10.1	12.0	55.3	10.5	12.1	3,071
30 to 40	5.1	7.7	62.8	14.4	10.1	5,275
40 to 50	5.6	9.2	66.5	9.9	8.8	4,822
50 to 60	5.3	9.0	71.0	9.0	5.6	2,342
> 60	11.3	19.1	58.3	6.2	5.0	756

Sample: F1

A10.11 Distribution of deciles of total consumption per unit floor area by household characteristics

(Row %/k households)

	0 to 10%	10 to 20%	20 to 80%	80 to 90%	90 to 100%	House-holds
a) Net income						
Under £4,500	18.0	15.2	53.7	6.6	6.5	4,011
£4,500 - £8,500	12.3	11.3	58.2	8.9	9.3	3,938
£8,500 - £13,500	6.3	10.4	60.3	11.0	12.0	3,713
£13,500 - £19,500	6.0	7.2	63.6	12.2	11.0	3,803
£19,500 or more	7.3	5.7	64.4	11.3	11.3	3,646
b) Household size						
1 person	20.5	16.1	50.7	7.3	5.4	4,455
2 persons	7.7	10.7	64.8	8.9	7.9	6,685
3 persons	9.8	7.4	59.1	11.5	12.2	3,189
4 persons	4.5	5.9	63.6	12.3	13.7	3,205
5 persons	4.2	2.3	59.7	15.5	18.3	1,139
6 or more persons	3.9	8.2	56.5	11.5	19.9	439

Sample: F1

A11.1 Total annual fuel expenditure by household type by tenure

(£/row %/k households)

Tenure and household type	Mean spend £	Row % of households whose fuel expenditure is					House-holds
		Under £400	£400 to £600	£600 to £800	£800 to £1000	£1000 or more	
Owner Occupiers	**715**	**8.1**	**30.0**	**34.3**	**14.8**	**12.7**	**12,872**
large family	897	0.6	11.9	36.9	22.3	28.3	1,505
large adult	865	3.2	16.3	35.4	20.9	24.3	1,698
small family	758	3.3	22.2	45.7	16.0	12.8	2,498
two adults	660	6.9	41.0	32.1	12.6	7.5	2,502
two older	681	6.2	35.5	35.5	14.2	8.5	2,132
lone parents	718	3.1	25.7	40.7	23.4	7.0	272
lone adult	521	31.7	41.7	16.1	5.6	4.8	827
lone older	521	25.1	46.2	20.3	5.6	2.8	1,439
Private tenants	**618**	**21.1**	**39.0**	**20.3**	**13.6**	**5.9**	**1,700**
large family	982	0	6.7	30.8	38.9	23.7	101
large adult	684	7.3	30.6	40.0	15.6	6.5	168
small family	675	4.9	37.7	31.1	19.4	6.9	224
two adults	658	16.4	47.0	19.8	9.3	7.5	371
two older	673	12.1	37.0	16.3	28.8	5.8	181
lone parents	598	13.1	41.6	21.3	24.0	0	71
lone adult	468	44.5	43.2	6.3	4.2	1.8	328
lone older	445	44.2	45.8	7.5	1.5	0.9	255
Council tenants	**521**	**31.4**	**37.2**	**22.3**	**6.6**	**2.5**	**3,877**
large family	751	2.8	21.3	42.4	20.9	12.6	370
large adult	642	5.9	36.8	39.9	14.5	2.8	365
small family	617	4.9	40.8	44.0	9.3	1.0	481
two adults	540	22.7	43.3	29.2	3.3	1.5	312
two older	487	28.3	56.1	11.9	2.6	1.2	698
lone parents	564	21.1	40.7	26.5	8.8	3.0	365
lone adult	401	58.7	31.6	5.5	3.4	0.8	333
lone older	379	65.4	26.7	6.1	1.1	0.7	953
HA tenants	**464**	**44.8**	**32.5**	**13.7**	**6.9**	**2.1**	**662**
large family	884	0	5.6	52.4	22.8	19.1	41
large adult	703	0	39.2	23.6	24.2	13.1	38
small family	618	5.1	36.3	47.7	10.9	0	68
two adults	534	23.3	48.5	6.3	21.9	0	39
two older	469	35.4	51.6	11.8	1.2	0	85
lone parents	466	41.7	52.1	3.3	1.5	1.5	71
lone adult	386	62.8	26.6	7.3	3.3	0	125
lone older	296	79.4	16.4	2.5	1.7	0	195
All households	**659**	**15.3**	**32.3**	**30.0**	**12.8**	**9.6**	**19,111**

Sample: F1

A11.2 Fuel expenditure per square metre by household type by tenure

(£/m²/row %/k households)

Tenure and household type	Mean spend £/m²	Under £6/m²	£6 to £8/m²	£8 to £10/m²	£10 to £12/m²	£12/m² or more	House-holds
Owner Occupier	**8.70**	**19.6**	**28.7**	**23.9**	**14.3**	**13.5**	**12,872**
large family	9.40	14.2	26.3	25.1	16.6	17.8	1,505
large adult	9.09	13.1	27.0	29.7	15.7	14.5	1,698
small family	9.28	14.9	22.5	27.3	18.0	17.3	2,498
two adults	8.72	16.9	27.6	27.6	15.1	12.8	2,502
two older	8.35	23.6	32.8	20.3	10.9	12.4	2,132
lone parents	8.29	29.8	27.8	19.6	10.0	12.7	272
lone adult	8.23	33.3	28.3	15.3	10.7	12.4	827
lone older	7.24	31.8	40.6	13.2	10.1	4.2	1,439
Private tenants	**9.03**	**22.5**	**27.0**	**20.9**	**13.1**	**16.5**	**1,700**
large family	9.55	6.1	30.3	30.9	22.4	10.3	101
large adult	8.88	18.6	29.9	19.6	15.7	16.3	168
small family	10.37	19.2	12.1	24.6	14.3	29.9	224
two adults	8.46	22.9	29.6	21.4	19.9	6.3	371
two older	9.82	10.7	23.4	17.4	17.6	30.9	181
lone parents	7.90	24.4	39.3	24.1	0	12.2	71
lone adult	10.08	27.4	29.2	14.9	3.8	24.6	328
lone older	7.38	35.1	28.7	21.0	8.4	6.9	255
Council tenants	**8.90**	**18.0**	**26.0**	**26.1**	**14.5**	**15.4**	**3,877**
large family	10.52	4.3	14.2	39.3	17.4	24.8	370
large adult	9.48	14.3	18.7	28.3	20.7	18.0	365
small family	10.13	6.9	17.7	32.3	19.8	23.2	481
two adults	8.91	13.4	29.5	29.7	15.6	11.9	312
two older	8.43	17.2	37.2	21.6	13.3	10.7	698
lone parents	8.93	15.0	29.8	25.4	16.9	12.8	365
lone adult	7.83	33.3	23.3	19.5	11.7	12.2	333
lone older	8.11	28.2	28.1	21.5	8.9	13.4	953
HA tenants	**8.60**	**25.1**	**25.3**	**21.0**	**14.1**	**14.5**	**662**
large family	11.73	0	6.7	6.2	62.2	25.0	41
large adult	9.59	16.3	30.3	1.0	31.4	21.1	38
small family	9.68	14.8	20.1	33.6	10.1	21.4	68
two adults	9.67	0.9	40.9	18.5	28.1	11.7	39
two older	8.08	24.0	36.9	15.6	8.3	15.2	85
lone parents	7.84	38.7	12.6	27.9	16.5	4.4	71
lone adult	9.82	26.7	15.2	30.0	1.3	26.8	125
lone older	7.32	33.9	31.7	18.9	6.0	9.5	195
All households	**8.77**	**19.7**	**27.8**	**24.0**	**14.2**	**14.2**	**19,111**

Sample: F1

A11.3 Mean fuel costs and fuel use by household type by tenure

(Pence/kWh/row %)

Tenure	Mains gas		Electricity			Other fuels		All fuels used	
	cost p/ kWh	use %	cost p/ kWh	on-peak %	off-peak %	cost p/ kWh	use %	cost p/ kWh	use %
Owner Occupiers	**1.82**	*70*	**8.55**	*18*	*4*	**1.42**	*8*	**3.02**	*(100)*
large family	1.77	77	8.44	16	2	1.51	5	2.82	(100)
large adult	1.75	67	8.27	18	3	1.26	12	2.91	(100)
small family	1.79	73	8.42	18	3	1.40	7	2.97	(100)
two adults	1.80	69	8.53	18	4	1.47	8	3.07	(100)
two older	1.80	69	8.60	16	5	1.36	11	2.93	(100)
lone parents	1.74	80	8.51	14	2	1.61	4	2.74	(100)
lone adult	1.95	63	9.10	19	7	1.28	11	3.36	(100)
lone older	2.07	63	8.93	19	10	1.66	8	3.40	(100)
Private tenants	**1.91**	*51*	**8.68**	*24*	*7*	**1.58**	*18*	**3.57**	*(100)*
large family	1.70	64	8.39	16	3	1.01	18	2.70	(100)
large adult	1.82	56	8.65	23	9	1.27	12	3.54	(100)
small family	1.90	45	7.74	24	12	1.26	19	3.45	(100)
two adults	1.91	45	8.57	31	6	1.60	19	3.99	(100)
two older	1.89	49	8.15	17	10	1.45	24	3.15	(100)
lone parents	1.81	64	9.02	27	4	2.47	5	3.88	(100)
lone adult	1.87	56	9.52	20	4	1.98	20	3.40	(100)
lone older	2.20	50	9.07	24	6	1.67	20	3.83	(100)
Council tenants	**2.15**	*64*	**9.24**	*24*	*6*	**1.87**	*6*	**3.77**	*(100)*
large family	1.83	70	8.58	23	2	1.73	5	3.39	(100)
large adult	1.85	67	8.80	22	3	1.91	9	3.36	(100)
small family	1.98	68	8.72	20	4	1.58	8	3.27	(100)
two adults	1.87	67	8.96	22	6	2.14	5	3.52	(100)
two older	2.08	63	9.10	24	10	1.95	8	3.69	(100)
lone parents	2.16	67	9.15	28	4	2.59	2	3.91	(100)
lone adult	2.68	62	10.24	27	6	1.72	5	4.46	(100)
lone older	2.48	59	9.82	25	10	1.68	5	4.16	(100)
HA tenants	**1.92**	*53*	**9.21**	*34*	*9*	**2.43**	*4*	**4.75**	*(100)*
large family	1.78	68	8.35	26	1	2.94	5	3.54	(100)
large adult	1.90	59	8.15	27	8	2.49	6	3.69	(100)
small family	1.81	74	8.64	20	3	2.94	2	3.32	(100)
two adults	1.97	74	9.26	21	0	1.99	5	3.42	(100)
two older	1.91	66	9.63	24	9	1.63	6	3.63	(100)
lone parents	1.91	69	8.99	20	10	2.79	1	3.52	(100)
lone adult	1.97	41	8.50	30	26	2.88	3	4.73	(100)
lone older	2.08	30	10.00	57	0	1.25	4	7.05	(100)
All households	**1.90**	*66*	**8.73**	*20*	*5*	**1.54**	*9*	**3.28**	*(100)*

Sample: F1-4

A11.4 Typical relationships between fuel costs, fuel use, dwelling sizes and total expenditures for household types in each main tenure

Tenure and household type	Fuel costs Median	p/kWh	Fuel use Median	kWh/m²	Dwelling size Median	m²	Total expenditure Median	£
Owner Occupiers								
large family	Low	2.63	High	329	Large	89	High	802
large adult	Low/med.	2.69	High	327	Large	85	High	768
small family	Medium	2.77	High	324	Med./large	78	High	696
two adults	Medium	2.77	Medium	290	Medium	73	Medium	615
two older	Low/med.	2.68	Medium	279	Med./large	78	Medium	644
lone parents	Low	2.53	Medium	290	Large	83	High	730
lone adult	Medium	2.82	Low	244	Small	64	Low	481
lone older	Medium	2.87	Low	232	Medium	68	Low	468
Private tenants								
large family	Low	2.48	High	321	Very large	112	Very high	911
large adult	Medium	2.87	Medium	264	Medium	75	Medium	661
small family	Med./high	3.02	Medium	307	Small/med	67	Medium	638
two adults	High	3.37	Low	225	Medium	71	Medium	564
two older	Medium	2.85	Medium	305	Small/med	64	Medium	611
lone parents	High	3.13	Medium	294	Med./large	80	Medium	583
lone adult	Medium	2.94	Medium	263	Small	57	Low	442
lone older	High	3.19	Low	216	Small	58	Low	451
Council tenants								
large family	Medium	2.94	High	339	Medium	71	High	711
large adult	Medium	2.92	Medium	304	Medium	70	Medium	629
small family	Medium	2.96	High	320	Small/med	64	Medium	617
two adults	Med./high	3.01	Medium	271	Small	62	Low	508
two older	Medium	2.95	Low	251	Small	61	Low	474
lone parents	High	3.28	Medium	258	Small	63	Low	527
lone adult	High	3.39	Low	225	Small	56	Very low	380
lone older	High	3.27	Low	228	Small	48	Very low	366
HA tenants								
large family	High	3.52	Med./high	315	Medium	70	High	778
large adult	High	3.54	Medium	296	Medium	74	High	696
small family	Medium	2.94	Medium	272	Small	63	Medium	607
two adults	High	3.57	Medium	277	Small	63	Low	463
two older	High	3.21	Medium	265	Small	63	Low	502
lone parents	High	3.57	V.low/low	192	Small	60	Low	458
lone adult	Very high	4.15	Very low	177	Very small	44	Very low	320
lone older	Very high	7.41	Very low	114	Very small	39	Very low	283
All households	(Median)	2.83		284		72		617
	(Mean)	3.28		305		83		659

Sample: F1

A11.5 Percentage of net household income spent on fuel by household type by tenure

(% of income/row %/k households)

Tenure and household type	Mean % income spent	Row % of households whose fuel spending is					House- holds
		Under 5% of income	5 to 10% of income	10 to 15% of income	15 to 20% of income	20% plus of income	
Owner Occupier	**7.14**	**52.8**	**28.3**	**10.3**	**4.0**	**4.6**	**12,872**
large family	5.67	55.9	35.5	6.2	1.3	1.1	1,505
large adult	8.10	45.1	31.2	12.7	4.6	6.5	1,698
small family	4.99	69.9	24.3	2.9	1.6	1.2	2,498
two adults	4.68	74.6	18.6	4.0	1.2	1.6	2,502
two older	8.13	36.1	39.0	14.4	5.8	4.6	2,132
lone parents	18.13	23.7	33.4	18.3	9.1	15.5	272
lone adult	7.89	54.9	25.0	5.5	3.1	11.4	827
lone older	12.28	36.1	39.0	14.4	5.8	4.6	1,439
Private tenants	**12.07**	**30.7**	**34.1**	**17.1**	**8.8**	**9.3**	**1,700**
large family	11.30	42.0	35.7	14.8	0	7.5	101
large adult	22.76	21.4	42.9	5.8	2.9	26.9	168
small family	6.71	31.3	53.5	12.0	3.2	0	224
two adults	10.56	45.3	25.8	11.1	9.5	8.2	371
two older	9.96	11.8	53.0	17.1	9.7	8.3	181
lone parents	15.33	0	0	62.6	27.1	10.3	71
lone adult	11.33	54.9	16.4	9.1	5.9	13.6	328
lone older	11.16	8.0	38.1	34.9	18.1	0.9	255
Council tenants	**10.49**	**16.9**	**39.3**	**26.7**	**9.9**	**7.3**	**3,877**
large family	9.41	16.6	45.0	28.9	6.9	2.6	370
large adult	11.30	19.6	33.5	26.2	8.4	12.4	365
small family	9.31	24.7	41.3	20.5	9.0	4.5	481
two adults	9.56	43.0	22.1	14.7	7.7	12.4	312
two older	8.06	17.5	59.8	15.2	6.3	1.2	698
lone parents	14.80	0	24.6	39.9	21.6	13.9	365
lone adult	12.93	10.5	32.4	27.4	15.0	14.6	333
lone older	10.82	10.3	37.8	36.8	9.2	6.0	953
HA tenants	**9.73**	**27.6**	**35.1**	**25.4**	**5.6**	**6.3**	**662**
large family	11.21	10.0	68.6	8.3	6.1	7.0	41
large adult	10.62	5.0	45.1	43.6	0	6.3	38
small family	8.07	29.0	40.3	24.1	3.2	3.4	68
two adults	12.67	26.3	28.8	29.4	0	15.5	39
two older	7.32	16.3	72.5	6.5	4.6	0	85
lone parents	12.47	1.0	45.9	29.1	17.7	6.4	71
lone adult	10.11	49.7	15.2	17.3	2.7	15.1	125
lone older	8.57	44.0	15.3	32.2	4.4	4.0	195
All households	**8.33**	**42.7**	**31.3**	**14.8**	**5.7**	**5.6**	**19,111**

Sample: F1

A11.6 **Comparison of fuel expenditures required for actual heating regime, minimum and standard regimes by household type by tenure**

(% of income/row %/k households)

Household type	% of income required for heating regime			Row % of households needing to spend 15% plus of income for			House-holds
	Actual	Minimum	Standard	Actual	Minimum	Standard	
Owner Occupier	**7.14**	**7.69**	**8.87**	**8.6**	**11.7**	**14.8**	**12,872**
large family	5.67	5.90	6.59	2.4	2.4	4.1	1,505
large adult	8.10	8.51	9.73	11.0	14.0	18.2	1,698
small family	4.99	4.86	5.49	2.9	2.5	3.3	2,498
two adults	4.68	4.38	5.04	2.8	2.2	3.0	2,502
two older	8.13	8.61	10.28	10.5	13.9	18.4	2,132
lone parents	18.13	18.85	21.13	24.5	26.1	26.8	272
lone adult	7.89	9.45	11.16	14.5	18.0	21.9	827
lone older	12.28	15.41	18.24	25.1	45.6	55.8	1,439
Private tenants	**12.07**	**16.53**	**19.58**	**18.0**	**30.5**	**38.9**	**1,700**
large family	11.30	12.95	14.89	7.5	17.1	37.5	101
large adult	22.76	31.21	36.22	29.9	36.7	39.1	168
small family	6.71	7.95	9.28	3.2	4.7	14.9	224
two adults	10.56	14.26	16.83	17.7	22.8	33.5	371
two older	9.96	12.32	14.64	18.1	23.4	35.9	181
lone parents	15.33	18.54	21.56	37.4	72.5	75.2	71
lone adult	11.33	15.01	17.95	19.5	23.5	24.0	328
lone older	11.16	20.29	24.78	19.0	62.0	74.3	255
Council tenants	**10.49**	**11.51**	**13.28**	**17.2**	**20.9**	**28.0**	**3,877**
large family	9.41	9.35	10.53	9.5	8.8	12.1	370
large adult	11.30	12.31	14.21	20.8	24.7	28.6	365
small family	9.31	9.37	10.69	13.5	12.2	18.2	481
two adults	9.56	9.86	11.38	20.2	20.3	24.4	312
two older	8.06	8.73	10.08	7.5	8.4	13.5	698
lone parents	14.80	15.15	17.36	35.5	37.4	49.8	365
lone adult	12.93	15.51	18.01	29.6	37.5	42.5	333
lone older	10.82	12.93	15.08	15.1	25.6	37.6	953
HA tenants	**9.73**	**11.64**	**13.43**	**12.0**	**24.6**	**31.6**	**662**
large family	11.21	10.25	11.43	13.1	9.8	18.3	41
large adult	10.62	12.86	15.14	6.3	8.5	23.0	38
small family	8.07	8.68	9.82	6.6	19.8	22.3	68
two adults	12.67	12.48	14.38	15.5	18.6	23.6	39
two older	7.32	9.58	11.13	4.6	11.8	19.7	85
lone parents	12.47	14.21	16.41	24.1	55.8	64.6	71
lone adult	10.11	10.80	12.47	17.7	25.8	33.4	125
lone older	8.57	12.40	14.37	8.5	20.5	26.0	195
All households	**8.33**	**9.36**	**10.84**	**11.3**	**15.6**	**20.1**	**19,111**

Sample: F1 & S1

A11.7 Percentage of household income required to achieve the standard heating regime by household type by tenure

(% of income/row %/k households)

Tenure and household type	Mean % income needed	% of households needing fuel spending of					House-holds
		Under 5% of income	5 to 10% of income	10 to 15% of income	15 to 20% of income	20% plus of income	
Owner Occupier	**8.87**	**44.8**	**30.8**	**9.5**	**5.3**	**9.5**	**12,872**
large family	6.59	42.7	46.9	6.3	2.2	1.9	1,505
large adult	9.73	41.6	29.0	11.2	8.7	9.6	1,698
small family	5.49	61.4	31.2	4.1	1.6	1.6	2,498
two adults	5.04	70.1	22.5	4.4	1.2	1.8	2,502
two older	10.28	27.2	38.4	16.0	8.2	10.1	2,132
lone parents	21.13	19.9	25.9	27.4	5.1	21.6	272
lone adult	11.16	40.3	30.3	7.5	4.6	17.3	827
lone older	18.24	5.4	20.3	18.4	16.2	39.6	1,439
Private tenants	**19.58**	**17.4**	**26.0**	**17.7**	**11.7**	**27.2**	**1,700**
large family	14.89	4.0	39.6	18.9	29.7	7.8	101
large adult	36.22	17.1	28.6	15.2	4.4	34.6	168
small family	9.28	19.3	43.9	21.9	10.1	4.7	224
two adults	16.83	28.3	29.8	8.5	12.4	21.1	371
two older	14.64	9.2	30.1	24.8	17.2	18.7	181
lone parents	21.56	0	9.5	15.3	22.9	52.3	71
lone adult	17.95	29.3	23.5	23.2	1.2	22.8	328
lone older	24.78	3.8	4.7	17.2	17.8	56.5	255
Council tenants	**13.28**	**12.0**	**30.0**	**30.0**	**13.8**	**14.1**	**3,877**
large family	10.53	11.8	47.5	28.5	7.3	4.9	370
large adult	14.21	14.1	31.9	25.4	11.1	17.5	365
small family	10.69	19.4	33.8	28.6	10.1	8.1	481
two adults	11.38	35.2	28.3	12.2	7.5	16.9	312
two older	10.08	10.9	50.6	25.0	9.2	4.3	698
lone parents	17.36	0	11.2	39.0	31.0	18.8	365
lone adult	18.01	11.4	17.7	28.5	13.8	28.7	333
lone older	15.08	3.8	17.1	41.4	19.2	18.4	953
HA tenants	**13.43**	**15.7**	**27.6**	**25.2**	**18.9**	**12.7**	**662**
large family	11.43	53.4	23.9	4.4	11.1	7.2	41
large adult	15.14	5.7	54.3	17.0	14.4	8.5	38
small family	9.82	33.4	39.3	4.9	5.2	17.1	68
two adults	14.38	13.5	51.8	11.1	7.1	16.5	39
two older	11.13	5.5	48.2	26.6	12.4	7.3	85
lone parents	16.41	0	6.0	29.4	60.4	4.1	71
lone adult	12.47	34.0	23.4	9.1	11.1	22.3	125
lone older	14.37	7.4	16.7	50.0	10.4	15.5	195
All households	**10.84**	**34.7**	**30.2**	**15.0**	**8.1**	**12.0**	**19,111**

Sample: S1

A11.8   Adequacy of existing fuel expenditure to achieve the minimum heating
regime by household type by tenure

(% overspend/row %/k households)

Tenure and household type	Mean % over-spend*	Row % of households whose fuel spending is						House-holds
		> adequate		adequate	< adequate			
		by >30%	10-30%	+/-10%	10-30%	30-50%	by >50%	
Owner Occupier	**1.89**	**14.5**	**22.0**	**27.8**	**23.0**	**8.7**	**4.1**	**12,872**
large family	1.07	13.1	16.6	31.7	26.5	10.1	1.9	1505
large adult	4.78	14.3	25.1	32.5	18.1	4.3	5.7	1698
small family	7.58	16.5	24.5	30.8	22.4	5.1	0.7	2498
two adults	6.89	18.7	26.8	28.7	16.5	7.2	2.1	2502
two older	0.13	11.9	22.3	25.5	25.9	9.8	4.7	2132
lone parents	1.77	9.9	23.7	39.8	19.0	6.5	1.0	272
lone adult	- 4.08	17.8	16.9	16.0	23.8	17.5	8.1	827
lone older	-14.76	6.9	12.6	18.5	34.5	15.0	12.5	1439
Private tenants	**-17.15**	**9.5**	**10.9**	**17.8**	**25.1**	**21.5**	**15.3**	**1,700**
large family	-22.17	11.8	0	7.6	36.5	25.8	18.3	101
large adult	-13.38	5.4	18.3	26.4	22.3	17.1	10.6	168
small family	-6.57	15.7	16.1	19.1	20.1	23.4	5.7	224
two adults	-16.36	10.9	9.9	15.5	26.1	25.3	12.3	371
two older	-9.13	17.1	2.9	25.5	38.1	9.0	7.4	181
lone parents	-15.55	9.5	13.1	16.6	19.1	28.8	12.8	71
lone adult	-14.08	9.1	11.9	22.6	25.9	17.6	12.9	328
lone older	-35.74	1.4	8.3	7.5	20.5	26.2	36.1	255
Council tenants	**- 1.37**	**15.1**	**17.2**	**27.1**	**23.3**	**10.3**	**7.0**	**3,877**
large family	4.64	16.1	19.9	34.0	20.0	6.8	3.2	370
large adult	1.77	13.6	22.5	33.8	15.9	9.2	5.0	365
small family	5.26	22.5	17.3	29.1	19.5	8.5	3.1	481
two adults	5.76	18.1	24.2	26.7	22.1	6.7	2.2	312
two older	- 4.12	10.8	16.9	32.0	26.0	9.0	5.4	698
lone parents	1.53	16.1	16.0	25.3	30.0	9.5	3.3	365
lone adult	- 1.68	17.5	14.5	19.7	24.8	10.9	12.6	333
lone older	-10.60	11.9	12.8	20.7	25.0	15.7	13.9	953
HA tenants	**- 2.90**	**18.7**	**20.4**	**18.9**	**12.7**	**17.9**	**11.3**	**662**
large family	18.65	14.1	58.9	20.4	3.4	3.2	0	41
large adult	7.40	46.4	5.3	3.1	28.2	9.8	7.1	38
small family	4.29	17.5	22.6	34.0	9.6	13.6	2.7	68
two adults	27.34	48.8	20.3	24.6	5.2	1.0	0	39
two older	-11.52	13.8	5.9	25.7	25.1	18.6	11.0	85
lone parents	- 7.17	16.4	12.1	14.0	19.7	37.3	0.5	71
lone adult	6.23	25.0	21.0	20.9	10.7	13.5	8.9	125
lone older	-20.66	5.7	24.9	13.1	5.9	19.4	31.1	195
All households	**- 0.53**	**14.3**	**20.0**	**26.5**	**22.9**	**10.4**	**5.9**	**19,111**

* minus sign denotes mean under-spend
Sample: S1

A12.1 Comparison of case study dwellings with mean for all households of same type, size and tenure

Case study figures/(mean for household type & size in tenure)

	Case 1 LA - 1 pension	Case 2 OO - 4p Hhold	Case 3 LA - 4p family	Case 4 OO - 4p family	All hholds
Physical standards					
Dwelling size m²	30 (50)	90 (109)	65 (66)	62 (95)	83
Space heating	Communal	Gas CH	Gas NCH	Gas CH	
Water heating	Communal	Gas CH	Electric NCH	Gas CH	
Insulation[3]	De	L,C	L	C	
Energy SAP rating	46 (31)	21 (37)	26 (33)	41 (43)	35
Heating price index	95 (112)	109 (92)	142 (105)	80 (90)	100
Heat loss index	89 (103)	115 (100)	83 (99)	106 (91)	100
Energy consumption					
Cooking fuels	Electricity	Electricity	Mains gas	Mains gas	
Total consumption					
KWh (000s)	- (11.6)	35.9 (41.9)	14.8 (22.6)	28.7 (29.2)	24.0
Unit consumption					
kWh/m²	- (244)	399 (384)	228 (353)	464 (324)	303
% gas	? (59)	77 (60)	64 (67)	89 (74)	66
% electricity	? (36)	20 (20)	36 (24)	11 (21)	26
% other fuels	? (5)	0 (20)	0 (9)	0 (5)	8
Unit fuel cost					
p/kWh	- (4.10)	3.09 (2.71)	4.26 (3.15)	2.54 (2.90)	3.23
Total expenditure £	665 (380)	1,110 (941)	632 (677)	732 (787)	661
Unit expenditure					
£/m²	22.17 (8.01)	12.33 (9.22)	9.73 (10.41)	11.81 (8.95)	8.68
% gas	? (39)	41 (39)	29 (41)	62 (47)	43
% electricity	? (58)	59 (50)	71 (55)	38 (51)	5
% other fuels	? (3)	0 (11)	0 (4)	0 (2)	4
Thermal conditions					
Outside temp °C	14.3 (10.9)	14.5 (10.9)	8.5 (10.6)	16.3 (10.9)	11.1
Living room temp °C	25.6 (20.0)	16.3 (19.7)	13.8 (19.7)	19.4 (19.4)	19.5
Hall/stairs temp °C	23.4 (18.5)	13.9 (18.8)	13.6 (18.0)	19.2 (18.5)	18.3
Mould growth index	0.0 (0.16)	2.5 (0.19)	1.0 (0.96)	3.5 (0.26)	0.34
Energy Action					
Adequacy of spend[1]	224 (77.9)	90.7 (93.8)	81.5 (94.6)	118 (94.5)	87.7
Target SAP rating	64	72	67	72	-
Improvement cost £	275	10,690	2,210	3,274	-
Energy saving[2] kWh	465	19,860	8,360	7,952	-
Cost saving[2] £	55	615	355	200	-
Simple payback yrs	5	17	6	16	-

[1] adequacy to achieve standard heating regime

[2] assuming standard heating regime and normal energy use for dwelling and household size

[3] Insulation: W=cavity wall fill, L=loft insulation, C=cylinder insulation, Dg=Double glazing, De=draught stripping.

A13.1 Mean living room, hall and external spot temperatures by month

(°Centigrade)

	Living room		Hall		External	
	Average	Std dev	Average	Std dev	Average	Std dev
February	19.27	2.38	17.87	3.08	8.36	3.52
March	19.22	2.43	17.90	2.84	9.77	2.67
April	19.58	2.25	18.33	2.61	11.52	3.48
May	20.29	2.20	19.36	2.34	15.32	3.78
Don't know	19.78	3.19	18.17	2.93	10.63	2.42

Sample: T4

A13.2 Mean room spot temperatures

(°Centigrade)

Room	Average	Standard deviation
Living room	19.52	2.39
Hall	18.26	2.75
Kitchen	18.89	2.61
Second living room	19.07	2.74
Other room	18.44	3.15
Unknown	19.17	2.54
Living room*	19.51*	2.37*
Hall*	18.26*	2.76*

* Common sample where both living room and hall temperatures were recorded.   Sample: T1

A13.3 Mean living room and hall spot temperatures by stock characteristics

(°C/k households)

	Living room		Hall		Households
	Average	Std dev	Average	Std dev	
a) Tenure					
Owner occupied	19.44	2.25	18.33	2.59	12,872
Private rented	19.13	2.61	17.59	3.03	1,700
Local authority	19.71	2.49	18.12	3.01	3,877
Housing association	20.54	2.80	19.40	3.14	662
b) Dwelling age					
Pre 1850	18.80	2.28	17.46	2.61	604
1850-1899	19.21	2.56	17.79	2.75	2,701
1900-1918	19.06	2.27	17.96	2.50	1,759
1919-1944	19.40	2.31	17.90	2.67	3,821
1945-1964	19.44	2.31	18.04	2.77	4,206
1965-1980	20.03	2.34	18.96	2.73	4,491
Post 1980	19.74	2.28	19.19	2.70	1,527
c) Dwelling type					
End terrace	19.44	2.47	17.84	2.92	1,853
Mid terrace	19.42	2.47	18.09	2.92	3,760
Semi detached	19.37	2.72	17.84	2.74	5,948
Detached	19.42	2.21	18.57	2.32	4,020
Temporary	18.36	1.73	14.47	4.14	86
Converted flat	19.82	2.70	18.85	2.49	1,034
Purpose-built flat	20.22	2.49	19.37	2.92	2,353
Non-residential	17.73	3.32	17.42	3.35	58
d) Region					
Northern	19.30	2.51	17.65	3.08	1,046
Yorks / Humb	19.28	2.40	17.84	2.66	1,937
North West	19.62	2.44	17.84	3.16	2,718
East Midlands	19.95	2.19	18.77	2.54	1,548
West Midlands	19.09	2.51	17.19	2.90	2,059
South West	19.25	2.63	18.07	2.73	1,912
Eastern	19.90	2.15	18.77	2.33	2,211
Greater London	19.69	2.31	19.07	2.57	2,863
South East	19.34	2.13	18.51	2.33	2,819
e) Dwelling location					
City centre	19.77	2.42	18.72	2.86	706
Urban residential	19.57	2.41	18.27	2.88	4,931
Suburban residential	19.60	2.32	18.37	2.69	9,298
Rural residential	19.38	2.36	18.15	2.71	2,657
Village centre	18.95	2.04	17.83	2.28	575
Rural isolated	18.78	2.59	17.18	2.83	944
f) Fitness of dwelling					
Fit	19.55	2.34	18.33	2.71	17,698
Unfit	18.95	2.69	17.24	3.16	1,414

Sample: T2

A13.4 **Mean room spot temperatures for centrally heated and non-centrally heated dwellings**

(°Centigrade)

Room	Average	Standard deviation
a) Centrally heated dwellings		
Living room	19.68	2.29
Hall	18.62	2.57
Kitchen	19.38	2.38
Second living room	19.42	2.47
Other room	18.92	3.01
Unknown	19.60	2.42
Living room*	19.65*	2.28*
Hall*	18.61*	2.58*
b) Non-centrally heated dwellings		
Living room	18.78	2.69
Hall	16.56	2.94
Kitchen	16.95	2.53
Second living room	17.51	3.32
Other room	16.16	2.84
Unknown	17.31	2.20
Living room*	18.84*	2.66*
Hall*	16.59*	2.95*

* Common sample where both living room and hall temperatures were recorded.   Sample: T1

A13.5 **Mean living room and hall spot temperatures by energy characteristics**

(°C/k households)

	Living room		Hall		Households
	Average	Std dev	Average	Std dev	
a) Provision for heating					
Unfit	18.03	2.43	15.84	2.87	191
Defective	18.76	2.60	16.41	3.00	540
Just satisfactory	19.02	2.73	17.12	3.06	1,733
Satisfactory	19.59	2.31	18.44	2.66	16,647
b) Central heating fuel					
Gas	19.65	2.23	18.68	2.47	12,709
Solid	19.13	2.50	17.34	2.90	900
Electric	19.90	2.27	18.55	2.85	1,492
Oil	19.64	2.58	18.68	2.81	594
Other	20.52	2.69	19.87	2.95	309
All fuels	19.65	2.28	18.61	2.58	16,003
c) Non-central heating fuel					
Gas	19.05	2.61	16.79	2.91	2,297
Solid	18.01	2.79	15.43	2.81	453
Electric	19.27	2.72	17.68	2.66	133
Portable / none	18.13	2.40	16.10	3.15	225
All fuels	18.84	2.65	16.59	2.95	3,108
d) Weekday heating pattern in living room					
All-day	19.72	2.32	18.19	2.92	6,918
Morning-and-evening	19.54	2.29	18.55	2.55	7,744
Evening-only	19.18	2.54	17.81	2.82	4,014
Not regular	18.51	1.98	17.73	2.14	270
Don't know	20.42	3.54	20.03	3.66	146
Not heated	18.15	4.47	18.00	4.91	19
e) SAP rating					
Less than 10	18.55	2.71	16.18	2.90	1,318
10-20	19.23	2.40	17.06	2.97	1,527
20-30	19.45	2.53	17.89	2.85	3,071
30-40	19.53	2.33	18.28	2.69	5,275
40-50	19.71	2.12	18.73	2.39	4,822
50-60	19.73	2.17	18.96	2.48	2,342
60-70	19.92	2.82	19.34	2.85	677
70+	20.37	1.99	19.85	2.67	79

Sample: T2

A13.6 Mean living room and hall spot temperatures by household characteristics

(°C/k households)

	Living room		Hall		Households
	Average	Std dev	Average	Std dev	
a) Household type					
Single person (not pensioner)	18.78	2.66	17.57	3.33	1,613
2 adults (not pensioners)	19.44	2.43	18.26	2.70	3,223
Lone parent	19.42	2.85	18.32	2.93	779
Small family	19.54	2.15	18.41	2.54	3,270
Large family	19.56	2.21	18.59	2.53	2,017
Large adult	19.44	2.36	18.22	2.61	2,270
2 adults (1+ pensioners)	19.78	2.23	18.24	2.68	3,096
Lone pensioner	19.69	2.42	18.23	2.97	2,842
b) Employment status of household					
2 in full-time	19.59	2.34	18.51	2.67	2,680
Minimum of 1 in full-time	19.47	2.16	18.42	2.44	5,039
Single full-time	19.16	2.66	18.16	2.95	1,450
Minimum of 1 part-time	19.01	2.48	17.67	2.96	1,471
2 not working	19.83	2.26	18.31	2.70	3,883
Single not working	19.49	2.53	18.07	3.03	4,539
Unknown	20.50	2.19	19.88	1.95	48
c) Net income					
Under £4,500	19.41	2.58	17.92	3.14	4,011
£4,500 - £8,500	19.55	2.44	17.95	2.82	3,938
£8,500 - £13,500	19.41	2.39	18.12	2.76	3,713
£13,500 - £19,500	19.65	2.19	18.56	2.49	3,803
£19,500 or more	19.52	2.20	18.75	2.40	3,646

Sample: T2

A13.7 Living room and hall comfort ratings and corresponding mean spot temperatures

(°C/Column % households)

Description		Living room			Hall		
Comfort rating		Mean temp.	Std dev	% House-holds	Mean temp.	Std dev	% House-holds
1	Much too cool	16.67	2.48	1.1	15.23	2.97	3.3
2	Too cool	17.81	2.34	5.1	16.42	2.62	11.4
3	Comfortably cool	18.20	2.14	9.7	17.22	2.43	18.0
4	Comfortable	19.36	2.21	52.4	18.65	2.49	49.0
5	Comfortably warm	20.46	2.17	29.6	19.86	2.23	17.2
6	Too warm	21.65	1.97	1.9	21.50	1.97	1.0
7	Much too warm	23.63	1.29	0.1	26.10	0	0.1

Sample: T3

A13.8 Comfort rating for the whole dwelling

(Column % of households)

Description	Respondent	Interviewer
Comfort rating	% Households	% Households
1 Much too cool	2.2	1.0
2 Too cool	6.9	7.0
3 Comfortably cool	9.4	16.3
4 Comfortable	56.5	44.7
5 Comfortably warm	24.0	22.9
6 Too warm	0.9	7.0
7 Much too warm	0.1	1.0

Sample: T3

A13.9 Whether usual temperatures for living room and hall

(°C/Row % households)

	Cooler than usual	Same as usual	Warmer than usual
Living room			
Mean temp.	18.33	19.63	20.48
Std. Dev.	2.24	2.26	2.45
Mean comfort rating	3.54	4.19	4.43
Std. Dev.	1.06	0.75	0.92
Households %	17.6	69.9	12.5
Hall			
Mean temp.	17.15	18.27	19.61
Std. Dev.	2.57	2.73	2.48
Mean comfort rating	3.10	3.73	4.06
Std. Dev.	1.08	0.97	1.09
Households %	12.4	77.4	10.2

Sample: T3

A13.10 Percentage of households achieving minimum and target standards for given external temperatures

(Row % of households)

External temperature less than or equal to;	Minimum standard	Target standard
16	47.3	22.5
15	47.2	21.7
14	46.7	21.6
13	47.1	20.9
12	47.1	19.7
11	46.6	19.0
10	45.6	17.3
9	47.1	15.7
8	47.2	14.8
7	48.9	11.7
6	50.0	9.0
5	37.9	10.9
4	33.0	10.7
3	26.4	21.1

Sample: T5

A13.11 **Percentage of households in dwellings of different tenures achieving minimum and target standards for given external temperatures**

(Row % of households)

Ext. temp.	Owner occupier		Private rented		Local authority		Housing association	
less than or equal to;	Min. stand.	Target stand.	Min. stand.	Target stand.	Min. stand.	Target stand.	Min. stand.	Target stand.
16	48.6	21.7	46.3	21.5	43.0	24.7	42.8	31.7
15	49.1	20.9	42.0	22.0	43.2	23.3	43.0	30.8
14	48.8	20.9	40.8	21.9	42.3	22.7	42.1	31.3
13	49.1	20.1	42.6	20.9	42.2	22.5	43.1	32.5
12	49.0	18.9	42.8	19.8	42.1	21.0	42.4	32.1
11	48.3	18.4	44.9	16.4	41.4	20.5	45.4	30.2
10	47.5	17.2	43.0	10.5	38.7	19.2	51.4	27.0
9	49.1	15.6	45.1	7.6	39.8	17.3	53.4	23.1
8	50.0	15.1	39.6	5.1	38.5	15.4	53.5	23.5
7	52.5	11.5	25.8	5.7	41.6	13.0	54.5	20.2
6	52.5	7.8	31.1	N.D	45.6	12.9	45.5	30.5
5	39.2	11.6	15.7	N.D	40.7	8.3	5.3	61.8
4	37.7	11.8	5.3	N.D	26.8	11.1	100.0	N.D
3	28.7	21.8	N.D	N.D	14.6	17.8	N.D	N.D

N.D = no data
Sample: T5

A13.12 **Percentage of households with and without central heating achieving minimum and target standards for given external temperatures**

(Row % of households)

External temp.	Central heating		Non-central heating	
less than or equal to;	Minimum standard	Target standard	Minimum standard	Target standard
16	49.9	24.5	32.4	11.6
15	50.1	23.6	31.3	11.4
14	49.9	23.6	29.4	10.5
13	50.4	22.8	29.0	10.5
12	50.4	21.8	28.6	8.1
11	49.9	21.3	28.4	6.4
10	49.5	19.3	23.7	6.3
9	51.3	17.2	20.8	6.0
8	52.4	15.8	11.0	8.2
7	54.7	11.7	7.4	11.9
6	55.5	9.7	5.0	3.6
5	42.4	11.9	4.5	3.5
4	36.3	11.2	0	0
3	29.1	23.3	0	0

Sample: T5

A13.13 Percentage of households living in dwellings with SAP less than or equal to 20 and SAP greater than 20 achieving minimum and target standards for given external temperatures

(Row % of households)

External temp.	SAP less than or equal to 20		SAP greater than 20	
less than or equal to;	Minimum standard	Target standard	Minimum standard	Target standard
16	36.5	13.5	48.3	23.6
15	36.0	12.5	48.4	22.8
14	34.7	12.1	48.1	22.5
13	34.5	12.3	48.1	22.0
12	33.9	11.2	48.0	20.9
11	32.6	9.4	47.8	20.1
10	29.8	9.6	46.8	18.3
9	29.0	7.3	48.7	16.3
8	22.6	8.5	48.4	15.8
7	15.4	9.3	50.8	12.6
6	7.0	6.4	52.2	9.4
5	2.2	3.1	36.3	12.9
4	100.0	0	31.1	12.6
3	100.0	0	28.6	23.3

Sample: T5

A13.14 Percentage of households achieving minimum and target standards for given external temperatures by income

(Row % of households)

Ext. temp.	Under £4,500		£4,500 - £8,500		£8,500 - £13,500		£13,500 - £19,500		£19,500 or more	
less than or = to;	Min. stand.	Target stand.	Min. stand.	Target stand.	Min. stand.	Target stand.	Min. stand.	Target stand.	Min. stand.	Target stand.
16	44.7	19.9	44.3	22.1	47.0	19.7	51.9	24.8	47.6	25.6
15	44.8	18.8	43.5	21.9	46.1	19.7	51.9	23.6	49.0	24.3
14	44.3	18.0	43.0	21.3	44.9	20.1	51.6	23.9	49.1	24.3
13	44.8	17.1	42.1	21.8	46.6	17.5	52.7	22.6	48.4	25.1
12	44.3	16.0	41.3	20.0	47.0	16.1	52.2	22.6	49.5	23.2
11	42.2	15.2	39.7	19.4	47.2	16.4	51.3	22.8	51.4	20.2
10	40.1	14.0	36.1	17.8	44.1	15.0	55.1	18.9	49.6	20.6
9	44.1	11.6	36.1	17.9	43.3	15.2	58.2	14.2	50.5	20.3
8	42.8	11.0	35.0	15.8	39.9	13.6	59.9	13.6	26.6	20.1
7	45.9	7.9	31.2	14.6	37.9	12.2	63.3	8.6	59.8	16.3
6	51.9	5.6	36.2	11.1	29.7	11.1	64.1	6.9	59.2	12.5
5	24.2	0	26.3	12.7	39.1	13.0	45.2	10.1	45.7	16.3
4	25.7	0	20.0	10.9	22.0	16.8	28.6	2.7	47.8	13.0
3	20.7	0	0	20.8	0	54.6	42.2	0	38.2	26.4

Sample: T5

A13.15 Percentage of households achieving minimum and target standards for given external temperatures by dependency on state benefit

(Row % of households)

Ext. temp.	75% or more of income from state benefits		Not on state benefits		No record of whether or not on state benefit	
less than or = to;	Min. stand.	Target stand.	Min. stand.	Target stand.	Min. stand.	Target stand.
16	44.6	22.8	47.7	22.5	50.6	21.9
15	44.7	21.8	47.6	21.8	51.1	21.1
14	44.2	20.9	46.9	22.0	51.5	20.9
13	44.2	19.9	47.3	21.6	52.6	19.6
12	43.7	18.5	47.3	20.7	52.8	17.1
11	42.7	17.0	47.1	20.0	52.2	17.8
10	41.3	14.8	46.8	18.3	48.7	17.6
9	44.3	13.0	47.3	16.4	52.9	18.3
8	42.3	13.2	47.3	16.2	59.0	10.5
7	46.2	10.6	47.7	13.2	59.5	7.5
6	54.2	5.6	47.3	10.6	52.7	9.7
5	32.9	1.3	35.9	14.0	51.9	10.0
4	27.6	0	32.8	13.5	41.5	13.3
3	13.7	0	31.9	23.5	0	51.7

Sample: T5

A14.1 Percentage of the stock affected by rising and penetrating damp by dwelling age by tenure

(% of dwellings)

	Owner Occupied	Private Rented	Local Authority	Housing Association	All tenures
a) Rising damp					
Pre 1850	23.5	39.5	30.1	0.0	26.7
1850-1899	15.2	32.6	18.3	12.0	18.0
1900-1918	11.4	28.9	6.7	12.6	14.0
1919-1944	3.4	8.6	8.9	14.4	5.0
1945-1964	1.7	2.7	3.6	0.9	2.3
1965-1980	0.3	0.0	2.4	3.7	0.8
Post 1980	1.3	0.0	0.4	1.6	1.2
All ages	**5.4**	**20.7**	**5.0**	**7.1**	**7.0**
b) Penetrating damp					
Pre 1850	17.8	45.3	31.7	0.0	24.8
1850-1899	19.3	26.9	25.9	10.1	19.2
1900-1918	14.4	27.1	21.8	9.7	15.7
1919-1944	5.8	12.8	10.0	8.0	7.1
1945-1964	2.8	5.4	6.8	11.2	4.4
1965-1980	2.0	1.7	5.8	3.5	3.0
Post 1980	1.9	0.9	0.7	5.0	1.8
All Ages	**7.2**	**20.6**	**7.7**	**6.7**	**8.0**

Sample: P2

A14.2 Percentage of stock with rising and penetrating damp by type of locality

(Row % of dwellings)

Type of locality	% with Penetrating Damp	% with Rising Damp	% built before 1918
Rural residential	5.1	3.5	16.3
Suburban residential	5.8	3.4	10.9
City centre	12.0	11.6	52.7
Village centre	12.5	11.0	49.5
Urban	13.4	10.3	46.4
Rural isolated	14.2	20.0	71.1

Sample: P2

A14.3 Percentage of stock with rising and penetrating damp by household type

(Row %/ k households)

Household Type	% with Penetrating Damp	% with Rising Damp	% built before 1918	% in worst 10%	House- holds
2 adult (not pens)	6.2	6.5	29.9	9.1	3,223
small fam/dep	6.5	3.7	23.1	9.1	3,270
2 adult (1+ pens)	7.8	7.0	20.7	7.6	3,096
1 adult (pens)	8.9	8.4	26.1	12.4	2,842
Large hhold/adult	8.9	5.4	26.2	7.6	2,270
Large fam/dep	9.1	5.7	23.1	8.3	2,017
Lone parent	10.7	10.5	25.4	11.2	779
1 adult (not pens)	15.3	8.0	39.8	17.5	1,613

Sample: H1

A14.4 Perception of the problem - households with a mould problem in each tenure

(Column % of households)

Perception of problem	Owner occupied	Private rented	Local authority	Housing association	All stock
No trouble	30.3	20.3	13.0	22.1	23.3
Inconvenient	48.2	39.3	37.2	23.6	42.5
Discomforting	8.1	20.5	18.3	30.0	14.1
Distressing	13.3	19.7	31.3	22.9	20.0
Don't know	0.1	0.2	0.2	1.4	0.2

Sample: H1

A14.5 Percentage of homes with different severities of mould growth by tenure

(Row %/k households)

Tenure	None	Slight	Moderate	Severe	Households
Owner occupied	82.9	10.9	4.8	1.4	12,872
Private rented	62.9	14.7	13.8	8.6	1,700
Local authority/NT	67.0	16.8	11.3	5.0	3,877
Housing association	71.6	13.5	11.7	3.3	662
Total	**77.6**	**12.5**	**7.1**	**2.8**	**19,111**

Sample: H1

A14.6 Numbers of homes with different severities of mould by tenure

(thousands/percent in each severity)

	Slight	Moderate	Severe	Total with mould
Owner occupied	1,401 (59)	622 (46)	176 (33)	2,200 (52)
Private rented	240 (10)	226 (17)	141 (27)	607 (14)
Local authority/NT	649 (27)	436 (32)	193 (36)	1,278 (30)
Housing association	84 (4)	73 (5)	20 (4)	177 (4)
All stock	**2,374 (100)**	**1,357 (100)**	**530 (100)**	**4,262 (100)**

Sample: H6

A14.7   Severity of mould growth by age of construction, dwelling type and age, and Met/non-Met region

(Row %/k households)

	None	Slight	Moderate	Severe	Hholds
a) Age of construction					
Pre 1850	68.5	13.6	13.6	4.3	604
1850-1899	73.3	11.3	10.5	4.9	2,701
1900-1918	75.0	12.3	9.3	3.5	1,759
1919-1944	75.8	13.8	7.7	2.8	3,821
1945-1964	76.1	13.6	7.5	2.8	4,206
1965-1980	82.8	10.9	4.5	1.9	4,991
Post 1980	85.0	12.9	1.6	0.4	1,527
b) Dwelling type and age					
1965-80 Detached	91.1	5.6	2.7	0.6	1,046
Post 1980 All flats	87.9	10.5	0.9	0.7	291
Post 1980 Bungalow	87.4	11.0	1.5	0.0	256
1945-1980 Bungalow	84.8	9.1	4.5	1.6	1,335
1965-80 High flats	84.0	5.6	6.2	4.3	158
Post 1980 All houses	83.5	14.2	1.9	0.4	980
1965-80 Small Terraced/Semi	81.9	12.7	4.8	0.5	1,233
1919-44 Detached	80.3	11.8	6.4	1.5	500
1945-64 Detached	78.3	12.7	7.8	1.2	394
Pre 1945 Bungalow	77.4	14.2	6.4	1.9	280
1945-64 Med/large Terrace/Semi	76.9	14.1	6.3	2.7	2,095
1965-80 Low flats/Conv.	76.6	12.7	6.4	4.2	886
1919-44 Semi	75.7	14.3	7.4	2.6	1,871
Pre 1919 Med/large terraced	75.1	12.1	10.0	2.8	1,286
1919-44 Med/large terraced	74.6	13.3	7.9	4.2	351
Pre 1919 Small terraced	74.6	11.6	10.9	2.9	1,140
Pre 1965 Low rise flats	73.1	14.2	8.9	3.9	943
1965-80 Med/large Terraced	72.8	17.1	6.5	3.7	456
Pre 1919 Semi & detached	71.5	12.8	10.0	5.7	1,420
Pre 1965 Conversion	71.3	10.3	11.9	6.6	1,037
1919-44 Small terraced	71.2	16.0	9.3	3.5	623
1945-64 Small Terraced	70.3	18.8	9.1	1.8	401
Pre 1965 High Flats	63.7	8.4	17.0	10.9	129
c) Met/non-Met Region					
Outer London	81.1	10.6	5.5	2.7	1,804
Inner London	80.6	8.1	7.4	3.9	1,059
Eastern	79.9	12.6	5.3	2.2	2,211
South East	79.1	11.2	7.8	1.9	2,819
S Yorks met	78.6	13.6	6.0	1.8	583
Y&H non-met	78.2	11.7	5.9	4.2	603
Northern non-met	78.0	15.6	4.7	1.7	649
Gt Manchester	77.3	13.9	6.0	2.8	1,019
East Midlands	76.9	13.8	7.7	1.7	1,548
NW non-met	76.7	11.9	8.8	2.6	1,172
South West	75.7	13.6	7.4	3.3	1,310
W Yorks met	75.6	13.0	7.1	4.2	752
W Mids non-met	75.0	13.8	7.7	3.6	1,096
Merseyside TF	74.5	12.9	8.6	4.0	526
Tyne & Wear met	73.9	16.7	7.3	2.1	397
Devon & Cornwall	72.4	9.5	12.2	5.8	602
W Mids met	70.8	14.8	10.7	3.7	963

Sample: H1

A14.8 Severity of mould growth by energy characteristics

(Row %/k households)

	None	Slight	Moderate	Severe	Hholds
a) Main heating system					
Oil - ch	85.3	8.4	3.0	3.2	594
Gas - ch	79.8	12.6	5.8	1.9	12,709
Electric - ch	78.2	12.4	6.8	2.7	1,492
Portable/none	73.4	5.5	13.8	7.3	225
Other - ch	71.6	18.4	9.0	1.0	309
Solid - ch	69.7	15.8	6.0	8.6	900
Solid - no ch	66.3	16.9	14.3	2.5	453
Gas - no ch	65.3	17.8	11.6	5.3	2,297
Electric - no ch	57.1	24.4	13.0	5.6	133
Any central heating	79.1	12.7	5.8	2.4	16,003
No central heating	65.7	17.0	12.2	5.0	3,108
b) SAP rating					
> 60	82.7	10.8	5.0	1.5	570
50 - 60	78.6	15.8	4.8	0.9	2,305
40 - 50	80.7	11.9	5.5	2.0	4,643
30 - 40	77.8	13.2	6.8	2.2	5,478
20 - 30	74.6	12.9	8.4	4.2	3,318
10 - 20	68.7	14.1	10.9	6.3	1,463
< 10	64.1	20.1	11.5	4.4	1,334

Sample: H1

A14.9 Consumption of all fuels in thousands of kWh by severity of mould growth

(thousand kWh/% contribution of each fuel)

	Gas		On peak		Off peak		Other		Total	
None	16.47	(69)	3.52	(15)	0.84	(3)	3.12	(13)	23.95	(100)
Slight	15.55	(65)	3.70	(15)	0.90	(4)	3.79	(16)	23.94	(100)
Moderate	15.43	(64)	4.01	(17)	0.82	(3)	3.80	(16)	24.05	(100)
Severe	14.15	(55)	3.85	(15)	0.81	(3)	6.86	(27)	25.67	(100)

Sample: F1

A14.10 Severity of mould growth by type of household

(Row %/k households)

Household type	None	Slight	Moderate	Severe	Hholds
Lone parent	62.0	16.0	15.1	7.0	779
Large fam/dep	66.4	18.2	11.2	4.2	2,017
Small fam/dep	72.4	15.6	8.0	4.0	3,271
Large adult	76.4	14.4	6.3	2.8	2,270
1 adult (not pens)	77.9	12.0	6.4	3.8	1,613
2 adult (not pens)	78.3	11.4	7.6	2.7	3,223
2 adult (1+ pens)	82.9	10.4	6.0	0.8	3,096
1 adult (pens)	89.5	5.9	3.6	1.0	2,842

Sample: H1

A15.1 Satisfaction with heating by number of complaints

(Row %/k households)

Number of complaints	Very satisfied	Fairly satisfied	Fairly unsatisfied	Very unsatisfied	All hholds
0	57.1	42.9	0	0	16,737
1	0	0	72.7	27.3	917
2	0	0	66.6	33.4	764
3	0	0	53.7	46.3	443
4	0	0	45.9	54.1	159
5+	0	0	30.6	69.4	91
All households	**50.0**	**37.4**	**8.0**	**4.6**	**19,111**

Sample: E1

A15.2 Satisfaction with heating by stock characteristics

(Row %/k households)

	Very satisfied	Fairly satisfied	Fairly unsatisfied	Very unsatisfied	All hholds
a) Tenure					
Owner occupier	54.7	37.9	5.6	1.8	12,872
Private rented	33.5	43.2	16.2	7.1	1,700
Local authority	42.9	35.1	9.8	12.2	3,877
Housing association	41.0	28.7	23.5	6.8	662
b) Dwelling type and age					
Pre-1965 conversions	42.3	32.2	18.5	7.0	1,037
Pre-1965 PB flats - low rise	41.4	39.4	8.1	11.1	943
Pre-1965 PB flats - high rise	36.2	33.8	15.4	14.6	129
1965-80 PB flats - low rise and conversions	51.5	32.7	10.7	5.1	886
1965-80 PB flats - high rise	46.5	26.3	13.2	14.0	158
Post-1980 All flats	73.6	21.4	5.0	0	291
Pre-1945 bungalow	59.4	30.6	6.1	3.9	280
1945-80 bungalow	66.7	28.8	3.4	1.1	1,335
Post-1980 bungalow	74.8	23.9	0.3	1.0	256
Pre-1919 small terrace	41.1	44.6	7.9	6.4	1,140
Pre-1919 med/large terrace	41.1	43.8	10.8	4.3	1,286
Pre-1919 semi/detached	44.2	43.4	8.7	3.7	1,420
1919-44 small terrace	44.6	33.9	13.1	8.4	623
1919-44 med/large terrace	42.6	45.6	8.5	3.3	351
1919-44 semi	49.0	39.5	6.7	4.8	1,871
1919-44 detached	49.6	44.8	5.6	0	500
1945-64 small terrace	47.4	33.3	8.0	11.3	401
1945-64 med/large ter./semi	49.3	36.2	8.3	6.2	2,095
1945-64 detached	48.4	44.8	6.1	0.7	394
1965-80 small terrace/semi	47.5	42.1	8.9	1.5	1,233
1965-80 med/large terrace	44.6	39.8	6.0	9.6	456
1965-80 detached	58.2	36.0	5.8	0	1,046
Post-80 All houses	68.8	28.1	2.5	0.6	980
c) Region					
Northern	49.4	37.3	7.8	5.5	1,046
Yorks. & Humberside	53.3	33.8	6.9	6.0	1,937
North West	47.4	39.9	8.4	4.3	2,718
East Midlands	47.2	38.6	9.4	4.8	1,548
West Midlands	49.1	38.6	6.5	5.8	2,059
South West	47.2	42.5	8.1	2.2	1,912
Eastern	51.4	37.1	9.1	2.4	2,211
Greater London	44.0	39.6	9.2	7.2	2,863
South East	59.5	31.0	6.4	3.1	2,819
d) Location					
City centre	33.9	49.0	10.2	6.9	706
Urban	47.3	36.7	8.8	7.2	4,931
Suburban residential	52.3	36.6	7.2	3.9	9,298
Rural residential	51.2	38.1	7.8	2.9	2,657
Village centre	49.1	39.9	7.5	3.5	575
Rural	48.3	39.7	10.3	1.7	944
All households	**50.0**	**37.4**	**8.0**	**4.6**	**19,111**

Sample: E1

A15.3 Main complaints *(grouped)* by stock characteristics

(Row %/k households)

	Insufficient heat	Partial heating	Problems with system	Cost of heating	Other/no answer	H/holds
a) Tenure						
Owner occupier	22.7	11.8	39.0	20.9	5.6	942
Private rented	38.0	22.1	21.6	16.9	1.4	383
Local authority	24.5	28.9	17.8	20.6	8.2	844
Housing association	20.6	32.6	23.0	20.8	3.0	205
b) Region						
Northern	23.8	20.8	20.4	27.2	7.8	139
Yorks. & Humberside	33.3	26.6	15.4	17.4	7.3	247
North West	28.6	21.6	23.3	24.1	2.4	344
East Midlands	19.9	13.8	35.8	20.8	9.7	218
West Midlands	29.0	21.9	26.5	19.0	3.6	251
South West	31.7	22.1	23.3	20.2	2.7	197
Eastern	26.4	24.1	37.6	11.6	0.3	254
Greater London	22.2	25.0	25.4	19.6	7.8	464
South East	17.7	12.1	37.4	23.7	9.1	262
c) Location						
City centre	47.4	14.0	21.9	12.3	4.4	105
Urban	26.3	21.5	23.7	23.7	4.8	757
Suburban residential	23.1	21.1	29.9	19.1	6.8	1,057
Rural residential	14.9	28.1	33.1	17.1	6.8	281
Village centre	22.1	23.0	44.8	7.3	2.8	66
Rural	53.7	11.4	9.2	25.7	0	109
All complaints	**25.6**	**21.3**	**27.3**	**20.2**	**5.6**	**2,375**

* excluded due to small sample size
Sample: E5

A15.4 Satisfaction with heating by energy characteristics

(Row %/k households)

	Very satisfied	Fairly satisfied	Fairly unsatisfied	Very unsatisfied	All hholds
a) Extent Of CH					
Full central heating	58.7	34.7	5.2	1.4	12,731
Partial central heating	43.6	40.0	11.1	5.3	3,090
No central heating	22.3	46.0	15.7	16.0	3,290
b) Type of heating					
Central Heating					
Single purpose boiler	60.1	34.8	3.9	1.2	9,274
Back boiler	57.2	35.1	5.1	2.6	2,790
Ducted air	30.7	42.7	13.6	13.0	567
Programmable convector	38.5	39.7	20.5	1.3	78
Total mains gas	**58.0**	**35.3**	**4.7**	**2.0**	**12,709**
Single purpose boiler	55.5	39.8	2.8	1.9	108
Back boiler	42.4	38.1	15.7	3.8	792
Total solid fuel	**44.0**	**38.3**	**14.1**	**3.6**	**900**
Off peak storage heaters	41.7	41.0	14.3	3.0	1,347
Electric under floor	39.4	37.9	17.9	4.8	145
Total electric	**41.5**	**40.7**	**14.6**	**3.2**	**1,492**
Oil	65.2	32.8	2.0	0	594
Other central heating	65.1	19.4	12.9	2.6	309
Total central heating	**56.1**	**35.5**	**6.2**	**2.2**	**16,004**
Other heating					
Mains gas fires/convectors	19.5	46.6	16.5	17.4	2,297
Solid fuel fires	12.7	47.7	22.3	17.3	346
Solid fuel stoves	21.7	60.4	11.3	6.6	106
Total solid fuel	**14.8**	**51.1**	**19.7**	**14.8**	**452**
Fixed electric fires	27.1	36.1	21.0	15.8	133
Portable/other	11.4	56.5	16.3	15.8	202
Total other heating	**18.6**	**47.4**	**17.1**	**16.9**	**3,084**
No heating	13.0	52.2	0	34.8	23
c) Age of heating system (years)					
25+	29.1	45.7	14.7	10.5	1,332
15 to 24	46.5	36.6	11.1	5.8	3,838
5 to 14	48.3	41.3	6.6	3.8	7,300
<5	58.0	32.2	6.3	3.5	6,641
d) Provision for heating					
Unfit	21.5	34.8	14.8	28.9	191
Defective	18.1	48.6	9.5	23.8	540
Just acceptable	25.4	46.2	16.5	11.9	1,733
Satisfactory	53.8	36.2	7.0	3.0	16,647
All households	**50.0**	**37.4**	**8.0**	**4.6**	**19,111**

Sample: E1

A15.5 Main complaints *(grouped)* by energy characteristics

(Row %/k households)

	Insufficient heat	Partial heating	Problems with system	Cost of heating	Other/no answer	All hholds
a) Extent of CH						
Full central heating	20.0	6.4	47.0	21.5	5.1	841
Partial central heating	22.0	20.0	27.6	24.0	6.4	504
No central heating	32.0	34.2	11.1	17.2	5.5	1,030
b) Type of heating						
Central Heating						
Single purpose boiler	20.0	6.9	41.3	25.1	6.7	466
Back boiler	17.2	23.8	33.2	19.1	6.7	215
Ducted air	22.1	8.7	58.4	6.1	4.7	149
Total mains gas	**19.2**	**11.3**	**43.1**	**20.3**	**6.1**	**847**
Back boiler	12.3	12.5	33.4	30.6	11.2	154
Total solid fuel	**12.0**	**12.0**	**35.4**	**29.8**	**10.8**	**158**
Off peak storage htrs.	38.9	12.2	28.3	16.9	3.7	230
Total electric	**34.4**	**10.7**	**29.3**	**21.4**	**4.2**	**262**
Total central heating	**21.7**	**11.3**	**39.0**	**22.0**	**6.0**	**1,326**
Other heating						
Mains gas fires/ convectors	30.8	38.2	9.1	16.9	5.0	773
Solid fuel fires	31.2	28.9	17.5	17.7	4.7	135
Total solid fuel	**30.5**	**29.9**	**19.5**	**15.6**	**4.5**	**154**
Fixed electric fires	45.3	3.3	28.5	22.9	0	50
Portable/other	18.1	21.2	27.3	27.3	6.1	65
Total other heating	**30.7**	**34.1**	**12.7**	**17.7**	**4.8**	**1,042**
TOTAL	**25.6**	**21.3**	**27.3**	**20.2**	**5.6**	**2,375**
c) SAP rating						
Low (< 20)	30.1	22.3	22.5	21.1	4.0	711
Average (20 - 50)	25.1	21.5	25.5	20.2	7.7	1,463
High (50 +)	18.0	16.1	45.5	20.4	0	201

Heating problems for types of heating where small numbers identified problems have been excluded. However, they have been included in totals and the relevant sub-total. These are: (central heating) gas programmable convectors, single purpose solid fuel boilers, electric ceiling/under floor, oil, and "other" central heating, (other heating) solid fuel stoves. Also homes with no heating. Sample: E5 & S4

A15.6 Satisfaction with heating by SAP, heat loss and heating price index

(Row %/k households)

SAP components	Very satisfied	Fairly satisfied	Fairly unsatisfied	Very unsatisfied	All hholds
a) SAP rating					
Low (<20)	27.3	46.8	15.1	10.8	2,845
Average (20 <50)	52.2	36.9	6.9	4.0	13,169
High (50+)	61.7	31.3	5.8	1.2	3,097
b) Heat loss index					
<80	55.4	35.0	6.3	3.3	4,291
80 up to 95	49.7	38.3	7.2	4.8	4,077
95 up to 105	55.2	34.2	6.2	4.4	3,191
105 up to 120	48.1	38.4	9.4	4.1	3,973
120+	41.4	41.3	10.8	6.5	3,579
c) Heating price index					
<85	61.0	33.0	4.4	1.6	4,979
85 up to 90	58.7	34.9	5.0	1.4	4,085
90 up to 95	49.4	38.6	9.8	2.2	2,781
95 up to 110	50.3	37.5	6.5	5.7	3,198
110+	28.1	44.7	15.1	12.1	4,068

Sample: E1 & S2

A15.7 Satisfaction with heating by household characteristics

(Row %/k households)

	Very satisfied	Fairly satisfied	Fairly unsatisfied	Very unsatisfied	All hholds
a) Age of household head (years)					
16 to 39	39.5	39.9	11.9	8.7	5,597
40 to 59	51.5	38.4	6.9	3.2	6,427
60 to 74	56.8	34.2	6.5	2.5	4,634
75+	57.5	35.4	4.4	2.7	2,452
b) Length of residence (years)					
Up to 2	42.6	38.5	12.3	6.5	2,601
2 to 4	46.3	37.5	9.8	6.4	3,690
5 to 9	54.0	34.5	6.8	4.7	4,021
10 to 19	51.7	38.5	6.3	3.5	4,220
20 or more	51.8	38.6	6.7	2.9	4,580
c) 75%+ of income from state benefits					
Yes	47.3	35.1	10.1	7.5	4,949
No	50.9	38.2	7.1	3.6	11,885
Not known	50.0	38.8	7.6	3.6	2,278
d) At or below income support level					
Yes	44.9	35.6	10.5	9.0	1,979
No	50.5	37.7	7.7	4.1	17,132
e) Household type					
Adult only (1 or 2 non pens)	45.9	40.2	9.0	4.9	4,836
Lone parent + children	28.7	40.9	15.5	14.9	779
2 parent + children	46.8	38.9	9.0	5.3	5,287
Large adult (3+)	51.6	37.5	6.8	4.1	2,270
Pensioner	58.7	33.3	5.5	2.5	5,938
f) Employment status					
Two+ 2+ full time	49.6	38.9	8.6	2.9	2,680
adults only 1 full time	51.9	36.8	7.8	3.5	5,039
part time only	41.9	44.2	7.9	6.0	966
2 unemployed	45.9	34.9	8.3	10.9	826
2 retired	58.4	35.1	4.7	1.8	2,788
2 students etc.	53.8	29.6	9.5	7.1	276
Lone full time work	39.2	48.2	7.6	5.0	1,450
adult part time	36.5	41.7	11.2	10.6	505
unemployed	25.9	41.8	19.8	12.5	401
retired	55.4	35.1	6.2	3.3	2,790
student etc.	45.1	32.0	13.4	9.5	1,342
g) Net household income					
Less than £4,500	48.4	34.3	10.4	6.9	4,011
£4,500 up to £8,500	47.3	37.0	8.9	6.7	3,938
£8,500 up to £13,500	44.4	40.7	9.2	5.7	3,713
£13,500 up to £19,500	54.9	36.6	6.1	2.4	3,803
£19,500 or more	54.7	39.0	5.2	1.1	3,646
All households	**50.0**	**37.4**	**8.0**	**4.6**	**19,111**

Sample: E1

A15.8   Main complaints *(grouped)* by household characteristics

(Row %/k households)

	Insufficient heat	Partial heating	Problems with system	Cost of heating	Other/no answer	All hholds
a) Household type						
Adult only (1 or 2)	32.4	18.3	24.1	20.0	5.2	671
Lone parent + children	16.5	35.0	16.1	25.3	7.1	238
2 parent + children	27.9	20.1	31.9	15.4	4.7	760
Large adult (3+)	16.1	19.1	31.3	28.6	4.9	247
Pensioner	21.9	21.9	27.9	21.0	7.3	458
b) Employment status						
Two+ 2+ full time	29.7	23.2	29.8	7.9	9.3	305
adults only 1 full time	31.6	17.0	32.1	16.9	2.4	584
part time only	25.6	22.7	35.0	12.3	4.3	124
2 unemployed	16.4	22.1	25.5	32.6	3.4	171
2 retired	17.7	31.8	25.8	14.1	10.5	170
2 students etc.	41.5	21.8	12.1	21.3	3.4	56
Lone full time work	21.3	10.9	44.6	16.2	6.9	181
adult part time	24.9	11.3	11.4	42.9	9.4	104
unemployed	40.0	14.2	15.1	24.2	6.5	106
retired	25.0	20.5	25.1	23.4	6.0	260
student etc.	15.8	35.0	19.2	25.7	4.3	303
c) Net household income						
Less than £4,500	21.8	26.5	19.0	27.9	4.8	674
£4,500 up to £8,500	22.4	22.6	23.2	25.5	6.3	586
£8,500 up to £13,500	31.9	19.6	30.1	13.7	4.7	545
£13,500 up to £19,500	29.1	20.2	32.4	12.1	6.2	343
£19,500 or more	25.0	8.6	48.2	11.7	6.5	227
All complaints	**25.6**	**21.3**	**27.3**	**20.2**	**5.6**	**2,375**

Sample: E5

A15.9   Annual fuel expenditure by satisfaction with heating

(Row %/k households)

	Very satisfied	Fairly satisfied	Fairly unsatisfied	Very unsatisfied	All hholds
Annual gas cost (£)					
<£210	35.7	39.8	13.9	10.6	3,166
£210 up to £280	50.6	36.9	7.8	4.7	3,044
£280 up to £355	52.8	36.3	7.0	3.9	2,246
£355 up to £450	56.9	36.8	4.9	1.4	3,089
£450+	54.2	37.6	6.1	2.1	3,109
Annual electricity cost (£)					
<£195	53.1	33.6	7.7	5.6	3,825
£195 up to £265	52.1	37.9	6.7	3.3	3,934
£265 up to £325	48.1	40.9	7.5	3.5	3,637
£325 up to £425	54.9	33.2	7.4	4.5	3,884
£425+	41.6	41.9	10.6	5.9	3,830
Annual fuel cost (£) ALL FUELS					
<£430	46.0	37.2	10.2	6.6	3,760
£430 up to £555	53.9	32.1	8.6	5.4	3,822
£555 up to £670	49.9	38.1	7.6	4.4	3,926
£670 up to £820	52.0	37.6	6.9	3.5	3,770
£820+	48.2	42.3	6.5	3.0	3,833

Sample: F1

A15.10 Satisfaction with heating by heating regime

(Row %/k households)

Heating regime (living room and hall)	Very satisfied	Fairly satisfied	Fairly unsatisfied	Very unsatisfied	All hholds
Standard	57.4	35.0	5.4	2.2	4,467
Minimum	52.6	37.5	7.4	2.5	8,957
Below minimum					
(living room or hall)	40.3	41.7	10.8	7.2	3,581
Below minimum (both)	37.8	40.6	11.5	10.1	2,106
All households	**50.0**	**37.4**	**8.0**	**4.6**	**19,111**

Sample: T5

A15.11 Main complaints *(grouped)* by heating regime

(Row %/k households)

	Insufficient heat	Partial heating	Problems with system	Cost of heating	Other/no answer	All hholds
Standard	13.4	27.0	47.8	10.3	1.5	348
Minimum	23.5	22.8	31.2	18.0	4.5	912
Below minimum						
(living room or hall)	25.7	26.8	26.3	15.1	6.2	655
Below minimum (both)	28.8	15.1	19.8	29.9	6.4	460
All households	**25.6**	**21.3**	**27.3**	**20.2**	**5.6**	**2,375**

Sample: T6

A15.12 Satisfaction with heating by condensation and mould growth

(Row %/k households)

Number of rooms affected by:	Very satisfied	Fairly satisfied	Fairly unsatisfied	Very unsatisfied	All hholds
Condensation					
None	55.8	35.8	5.7	2.7	12,163
1 to 3	43.4	39.6	9.9	7.1	4,759
4 or more	32.1	42.3	16.3	9.3	2,189
Mould growth					
None	54.3	36.4	6.4	2.9	15,770
1 to 4	30.4	43.0	15.7	10.9	3,175
5 or more	16.3	31.9	9.0	42.8	166
All households	**50.0**	**37.4**	**8.0**	**4.6**	**19,111**

Sample: E1

A16.1 Comparison of case study dwellings with mean for all households of same type, size and tenure

Case study figures/(mean for household type & size in tenure)

	Case 16.1 LA - 1 pension	Case 16.2 OO - 2p Hhold	Case 16.3 OO - 1 pension	Case 16.4 PR - 4p family	All hholds
Physical standards					
Dwelling size m^2	53 (50)	97 (86)	203 (78)	63 (88)	**83**
Space heating	Gas CH	Electric CH	Electric NCH	Gas NCH	
Water heating	Gas CH	Electric NCH	Gas NCH	Gas NCH	
Insulation^3	W,L,C,Dg	W,L,C,Dg	None	None	
Energy SAP rating	49 (31)	41 (37)	37 (29)	9 (23)	**35**
Heating price index	88 (112)	121 (94)	86 (104)	110 (117)	**100**
Heat loss index	83 (103)	68 (99)	102 (110)	157 (115)	**100**
Energy consumption					
Cooking fuel	Mains gas	Electricity	Mains gas	Mains gas	
Total consumption KWh (000s)	20.1 (11.6)	11.2 (24.8)	7.5 (18.5)	34.2 (32.2)	**24.0**
Unit consumption kWh/m^2	379 (244)	115 (308)	53 (249)	543 (388)	**303**
% gas	90 (59)	0 (69)	48 (64)	94 (52)	**66**
% electricity	10 (36)	100 (23)	34 (29)	6 (28)	**26**
% other fuels	0 (5)	0 (8)	18 (7)	0 (20)	**8**
Unit fuel cost p/kWh	2.49 (4.10)	2.58 (3.02)	3.92 (3.34)	2.17 (3.02)	**3.23**
Total expenditure £	501 (380)	287 (661)	292 (523)	742 (858)	**661**
Unit expenditure £/m^2	9.45 (8.01)	2.96 (8.64)	2.06 (7.27)	11.77 (10.61)	**8.68**
% gas	64 (39)	0 (45)	33 (43)	72 (34)	**43**
% electricity	36 (58)	100 (51)	55 (53)	28 (58)	**53**
% other fuels	0 (3)	0 (4)	12 (4)	0 (8)	**4**
Thermal conditions					
Outside temp °C	16.7 (10.9)	15.0 (10.8)	10.8 (11.0)	9.8 (11.0)	**11.1**
Living room temp °C	24.3 (20.0)	20.0 (19.5)	16.6 (19.4)	18.9 (19.5)	**19.5**
Hall/stairs temp °C	22.1 (18.5)	18.5 (18.4)	15.5 (18.1)	14.1 (18.6)	**18.3**
Mould growth index	0.0 (0.16)	0.0 (0.22)	0.0 (0.09)	2.5 (1.21)	**0.34**
Energy Action					
Adequacy of spend^1	119 (77.9)	38.1 (93.9)	26.7 (74.2)	68.5 (81.4)	**87.7**
Target SAP rating	66	75	59	45	
Improvement cost £	150	2660	810	5,160	-
Energy saving^2 kWh	375	12,765	13,060	21,595	-
Cost saving^2 £	95	330	530	468	-
Simple payback yrs	2	8	2	11	-

^{1} adequacy to achieve standard heating regime

^{2} assuming standard heating regime and normal energy use for dwelling and household size

^{3} Insulation: W=cavity wall fill, L=loft insulation, C=cylinder insulation, Dg=Double glazing, De=draught stripping.

A17.1 Owner occupiers: mean value *(£)* of energy related work in 1991 by dwelling type and age *(over whole sector)*

(mean £/% households)

Dwelling type	Pre 1919	1919-44	1945-64	Post 1964	All ages
All energy related work (mean (£))					
Mid-terrace house	275	332	425	266	294
Semi-detached house	286	438	371	366	375
Detached house	442	511	382	361	400
Flat	71	148	192	154	115
All dwellings	**265**	**429**	**370**	**332**	**341**
Insulation (mean (£))					
Mid-terrace house	133	216	240	199	166
Semi-detached house	131	296	236	249	239
Detached house	163	326	245	233	240
Flat	11	1	161	82	49
All dwellings	**116**	**282**	**235**	**220**	**206**
Central heating (mean (£))					
Mid-terrace house	73	63	64	45	66
Semi-detached house	79	79	82	59	75
Detached house	162	108	82	90	102
Flat	39	141	18	19	37
All dwellings	**80**	**84**	**78**	**67**	**77**
Energy inefficient dwellings (% SAP <20)					
Mid-terrace house	14.1	10.6	9.9	1.6	11.0
Semi-detached house	21.6	13.1	7.7	4.0	10.9
Detached house	19.4	15.1	8.5	2.2	7.8
Flat	7.8	24.6	6.1	21.2	13.1
All dwellings	**15.8**	**13.5**	**8.0**	**4.6**	**10.3**

Sample: H7

A17.2 Owner occupiers: mean value *(£)* of energy related work in 1991 by income by household type *(over whole sector)*

(mean £/% households)

Income	1(non -pens)	2 (non -pens)	lone parent	small family	large family	large hhold	1 or> pens	1 pens	All types
Insulation (mean (£))									
lowest income quintile	14	38	63	255	61	270	99	100	105
second income quintile	148	324	49	363	108	206	241	229	231
third income quintile	164	160	407	286	330	215	128	0	220
fourth income quintile	154	228	0	251	222	292	239	0	238
highest income quintile	0	233	4	195	315	338	158	0	239
All incomes	**108**	**215**	**92**	**252**	**262**	**261**	**177**	**119**	**206**
Central heating (mean (£))									
lowest income quintile	16	57	4	55	0	44	38	27	31
second income quintile	39	147	127	78	92	39	80	26	76
third income quintile	80	95	114	81	145	66	71	91	89
fourth income quintile	20	116	0	76	61	148	201	0	99
highest income quintile	0	74	25	110	113	77	0	0	88
All incomes	**39**	**98**	**63**	**87**	**101**	**78**	**72**	**28**	**77**
Energy inefficient dwellings (% SAP <20)									
lowest income quintile	25	20	11	16	20	10	18	20	19
second income quintile	30	11	3	11	13	12	14	9	14
third income quintile	16	15	12	8	6	13	8	31	11
fourth income quintile	11	7	0	4	6	4	0	18	5
highest income quintile	6	3	0	3	4	5	0	0	3
All incomes	**21**	**8**	**6**	**5**	**7**	**9**	**13**	**18**	**10**

Sample: H7

A17.3 Tenants: mean value (£) of energy related work in 1991 by dwelling type by dwelling age *(over whole sector)*

(mean £)

Dwelling type	Pre 1919	1919-44	1945-64	Post 1964	All ages
Insulation (mean (£))					
Mid-terrace house	2	0	4	7	3
Semi-detached house	0	11	3	12	7
Detached house	7	0	0	0	3
Flat	1	0	20	0	6
All dwellings	**1**	**7**	**9**	**4**	**6**
Central heating (mean (£))					
Mid-terrace house	2	0	23	0	6
Semi-detached house	2	8	11	5	8
Detached house	115	0	499	0	103
Flat	2	20	7	6	7
All dwellings	**12**	**8**	**18**	**4**	**11**

Sample: H8

A17.4 Tenants: mean value (£) of energy related work in 1991 by income by household type *(over whole sector)*

(mean £)

Income	1 (non -pens)	2 (non -pens)	lone parent	small family	large family	large hhold	1 or> pens	1 pens	All hholds
Insulation (mean (£))									
lowest income quintile	9	0	0	2	2	5	0	1	3
second income quintile	0	0	13	123	0	0	0	3	13
third income quintile	3	0	3	4	0	2	2	0	2
fourth income quintile	7	0	0	15	8	0	4	0	5
highest income quintile	0	3	0	2	20	0	0	0	5
All incomes	**5**	**1**	**7**	**19**	**11**	**1**	**2**	**1**	**6**
Central heating (mean (£))									
lowest income quintile	0	0	0	0	0	0	0	0	0
second income quintile	22	1	14	0	0	0	0	0	5
third income quintile	0	0	28	2	10	49	1	0	9
fourth income quintile	13	0	0	76	0	39	0	0	16
highest income quintile	9	14	0	11	65	34	13	0	25
All incomes	**7**	**6**	**13**	**22**	**30**	**29**	**2**	**0**	**11**

Sample: H8

A17.5 **Energy related work by social sector landlords during 1987-91**

Sector and Type of work	Value of work			Dwellings affected	
	Value (£m)	% of all rehab spend	% of all energy spend	Number (000s)	As % of stock
Local authorities *(capital spend)*					
Overcladding	70	1.5	3.6	38	1
Double glazing, secondary glazing	650	12.8	33.2	309	8
Roof, cavity and wall insulation	60	1.3	3.1	424	11
Insulation to water tanks & pipework	20	0.4	1.0	232	6
Other and non-specified insulation	120	2.3	6.1	77	2
Improvements to heating systems	270	5.2	13.8	232	6
New heating systems	650	12.7	33.2	424	11
Other & non-specified measures	120	2.2	6.1	77	2
All LA energy measures	**1,950**	**38.4**	**100.0**	**1,003**	**26**
Housing association *(programme spend)*					
Overcladding	0	0	0	0	0
Double glazing, secondary glazing	81.4	9.3	37.9	39	6.3
Roof, cavity and wall insulation	15.2	1.7	7.1	34	5.4
Insulation to water tanks & pipework	3.5	0.4	1.6	29	4.6
Other and non-specified insulation	9.4	1.1	4.4	5	0.8
Improvements to heating systems	42.9	5.0	20.0	23	3.7
New heating systems	35.4	4.0	16.5	25	4.0
Other & non-specified measures	26.7	3.0	12.4	12	2.0
All HA energy measures	**214.5**	**25.0**	**100.0**	**74**	**11.8**

Sample: Q1 and Q2

A18.1 **'Improvers' and 'non-improvers' by stock characteristics**

(Row %/k households)

	Improver	Non-improver	Already efficient	House-holds
a) Tenure				
Owner occupier	76.3	18.3	5.4	12,872
Private rented	29.3	66.4	4.3	1,700
Local authority	20.7	66.6	12.7	3,877
Housing association	12.4	71.9	15.7	662
b) Location				
City Centre	43.4	41.1	15.5	706
Urban	49.6	40.9	9.4	4,931
Suburban residential	62.9	30.2	6.8	9,298
Rural residential	67.4	29.2	3.4	2,657
Village centre	68.6	28.7	2.7	575
Rural	74.8	24.3	0.9	944
c) Region				
Northern	50.0	43.4	6.6	1,046
Yorkshire & Humb.	55.1	38.5	6.4	1,937
North West	63.3	31.6	5.2	2,718
East Midlands	63.6	32.8	3.7	1,548
West Midlands	59.9	33.2	6.9	2,059
South West	64.8	29.0	6.3	1,912
Eastern	66.5	28.7	4.8	2,211
London	50.4	36.9	12.7	2,863
South East	65.4	27.5	7.1	2,819

Sample: E1

A18.2 Landlord improvements by tenure

(Column %/k households)

	Owner occupier	Private rented	Local authority	Housing Association
Improver				
Improver only	74.8	22.1	9.8	8.6
Improver and landlord	1.5	7.2	10.9	3.8
Non-improver				
No improvement	17.5	54.7	31.8	48.4
Landlord improvement	0.8	11.7	34.8	23.5
Already efficient				
No improvement	5.3	3.7	7.5	11.8
Landlord improvement	0.1	0.6	5.2	3.9
Households	**12,872**	**1,700**	**3,877**	**662**

Sample: E1

A18.3 'Improvers': insulation improvements made

(Column % /k households)

Combination	Owner occupier		Private rented		Local authority		Housing association	
	Since 1986	All	Since 1986	All	Since 1986	All	Since 1986	All
Wall	1.5	0.8	0	0	0	0	*	0
Loft	5.6	4.1	9.7	9.5	7.0	6.7	*	2.1
Cylinder (cyl)	6.8	4.5	10.4	20.0	8.7	17.2	*	9.4
Double glazing (dg)	33.9	15.0	6.3	5.5	5.9	4.9	*	1.1
Draught excluders (de)	11.1	7.1	50.5	29.0	71.5	53.3	*	58.4
Wall + 1 other	2.6	2.1	0	0.9	0.4	0.6	*	0
Loft + cyl	2.1	6.8	4.6	4.2	1.3	4.3	*	4.6
Loft + dg	4.5	6.2	0	2.5	1.4	1.5	*	0
Loft + de	2.1	1.7	0.5	4.2	0.4	3.9	*	1.6
Cyl + dg	5.9	5.3	0	4.9	0.4	1.0	*	0
Cyl + de	2.5	2.0	7.8	7.6	0.6	2.4	*	11.9
Dg + de	8.6	4.5	1.5	0	0	1.8	*	8.6
Wall + 2 others	2.2	3.2	0	0	0	0.4	*	0
Loft + cyl + dg	2.3	11.0	0	1.2	0	0	*	0
Loft + cyl + de	0.8	3.3	6.4	6.7	0	1.3	*	2.1
Loft + dg + de	2.1	2.9	2.3	1.2	1.3	0	*	0
Cyl + dg + de	2.3	3.2	0	2	0	0	*	0
Wall + 3 others	1.3	4.5	0	0	0	0	*	0
Loft + cyl + dg + de	1.2	7.7	0	0.2	0.9	0.8	*	0
All	0.3	3.9	0	0	0	0	*	0
Households	**6,398**	**9,823**	**258**	**498**	**460**	**801**	*****	**82**

* excluded due to small sample size
Sample: E6 & E7

A18.4   'Improvers': reasons for insulation, main combinations since 1986

(Column %/k households)

Owner occupiers	Main combination			
Reason for insulation	Loft	Cylinder (Cyl)	Double glazing (Dg)	Draught excluders (De)
Keep home warmer	78.2	2.8	56.6	91.3
Reduce fuel bills	10.1	17.9	4.6	4.6
Keep water hot	0	65.1	0	0
Included in other work	4.0	7.1	4.9	0
Ease of maintenance	0	1.0	10.8	0
No one main reason	0	0.5	5.5	1.0
Other	1.7	0.9	13.9	1.2
Don't know/no answer	6.0	4.7	3.6	1.8
Households	**361**	**437**	**2,166**	**707**

Owner occupiers	Loft + Dg		Cyl + Dg		Dg +De	
Reason for insulation	Loft	Dg	Cyl	Dg	Dg	De
Keep home warmer	73.1	58.3	8.9	64.4	47.9	79.7
Keep noise down	1.0	15.9	0	2.2	9.6	1.4
Reduce fuel bills	15.4	4.2	16.7	3.3	9.7	8.3
Keep water hot	0	0	51.8	0	0	0
Grant available	5.0	0	0	0	0	0
Reduce condensation	0	7.0	0	0	7.1	0
Included in other work	1.2	0.7	15.4	8.7	7.8	6.2
Ease of maintenance	4.2	9.8	1.8	17.0	11.2	0
No one main reason	0	1.4	0	1.8	1.3	1.3
Other	0	2.6	1.3	1.1	1.8	0
Don't know/no answer	0	0	4.1	1.5	3.6	3.2
Households	**286**		**378**		**550**	

Local authority & Private rented	Main combination			
Reason for insulation	Loft	Cylinder (Cyl)	Double glazing (Dg)	Draught excluders (De)
Local authority				
Keep home warmer	60.5	0	63.8	90.0
Reduce fuel bills	0	20.8	0	2.4
Keep water hot	0	70.8	0	0
Grant available	16.0	0	0	0
Recommended by acquaintance	0	8.4	12.4	0
No one main reason	4.7	0	10.6	1.7
Other	0	0	0	1.6
Don't know/no answer	18.7	0	13.2	4.3
Households	**32**	**40**	**27**	**329**
Private rented				
Keep home warmer	100.0	0	*	100.0
Reduce fuel bills	0	32.6	*	0
Keep water hot	0	60.0	*	0
Persuaded by salesperson	0	7.4	*	0
Households	**25**	**27**	*	**130**

Housing association (pre- and post-1986)	Draught excluders
Reason for insulation	(De)
Keep home warmer	91.9
Other	7.1
Don't know/no answer	1.0
Households	**48**

* Other main combinations (loft + cylinder, cylinder + draught excluders, loft + cylinder + draught excluders) are not shown because these were small samples. Sample: E7

A18.5 Owner occupier households without particular measures: future insulation intentions

(Column %/k households)

Intend to insulate in future	Wall	Loft	Cylinder	Double glazing	Draught excluder
(a) Improvers					
Yes	3.3	23.0	10.8	14.9	7.0
No	67.9	48.1	64.9	60.4	68.3
Don't know/no answer	28.8	28.9	24.3	24.7	24.7
H/hlds without insulation	**3,950**	**569**	**472**	**2,476**	**5,610**
Reasons for non-installation					
Moving soon	9.6	19.1	2.4	11.7	5.3
Can't afford	23.4	31.9	2.2	47.7	5.9
No space	4.4	14.3	8.6	0.7	0.9
Never considered	16.3	12.9	0	2.8	17.1
No need	34.3	26.3	58.3	29.0	61.8
Don't want	20.3	4.1	0.4	11.4	5.4
Other	12.2	9.3	28.1	20.4	7.9
Households	**2,681**	**274**	**307**	**1,495**	**3,834**
(b) Already efficient					
Yes	0	*	*	5.6	5.5
No	88.7	*	*	62.9	76.3
Don't know/no answer	11.3	*	*	31.5	18.2
H/hlds without insulation	**80**	*	*	**332**	**391**
Reasons for non-installation					
Moving soon	11.2	*	*	11.2	10.9
Can't afford	33.1	*	*	63.5	6.2
Never considered	5.3	*	*	4.1	22.2
No need	27.0	*	*	43.1	55.2
Don't want	0	*	*	8.2	9.8
No grant available	19.0	*	*	0	0
Not responsible	37.5	*	*	0.9	0
Other	0	*	*	5.7	1.4
Households	**71**	*	*	**209**	**298**
(c) Non-improvers					
Yes	2.6	31.0	12.2	16.0	14.2
No	69.0	49.6	71.8	60.1	59.3
Don't know/no answer	28.4	19.4	16.0	23.8	26.4
H/hlds without insulation	**777**	**228**	**133**	**1,317**	**1,741**
Reasons for non-installation					
Moving soon	10.2	14.4	14.2	19.3	14.2
Can't afford	20.9	33.2	23.3	43.3	14.7
No space	5.6	5.6	3.8	0.2	0
Never considered	19.5	12.3	12.8	5.6	26.8
No need	27.4	28.7	30.9	26.0	36.1
Don't want	18.2	0	0	6.8	3.9
Other	12.6	10.9	23.0	16.1	5.8
Households	**536**	**113**	**95**	**792**	**1,033**

* excluded due to small sample size

Reasons for non-installation: Percentages may sum to more than 100 (survey allowed for more than one response).

Sample: E8

A18.6 Tenant households without particular measures: future insulation intentions

(Column %/k households)

Intend to insulate in future	Local authority				Private rented			Housing association	
	Wall	Cyl	Dg	De	Loft	Dg	De	Dg	De
a) Improver									
Yes	2.2	7.5	0.8	6.7	17.6	2.7	12.5	10.1	*
No	74.0	64.7	76.4	66.1	67.5	74.8	62.0	68.6	*
Don't know/no answer	23.9	27.8	22.9	27.2	14.9	22.5	25.5	21.3	*
H/hlds without insulation	442	72	621	218	167	360	220	65	*
Reasons for non-installation									
Moving soon	0	0	0	0	18.2	10.3	0	7.9	*
Can't afford	26.8	22.6	31.0	22.3	3.5	18.1	3.6	16.9	*
No space	0	0	0.4	0	6.1	0	3.4	0	*
Never considered	2.7	4.4	0.6	9.7	0	0.8	5.5	0	*
No need	5.2	36.1	2.7	16.1	14.9	10.3	34.8	10.3	*
No grant available	0	0	0	0	0	0	0	6.7	*
Don't want	0	0	0	0	6.0	5.5	0	0	*
Not responsible	72.4	29.7	75.9	51.8	57.8	64.4	63.1	69.9	*
Other	11.1	12.7	11.3	6.2	4.0	7.6	9.0	39.9	*
Households	**327**	**47**	**474**	**144**	**113**	**269**	**136**	**45**	*
b) Already efficient									
Yes	0	0	0.9	5.6	*	0	2.9	0	4.3
No	92.2	81.9	82.2	82.8	*	65.5	82.0	84.2	81.1
Don't know/no answer	7.8	18.1	16.9	11.7	*	34.5	15.1	15.8	14.6
H/hlds without insulation	101	32	322	359	*	45	53	63	74
Reasons for non-installation									
Moving soon	0	0	0	0	*	8.8	6.0	0	0
Can't afford	10.8	8.2	21.5	6.4	*	0	0	52.0	30.8
Never considered	0	0	1.5	6.5	*	0	30.5	0	24.3
No need	14.0	0	7.5	22.9	*	36.4	27.5	0	22.7
Not responsible	77.0	56.5	78.9	64.1	*	54.7	35.9	63.3	29.1
Other	5.5	35.3	7.3	7.3	*	0	0	0	0
Households	**93**	**84**	**265**	**297**	*	**30**	**43**	**53**	**60**
c) Non-improver									
Yes	1.2	3.5	1.8	6.5	2.4	3.9	8.0	3.9	8.9
No	72.1	65.1	74.0	68.1	83.0	81.8	78.0	67.1	61.8
Don't know/no answer	26.8	31.4	24.1	25.4	14.6	14.3	14.0	29.0	29.3
H/hlds without insulation	1116	307	2,042	1,748	201	779	805	266	259
Reasons for non-installation									
Moving soon	4.1	5.8	4.1	4.0	9.7	15.2	15.7	7.8	4.2
Can't afford	19.9	15.3	24.5	13.3	18.4	16.7	13.0	26.4	15.5
Never considered	5.2	9.7	1.5	10.0	7.5	4.6	6.0	1.3	9.5
No need	5.1	7.3	5.3	13.5	3.6	12.1	18.1	20.1	28.0
Not responsible	80.3	65.2	81.6	66.0	76.4	73.1	60.6	65.7	55.4
Other	8.9	8.6	4.9	8.4	3.5	5.5	9.0	10.8	4.8
Households	**804**	**200**	**1512**	**1190**	**167**	**637**	**628**	**179**	**160**

* excluded due to small sample size.

Reasons for non-installation: Percentages may sum to more than 100 (survey allowed for more than one response).

Types of insulation have been excluded where smaller numbers lack these, for example, of non-improvers 168 thousand local authority tenants lack loft insulation and 180 thousand private rented tenants lack cylinder insulation.

Sample: E9

A18.7 'Improvers' and 'non improvers' by dwelling type by tenure

(Column %/k households)

Dwelling type	Improver		Non- improver	Already efficient
	Since 1986	All		
Owner occupiers				
All flats	5.2	4.7	11.7	17.4
All bungalows	10.4	10.8	8.4	5.5
Pre-1919 small terrace	6.3	6.4	13.3	3.4
Pre-1919 medium/large terrace	7.1	7.7	10.2	7.8
Pre-1919 semi/detached house	7.6	10.1	8.3	0.4
1919-44 semi-detached house	12.1	11.9	7.9	1.3
1945-64 med/large terrace and semi	11.3	10.9	7.4	2.2
1965-80 small terrace and semi	9.5	8.3	9.4	4.9
1965-80 detached	8.0	7.9	5.6	2.3
Post-1980 all houses	5.7	5.2	5.8	50.9
All other houses	16.9	16.2	12.2	3.9
Households	**6,398**	**9,823**	**2,352**	**697**
Local authority				
Pre-1965 PB low-rise flat	12.1	11.4	15.3	18.2
1965-80 PB low-rise/converted flat	4.8	5.1	11.3	27.1
All other flats	5.6	4.6	6.0	23.8
All bungalows	7.7	9.0	11.9	1.1
1919-44 small terrace	10.8	8.5	7.9	0.9
1919-44 semi-detached house	9.4	8.8	12.4	3.6
Other pre-1945 houses	3.2	4.0	4.7	6.1
1945-64 small terrace	9.5	9.6	6.6	2.2
1945-64 med/large terrace and semi	24.9	29.0	16.7	4.1
Other post-1945 houses	12.0	10.3	7.2	12.8
Households	**460**	**801**	**2,583**	**493**
Private rented				
Pre-1965 converted flat	4.4	5.1	17.8	22.9
Pre-1965 PB low-rise flat	5.0	5.3	5.7	22.9
All other flats	1.4	0.7	3.2	15.1
Pre-1945 bungalow	14.7	7.9	2.4	0
Post-1945 bungalow	5.2	2.8	3.8	0
Pre-1919 small terrace	12.8	12.8	15.7	6.7
Pre-1919 medium/large terrace	9.0	6.2	13.9	12.0
Pre-1919 semi/detached house	25.4	29.5	14.9	0
1919-44 semi-detached house	10.0	10.7	6.1	0
Post-1980 all houses	0	0	1.7	20.4
All other houses	12.0	19.1	14.7	0
Households	**258**	**498**	**1,128**	**74**
Housing association				
Pre-1965 converted flat	*	2.4	20.0	19.6
Pre-1965 PB low-rise flat	*	10.0	10.8	11.2
1965-80 PB low-rise/converted flat	*	7.5	16.6	32.3
All other flats	*	2.5	11.4	10.9
All bungalows	*	3.8	6.4	0
Pre-1919 small terrace	*	11.4	7.1	0
Pre-1919 medium/large terrace	*	5.7	3.9	9.6
1919-44 medium/large terrace	*	7.2	0.3	0
1919-44 semi-detached house	*	6.0	4.0	8.7
1945-64 med/large terrace and semi	*	18.7	6.2	0
1965-80 small terrace and semi	*	21.2	2.7	0
All other houses	*	3.6	10.7	7.6
Households	*	**82**	**477**	**104**

* Excluded due to small sample size
Sample: E1 & E7

A18.8 **Household characteristics of owner occupier 'improvers' and 'non improvers'**

(Column %/k households)

Household characteristics	Improver		Non-improver	Already efficient
	Since 1986	All		
a) Income				
< £4,500	10.0	12.1	13.3	2.1
£4,500 up to £8,500	12.4	15.4	12.2	10.5
£8,500 up to £13,500	19.5	19.0	23.2	13.9
£13,500 up to £19,500	30.0	28.2	25.2	29.7
£19,500 +	28.0	25.4	26.1	43.7
b) Age of household head				
16 up to 39	28.6	22.9	45.2	39.9
40 up to 59	41.7	40.3	32.6	43.1
60 up to 74	22.0	25.6	15.6	13.8
75 +	7.6	11.2	6.5	3.2
c) Household type				
One adult (not pensioner)	4.2	4.2	12.6	10.1
Two adult (not pensioner)	21.9	19.4	26.7	17.6
Lone parent	1.7	2.2	1.4	3.6
Small family/dependent children	22.3	19.0	18.8	30.1
Large family/dependent children	13.1	11.3	11.8	17.5
Large adult only household	13.4	14.0	10.2	6.3
Two adult (1 or more pensioner)	15.4	19.1	8.4	9.9
One adult (pensioner)	8.1	10.8	10.0	4.9
d) Length of residence (years)				
Up to 2	7.1	4.9	24.1	18.2
2 up to 5	20.6	13.8	35.5	56.1
5 up to 10	26.1	23.8	21.9	18.4
10 up to 20	24.0	28.6	9.2	5.9
20 +	22.2	28.8	9.2	1.5
e) Employment status				
Two full-time	19.9	16.5	24.1	22.8
Minimum one full-time	38.0	33.9	30.1	38.6
Single full-time	5.9	5.8	13.3	18.0
Minimum one part-time	5.8	7.0	7.3	2.7
Two not working	18.3	21.6	10.2	12.2
Single not working	12.0	15.2	14.3	5.7
Unknown	0.1	0.1	0.7	0
f) Socio-economic group				
Professional	9.1	8.6	5.4	15.7
Employers and managers	26.6	26.3	26.0	29.1
Intermediate non-manual	13.9	14.1	13.5	6.2
Junior non-manual	7.4	8.2	9.9	9.7
Skilled manual	30.2	29.9	30.7	20.0
Semi-skilled manual	8.4	8.7	9.1	9.1
Unskilled manual	2.6	2.6	3.5	6.3
Armed forces	0.3	0.4	0.4	2.0
Never worked etc	1.4	1.2	1.5	1.8
Households	**6,398**	**9,823**	**2,352**	**697**

Sample: E8

A18.9 Household characteristics of tenant 'improvers' and 'non improvers'

(Column %/k households)

Household characteristics	Local authority			Private rented			Housing association		
	All improvers	Non-improver	Already efficient	All improvers	Non-improver	Already efficient	All improvers	Non-improver	Already efficient
a) Income									
< £4,500	33.9	43.3	42.0	22.3	35.8	18.3	25.3	49.2	38.0
£4,500 up to £8,500	40.0	34.0	29.9	17.4	21.4	26.9	35.0	31.6	46.1
£8,500 up to £13,500	15.4	15.6	17.1	37.2	26.0	34.2	9.4	13.9	3.5
£13,500 up to £19,500	8.9	5.7	9.1	17.4	11.1	16.3	27.6	4.5	12.5
£19,500 +	1.8	1.4	2.0	5.8	5.7	4.3	2.7	0.8	0
b) Age of household head (years)									
16 up to 39	25.0	27.4	36.0	28.5	50.2	62.8	18.9	36.1	41.7
40 up to 59	24.9	24.0	24.0	23.8	28.1	13.7	38.5	16.4	34.3
60 up to 74	35.9	27.7	25.8	28.5	11.2	18.5	26.1	27.9	17.5
75 +	14.2	20.8	14.1	19.2	10.4	5.0	16.5	19.6	6.5
c) Household type									
One adult (not pensioner)	6.7	9.3	16.7	6.8	22.8	13.3	7.7	12.2	11.7
Two adult (not pensioner)	10.2	8.7	9.1	13.7	24.2	16.6	4.0	5.8	18.8
Lone parent	6.9	9.1	11.8	1.1	4.6	8.0	0.4	19.8	23.0
Small family/dep. children	12.2	12.9	11.4	17.9	11.4	31.2	18.3	11.2	16.0
Large family/dep. children	12.8	9.2	9.1	7.1	4.7	0	21.3	4.4	1.8
Large adult only household	9.7	9.2	10.0	14.6	13.2	7.4	13.8	5.4	4.8
Two adult (1 or more pens.)	23.3	16.3	12.8	12.6	5.9	21.4	16.6	11.4	6.0
One adult (pensioner)	18.2	25.5	18.9	26.2	13.2	2.1	18.0	29.9	18.0
d) Length of residence (years)									
Up to 2	5.5	15.9	22.3	10.2	47.5	60.3	14.0	19.2	38.6
2 up to 5	16.1	20.6	23.8	14.3	12.1	10.5	9.4	35.6	13.7
5 up to 10	20.4	19.4	14.6	12.1	8.7	14.6	26.2	16.9	32.0
10 up to 20	22.3	19.0	22.8	20.8	12.8	9.1	30.9	10.9	12.4
20 +	35.7	25.0	16.5	42.6	18.9	5.5	19.5	17.4	3.4
e) Employment status									
Two full-time	4.6	3.3	4.2	12.2	8.0	15.2	3.2	0.7	4.8
Minimum one full-time	14.8	12.8	10.7	27.2	15.0	30.5	28.5	9.3	4.9
Single full-time	2.7	3.7	9.4	6.6	22.9	11.0	1.2	4.7	3.8
Minimum one part-time	9.3	7.7	5.3	12.5	8.8	8.9	5.9	10.4	20.7
Two not working	30.5	26.7	27.0	15.1	13.4	11.7	32.7	15.3	16.5
Single not working	38.0	45.7	43.5	26.5	32.0	22.7	28.4	59.6	49.3
f) Socio-economic group									
Professional	0.8	0.8	1.9	1.1	4.7	1.8	5.2	1.5	0
Employers and managers	7.6	6.0	7.9	19.1	15.6	8.9	4.2	7.3	2.1
Intermediate non-manual	3.2	3.5	1.6	6.4	7.6	6.7	7.8	3.1	5.6
Junior non-manual	10.7	8.9	11.7	5.9	10.6	10.6	6.7	9.2	21.9
Skilled manual	40.9	36.2	36.6	28.3	21.2	0	55.5	31.1	26.1
Semi-skilled manual	24.0	26.5	24.7	30.5	16.3	22.3	17.4	23.6	32.9
Unskilled manual	9.3	13.9	11.5	8.6	7.6	38.2	3.3	11.5	11.4
Armed forces	0.4	0	0	0	1.4	0	0	0	0
Never worked etc	3.2	4.0	4.2	0	15.0	11.4	0	12.7	0
All tenants (thousands)	**801**	**2,583**	**493**	**498**	**1,128**	**74**	**82**	**477**	**104**

Sample: E9

A18.10 Landlords and the rented sector: insulation improvements made

(Column %/k households)

Combination	Local authority			Private rented			Housing association		
	Imp-prover	Non imp.	Already efficient	Imp-prover	Non imp.	Already efficient	Imp-prover	Non imp.	Already efficient
Wall	7.9	3.1	1.1	0	0	*	*	6.9	*
Loft	20.5	10.7	3.3	26.0	18.9	*	*	6.0	*
Cylinder (cyl)	11.1	13.7	13.4	39.3	21.7	*	*	8.1	*
Double glazing (dg)	3.5	6.8	16.4	17.8	2.8	*	*	14.2	*
Draught excluders (de)	6.3	9.7	12.1	3.8	7.7	*	*	11.9	*
Wall + loft	5.2	1.4	5.4	2.7	0	*	*	3.3	*
Wall + cyl	2.3	0.9	3.1	0	0	*	*	1.4	*
Wall + dg	1.9	0.8	4.3	0	0	*	*	0	*
Loft + cyl	16.1	17.4	5.4	4.9	10.0	*	*	17.0	*
Loft + dg	3.1	2.0	0	4.2	16.7	*	*	1.9	*
Loft + de	3.8	3.3	0	0	0	*	*	6.7	*
Cyl + dg	5.3	2.0	2.7	1.3	1.5	*	*	0	*
Cyl + de	1.7	1.3	0.9	0	6.5	*	*	0	*
Dg + de	1.1	2.4	2.3	0	0	*	*	4.9	*
Wall + loft + cyl	4.4	3.1	7.3	0	5.3	*	*	0	*
Wall + loft + dg	2.1	0	1.2	0	0	*	*	0	*
Wall + loft + de	0	2.4	2.3	0	0	*	*	0	*
Wall + cyl + dg	0	0.2	3.0	0	0	*	*	0	*
Loft + cyl + dg	3.0	2.6	1.3	0	0	*	*	9.0	*
Loft + cyl + de	0.6	6.8	2.8	0	3.6	*	*	0.9	*
Wall + loft +cyl + dg	0	2.1	5.2	0	0	*	*	0	*
Wall +loft + cyl +de	0	1.6	4.7	0	0	*	*	0.4	*
Loft + cyl + dg + de	0	1.3	0	0	5.5	*	*	3.9	*
All	0	1.2	1.8	0	0	*	*	3.5	*
Other combinations	0	3.1	0	0	0	*	*	0	*
Households	424	1,307	196	119	175	*	*	126	*

* excluded due to small sample size
Sample: E10

A19.1 Potential for energy up-grading: Mean annual cost of heating (over whole stock) before and after improvement and % reduction in cost

(mean annual cost/see footnote)

Tenure	Dwellings included									
	SAP<10		SAP<20		SAP<30		SAP<40		SAP<50	
Owner occupier										
Before upgrading	621.0		621.0		621.0		621.0		621.0	
Target SAP 30	592.0	(5)	569.4	(8)	532.9	(14)	474.3	(24)	431.3	(31)
Target SAP 35	591.4	(5)	566.8	(9)	529.7	(15)	471.1	(24)	428.1	(31)
Target SAP 40	590.4	(5)	564.2	(9)	524.5	(16)	465.9	(25)	422.9	(32)
Target SAP 50	588.3	(5)	559.1	(10)	512.0	(18)	446.0	(28)	403.0	(35)
Target SAP 60	586.0	(6)	552.2	(11)	494.5	(20)	406.5	(35)	355.4	(43)
Target SAP 70	585.3	(6)	549.9	(11)	487.9	(21)	383.0	(38)	314.2	(49)
Privately rented										
Before upgrading	792.3		792.3		792.3		792.3		792.3	
Target SAP 30	581.2	(27)	518.5	(35)	474.8	(40)	443.1	(44)	423.0	(47)
Target SAP 35	576.7	(27)	504.3	(36)	459.0	(42)	427.3	(46)	407.2	(49)
Target SAP 40	570.9	(28)	494.8	(38)	444.1	(44)	412.3	(48)	392.2	(50)
Target SAP 50	555.2	(30)	469.7	(41)	410.7	(48)	371.3	(53)	351.2	(56)
Target SAP 60	539.8	(32)	441.5	(44)	370.8	(53)	321.2	(59)	296.5	(63)
Target SAP 70	535.5	(32)	432.6	(45)	354.9	(55)	295.7	(63)	264.0	(67)
Local authority										
Before upgrading	507.1		507.1		507.1		507.1		507.1	
Target SAP 30	459.5	(9)	428.4	(16)	392.3	(23)	353.4	(30)	325.7	(36)
Target SAP 35	458.4	(10)	425.2	(16)	388.1	(23)	349.2	(31)	321.6	(37)
Target SAP 40	457.2	(10)	421.5	(17)	382.6	(25)	343.7	(32)	316.0	(38)
Target SAP 50	454.9	(10)	414.2	(18)	369.2	(27)	326.0	(36)	298.4	(41)
Target SAP 60	451.5	(11)	405.0	(20)	351.6	(31)	297.4	(41)	265.3	(48)
Target SAP 70	450.1	(11)	402.3	(21)	345.0	(32)	281.8	(44)	241.2	(52)
Housing association										
Before upgrading	472.0		472.0		472.0		472.0		472.0	
Target SAP 30	431.1	(9)	401.8	(15)	369.6	(22)	333.9	(29)	308.3	(35)
Target SAP 35	430.4	(9)	399.4	(15)	365.3	(23)	329.6	(30)	304.0	(36)
Target SAP 40	429.6	(9)	397.5	(16)	362.3	(23)	326.6	(31)	301.0	(36)
Target SAP 50	427.4	(9)	387.8	(18)	343.9	(27)	302.6	(36)	277.0	(41)
Target SAP 60	424.4	(10)	381.9	(19)	331.5	(30)	281.4	(40)	252.7	(46)
Target SAP 70	423.3	(10)	379.0	(20)	324.1	(31)	268.0	(43)	231.3	(51)
All tenures										
Before upgrading	606.2		606.2		606.2		606.2		606.2	
Target SAP 30	558.2	(8)	530.3	(13)	493.5	(19)	441.9	(27)	404.5	(33)
Target SAP 35	557.2	(8)	526.7	(13)	489.0	(19)	437.5	(28)	400.1	(34)
Target SAP 40	555.7	(8)	523.4	(14)	483.0	(20)	431.5	(29)	394.1	(35)
Target SAP 50	552.5	(9)	516.0	(15)	468.5	(23)	410.2	(32)	372.8	(39)
Target SAP 60	548.9	(9)	506.9	(16)	449.3	(26)	372.7	(39)	328.5	(46)
Target SAP 70	547.7	(10)	504.0	(17)	441.9	(27)	351.0	(42)	292.2	(52)

Averages are taken over all dwellings in the stock, whether or not they are included in the improvement. After upgrading, the % reduction in heating costs is given in brackets.
Sample: Sp1

A19.2 Potential for energy up-grading: Mean cost of upgrading per dwelling improved and mean cost over whole stock

(Cost £/dwelling)

Tenure & target SAP	SAP<10 mean cost:		SAP<20 mean cost:		SAP<30 mean cost:		SAP<40 mean cost:		SAP<50 mean cost:	
	per dwelling	whole stock	per dwelling	whole stock	per dwelling	whole stock	per dwelling	whole stock	per dwelling	whole stock
Owner occupier										
30	2,012	(90)	1910	(201)	1,994	(513)	2,033	(1,121)	2,064	(1,705)
35	2,252	(101)	2,209	(233)	2,151	(554)	2,104	(1,160)	2,111	(1,744)
40	2,634	(118)	2,586	(272)	2,447	(630)	2,239	(1,234)	2,201	(1,819)
50	3,664	(164)	3,617	(381)	3,492	(899)	2,969	(1,637)	2,690	(2,222)
60	5,470	(245)	5,514	(580)	5,492	(1,414)	5,095	(2,809)	4,361	(3,602)
70	6,089	(273)	6,345	(668)	6,476	(1,667)	6,625	(3,654)	6,180	(5,105)
Private rented										
30	2,107	(553)	1,869	(796)	1,756	(1,107)	1,739	(1,398)	1,779	(1,659)
35	2,360	(619)	2,205	(939)	2,026	(1,278)	1,949	(1,566)	1,959	(1,827)
40	2,873	(753)	2,580	(1,098)	2,398	(1,513)	2,237	(1,797)	2,205	(2,056)
50	4,251	(1,115)	3,787	(1,612)	3,543	(2,235)	3,300	(2,651)	3,116	(2,906)
60	5,817	(1,526)	5,402	(2,299)	5,111	(3,224)	4,903	(3,939)	4,634	(4,321)
0	6,387	(1,675)	6,048	(2,575)	5,954	(3,756)	5,945	(4,777)	5,811	(5,419)
Local authority										
30	1,674	(121)	1,590	(285)	1,671	(585)	1,694	(1,045)	1,647	(1,402)
35	1,880	(136)	1,815	(325)	1,816	(636)	1,776	(1,096)	1,707	(1,452)
40	2,160	(156)	2,113	(379)	2,048	(717)	1,906	(1,176)	1,801	(1,532)
50	2,735	(198)	2,856	(512)	2,751	(964)	2,455	(1,515)	2,196	(1,869)
60	4,071	(294)	4,393	(788)	4,173	(1,462)	3,822	(2,358)	3,323	(2,828)
70	4,831	(349)	5,050	(906)	4,927	(1,726)	4,736	(2,922)	4,372	(3,721)
Housing association										
30	1,881	(127)	1,458	(253)	1,405	(457)	1,494	(831)	1,520	(1,162)
35	2,076	(140)	1,727	(299)	1,670	(543)	1,648	(917)	1,632	(1,247)
40	2,372	(160)	2,063	(357)	1,929	(627)	1,799	(1,000)	1,741	(1,330)
50	3,071	(208)	2,844	(493)	2,795	(909)	2,509	(1,395)	2,255	(1,723)
60	4,132	(280)	3,770	(653)	3,744	(1,217)	3,518	(1,957)	3,141	(2,400)
70	4,647	(314)	4,355	(755)	4,439	(1,443)	4,284	(2,382)	4,102	(3,134)
All tenures										
30	1,964	(137)	1,804	(270)	1,857	(576)	1,909	(1,120)	1,933	(1,621)
35	2,200	(153)	2,093	(313)	2,034	(631)	2,001	(1,173)	1,997	(1,674)
40	2,598	(181)	2,448	(367)	2,325	(722)	2,152	(1,262)	2,103	(1,763)
50	3,628	(253)	3,442	(515)	3,298	(1,023)	2,878	(1,688)	2,610	(2,188)
60	5,233	(364)	5,146	(771)	5,052	(1,568)	4,745	(2,782)	4,128	(3,460)
70	5,864	(408)	5,881	(881)	5,948	(1,846)	6,063	(3,555)	5,700	(4,778)

Sample: Sp1

A19.3 **Percentage of dwellings with SAP <50 requiring particular upgrading packages by tenure**

(% of dwellings)

Tenure	Owner occupied	Private rented	Local authority	Housing association
1) Heating and insulation to highest standard	0.1	0.5	0.1	0.2
2) Heating and insulation to high intermediate standard	0.7	1.9	0.8	1.6
3) Heating and insulation to low intermediate standard	1.6	2.1	0.8	1.6
4) Heating and insulation to minimum standard	14.2	26.4	23.5	31.3
5) Heating only to highest standard	55.7	52.6	49.6	37.9
6) Insulation only to highest standard	3.2	4.2	2.2	4.9
7) Heating to high intermediate/insulation to minimum	1.6	6.1	2.2	1.3
8) Heating to minimum/ insulation to high intermediate	22.9	6.2	17.8	16.7

Sample: Sp5

A19.4 **Cost of upgrading (£) for each tenure for improvement options (target SAP 30)**

(% of dwellings falling within each cost band)

Cost of up-grading (£)	Dwellings included			
	SAP<10	SAP<20	SAP<30	SAP<50
Owner occupier				
Under £250	1.3	2.2	2.8	2.2
250-500	1.8	9.0	11.5	10.4
500-1000	1.4	2.9	3.7	3.9
1000-1500	33.8	25.1	17.8	14.0
1500-2500	41.7	42.3	39.7	39.7
2500-4000	16.3	14.6	20.7	26.9
4000-6000	2.2	3.1	3.0	2.5
Over £6000	1.6	0.8	0.8	0.4
Private rented				
Under £250	0.5	7.1	8.9	9.7
250-500	4.2	10.5	13.9	15.8
500-1000	1.9	1.4	2.8	2.9
1000-1500	16.9	17.2	16.4	13.5
1500-2500	49.2	39.9	35.5	33.8
2500-4000	24.7	20.7	19.4	20.9
4000-6000	2.5	3.2	2.7	3.2
Over £6000	0	0	0.3	0.3
Local authority				
Under £250	2.6	6.5	9.6	14.7
250-500	5.7	12.9	12.7	12.4
500-1000	2.5	1.6	1.9	3.1
1000-1500	35.8	28.7	22.3	14.4
1500-2500	48.9	44.4	41.9	40.8
2500-4000	4.1	4.8	9.0	12.1
4000-6000	0.4	1.2	2.2	2.2
Over £6000	0	0	0.3	0.3
Housing association				
Under £250	1.4	23.3	24.7	22.1
250-500	2.9	5.9	8.9	12.8
500-1000	6.3	3.7	8.1	4.7
1000-1500	32.9	24.8	19.1	12.8
1500-2500	36.5	30.4	26.5	28.7
2500-4000	19.3	10.9	10.1	16.6
4000-6000	0.7	1.0	1.5	1.1
Over £6000	0	0	0.9	1.0

Sample: Sp2 - 5

A19.5 SAP distribution before and after energy upgrading *(target SAP 30)*

(Column % of dwellings)

SAP rating	whole stock before upgrading	Dwellings improved (all tenures)				Whole stock (all tenures)			
		SAP<10	SAP<20	SAP<30	SAP<50	SAP<10	SAP<20	SAP<30	SAP<50
<10	6.5	0	0	0	0	0	0	0	0
10-20	8.3	0	0	0	0	8.3	0	0	0
20-30	15.8	0	0	0	0	15.8	15.8	0	0
30-40	28.4	41.5	42.7	30.9	11.2	31.1	34.8	37.8	9.4
40-50	25.3	32.9	36.4	42.3	27.1	27.5	30.7	38.3	22.8
50-60	12.1	18.7	16.9	22.2	39.5	13.3	14.6	18.9	45.3
60-70	3.2	5.8	3.4	4.3	20.0	3.5	3.7	4.5	20.2
70-80	0.3	1.0	0.6	0.4	2.1	0.4	0.4	0.5	2.1
>80	0.1	0	0	0	0.1	0.1	0.1	0.1	0.2
Mean SAP before upgrading		-2.8	7.6	17.0	31.4	35.4	35.4	35.4	35.4
Mean SAP after upgrading		43.7	42.9	44.9	52.5	38.4	40.6	43.9	53.2
% below target SAP		0	0	0	0	24.1	15.8	0	0

Sample: Sp1 - 5

A19.6 Household resources for energy upgrading *(owner occupiers)*

(Col % of households)

	Homes included					
	SAP<10		SAP<20	SAP<30	SAP<50	
	all	(on benefit)	all	all	all	(on benefit)
Upgrading cost/annual income						
under 2%	2	(0)	3	3	4	(0)
2-5%	2	(0)	5	8	8	(1)
5-10%	9	(1)	12	11	17	(1)
10-20%	23	(4)	25	28	33	(2)
20-30%	14	(4)	15	15	14	(1)
30-40%	10	(4)	9	9	8	(2)
40-50%	15	(6)	10	7	5	(3)
50-70%	10	(7)	9	7	5	(3)
70-100%	10	(9)	9	6	5	(4)
over 100%	5	(1)	4	6	3	(2)
Dependent on state benefits?						
Total %	35	(35)	33	28	18	(18)
Below income support level?						
Total %	9	(9)	9	9	6	(6)

Sample: Sp2 - 5

A19.7 SAP ratings for each tenure before and after energy upgrading
(target SAP 30)

(% of dwellings falling within each SAP rating band)

SAP rating of whole stock	Before upgrading	After upgrading dwellings with:			
		SAP<10	SAP<20	SAP<30	SAP<50
Owner occupiers					
Under 10	4.2	0	0	0	0
10-20	6.2	6.2	0	0	0
20-30	15.0	15.0	15.0	0	0
30-40	30.4	32.2	34.8	37.5	7.1
40-50	27.5	28.8	31.3	39.1	22.2
50-60	13.4	14.1	15.2	18.9	47.7
60-70	3.2	3.4	3.5	4.3	21.4
70-80	0.2	0.2	0.3	0.3	1.6
Over 80	0	0	0	0	0
Private rented					
Under 10	25.1	0	0	0	0
10-20	18.4	18.4	0	0	0
20-30	18.0	18.0	18.0	0	0
30-40	18.1	29.2	39.4	45.5	27.3
40-50	13.2	21.8	28.4	34.5	29.8
50-60	3.5	7.5	8.8	13.8	29.0
60-70	3	4.3	4.7	5.5	11.8
70-80	0.5	0.7	0.7	0.7	1.9
Over 80	0	0	0	0	0.3
Local authority					
Under 10	6.7	0	0	0	0
10-20	10.5	10.5	0	0	0
20-30	17.2	17.2	17.2	0	0
30-40	26.6	28.9	33.0	36.0	9.4
40-50	23.4	25.7	30.0	37.2	21.9
50-60	11.5	13.1	15.0	21.1	44.8
60-70	3.2	3.6	3.6	4.5	19.8
70-80	0.6	0.7	0.8	0.9	3.4
Over 80	0.3	0.3	0.3	0.3	0.6
Housing association					
Under 10	6.7	0	0	0	0
10-20	11.7	11.7	0	0	0
20-30	17.0	17.0	17.0	0	0
30-40	25.5	27.9	34.1	37.4	11.9
40-50	23.1	24.7	28.5	37.4	24.9
50-60	11.4	12.4	13.5	17.8	38.9
60-70	2.9	4.5	5.1	5.7	18.2
70-80	1.6	1.7	1.8	1.8	6.1
Over 80	0	0	0	0	0.1

Sample: Sp1

A19.8 **Payback period (in years) for each tenure for improvement options**
(target SAP 30)

(% of dwelling falling within each period)

Payback period (years)	Dwellings included			
	SAP<10	SAP<20	SAP<30	SAP<50
Owner occupier				
under 2	22	19	13	7
2-4	47	25	17	12
4-6	25	35	20	8
6-8	3	14	19	12
8-10	0	3	9	10
10-12	0	1	6	9
12-15	0	1	7	14
15-20	2	2	7	19
over 20	0	0	3	10
Private rented				
under 2	35	35	33	26
2-4	45	29	24	23
4-6	15	21	19	14
6-8	1	8	10	9
8-10	2	3	5	6
10-12	2	2	2	3
12-15	1	0	3	6
15-20	1	1	2	6
over 20	0	1	2	8
Local authority				
under 2	30	27	24	21
2-4	53	23	14	11
4-6	14	28	17	8
6-8	3	15	22	12
8-10	0	2	6	7
10-12	0	1	2	4
12-15	0	0	3	7
15-20	0	2	4	22
over 20	0	3	8	17
Housing association				
under 2	11	30	33	24
2-4	56	23	13	14
4-6	21	25	15	8
6-8	5	13	18	11
8-10	6	2	2	3
10-12	0	1	5	5
12-15	0	2	7	6
15-20	0	4	3	13
over 20	0	1	5	15

Sample: Sp2 - 5

A19.9 Mean actual fuel expenditure compared with theoretical heating and appliance costs required to meet standard heating regime

(£/% of households)

SAP Rating	Mean actual fuel expenditure (£)	For standard regime		Surplus (£)*	% of households spending more than requirement
		Mean heating requirement (£)	Mean other requirement (£)		
Under 0	537	1,091	138	-692	7
0-10	599	864	139	-404	4
10-20	558	644	155	-241	15
20-30	592	557	172	-137	22
30-40	674	532	222	-79	32
40-50	652	468	234	-50	42
50-60	666	405	252	9	58
60-70	625	325	224	77	69
70-80	616	357	270	-11	46

Surplus: the difference in £ between actual annual fuel expenditure and that required to meet the standard heating regime - may be positive or negative.
Sample: S1

A19.10 Distribution of 'surplus' expenditure on fuel for low, intermediate and high SAP ratings

(Expenditure £)

Percentiles of households	SAP<10	SAP30-40	SAP>60
5th (low)	-1,177	-408	-198
10th	-997	-319	-127
lower quartile	-704	-208	-46
median	-445	-77	72
upper quartile	-229	15	186
90th	-97	139	335
95th (high)	29	220	335

Sample: S1

A19.11 Surplus of annual fuel expenditure over that theoretically required (for whole stock) to meet standard heating regime

(£/£m/k households)

SAP rating	Negative surplus			Positive surplus			Net Surplus (£m)
	Mean (£)	H/holds	Surplus (£m)	Mean (£)	H/holds	Surplus (£m)	
Under 0	-744	71	-53	41	5	0	-53
0-10	-495	302	-149	1,543	14	22	-127
10-20	-303	779	-236	120	135	16	-220
20-30	-216	2,347	-507	145	655	95	-412
30-40	-183	4,226	-773	138	2,029	280	-493
40-50	-164	3,141	-515	109	2,251	245	-270
50-60	-138	1,056	-146	116	1,452	168	23
60-70	-90	158	-14	153	346	53	39
70-80	-123	51	-6	116	44	5	-1
Total		12,132	-2,400		6,934	885	-1,515

Data are given for those households spending more than the theoretical requirement, for those spending less, and for all households
Sample: S1

A19.12 Annual standard heating costs for each tenure before and after upgrading *(target SAP 30)*

(% of dwellings falling within each cost band)

Annual heating cost (£)	Before	After upgrading homes with:			
		SAP<10	SAP<20	SAP<30	SAP<50
Owner occupiers					
Under £100	0	0	0	0	0
100-200	0.2	0.2	0.3	0.4	0.8
200-300	2.9	3.8	4.1	5.5	14.7
300-500	32.9	35.1	38.9	46.5	62.0
500-750	42.8	42.8	41.6	35.7	18.0
750-1000	13.6	12.4	10.4	8.5	3.7
1000-1500	6.1	4.9	4.2	3.1	0.7
1500-2000	1.1	0.6	0.4	0.3	0.1
Above £2000	0.4	0.2	0.1	0	0
Private rented					
Under £100	0	0	0	0	0
100-200	2.3	3.4	3.4	4.1	5.1
200-300	3.1	7	8.3	10.4	15.8
300-500	21.6	34.3	42.8	48.1	53.7
500-750	34.0	36.8	35.8	32.3	23.2
750-1000	15.3	11.6	6.1	3.6	1.6
1000-1500	15.0	5.6	2.8	1.1	0.3
1500-2000	5.6	1.0	0.6	0.4	0.2
Above £2000	3.0	0.3	0.1	0.1	0.1
Local authority					
Under £100	0	0	0	0	0
100-200	1.0	1.3	1.4	2.0	5.5
200-300	11.8	13.3	15.0	19.2	36.6
300-500	48.0	51.9	57.3	62.8	54.7
500-750	28.6	27.6	24.3	15.6	3.0
750-1000	7.1	5.6	1.9	0.4	0.2
1000-1500	2.8	0.4	0.1	0	0
1500-2000	0.6	0	0	0	0
Above £2000	0.1	0	0	0	0
Housing association					
Under £100	0	0	0	0	0
100-200	3.6	4.1	4.6	6.0	11.2
200-300	18.7	21.1	25.6	28.0	41.4
300-500	44.3	46.6	47.7	53.2	43.5
500-750	22.9	21.8	19.0	11.3	3.6
750-1000	8.2	5.8	2.8	1.2	0.3
1000-1500	1.6	0.5	0.3	0.3	0
1500-2000	0.4	0	0	0	0
Above £2000	0.3	0	0	0	0

Sample: Sp1

A19.13   Potential impact on affordable warmth of a wide range of improvement options

(Mean %/column % households/SAP rating/Cost £b)

% of income needed for standard regime	Before improve-ment	After improvement by at least 10 SAP points							
		to target of 30, all dwlgs				to target of 70, all dwlgs			
		<10	<20	<30	<50	<10	<20	<30	<50
(mean % needed)	*(10.8)*	*(9.5)*	*(9.1)*	*(8.6)*	*(7.6)*	*(9.3)*	*(8.7)*	*(7.8)*	*(6.2)*
% of hhlds needing									
under 5% of income	34.7	38.8	40.0	42.0	48.7	40.0	42.4	46.5	58.1
5 to 10%	30.2	30.1	30.5	30.8	28.7	30.0	30.8	31.0	26.8
10 to 15%	15.0	14.7	14.9	15.1	13.1	14.3	13.7	12.8	9.8
15% or more	20.1	16.4	14.6	12.1	9.5	15.7	13.1	9.7	5.3
Adequacy of spend for minimum regime									
(mean % over-spend)	*(-1)*	*(12)*	*(14)*	*(19)*	*(31)*	*(14)*	*(20)*	*(29)*	*(52)*
% of hhlds spending									
over 10% more	34.3	40.9	43.4	48.8	64.9	42.7	47.3	56.8	82.5
within 10%	26.5	26.1	26.4	26.0	21.1	25.2	25.0	22.6	11.4
10 to 30% less	22.9	21.4	20.7	17.9	9.5	20.9	19.1	14.8	4.0
over 30% less	16.3	11.6	9.5	7.3	4.5	11.2	8.6	5.7	2.0
Mean SAP of stock	35.4	38.4	40.6	43.9	53.2	40.1	44.6	51.5	69.3
Capital costs (£b)		**2.4**	**5.1**	**10.8**	**31.1**	**7.3**	**16.7**	**34.7**	**91.7**

Sample: S1

A20.1   **Energy upgrading capital costs and percentage savings in heating costs**

(% saving/cost £b)

Dwellings included	Energy upgrading target	% saving	Capital cost (£bn)	Cost (£bn) for each % saving
SAP<10	Target SAP 30	8	2.6	0.33
	Target SAP 35	8	2.9	0.36
	Target SAP 40	8	3.5	0.41
	Target SAP 50	9	4.8	0.54
	Target SAP 60	9	7.0	0.74
	Target SAP 70	10	7.8	0.81
SAP<20	Target SAP 30	13	5.2	0.41
	Target SAP 35	13	6.0	0.46
	Target SAP 40	14	7.0	0.51
	Target SAP 50	15	9.8	0.66
	Target SAP 60	16	14.7	0.90
	Target SAP 70	17	16.8	1.00
SAP<30	Target SAP 30	19	11.0	0.59
	Target SAP 35	19	12.0	0.62
	Target SAP 40	20	13.8	0.68
	Target SAP 50	23	19.5	0.86
	Target SAP 60	26	29.9	1.16
	Target SAP 70	27	35.2	1.30
SAP<40	Target SAP 30	27	21.4	0.79
	Target SAP 35	28	22.4	0.80
	Target SAP 40	29	24.1	0.84
	Target SAP 50	32	32.2	1.00
	Target SAP 60	39	53.1	1.38
	Target SAP 70	42	67.9	1.61
SAP<50	Target SAP 30	33	30.9	0.93
	Target SAP 35	34	32.0	0.94
	Target SAP 40	35	33.6	0.96
	Target SAP 50	39	41.8	1.08
	Target SAP 60	46	66.0	1.44
	Target SAP 70	52	91.2	1.76

Sample: Sp1

Annex B

Survey schedules

This annex reproduces those sections of the EHCS survey schedules which contained the main heating and energy related questions, as follows:

B.1   **Physical survey, pages 3 to 5**   *(Pages 348 to 349)*

B.2   **Interview survey, pages 5 to 7, 29 to 52**   *(Pages 349 to 362)*

B.3   **Postal survey, Private sector stock**   *(Pages 363 to 367)*
              Public sector stock*

B.4   **Gas and electricity permission sheets**   *(Pages 368 to 371)*
          and consumption and tariff pro formae

* Relevant pages from the postal survey to housing associations are very similar to those shown for the public sector stock.

A copy of the full physical survey schedule can be found in the first EHCS report and copies of the interview and postal survey schedules will be included in a further report.[1]

---

1   *Department of the Environment, 1993 and 1996, op. cit.*

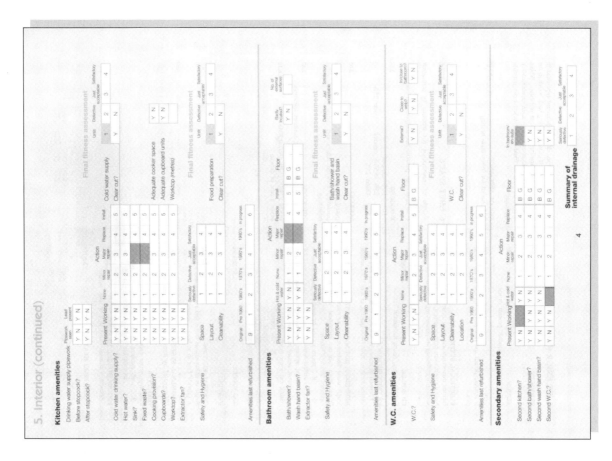

B.1   Physical survey, pages 3 and 4

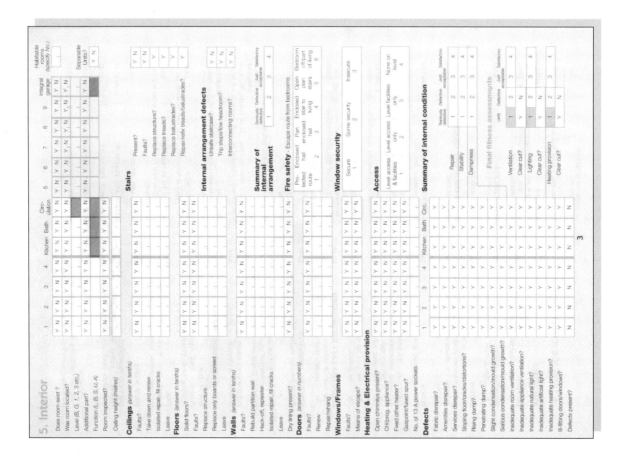

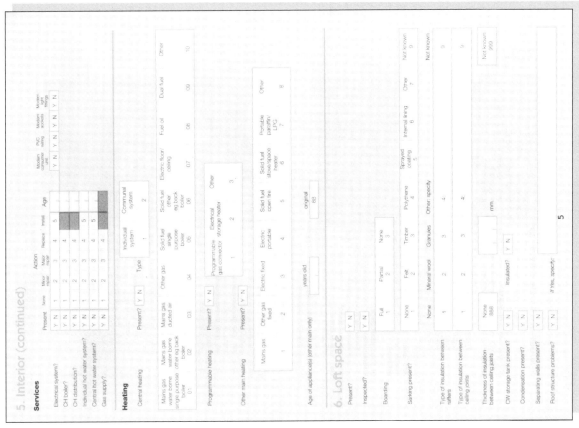

B.1   Physical survey, page 5

B.2   Interview survey, page 5

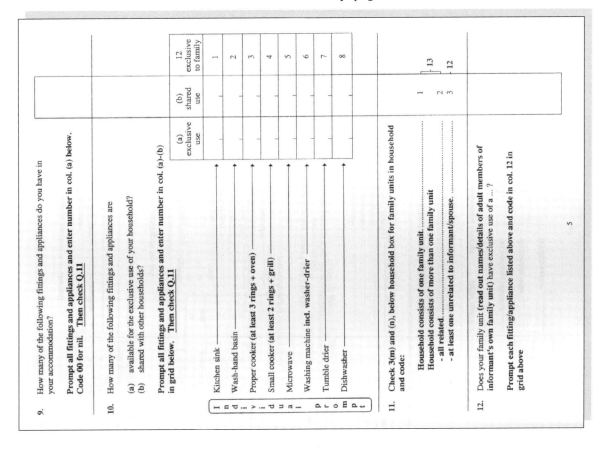

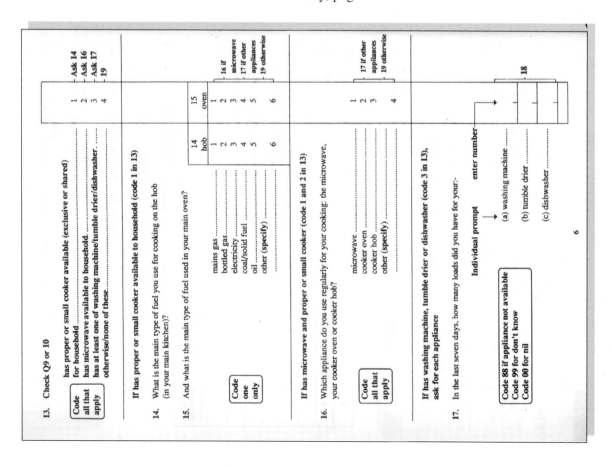

18. Are you on Economy 7/the white meter/the cheap/off-peak rate for your electricity?

yes .... 1 (a)
no .... 2 → 19
don't know 3

(a) When you use your .... (name appliance), do you use it at the cheap rate ....?
Ask for each appliance

	washing machine	tumble drier	dish-washer
does not have use of	9	9	9
always	1	1	1
occasionally	2	2	2
never	3	3	3
other (specify)	4	4	4

→ 19

Running prompt

Code one only

19. Check 3, household box, for lodgers/boarders in household and code:

household contains no lodgers/boarders .... 1 → 21
household contains lodgers/boarders .... 2 → 20

20. Does your lodger/boarder) usually prepare
Do any of your lodgers/boarders) their own evening meal during the week?

yes .... 1 (a)
no, none do .... 2 → 21
don't know 3

(a) What does he/she usually do? Does he/she prepare meals: ...?

in the same kitchen as your household 1
in a separate kitchen for the use of lodgers 2
in a cooking area in their own rooms 3
or doesn't he/she have access to cooking facilities 4
other (specify) 5

→ 21

Running prompt

Code all that apply

7

B.2 Interview survey, pages 6 and 7

---

13. Check Q9 or 10

has proper or small cooker available (exclusive or shared) for household .... 1 Ask 14
has microwave available to household .... 2 Ask 16
has at least one of washing machine/tumble drier/dishwasher .... 3 Ask 17
otherwise/none of these 4 19

Code all that apply

If has proper or small cooker available to household (code 1 in 13)

14. What is the main type of fuel you use for cooking on the hob (in your main kitchen)?

15. And what is the main type of fuel used in your main oven?

	14 hob	15 oven
mains gas	1	1
bottled gas	2	2
electricity	3	3
coal/solid fuel	4	4
oil	5	5
other (specify)	6	6

16 if microwave
17 if other appliances
19 otherwise

Code one only

If has microwave and proper or small cooker (code 1 and 2 in 13)

16. Which appliance do you use regularly for your cooking: the microwave, your cooker oven or cooker hob?

microwave 1
cooker oven 2
cooker hob 3
other (specify) 4

17 if other appliances
19 otherwise

Code all that apply

If has washing machine, tumble drier or dishwasher (code 3 in 13), ask for each appliance

17. In the last seven days, how many loads did you have for your:-

Individual prompt   enter number

(a) washing machine ...... → 18
(b) tumble drier ....
(c) dishwasher ....

Code 88 if appliance not available
Code 99 for don't know
Code 00 for nil

6

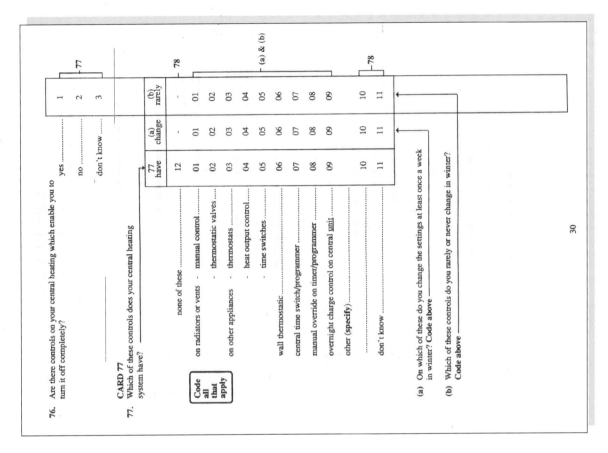

76. Are there controls on your central heating which enable you to turn it off completely?

yes .... 1 → 77
no 2
don't know 3

CARD 77
77. Which of these controls does your central heating system have?

Code all that apply

	77 have	(a) change	(b) rarely
none of these	12	-	-
on radiators or vents - manual control	01	01	01
- thermostatic valves	02	02	02
on other appliances - thermostats	03	03	03
- heat output control	04	04	04
- time switches	05	05	05
wall thermostatic	06	06	06
central time switch/programmer	07	07	07
manual override on timer/programmer	08	08	08
overnight charge control on central unit	09	09	09
other (specify)	10	10	10
don't know	11	11	11

(a) & (b) → 78

(a) On which of these do you change the settings at least once a week in winter? Code above
(b) Which of these controls do you rarely or never change in winter? Code above

30

B.2   Interview survey, pages 29 and 30

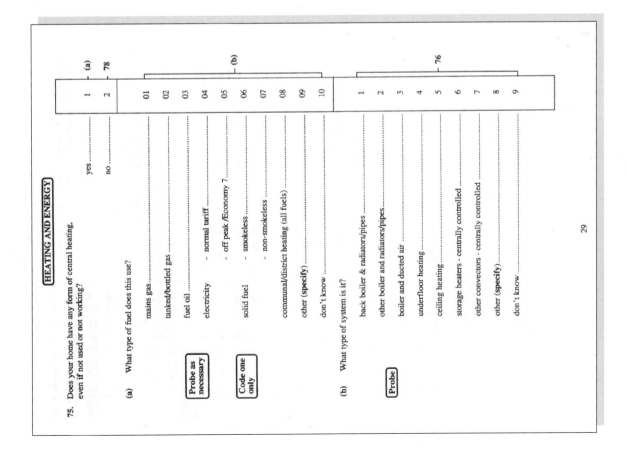

HEATING AND ENERGY

75. Does your home have any form of central heating, even if not used or not working?

yes .... 1 (a)
no .... 2 → 78

(a) What type of fuel does this use?

Probe as necessary

Code one only

mains gas	01
tanked/bottled gas	02
fuel oil	03
electricity - normal tariff	04
- off peak /Economy 7	05
solid fuel - smokeless	06
- non-smokeless	07
communal/district heating (all fuels)	08
other (specify)	09
don't know	10

(b) → (b)

(b) What type of system is it?

Probe

back boiler & radiators/pipes	1
other boiler and radiators/pipes	2
boiler and ducted air	3
underfloor heating	4
ceiling heating	5
storage heaters - centrally controlled	6
other convectors - centrally controlled	7
other (specify)	8
don't know	9

→ 76

29

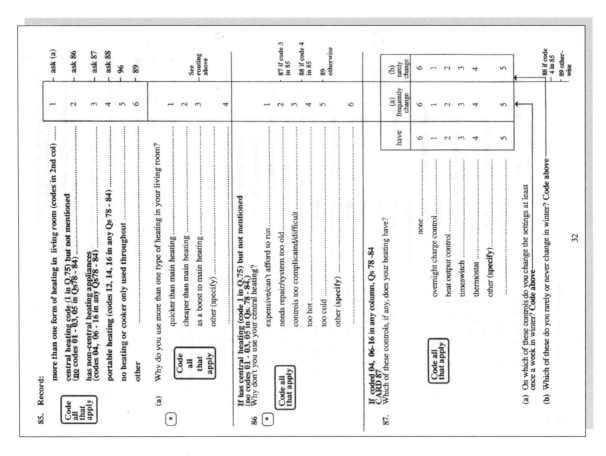

85. Record:

Code all that apply		
more than one form of heating in living room (1 in Q.75) but not mentioned	1	ask (a)
central heating code (1 in Q.75) but not mentioned (no codes 01 - 03, 05 in Qs78 - 84)	2	ask 86
has non-central heating appliances (codes 04, 06 - 16 in any Qs78 - 84)	3	ask 87
portable heating (codes 12, 14, 16 in any Qs 78 - 84)	4	ask 88
no heating or cooker only used throughout	5	96
other	6	89

(a) Why do you use more than one type of heating in your living room?

Code all that apply		
quicker than main heating	1	See routing above
cheaper than main heating	2	
as a boost to main heating	3	
other (specify)	4	

86. If has central heating (code 1 in Q.75) but not mentioned (no codes 01 - 03, 05 in Qs. 78 - 84.) Why don't you use your central heating?

Code all that apply		
expensive/can't afford to run	1	87 if code 3 in 85
needs repair/system too old	2	
controls too complicated/difficult	3	88 if code 4 in 85
too hot	4	
too cold	5	89 otherwise
other (specify)	6	

87. If coded 04, 06-16 in any column, Qs 78 -84
CARD 87
Which of these controls, if any, does your heating have?

Code all that apply	have	(a) frequently change	(b) rarely change
none	6	6	6
overnight charge control	1	1	1
heat output control	2	2	2
timeswitch	3	3	3
thermostat	4	4	4
other (specify)	5	5	5

(a) On which of these controls do you change the settings at least once a week in winter? Code above
(b) Which of these do you rarely or never change in winter? Code above

88 if code 4 in 85
89 otherwise

32

B.2 Interview survey, pages 31 and 32

78. What is the main way of heating your main (not 'best') living room in the winter? (Code one only below)
79. Do you use any other form of heating in this living room? What kind? (Code all that apply below, including 'no other form of heating')
80. How do you heat your bedroom in the winter (Code all that apply)
81. How do you heat your other bedrooms in the winter (Code all that apply, including 'no heating used')
82. How do you heat the hall in the winter (Code all that apply)
83. How do you heat the kitchen in the winter (Code all that apply)
84. How do you heat the bathroom in the winter (Code all that apply)

	Main Living Main heating	Other heating	Your bed	Other bed	Hall	Kitchen	Bathroom
room does not exist	19	19	19	19	19	19	19
no heating used	20	20	20	20	20	20	20
no other form of heating used	-	21	-	-	-	-	-
central heating boiler only	01	01	01	01	01	01	01
central heating outlets (radiators/vents)	02	02	02	02	02	02	02
programmable gas convector - centrally controlled	03	03	03	03	03	03	03
- separate	04	04	04	04	04	04	04
electric storage heater - centrally controlled	05	05	05	05	05	05	05
- separate	06	06	06	06	06	06	06
mains gas fire - fire/convector	07	07	07	07	07	07	07
- radiant fire only	08	078	08	08	08	08	08
solid fuel - open fire	09	09	09	09	09	09	09
- enclosed grate/stove	10	10	10	10	10	10	10
electric oil-filled radiator - fixed	11	11	11	11	11	11	11
- portable	12	12	12	12	12	12	12
electric fire/convector/heater -fixed	13	13	13	13	13	13	13
-portable	14	14	14	14	14	14	14
bottled gas/paraffin heater -fixed	15	15	15	15	15	15	15
-portable	16	16	16	16	16	16	16
cooker (heating only)	17	17	17	17	17	17	17
other (specify)	18	18	18	18	18	18	18

Probe as necessary

31

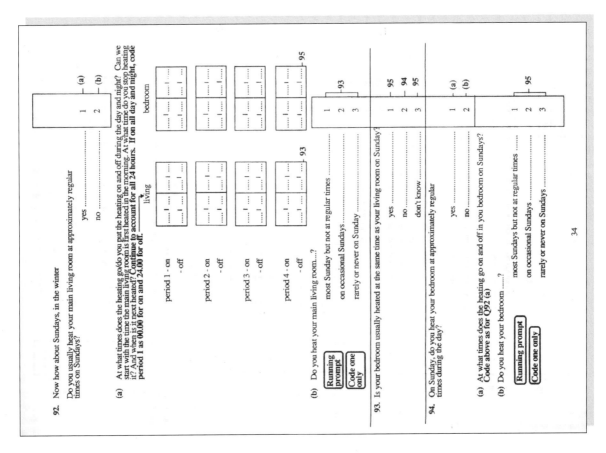

B.2   Interview survey, pages 33 and 34

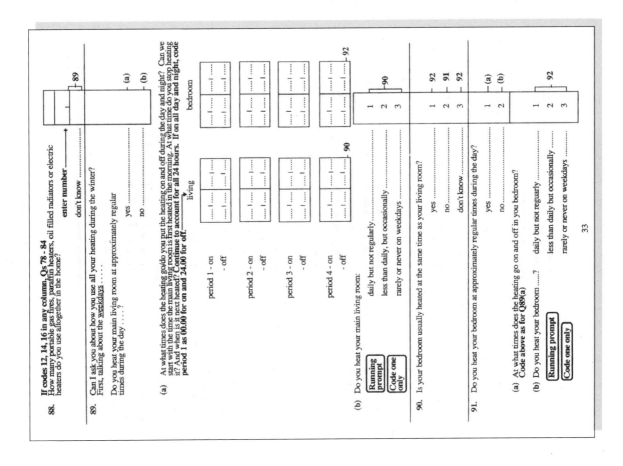

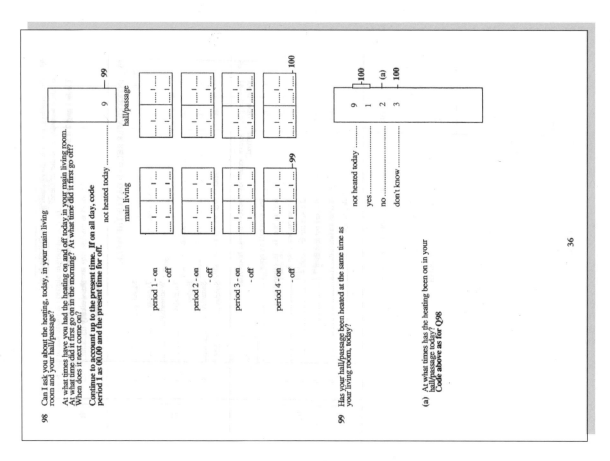

B.2   Interview survey, pages 35 and 36

98 Can I ask you about the heating, today, in your main living room and your hall/passage?

At what times have you had the heating on and off today in your main living room. At what time did it first go on in the morning? At what time did it first go off? When does it next come on?

Continue to account up to the present time. If on all day, code period 1 as 00.00 and the present time for off.

	main living			hall/passage		
period 1 - on	I__I__I	I__I__I		I__I__I	I__I__I	
- off	I__I__I	I__I__I		I__I__I	I__I__I	
period 2 - on	I__I__I	I__I__I		I__I__I	I__I__I	
- off	I__I__I	I__I__I		I__I__I	I__I__I	
period 3 - on	I__I__I	I__I__I		I__I__I	I__I__I	
- off	I__I__I	I__I__I		I__I__I	I__I__I	
period 4 - on	I__I__I	I__I__I		I__I__I	I__I__I	
- off	I__I__I	I__I__I 99		I__I__I	I__I__I 100	

not heated today .... 9 → 99

99 Has your hall/passage been heated at the same time as your living room, today?

not heated today .... 9 → 100
yes .... 1 → (a)
no .... 2 → 100
don't know .... 3 → 100

(a) At what times has the heating been on in your hall/passage today?
Code above as for Q98

36

---

95 On Saturdays, is your heating pattern generally like Sundays or like a weekday or neither of these?

Code **1 and 2** if Sundays and weekdays are similar

like Sunday 1
like weekday 2   96
like neither 3

96 INTERVIEWER RECORD DAY OF THE WEEK

Monday 1
Tuesday 2
Wednesday 3
Thursday 4   97
Friday 5
Saturday 6
Sunday 7

97 How long have you or somebody else been in your house/flat today, before I arrived?

less than half an hour 1
half an hour but less than 1 hour 2
1 hour but less than 2 3
2 hours but less than 4 4   98
4 hours but less than 7 5
7 or more hours 6
don't know 7

35

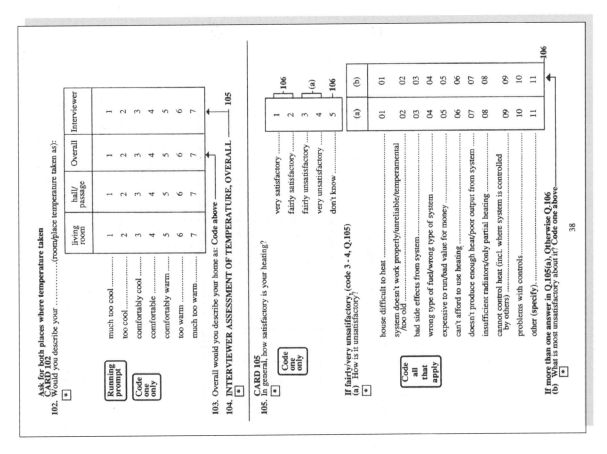

B.2   Interview survey, pages 37 and 38

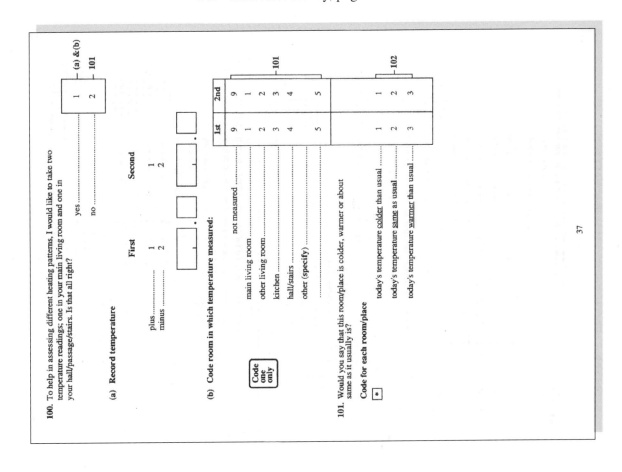

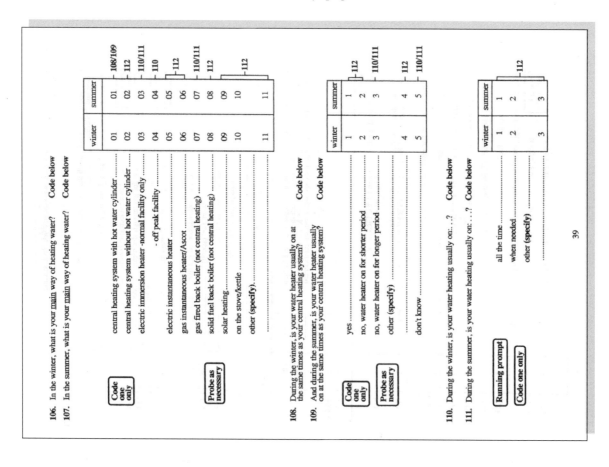

112. Now, I would like to ask you about how you pay your fuel bills and what your costs are. . . .

Would you tell me which are all the ways you pay for your heating and fuel bills...

Probe as necessary

Code all that apply

pays direct to gas board	01
pays direct to electricity board	02 — 113
pays for gas through slot meter - coin	03
- token/card/key	04
pays for electricity through meter - coin	05
- token/card/key	06
buys fuel - oil/coal/bottled gas from supplier	07 — Ask 121
-other fuel (specify)	08
fuel bill incl. in rent	09 — 124
fuel bills paid direct by DSS	10
other (specify)	11

113. Would you be prepared to give your permission for the Electricity Company and the British Gas Region to tell the Department about the fuel consumption of this house/flat? The details would just be used solely for research purposes and would remain confidential.

	(a) ELEC.	(b) GAS	
dna - no gas/electricity	9	9	
yes	1	1	— 114
no	2	2	

Record:

114(i). Complete (i) GAS PERMISSION SHEET and (ii) ELECTRICITY PERMISSION SHEET, as relevant

(a) pays directly for electricity .... 1 — (a)

(b) pays directly for gas .... 2 — (b)

pays through slot meter for electricity .... 1 — (c)

pays throught slot meter for gas .... 2 — 118

.... 3 — 119

(c) buys fuel (codes 07, 08 in Q112) 4

does not buy fuel .... 1 — 121

.... 2 — 124

(ii) Permission not given for either GAS or ELECTRICITY or BOTH

Code all that apply

- and pays directly for it (them) .... 2 — 115

- and pays through meter for it (them) .... 3 — 118

40

B.2   Interview survey, pages 39 and 40

106. In the winter, what is your main way of heating water?   Code below

107. In the summer, what is your main way of heating water?   Code below

Code one only

	winter	summer	
central heating system with hot water cylinder	01	01	108/109
central heating system without hot water cylinder	02	02	112
electric immersion heater - normal facility only	03	03	110/111
- off peak facility	04	04	110
electric instantaneous heater	05	05	— 112
gas instantaneous heater/Ascot	06	06	
gas fired back boiler (not central heating)	07	07	110/111
solid fuel back boiler (not central heating)	08	08	112
solar heating	09	09	
on the stove/kettle	10	10	— 112
other (specify)	11	11	

108. During the winter, is your water heater usually on at the same times as your central heating system?   Code below

109. And during the summer, is your water heater usually on at the same times as your central heating system?   Code below

Code one only

Probe as necessary

	winter	summer	
yes	1	1	— 112
no, water heater on for shorter period	2	2	
no, water heater on for longer period	3	3	110/111
other (specify)	4	4	112
don't know	5	5	110/111

110. During the winter, is your water heating usually on: ...?   Code below

111. During the summer, is your water heating usually on: ...?   Code below

Running prompt

Code one only

	winter	summer	
all the time	1	1	
when needed	2	2	— 112
other (specify)	3	3	

39

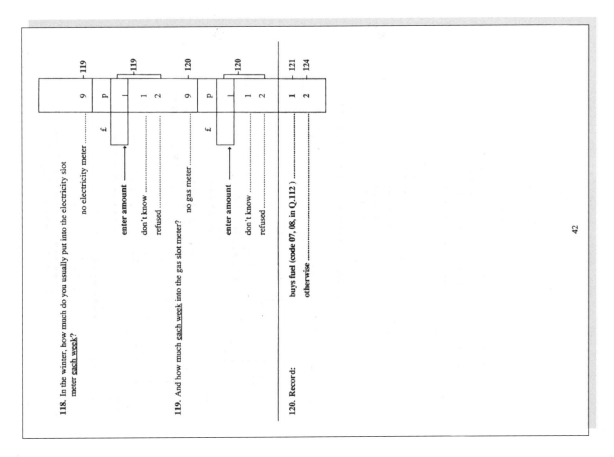

118. In the winter, how much do you usually put into the electricity slot meter each week?

no electricity meter	9	— 119
£ p		
enter amount —	—	— 119
don't know	1	
refused	2	

119. And how much each week into the gas slot meter?

no gas meter	9	— 120
£ p		
enter amount —	—	— 120
don't know	1	
refused	2	

120. Record:

buys fuel (code 07, 08, in Q.112)	1	— 121
otherwise	2	— 124

42

B.2   Interview survey, pages 41 and 42

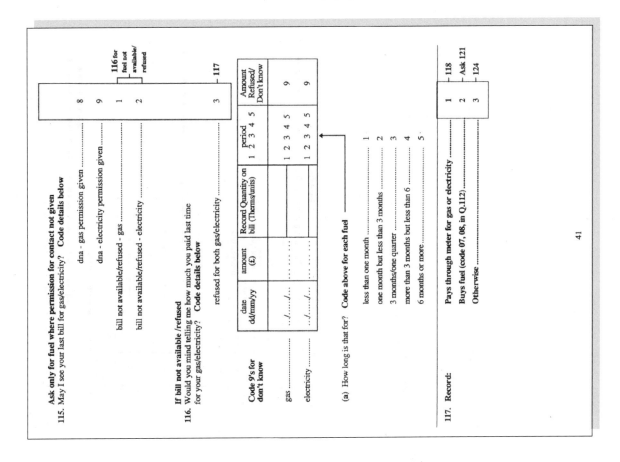

Ask only for fuel where permission for contact not given
115. May I see your last bill for gas/electricity?   **Code details below**

dna - gas permission given	8	
dna - electricity permission given	9	
bill not available/refused - gas	1	116 for fuel not available/ refused
bill not available/refused - electricity	2	

If bill not available /refused
116. Would you mind telling me how much you paid last time for your gas/electricity?   **Code details below**

refused for both gas/electricity	3	— 117

Code 9's for don't know	date dd/mm/yy	amount (£)	Record Qnantity on bill (Therms/units)	period 1 2 3 4 5	Amount Refused/ Don't know
gas	../...../..	· · · · · · ·		1 2 3 4 5	9
electricity	../...../..	· · · · · · ·		1 2 3 4 5	9

(a) How long is that for?   **Code above for each fuel**

less than one month	1
one month but less than 3 months	2
3 months/one quarter	3
more than 3 months but less than 6	4
6 months or more	5

117. Record:

Pays through meter for gas or electricity	1	— 118
Buys fuel (code 07, 08, in Q.112)	2	— Ask 121
Otherwise	3	— 124

41

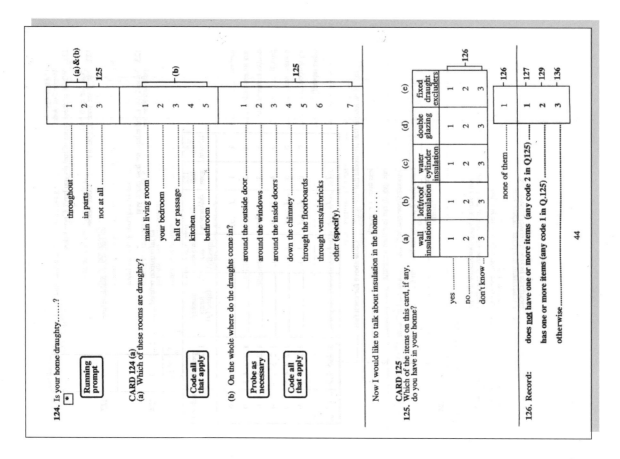

B.2   Interview survey, pages 43 and 44

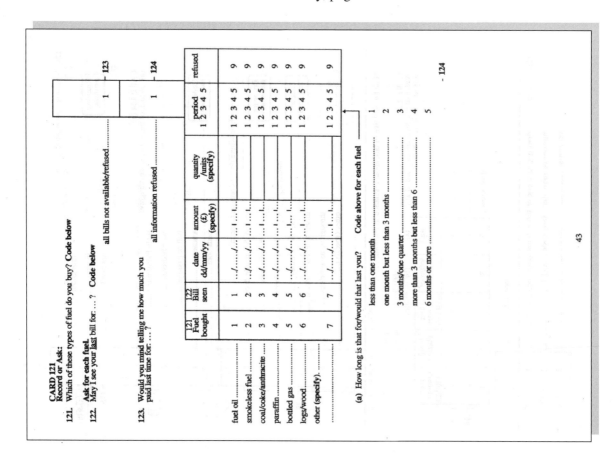

Page 46

Ask for each item partly/entirely put in by self

129. (a) When did you last add to or put in ....?
Code one only

	wall insulation	loft/roof insulation	water cylinder insulation	double glazing	fixed draught excluders	
up to 2 yrs ago	1	1	1	1	1	
2 yrs but less than 5	2	2	2	2	2	
5 yrs but less than 10	3	3	3	3	3	
10 yrs or more ago	4	4	4	4	4	
don't know	5	5	5	5	5	→ (b)

CARD 129 (b)

129. (b) Which of these was the <u>main</u> reason why <u>you</u> put in ....? [*]
Code one only

	wall insulation	loft/roof insulation	water cylinder insulation	double glazing	fixed draught excluders	
to keep home warmer	01	01	01	01	01	
to keep noise down	02	02	02	02	02	
to reduce fuel bills	03	03	03	03	03	
to keep water hot	04	04	04	04	04	
grant was made available	05	05	05	05	05	
to reduce condensation	06	06	06	06	06	
included when other repairs done	07	07	07	07	07	
persuaded by salesman	08	08	08	08	08	
neighbour /friend/relations recommended	09	09	09	09	09	
to increase value of house	10	10	10	10	10	
security	11	11	11	11	11	
ease of maintenance	12	12	12	12	12	
no one main reason	13	13	13	13	13	
don't know	14	14	14	14	14	→ 130

130. Record: *Code all that apply*

If wall insulation	1	Ask 131
If hot water cylinder insulation	2	Ask 132
If double glazing	3	Ask 133 &134
If draught excluders	4	Ask 135
Otherwise	5	136

46

B.2   Interview survey, pages 45 and 46

Page 45

For each item does not have
127. Do you intend to put .... in your home?

	Wall insulation	loft/roof insulation	water cylinder insulation	double glazing	fixed draught excluders	
dna - has item	8	8	8	8	8	→ 129
yes	1	1	1	1	1	→ 128
no	2	2	2	2	2	→ 129
don't know	3	3	3	3	3	

Ask Q128 for each item <u>not</u> intending to install. Ask Q.129 for each item already in home, Q.130 otherwise.

128. Why don't you intend installing ....?
[*] *Code all that apply*

	Wall insulation	loft/roof insulation	water cylinder insulation	double glazing	fixed draught excluders	
intend to move soon	1	1	1	1	1	
too expensive/can't afford	2	2	2	2	2	
no space/no room/no access difficult to get to	3	3	3	3	3	129 for items in the home
never thought about it/not got round to it/just moved in	4	4	4	4	4	
no need for it/warm enough	5	5	5	5	5	130 if none in home
don't believe in it/it makes problems	6	6	6	6	6	
can't get a grant for it	7	7	7	7	7	
not my responsibility	8	8	8	8	8	
other (specify)	9	9	9	9	9	

CARD 129
For each item of insulation in the home
129. When you moved in, was/were the:
Running prompt — Code one only

	Wall insulation	loft/roof insulation	water cylinder insulation	double glazing	fixed draught excluders	
already here	1	1	1	1	1	→ 130
partly put in, which you added to	2	2	2	2	2	(a) & (b)
put in/replaced entirely by you	3	3	3	3	3	
put in by landlord/council etc..	4	4	4	4	4	
other (specify)	5	5	5	5	5	→ 130

45

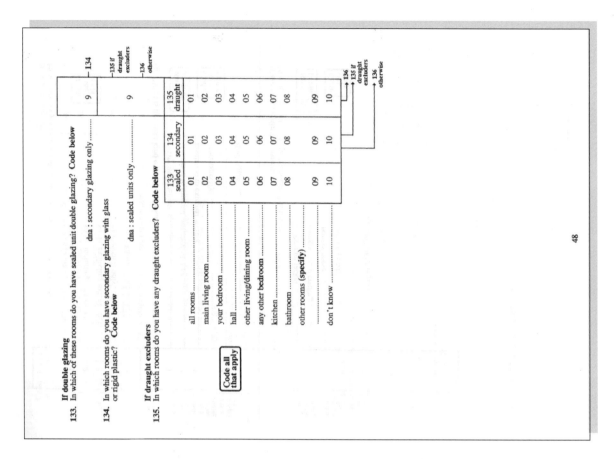

If double glazing
133. In which of these rooms do you have sealed unit double glazing? Code below
dna : secondary glazing only ...... → 134
dna : sealed units only ...... → 136

134. In which rooms do you have secondary glazing with glass or rigid plastic? Code below

135 if draught excluders
136 otherwise

If draught excluders
135. In which rooms do you have any draught excluders? Code below

	133 sealed	134 secondary	135 draught
all rooms	01	01	01
main living room	02	02	02
your bedroom	03	03	03
hall	04	04	04
other living/dining room	05	05	05
any other bedroom	06	06	06
kitchen	07	07	07
bathroom	08	08	08
other rooms (specify)	09	09	09
don't know	10	10	10

Code all that apply

→ 136
→ 135 if draught excluders
→ 136 otherwise

B.2　Interview survey, pages 47 and 48

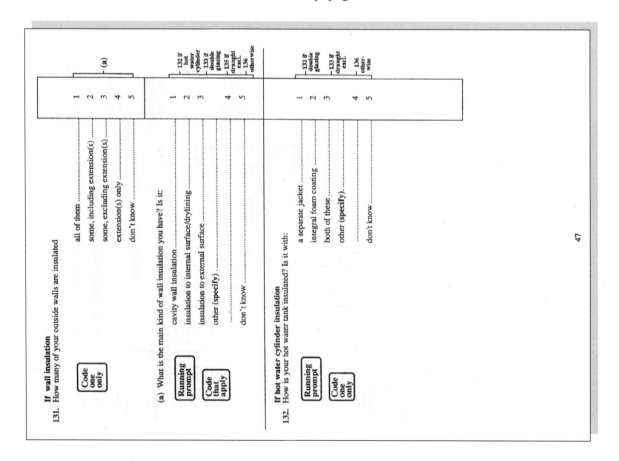

If wall insulation
131. How many of your outside walls are insulated

Code one only
all of them 1
some, including extension(s) ...... 2 (a)
some, excluding extension(s) 3
extension(s) only 4
don't know 5

(a) What is the main kind of wall insulation you have? Is it:

Running prompt
cavity wall insulation ...... 1　132 if hot water cylinder
insulation to internal surface/drylining ...... 2　133 if double glazing
insulation to external surface 3
other (specify) ...... 4　135 if draught excl.
don't know ...... 5　136 otherwise

Code that apply

If hot water cylinder insulation
132. How is your hot water tank insulated? Is it with:

Running prompt
a separate jacket ...... 1　132 if double glazing
integral foam coating ...... 2　133 if draught excl.
both of these 3
other (specify) ...... 4　136 otherwise
don't know 5

Code one only

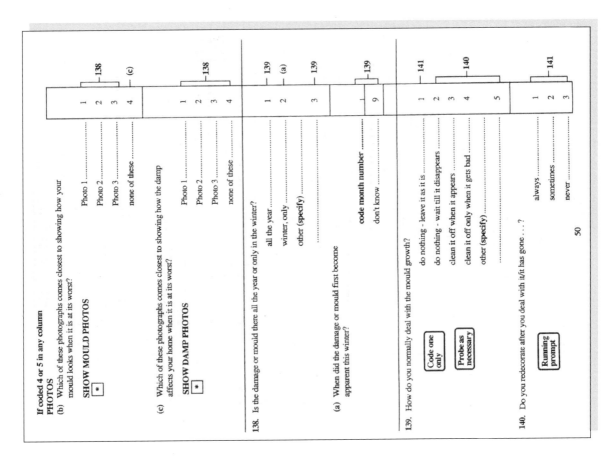

B.2   Interview survey, pages 49 and 50

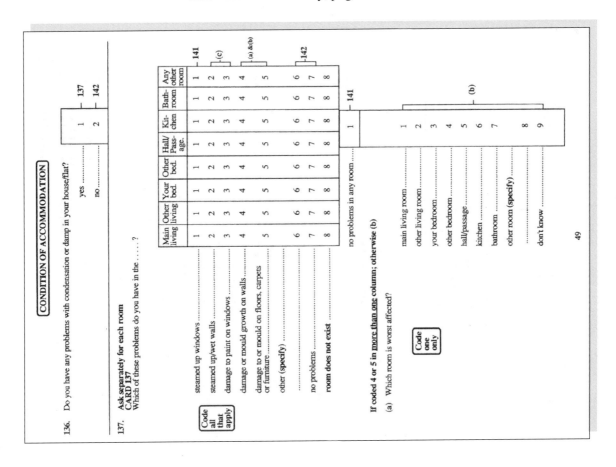

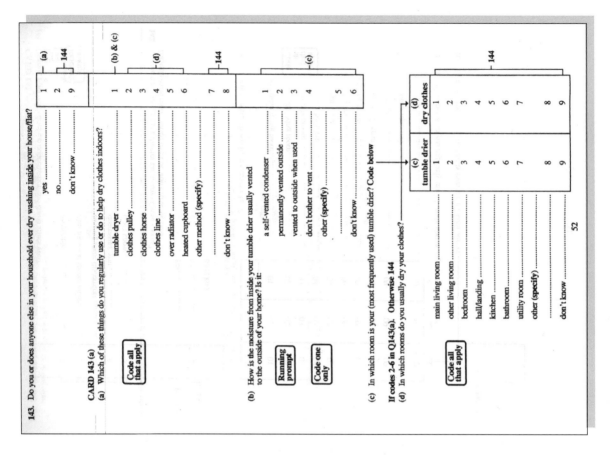

143. Do you or does anyone else in your household ever dry washing inside your house/flat?

yes ... 1 — (a)
no ... 2 | 144
don't know ... 9 |

CARD 143 (a)
(a) Which of these things do you regularly use or do to help dry clothes indoors?

Code all that apply

tumble dryer ... 1 — (b) & (c)
clothes pulley ... 2
clothes horse ... 3
clothes line ... 4 — (d)
over radiator ... 5
heated cupboard ... 6
other method (specify) ... 7 | 144
... 8 |

(b) How is the moisture from inside your tumble drier usually vented to the outside of your home? Is it:

Running prompt

a self-vented condenser ... 1
permanently vented outside ... 2
vented to outside when used ... 3 — (c)
don't bother to vent ... 4

Code one only

other (specify) ... 5
don't know ... 6

(c) In which room is your (most frequently used) tumble drier? Code below

If codes 2-6 in Q143(a). Otherwise 144
(d) In which rooms do you usually dry your clothes?

Code all that apply

	(c) tumble drier	(d) dry clothes
main living room	1	1
other living room	2	2
bedroom	3	3
hall/landing	4	4
kitchen	5	5
bathroom	6	6
utility room	7	7
other (specify)	8	8
don't know	9	9

(c) and (d) → 144

52

B.2 Interview survey, pages 51 and 52

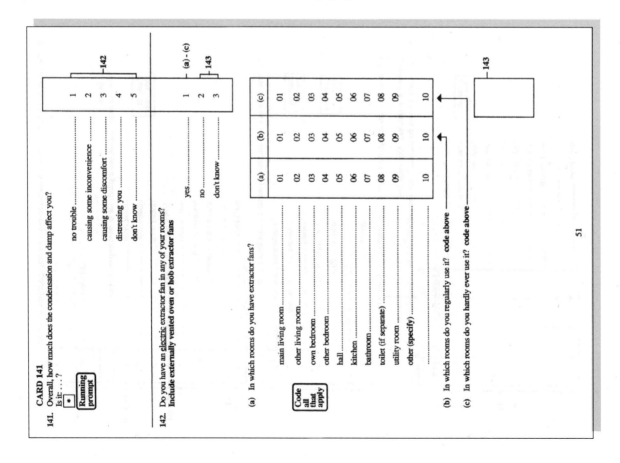

CARD 141
141. Overall, how much does the condensation and damp affect you?
Is it: ...?

Running prompt

no trouble ... 1
causing some inconvenience ... 2
causing some discomfort ... 3 | 142
distressing you ... 4
don't know ... 5

142. Do you have an electric extractor fan in any of your rooms?
Include externally vented oven or hob extractor fans

yes ... 1 — (a) - (c)
no ... 2 | 143
don't know ... 3

(a) In which rooms do you have extractor fans?

Code all that apply

	(a)	(b)	(c)
main living room	01	01	01
other living room	02	02	02
own bedroom	03	03	03
other bedroom	04	04	04
hall	05	05	05
kitchen	06	06	06
bathroom	07	07	07
toilet (if separate)	08	08	08
utility room	09	09	09
other (specify)	10	10	10

(b) In which rooms do you regularly use it? code above
(c) In which rooms do you hardly ever use it? code above

143

51

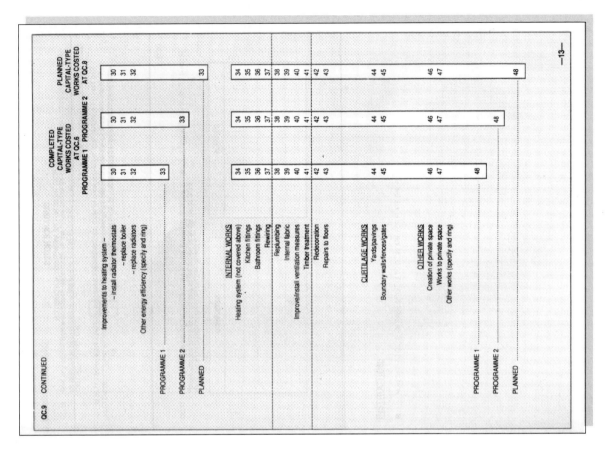

B.3   Postal survey, Public Sector stock, pages 12 and 13

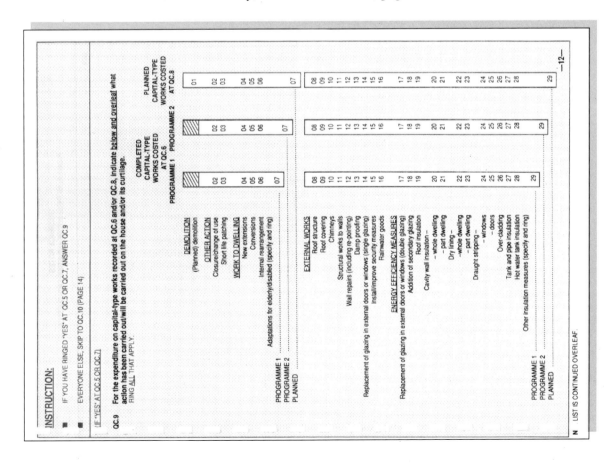

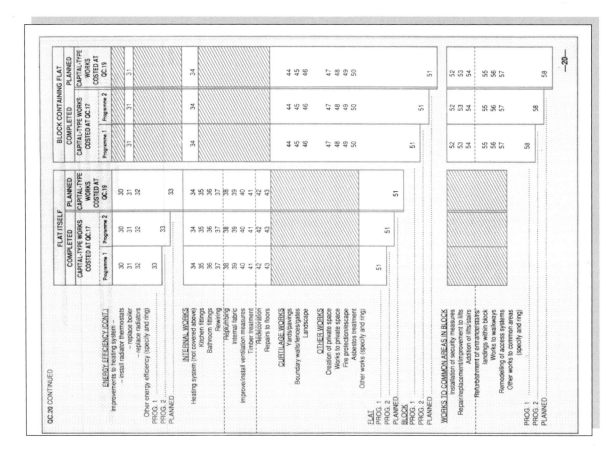

B.3   Postal survey, Public Sector stock, pages 19 and 20

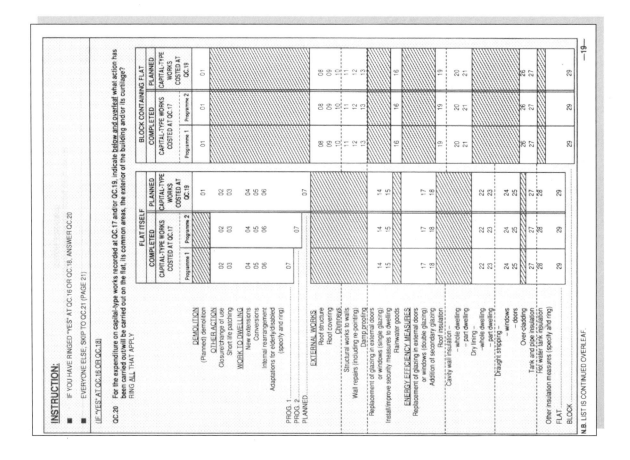

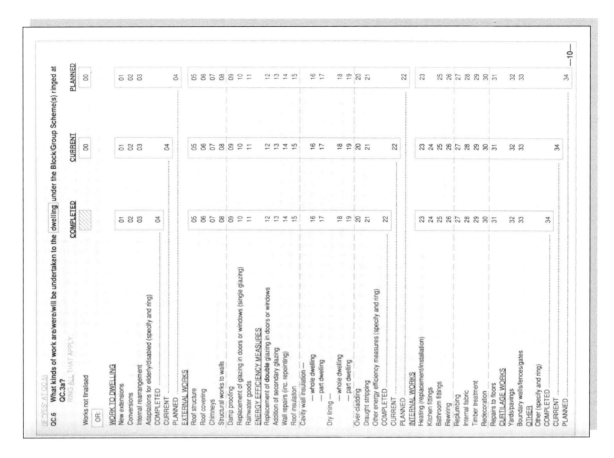

B.3   Postal survey, Private Sector stock, pages 5 and 10

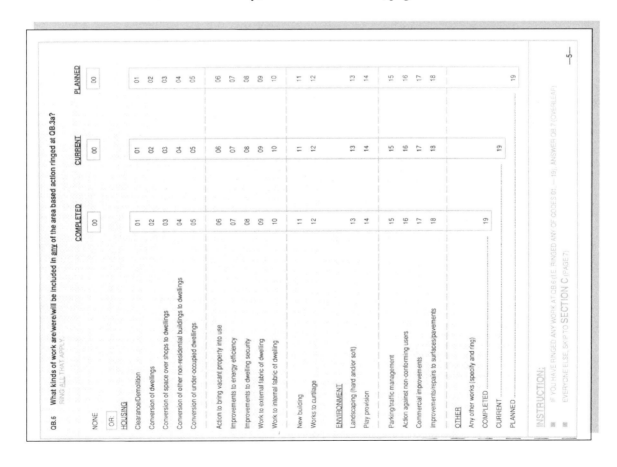

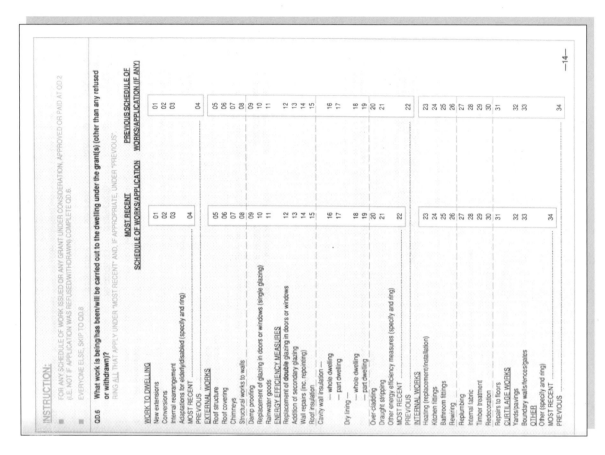

B.3   Postal survey, Private Sector stock, pages 12 and 14

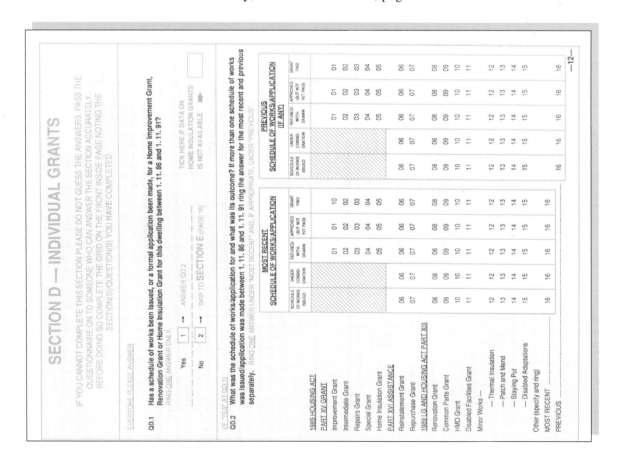

(IF 'YES' AT QE.5)

QE.6 What work is being/has been/will be undertaken to the dwelling in default or without grant assistance as a result of this compulsory purchase or enforcement action?

RING ALL THAT APPLY.

	COMPLETED	CURRENT	PLANNED
WORK TO DWELLING			
New extensions	01	01	01
Conversions	02	02	02
Internal rearrangement	03	03	03
Adaptations for elderly/disabled (specify and ring)			
COMPLETED	04		
CURRENT		04	
PLANNED			04
EXTERNAL WORKS			
Roof structure	05	05	05
Roof covering	06	06	06
Chimneys	07	07	07
Structural works to walls	08	08	08
Damp proofing	09	09	09
Replacement of glazing in doors or windows (single glazing)	10	10	10
Rainwater goods	11	11	11
ENERGY EFFICIENCY MEASURES			
Replacement of **double** glazing in doors or windows	12	12	12
Addition of secondary glazing	13	13	13
Wall repairs (inc. repointing)	14	14	14
Roof insulation	15	15	15
Cavity wall insulation —			
— whole dwelling	16	16	16
— part dwelling	17	17	17
Dry lining —			
— whole dwelling	18	18	18
— part dwelling	19	19	19
Over-cladding	20	20	20
Draught stripping	21	21	21
Other energy efficiency measures (specify and ring)			
COMPLETED	22		
CURRENT		22	
PLANNED			22
INTERNAL WORKS			
Heating (replacement/installation)	23	23	23
Kitchen fittings	24	24	24
Bathroom fittings	25	25	25
Rewiring	26	26	26
Replumbing	27	27	27
Internal fabric	28	28	28
Timber treatment	29	29	29
Redecoration	30	30	30
Repairs to floors	31	31	31
CURTILAGE WORKS			
Yards/pavings	32	32	32
Boundary walls/fences/gates	33	33	33
OTHER			
Other (specify and ring)			
COMPLETED	34		
CURRENT		34	
PLANNED			34

INSTRUCTION:

■ NOW RETURN TO THE FIRST FACING PAGE OF THE QUESTIONNAIRE TO COMPLETE THE GRID

—18—

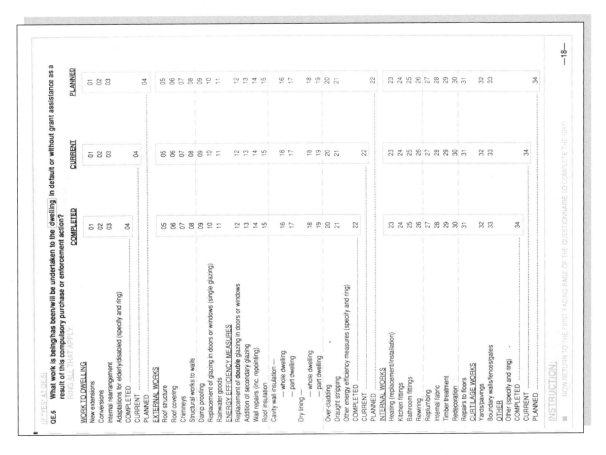

B.3 Postal survey, Private Sector stock, page 18

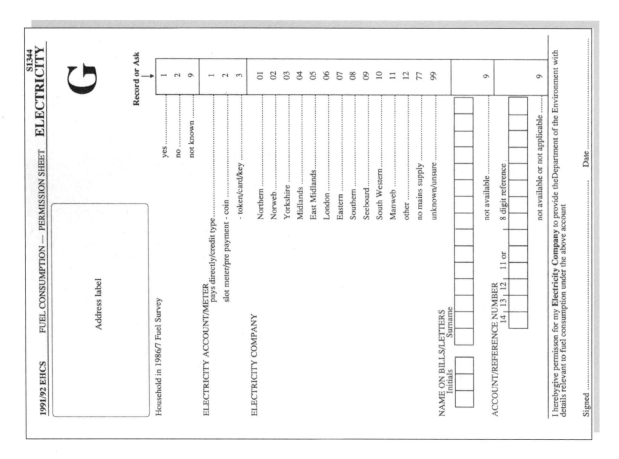

B.4   Gas and electricity permission sheets

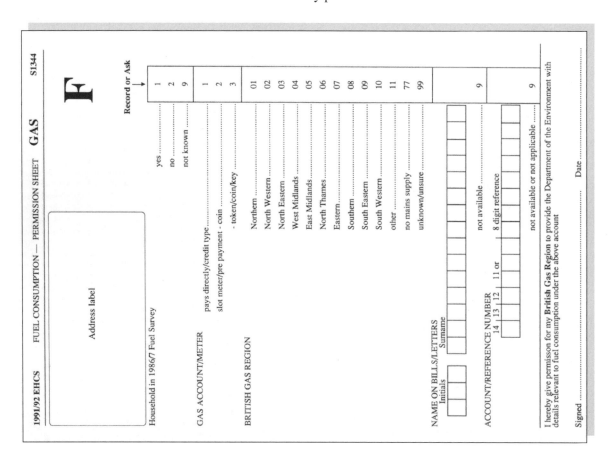

Electricity Consumption Form

ELECTRICITY CONSUMPTION   Meter type   Company   ENGLISH HOUSE CONDITION SURVEY 91/92

ACCOUNT NUMBER >

CUSTOMER'S NAME >

ADDRESS >

POST CODE >

Please include ACCOUNT NUMBER if not on label

14 13 12 11   8 DIGIT REFERENCE

IF NO DATA AVAILABLE, RING 9 AND SPECIFY REASON   9

QUARTERLY CONSUMPTIONS	A DATE OF ACCOUNT READING OR ESTIMATE	B LENGTH OF 'QUARTER	C TYPE OF READING	D DAY/NORMAL TARIFF		E NIGHT/OFF-PEAK TARIFF		F N/A
	DAY MONTH YEAR	IN DAYS	fuel co. estimate customer	1.TARIFF CODE	2.NUMBER OF UNITS 10k k 100 10 1	1.TARIFF CODE	2.NUMBER OF UNITS 10k k 100 10 1	
MOST RECENT QUARTER 1st			f e c					9
PREVIOUS 4 QUARTERS 2nd			f e c					9
3rd	OR		f e c					9
4th			f e c					9
5th			f e c					9
6TH QUARTER DATE AND TYPE 6th		--------	f e c	CONSUMPTION FOR 6TH QUARTER NOT REQUIRED				

NOTES:-
A Please give date of most recent reading in 1st row A&B Give preceding dates OR periods covered, if known.
B Include 91 day quarters Enter period eg 70 days as [|7|0]
C Ring f,e or c. Include initial & any other types in f.
D1 & E1 Enter current tariff code in 1st row, and any different codes in previous rows. If no off peak enter code in E1 as [0|0|0|0].
D2 & E2 Enter consumptions in boxes e.g. 903 units as [| |9|0|3]. Enter recorded nil consumptions as [0|0|0|0|0]

B.4 Gas and electricity quarterly consumption sheets

GAS CONSUMPTION   Meter type   Region   ENGLISH HOUSE CONDITION SURVEY 91/92

ACCOUNT NUMBER >

CUSTOMER'S NAME >

ADDRESS >

POST CODE >

Please include ACCOUNT NUMBER if not on label

15 14 13 12 11   8 DIGIT REFERENCE

IF NO DATA AVAILABLE, RING 9 AND SPECIFY REASON   9

QUARTERLY CONSUMPTIONS	A DATE OF ACCOUNT READING OR ESTIMATE	B LENGTH OF 'QUARTER'	C TYPE OF READING	D TYPE OF GAS UNITS	E TARIFF CODE	F NUMBER OF UNITS CONSUMED	G QURTR NO AVAILABL
	DAY MONTH YEAR	IN DAYS	fuel co. estimate customer	Cu Ft Therms kWh (100) (1s) (1s)		10k k 100 10 1	
MOST RECENT QUARTER 1st			f e c	1 2 3			9
PREVIOUS 4 QUARTERS 2nd			f e c	1 2 3			9
3rd	OR		f e c	1 2 3			9
4th			f e c	1 2 3			9
5th			f e c	1 2 3			9
6TH QUARTER DATE AND TYPE 6th		----	f e c	CONSUMPTION FOR 6TH QUARTER NOT REQUIRED			

NOTES:-
A Please give date of most recent reading in 1st row A&B Give preceding dates OR periods covered, if known.
B Include 91 day quarters Enter period eg 70 days as [|7|0]
C Ring f,e or c. Include initial & any other types in f.
D Give units: Ring :- 1 if 100 Cu ft 2 if Therms 3 if kWh
E Enter code of tariff in force in first row, and any different codes below.
F Enter consumption in boxes eg. 203 as [| |2|0|3]. and specify to nearest unit. Enter recorded nil consumptions as [0|0|0|0|0]

GAS TARIFFS: PART 2 - STANDING CHARGES   ENGLISH HOUSE CONDITION SURVEY 91/92

GAS REGION .... Office code ☐☐

Please provide details of all standing charges available in last 2 years

A TARIFF CODE	B STANDING CHARGE £ per quarter	C TYPE OF ACCOUNT/METER/S Normal Pre-payment Other Credit Coin Token Card Key	D DATES CHARGE CHANGED Date Introduced Date replaced Day Month Year Day Month Year	F CHANGE APPLIED Immediately? On billing?
1 ☐☐☐☐	☐☐☐ 10 1s .1 .01	1 2 3 4 5 6 + specify	☐☐☐☐☐☐ ☐☐☐☐☐☐	1 2
2 ☐☐☐	☐☐☐	1 2 3 4 5 6 + specify	☐☐☐☐☐☐ ☐☐☐☐☐☐	1 2
3 ☐☐☐	☐☐☐	1 2 3 4 5 6 + specify	☐☐☐☐☐☐ ☐☐☐☐☐☐	1 2
4 ☐☐☐	☐☐☐	1 2 3 4 5 6 + specify	☐☐☐☐☐☐ ☐☐☐☐☐☐	1 2
5 ☐☐☐	☐☐☐	1 2 3 4 5 6 + specify	☐☐☐☐☐☐ ☐☐☐☐☐☐	1 2

B.4   Gas tariffs: fuel prices and standing charge forms

GAS TARIFFS: PART 1 - FUEL PRICES   ENGLISH HOUSE CONDITION SURVEY 91/92

GAS REGION .... Office code ☐☐

Please provide details of all Tariffs/Fuel Prices available for domestic use in last 2 years.

A TARIFF CODE	B UNITS Cu Ft (100) Therms kWh	C COST pence per unit 10 1s .1 .01	D TYPE OF TARIFF Normal domestic Other type	E DATES TARIFF CHANGED Date Introduced Date replaced Day Month Year Day Month Year	F CHANGE APPLIED Immediately? On billing?
1 ☐☐☐	1 2 3	☐☐☐	1 2 + specify	☐☐☐☐☐☐ ☐☐☐☐☐☐	1 2
2 ☐☐☐	1 2 3	☐☐☐	1 2 + specify	☐☐☐☐☐☐ ☐☐☐☐☐☐	1 2
3 ☐☐☐	1 2 3	☐☐☐	1 2 + specify	☐☐☐☐☐☐ ☐☐☐☐☐☐	1 2
4 ☐☐☐	1 2 3	☐☐☐	1 2 + specify	☐☐☐☐☐☐ ☐☐☐☐☐☐	1 2
5 ☐☐☐	1 2 3	☐☐☐	1 2 + specify	☐☐☐☐☐☐ ☐☐☐☐☐☐	1 2

ELECTRICITY TARIFFS: PART 2 - STANDING CHARGES   ENGLISH HOUSE CONDITION SURVEY 91/92

ELECTRICITY COMPANY .... Office code ☐☐

Please provide details of all standing charges available in last 2 years for Tariff Codes in Part 1.

A TARIFF CODE	B STANDING CHARGE £ per quarter	C TYPE OF ACCOUNT/METER/S Normal Pre-payment Other Credit Coin Token Card Key	D DATES CHARGE REVISED Date Date Introduced replaced Day Month Year Day Month Year	E CHANGE APPLIED Immediately? On billing?
1 ☐☐☐	☐☐☐	1 2 3 4 5 6 + *specify*	☐☐☐☐☐☐ ☐☐☐☐☐☐	1 2
2 ☐☐☐	☐☐☐	1 2 3 4 5 6 + *specify*	☐☐☐☐☐☐ ☐☐☐☐☐☐	1 2
3 ☐☐☐	☐☐☐	1 2 3 4 5 6 + *specify*	☐☐☐☐☐☐ ☐☐☐☐☐☐	1 2
4 ☐☐☐	☐☐☐	1 2 3 4 5 6 + *specify*	☐☐☐☐☐☐ ☐☐☐☐☐☐	1 2
5 ☐☐☐	☐☐☐	1 2 3 4 5 6 + *specify*	☐☐☐☐☐☐ ☐☐☐☐☐☐	1 2

Standing charge box header: 10 1s .1 .01

B.4   Electricity tariffs: fuel prices and standing charge forms

ELECTRICITY TARIFFS: PART 1 - FUEL PRICES   ENGLISH HOUSE CONDITION SURVEY 91/92

ELECTRICITY COMPANY .... Office code ☐☐

Please provide details of all Tariffs/Fuel Prices available for domestic use in last 2 years.

A TARIFF CODE	B COST pence per kWh	C TYPE OF TARIFF Normal domestic On-peak rate Off-peak rate Other	D TIME/S TARIFF AVAILABLE ON OFF hour min hour min	TARIFF USE/S Rm. heating H. water Other	E DATES TARIFF CHANGED Date Date Introduced replaced Day Month Year Day Month Year	F CHANGE APPLIED Immediately? On billing?
1 ☐☐☐	☐☐☐	1 2 3 4 + *specify*	1st ☐☐☐ ☐☐☐ 2nd ☐☐☐ ☐☐☐	1 2 3 1 2 3	☐☐☐☐☐☐ ☐☐☐☐☐☐	1 2
2 ☐☐☐	☐☐☐	1 2 3 4 + *specify*	1st ☐☐☐ ☐☐☐ 2nd ☐☐☐ ☐☐☐	1 2 3 1 2 3	☐☐☐☐☐☐ ☐☐☐☐☐☐	1 2
3 ☐☐☐	☐☐☐	1 2 3 4 + *specify*	1st ☐☐☐ ☐☐☐ 2nd ☐☐☐ ☐☐☐	1 2 3 1 2 3	☐☐☐☐☐☐ ☐☐☐☐☐☐	1 2
4 ☐☐☐	☐☐☐	1 2 3 4 + *specify*	1st ☐☐☐ ☐☐☐ 2nd ☐☐☐ ☐☐☐	1 2 3 1 2 3	☐☐☐☐☐☐ ☐☐☐☐☐☐	1 2
5 ☐☐☐	☐☐☐	1 2 3 4 + *specify*	1st ☐☐☐ ☐☐☐ 2nd ☐☐☐ ☐☐☐	1 2 3 1 2 3	☐☐☐☐☐☐ ☐☐☐☐☐☐	1 2

Cost box header: 10 1s .1 .01

Annex C
Methodological aspects

Preamble

C.1 *The general methodology and data quality of the main EHCS surveys are discussed in Appendices B, C and E of the first Report[1]. This annex covers methodological aspects related specifically to the energy data and particularly to the temperature and fuel consumption surveys and modelling of energy efficiency.*

Energy components of 1991 survey

C.2 A total of 24,638 addresses were issued in the Physical Survey, of which 12,245 were from the 1986 Survey and 12,393 a new sample drawn in 1991. However, only 13,986 of the total provided full surveys and energy related data, for example, on heating facilities and standards of insulation. Some 14% were refusals, demolished or untraceable and a further 29% were partial surveys mainly of only the exterior of the dwelling.

Figure C.1   Sample structure for energy related questions

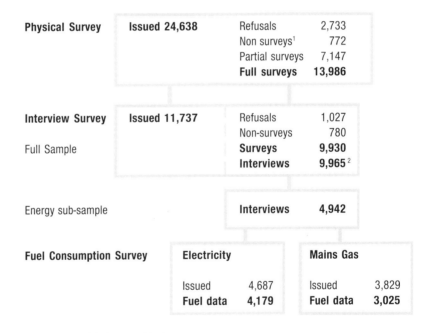

1 dwelling demolished, untraceable etc
2 includes interviews at multi-occupied dwellings where up to 4 households could be interviewed

Interview survey

C.3 The Interview sample was drawn from the addresses in the Physical Survey for which there was an early record of a full survey, a total of 11,737 addresses being issued. Of these, a further 14% were refusals or not surveyed for one reason or another, producing a total of 9,965 interviews, including those in multi-occupied dwellings where up to four separate households were interviewed.

C.4 As for the 1986 EHCS energy component, the 1991 Interview sample was randomly divided into two roughly equal parts. The main questions on

---

1   *Department of the Environment, English House Condition Survey 1991, HMSO, London, 1993*

heating systems and insulation measures required to determine energy efficiency ratings (in addition to the data provided by the Physical Survey) were asked of both parts, as were the questions on condensation and mould growth. However, other energy questions, for example, on heating controls and heating regimes, fuel consumption, temperatures and attitudes to energy measures, were limited to the one part comprising the energy sub-sample. This part yielded 4,942 interviews or 49.6 % of the total in the full Interview Survey.

Temperature survey

C.5   In the Interview Survey, interviewers were issued with digital thermometers and instructed to take three temperature readings at each dwelling in the energy sub-sample. The first reading was taken in the 'living room' used by the occupant, which was not necessarily the main living room or room used for the interview. The second spot temperature was taken in the hall or at the foot of the stairs, and only failing this in some other room, the hall or stairs having been shown by an earlier survey[2] to be a good proxy for the mean of all rooms. The third reading was taken in the open air outside the building. Interior temperatures were taken approximately half-way through and the outside reading at the end of the generally 85 minute interview. For room temperatures, the interviewers were instructed to take readings at 'worktop' height and to avoid unusually cold positions near doors and windows.

C.6   In total, room temperature readings were recorded at some 4,853 or 98% of addresses. However, the validation of this sample for incomplete or erroneous data and the subsequent grossing procedure resulted in some reduction in the sample for the analysis. The final number of sample addresses yielding valid home temperature data was 4,788. Of these, some 96% of first temperatures were taken in the living room and 92% of second readings in the hall, giving both living room and hall temperatures in almost 90% of the sample.

Fuel consumption survey

Electricity and gas data

C.7   During the Interview Survey, all households in the energy sub-sample were requested to sign separate 'permission sheets' authorising the Department to obtain details of their fuel consumption directly from the local electricity company and, where applicable, local British Gas region. These sheets also recorded the customer name and account number, enabling the Department to compile a sample list of electricity and gas consumers for each company and region. In total, permission to obtain consumption data from the local electricity companies was obtained for 4,687 households or 95% of the energy sub-sample, and to approach the British Gas Regions from 3,829 or 93% of those using gas.

C.8   Most electricity companies and gas regions were then sent the authorisation sheets together with pre-addressed proformae for recording the fuel consumption and relevant tariffs at each sample dwelling in their area. However, a few companies had previously opted to provide this information by means of a computer printout and disc. All companies and regions were asked to provide the consumptions of all fuel supplies to each particular customer over the previous five metered periods - usually quarters - together with details of the relevant fuel tariffs, including standing charges, in force during that period.

2   *Hunt and Gidman M.I, 1982, A National Field Survey of House Temperatures, Building and Environment, Vol 17, No 2, pp. 107-184.*

C.9   In total, the 11 electricity companies provided consumption data for 4,179 households (89% of the cases issued) and the 10 gas regions for 3,025 households (79%). The remaining cases were households who had moved since the Interview Survey or whom the fuel suppliers could not trace from the information supplied.

C.10 For the analysis of fuel consumption, all consumption figures were converted to kilowatt hours (kWh), using the calorific value of gas. For gas and both on and off-peak electricity, total consumption over exactly 1 year was calculated from the last four 'quarterly' figures or, if these covered significantly less than 12 months, from five periods. The small number of cases in which less than 270 days of data were available were omitted, as it was felt that a full missing season could not be accurately estimated from the remaining 'quarterly' figures. For the analysis of fuel expenditure, the total costs to the household were calculated from the annual consumption and specific tariffs and standing charges.

Imputing
missing fuel
data

C.11 The achieved sample for electricity and gas consumption amounted to some 85% and 75% respectively of the relevant addresses in the full energy sub-sample. To eliminate the distortions that these partial samples might introduce, after grossing, into the distributions of fuel consumption within the national stock, consumption figures were estimated for the missing data by a process of imputing.

C.12 It was assumed that all dwellings used on-peak electricity, while those using gas or off-peak electricity were identified from the information on appliance use collected in the Interview Survey. Regression models were constructed between the known consumption of gas, on-peak and off-peak electricity and the housing and occupancy characteristics of the particular sample addresses concerned. These models were then used to predict the fuel consumption in the remainder of the sample. Inevitably, this process produces a distribution with fewer extreme values than the real data and to allow for this the percentiles of the imputed data were adjusted to make them equal to the recorded data.

Unmetered
fuels

C.13 During the Interview Survey, the households in the energy sub-sample were also asked if they used any unmetered fuels, such as coal, wood, oil, calor gas or paraffin, and if so, the cost of their most recent bill and the period of use it covered. The data covering various periods were converted into weekly expenditure. Information on typical costs and calorific values of these fuels was then used to calculate weekly consumptions in kWh. As the interview was carried out during winter months, when consumption would be higher, annual consumptions and costs are calculated by multiplying the weekly figure by 36.

C.14 Although these fuel figures are inevitably less accurate than those for the main metered fuels, overall they give reasonably good agreement with consumption and expenditure data from other sources such as the Family Expenditure Survey.

Grossing and
estimates

C.15 The grossing procedure for the main Physical, Interview and Postal survey samples is explained in the first EHCS report[3]. The energy sub-sample was separately grossed to the same national stock totals for tenure, and

3   *Department of the Environment, 1993, op.cit.*

Samples and grossing

region as used in grossing the full Interview Survey sample. As the response rate for the fuel consumption survey was high it was not found necessary to separately gross this survey sample, as done in 1986. A number of analyses, which required comprehensive and reliable data from a number of sources, produced particular samples short of the full interview or energy-sub-samples. After grossing, these partial samples were checked against the main key variables to ensure that they remained broadly representative of the national stock.

C.16 Table C.1 compares the sample sizes and grossed estimates for the controlling variables of tenure and region for the main samples used in this report - the physical (full-survey), interview and energy sub-samples. While matched exactly on tenure and region, the grossing of the energy sub-sample produces marginally different household estimates for other key variables, such as dwelling age and type, from those produced by the grossing of the full interview sample. (There are similar small discrepancies between the dwelling estimates produced by the physical samples including and excluding partial surveys). Where quoted in the report, the control totals are normally those generated by the largest sample available, which for dwellings are generally those provided by the physical survey sample including partial surveys, and for household totals by the full interview sample.

Table C.1   **Comparison of sample sizes and grossed estimates generated by the physical (full-survey) sample, full interview and energy sub-samples**

| Control variables | Physical (full-survey) sample number | Grossed occupied dwellings[1] (thous) | Interview survey | | Grossed household totals (thous) |
			Full sample number	Energy sub-sample number	
Tenure[2]					
Owner occupied	7,580	12,872	5,535	2,762	12,872
Private rented	1,256	1,626	· 792	361	1,700
Local authority	4.101	3,851	2,930	1,463	3,877
Housing association	1,049	591	708	356	662
Region					
Northern	1,483	1,042	1,068	518	1,046
Yorks & Humberside	1,619	1,926	1,150	547	1,937
North West	1,754	2,706	1,337	669	2,718
East Midlands	1,301	1,535	910	462	1,548
West Midlands	1,569	2,032	1,141	590	2,059
South West	1,269	1,906	924	455	1,912
Eastern	1,346	2,193	984	484	2,211
Greater London	2,455	2,825	1,624	809	2,863
South East	1,190	2,775	827	408	2,819
Totals	**13,986**	**18,940**	**9,965**	**4,492**	**19,111**

1 Excluding new housing (see para. C.17 below)

2 A few addresses are recorded with different tenures in the physical and interview surveys

Estimates

Exclusion of new dwellings

C.17 As in the 1986 energy report, the estimates exclude new dwellings built between the date the sample was drawn and the EHCS fieldwork in 1991/92. The exclusion of these dwellings has little or no effect on the estimates provided. For example, assuming these new dwellings were built to then current Building Regulations and have an average energy efficiency (SAP) rating of around 60, their addition raises the average rating for the total stock from 34.8 to 35.0 and the rating of dwellings built since 1980 from 49 to 50. Such differences are not significant being within the methodological errors of the survey.

Occupied   C.18 Due to problems of access, details of heating systems, insulation and other
dwellings   physical energy data is generally not available for vacant dwellings and, of course, neither is any data available here on energy consumption. Consequently, the estimates in this report are limited to those for either occupied dwellings or households. In the description of 'physical standards' (i.e. the whole of Part I apart from the last chapter on 'households and standards') the estimates refer to occupied dwellings and come mainly from the Physical Survey. Where any estimate regarding heating facilities, insulation standards or the energy efficiency of dwellings comes from the household based Interview Survey (for example, information on cavity wall insulation) it has been converted to a dwelling based estimate by limiting the interview sample for analysis to only one household in each dwelling.

Treatment of   C.19 Unless imputed, as in the case of the fuel consumption data, missing data
missing data   is treated in two ways. Where missing data for any variable amounts to a small proportion of the total, being not significantly greater than the sampling and other methodological errors associated with that variable, it has been re-allocated within any cross-tabulation in the most appropriate manner. This is done, to conform to any existing control totals, generally by reference to those known variables found to be most strongly correlated with the particular variable for which data is missing.

C.20 For variables where the missing data accounts for a substantial proportion of the whole, the missing data is recorded separately in the tables. In such cases, it was felt that the numbers involved were too great to enable the missing data to be attributed, in any manner, with sufficient confidence.

Energy   C.21 The Standard Assessment Procedure (SAP) is based on the calculated
modelling   energy cost for space and water heating and is the Government's recommended method of producing an energy rating for a dwelling[4]. The
EHCS energy   calculation assumes a standard occupancy pattern, derived from the
rating model   measured floor area of the dwelling, and a standard heating pattern. The rating is normalised for floor area so that the size of the dwelling does not strongly affect the result. The rating is normally expressed on a scale of 1 to 100; the higher the number the better the standard.

Factors   C.22 The rating obtained from following the procedure depends upon a range
considered   of factors that contribute to energy efficiency:

❑   thermal insulation of the building fabric;

❑   efficiency and control of the heating system;

❑   ventilation characteristics of the dwelling;

❑   solar gain characteristics of the dwelling;

❑   the price of fuels used for space and water heating.

---

4   *For full details of the procedure see Department of the Environment Energy Efficiency Office, 'The Government's Standard Assessment Procedure for energy rating of dwellings', BRECSU, Building Research Establishment, Garston, 1994*

C.23 The rating is not affected by factors that depend on the individual characteristics of the household occupying the dwelling when the rating is calculated, such as:

- ❑ household size and composition;

- ❑ the possession and efficiency of non-heating domestic appliances;

- ❑ individual heating patterns and temperatures.

It is also not affected by the geographical location of the dwelling; a particular dwelling will have the same rating whether it is built in Penzance or Berwick upon Tweed.

Data sources

C.24 A computerised version of the standard worksheet for the Standard Assessment Procedure is used to calculate the SAP rating for each dwelling in the 1991 EHCS sample. Most of the data required for the calculation of SAP is available from the Survey, either directly from the questions asked or as a result of further computation. The only items not collected were those shown in advance, by a sensitivity analysis, to have very little impact on the rating. It is estimated that including all of the primary data demanded by the worksheet would not change the calculated rating by more than 1 or 2 units, which is probably a smaller discrepancy than would be expected from errors in the data collected (for example, errors in the measured dimensions of the building).

C.25 Some primary data relating to the heating systems and controls, and to insulation measures, were collected in both the Physical and Interview Surveys. In such cases the source is chosen which offers the most reliable or most detailed data. When data are not available from the preferred source, for whatever reason, the alternative source is used. This means that there are relatively few cases in which an estimate of the SAP rating is not possible.

Components of
SAP rating

C.26 As explained in Chapter 3, the overall SAP rating depends on two separate factors:-

i) the rate of heat loss, which depends on the thermal properties of the structure, the degree of insulation and the level of ventilation, and

ii) the cost of supplying the lost heat, which in turn depends on the efficiency of the heating system and the price of the particular fuel used.

C.27 An individual dwelling can have a low rating because it is defective in both of these characteristics, or because it scores very badly on just one of them. How in practice the two factors combine to determine the overall rating is illustrated in Figure C.2. The plots show, for the total housing stock, the range of values of the heat loss index and heating price index corresponding to each value of SAP.

C.28 The plot for the heat loss index shows a steady gradient over the whole range of SAP, while the heating price index tends to be relatively independent of SAP except at values below about 30, when it rises increasingly sharply with decreasing values of SAP. This indicates that dwellings with high SAP ratings gain their main advantage from their low values of the heat loss index, that is from their superior insulation properties, and not because of any particularly outstanding heating systems.

Figure C.2   Relationship between heat loss and heating price indices and SAP rating

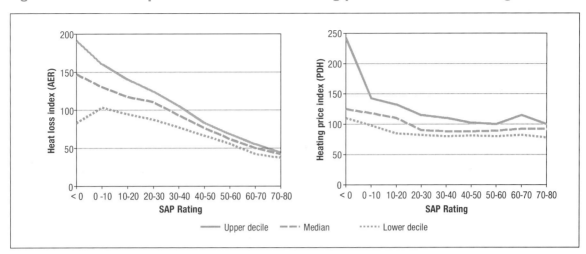

Dwellings with low SAP ratings tend to have both poor insulation properties and poor heating systems, with perhaps the latter having the dominant effect.

Calculation of standardised fuel costs

Heating costs

C.29   To determine, on the one hand, the lack of affordable warmth in the housing stock and on the other, the potential for overall energy savings, it is necessary to estimate for each dwelling in the sample the total fuel costs required to achieve the standard or minimum heating regimes, irrespective of the actual fuel expenditure of the household. Such an estimate can be calculated directly from the energy efficiency (SAP) rating, as this provides a measure of the unit cost of heating the dwelling to a set heating regime. Thus, the annual cost of space and water heating depends on:-

❏   Energy Efficiency (SAP) Rating;

❏   Total Floor Area; and

❏   Heating Regime required

and is calculated for the two heating regimes using the equations below.

Equations C.1   Calculation of annual heating costs for standard and minimum heating regimes

Heating cost of dwelling (£)

$$\text{Cost} = (\text{Energy Cost Factor} \times \text{Total Floor Area} + 40) / 0.97$$

where the Energy Cost Factor (ECF) is given by

$$\text{ECF}_{\text{for Standard Regime}} = 10^{(1.15 - \text{SAP}/100)}$$
$$\text{ECF}_{\text{for Minimum Regime}} = 10^{(1.097 - \text{SAP}/105.3)}$$

Non-heating costs

C.30   To compare the actual fuel expenditure of households with the total fuel cost required for heating a dwelling to the standard regime, we need to add to these standardised heating costs equivalent estimates for the fuel costs attributable to cooking, lighting and domestic appliances. These non-heating costs are calculated using the Building Research Establishment Domestic Energy Model (BREDEM-12) fuel use algorithms[5] for cookers, lights and appliances and associated fuel costs.

5   *B R Anderson et al, Building Research Establishment Laboratory Report, BRE 315, BRE, Garston, August 1996*

C.31   For each dwelling in the sample, the estimate of the fuel costs associated with cooking is calculated from the type of cooker used and the number of occupants, using the first set of equations in box C.2 below. Similarly, the fuel expenditure associated with lights and appliances depends upon the floor area of the dwelling and the number of occupants, and is calculated from the second set of equations shown below. In addition, as these fuel costs do not include the standing charges for normal tariff electricity, a nominal £42 is added to take this into account.

Equations C.2   Calculation of annual standardised costs for cooking, lighting and appliances

Cooking costs (£) for type of cooker

Electric cooker	$\text{Cost} = (1.70 + 0.34\,N) \times 21.08$
Gas cooker	$\text{Cost} = (2.98 + 0.60\,N) \times 4.26$
Gas hob and	$\text{Cost} = (1.49 + 0.30\,N) \times 4.26$
electric oven	$\text{Cost} = (0.85 + 0.17\,N) \times 21.08$

Lighting and appliance costs for size of 'home' (£)

Small	(TFA x N < 750)	$\text{Cost} = (2.16 + 0.0221\,\text{TFA} \times N) \times 21.08$
Moderate	(750 <TFA x N <2475)	$\text{Cost} = (9.49 + 0.0143\,\text{TFA} \times N$ $-2.63 \times 10^{-6}\,(\text{TFA} \times N)^2 \times 21.08$
Large	2475 < TFA x N	$\text{Cost} = (28.77) \times 21.08$
where		N = number of occupants, and TFA = Total floor area

C.32   The resultant overall estimate of fuel costs for lights, cooking and appliances is considered to be that required by an average household with the same number of occupants living in a dwelling of the same floor area as the sample dwelling. However, if the particular household has an above average actual fuel consumption, this notional average is increased by 20%, while if the actual consumption is below average, it is reduced by 20% and if particularly low, for example due to low income, reduced by 40%.

Fuel costs relative to income

Joint income

C.33   In the assessment of affordable warmth, the total fuel expenditure required to meet the standardised costs for cooking, lighting and appliances and also achieve the standard heating regime is determined as a proportion of household income. The household income given by the 1991 EHCS is the net income after tax of just the nominated head of household and any partner. Consequently, the total incomes of some large families and large adult households may be underestimated. However, this possible underestimation was not found to be critical to the assessment of affordable warmth. Apart from the contributions made by other household members to fuel expenditure being unclear, large households are not generally amongst those groups most affected by fuel poverty. The relatively favourable position of large households is similar whether affordable warmth is measured relative to household income or in terms of the adequacy of existing fuel expenditure - irrespective of the proportion of income spent.

Modelling of investment income

C.34   A potentially more serious problem in this respect was the fact that the EHCS did not ask specifically about income from savings or other investments. This can comprise a significant source of income for some elderly households and, consequently, if omitted could have significantly underestimated the disposable income available to such households for expenditure on fuel. For example, retired households who are not mainly dependent on state benefits derive, on average, over a fifth of their total gross income from such sources. To overcome this problem, published results from the 1991 Family Expenditure Survey (FES), indicating how investment income varies with household type, household income, age of head of household and tenure, were used to produce estimates of investment income for the 1991 EHCS.

C.35 Each household was first allocated the mean amount of income from investments for the particular household type. This was then weighted to take account of the household's actual income from other sources. For most types of household, this produced satisfactory results but for certain types of households further adjustments improved the estimates. For example, additional weightings for tenure produced results closer to the FES figures for lower income retired households, while additional weightings for the age of head of household improved the results for couples without children and households with 3 or more adults and at least one dependent child. (Table C.2) To arrive at the net income from investments, tax at the basic rate (25% in 1991) was deducted assuming a 'realistic scenario' that everyone pays basic rate tax on the returns from 50% of their savings and/or investments, only a proportion of their savings being organised as TESSA (tax exempt) up to the maximum limit of £9,000. Finally, this modelled data on investment income was added to the existing EHCS figures on income from earnings, pensions and benefits, which already matched closely those from the 1991 FES.

Table C.2 Comparison between FES published data and EHCS modelled data for mean weekly gross income from investments, by household type

Mean investment income for household type	1991 FES £/week	1991 EHCS £/week
Retired households		
Single retired, mainly dependent on benefit	1.80	1.61
Other single retired	41.87	43.04
Retired couple, mainly dependent on benefit	4.05	3.51
Other retired couple	69.43	62.17
Non retired households		
Single adult	17.70	13.19
Single parent, 1 child	2.56	2.26
Single parent, 2 or more children	2.29	2.45
Couple, no children	36.62	38.52
Couple, 1 child	11.96	14.50
Couple, 2 children	10.71	13.05
Couple, 3 children	8.83	8.78
Couple, 4 or more children	9.98	10.28
Three adults	28.88	31.59
Three adults, 1 or more children	23.65	22.80
Four adults	31.07	33.05
Four adults, 1 or more children	15.05	13.39
All households	**23.57**	**22.80**

Other modelling

C.36 Domestic fuel consumption fluctuates considerably with weather conditions and needs to be 'temperature corrected' if meaningful comparisons are to be drawn from differences in consumption between years. As shown in

Temperature corrections of 1986 and 1991 fuel data

Table C.3, external temperatures during the period covered by the 1986 EHCS fuel consumption survey were below average (as measured against the long term mean temperatures for 1975 to 1995), while those for the period covered by the equivalent 1991 survey were generally above average.

Table C.3   External temperatures 1986 to 1992 *(average of recordings at Heathrow, Manchester, Newcastle and Plymouth)*

Year	Qtr	External temperature °C	Correction from 75-95 mean °C	Year	Qtr	External temperature °C	Correction from 75-95 mean	1975-1995 mean temp. °C
1986	1	3.5	-1.9	1991	1	4.9	-0.5	5.4
	2 *	10.7	-0.5		2 *	10.7	-0.5	11.2
	3 *	13.9	-1.6		3 *	16.3	+0.7	15.5
	4 *	8.9	+0.7		4 *	7.9	-0.3	8.2
1987	1 *	3.7	-1.7	1992	1 *	6.1	+0.7	5.4
	2	11.2	+0.0		2	12.7	+1.5	11.2
	3	15.3	-0.2		3	15.1	-0.4	15.5
	4	8.2	+0.0		4	6.9	-1.3	8.2

C.37 The fuel data collected were generally for the four quarters highlighted in the table, when the average temperature was 0.8°C below the long term mean during the 1986/97 survey and 0.2°C above in 1991/92. The gas and electricity consumptions were corrected using a methodology developed by the Building Research Establishment.[6] The quarterly consumptions for both surveys were corrected to what they would have been if the temperature had remained the same as the long-term mean, by applying the equation:

Equation C.3   Calculation of fuel consumption corrected for external temperature

$$Dqc = \frac{Dq}{(1 + (Tq - Tqm) * Fq/100)}$$

Where

Dqc	is the corrected consumption
Dq	is the metered consumption
Tq	is the actual quarterly temperature
Tqm	is the mean quarterly temperature
Fq	is the quarterly temperature correction factor

C.38 The values of the quarterly temperature correction factor have been derived by BRECSU for each fuel from metered consumption data and are as follows:

Table C.4   Quarterly temperature correction factors

	Quarter 1	Quarter 2	Quarter 3	Quarter 4
Gas	-5.47	-9.05	-5.53	-5.04
Electricity	-2.21	-0.00	-2.82	-1.36

C.39 Corrected fuel consumptions for the total stock are calculated for quarterly gas and electricity consumptions using the above equation and applying the correction factors (Tq-Tqm) and Fq in Tables C.3 and C.4 respectively. The corrected annual consumption was then calculated from the sum of the four quarters. It is possible that consumption may vary with temperature

6   *George Henderson and Christine Pout, Building Research Establishment Client Report 21/93, BRECSU, 1993 (unpublished).*

in different ways in different sectors, but, in the absence of any information on this, it is assumed that the relationship is the same for all tenures. Consequently, the corrected values for the individual tenures are calculated by assuming that the proportion of the total consumption taken by each tenure is the same both before and after correction.

Comparison of 1986 and 1991 home temperatures

C.40 To compare home temperatures in 1991 with those recorded in 1986, a common sample of addresses having living room and hall temperatures in both years has been analysed. Table C.5 shows the mean internal and external temperatures for these particular homes.

Table C.5   Average spot temperature for common sample, 1986 and 1991

Location	Mean temperature °C		Standard deviation °C	
	1986	1991	1986	1991
Living room	18.3	19.3	2.83	2.39
Hall	16.2	17.9	3.69	2.72
External	6.0	11.2	4.29	3.81

C.41 To control for the effects of outside temperatures, three simple linear regressions have been constructed. (Figure C.3) For each address in the sample, the difference between the living room and the external temperature has been plotted against the external temperature to produce three scatter diagrams for:-

  1) all the temperature readings obtained in 1986

  2) all the temperature readings obtained in 1991

  3) all the temperature readings obtained in 1986 and 1991.

C.42 The regressions 1 and 2 were compared with regression model 3 to establish whether fitting the two separate regression models (one for each year) explains more of the variation than fitting the single regression model for all the data. This was done by comparing the residual sum of squares. The same statistical test was repeated with the equivalent data for the hall temperatures.

C.43 The results of these statistical tests show that we are 95% confident that any difference in the relationship between the external temperature and the difference between the external and internal temperature for the two years is by chance.

Classification of mould growth

C.44 The severity of condensation and mould growth varies widely from steamed up windows in a kitchen or slight mould around a bath to extensive and dense growths on the walls and ceilings of the main habitable rooms. Information on condensation and mould collected in the 1991 EHCS has been combined to give a 'mould severity index' and to classify the problem into 'slight', 'moderate' and 'severe'.

Data sources

C.45 The Interview Survey contained a number of questions relevant to the severity of condensation and mould growth, namely on:

  ❑ Whether rooms were affected by:
      a) "steamed up windows";

Figure C.3   Linear regression models for 1986, 1991 and 1986/ 1991 living room spot temperatures

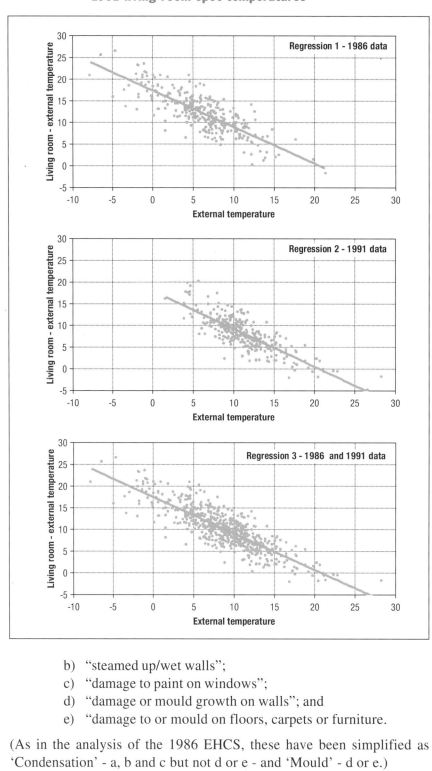

b) "steamed up/wet walls";

c) "damage to paint on windows";

d) "damage or mould growth on walls"; and

e) "damage to or mould on floors, carpets or furniture.

(As in the analysis of the 1986 EHCS, these have been simplified as 'Condensation' - a, b and c but not d or e - and 'Mould' - d or e.)

❏   The number affected of 7 specified rooms and one "other" room.

❏   Which of these room was worst affected.

❏   Which of three photographs of mould (opposite) most resembled the problem. (To provide a more objective assessment of the severity of mould growth, the occupants were asked to select the photograph most like their worst affected area).

❏   How much the condensation and damp affects the occupants.

Photograph C.1   Photographs of mould used in interview survey

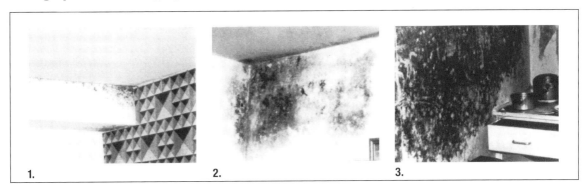

1.   2.   3.

Mould severity   C.46   The first four of these factors were combined in the Mould Severity Index
index   on the basis of the following assumptions:-

❑   Mould is generally more serious than condensation. (Mould growth
is a much more important cause of dissatisfaction than condensation
on windows and is associated with health problems such as asthma
and other respiratory illnesses).

❑   The more rooms affected the worse the problem. (Most homes
affected had mould growth in only one room and very few had mould
in over four rooms).

❑   Mould growth is more serious in some rooms than others; the various
rooms can be divided into three categories:

a)   Living rooms: As these are generally well heated and not a
source of moisture production, problems may indicate specific
defects or a poor environment in the dwelling as a whole. As
they are the main habitable rooms, mould growth is of more
concern here than elsewhere.

b)   Bedrooms: These are often poorly heated but have little
moisture production other than the respiration of occupants.
Here, condensation on windows overnight is often regarded
as a 'fact of life', although mould growth in a child's bedroom
may be of more concern.

c)   Kitchens and bathrooms: Here moisture production is high
but heating is also frequently high in kitchens. Condensation
on windows is accepted as common as is slight mould in
bathrooms, but mould in kitchens may be a more serious health
hazard.

❑   The severity of the problem increases with the density of growth, as
indicated by the number of the photograph selected.

C.47   The mould severity index is calculated for each sample address, to reflect
the extent, location and density of any condensation and mould, with the
following equation. (Equation C.4)

Equation C.4   Calculation of mould growth severity index

> **Mould Severity Index** = Number of rooms with mould growth / 2
> +1 if condensation in more than four rooms
> +1 if mould in living room
> +1 if second mould photograph identified
> +2 if third mould photograph identified

C.48 The occupants attitude to the problem was not included in the index, as this is more subjective and also strongly correlated with both the number of rooms affected and the photograph selected.

C.49 About half of the total stock with mould growth have values of the index ≤ 1, three-quarters ≤ 2 and nine-tenths ≤ 3. The index therefore, gives a useful division of the degree of mould growth into the broad categories of slight, moderate and severe, as shown in Table C.6.

Table C.6   Classification of mould growth using mould severity index

Value of Index	% of stock with mould	Severity of mould growth
0.5 to 1.0	50	Slight Mould
1.5 to 2.5	40	Moderate Mould
3 and over	10	Severe Mould

Annex

Glossary

| Preamble | D.1 | *This Annex gives the survey definitions used in the report (in order of appearance in the main chapters) firstly for the energy variables and then for some main stock and household variables. It ends with some statistical terms used. Descriptions are based either on the surveyors or interviewers instructions for questions in the original surveys or are those determined subsequently for the analysis of the data. With reference to Annex B, it also gives the pages of the physical schedule (e.g. P5) and sections of the household interview (e.g. H75) or other survey parts, containing questions on which the variables are based. For some derived variables, reference is made to paragraphs in the text of the main chapters and/or of Annex C.* |

Energy variables

D.2 Central heating is categorised into the following 12 types, types are combined in a number of the tables:-

Central heating (P5, H75)

Mains gas	· Dedicated boiler and radiators	A mains gas-fired, single purpose free-standing or wall hung boiler, heating water piped to one or more radiators.
	· Back boiler and radiators	A water borne distribution system as above, but run from a back boiler behind a gas radiant or an Aga type range.
	· Ducted air	Warm air system, powered by a mains gas-fired heater.
	· Programmable convector	A modern gas-fired room convector which can be controlled/programmed, either centrally or at the heater.
Solid fuel	· Dedicated boiler & rads	A solid fuel fired, single purpose free standing boiler, heating water piped to one or more radiators.
	· Back boiler and radiators	A distribution system as above, but run from a back boiler behind a solid fuel open fire or stove or an Aga type range.
Elect-ricity	· Off-peak storage heaters	Electric convector storage heaters which can be programmed, either centrally or at the heater, to run on off-peak electricity.
	· Underfloor & ceiling heaters	All other forms of electric central heating (e.g. cabling providing electric underfloor or ceiling heating).
Oil	· All systems	Usually, an oil fired dedicated boiler and radiators.
LPG	· All systems	Usually, a propane fired dedicated boiler and radiators.
Com-munal	· All systems	A district/estate heating scheme serving several buildings; communal heating to several flats in one building.
Other	· Dual fuel etc.	Dual fuel, solar heating and other less conventional systems.

Other heating (P5, H78-84)	D.3	Other heating is categorised into 4 types of fixed heating and portable heating:-	

Gas	· All heaters	Mains gas fired radiant fire, convector or Aga type gas range.
Solid fuel	· Open fires	Traditional open fire burning coal or other solid fuels.
	· Enclosed stove	Enclosed solid fuel stove or solid fuel fired range.
Elect-ricity	· Electric heaters	Electric radiant fires and convectors fixed to the wall and/or wired direct to a fused spur; large electric oil filled radiators.
Port-able	· All types	Portable electric fires and heaters, portable paraffin & bottled gas heaters etc.; includes those recording no heating appliances.

Extent of central heating (P3, H78-84)	D.4	A room is deemed to be centrally heated if it possesses a heating outlet/appliance from any of the above 12 systems, including a dedicated boiler likely to emit sufficient incidental heat. However, if the room contains a back boiler behind a gas radiant fire or convector or solid fuel fire or stove, but there are no radiators or warm air outlets also in that room, the room is regarded as having only fixed other heating. A dwelling has:-

Full central heating	where 70% or more rooms are centrally heated.
Partial central heating	30 to 70% (e.g. ground floor or 'half house' centrally heated).
Limited central heating	less than 30% (e.g. only 1 or 2 rooms 'centrally heated').

Heating controls (H77, H87)	D.5	Controls for central and programmable heating are defined as follows:-

CH	Central timer	A programmer controlling time at which the system operates.
	Manual override	Allows heating to be manually switched on or off at times other than those specified by the timer.
	Wall thermostat	Shuts off whole system when set room temperature is reached.
	Manual valves	Allows individual radiators to be manually turned on or off.
	TRVs	Thermostatic radiator valves which automatically shut off radiators when set temperature is reached in room.
	Appl. thermostat	Controls boiler/appliance to achieve a set temperature.
Prog.	Overnight charge	Controls the length of time overnight charge operates.
	Heat output	Controls the rate at which heat is released into room.
	Appliance timer	A programmer controlling time at which the appliance operates.

Water heating (H106)	D.6	The main hot water systems analysed in the report are:-

Central heating	Water is heated by system which also provides space heating.
Electric immersion	· On-peak only, where not wired to secondary 'white meter'.
	· Wired to take advantage of 'off peak' tariff.

	Individual electric	Electric instantaneous heater usually providing hot water to single amenity, i.e. sink, bath/shower or washbasin.
	Individual gas	Gas-fired instantaneous (Ascot type) heater usually serving single amenity; or back boiler (non-central heating) system.

Wall construction (P12,15)   D.7   Whilst detailed within the SAP model, the report refers to only 3 categories of wall construction. The predominant type, usually of the oldest part of the dwelling, is given.

	Masonry cavity	All masonry double leaf walls (i.e. brick, block or stone).
	Masonry solid	All types of masonry single leaf walls (i.e. brick, block, stone, flint etc.) of any thickness.
	Non masonry walls	All other types, including prefabricated and insitu concrete, timber frame, metal or asbestos cement sheeting etc.

Wall insulation (P7 house, H131)   D.8   With reference to the construction, wall insulation is also banded into three categories:-

	Cavity wall insulation/fill	Masonry cavity insulation, whether built in at the time of construction or injected subsequently.
	Solid wall insulation	Internal dry lining and external insulation to solid masonry and non-masonry walls; new cladding to high rise flats.
	Other wall insulation	e.g. cavity insulation in modern timber-framed construction.

Double glazing & draught proofing (H133-135)   D.9   Double glazing and draught proofing are regarded as 'full' installations if fitted in all rooms, and 'partial' if otherwise. Double glazing is divided into two types, as follows:-

	Sealed units	Factory made sealed double glazed units.
	Secondary glazing	Secondary glazing of glass/rigid plastic, not flexible sheeting.

Loft insulation (P5 house, H129)   D.10   Detailed data on the type and thickness of loft insulation was collected only at houses with accessible lofts. The general variable used classifies houses as with loft insulation, without insulation or as having no accessible loft and divides flats between those on the top floor and those located on lower floors.

Building Regulations standard (Text, 5.3-4 & 5.30)   D.11   Data collected on construction and thermal insulation has also been combined with information on the age of the dwelling to determine which standard of wall and roof insulation, as set progressively by the 1965, 1974 and 1981 amendments to the Building Regulations, is met by any particular house or flat.

Cylinder insulation (H106-107 & H132)   D.12   For households with hot water cylinders, two forms of insulation were recorded:-

	Foam	Firm integral foam coating applied to the cylinder in the factory.
	Jacket	Insulating jacket strapped around the cylinder.

SAP rating, Heat loss index & Heating price index (Text, 3,3-3.8,C.21-28)	D.13	The main measure of energy efficiency used in the report is the energy rating as determined by the Government's Standard Assessment Procedure (SAP). Indexes for the two main components of energy efficiency, the heat loss and heating price are also used in the analyses.
Cooking facilities (H10 & H13-16)	D.14	Cooking facilities are categorised according to the size of cooker and type of fuel used. Dual fuel cookers refer to cases where the oven and hob use different fuels, whether or not these form separate/'split level' appliances.
Fuel types (H112-123 & Fuel survey)	D.15	Types of domestic fuel are categorised as metered and un-metered fuels as follows:-

Gas	Mains supply provided through credit or pre-payment meters.
Electricity	Mains supply provided through credit or pre-payment meters, at · on-peak/normal/day-rate tariffs. · off-peak/night/while meter/'Economy 7' tariffs, defined as including all lower tariffs determined by time of day of supply.
Solid fuel	Includes coal, coke, anthracite, smokeless fuels, logs/wood etc.
Fuel oil	Petroleum oil normally stored in large fixed tank near dwelling.
LPG	Liquid petroleum gas/tanked or bottled gas - propane or 'calor' gas, stored in a large fixed tank or purchased in smaller 'portable' canisters.
Paraffin	e.g. as used in portable paraffin heaters.

Fuel consumption (H121-123 & Fuel survey)	D.16	The fuel consumption given is generally the annual consumption per household and is measured for all fuel types in kilowatt hours (kWh). In keeping with convention, national fuel consumption is given in Peta joules (PJ), one PJ being equal to 278 million kWh.
Fuel expenditure (H121-123 & Fuel survey)	D.17	The fuel expenditure for any given fuel is generally the total annual expenditure per household and includes the cost of fuel and any standing charges. It does not include VAT on fuel, as at the time of the survey in 1991/92 this was zero rated.
Standard heating regime (Text, 8.2-8.8)	D.18	The standard heating regime is that used in calculating SAP ratings and is summarised as follows:-

Room temperatures	Living room - 21°C; other rooms - 18°C
Duration of heating	Morning and evening
Extent of heating	Full-house

Minimum heating regime (Text, 8.2-8.8)	D.19	The minimum heating regime is a lower standard safeguarding health (see also chapter 8, paras 8.2-8.7) and may be summarised as:-

Room temperatures	Living room - 18°C; other heated rooms - 16°C
Duration of heating	All-day
Extent of heating	Half-house

Rising damp (P3)	D.20	Damp caused by ground water rising up a wall or floor of a ground floor or basement room due to the absence of, or faults in, a damp-proof course or membrane (DPC).

Penetrating damp (P3)	D.21	Damp in any room caused by rainwater penetrating the roof, flashing, walls, cills, reveals or other joins in the building fabric making up the external envelope.

Condensation and mould growth (Annex, C.44-49)	D.22	In the analysis, data collected on condensation and mould was used to produce a 'severity index'. This index was used to determine three broad categories of problem, describing the following circumstances:-

Slight	Condensation on windows and/or limited mould in bathrooms and kitchens.
Moderate	Larger areas of mould, especially in bedrooms and/or widespread condensation.
Severe	Widespread mould, especially in living rooms.

Cold bridges	D.23	Cold bridges are formed when building elements such as concrete frames or lintels bridge cavities or other forms of insulation so as to produce relatively cold internal surface areas, on which moisture vapour can more easily condense.

Stock variables[1]	D.24	The following four tenure categories are used throughout the report. Occasionally the local authority and housing association sectors are combined as 'social rented':-

Housing tenure (P2, 7 & H24-31)	
Owner-occupied	Occupied by outright owners, those buying on a mortgage or those in shared ownership schemes (e.g. part buying and part renting their homes from a local authority or housing association).
Private rented	Rented from a private landlord, private company or other organisation, relative or friend; includes accommodation provided free with employment.
Local authority	Rented from the local authority, new town or development corporation.
Housing association	Rented from a housing association, including housing charitable trusts and co-operatives.

Dwelling types (P2)	D.25	Types of dwelling are sometimes described separately or combined with dwelling age to provide a more detailed typology. The main categories used are:-

Converted flat	Flat in building converted from a house or some other use; includes dwellings associated with a non-residential use, such as flats over shops and pubs (unless separately listed).
Low-rise flat	Flat in purpose-built block of less than 6 storeys.
High-rise flat	Flat in purpose built block of 6 or more storeys.
Detached	Detached house, of two or more storeys (if bungalows also listed).
Semi-detached	Semi-detached house, of two or more storeys (if bungalows also listed).
Larger terraced	Middle or end terraced house of two or more storeys with a useable floor area of 70 m^2 or more.
Small terraced	Middle or end terraced house of two or more storeys with a useable floor area of less than 70 m^2.
Bungalow	Single storey detached, semi-detached or terraced house, excluding chalet bungalows or bungalows with lofts converted to habitable accommodation.

[1] *The stock and household variables are generally those used in the other EHCS reports. For further details of these variables and the relevant survey questions (where not included in Annex B) see Department of the Environment, 1993 and 1996, op.cit.*

Region and Metropolitan area (from address)	D.26	The main geographical categories used refer to the 10 administrative regions of the unified Government Offices, including Merseyside. In a number of figures and tables each relevant region has been further sub-divided into its metropolitan area(s) and remaining non-metropolitan area, into Inner and Outer London and into the sub-regions of Devon and Cornwall and the rest of the South West.

Dwelling location (P25)

D.27 The surveyors recorded dwellings as being located in one of six types of area:-

City centre	Areas immediately around the core of large cities.
Urban	Areas around the core of towns and small cities, or older urban areas which have been swallowed up by a metropolis.
Suburban residential	Outer areas of towns or cities, characterised by large private or public housing estates.
Rural residential	Suburban areas of villages, often meeting the housing needs of people who work in nearby towns or cities.
Village centre	Traditional villages or the old centre of villages which have been suburbanised.
Rural isolated	Predominantly rural areas, e.g. agricultural with isolated dwellings or small hamlets.

Dwelling fitness (See first EHCS report)

D.28 A number of analyses assess energy related aspects against whether dwellings are judged 'fit' or 'unfit' on the statutory standard set down in the Housing Act 1985, as amended by section 83 of Schedule 9 to the 1989 Local Government and Housing Act. (For a full description of the fitness standard, see DOE Circular 6/90, Annex A)

Adequate provision for heating (P3)

D.29 One requirement of the fitness standard is that a dwelling shall have 'adequate provision for heating'. As a minimum, this may be interpreted as a suitably located 13 amp outlet or gas point in all main habitable rooms, which in the living room can be dedicated, together with wall space, to a fixed heater. On this requirement, a dwelling is regarded as being:-

Unfit	if there are major problems such that the dwelling fails to meet this requirement and by that failure is not suitable for occupation.
Defective	if there are major problems with the provision for heating, but they are not sufficient to make the dwelling unfit.
Acceptable	if there are some problems but on a small scale and not likely to inconvenience the occupants.
Satisfactory	if there are no problems of note.

General condition (See first EHCS report)

D.30 Some analyses refer to the best and worst housing in the stock, this being defined as:-

Worst	The worst 10% of dwellings, according to the cost of carrying out urgent repairs and any additional costs to make the dwelling fit. These have the highest unit repair costs, the cut-off being £26 per square metre (equivalent to £2,080 or more for an average 80 sq.m. dwelling).
Best	The 30% of homes with no or only minimal repair costs, the threshold being £1.45 per square metre.
The rest	The remaining 60% of dwellings are those which require some work, ranging from a few non-urgent repairs to urgent repairs up to the value of £26 square metre.

Household variables[1]	D.31	Households are classified into eight types which are defined as follows:-

Household type (H3)

Lone parent	One adult living with dependent children (less than 16 year of age).
Two adults	Two persons (related or unrelated) both below pensionable age.
Small family	More than one adult living with 1 or 2 dependent children.
Large family	More than one adult living with more than 2 dependent children.
Large adult	Three or more adults with no dependent children.
Lone adult	One person below pensionable age (65 for men, 60 for women).
Two older	Two persons at least one of whom is of pensionable age.
Lone older	Lone persons of pensionable age.

Household income (H189-205)

D.32 Household income is defined as the net income after tax of the nominated head of household and any partner. As used in this report, it includes:-

· earnings from employment or self employment;
· earnings from any second jobs (as employee or self employed);
· social security benefits;
· state pensions, private pensions and annuities;
· income from shares or other investments (see Annex C, para C.34-35); and
· any other regular income such as rent from lodgers, maintenance payments etc.

Dependent on benefit (H203)

D.33 In the report, households are said to be dependent on benefit if they derive 75% or more of their annual income from the following state benefits:-

· National Insurance retirement or old age pensions;
· income support;
· family credit;
· child benefit, including one-parent benefit;
· National Insurance sickness benefit; and
· unemployment benefit.

Vulnerable households (H3, H183-184)

D.34 In the analysis, vulnerable households are classified as those including:-

Young children	Children under the age of 11 years, sub divided into under 4, 5 & 6, and 7 to 10 years.
Elderly persons	Persons aged 65 or over, sub-divided into 65 to 74, 75 to 84 and 85 years or more.
Persons with respiratory problems	Those reporting a household member (including children) with a long standing illness and suffering from:-

· asthma;
· rhinitis;
· bronchitis;
· pneumonia; and/or
· chest wheezing and whistling.

Persons with mobility problems	Those indicating (for a series of questions on mobility) that a household member is:-

· unable to walk; or
· has difficulty with walking.

---

[1] *The stock and household variables are generally those used in the other EHCS reports. For further details of these variables and the relevant survey questions (where not included in Annex B) see Department of the Environment, 1993 and 1996, op.cit.*

Under - *occupation* *(P6/15 & H3)*	D.35		Under-occupation is measured as a multiple of the 1968 'Parker Morris' (PM) minimum space standard for local authority housing. For each number of occupants, calculations are based on the largest dwelling types specified in the Standard - excluding less common 3 storey houses - and assuming that storage space is internal, as follows:-

1 person	33.0 m², bungalow (PM range 32.5 m² - for flat - to 33.0 m²).
2 persons	48.5 m², bungalow (PM range 47.5 to 48.5 m²).
3 persons	61.0 m², bungalow (PM range 60.0 to 61.0 m²).
4 persons	79.0 m², two-storey terraced house (PM range: 70.5 to 79.0 m²).
5 persons	89.5 m², two-storey terraced house (PM range: 82.5 to 98.5 m²).
6 persons	97.0 m², two-storey terraced house (PM range: 90.0 to 102.5 m²).
7 persons	114.5 m², two-storey terraced house (PM range: 111.5 to 118.5 m²).

Statistical terms	D.36	Mean	The average value of a distribution, i.e. the sum of all the values divided by the number of cases.
		Median	The value that divides a distribution into two equal parts, such that half the cases have a value above the median and half below the median.
		Percentiles	The values that divide a distribution such that a set percentage of cases fall below that value, e.g. 5%, 10%, 90%, 95% of cases etc.; the median is the 50% percentile.
		Quintiles	Categories formed by ordering cases according to their value and then dividing the cases into five equal parts, each containing 20% of cases.
		Deciles	Categories formed by ordering cases according to their value and then dividing the cases into ten equal parts, each containing 10% of cases.
		Standard deviation	A common measure of the scatter or dispersion of a set of measurements, equal to the square root of the mean value of the squares of all the deviations from the mean.

Annex E

E.1 Main index to text and figures

E.2 Tables in text & Annex C

E.3 Main tables in Annex A

Printed in the United Kingdom for The Stationery Office.
Dd.0301663, 11/96, C6, 3396/4, 5673, 362859.